Third World
Women's Literatures

Third World Women's Literatures

A Dictionary and Guide to Materials in English

BARBARA FISTER

GREENWOOD PRESS
Westport, Connecticut • London

Library of Congress Cataloging-in-Publication Data

Fister, Barbara.
   Third world women's literatures : a dictionary and guide to
materials in English / Barbara Fister.
      p.   cm.
   ISBN 0–313–28988–3 (alk. paper)
   1. Developing countries—Literatures—History and criticism—
Dictionaries.   2. Developing countries—Literatures—Women authors—
Dictionaries.   I. Title.
PN849.U43F58   1995
809'.891724'082—dc20   95–7479

British Library Cataloguing in Publication Data is available.

Library of Congress Catalog Card Number: 95–7479
ISBN: 0–313–28988–3

First published in 1995

Greenwood Press, 88 Post Road West, Westport, CT 06881
An imprint of Greenwood Publishing Group, Inc.

Printed in the United States of America

The paper used in this book complies with the
Permanent Paper Standard issued by the National
Information Standards Organization (Z39.48-1984).

10   9   8   7   6   5   4   3   2   1

Contents

Introduction

This book is a companion for readers, librarians, teachers, and students who have an interest in third world women's literatures or who are seeking information unavailable in other literary companions. It includes brief descriptive entries on writers, works, and topics as well as bibliographic leads to works and criticism in English or English translation.

I started work on this book when a teacher complained that he was having trouble finding literature by third world women to include in a course reading list. Since that conversation, a great deal has been published, including literary works, criticism, and excellent reference books such as the *Bloomsbury Guide to Women's Literature* that have provided far more information than was heretofore available on women writers from the third world. However, there has been no other reference work published to date that focuses exclusively on third world women's literatures and that provides extensive bibliographies of works and criticism, a need this book addresses.

The terms used in the title—*third world*, *women's literatures*, and even the category *literature*—are problematic and require some explanation. The term *third world* is not only anachronistic since the withering away of the second world, but is also a phrase some find offensive. Nevertheless, I find it preferable to terms such as *developing countries*, the subject heading used by the Library of Congress. In the past ten years, *postcolonial* has been in frequent use, but I agree with Ama Ata Aidoo that the prefix is unduly optimistic: "[T]he term 'postcolonial' makes me uncomfortable. Post what? . . . because it has not gone yet" (George, 308). Terminology aside, the third world is not a place with defined boundaries but is, in Sara Suleri's phrase, "locatable only as a discourse of convenience'' (20) rather than as a readily definable political, economic, or geographical entity. Gayatri Spivak has critiqued the concept, saying it was generated out of ''a new organization of the international division of labor after the Second World War,'' and goes on to say pointedly that ''we who are from the other side of the globe very much fight against that labelling of all of us under one rubric, which follows from the logic of neo-colonialism. . . . [I]t actually reflects the site of a desire for people in the First World . . . to have a manageable other'' (114). At the risk of participating in the logic of neocolonialism, I am using the term as a convenience and mean by it the countries of the Caribbean, Central and Latin America, Africa, the Middle East, South Asia, and Asia, excluding Japan, Australia, and New Zealand. My object is not to invent a unity where there is none, or to make out of the majority of the world's population a manageable other, but simply to attend to women writers in parts of the world often left out of reference works produced in the West.

The term *women's literatures* similarly suggests a singularity that does not exist and implies that women are a peculiar subcategory of the class ''writer.'' While there are conditions for cultural production shared by women in many cases, and while critics may see common stylistic elements in many women's texts, I am making no such claims but rather am focusing on women in order to pay attention to writers who deserve it and may not receive it elsewhere.

Furthermore, the category *literature* has at times been narrowly defined as a body of high cultural texts appealing to a select audience attuned to its demands and residing exclusively in certain genres endorsed by the guardians of the literary canon. The narrower the definition, the more likely women's texts and postcolonial texts will be excluded. I have defined the term broadly, including not only novels, poetry, short fiction, and plays but also autobiography, life stories, testimonial works, transcribed oral literature, and to a limited extent, children's literature. I also prefer the plural *literatures* because it suggests the multiplicity of traditions from which this book draws its material and does not presuppose a grand unified theory of culture that is, inevitably, based on Western cultural assumptions.

The majority of the book is a dictionary with three types of entries. *Biographical entries* give some information about the writer's life, a very brief discussion of her writings, and some notion of their significance. Length of entries varies depending on the amount of information available, not on the writer's importance. In compiling this information, I have relied on standard reference works, autobiographical writings, publishers' information, and information provided in literary criticism and interviews.

Though the argument can be made that minorities, immigrants, or people of color living in the first world have, essentially, residence in a political and economic third world within the first, I am limiting the focus of this book, for reasons of convenience rather than ideology, to the geographical limits given above. Entries cover selected writers who were born in the regions included or spent substantial time in third world countries. Colonial writers are included selectively, including writers such as Marguerite Duras, who is more properly identified as a French writer but whose colonial childhood is significant to her work. Also included are writers such as Paule Marshall, who was born in the United States of Barbadian parents and who has spent much time in, and written much about, the Caribbean. I have, with some reluctance, decided to list the names of writers under the spelling accepted by the Library of Congress, providing cross-references as necessary. This means that many Arabic and almost all Chinese writers will be listed under a spelling that does not match that given on most title pages—the transliteration systems employed by the Library of Congress for these languages rarely coincide with the usage followed by translators—but it should make it easier for the reader to search library catalogs, particularly those that do not provide adequate cross-references for authors' names.

Each biographical entry is followed by a selective list of works and criticism published through 1994. The bibliographies of works are limited for the most part to separately published monographs and do not include work published in anthologies, literary magazines, or journals. The only exception made to this rule is in the case of plays appearing in anthologies and not available elsewhere that have been selectively included. No effort was made to be exhaustive, and works that have appeared in many editions are only listed once. An asterisk (*) in the list of works indicates those books that have an entry of their own in the dictionary. Bibliographies of criticism are selective, intended to provide useful leads for the interested reader. Journal articles, books, and essays appearing in monographs are included, but book reviews, dissertations and theses, and non-print materials are not. Enough essential publication information has been included to make it possible for researchers to find the works either locally or through interlibrary loan channels. Works published in the third world are not as thoroughly represented as would be ideal. Since my research was conducted through libraries in the United States, relying heavily on regional interlibrary loan services, resources were limited. However, an effort was made to include as many literary and critical works as feasible that would be accessible to researchers in most academic libraries served by interlibrary loan.

A second type of entry describes *individual works of literature*. These entries are based entirely on my readings of the works involved and, as such, are highly subjective. Entries generally include a description of the work and some commentary on its style and its significance. A great many worthy books do not have entries of their own. Choices were made on the basis of availability and, to some extent, my own interests, and an effort was made to select works in a variety of genres and styles by writers from various regions rather than to make selections on the basis of an elusive notion of literary quality. Whenever possible, a bibliography of related criticism has been included.

A third type of entry is *thematic*, intended to pull together literary works and commentary on issues, themes, or ideas relevant to third world women's literature. The number of these entries is limited; subjects were suggested by the literature itself or by the body of criticism relating to it. It is hoped that these entries will serve the reader both to clarify issues and to recommend relevant literature and criticism.

Finally, there are *appendixes* to cover material that did not fit conveniently into a dictionary format. Writers are listed in geographic and chronological order, and there are three bibliographies covering research resources, anthologies of third world women's literatures, and general criticism.

It needs to be noted that there are a great many writers of quality left out for reasons of space or lack of information. It would have been a very different project if exhaustiveness had been the object. Selection is not based only on significance of writers (whatever that might mean) but on providing a mix of writers from different regions with various styles and genres. My object is not to create an alternate canon of essential literature but to call the reader's attention to the variety and extent of literature available, hoping that the inquiring reader will find it a useful starting point.

I am grateful to the interlibrary loan staff of the Folke Bernadotte Memorial Library in St. Peter, Minnesota, and the MINITEX regional library consortium, who graciously coped with my unreasonable demands; for the help of students Ann Delgehausen, Marisa Squadrito, and others who have contributed enthusiasm, time, and effort to this project; and to Terry Flaherty for prompting my curiosity.

REFERENCES

George, Rosemary Marangoly, and Helen Scott. " 'A New Tail to an Old Tale': An Interview with Ama Ata Aidoo." *Novel* 26.3 (spring 1993): 297–308.

Spivak, Gayatri Chakravorty. *The Post-Colonial Critic: Interviews, Strategies, Dialogues.* New York: Routledge, 1989.

Suleri, Sara. *Meatless Days.* Chicago, IL: University of Chicago, 1989.

A

Abeng by Michelle Cliff (Trumansburg, NY: Crossing Press, 1984). Two stories, two times, are retold, the past slowly emerging through the present. Clare Savage, daughter of a black woman and a man who is descended from a slave-owning plantation family, searches for an identity in a divided world, one in which "proper" people keep dogs to attack blacks, one where a salt-rimed abandoned mansion has become the focal point of a new tourist development for Americans—and another world, that of her grandmother in the country where the Creole language and the natural world are new discoveries for Clare. The history of Jamaica, of the Maroon warrior woman Nanny and her trek across the island to unite the rebel forces, is interpolated in Clare's growing sense of self.

Commentary

Cliff, Michelle. "Caliban's Daughter: The Tempest and the Teapot." *Frontiers* 12.2 (summer 1991): 36–51.

Gikandi, Simon. "Narration at the Postcolonial Moment: History and Representation in *Abeng*." *Writing in Limbo: Modernism and Caribbean Literature*. Ithaca, NY: Cornell University, 1992. 231–251.

Johnson, Lemuel. "A-beng: (Re)calling the Body in(to) Question." *Out of the Kumbla: Women and Literature in the Caribbean*. Trenton, NJ: Africa World Press, 1990. 111–142.

Lionnet, Françoise. "Of Mangoes and Maroons: Language, History, and the Multicultural Subject of Michelle Cliff's *Abeng*." *De/Colonizing the Subject: The Politics of Gender in Women's Autobiography*. Minneapolis: University of Minnesota, 1992. 321–345.

Abouzeid, Leila. Born in 1950 in El Ksiba, a Moroccan village where her father worked as an interpreter for the French government, a government he later opposed during the liberation movement. She attended a Moroccan lycée, learning both French and Arabic, then studied at Mohammed V University in Rabbat and at the London School of Journalism. Returning home, she began to write for Arabic-language newspapers and magazines, served as press assistant for the Moroccan government, wrote and directed a radio talk show, and was anchorwoman for the newly created Moroccan television station. She writes in Arabic, using in her fiction a modified Moroccan vernacular that is innovative. Her novella *Year of the Elephant*, first published in 1983, is available in English translation, accompanied by several short stories that are brief, pointed, and ironic.

Work

*Year of the Elephant: A Moroccan Woman's Journey Toward Independence. Translated by Barbara Parmenter. Austin, TX: Center for Middle Eastern Studies, 1989.

Accad, Evelyne. Born to a Swiss mother and an Egyptian-Lebanese father, she had a strict Protestant religious upbringing in Beirut. At age four, she began to perform songs and stories, later writing in school and outside of it for her own pleasure. She attended a French Protestant school in Beirut, then studied at the Beirut College for Women. When the war in Lebanon broke out in 1975, she began to compose songs to work through the feelings she had about it and found that audiences, particularly in Lebanon, responded to them, giving her a sense of the power of words. She studied in the United States, earning a doctorate at Indiana University in 1973, where she wrote her dissertation on the role of Arab women in the writings of women and men in the French and Arabic literatures of the Maghreb and the Mashrek, including a critique of conditions for women in the Middle East that was controversial with her committee, who wondered what it had to do with literature; this was the basis for her book *Veil of Shame*. She has taught French and comparative literature at the University of Illinois since 1974. She wrote her novel *L'Excisée* based on the research she had done for her thesis on female circumcision and based on her own childhood and adolescence in Lebanon. She is the author of criticism, commentary, and fiction.

Work

*L'Excisée. Washington, DC: Three Continents, 1989.

Commentary

Accad, Evelyne. *Veil of Shame: The Role of Women in the Contemporary Fiction of North Africa and the Arab World*. Sherbrooke, Quebec: Naaman, 1978.
Accad, Evelyne. *Sexuality and War: Literary Masks of the Middle East*. New York: New York University, 1990.
Accad, Evelyne. "Sexuality and Sexual Politics: Conflicts and Contradictions for Con-

temporary Women in the Middle East." *Third World Women and the Politics of Feminism*. Bloomington: Indiana University, 1991. 237–250.

Accad, Evelyne. "Sexuality, War, and Literature in Lebanon." *Feminist Issues* 11 (fall 1991): 27–42.

Accad, Evelyne. "Writing to Explore (W)Human Experience." *Research in African Literatures* 23.1 (spring 1992): 179–185.

Marx-Scouras, Danielle. "Muffled Screams/Stifled Voices." *Yale French Studies* 82 (May 1993): 172–182.

Acholonu, Catherine Obianuju. Born October 26, 1951, in Orlu, Imo State, Nigeria, she attended school in Nigeria and then earned master's and doctoral degrees in English and African literatures from the University of Düsseldorf. She teaches in the English Department of the Alvan Ikoku College of Education, Owerri, where she is involved in many arts and literary organizations. She has published volumes of poetry, numerous plays, and essays on literature.

Works

The Deal and Who Is the Head of State? Owerri, Nigeria: Totan, 1986.
Into the Heart of Biafra: A Play in Three Acts. Owerri, Nigeria: C. Acholonu, 1970.
Nigeria in the Year 1999. Owerri, Nigeria: Totan, 1985.
The Spring's Last Drop. Owerri, Nigeria: Totan, 1985.
Trial of the Beautiful Ones: A Play in One Act. Owerri, Nigeria: Totan, 1985.

Commentary

Maduakor, Obi. "Female Voices in Poetry: Catherine Acholonu and Omolara Ogundipe-Leslie as Poets." *Nigerian Female Writers: A Critical Perspective*. Lagos, Nigeria: Malthouse, 1989. 75–91.

Adisa, Opal Palmer. Born in Kingston, Jamaica, in 1954, she earned a B.A. in communications from Hunter College, New York City, and an M.A. in creative writing from San Francisco State University. She has taught at the City College of San Francisco and the University of California at Berkeley, has written books for children, written and directed plays for the Black Repertory and other theaters in the Bay area, and has written and produced for television. In Jamaica, she has been a producer with the Educational Broadcasting Service of the Jamaican Ministry of Education and has published poetry and short stories.

Works

Bake-Face and Other Guava Stories. Berkeley, CA: Kelsey Street Press, 1986.
Pina, the Many-Eyed Fruit. San Francisco: Julian Richardson, 1985.
Travelling Women. Oakland, CA: Jukebox, 1989.

Commentary

Flockemann, Miki. "Language and Self in Opal Palmer Adisa's *Bake-Face and Other Guava Stories*." *Ariel* 24.1 (January 1993): 59–73.

Adnan, Etel. Daughter of a Syrian father and a Greek mother, she was born in 1925, grew up in Beirut, attended a French convent school, and in 1947 moved to Paris to study at the Sorbonne with the help of a scholarship. She later studied at Berkeley and Harvard, and she taught philosophy at Dominican College, San Rafael, California, leaving in 1972 to work as literary editor for a French-language newspaper. She taught for two years, 1957–1959, at the Ahliya School in Beirut, where many Lebanese women writers studied. At the outbreak of the civil war, she left Lebanon to live in France and in the United States; after thirty years abroad, she finally decided to take U.S. citizenship. She writes in French and English, though not in Arabic; she was punished for speaking Arabic as a child, so it is not a language in which she expresses herself naturally; however, many of her works are translated into Arabic with her encouragement. In some cases, she intermingles her poetry with images, as in *The Arab Apocalypse*. She has published many collections of poetry and the novel *Sitt Marie Rose*.

Works

The Arab Apocalypse. Sausalito, CA: Post-Apollo, 1989.
Five Senses for One Death. New York: The Smith, 1978.
From A to Z. Sausalito, CA: Post-Apollo, 1982.
The Indian Never Had a Horse and Other Poems. Sausalito, CA: Post-Apollo, 1986.
Journey to Mount Tamalpais. Sausalito, CA: Post-Apollo, 1986.
Moonshots. Beirut, Lebanon: Reveil, 1966.
Of Cities and Women: Letters to Fawwaz. Sausalito, CA: Post-Apollo, 1993.
Pablo Neruda Is a Banana Tree. Lisbon, Portugal: Da Almeda, 1982.
Paris, When It's Naked. Sausalito, CA: Post-Apollo, 1993.
Sitt Marie Rose. Translated by Georgina Kleege. Sausalito, CA: Post-Apollo, 1982.
The Spring Flowers Own: And the Manifestations of the Voyage. Sausalito, CA: Post-Apollo, 1990.

Commentary

Accad, Evelyne. *Sexuality and War: Literary Masks of the Middle East*. New York: New York University, 1990.
Accad, Evelyne. "Sexuality, War, and Literature in Lebanon." *Feminist Issues* 11 (fall 1991): 27–42.
Adnan, Etel. "To Write in a Foreign Language." *Connexions* 2.2 (fall 1986–winter 1987): 13–17.
Adnan, Etel. "Growing Up to Be a Woman Writer in Lebanon." *Opening the Gates: A Century of Arab Feminist Writing*. Bloomington: Indiana University, 1990. 5–20.
Cooke, Miriam. *War's Other Voices: Women Writers on the Lebanese Civil War, 1975–82*. Cambridge: Cambridge University, 1988.
Fernea, Elizabeth. "The Case of *Sitt Marie Rose*: An Ethnographic Novel from the Modern Middle East." *Literature and Anthropology*. Lubbock: Texas Tech, 1989. 153–164.

African Diaspora. Many of the writers of the African Diaspora—notably Paule Marshall, Michelle Cliff, Merle Collins, Grace Nichols, Simone Schwarz-

Bart, and Maryse Condé—write about the Diaspora in terms both of exile and dispossession and as a theme of the recovery of history, connectedness, and identity. The novel *No Telephone to Heaven* by Michelle Cliff, for example, follows the travels of a young woman living in America and receiving in Britain a solid education in the Western tradition, who returns to Jamaica to find her past; as she excavates her own family's history, she connects to her West Indian and ultimately her African forebears. Cliff explores the same ground in her book *Claiming an Identity They Taught Me to Despise*. The heroine of Paule Marshall's *Praisesong for the Widow* is another traveler, a well-to-do suburban American housewife who responds to an overwhelming sense of the past implanted in childhood by her grandmother and revived by disturbing dreams. She finally reconnects to her African ancestors through a traditional "pardon dance" on a Caribbean island. In *Heremakhonon* by Maryse Condé, a West Indian woman travels to Africa to find her past and to try to come to terms with her ancestors' slavery. Her encounter with modern African politics leaves her, if anything, more ambivalent, and her divided identity is a symptom of the continuing costs of the Diaspora. Simone Schwarz-Bart tells of a mythic journey in which Ti Jean L'Horizon must travel not only to Africa but to the land of the dead to recover the sun in her novel *Between Two Worlds*. Grace Nichols personalizes the historical—and historicizes her personal experience—when she says she must gather her life together like scattered beads (*I Is a Long-Memoried Woman*, 20). In the collection *Rotten Pomerack*, Merle Collins gathers those fragments in her poem "Where the Scattering Began," in which she returns to Africa to examine the Diasporic experience.

Critic Abena Busia describes this common theme of black literature as "reversing the middle passage" (209). There are several common features of Diasporic literature, which include the use of oral tradition, the recovery of a history that has been erased, a sense of bonding with a once-scattered community, and the development of an authentic voice. Critic Karla Holloway explores these features in *Moorings and Metaphors*, arguing that such works of literature "indicate the places where culture and memory converge in African and African-American women's texts" and it is where readers will find "ancestrally mediated places and voices" (169). The notion of ancestors being present, of time being not linear but layered, often creates the conditions for layered and nonlinear narrative techniques, which, Toni Morrison argues, is one distinctive feature of black literature. Gay Wilentz argues that black women's literature has a particular approach to the past, that the connections between African women writers and African-American women writers are invisible threads binding together foremothers and their children through oral literature, through storytelling that is, like childbearing, a means of continuing the cultural ties through which black women define themselves, rediscover their past, and pass it on to their children. These binding threads, reversals of the middle passage, are both a common theme of literature by women of the African Diaspora and a critical approach for seeking and interpreting connections among Diasporic texts.

Works

*Cliff, Michelle. *No Telephone to Heaven*. New York: Dutton, 1987.
*Cliff, Michelle. *Claiming an Identity They Taught Me to Despise*. Watertown, MA: Persephone Press, 1980.
*Collins, Merle. *Rotten Pomerack*. London, England: Virago, 1992.
*Condé, Maryse. *Heremakhonon*. Translated by Richard Philcox. Washington, DC: Three Continents, 1981.
*Marshall, Paule. *Praisesong for the Widow*. New York: Dutton, 1984.
*Nichols, Grace. *I Is a Long Memoried Woman*. London, England: Karnak House, 1983.
*Schwarz-Bart, Simone. *Between Two Worlds*. Translated by Barbara Bray. New York: Harper, 1981.

Commentary

Busia, Abena P. A. "What Is Your Nation? Reconnecting Africa and Her Diaspora Through Paule Marshall's *Praisesong for the Widow*." *Changing Our Own Words: Essays on Criticism, Theory, and Writing by Black Women*. New Brunswick, NJ: Rutgers University, 1989. 196–211.
Holloway, Karla. *Moorings and Metaphors: Figures of Culture and Gender in Black Women's Literature*. New Brunswick, NJ: Rutgers University, 1992.
Morrison, Toni. "Rootedness: The Ancestor as Foundation." *Black Women Writers (1950–1980): A Critical Evaluation*. New York: Anchor, 1984. 339–345.
Wilentz, Gay. *Binding Cultures: Black Women Writers in Africa and the Diaspora*. Bloomington: Indiana University, 1992.

Agosín, Marjorie. Poet, critic, and human rights activist. Born in the United States of Chilean parents in 1955, the descendants of Russian and Austrian Jewish émigrés, she spent her childhood and adolescence in Chile, then returned to the United States in 1973 when her family fled Pinochet's repressive military regime. She earned a B.A. in philosophy, an M.A. in Latin American literature, and a Ph.D. from Indiana University. She has taught for several years at Wellesley and has published many volumes of poetry and works of literary criticism, including books on the works of Violeta Parra, María Luisa Bombal, and Pablo Neruda, as well as poetry that explores the intertwined imagery of history and current political realities. In some of her work, she traces women's history (as in *Brujas y algo mas* and *Women of Smoke*) and in others focuses on the fate of the "disappeared" victims of military violence. Recent work has explored family history and her peculiar vantage point as a product of two exiles and two holocausts, seeing parallels in her European Jewish roots and the more recent turmoil in Chile.

Works

Brujas y algo mas: Witches and Other Things. Translated by Cola Franzen. Pittsburgh, PA: Latin American Literary Review, 1984.
Circles of Madness: Circulos de locura: Mothers of the Plaza de Mayo: Madres de la Plaza de Mayo. Translated by Celeste Kostopulos-Cooperman. Fredonia, NY: White Pine, 1992.

From the Midwest to the West. Bloomington: Indiana University, 1980.
Happiness. Translated by Elizabeth Horan. Fredonia, NY: White Pine, 1993.
Hogueras: Bonfires. Translated by Naomi Lindstrom. Tempe, AZ: Bilingual Press, 1990.
Sargazo: Sargasso. Translated by Cola Franzen. Fredonia, NY: White Pine, 1993.
Scraps of Life: Chilean arpilleras. Translated by Cola Franzen. Trenton, NJ: Red Sea, 1987.
Toward the Splendid City. Translated by Richard Schaaf. Tempe, AZ: Bilingual Press, 1994.
Women of Smoke. Translated by Naomi Lindstrom. Pittsburgh, PA: Latin American Literary Review, 1988.
Zones of Pain: Las zonas del dolor. Translated by Cola Franzen. Fredonia, NY: White Pine, 1988.

Commentary

Mujica, Barbara. "Marjorie Agosín Weaves Magic with Social Vision." *Américas* 45.1 (January-February 1993): 44–49.

Ai Bei. See **Bei, Ai.**

Aidoo, Ama Ata. Born March 23, 1942, in the Fante town of Abeadzi Kyiako in Ghana's Central Region, the daughter of a chief. She attended Wesley Girl's School in Cape Coast, then earned a B.A. in English from the University of Ghana in 1964, where, in her final year, she wrote her play *Dilemma of a Ghost*. During that time, she worked with dramatist Efua Sutherland in the Drama Studio. She was made a fellow of the Institute of African Studies at the University of Ghana and has held academic positions at various institutions in Africa and in the United States. In 1981, she was briefly the minister of education in the government of Jerry Rawlings. She later settled in Harare, Zimbabwe, where she has lived since 1983 and where she is active in the Zimbabwe Women Writers Group. She recently has been a visiting professor at Hamilton College, New York. Aidoo is a leading African voice in the critique of neocolonialism and of the treatment of women. She argues that sexism is not inherent to African cultures but rather is a colonialist import. Her novels, plays, and poetry are all accomplished and innovative explorations of identity, politics, and history. She typically mixes genres and employs aspects of oral tradition along with deadly satire in her work.

Works

Anowa. Harlow, England: Longman, 1970.
Birds and Other Poems. Harare, Zimbabwe: College Press, 1987.
Changes. London, England: Women's Press, 1991.
Dilemma of a Ghost. New York: Collier Books, 1971.
Dilemma of a Ghost; Anowa: Two Plays. Harlow, England: Longman, 1987.
The Eagle and the Chickens: And Other Stories. Accra, Ghana: Afram, 1989.
No Sweetness Here. Garden City, NY: Doubleday, 1972.

Our Sister Killjoy: Or Reflections from a Black-Eyed Squint. London, England: Longman, 1981.
Someone Talking to Sometime. Harare, Zimbabwe: College Press, 1985.
*A Very Angry Letter in January. Sydney, Australia: Dangaroo, 1992.

Commentary

Adelugba, Dapo. "Language and Drama: Ama Ata Aidoo." *African Literature Today* 8 (1976): 72–84.
Aidoo, Ama Ata. "Ghana: To Be a Woman." *Sisterhood Is Global: The International Women's Movement Anthology.* New York: Doubleday, 1984. 258–265.
Aidoo, Ama Ata. "To Be an African Woman Writer—An Overview and a Detail." *Criticism and Ideology: Second African Writers Conference, Stockholm 1986.* Uppsala, Sweden: Scandinavian Institute of African Studies, 1988. 155–172.
Aidoo, Ama Ata. [untitled essay]. *Critical Fictions: The Politics of Imaginative Writing.* Seattle, WA: Bay Press, 1991. 151–154.
Brown, Lloyd W. *Women Writers in Black Africa.* Westport, CT: Greenwood, 1981.
Bruner, Charlotte. "Been-To or Has-Been: A Dilemma for Today's African Woman." *Ba Shiru* 8.2 (1977): 21–30.
Bruner, Charlotte. "Child Africa as Depicted by Bessie Head and Ama Ata Aidoo." *Studies in the Humanities* 7.2 (1979): 5–11.
Cliff, Michelle. "A Journey into Speech." *Graywolf Annual Five: Multi-Cultural Literacy.* St. Paul, MN: Graywolf, 1988. 57–62.
Condé, Maryse. "Three Female Writers in Modern Africa: Flora Nwapa, Ama Ata Aidoo and Grace Ogot." *Présence Africaine* 82 (1972): 132–144.
Duerden, Dennis, and Cosmo Pieterse. *African Writers Talking.* London, England: Heinemann, 1972.
Eke, Ebele. "Beyond the Myth of Confrontation: A Comparative Study of African and African-American Female Protagonists." *Ariel* 17.4 (1986): 139–152.
Elder, Arlene. "Ama Ata Aidoo and the Oral Tradition: A Paradox of Form and Substance." *African Literature Today* 15 (1985): 109–118.
George, Rosemary Marangoly, and Helen Scott. " 'A New Tail to an Old Tale': An Interview with Ama Ata Aidoo." *Novel* 26.3 (spring 1993): 297–308.
Grandqvist, Raoul, and John Stotesbury, editors. *African Voices: Interviews with Thirteen African Writers.* Sydney, Australia: Dangaroo, 1990.
Innes, C. L. "Mothers or Sisters? Identity, Discourse, and Audience in the Writing of Ama Ata Aidoo and Mariama Bâ." *Motherlands: Women's Writings from Africa, the Caribbean, and South Asia.* New Brunswick, NJ: Rutgers University, 1992. 129–151.
James, Adeola, editor. *In Their Own Voices: African Women Writers Talk.* London, England: James Currey, 1990.
Kilson, Marion. "Women and African Literature." *Journal of African Studies* 4.2 (1977): 161–166.
Korang, Kwaku Larbi. "Ama Ata Aidoo's Voyage Out: Mapping the Coordinates of Modernity and African Selfhood in *Our Sister Killjoy*." *Kunapipi* 14.3 (1992): 50–61.
Mackay, Mary. "Ama Ata Aidoo." *Belles Lettres* 9.1 (fall 1993): 32–35.
Nwankwo, Chimalum. "The Feminist Impulse and Social Realism in Ama Ata Aidoo's

No Sweetness Here and *Our Sister Killjoy.*" *Ngambika: Studies of Women in African Literature.* Trenton, NJ: Africa World Press, 1986. 151–159.

Odamtten, Vincent O. *The Art of Ama Ata Aidoo: Polylectics and Reading Against Colonialism.* Gainesville: University of Florida, 1994.

Owusu, Kofi. "Canons Under Siege: Blackness, Femaleness, and Ama Ata Aidoo's *Our Sister Killjoy.*" *Callaloo* 13.2 (spring 1990): 341–363.

Park, Christine, and Caroline Heaton, editors. *Close Company: Stories of Mothers and Daughters.* London, England: Virago, 1987.

Phillips, Maggi. "Engaging Dreams: Alternative Perspectives on Flora Nwapa, Buchi Emecheta, Ama Ata Aidoo, Bessie Head, and Tsitsi Dangarembga." *Research in African Literatures* 25.4 (winter 1994): 89–103.

Rooney, Carolyn. " 'Dangerous Knowledge' and the Poetics of Survival: A Reading of *Our Sister Killjoy* and *A Question of Power.*" *Motherlands: Women's Writings from Africa, the Caribbean, and South Asia.* New Brunswick, NJ: Rutgers University, 1992. 99–126.

Wilentz, Gay. *Binding Cultures: Black Women Writers in Africa and the Diaspora.* Bloomington: Indiana University, 1992.

Aikath-Gyaltsen, Indrani. Born in Chaibasa, Bihar, India, in 1952, she attended school in Jamshedpur and later moved to New York and studied at Barnard. She returned to India, to own and manage a hotel in Darjeeling. She worked as a freelance journalist as well as being a novelist. She died in 1993 after publishing her first novel, *Daughters of the House*, and before her second novel, *Cranes' Morning*, was published. Both were well received by critics; however, her second novel was withdrawn from the market by its American publisher when a complaint was made that it was plagiarized from a novel by Elizabeth Goudge, *The Rosemary Tree*, published in 1956. (See *The New York Times*, April 19, 1994, p. C19.)

Works

*Daughters of the House. New York: Ballantine, 1991.
Cranes' Morning. New York: Ballantine, 1993.

Akello, Grace. Born in eastern Uganda, she was brought up by her grandmother, who was a midwife. She attended Makerere University and worked in Kenya and Tanzania. She married and had four sons, was widowed, and remarried, moving to England in 1981. Her poetry is feminist and political, as well as highly personal.

Work

*My Barren Song. Dar es Salaam, Tanzania: Eastern African Publications, 1979.

Commentary

Akello, Grace. "We Too Have Hands." *A Double Colonization: Colonial and Post-Colonial Women's Writing.* Mundelstrup, Denmark: Dangaroo, 1986. 87–89.

Alamuddin, Rima. Lebanese author of a novel, short stories, and poetry. Born in 1941, daughter of Sheik Naijib Alamuddin, a prominent Druse who had married the daughter of a Swiss missionary, she was raised in Beirut. She was the eldest child in a prosperous family with a family estate in central Lebanon, a home in Beirut, and a summer house in Shemlan, in the mountains. She attended the Protestant School for Girls and the Ahliya College, earning a degree from the American University of Beirut, during which time she published her novel *Spring to Summer* as well as several stories and poems in Lebanese magazines. She then went to England, where she studied English literature at Girton College, Cambridge. After her first year there, she went home for summer holidays in 1963 and was murdered, outside the gates of her parents' Beirut house, by a man whom she had refused to marry and who committed suicide after shooting her. A collection of stories was published after her death.

Works

Spring to Summer. Beirut, Lebanon: Khayyat, 1963.
The Sun Is Silent. London, England: Hodder and Stoughton, 1964.

Alegría, Claribel. Born on May 12, 1924, in Esteli, Nicaragua. Her family moved to Santa Ana, El Salvador, when she was only nine months old, when her father was forced to flee the country. She earned a degree in philosophy from George Washington University and is married to the American writer Darwin J. Flakoll, who has translated many of her works into English. She has been an active writer, publishing many works that have documented the political and social turmoil of El Salvador. She has also translated works of Morris West and Robert Graves into Spanish and, with her husband, works of Benedetti and Asturias into English. She has lived in many countries in Europe and the Americas, writing poetry, fiction, and historical-political analysis of affairs in Central America. Most of her books have been banned in El Salvador.

Works

Ashes of Izalco. Translated by Darwin J. Flakoll. Willimantic, CT: Curbstone, 1989.
*Family Album. Translated by Amanda Hopkinson. Willimantic, CT: Curbstone, 1991.
*Flowers from the Volcano. Translated by Carolyn Forche. Pittsburgh, PA: University of Pittsburgh, 1982.
Fugues. Translated by Darwin J. Flakoll. Willimantic, CT: Curbstone, 1993.
*Luisa in Realityland. Translated by Darwin J. Flakoll. Willimantic, CT: Curbstone, 1987.
*They Won't Take Me Alive. Translated by Amanda Hopkinson. London, England: Women's Press, 1986.
Woman of the River. Translated by D. J. Flakoll. Pittsburgh: University of Pittsburgh, 1989.

Commentary

Alegría, Claribel. "The Writer's Commitment." *Lives on the Line: The Testimony of Contemporary Latin American Authors*. Berkeley: University of California, 1988. 308–311.

Boschetto-Sandoval, Sandra M., and Marcia P. McGowan, editors. *Claribel Alegría and Central American Literature: Critical Essays.* Athens: Ohio University Center for International Studies, 1993.

Longo, Teresa. "Claribel Alegría's 'Sorrow': In Defiance of the Space Which Separates." *Latin American Literary Review* 20 (January-June 1992): 18–27.

Shea, Maureen. "Latin American Women and the Oral Tradition: Giving Voice to the Voiceless." *Critique* 34.3 (Spring 1993): 139–153.

Sommer, Doris. "Not Just a Personal Story: Women's *Testimonios* and the Plural Self." *Life/Lines: Theorizing Women's Autobiography.* Ithaca, NY: Cornell University, 1988. 107–130.

Alexander, Meena. Born in Allahabad, India, on February 17, 1951, the eldest of three children. Her father was a civil servant, and he was sent on assignment abroad when Alexander was five years old. She lived part of the year with her parents in Khartoum and part of it in India in the Kerala home of her grandparents. She was a precocious child, learning to read early and publishing her poetry (in Arabic translation) at age fifteen in Sudanese newspapers. She entered the University of Khartoum at age thirteen and at eighteen was awarded a scholarship for graduate study at the University of Nottingham, where she completed a dissertation on the English romantic poets. Returning to India in 1974, she taught English literature at the University of Delhi, Jawaharlal Nehru University, and the Central Institute of English in Hyderabad. She moved to New York in 1979, married, expecting her first child, and with a job as assistant professor of English at Fordham University, far from her husband's academic job in Minnesota. She has taught at several U.S. institutions since and lives in New York with her husband and two children. She has published several volumes of poetry, criticism, a play, a novel, and an autobiography. She is a writer who is very at home with the English literary canon and whose poetry draws on classic literature but who is particularly interested in "fault lines," the areas of fracture between one cultural tradition and another.

Works

The Bird's Bright Ring: A Long Poem. Calcutta, India: Writers' Workshop, 1976.

*Fault Lines: A Memoir. New York: Feminist Press, 1992.

House of a Thousand Doors: Poems and Prose Pieces. Washington, DC: Three Continents, 1988.

I Root My Name. Calcutta, India: United Writers, 1977.

In the Middle Earth. New Delhi, India: Entact, 1977.

Nampally Road. San Francisco: Mercury House, 1991.

*Night-Scene, the Garden. New York: Red Dust, 1992.

Stone Roots. New Delhi, India: Arnold Heinemann, 1980.

The Storm: A Poem in Five Parts. New York: Red Dust, 1989.

Without Place. Calcutta, India: Writers' Workshop, 1978.

Commentary

"Interview with Meena Alexander." *Dispatch* [Center for American Culture Studies, Columbia University] (spring 1988): 23–26.

Daruwalla, Keki. "Confessional Poetry as Social Commentary: A View of English Poetry by Indian Women Poets." *Indian Horizons* 35.3–4 (1986): 15–24.
Tharu, Susie. "Almost Literally Making Ground: A Conversation with Meena Alexander." *Chandrabhaga* 7 (summer 1982): 69–74.
Tharu, Susie. "Meena Alexander." *Journal of South Asian Literature* 21 (1986): 11–14.

Alfon, Estrella. Born in 1917 in Cebu, Philippines, a daughter of a grocer, she won a literary prize at age twelve. She attended the University of the Philippines and there joined several writing circles, including the avant-garde Veronicans. Her marriage broke up, and she had several common-law relationships with men, trying to find a way of life in which she was free to create and live without hypocrisy. For the most part, she wrote in English, though some of her stories were written in Cebuano. Most are autobiographical, set in Espeleta, the street where she grew up, focusing on women and children and the community of the street, which serves as a character in its own right, a kind of chorus to the events of the stories. She was found guilty of obscenity in 1957, the result of a suit filed by conservative Catholic groups, more because of her lifestyle, considered unconventional, than for the sexual content of the story in question. After that incident, she wrote less and devoted more time to a career in public relations. She died in 1982.

Work

Magnificence, and Other Stories. Manila, Philippines: Regal, 1960.

Commentary

Arambulo, Thelma A. "The Filipina as Writer: Against All Odds." *Women Reading . . . Feminist Perspectives on Philippine Literary Texts.* Quezon City: University of the Philippines, 1992. 163–186.
Grow, L. M. "Brutality in the Fiction of Estrella D. Alfon." *Dalhousie Review* 70.2 (summer 1990): 238–254.

Ali, Hauwa. Born in Gusau, Sokoto State, Nigeria, Ali was educated in Nigeria and the United States, earning a Nigerian Certificate of Education in 1969, a B.A. in education from Ohio University in 1972, an M.A. in international affairs at Ohio in 1973, an M.Ed. in 1979, and a Ph.D. in curriculum and instruction, University of Maiduguri, in 1987, where she is currently a senior lecturer in education. She has published two novels, *Destiny*, which was awarded the Delta Fiction Award, and *Victory*, a short novel about a young woman who goes to work as a physician at a hospital in Kano, where she encounters a new love and lays to rest an old one. Her fiction is unpretentious romance that touches on regional, cultural, religious, gender, and class differences without attempting to penetrate very deeply.

Works

Destiny. Enugu, Nigeria: Delta, 1988.
Victory. Enugu, Nigeria: Delta, 1989.

Alkali, Zaynab. Born on February 3, 1950, in Borno State, Nigeria, she was brought up in Gongola State. She earned a B.A. in 1973 from Bayero University, Kano, and an M.A. in African literature in English in 1979, teaching classes while earning her degree. Since 1980, she has taught English and African literature at the University of Maiduguri, where she serves as the coordinator of English and General Studies for the Modibbo Adama College, Yola Campus. She is married to Mohammed Nur Alkali, the university's vice chancellor. She was the first Muslim woman from northern Nigeria to publish fiction in English. The novels she has published to date deal with the various choices facing young women and what their decisions entail.

Works

The Stillborn. Harlow, England: Longman, 1989.
The Virtuous Woman. Harlow, England: Longman, 1987.

Commentary

James, Adeola, editor. *In Their Own Voices: African Women Writers Talk.* London, England: James Currey, 1990.
Koroye, Seiyifa. "The Ascetic Feminist Vision of Zaynab Alkali." *Nigerian Female Writers: A Critical Perspective.* Lagos, Nigeria: Malthouse, 1989. 47–51.
Maya Pearce, Adewale. *A Mask Dancing: Nigerian Novelists of the Eighties.* London, England: Zell, 1992.

Allende, Isabel. Born in Lima, Peru, on August 2, 1942, where her father was a diplomat; her parents divorced, and she moved with her mother to Santiago, where they lived with her grandparents. Her grandmother, a storyteller who held seances and who was an astrologer, was present even after her death—her grandfather summoned her and spoke with her daily. Her mother encouraged her creativity and gave her both a notebook to write in and a wall of her bedroom to draw on. After her mother married a second time, to another diplomat, she traveled with them to Europe and the Middle East. In 1967, they were posted to Lebanon, and she was soon sent home because of the civil war there. That year she left school and went to work for the United Nations, began to write for magazines (including a popular humor column called "Civilize Your Troglodyte"), and worked as a host on television talk shows doing interviews and newscasts. At twenty, she married and started to write for children. The death of her father's first cousin and her godfather, Salvador Allende, and the repression following, was a turning point in her life, and after assisting victims of the coup for a period of several months, she moved to Venezuela with her husband and children; though not personally targeted by the new regime, she could not live with the torture and terror it imposed on the country. In 1981, her grandfather, approaching his hundredth birthday, called her and said he had decided to die; it was to preserve his spirit and the spirit of the family household that she started to write *The House of the Spirits*, which became the first international best-seller by a Latin American woman. After some fifteen years in Venezuela, she moved to the United States, where she now lives in San Rafael, California. The style of her first novel was likened by some critics to that of *One Hundred Years of Solitude*, with its whimsical magic realism combined with historical testimony. Her second novel, *Of Love and Shadows*, also set in Chile, is a combination of testimonial literature and romance. *Eva Luna* is a picaresque novel about storytelling, carried out in *The Stories of Eva Luna*, and her latest work, *The Infinite Plan*, is her only work set in North America. Her books are international best-sellers and have been translated into many languages.

Works

Eva Luna. Translated by Margaret Sayers Peden. New York: Knopf, 1988.
*The House of the Spirits. Translated by Magda Bogin. New York: Knopf, 1985.
The Infinite Plan. Translated by Margaret Sayers Peden. New York: HarperCollins, 1993.
*Of Love and Shadows. Translated by Margaret Sayers Peden. New York: Knopf, 1987.
The Stories of Eva Luna. Translated by Margaret Sayers Peden. New York: Atheneum, 1991.

Commentary

Allende, Isabel. "The World Is Full of Stories." *Review: Latin American Literature and Arts* 34 (January-June 1985): 18–20.
Allende, Isabel. "The Spirits Were Willing." *Lives on the Line: The Testimony of Contemporary Latin American Authors*. Berkeley: University of California, 1988. 237–242.
Allende, Isabel, et al. "Writing as an Act of Hope." *Paths of Resistance: The Art and Craft of the Political Novel*. Boston: Houghton Mifflin, 1989. 41–63.
Boschetto, Sandra M. "Threads, Connections, and the Fairy Tale: Reading the Writing in Isabel Allende's *La casa de los espíritus*." *Continental, Latin-American, and Francophone Women Writers*. Lanham, MD: University Press of America, 1990. 51–63.
Crustall, Elyse, Jill Kuhnheim, and Mary Layoun. "An Interview with Isabel Allende." *Contemporary Literature* 33.4 (winter 1992): 585–600.
Gautier, Marie-Lise Gazarian. *Interviews with Latin American Writers*. Elmwood Park, IL: Dalkey Archive, 1989.
Hart, Patricia. *Narrative Magic in the Fiction of Isabel Allende*. Rutherford, NJ: Farleigh Dickinson, 1989.
Levine, Linda Gould. "A Passage to Androgyny: Isabel Allende's *La casa de los espíritus*." *In the Feminine Mode: Essays on Hispanic Women Writers*. Lewisburg, PA: Bucknell University, 1990. 164–176.
Magnarelli, Sharon. "Framing Power in Luisa Valenzuela's *Cola de lagartija [The Lizard's Tail]* and Isabel Allende's *Casa de los espíritus [The House of the Spirits].*" *Splintering Darkness: Latin American Women Writers in Search of Themselves*. Pittsburgh, PA: Latin American Literary Review, 1990. 43–62.

Moody, Michael. "Isabel Allende and the Testimonial Novel." *Confluencia* 2.1 (fall 1986): 39–43.

Parkinson, Lois. "The Magic Tables of Isabel Allende and Remedios Varo." *Comparative Literature* 44.2 (spring 1994): 113–144.

Pinto, Magdalena Garcia. *Women Writers of Latin America: Intimate Histories.* Austin: University of Texas, 1991.

Price, Greg, editor. *Latin America: The Writer's Journey.* London, England: Hamish Hamilton, 1990.

Rivero, Eliana S. "Scheherazade Liberated: *Eva Luna* and Women Storytellers." *Splintering Darkness: Latin American Women Writers in Search of Themselves.* Pittsburgh, PA: Latin American Literary Review, 1990. 143–156.

Rojas, Sonia Riquelme, and Edna Aguirre Rehbein, editors. *Critical Approaches to Isabel Allende's Novels.* New York: P. Lang, 1991.

Allfrey, Phyllis Shand. Born in Dominica in 1915, one of four daughters of Elfreda Nicholls and Francis Byam Berkeley Shand, a descendant of the early settlers of the white Caribbean ruling class. She was educated at home by tutors and an aunt and, as a child, was a voracious reader and writer, publishing a juvenile story in *Tiger Tim's Weekly* at the age of thirteen. After age seventeen she studied in England, Belgium, Germany, and France. Living in London, she joined the Labour Party and the Fabian society and worked with the Parliamentary Committee for West Indian Affairs. She married Robert Allfrey, with whom she had two children; they later adopted three more children in Dominica. Returning to the West Indies in the 1950s, she found the island of Dominica embroiled in a struggle for independence. In this atmosphere, she wrote *The Orchid House*, a novel with something of a *Cherry Tree* ambiance, the story of a once well-to-do family faced with uncertainty in a newly forming society. By 1955 she became active in political affairs, founding the Labour Party of Dominica, then in 1958 was named the minister of labour and social affairs in the federal government of the West Indies. After the federation failed in 1962, she and her husband ran *The Dominica Herald* and a few years later founded their own paper, *The Star*. The end of her life was marred by the violent death of her daughter Josephine and by poverty and neglect. She died in February 1986.

Works

In Circles, Poems. Harrow Weald, England: Raven Press, 1940.
*The Orchid House. London, England: Constable, 1953.
Palm and Oak: Poems. Fulham, England: Copyotype Company, 1967.
Palm and Oak II. Roseay, Dominica: Star Printery, 1973.

Commentary

Campbell, Elaine. " 'In the Cabinet': A Novelistic Rendition of Federation Politics." *Ariel* 17.4 (October 1986): 117–125.

"Neglected West Indian Writers, No. 1: Phyllis Allfrey's *The Orchid House*." *World Literature Written in English* 11.1 (1972): 81–83.

Nuñez-Harrell, Elizabeth. "The Paradoxes of Belonging: The White West Indian Woman in Fiction." *Modern Fiction Studies* 31.2 (summer 1985): 281–293.

Williamson, Karina. *Voyages in the Dark: Jean Rhys and Phyllis Shand Allfrey.* Warwick, England: University of Warwick, 1987.

Wylie, Herb. "Narrator/Narrated: The Position of Lally in *The Orchid House.*" *World Literature Written in English* 31.1 (spring 1991): 21–33.

The Alphabet in the Park: Selected Poems of Adélia Prado by Adélia Prado (Middletown, CT: Wesleyan University, 1990). Lyrical, existential, and surprising poetry that juxtaposes images in surprising ways. In "Some Other Names for Poetry," she makes a case for poetry, addressing issues of importance, including the power of imagination. The title poem is also about poetry and how it approaches and touches reality—words not being simply words but being things themselves. Prado cannot be assigned to a particular school or be said to be attempting any particular project; her poetry is observant and exploratory, stylish without being in a particular style.

Al-Saadawi, Nawal. See **Sa'dawi, Nawal.**

Al-Shaykh, Hanan. See **Shaykh, Hanan.**

Alvarado, Elvira. A Honduran activist who grew up in poverty, having to fend for herself from the age of thirteen. She became involved in the *campesinos'* struggle for land and rights and has told how she organized her neighbors for resistance in a straightforward, outspoken *testimonio.*

Work

*Don't Be Afraid, Gringo: A Honduran Woman Speaks from the Heart. Translated and edited by Medea Benjamin. San Francisco, CA: Institute for Food and Development, 1987.

Ambai. See **Lakshmi, C. S.**

An American Brat by Bapsi Sidhwa (Minneapolis, MN: Milkweed, 1993). A novel about intergenerational and intercultural differences as reflected in the experiences of Feroza, a bold young Parsi woman who travels to America. She is introduced to the brave new world by her young cousin Manek, a college student. Americans' bewildered hostility to foreigners is provoked under the most innocent of circumstances. Small tasks—even buying hair spray in a Walmart—become an occasion for miscommunication, just as American assumptions prompt reexamination of Parsi customs and values. Feroza's mother comes to America when her daughter plans to marry, and the fissures between cultures grow wider, given a generational twist. A comedy of manners that puts all habits and customs up for examination.

Amrita Pritam. Born in 1919 in Gujranwala in a part of India that later became Pakistan, she was the only child of a schoolteacher and a poet. Her mother died when she was eleven, and she grew up with adult responsibilities. She began to write at an early age, and her first collection was published when she was only sixteen years old, the year she married an editor to whom she was engaged in early childhood. In 1947 at the time of the Partition, she moved to New Delhi, where she began to write in Hindi as opposed to Punjabi, her mother tongue. She worked until 1961 for All India Radio. She was divorced in 1960, and since then, her work has become more explicitly feminist, drawing on her unhappy marriage in many of her stories and poems. A number of her works have been translated into English, including her autobiographical works *Black Rose* and *The Revenue Stamp.*

Works

The Aerial and Other Stories. Calcutta, India: United Writers, 1968.
Alone in the Multitude: Selected Poems. Translated by Suresh Kohli. New Delhi, India: Indian Literary Review, 1979.
Black Rose. New Delhi, India: Nagmani, 1967.
Blank Sheets. Delhi, India: B. R. Publishing Company, 1992.
Death of a City. New Delhi, India: Arnold Heinemann, 1976.
Existence and Other Poems. New Delhi, India: Nagmani, 1968.
Flirting with Youth. New Delhi, India: Sterling, 1973.
49 Days. Delhi, India: Chanakya, 1981.
Life and Times. New Delhi, India: Vikas, 1989.
A Line in Water. New Delhi, India: Arnold Heinemann, 1975.
Nobody Knows; and Time and Beyond. New Delhi, India: Himalaya, 1977.
Profiles. Delhi, India: Raj Deep, 1983.
The Revenue Stamp: An Autobiography. Translated by Krishna Gorowara. New Delhi, India: Vikas, 1977.
The Rising Sun. New Delhi, India: India Paperbacks, 1977.
Selected Poems. Calcutta, India: Dialogue Calcutta, 1970.
The Skeleton; and That Man. New Delhi, India: Sterling, 1987.
A Slice of Life: Selected Works. New Delhi, India: Vikas, 1990.
A Statement of Agony. New Delhi, India: Vision, 1979.
The Thirteenth Sun: Teheruan Suraj. Delhi, India: Vikrant, 1982.
Time and Again and Other Poems. Calcutta, India: United Writers, 1975.
Two Faces of Eve. Delhi, India: Hind Pocketbooks, 1971.

Commentary

Ash, Ranjana. "The Search for Freedom in Indian Women's Writing." *Motherlands: Women's Writings from Africa, the Caribbean, and South Asia.* New Brunswick, NJ: Rutgers University, 1992. 152–174.

Amritvela by Leena Dhingra (London, England: Women's Press, 1988). A novel about the quest of an Indian woman who lives in Britain and returns to India seeking the clarity and calm of *amritvela*, "nectar time"—the time when the sun is not yet up, but the sky is light. She makes the journey in order to find meaning in her life, both her past and her complicated present, as well as to sort out just where she belongs. Through her connection with her aunt and her large extended family, and through her encounters with a country that enchants her and enrages her—the extraordinary trouble it takes to mail a package is a revelation to her—she comes to a reconciliation with herself that sends her back to her English husband and her daughter, feeling more at peace, more whole.

Amrouche, Fadhma. A Kabyle Berber woman, born in Taourirth-Moussa-ou-Amar, Algeria, in 1882 to an unmarried mother. She grew up rejected and persecuted by the Kabyle villagers, and her mother finally sent her to live in a convent school. She eventually moved to Tunisia, and then France, where she died in 1967. She felt an exile from her own culture and never at home elsewhere, though her autobiography is a telling and detailed record of Kabyle culture. She was the mother of Jean Amrouche, a poet, and Marguerite Taos Amrouche, an ethnomusicologist. According to an interview published in 1993, the Algerian writer Assia Djebar is planning to make her next film on the life of Fadhma Amrouche (Djebar, 200).

Work

My Life Story: The Autobiography of a Berber Woman. New Brunswick, NJ: Rutgers University, 1988.

Commentary

Djebar, Assia. *Women of Algiers in Their Apartment.* Charlottesville: University of Virginia, 1992.

Anancy and Miss Lou by Louise Bennett (Kingston, Jamaica: Sangster's, 1979). Traditional Jamaican versions of the Anancy stories, descendants of the Ashanti tales of a spider-trickster, rendered in a Jamaican patois or Creole. The text is followed by music commonly associated with the stories, giving a sense of the performance that is a vital part of the art of Louise Bennett.

And They Didn't Die by Lauretta Ngcobo (New York: Braziller, 1991). A novel that recognizes and reclaims the contributions of rural women to the struggle against apartheid in South Africa. The narrative centers around Jezile, a strong, independent, morally indignant young woman who rebels against restrictions imposed on her community by the government. Yet her rebellion is tempered by the factors that the apartheid system exploits to keep rebellion in check. Her husband must work in the city once the land is taken away, but he can only work there without his family and can only visit briefly each year. Since the bearing of children is a function much valued by the African community, Jezile must bow to the hated pass laws if she is to visit her husband and fulfill her traditional duty of motherhood. She brews beer for road workers and travels to a remote region to do domestic work, leaving her children with their grand-mother, because if she doesn't, they will starve; yet she knows these are also capitulations that will, in the long run, work against her people. Jezile's story contains the cruel twists that apartheid used to demoralize the African majority but also depicts the strength and courage that kept resistance alive, particularly among women in the rural areas.

Commentary

Farred, Grant. " 'Not Like Women at All': Black Female Subjectivity in Lauretta Ngco-bo's *And They Didn't Die.*" *Genders* 16 (spring 1993): 94–112.

Ang, Li. See Li Ang.

Angel by Merle Collins (London, England: Women's Press, 1987). This novel deals with a family's experiences in Grenada from independence through the U.S. invasion. It follows the life of Angel from infancy through adulthood, examining the educational process for a Caribbean child, relations between men and women, colonialism, and the struggle for power in a postcolonial world. The political situation in the country is a backdrop for the day-to-day life of the main characters. Language plays an important role in the narrative; dialogue and much of the narration are written in Grenadian Creole. The author slips grace-fully between standard English and Creole, letting the characters speak in their own voices and enriching the narrative with multiple linguistic strands.

Commentary

Lima, Maria Helena. "Revolutionary Developments: Michelle Cliff's *No Telephone to Heaven* and Merle Collins's *Angel.*" *Ariel* 24.1 (January 1993): 35–56.

Annie John by Jamaica Kincaid (New York: Farrar, Straus, Giroux, 1985). This novel is a beautiful, intense, and sensitive *bildungsroman* about childhood in Antigua, recounting the close relationship between a child and her mother and their gradual disaffection as the child approaches adulthood. Annie John is bright at school, able to do what her English teachers want without seeming to work very hard, but her insubordination continually gets her in trouble. At home, her mother nudges her toward independence and away from closeness, leaving her angry and bewildered. Her feelings for her mother are echoed in her feelings about the island: She wants to leave home but mourns for the loss of home. The novel interestingly mixes mother/daughter relationships and the scars of colonization.

Commentary

de Abruna, Laura Niesen. "Family Connections: Mother and Mother Country in the Fiction of Jean Rhys and Jamaica Kincaid." *Motherlands: Women's Writings* from Africa, the Caribbean, and South Asia. New Brunswick, NJ: Rutgers University, 1992. 257–289.

Ismond, Patricia. "Jamaica Kincaid: 'First They Must Be Children.' " *World Literature Written in English* 28.2 (1988): 336–341.

Tapping, Craig. "Children and History in the Caribbean Novel: George Lamming's *In the Castle of My Skin* and Jamaica Kincaid's *Annie John.*" *Kunapipi* 11.2 (1989): 51–59.

Another Birth: Selected Poems of Forugh Farrokhzad by Furugh Farrukhzad (Emeryville, CA: Albany, 1981). Personal poems expressing loneliness, disaffection, disconnectedness from modern Iran. "Let Us Believe in the Beginning of a Cold Season" contains references to—and emulates the mood of—Eliot's "Hollow Men." "Mechanical Doll" is a criticism of women who behave according to norms without thinking for themselves.

Another Country and Other Stories by Shirley Lim (Singapore: Times Books International, 1982). Stories that reflect the author's experiences as an exile and explore other worlds, touching also on such subjects as tradition and the many forces that attack it, the dark side of tradition, and physical and psychological dislocation. "All My Uncles" is a story about an extended family and the relationship between several women related through marriage, holding their family together while the men abdicate responsibility for their numerous children. In "Another Country" a young woman of Chinese descent befriends a Muslim woman while staying in a hospital. The Muslim woman, hospitalized for manic depression, encourages patients to break all the rules and become friends. Though modest in scope, these stories tackle the complexities of Peninsular culture.

Antonius, Soraya. Born in Jerusalem when it was still the capital of Palestine, she has worked as a columnist, editor, and publisher in Beirut, where she now lives. She was editor of the *Middle East Forum* and served on committees of the General Union of Palestinian Women. Her novels are densely plotted dramas of the political and social upheaval surrounding the founding of the state of Israel.

Works

*The Lord. New York: Henry Holt, 1986.
*Where the Jinn Consult. London, England: Hamish Hamilton, 1987.

Commentary

Antonius, Soraya. "Fighting on Two Fronts: Conversations with Palestinian Women." *Third World, Second Sex*. London: Zed, 1983. 63–77.

Appachana, Anjana. A graduate of Delhi University and Jawaharlal Nehru University, she left India in 1984 to study in the United States, where she earned a degree from Pennsylvania State University. She now lives in Tempe, Arizona, where she writes short stories and is working on a novel.

Work

Incantations and Other Stories. London, England: Virago, 1991.

Appiah, Peggy. Born in England, she settled in Ghana after her marriage in 1953. She is the author of several books and articles, including a retelling of Ananse stories for children, a collection of gentle stories of village life, and works on Ghanaian history and culture.

Works

Ananse the Spider: Tales from an Ashanti Village. New York: Pantheon, 1966.
A Smell of Onions. Harlow, England: Longman, 1979.
Tales of an Ashanti Father. London, England: Deutsch, 1967.

An Apprenticeship, or the Book of Delights by Clarice Lispector (Austin: University of Texas, 1986). This novel chronicles the existential awakening of a young woman under the apprenticeship of a man named Ulysses. Unlike the existentialist awakenings of Sartre's characters, the woman experiences a kind of mystical merging with the world, a religious experience of a kind. The novel ends in midsentence, with Ulysses saying, ''What I think is this.'' The search, it seems, isn't over, but the search has become an occasion for enlightenment, the lack of resolution a transcendent gesture of consciousness.

The Arab Apocalypse by Etel Adnan (Sausalito, CA: Post-Apollo, 1989). Translated by the author from the French work, first published in 1980, a collection of idiosyncratic and interesting poems, all interrelated, that explore the Palestinian question from an abstract and deconstructed viewpoint. The text, full of images of violence, is evocative rather than descriptive and includes hieroglyphic ink-brush symbols.

Arasanayagam, Jean. Born in Kandy, Sri Lanka, in 1934, a ''Burgher''—of Dutch and Sri Lankan origin. She was educated at the University of Ceylon, Peradeniya. She is married to a Tamil and has two daughters. She is a poet, especially noted for her poetry of ethnic conflict in her country as well as on interethnic marriage and the colonial heritage of Sri Lanka.

Works

Fragments of a Journey. Kandy, Sri Lanka: Jean Arasanayagam, 1992.
Reddened Water Flows Clear: Poems from Sri Lanka. London: Forest Books, 1991.
Trial by Terror: Sri Lankan Poems. Hamilton, New Zealand: Rimu, 1987.

Commentary

Sjobohm, Anders. " 'Someone Smashed in the Door and Gave Me My Freedom': On the Writings of Jean Arasanayagam." *World Literature Today* 66.1 (winter 1992): 35–38.

Arrival of the Snake Woman and Other Stories by Olive Senior (Harlow, England: Longman, 1989). The title story is a sympathetic account of a friendship between members of two different ethnic groups—the "snake woman" is an Indian woman who walks with the sinuous movements of a snake and dresses in a sari that reveals her long, lithe shape. Several of the stories play with narration in interesting ways, such as seeing the world from the point of view of a small child, whose observations make the reader see the world from a fresh angle.

As Long as Nothing Happens, Nothing Will by Chang Chieh (London, England: Virago, 1988). Five stories that blur the distinction between omniscient narration and personal experience. In "What's Wrong with Him?" the lives of a large number of characters intersect in casual ways, the narration weaving among them without bringing them together. The collection is critical and ironic in tone, with a number of experimental surprises in its narrative structure.

As the Sorcerer Said by Myriam Warner-Vieyra (Harlow, England: Longman, 1982). A short, dramatic novel about a young black girl who is taken by her long-absent mother, long resident in the metropole, to live with her in France. There she finds herself in a foreign world where she is treated like a servant and worse, and eventually she ends up in a psychiatric ward, where she narrates her life story. The author explores, as she did in her novel *Juletane*, the personal pain caused by the fractures between cultures, revealing the mined terrain, the no-man's land, distancing the colonial power from its colonies.

Commentary

O'Callaghan, Evelyn. "Interior Schisms Dramatised: The Treatment of the 'Mad' Woman in the Work of Some Caribbean Novelists." *Out of the Kumbla: Women and Literature in the Caribbean.* Trenton, NJ: Africa World Press, 1990. 89–109.

At the Still Point by Mary Benson (Boston, MA: Gambit, 1969). The narrator of the novel returns to her home, South Africa, where she becomes politically involved in the fight against apartheid and personally involved with a lawyer who is devoting his life to the struggle. The narrative reveals many of the small details of life that demonstrate the apathy of many whites and the petty and large indignities inflicted on the majority. Many of the most vivid details are apparently autobiographical, reappearing in the author's memoir, *A Far Cry*.

Autobiography. Critic Georges Gusdorf once declared that "autobiography is essentially European" (quoted in Kaplan, 118) and that it is closely identified with a European notion of identity and the individual. Other critics disagree: In Linda Warley's estimation, "[i]f the notion of identity is a problematic one for all autobiographers, it is perhaps the obsession of post-colonial autobiographies" (107). Certainly many third world women have produced personal narratives that explore identity in terms that relate particularly to their status as women in a postcolonial world. Sara Suleri and Meena Alexander have produced eloquent meditations on their lives, depicting the fissures and fault lines produced by a postcolonial consciousness, as have Nafissatou Diallo, Ken Bugul, and Sharan-Jeet Shan. The writers Buchi Emecheta, Han Suyin, Kamala Das, and Jean Rhys have published autobiographies. Women in politics, such as Andrée Blouin, Ruth First, Gisèle Halimi, Helen Joseph, and Mary Benson, have written about their part in history; Eva Peron published an autobiography with a strongly didactic slant. Others have chronicled their involvement in historical events, as in the case of Cheng Nien, who was imprisoned during the Cultural Revolution, and Zhai Zhenhua, who was a member of the Red Guard at the time. Some writers have constructed family memoirs, notably Margo Glantz, Yasmine Gooneratne, and Jung Chang. Early autobiographers include Sor Juana Inés de la Cruz, whose *Answer* constitutes an intellectual autobiography, Mary Prince, author of a slave narrative, and the colorful Mrs. Seacole, whose picaresque adventures were popular in the nineteenth century. More recently, historian Shula Marks found and compiled autobiographical writings of three South African women whose lives were interrelated, filling out the ellipses in their stories with her own research.

Life story production is related to autobiography, though it is generally mediated by a writer who takes down and reorders a subject's life history, often with anthropological aims. Examples of this are Marjorie Shostak's *Nisa: The Life and Words of a !Kung Woman*, Mary Smith's *Baba of Karo*, Ruth Behar's *Translated Woman*, Daphne Patai's *Brazilian Women Speak*, and Ning Lao-T'ai-t'ai and Ida Pruitt's *A Daughter of Han*. An interesting example of a collection of intermediated personal narratives is the Sistren Theatre Collective's *Lionheart Gal*, with a thoughtful introduction by Honor Ford Smith that explores the problems of producing "authentic" life stories. See also **Testimonios** for related works.

Works

*Alexander, Meena. *Fault Lines: A Memoir*. New York: Feminist Press, 1992.
*Amrouche, Fadhma. *My Life Story: The Autobiography of a Berber Woman*. New Brunswick, NJ: Rutgers University, 1988.
*Andreski, Iris. *Old Wives' Tales: Life-Stories from Ibibioland*. New York: Schocken, 1970.
Atiya, Nayra. *Khul-Khaal: Five Egyptian Women Tell Their Stories*. Syracuse, NY: Syracuse University, 1982.

Behar, Ruth. *Translated Woman: Crossing the Border with Esperanza's Story.* Boston, MA: Beacon, 1992.

*Benson, Mary. *A Far Cry: The Making of a South African.* New York: Viking, 1989.

*Blouin, Andrée, with Jean MacKellar. *My Country, Africa: Autobiography of the Black Pasionaria.* New York: Praeger, 1983.

Brinda, Maharani of Kapurthala, with Elaine Williams. *The Story of an Indian Princess.* New York: Holt, 1954.

Bugul, Ken. *The Abandoned Baobab: The Autobiography of a Senegalese Woman.* Translated by Marjolijn de Jager. Brooklyn, NY: Lawrence Hill, 1991.

*Chang, Jung. *Wild Swans: Three Daughters of China.* London, England: HarperCollins, 1992.

Ch'en Hsueh-Chao. *Surviving the Storm: A Memoir.* Translated by Ti Hua and Caroline Greene. Armonk, NY: M. E. Sharpe, 1991.

Cheng Nien. *Life and Death in Shanghai.* New York: Grove, 1986.

*Creider, Jane Tapsubei. *Two Lives: My Spirit and I.* London, England: Women's Press, 1986.

Das, Kamala. *My Story.* New York: Quartet Books, 1978.

*Diallo, Nafissatou. *A Dakar Childhood.* Translated by Dorothy S. Blair. Harlow, England: Longman, 1982.

Emecheta, Buchi. *Head Above Water.* London, England: Ogwugwu Afor, 1986.

*Farman-Farmaian, Sattareh, and Dona Munker. *Daughter of Persia: A Woman's Journey from Her Father's Harem Through the Islamic Revolution.* New York: Anchor/Doubleday, 1993.

First, Ruth. *117 Days.* New York: Stein and Day, 1965.

*Glantz, Margo. *The Family Tree: An Illustrated Novel.* Translated by Susan Bassnett. London, England: Serpent's Tail, 1990.

*Gooneratne, Yasmine. *Relative Merits: A Personal Memoir of the Bandaranaike Family of Sri Lanka.* New York: St. Martin's, 1986.

*Guppy, Shusha. *The Blindfold Horse: Memories of a Persian Girlhood.* London, England: Heinemann, 1988.

Halimi, Gisèle. *Milk for the Orange Tree.* Translated by Dorothy S. Blair. London, England: Quartet, 1990.

Han Suyin. *The Crippled Tree.* New York: Putnam, 1965.

Hayslip, Le Ly, and Jay Wurts. *When Heaven and Earth Changed Places.* New York: Doubleday, 1989.

*Hsieh Ping-ying. *The Autobiography of a Chinese Girl.* Translated by Tsui Chi. London, England: Pandora, 1986.

Huxley, Elspeth Joscelin (Grant). *The Flame Trees of Thika.* New York: Morrow, 1959.

Joseph, Helen. *Tomorrow's Sun: A Smuggled Journal from South Africa.* New York: John Day, 1966.

Juana Inés de la Cruz. *The Answer: La repuesta.* Translated by Electa Arenal and Amanda Powell. New York: Feminist, 1994.

Khaled, Leila, with George Hajjar. *My People Shall Live: The Autobiography of a Revolutionary.* London, England: Hodder and Stoughton, 1973.

Kitson, Norma. *Where Sixpence Lives.* London, England: Chatto and Windus, 1986.

Kuzwayo, Ellen. *Call Me Woman.* Johannesburg, South Africa: Ravan, 1985.

*Lim, Janet. *Sold for Silver.* Cleveland, OH: World, 1958.

Makdisi, Jean Said. *Beirut Fragments: A War Memoir.* New York: Persea, 1990.

Makeba, Miriam, with James Hall. *Makeba: My Story*. Johannesburg, South Africa: Skotaville, 1988.

Markham, Beryl. *West with the Night*. Boston, MA: Houghton Mifflin, 1942.

*Marks, Shula. *"Not Either an Experimental Doll"*: The Separate Worlds of Three South African Women. Bloomington: Indiana University, 1987.

*Mi Mi Khaing. *Burmese Family*. London, England: Longmans, Green, 1946.

Mizra, Sarah, and Margaret Strobel, editors. *Three Swahili Women: Life Histories from Mombasa, Kenya*. Bloomington: Indiana University, 1989.

*Ning Lao-T'ai-t'ai and Ida Pruitt. *A Daughter of Han: The Autobiography of a Chinese Working Woman*. Stanford, CA: Stanford University, 1967.

Nzenza, Sekai. *Zimbabwean Woman: My Own Story*. London, England: Karia, 1988.

Patai, Daphne, editor. *Brazilian Women Speak: Contemporary Life Stories*. New Brunswick, NJ: Rutgers University, 1988.

Peron, Eva Duarte. *My Mission in Life*. New York: Vantage, 1953.

Prince, Mary. *The History of Mary Prince, a West Indian Slave, Related by Herself*. London, England: Pandora, 1987.

Rhys, Jean. *Smile Please: An Unfinished Autobiography*. New York: Harper and Row, 1979.

*Richards, Hylda. *Next Year Will Be Better*. Lincoln: University of Nebraska, 1985.

Romero, Patricia W. *Life Histories of African Women*. London, England: Ashfield, 1988.

Schreiner, B., editor. *A Snake with Ice Water: Prison Writings by South African Women*. Johannesburg, South Africa: COSAW, 1992.

*Seacole, Mary. *The Wonderful Adventures of Mrs. Seacole in Many Lands*. London, England: Oxford University, 1988.

Shan, Sharan-Jeet. *In My Own Name*. London, England: Women's Press, 1985.

*Sha'rawi, Huda. *Harem Years: The Memoirs of an Egyptian Feminist*. Translated by Margot Badran. London, England: Virago, 1986.

Shostak, Marjorie. *Nisa: The Life and Words of a !Kung Woman*. New Haven, CT: Harvard University, 1981.

*Sistren Theatre Collective. *Lionheart Gal: Life Stories of Jamaican Women*. London, England: Women's Press, 1986.

Smith, Mary Felice. *Baba of Karo: A Woman of the Muslim Hausa*. New Haven, CT: Yale University, 1980.

*Suleri, Sara. *Meatless Days*. Chicago, IL: University of Chicago, 1989.

Sunity Devee, Maharani of Cooch Behar. *The Autobiography of an Indian Princess*. London, England: J. Murray, 1921.

Suzman, Helen. *In No Uncertain Terms: A South African Memoir*. New York: Knopf, 1993.

Tabbara, Lina Mikdadi. *Surviving the Siege of Beirut: A Personal Account*. London, England: Onyx, 1983.

Tawil, Raymonda Hawa. *My Home, My Prison*. New York: Holt, 1980.

Tergeman, Sihan. *Daughter of Damascus: A memoir*. Translated by Andrea Rugh. Austin: University of Texas, 1994.

Waciuma, Charity. *Daughter of Mumbi*. Nairobi, Kenya: East African, 1974.

*Yu Lo-chin. *A Chinese Winter's Tale: An Autobiographical Fragment*. Translated by Rachel May and Zhu Zhiyu. Hong Kong: Renditions, 1986.

*Zhai Zhenhua. *Red Flower of China*. New York: Soho, 1993.

Commentary

Behar, Ruth. "Rage and Redemption: Reading the Life Story of a Mexican Marketing Woman." *Feminist Studies* 16.2 (summer 1990): 223–258.

Clayton, Cherry. "Post-Apartheid, Post-Feminist: Family and State in Prison Narratives by South African Women." *Kunapipi* 13.1–2 (1991): 136–144.

Foster, David William. "Narrative Persona in Eva Peron's *La razon de mi vida*." *Woman as Myth and Metaphor in Latin American Literature.* Columbia: University of Missouri, 1985. 63–77.

Geiger, Susan N. G. "Women's Life Histories: Method and Content." *Signs* 11.2 (winter 1986): 334–351.

Ibrahim, Huma. "The Autobiographical Content in the Works of South African Women Writers: The Personal and the Political." *Biography East and West: Selected Conference Papers.* Honolulu: University of Hawaii, 1989. 122–126.

Kaplan, Caren. "Resisting Autobiography: Out-Law Genres and Transnational Feminist Subjects." *De/Colonizing the Subject: The Politics of Gender in Women's Autobiography.* Minneapolis: University of Minnesota, 1992. 115–138.

Lambrech, Regine. "Three Black Women, Three Autobiographers." *Présence Africaine* 123 (1982): 136–143.

Lim, Shirley. "Semiotics, Experience, and the Material Self: An Inquiry into the Subject of the Contemporary Asian Woman Writer." *Women's Studies* 18 (1990): 153–175.

Lim, Shirley. "Up Against the Nationalist Canon: Women's War Memoirs from Malaysia and Singapore." *Journal of Commonwealth Literature* 29.1 (August 1993): 47–64.

Lionnet, Françoise. *Autobiographical Voices: Race, Gender, Self-Portraiture.* Ithaca, NY: Cornell University, 1989.

Marks, Shula. "The Context of Personal Narrative: Reflections on *Not Either an Experimental Doll: The Separate Worlds of Three South African Women*." *Interpreting Women's Lives: Feminist Theory and Personal Narratives.* Bloomington: Indiana University, 1989. 39–58.

Miaz, Magdalena, and Luis H. Pena. "Between Lines: Constructing the Political Self." *A/B: Auto/Biography Studies* 3.4 (summer 1988): 23–36.

Molloy, Sylvia. *At Face Value: Autobiographical Writing in Spanish America.* New York: Cambridge, 1991.

Neubauer, C. E. "Tradition and Change in Charity Waciuma's Autobiography *Daughter of Mumbi*." *World Literature Written in English* 25.2 (1985): 211–221.

Patai, Daphne. "Constructing a Self: A Brazilian Life Story." *Feminist Studies* 14.1 (spring 1988): 143–166.

Smith, Sidonie, and Julia Watson, editors. *De/Colonizing the Subject: The Politics of Gender in Women's Autobiography.* Minneapolis: University of Minnesota, 1992.

Warley, Linda. "Assembling Ingredients: Subjectivity in *Meatless Days*." *A/B: Auto/Biography Studies* 7.1 (spring 1991): 107–123.

Wright, Marcia. "Personal Narratives, Dynasties, and Women's Campaigns: Two Examples from Africa." *Interpreting Women's Lives: Feminist Theory and Personal Narratives.* Bloomington: Indiana University, 1989.

The Autobiography of a Chinese Girl by Hsieh Ping-ying (London, England: Pandora, 1986). First published in Chinese in 1936 and in this translation in 1943, this autobiography retells the life of a woman who grew up on the cusp of two worlds. Her father, a classical scholar, taught her to read, but she was nevertheless expected to follow the traditional path for women, including having her feet bound, an excruciating experience. She was an independent young woman, pursuing her education despite family objections, and became involved in politics, joining the army and becoming a propagandist. She describes being imprisoned by Chiang Kai-shek, her reentry into the military during the Japanese war, her motherhood, and the conflicts she felt, both personal and political. (This work was also translated as *Girl Rebel* by Adet and Anor Lin, the young daughters of Lin Yutang, and published in New York in 1940.)

Avellaneda, Gertrudis Gómez de. See **Gómez de Avellaneda, Gertrudis.**

B

Bâ, Mariama. Born in Dakar, Senegal, in 1929. Her mother died when she was young, and she was raised by maternal grandparents. Her father, who worked for the civil service and was the first minister of health appointed in Senegal, insisted she have a French education, and she did her first publishing—of two essays—when she attended the École Normal in Rufisque. She became involved in women's associations and issues and worked as a secretary and as a primary school teacher. She married Obeye Diop, a prominent politician, and had nine children before separating from him. Her novel *So Long a Letter* is said to be autobiographical. It won the first Noma Award for Publishing in Africa; she was celebrated as a representative of African writers at the Frankfurt Book Fair in October 1980, where she received the award. Her second novel, *Scarlet Song*, written while she was suffering from cancer, was published post-humously. She died in August 1981, less than a year after Europe discovered her. Many critics focus on the fact that both of her novels critique polygamous marriages, but those same works are also very much appreciative of Senegalese culture and critical of Western assumptions. Yet her feminism is undeniable: She describes *So Long a Letter* as "a cry coming from the heart of all women everywhere . . . there is a fundamental unity in all [women's] sufferings and in our desire for liberation and in our desire to cut off the chains which date from antiquity" (Harrell-Bond, 213).

Works

Scarlet Song. Translated by Dorothy S. Blair. Harlow, England: Longman, 1986.
So Long a Letter. Translated by Modupe Bode-Thomas. London, England: Heinemann, 1981.

Commentary

Bazin, Nancy Topping. "Feminism in the Literature of African Women." *The Black Scholar* 20.3–4 (summer-fall 1989): 8–17.

Blair, Dorothy S. *Senegalese Literature: A Critical History.* Boston, MA: Twayne, 1984.

Busia, Abena P. A. "Words Whispered Over Voids: A Context for Black Women's Rebellious Voices in the Novel of the African Diaspora." *Black Feminist Criticism and Critical Theory.* Greenwood, FL: Penkevill, 1988. 1–41.

Busia, Abena P. A. "Rebellious Women: Fictional Biographies—Nawal el Sa'adawi's *Woman at Point Zero* and Mariama Bâ's *So Long a Letter.*" *Motherlands: Women's Writings from Africa, the Caribbean, and South Asia.* New Brunswick, NJ: Rutgers University, 1992. 88–98.

Cham, Mbye Baboucar. "The Female Condition in Africa: A Literary Exploration by Mariama Bâ." *Current Bibliography on African Affairs* 17.1 (1985): 29–51.

Cham, Mbye B. "Contemporary Society and the Female Imagination: A Study of the Novels of Mariama Bâ." *African Literature Today* 15 (1987): 89–101.

d'Almeida, Irene Assiba. "The Concept of Choice in Mariama Bâ's Fiction." *Ngambika: Studies of Women in African Literature.* Trenton, NJ: Africa World Press, 1986. 161–171.

Flewellen, Elinor C. "Assertiveness vs. Submissiveness in Selected Works by African Women Writers." *Ba Shiru* 12.2 (1985): 3–18.

Harrell-Bond, Barbara. "Mariama Bâ, Winner of the First Noma Award for Publishing in Africa for Her Novel *Une si longue lettre.*" *African Book Publishing Record* 6.3–4 (1980): 209–214.

Innes, C. L. "Mothers or Sisters? Identity, Discourse, and Audience in the Writing of Ama Ata Aidoo and Mariama Bâ." *Motherlands: Women's Writings from Africa, the Caribbean, and South Asia.* New Brunswick, NJ: Rutgers University, 1992. 129–151.

McElaney-Johnson, Ann. "The Place of the Woman or the Woman Displaced in Mariama Bâ's *Une si longue lettre.*" *CLA Journal* 37.1 (September 1993): 19–28.

Makward, Edris. "Marriage, Tradition and Woman's Pursuit of Happiness in the Novels of Mariama Bâ." *Ngambika: Studies of Women in African Literature.* Trenton, NJ: Africa World Press, 1986. 271–281.

Miller, Christopher L. *Theories of Africans: Francophone Literature and Anthropology in Africa.* Chicago, IL: University of Chicago, 1990.

Mortimer, Mildred. *Journeys Through the French African Novel.* Portsmouth, NH: Heinemann, 1990.

Nwachukwu-Agbada, J. O. J. " 'One Wife for One Man': Mariama Bâ's Doctrine for Matrimony." *Modern Fiction Studies* 37.3 (autumn 1991): 561–573.

Ojo-Ade, Femi. "Still a Victim? Mariama Bâ's *Une si longue lettre.*" *African Literature Today* 12 (1987): 71–87.

Riesz, Janos, and Richard Bjornson. "Mariama Bâ's *Une si longue lettre*: An *Erziehungsroman.*" *Research in African Literatures* 22.1 (spring 1991): 27–43.

Schipper, Mineke. " 'Who Am I?' Fact and Fiction in African First-Person Narrative." *Research in African Literatures* 16.1 (spring 1985): 53–79.

Staunton, Cheryl Wall. "Mariama Bâ: Pioneer Senegalese Woman Novelist." *CLA Journal* 37.3 (March 1994): 328–335.

Stratton, Florence. "The Shallow Grave: Archetypes of Female Experience in African Fiction." *Research in African Literatures* 19.2 (1988): 143–169.

Baby Mother and the King of Swords: Short Stories by Lorna Goodison (Harlow, England: Longman, 1990). A collection of stories that explore the relations between men and women. In "The King of Swords" the narrator confronts an abusive man, knowing that once she has found a name for him, she will no longer be under his control. Other stories, such as "The Dolly Funeral," deal with childhood and others with what happens to children to make them into the dregs of society—as in "Shilling," which delves into a prostitute's past to find the wrenching origin of her current status. "The Big Shot" and "Bella Makes Life" are two approaches to the same theme, materialism and American values taking over and transforming Jamaicans' better natures. In the first story, a man goes to America to improve his fortunes and refuses to recognize the child he fathered or the woman he ran away from—though he will be haunted by them in spite of his rejection. Bella goes to America and comes back greedy and obsessed with getting money, abandoning her family in her mad dash toward heaven in the form of material culture. Funny, poignant, and compassionate stories full of fully realized characters and a narrative voice that speaks with Chekhovian wit.

Badr, Liyanah. Born in Jerusalem in the early 1950s to parents who were intellectuals and activists, she grew up in a turbulent world. In 1957, her father was arrested for his political beliefs, and her mother escaped to Syria. After some months, she and her sister were able to join her mother there, after which they moved to Egypt and Jordan, finally reuniting with her father after a general amnesty. She spent three years, 1960–1963, in an orphanage for Arab children, where she began to write. In 1969, she joined the Palestine Liberation Organization (PLO), working with Palestinian women in refugee camps in Jordan. She later worked as a journalist in Beirut while studying English literature at the university. She currently lives in Tunisia, where she writes stories, children's literature, and novels.

Works

A Balcony over the Fakihani. Translated by Peter Clark with Christopher Tingley. New York: Interlink, 1993.
A Compass for the Sunflower. Translated by Catherine Cobham. London, England: Women's Press, 1989.

Bakr, Salwa. Born in Egypt, she took degrees in management and drama criticism and has worked in such diverse positions as rationing inspector for the government and journalist. While a student, she was arrested for political activities and spent a short time in jail, an experience that she used as the basis for her first novel. She has lived in Beirut and Cyprus and currently lives in a suburb of Cairo, with her husband and daughter. Her fiction is feminist and politically acute, observant of gender and class relations in modern Egypt, making subtle use of irony and ambiguity.

Work

The Wiles of Men and Other Stories. London, England: Quartet, 1992.

A Balcony over the Fakihani by Liyanah Badr (New York: Interlink, 1993). Translation of *Shurfah 'ala al-Fakihani*, originally published in Arabic in 1983. Three novellas, with interwoven stories that deal with Palestinians living in war-torn Lebanon, recounting lives of three men and three women. One is a wounded prisoner of war, another a young woman who spends hours on end waiting for her turn at a water tap; others spend anxious days seeking missing loved ones. The book makes the war experience tangible by depicting the quotidian experiences of getting food and water, seeking shelter, caring for children, under horrific conditions, doing so in a narrative that weaves narrative voices in complex ways.

Bao Lord, Bette. See **Lord, Bette Bao.**

Baotown by Wang An-i (New York: W.W. Norton, 1989). "Naturally, this is just a tall tale, nothing to believe. It is only a story for one generation to tell the next" (vii). This deceptively simple tale, almost folkloric in tone, inter-weaves the lives of villagers in a Chinese town—Bao Renwen, the aspiring writer; Little Jade, homeless and resourceful; Picked-Up, the peddler; and Dregs, the child hero. The modern history of China subtly flows beneath the surface of the story, not related by dates or events so much as by the ways in which political and social upheaval are manifested in the daily life of villagers.

The Barren Years and Other Short Stories and Plays by Shih Shu-Ch'ing (San Francisco, CA: Chinese Materials Center, 1975). A collection that features stories and two plays. Barrenness is a recurrent theme in the work, as is cross-cultural tension and the absurdity of modern life. "Following the Clue" is a play that has a helpless, confused woman at its center; she is told by her husband to play the Boy Scout game of "follow the clue" to a location that doesn't exist. "When the Cowbell Rings" is about an intercultural marriage, in which an American academic uses his Chinese wife as an exhibit in his anthropology classroom; their friend, another anthropologist, fails to find a resting place between cultures. In her work, there is a pervasive sense of displacement and loss.

Barrios de Chungara, Domitila. Bolivian activist born in 1937, wife of a mine worker, mother of seven, and representative to the United Nations from the "Housewives' Committee of Siglo XX." Her testimony before the International Women's Year Tribunal, held in Mexico in 1975, bore dramatic witness to the ways that workers and their families are exploited in the Bolivian tin mines. Her *testimonio*, based on interviews and dialogues held at the time of the meeting in Mexico, exposes the effects of economic oppression on every aspect of the workers' lives and describes why and how she became an activist among the women of the mining village.

Work

Let Me Speak! Testimony of Domitila, A Woman of the Bolivian Mines. With Moema Viezzer. Translated by Victoria Ortiz. New York: Monthly Review, 1978.

Baumgartner's Bombay by Anita Desai (New York: Knopf, 1989). A story of an elderly Jewish exile who kindly takes in stray cats, relying on handouts from restaurants to feed them. When he reluctantly takes in a dangerous, drug-addicted German youth, he comes up against his past, back to the memories of his escape from the holocaust (in which his mother was not spared) and his years of internment as an enemy alien in British India. The intervention of the sullen and violent young addict puts an abrupt end to his life in exile. The view of India through Baumgartner's template, and the ironies created by its strange juxtapositions, makes for a moving and deeply interesting novel.

Bedford, Simi. Born in Nigeria, she now lives in London, where she has worked as a model and a writer for television and film. Her children's book *Yoruba Girl Dancing* explores the ways Africa is represented in English childhood culture and how an African girl adapts to and overcomes the racism and willful ignorance of stereotypes.

Work

Yoruba Girl Dancing. New York: Viking, 1992.

The Beggars' Strike, or, The Dregs of Society by Aminata Sow Fall (Harlow, England: Longman, 1986). The ironic story of a strike by beggars, a disenfranchised group who are able to destroy the dreams of a powerful politician. The beggars are all cleared from the streets in the interests of promoting the tourist trade, but the politician in charge finds he must observe the Islamic tradition of giving them alms if he is to realize his goal of high office. Caught in a double-bind—he has been ordered to remove the beggars by the president, but in order to gain his favor, he must distribute alms to them—he meets with failure. Ironically, it is the functionary who clears the beggars from the street who is most morally conflicted by the oppression implicit in the institutions of begging and of earning virtue through charity; he remembers with pain the poverty he and his mother endured when he was young. Fall reveals the self-serving nature of most social transactions in a book that is sharply funny and, while very short, rich with detail of place and character.

Commentary

Ajala, John D. "*The Beggars' Strike*: Aminata Sow Fall as a Spokeswoman for the Underprivileged." *CLA Journal* 34.2 (December 1990): 137–152.

Okeke-Ezigbo, Emeka. "Begging the Beggars: Restoration of the Dignity of Man in *The Beggars' Strike.*" *Neohelicon* 19.1 (1992): 307–322.

Trinh T. Minh-ha. "Aminata Sow Fall and the Beggars' Gift." *When the Moon Waxes Red: Representation, Gender, and Cultural Politics.* New York: Routledge, 1991. 169–183.

Bei, Ai. Born in Beijing, she practiced as a doctor in a provincial hospital before turning to writing full-time. She has published stories and novellas in prominent Chinese literary journals. In 1989, she traveled to the United States for an exchange visit sponsored by the U.S. Information Agency, and—at the time of the Tiananmen Square rebellion—she spoke out against the government's actions. In response, she was ordered to return to China, and the government suspended her wages. Rather than return, she has remained in the United States. A collection of her short stories that illustrate her dreamlike, highly subjective style is available in English translation.

Work

Red Ivy, Green Earth Mother. Translated by Howard Goldblatt. Salt Lake City, UT: Peregrine Smith Books, 1990.

Beka Lamb by Zee Edgell (London, England: Heinemann, 1982). The story of a young girl in Belize, told in flashback as she remembers the events leading to the death of a friend. She is having trouble in school and is in the habit of lying her way out of awkward situations, a habit her mother helps her cure by giving her a notebook to write in. Her friend, made pregnant by a young man who abandons her, loses her mind and is eventually killed in a hurricane. Beka's growing sense of self and of her critical ability to examine the world around her, fostered by her developing identity as a writer, is unfolded in a setting that reflects the many cultures of Belize.

Commentary

Brown, Bev E. L. "Mansong and Matrix: A Radical Experiment." *A Double Colonization: Colonial and Post-Colonial Women's Writing.* Mundelstrup, Denmark: Dangaroo, 1986. 68–79.

Down, Lorna. "Singing Her Own Song: Women and Selfhood in Zee Edgell's *Beka Lamb.*" *Ariel* 18.4 (October 1987): 39–50.

Flockemann, Miki. " 'Not-Quite Insiders and Not-Quite Outsiders': The 'Process of Womanhood' in *Beka Lamb, Nervous Conditions* and *Daughters of the Twilight.*" *Journal of Commonwealth Literature* 27.1 (1992): 37–47.

Gikandi, Simon. "Writing After Colonialism: *Crick Crack, Monkey* and *Beka Lamb.*" *Writing in Limbo: Modernism and Caribbean Literature.* Ithaca, NY: Cornell University, 1992. 197–230.

O'Callaghan, Evelyn. "Interior Schisms Dramatised: The Treatment of the 'Mad' Woman in the Work of Some Caribbean Novelists." *Out of the Kumbla: Women and Literature in the Caribbean.* Trenton, NJ: Africa World Press, 1990. 89–109.

Woodcock, Bruce. "Post-1975 Caribbean Fiction and the Challenge to English Litera-
    ture." *Critical Quarterly* 28 (winter 1986): 79–95.

Belgrave, Valerie. Born and raised in Trinidad, she studied at Sir George
Williams (Concordia) University in Montreal, Canada, earning a B.A. in painting and literature. She lives in Trinidad, where she is an artist and fabric designer, specializing in batik. Her one novel, *Ti Marie*, is a historical romance.

Work

Ti Marie. London, England: Heinemann, 1988.

Commentary

Harney, Steve. "Men Goh Respect All o' We: Valerie Belgrave's *Ti Marie* and the
    Invention of Trinidad." *World Literature Written in English* 30.2 (autumn 1990):
    110–119.
Tanifeani, William. "Interview with Valerie Belgrave, Novelist, Visual Artist." *Wasafiri*
    11 (1990): 24–25.

Belli, Gioconda. Born in Managua, Nicaragua, in 1948. At age fourteen she
went to Spain to finish her secondary education and then studied advertising in
Philadelphia, returning to Nicaragua after a four-year absence. She worked in
advertising until she became involved in the effort to overthrow the Somoza
dictatorship. She was also writing poetry, publishing her first collection, *Sobre
la grama,* in 1974. In 1975 she was forced into exile, living in Costa Rica with
her two daughters and there bearing a son and a second book of poetry, *Línea
de fuego.* After the Sandinista victory, she returned to Nicaragua and worked in
the party and for the government until 1986, when she started her novel *La
mujer habitatada* (*The Inhabited Woman*, 1994) and devoted herself to writing
full-time. Her poetry is at once feminist and political and concerned with the
body, sometimes drawing parallels between the urgency of sexual passion and
the desire for a woman's—and a country's—self-determination.

Works

From Eve's Rib. Translated by Steven White. Willimantic, CT: Curbstone Press, 1989;
    second edition, 1993.
The Inhabited Woman. Translated by Kathleen March. Willimantic, CT: Curbstone Press,
    1994.
Nicaragua in Reconstruction and at War: The People Speak. Translated by Marc Zim-
    merman. Minneapolis, MN: MEP Publications, 1985.
Nicaragua Water Fire. Warwick, England: Greville Press, 1989.

Commentary

Dawes, Greg. *Aesthetics and Revolution: Nicaraguan Poetry, 1979–1990*. Minneapolis:
    University of Minnesota, 1993.
Murray, Patricia. "A Place for Eve in the Revolution: Gioconda Belli and Rosario Mu-

rillo.'' *Knives and Angels: Women Writers in Latin America.* London, England: Zed, 1990. 176–197.

Randall, Margaret. *Risking a Somersault in the Air: Conversations with Nicaraguan Writers.* San Francisco: Solidarity, 1984.

Benitez, Sandra. A writer of Puerto Rican heritage, she grew up in Mexico, El Salvador, and Missouri. She is currently living in Edina, Minnesota, where she works as a creative writing teacher and is the author of a novel and several stories and essays.

Work

*A Place Where the Sea Remembers. Minneapolis, MN: Coffee House, 1993.

Bennett, Louise. Known fondly as ''Miss Lou,'' born on September 7, 1919, in Kingston, Jamaica, the only child of a dressmaker and a baker, all members of a lively extended family. Her father died when she was seven. Her mother was supportive of her interest in poetry, which she started to perform while at school; by 1943, she was performing her poetry on the first Jamaican radio station and began to publish a column for the *Gleaner.* In 1945, she won a British Council scholarship to study at the Royal Academy of Dramatic Art in London, where she later produced a Caribbean radio program for the British Broadcasting Corporation (BBC). Returning to Jamaica in 1955, she served as drama specialist for the Jamaica Social Welfare Commission. She has been awarded an M.B.E., the Order of Jamaica, and a D.Litt. from the University of the West Indies. She was one of the first writers to use Creole in her works and has had an enormous impact on Caribbean poetry and drama, though she was not recognized by the literary establishment as a poet until the 1960s.

Works

*Anancy and Miss Lou. Kingston, Jamaica: Sangster's, 1979.
Anancy Stories and Poems in Dialect Verse. Kingston, Jamaica: Gleaner, 1944.
Aunty Roachy Seh. Kingston, Jamaica: Sangster's, 1993.
Dialect Verses. Kingston, Jamaica: Herald, 1942.
Jamaica Labrish. Kingston, Jamaica: Sangster's, 1966.
Jamaican Dialect Poems. Kingston, Jamaica: Gleaner, 1948.
Jamaican Humour in Dialect. Kingston, Jamaica: Jamaica Press, 1943.
Laugh with Louise. Kingston, Jamaica: City Printery, 1961.
Lulu Says: Dialect Verse with Glossary. Kingston, Jamaica: Gleaner, 1952.
Miss Lulu Sez: A Collection of Dialect Poems. Kingston, Jamaica: Gleaner, 1949.
Selected Poems. Kingston, Jamaica: Sangster's, 1982.

Commentary

Cooper, Carolyn. ''Noh Lickle Twang: An Introduction to the Poetry of Louise Bennett.'' *World Literature Written in English* 17 (April 1978): 317–327.

Gloudon, Barbara. "The Hon. Louise Bennett, O. J.: Fifty Years of Laughter." *Jamaica Journal* 19.3 (1986): 2–10.
Scott, Dennis. "Bennett on Bennett." *Caribbean Quarterly* 14.1–2 (1968): 97–101.

Benson, Mary. Born in Pretoria, South Africa, in 1919. After serving in North Africa during World War II, she became a political activist, living in London and New York as well as South Africa, working for political rights of blacks in South Africa and South West Africa (later Namibia), and earning her keep as a journalist. Because of her political stance, she was forced into exile in 1966. She wrote a number of nonfiction works on the South African situation, wrote political plays and documentaries for the BBC, and published one novel and an autobiography.

Works

At the Still Point. Boston, MA: Gambit, 1969.
A Far Cry: The Making of a South African. New York: Viking, 1989.

Berji Kristin: Tales from the Garbage Hills by Latife Tekin (New York: Marion Boyars, 1993). A magical realist variation on the social realism frequently favored by Turkish novelists. Tekin's story takes place in a community that arises overnight from the detritus of urban life, forming up houses and streets out of scrap on the hills of garbage at the periphery of a large city. Here the wind blows constantly, sometimes lifting the roofs off the houses and carrying away the babies whose cradles are suspended from them. The chemical factories nearby supply the community with warm, blue-tinted water, and a snow of white flakes falls from their chimneys, making the residents sick. But like all communities, this one has its characters, its leaders, and its storytellers. In spite of its illegal and impermanent status, and the government's efforts to destroy it, it becomes anchored firmly through the stories that its inhabitants spin. This novel, unusual both in its folkloric, magic realist style and in its use of colloquial language, was very popular in Turkey when it was published in 1984.

Between Two Worlds by Simone Schwarz-Bart (New York: Harper, 1981). Translation of *Ti Jean L'Horizon*, first published in French in 1979. This novel follows the adventures of Ti Jean L'Horizon, who seeks to find the sun and, to do this, must travel from Guadeloupe to Africa, France, and finally through the land of the dead to bring it back. It is an epic that explores the notion of alienation, rootedness, and renewal as variant responses to the displacements of the African Diaspora, written in a style that is poetic, mythic, and rich in imagery and allusions.

Commentary

Mudimbe-Boyi, Elisabeth. "The Poetics of Exile and Errancy in *Le Baobab fou* by Ken Bugul and *Ti Jean L'Horizon* by Simone Schwarz-Bart." *Yale French Studies* 83 (June 1993): 196–212.

Shelton, Marie-Denise. "Literature Extracted: A Poetic of Daily Life." *Callaloo* 15.1 (winter 1992): 167–178.

A Bewitched Crossroad by Bessie Head (New York: Paragon House, 1986). This historical novel retells the history of Botswana, "bewitched" because in spite of the crossing and recrossing of tribes and the machinations of colonial powers it remained "black man's country." "The land eluded the colonial era. The forces of the scramble for Africa passed through it like a huge and destructive storm that passed on to other lands" (196). Her tale draws on accounts of the past, both oral and written, and though it involves fictional characters and their lives, the drama belongs to history itself. Head uses her characters to demonstrate historical events rather than use history as a backdrop. This unusual mingling of forms, which often violates the reader's expectations, challenges Western notions of the past and how we come to know it.

Bildungsroman. A number of works by third world women might be classified as *bildungsromane*, novels about the education and moral upbringing of a child, about coming of age and making the ethical choices that growing up entails. However, unlike the classic European *bildungsroman*, one choice that most heroines of third world coming of age stories must make is a conscious decision about which culture they will claim as their own. In many cases, their educations—based on European models and part of the colonial enterprise—are pulling them away from their roots, and they must choose whether to accept uprooting or fight it. Merle Hodge's books are particularly concerned with the child who must fight to affirm her cultural background against the claims of an educational establishment that seeks to improve her lot in life by erasing her own cultural identity. In other cases, their families expect their children to comply with traditional strictures or parental authority that are stifling or conflict with their growing sense of self. The heroine of Zaynab Alkali's novel *The Stillborn* must struggle to realize her potential against expectations that could render her dreams stillborn. Other heroines cope with the conflicting claims made on them by different constituencies within their cross-cultural lives lived on the boundaries, often a battle waged at school, where those claims become insistent. Merle Hodge finds this a natural setting for a postcolonial narrative. In an interview about her own books, she argues, "I've often thought of those child protagonists as symbols, as representative of the Caribbean culture in its infancy. So the impact of the educational system on the child is really an exploration of the impact of the educational system on the budding culture, because the culture is new and it hasn't been given a name and it didn't get recognized as a culture" (Balutansky, 653). In that sense, then, the postcolonial *bildungsroman* can be seen as a novel about the postcolonial culture affirming its own identity as well as about individuals achieving independence and a sense of self.

Works

*Alkali, Zaynab. *The Stillborn*. Harlow, England: Longman, 1989.
*Bedford, Simi. *Yoruba Girl Dancing*. New York: Viking, 1992.
*Cheong, Fiona. *The Scent of the Gods*. New York: Norton, 1991.
*Cliff, Michelle. *Abeng*. Trumansburg, NY: Crossing Press, 1984.
*Collins, Merle. *Angel*. London, England: Women's Press, 1987.
*Dangarembga, Tsitsi. *Nervous Conditions*. Seattle, WA: Seal, 1989.
*Edgell, Zee. *Beka Lamb*. London, England: Heinemann, 1982.
*Freed, Lynn. *Home Ground*. New York: Summit, 1986.
*Hodge, Merle. *Crick Crack, Monkey*. London, England: Heinemann, 1981.
*Hodge, Merle. *For the Life of Laetitia*. New York: Farrar, Straus, Giroux, 1993.
*Kincaid, Jamaica. *Annie John*. New York: Farrar, Straus, Giroux, 1985.
*Marshall, Paule. *Brown Girl, Brownstones*. New York: Random House, 1959.

Commentary

Balutansky, Kathleen M. "We Are All Activists: An Interview with Merle Hodge."
    Callaloo 12 (fall 1989): 651–662.

The Blindfold Horse: Memories of a Persian Girlhood by Shusha
Guppy (London, England: Heinemann, 1988). A nostalgic memoir of a privileged childhood in a wealthy household in Teheran. She likens her home to one
in a nineteenth-century Russian novel, and her memoir contains a certain lingering wistfulness for the grandeur of prerevolutionary times. Her upbringing
was traditional, and its ceremonies and textures are lovingly re-created, but she
was also educated along Western lines and sympathetic to the modernization
schemes of the shah. She mentions the growing political restiveness without
commenting much on it and in retrospect finds nothing good in the revolution.
There is a sense that she is longing for a vanished way of life, and she says, of
her leaving for higher education in Paris and almost turning back, "I just did
not have the courage to change my mind. All my future life was shaped by that
one piece of cowardice. . . . I did not know how hard I would have to work ever
after to earn a fraction of that love from others, which was given to me freely
without asking, and which I was leaving behind and discarding carelessly"
(242). The book is most interesting in describing experiences such as the family's summer camp in the countryside or visits to the women's baths, least
satisfying in the strange absences of political or social analysis. Iran's past is
colored with the nostalgic glow of a fondly remembered childhood.

Bloom, Valerie. Born in Clarendon, Jamaica, in 1956, she went to school in
Frankfield and worked as a librarian for a year before attending teacher's college
in Kingston, after which she taught for several years. She won a national medal
for a poem written in Jamaican Creole in 1978. She then went to England in
1979, earned a B.A. at the University of Kent, specializing in African and Caribbean literature, and then became a multicultural arts officer in Manchester,

teaching and lecturing on folk traditions in the arts. She has performed her work in England and Jamaica.

Work

Teach Mi, Tell Mi. London, England: Bogle l'Ouverture, 1983.

Blouin, Andrée. Born in the Congo in 1921, she was the daughter of a Belgian father and an African mother, who was forced to place her in a Dickensian orphanage in Brazzaville, where she first became a rebel against colonial domination. She was an activist in the Congolese independence movement, the subject of her memoir.

Work

*My Country, Africa: Autobiography of the Black Pasionaria. With Jean MacKellar. New York: Praeger, 1983.

Bodies of Water by Michelle Cliff (London, England: Methuen, 1990). Stories told in a spare but intense style, full of clear moments of images recollected, human gestures made or not made. Though each is a separate story, they overlap in interesting ways, each one carrying within it buried remnants of the others. The title story is a touching and vivid retelling of love and separation, about an elderly woman whose friend and lover has died, and about a woman who moves into her elderly brother's house, contemplating ways in which she betrayed him in childhood, when she didn't defend him against their homophobic parents. The last, brief story tells how a man keeps the small relics of buried pasts on an altar, maintains a Book of the Dead, and sings the ghosts to sleep. A poetic and delicately intersecting set of stories that explore the connections and disconnections of people's lives and the necessity of telling one's history.

Bombal, María Luisa. Born in Viña del Mar, Chile, on June 8, 1909 (some sources say 1910), to a family of Argentines who had fled political oppression in the midnineteenth century. She lived in Paris from 1922 to 1931, where she studied at the Sorbonne, moving to Buenos Aires after a short stay in Chile (where she met Neruda, who teased her about her French elegance), and finally settling in the United States. Her most famous work, *The Final Mist*, was published in Argentina by Victoria Ocampo's press, Sur. In Argentina, she was a part of the circle that formed around Sur and was acquainted with Alfonsina Storni, Ocampo, and Borges. After a couple of failed marriages and a scandalous incident in which she shot a man in the street in Santiago, she moved to New York, where she wrote film scripts, worked as a translator, and eventually remarried. After spending the years 1940 to 1973 in the United States, she returned to live in Chile in her last years of life, where she died in 1980. She is remembered as an important figure of the Latin American avant-garde.

Works

House of Mist. New York: Farrar, Straus, 1947.
*New Islands and Other Stories. New York: Farrar, Straus, Giroux, 1982.
The Shrouded Woman. New York: Farrar, Straus, 1948.

Commentary

Adams, Michael Ian. *Three Authors of Alienation: Bombal, Onetti, Carpentier.* Austin:
University of Texas, 1975.
Agosín, Marjorie. "María Luisa Bombal: Biography of a Story-Telling Woman." *Knives
and Angels: Women Writers in Latin America.* London, England: Zed, 1990. 26–
35.
Borinsky, Alicia. "The Lucidity of Inaction: María Luisa Bombal." *Theoretical Fables:
The Pedagogical Dream in Contemporary Latin American Fiction.* Philadelphia:
University of Pennsylvania, 1993. 104–117.
Ichiishi, Barbara F. "Death and Desire in *The Shrouded Woman*." *Latin American Lit-
erary Review* 17.33 (January-June 1989): 17–28.
Kostopulos-Cooperman, Celeste. *The Lyrical Vision of Maria Luisa Bombal.* London,
England: Tamesis, 1988.
Levine, Linda Gould. "María Luisa Bombal from a Feminist Perspective." *Revista In-
teramericana* 4 (1974): 148–161.
Meyer, Doris. " 'Feminine' Testimony in the Works of Teresa de la Parra, María Luisa
Bombal, and Victoria Ocampo." *Contemporary Women Authors of Latin Amer-
ica.* New York: Brooklyn College, 1983. 3–15.
Smith, Verity. "Dwarfed by Snow White: Feminist Revisions of Fairy Tale Discourse
in the Narrative of María Luisa Bombal and Dulce Maria Loynaz." *Feminist
Readings on Spanish and Latin American Literature.* Lewiston, NY: Mellon,
1991. 137–149.
Williams, Lorna V. "*The Shrouded Woman*: Marriage and Its Constraints in the Fiction
of María Luisa Bombal." *Latin American Literary Review* 10.20 (1982): 21–30.

Borinsky, Alicia. Poet, novelist, and critic, born and raised in Buenos Aires,
Argentina, in a family of East European exiles who fled the pogroms in Russia
and the Nazis in Poland. She began to write poetry at an early age. In 1966,
she left the country in the wake of a military coup and studied literature in the
United States. She maintains literary and family ties in Argentina and is at home
in the United States, Argentina, and Europe. She has published works of criticism, poetry, and novels.

Works

*Mean Woman. Translated by Cola Franzen. Lincoln: University of Nebraska, 1993.
Timorous Women. Translated by Cola Franzen. Peterborough, England: Spectacular Diseases, 1992.

Borrowed Tongue by T'ao Yang (Hong Kong: Renditions, 1986). An autobiographical narrative told by a woman to her children about her difficult relationship with her own mother and her search for a sense of belonging—

belonging to a place, to a culture, to a family. The revolution split her family, her mother and some siblings remaining on the mainland, her father and several children moving to Taiwan. She even has difficulty knowing what language is her own, as her mother spoke Suchowese and her father Mandarin. The book chronicles her life, in a highly personal, intimate style, and ends with her returning to see her dying mother, seeking but not finding a reconciliation. She finally turns to her children and their future for a sense of place and belonging.

The Boy Sandwich by Beryl Gilroy (London, England: Heinemann, 1989). Portrays the effects of life in Britain on three generations of a West Indian family, scarred by racial conflict and a longing for their past sense of security in the Caribbean. A series of events—the sale of an old painting, which brings in money, an arsonist's fire, which kills many and injures the narrator's girl-friend—prompts the family's return to the island. However, once there, the hero finds he does not belong there, that he is an outsider, and admits to himself, "I want to call myself British for the first time in my life." An engaging story, written for young readers, which explores the conflicts of identity among second-generation blacks in Britain.

Brand, Dionne. Born in 1953 in Guayguayare, Trinidad, where she was educated through high school. In 1970, she moved to Canada, where she graduated from the University of Toronto in 1975 with a degree in English and philosophy. She worked as information and communications coordinator in Grenada for a year until the American invasion of October 1983. Returning to Canada, she worked as an activist in black community work in Toronto, providing advocacy, education, and counseling for women immigrants. She has given readings of her poetry on stage, television, and radio and has published poems in publications such as *Spear* as well as collections of her poetry and fiction. Her work is critical, poetic and political, concerned with the erasures of history and the dislocations of the African Diaspora.

Works

Chronicles of the Hostile Sun. Toronto, Canada: Williams-Wallace, 1984.
Earth Magic. Toronto, Canada: Kids Can Press 1979.
'Fore Day Morning. Toronto, Canada: Khoisan Artists, 1987.
No Language Is Neutral. Toronto, Canada: Coach House, 1990.
Rivers Have Sources, Trees Have Roots: Speaking of Racism. With Krisantha Sri Bhag-
    giyadatta. Toronto, Canada: Cross Cultural Communications, 1986.
Sans Souci and Other Stories. Ithaca, NY: Firebrand, 1989.
Winter Epigrams and Epigrams to Ernesto Cardinal in Defense of Claudia. Toronto,
    Canada: Williams-Wallace, 1983.

Commentary

Brathwaite, Edward Kamau. "Dionne Brand's *Winter Epigrams*." *Canadian Literature*
    105 (summer 1985): 18–30.

Hunter, Lynette. "After Modernism: Alternative Voices in the Writings of Dionne Brand, Clair Harris and Marlene Philip." *University of Toronto Quarterly* 62.2 (winter 1992): 256–280.

Breath, Eyes, Memory by Edwidge Danticat (New York: Soho, 1994). A novel about the loss of trust and the lingering effects of sexual abuse among four generations of Haitian women. The narrator, raised in Haiti by a loving aunt, unwillingly joins her mother in New York, where she has been trying to escape painful memories of Haiti and earn a living for herself and her daughter. Sophie learns that she is a child of a brutal rape that still haunts her mother; she herself is traumatized when her mother, carrying on tradition, tests her virginity repeatedly, a practice Sophie opposes by breaking her own hymen forcibly, scarring herself so that sexual relations become unbearably painful. After marriage she returns to the island with her infant daughter to come to terms with the sense of belonging she has lost, but her relationship with her mother— and her mother's own brutalized sense of self—cannot be healed. The storytelling traditions passed down from mother to daughter carry not only a sense of connection but also a shared pain. "There is always a place where nightmares are passed on through generations like heirlooms" (234). The sharing, though, has a liberating function: The grandmother tells the narrator, "[I]f you listen closely in the night, you will hear your mother telling a story and at the end of the tale, she will ask you this question: '*Ou libéré?*' Are you free, my daughter?" (234). An impressive debut novel.

Breeze, Jean Binta. First female "dub" poet, born on March 11, 1956, in Pattyhill, Jamaica, one of four sisters. She spent her early years with her grandparents who were farmers; her mother studied to be a midwife and her father worked as a public health inspector. She attended school in Hanover, studying Spanish, geography, and English literature, topics in which she took A level exams. She married one of her former teachers, the Welshman Brian Breese, and they had a son before divorcing in 1978. She studied drama at the Jamaican School of Drama, became a teacher of English, geography, Spanish, and drama for five years, and worked two years with the Jamaican Cultural Development Commission as a coordinator of their speech and literacy program. She became a Rastafarian for a time and moved to the Clarendon Hills to live a deliberately traditional and politically aware life; there she had a daughter. She began to perform her work in 1983, earning a reputation as a dub poet in Jamaica before performing for the first time in Britain in 1985. She has since toured in Europe, North America, and the Caribbean. She has also recorded her poetry and written for television and theater and was featured in a film, *Moods and Moments*, about her life and work. She now divides her time between London and the Caribbean.

Works

Riddym Ravings and Other Poems. London, England: Race Today, 1988.
*Spring Cleaning. London, England: Virago, 1992.

Commentary

"An Interview with Jean Breeze." *Commonwealth Essays and Studies* 8.2 (spring 1986): 51–58.

Cooper, Carolyn. "Words Unbroken by the Beat: The Performance Poetry of Jean Binta Breeze and Mikey Smith." *Wasafiri* 8–9.11 (1989): 7–13.

Morris, Mervyn. "Gender in Some Performance Poems." *Critical Quarterly* 35.1 (spring 1993): 78–84.

Stuart, Andrea. "Riddym Ravings" [interview with Jean Binta Breeze]. *Marxism Today* (November 1988): 44–45.

The Bride Price by Buchi Emecheta (New York: Braziller, 1976). The story of an Igbo girl and her coming of age. She wants to be a teacher and plans to marry a teacher who is descended from slaves, a man who, because of his heritage, is an outcast. She opposes village wisdom and marries the teacher and unwittingly becomes the basis of stories that reinforce traditional ways in her village, a narrative twist that turns the subject around at the conclusion. The woman who tried to create her own story has become the proof of the traditional wisdom she struggled against.

The Bridge of Beyond by Simone Schwarz-Bart (New York: Atheneum, 1974). Translation of *Pluie et vent sur Télumée Miracle,* first published in 1972. A novel that focuses on the strength and endurance of island women who counter poverty with self-reliance, female solidarity, and love for life. The plot is intricately threaded with multiple strands of the cycle of birth, struggle, and rebirth. Themes include slavery and its persistence in modern times, black identity, and the matrilineal nature of Caribbean society. The language of the novel is remarkable in its allusiveness and poetry.

Commentary

Busia, Abena P. A. "Words Whispered over Voids: A Context for Black Women's Rebellious Voices in the Novel of the African Diaspora." *Black Feminist Criticism and Critical Theory.* Greenwood, FL: Penkevill, 1988. 1–41.

Omerod, Beverley. "The Boat and the Tree: Simone Schwarz-Bart's *The Bridge of Beyond.*" *An Introduction to the French Caribbean Novel.* London, England: Heinemann, 1985. 108–131.

Scarboro, Ann Armstrong. "A Shift Toward the Inner Voice and Creolité in the French Caribbean Novel." *Callaloo* 15.1 (winter 1992): 12–29.

Scharfman, Ronnie. "Mirroring and Mothering in Simone Schwarz-Bart's *Pluie et vent sur Télumée Miracle* and Jean Rhys's *Wide Sargasso Sea.*" *Yale French Studies* 62 (1981): 88–106.

Wilson, Elizabeth Betty. "History and Memory in *Un Plat de porc aux bananes vertes* and *Pluie et vent sur Télumée Miracle.*" *Callaloo* 15.1 (winter 1992): 179–189.

Brodber, Erna. Sister of Velma Pollard, born in Woodside, Jamaica, in 1940, the daughter of a farmer and a teacher, both of whom were active in local community affairs and cultural activities. Before starting secondary school, she already had published three stories in the *Weekly Times*. After high school, she worked in the civil service, took a B.A. honors degree from the University of the West Indies in history, taught history in Trinidad at a high school for girls, then returned to Jamaica to become a social worker and children's officer for the Ministry of Youth and Community Development. In 1967 she went to the United States with a Ford Foundation predoctoral scholarship and earned an M.Sc. in sociology, joining the Institute of Social and Economic Research as a lecturer. In connection with her work as a sociologist, she has written several sociological studies focusing on children, reggae, housing, and the perception of women in Jamaica. She has written for radio and theater as well as publishing her two well-received novels. The stream-of-consciousness style of her first novel is striking; her second won the 1989 Commonwealth Writers' Prize. Her novels are accomplished both in their embodiment of Caribbean experiences and landscapes and in their literary inventiveness.

Works

*Jane and Louisa Will Soon Come Home. London, England: New Beacon Books, 1980.
Myal. London, England: New Beacon Books, 1988.

Commentary

Brodber, Erna. *Perceptions of Caribbean Women: Towards a Documentation of Stereotypes.* Cave Hill, Barbados: University of the West Indies, 1982.
Cooper, Carolyn. "The Fertility of the Gardens of Women." *New Beacon Review* 2–3 (1986): 139–147.
Nelson-McDermott, Catherine. "Myal-ing Criticism: Beyond Colonizing Dialectics." *Ariel* 24.4 (October 1993): 53–67.
O'Callaghan, Evelyn. "Rediscovering the Natives of My Person." *Jamaica Journal* 16.3 (1984): 61–64.
Puri, Shalini. "An 'Other' Realism: Erna Brodber's *Myal.*" *Ariel* 24.3 (July 1993): 95–115.
Tiffin, Helen. "Cold Hearts and (Foreign) Tongues: Recitation and the Reclamation of the Female Body in the Works of Erna Brodber and Jamaica Kincaid." *Callaloo* 16.4 (fall 1993): 909–921.
Walker-Johnson, Joyce. "Autobiography, History and the Novel: Erna Brodber's *Jane and Louisa Will Soon Come Home.*" *Journal of West Indian Literature* 3.1 (January 1989): 47–59.
Woodcock, Bruce. "Post-1975 Caribbean Fiction and the Challenge to English Literature." *Critical Quarterly* 28 (winter 1986): 79–95.

Brown Girl, Brownstones by Paule Marshall (New York: Random House, 1959). The story of Selina Boyce, daughter of Barbadian immigrants to New York, her coming of age, and growing awareness of the tensions she and her community face. Her father, a weak-willed and pleasure-loving man, is unable to make his way; his wife, the strong and unswerving Sella, works constantly, driven to buy a brownstone and rent out rooms to maximize her investment, planning professional futures for her daughters. Selina, who rejects her mother's eagerness to make herself successful in a white world, still is her mother's daughter, and it is with her strength and endurance that Selina weathers her first encounter with racism. She ultimately decides to return to Barbados to claim her identity.

Commentary

Christian, Barbara. "Sculpture and Space: The Interdependency of Character and Culture in the Novels of Paule Marshall." *Black Women Novelists: The Development of a Tradition, 1892–1976.* Westport, CT: Greenwood, 1980. 80–136.

Eke, Ebele. "Beyond the Myth of Confrontation: A Comparative Study of African and African-American Female Protagonists." *Ariel* 17.4 (1986): 139–152.

Schneider, Deborah. "A Feminine Search for Selfhood: Paule Marshall's *Brown Girl, Brownstones.*" *The Afro-American Novel Since 1960.* Amsterdam, Netherlands: Gruner, 1982. 53–74.

Bugul, Ken. The pen name of Marietou M'Baye, a Senegalese sociologist. Born on November 28, 1948, in Louga, Senegal, she attended the University of Dakar and studied in Paris. She now lives in Togo, where she has worked as a program officer for the International Planned Parenthood Foundation. She is the author of an autobiography that explores her status as both a woman and a colonial subject and one novel, thus far unavailable in English translation, *La Chute des nuages.*

Work

The Abandoned Baobab: The Autobiography of a Senegalese Woman. Translated by Marjolijn de Jager. Brooklyn: Lawrence Hill, 1991.

Commentary

Mortimer, Mildred. *Journeys Through the French African Novel.* Portsmouth, NH: Heinemann, 1990.

Mudimbe-Boyi, Elisabeth. "The Poetics of Exile and Errancy in *Le Baobab fou* by Ken Bugul and *Ti Jean L'Horizon* by Simone Schwarz-Bart." *Yale French Studies* 83 (June 1993): 196–212.

The Bungalow by Lynn Freed (New York: Poseidon, 1993). Sequel to *Home Ground,* this novel recounts the return of the now-grown-up Ruth to South Africa and the arms of her aging parents. She is escaping again, this time from a disastrous marriage. She meets and falls in love with Hugh, an older academic with a bungalow by the sea, where she goes to live. He is murdered, senselessly, by a servant's drunken husband, and Ruth discovers she is pregnant. She stays on in South Africa until Hugh's grown son arrives to take possession, and she goes on to a new life in England. The novel is told in a series of nested flashbacks, from the point in the present when Ruth brings her grown daughter back to see the bungalow. As in *Home Ground,* the novelist is concerned with identity and with family relationships more than she is with politics or race issues in

South Africa. The final image of the bungalow, inhabited by a wealthy Lebanese family that has fortified it with security alarms and shark nets at the beach, has a kind of ironic nostalgia to it, a Cherry Orchard sense of the loss of privilege.

Burmese Family by Mi Mi Khaing (London, England: Longmans, Green, 1946). This autobiography is an account of Burmese life, written for the outsider. The author is more concerned with describing the Burmese culture in ethnographic terms than in developing her own life story. Still, it is a sure-footed and interesting account of life in a country that is little known to most Westerners. Interestingly, she comments that women have always enjoyed civil and property rights in traditional Burmese society. This account ends with the Japanese invasion in 1942.

Busia, Abena P. A. Born in Accra, Ghana, in 1953 and as a child lived in Ghana, Holland, and Mexico before her family settled in England. Her secondary schooling was in Oxford, after which she read for a B.A. in English at St. Anne's College, earning a degree in 1976. She earned a Ph.D. in social anthropology at St. Antony's College. She currently teaches at Rutgers in the English Department and is the author of short stories and poetry as well as criticism.

Work

*Testimonies of Exile. Trenton, NJ: Africa World Press, 1990.

Commentary

Busia, Abena P. A. ''Words Whispered Over Voids: A Context for Black Women's Rebellious Voices in the Novel of the African Diaspora.'' *Black Feminist Criticism and Critical Theory.* Greenwood, FL: Penkevill, 1988. 1–41.
Peterson, Kirsten Holst and Anna Rutherford, editors. *A Double Colonization: Colonial and Post-Colonial Women's Writing.* Mundelstrup, Denmark: Dangaroo, 1986.

The Butcher's Wife by Li Ang (San Francisco, CA: North Point, 1986). Translation from Chinese of *Sha Fu.* A brutal and powerful tale of cruelty, hunger, culminating in an act of murder by a brutalized wife against her cruelly abusive husband. Set in coastal Taiwan and based on a news account of an event that happened in Shanghai in the 1930s, this frank novel was criticized for its vivid portrayal of sexual violence but was awarded a prize by the *United Daily News,* which named it the best novel of the year.

Commentary

Chien, Ying-ying. ''From Utopian to Dystopian World: Two Faces of Feminism in Contemporary Taiwanese Women's Fiction.'' *World Literature Today* (winter 1994): 35–42.

C

Cambridge, Joan. Born and still lives in Guyana, where she has worked as a journalist and public relations officer. She has traveled extensively and has lived in the United States, Germany, and the United Kingdom. She has published one novel thus far, a funny and touching look at an immigrant's experience in New York.

Work

*Clarise Cumberbatch Want to Go Home. New York: Ticknor and Fields, 1987.

Campobello, Nellie. Born on November 7, 1909 (some sources say 1912), in Villa Ocampo, Mexico, a town her landowning family had helped to settle in the seventeenth century. Her father died in battle in the revolution, and her mother remarried Stephen Campbell, a doctor from Boston, whose last name Nellie adapted to Campobello. Because of the unsettled times and frequent moves, Nellie was taught at home by her mother, but in 1922 she entered the Escuela Inglesa in Mexico City, where she developed an interest in ballet. She became an authority on dance and traveled the country, giving performances and collecting indigenous dances. She founded the National School of Dance and the Ballet of Mexico City as well as the renowned Ballet Folklorico. She is the author of one of the first books to be published on folkloric dance and contributed much research to the field; she also wrote some poetry, a history of Pancho Villa's military campaigns, a memoir of her mother, and a powerful and poetic account of the Mexican revolution seen from a child's viewpoint; these last two works have been published together in English translation.

Work

Cartucho; and, My Mother's Hands. Translated by Doris Meyer and Irene Matthews. Austin: University of Texas, 1988.

Commentary

Meyer, Doris. "Divided Against Herself: The Early Poetry of Nellie Campobello." *Revista de Estudios Hispánicos* 20.2 (May 1986): 51–63.

Campos, Julieta. Born in Cuba in 1932, Campos was educated in France and moved to Mexico when she was twenty-three; she has remained there ever since. She has published volumes of literary criticism and several novels and has translated works on history and psychology from French and English. She served as president of the PEN club of Mexico and was editor of the *Revista de la Universidad de Mexico*. Literature and literary criticism are permeable categories in her work, not readily distinguishable; her novels are experiments that test literature and language in challenging ways.

Works

The Fear of Losing Eurydice. Translated by Leland H. Chambers. Normal, IL: Dalkey Archive Press, 1993.
She Has Reddish Hair and Her Name Is Sabina. Translated by Leland H. Chambers. Athens: University of Georgia, 1993.

Can Xue. See **Ts'an-hsueh.**

Cardinal, Marie. French novelist, born in Algeria in 1929. She has written a number of novels that treat the theme of women, language, and identity, the most famous of which is *Les mots pour le dire* (*The Words to Say It*) in which her colonial childhood, and its loss, is an important aspect of the narrator's growing mental illness, something she has to come to terms with in order to heal.

Work

The Words to Say It. Translated by Pat Goodheart. Cambridge, MA: VanVactor and Goodheart, 1983.

Commentary

Lionnet, Françoise. "Métissage, Emancipation, and Female Textuality in Two Franco-phone Writers." *Life/Lines: Theorizing Women's Autobiography*. Ithaca, NY: Cornell University, 1988. 260–278.
Lionnet, Françoise. *Autobiographical Voices: Race, Gender, Self-Portraiture*. Ithaca, NY: Cornell University, 1989.
Woodhull, Winifred. *Transfigurations of the Maghreb: Feminism, Decolonization, and Literatures*. Minneapolis: University of Minnesota, 1993.

Cartucho; and, My Mother's Hands by Nellie Campobello (Austin: University of Texas, 1988). Two short novels, written in brief vignettes, that convey the extraordinary events the author witnessed during the Mexican revolution in the north of Mexico, where Pancho Villa was a personal hero and a presence in the village where she lived. *Cartucho,* originally published in 1931, means literally "cartridge," referring to the emotions at the time of the revolution, always unpredictable and ready to blow up; the character of that name is both sentimental and victim of a random and violent act. The second, shorter novella, *My Mother's Hands,* is an elegiac and almost hagiographic memorial to the author's mother, in which the horror of war is always near at hand. Campobello, the only woman among the most well-known chroniclers of the revolution, uses a disconcertingly delicate touch as she portrays horrifying images of war.

Casely-Hayford, Adelaide. Born in 1868 in Sierra Leone of a Fanti mother and a Yorkshireman father. They moved to England in 1872, settling in Jersey, where she was educated first by a governess and later at the Jersey Ladies' College. At seventeen she went to study music in Germany for three years at a branch of the Stuttgart Conservatory before returning to Sierra Leone in 1879. There with her sister she founded a Girls' Vocational School in Freetown for adult African women. In 1903 she married Joseph E. Casely-Hayford, a lawyer, writer, and activist. Their daughter, Gladys, was born a year later in Axim, Gold Coast, and the marriage virtually ended a few years later, though they never actually divorced. She worked hard to raise funds in both England and America (where she lived from 1920 to 1923) for an Industrial and Technical Training School for Girls, which was in operation from 1923 to 1940. She wrote a few short stories (including "Mista Courifer," frequently anthologized) and articles as well as her memoirs and poems. She died in 1959.

Work

Mother and Daughter: Memoirs and Poems. With Gladys Casely-Hayford. Sierra Leone: Sierra Leone University, 1983.

Commentary

Cromwell, Adelaide M. *An African Victorian Feminist: The Life and Times of Adelaide Smith Casely-Hayford, 1868–1960.* London: F. Cass, 1986.

Casely-Hayford, Gladys May. She wrote under the name Aquah Laluah. Born in Axim, Ghana, in 1904, the only child of Adelaide Casely-Hayford, she was educated in Great Britain where, for a time, she was hospitalized with a mental breakdown. She returned to teach in Africa, first at her mother's school in Sierra Leone, then at the Achimota School in the Gold Coast. She married, bore a son, wrote for such publications as *Atlantic Monthly* and *Opportunity,* and performed as a musician in Freetown and in Europe. She was one of the first Sierra Leoneans to write in Krio. She died of blackwater fever in Freetown in 1950.

Work

Take 'Um So. Freetown, Sierra Leone: New Era, 1948.

Commentary

Cromwell, Adelaide M. *An African Victorian Feminist: The Life and Times of Adelaide Smith Casely-Hayford, 1868–1960.* London: F. Cass, 1986.

Castellanos, Rosario. Born on May 24, 1924 (some sources say 1925), in Mexico City, she grew up in Comitan, Chiapas. In 1942 her family, which had lived as neofeudal landowners, was forced to move to Mexico City after losing their landholdings in agrarian reform. In 1950 she earned a master's degree from the National Autonomous University in philosophy with a thesis entitled "On Feminine Culture." She studied further on scholarship in Madrid, then worked for the Institute of Indian Affairs in Chiapas and Mexico City. In Chiapas, she was particularly interested in the Tzeltal-speaking Indians of the area, an interest that influenced her work. She eventually became a professor of comparative literature at the National Autonomous University; she wrote a weekly column and other pieces for the newspapers *Excelsior, Novedades,* and *Siempre!* In 1958, she married and had a son, Gabriel, later divorcing. She resigned from the university in 1966, spent some years teaching at various universities in the United States, and then was appointed ambassador to Israel in 1971, where she also taught classes at the University of Tel Aviv. She died in 1974, a victim of accidental electrocution. She was renowned as one of Mexico's foremost writers and feminists, the author of poetry, essays, plays, and novels.

Works

Another Way to Be: Selected Work of Rosario Castellanos. Translated by Myralyn F. Allgood. Athens: University of Georgia, 1990.
*City of Kings. Translated by Robert S. Rudder and Gloria Chacon de Arjonar. Pittsburgh, PA: Latin American Literary Review, 1993.
Meditation on the Threshold: A Bilingual Anthology of Poetry. Translated by Julian Palley. Tempe, AZ: Bilingual Press, 1988.
*The Nine Guardians. Translated by Irene Nicholson. London, England: Faber and Faber, 1959.
A Rosario Castellanos Reader. Translated by Maureen Ahern and others. Austin: University of Texas, 1988.
The Selected Poems of Rosario Castellanos. Translated by Magda Bogin. St. Paul, MN: Graywolf Press, 1988.

Commentary

Anderson, Helene M. "Rosario Castellanos and the Structures of Power." *Contemporary Women Authors of Latin America.* New York: Brooklyn College, 1983. 22–32.

Bonifaz Caballero, Oscar. *Remembering Rosario: A Personal Glimpse into the Life and Works of Rosario Castellanos*. Potomac, MD: Scripta Humanistica, 1990.

Castellanos, Rosario. "Early Writings." *Lives on the Line: The Testimony of Contemporary Latin American Authors*. Berkeley: University of California, 1988. 86–89.

Castillo, Debra A. "Rosario Castellanos: 'Ashes Without a Face.'" *De/Colonizing the Subject: The Politics of Gender in Women's Autobiography*. Minneapolis: University of Minnesota, 1992. 242–269.

Cypess, Sandra Messinger. "*Balun-Canan*: A Model Demonstration of Discourse as Power." *Revista de Estudios Hispánicos* 19 (1985): 1–15.

Fox-Lockert, Lucía. *Women Novelists in Spain and Spanish America*. Metuchen, NJ: Scarecrow Press, 1979.

Furnival, Chloe. "Confronting Myths of Oppression: The Short Stories of Rosario Castellanos." *Knives and Angels: Women Writers in Latin America*. London, England: Zed, 1990. 52–73.

Kintz, Linda. *The Subject's Tragedy: Political Poetics, Feminist Theory, and Drama*. Ann Arbor: University of Michigan, 1992.

Lindstrom, Naomi. "Narrative Technique and Women's Expression in a Novel by Rosario Castellanos." *Modern Language Studies* 8.3 (1983): 71–80.

Lindstrom, Naomi. *Women's Voice in Latin America*. Washington, DC: Three Continents, 1989.

Nigro, Kirsten F. "Rosario Castellanos' Debunking of the Eternal Feminine." *Journal of Spanish Studies* 8.1–2 (spring-fall 1980): 89–102.

Rodriguez-Peralta, Phyllis. "Images of Women in Rosario Castellanos' Prose." *Latin American Literary Review* 6.11 (1977): 68–80.

Steele, Cynthia. "The Fiction of National Formation: The *Indigenista* Novels of James Fenimore Cooper and Rosario Castellanos." *Reinventing the Americas: Comparative Studies of Literature of the United States and Spanish America*. Cambridge: Cambridge University, 1986. 60–67.

Censorship. Many third world women have had their work as writers subjected to censorship. In many cases, their governments find their works politically threatening. Writers in Latin America, the Middle East, and notably, South Africa have frequently had their writing banned. Recently, the Bangladeshi writer Taslima Nasreen became the object of a *fatwa* and had to go into hiding; she criticized the fundamentalists' strict interpretation of the Koran and enforcement of Sharia law in newspaper interviews and in her 1993 novel *Lajja* (*Shame*), in which she addresses the lives of the Hindu minority in Bangladesh. Even Nobel Prize–winning writer Nadine Gordimer, who herself considers her work too difficult and out of the popular mainstream to be considered dangerous to the public, has had works censored and has been a champion of African writers in general, arguing that censorship is harmful to the nation. "[N]o one can be well-read or well-informed or fitted to contribute fully to the culture and development of his own society in the democratic sense while he does not have absolutely free access to the ideas of his time as well as to the accumulated thought of the past, nor while, in particular, there are areas of experience in the life of his own society and country which, through censorship, are left out of his reading. . . .

[C]an South Africans in general boast of a 'literature' while, by decree, in their own country, it consists of *some* of the books written by its black and white, Afrikaans- and English-speaking writers?" (67). Luisa Valenzuela has pointed out that censorship is a many-headed hydra that works not only through direct governmental agency but through cultural and economic means—by publishers and critics ignoring or misinterpreting works and by readers and writers censoring themselves, not only for reasons of self-preservation but out of a fear of confronting the truth, a "Freudian negation of reality. You cannot see things because you do not allow yourself to see them" (56). Censorship can be gendered; Buchi Emecheta's husband was so threatened by his wife's writing that he burned the only manuscript of her first novel, and Alifa Rif'at was forbidden by her husband to write—making her wait until his death to publish her stories.

Yet some writers find that censorship, paradoxically, is a sign that the word carries enormous power. Nawal Sa'dawi has found some gratification in the fact that her work is threatening enough to warrant censorship. "In 1972, all of my books—novels and nonfiction—were censored. I went to jail under President Sadat because of the content of my work, because I am a writer—not because I am a member of any particular political party or group, but simply because I expressed myself in written form on a variety of subjects having to do with Arab women. My arrest proved to me the tremendous power of the pen. It was actually exhilarating to know that Sadat was afraid of one woman with a pen! And the state's fear was demonstrated to me every morning when the jailer would search my cell and say to me, 'If I find a pen or paper in your cell, it is much more dangerous to you than if I find a gun.' I understood then the power of the word" (156). Bapsi Sidhwa, too, feels that the word is simply more valued, and therefore more powerful, in the third world. "In Islam, the word 'book' means more than it means in the West. Perhaps all over the East it means more. For example, the Moslems call the Jews and the Christians 'those of the book.' The printed word in Third World Countries is still rather dear. A book is seldom destroyed. And all this gives the printed word and a book more power than it has in the West. In the West, one is used to reading profanity in books, but the same thing in an Islamic country or a Third World country has a different connotation. Anything written down there is so much more powerful" (Montenegro, 515–516).

Censorship, too, can have its absurd side. Sidhwa remarks that her works translated into Urdu would come under much more careful examination by the censors and would probably have to be modified to be published. "It is of great advantage to write in English and be in Pakistan . . . you can get away with writing in English what you can't writing in Urdu" (523). Sheila Roberts, a white South African writer whose work is not notably political in nature, found her value—both as a writer and as an academic—much increased in the United States once it was learned that one of her novels had been banned in South Africa. The absurdity and the grim violence of censorship is the subject of a short story by Luisa Valenzuela ("The Censors" in *Open Door*) in which a hapless citizen schemes to get a job as a censor so he can intercept an ill-considered letter he wrote, only to become so caught up in the strange logic of the system that he denounces himself.

Work

Valenzuela, Luisa. "The Censors" in *Open Door*. Translated by Hortense Carpentier and others. San Francisco: North Point Press, 1988.

Commentary

Gordimer, Nadine. "Censored, Banned, Gagged." *The Essential Gesture: Writing, Politics, and Places*. New York: Knopf, 1988. 58–67.
Magnarelli, Sharon. "Censorship and the Female Writer: An Interview-Dialogue with Luisa Valenzuela." *Letras Femeninas* 10.1 (1984): 55–64.
Montenegro, David. "Bapsi Sidhwa: An Interview." *Massachusetts Review* 31 (winter 1990): 513–533.
Rive, Richard. "Miriam Tlali." *Index on Censorship* 13.6 (December 1984): 23.
Roberts, Sheila. [untitled autobiographical sketch]. *Momentum: On Recent South African Writing*. Pietermaritzburg, South Africa: University of Natal, 1984. 305–306.
Sa'dawi, Nawal. [untitled essay]. *Critical Fictions: The Politics of Imaginative Writing*. Seattle, WA: Bay Press, 1991. 155–156.
Tlali, Miriam. "Remove the Chains: South African Censorship and the Black Writer." *Index on Censorship* 13.6 (December 1984): 22–26.
What Happened to Burger's Daughter *or How South African Censorship Works*. Emmarentia, South Africa: Taurus, 1980.

Chang, Ai-ling. Born in Shanghai in 1921, she grew up in a cosmopolitan atmosphere, in a wealthy family that was headed by an abusive, opium-addicted father. When he took a concubine, her mother moved to France for several years, taking her children with her. Later Ai-ling lived with her father and a stepmother for a time, but they followed tradition and confined her to the house, a restriction she could not live with, and she moved out as soon as possible. She attended the University of Hong Kong and then, after moving to Shanghai again, began to write, gaining a wide audience. After the war ended, she took up film writing but found the political climate increasingly hostile, so she moved to Hong Kong in 1950 and then, after a few years, the United States, where she married a friend of Berthold Brecht and continued to write under the name Eileen Chang. Her works have had a popular following in Taiwan.

Works

Naked Earth. Hong Kong: Union Press, 1954.
Rice Sprout Song. New York: Scribner, 1955.
The Rouge of the North. London, England: Cassell, 1967.

Commentary

Chang, Ai-ling. "International Shanghai, 1941: Coffee House Chat About Sexual Intimacy and the Childlike Charm of the Japanese." *Modern Chinese Writers: Self-Portrayals*. Armonk, NY: M. E. Sharpe, 1992. 296–301.

Miller, Lucien, and Hui-chuan Chang. "Fiction and Autobiography: Spatial Form in 'The
    Golden Cangue' and *The Woman Warrior.*" *Modern Chinese Women Writers:
    Critical Appraisals.* Armonk, NY: M. E. Sharpe, 1989. 25–43.

Chang Chieh. Born in 1937 to a father who was director of a literary review
and a mother who was a teacher, a family setting that led to her receiving a
liberal education. During World War II, her parents separated, and she moved
with her mother to a village in Liaoning Province, where they lived in straight-
ened circumstances. She wanted to study music and literature but was persuaded
to study economics at the People's University as a more useful subject. After
graduation, she worked for several years at an industrial bureau, then became
employed by a film studio, where she had the chance to write two film scripts.
She was married and divorced, and then, in middle age, fell in love with a
married public official. He would not seek a divorce, fearing the scandal would
injure his career; he waited until his retirement to marry her. This situation was
recalled in a number of her works, which often deal with conflicts between
lovers and social expectations. She began to write after the end of the Cultural
Revolution at age forty. In 1978 she won a prize for the best short story of the
year with "The Music of the Forests" and later won the Mao Dun Literary
Prize for her novel *Leaden Wings.* Now she is a full-time writer and enjoys a
large following in China. She counts among her literary influences Virginia
Woolf and Jorge Luis Borges. She says in her essay "The Boat I Steer" that
she was criticized publicly for being "too deeply poisoned by eighteenth- and
nineteenth-century novels from the West" (120). Her novel *Fangzhou* (*The Ark,*
1981) is considered one of the most strongly feminist novels in Chinese literature.

Works

*As Long as Nothing Happens, Nothing Will. Translated by Gladys Yang et al. London,
    England: Virago, 1988.
*Leaden Wings. Translated by Gladys Yang. London, England: Virago, 1987.
Love Must Not Be Forgotten. Translated by Gladys Yang et al. Beijing, China: Panda,
    1986.

Commentary

Bailey, Allison. "Travelling Together: Narrative Technique in Zhang Jie's *The Ark.*"
    Modern Chinese Women Writers: Critical Appraisals. Armonk, NY: M. E.
    Sharpe, 1989. 96–111.
Chan, Sylvia. "Chang Chieh's Fiction: In Search of Female Identity." *Issues and Studies*
    25.9 (November 1989): 85–104.
Chang Chieh. "The Time Is Not Yet Ripe." *Chinese Literature* (autumn 1984): 25–39.
Chang Chieh. "The Boat I Steer: A Study in Perseverance." *Modern Chinese Writers:
    Self-Portrayals.* Armonk, NY: M. E. Sharpe, 1992. 119–122.
Hitchcock, Peter. *Dialogics of the Oppressed.* Minnesota: University of Minnesota, 1993.
Knapp, Bettina. "The New Era for Women Writers in China." *World Literature Today*
    65 (summer 1991): 432–439.

Liu, Lydia H. "The Female Tradition in Modern Chinese Literature: Negotiating Feminisms Across East/West Boundaries." *Genders* 12 (winter 1991): 22–44.

Chang, Eileen. See **Chang, Ai-ling.**

Chang, Jung. Born in China in 1952 to politically prominent parents who had been active in the revolution, she lost her comfortable station in life during the Cultural Revolution, when her family came under attack as rightists and its members were sent to different labor camps for reeducation. While working as a technically uninformed electrician—nearly electrocuting herself in the process—and as a "barefoot doctor" in rural areas, the Cultural Revolution ran its course, and she was able to enroll at Sichuan University, where she earned a degree in English language and literature. She then emigrated to England, where she earned a Ph.D. in linguistics from York University. She has recounted her life story and the lives of her mother and grandmother in a family memoir.

Work

Wild Swans: Three Daughters of China. London, England: HarperCollins, 1992.

Changes by Ama Ata Aidoo (London, England: Women's Press, 1991). A novel about three women and the choices they face in marriage and in work. Esi is a successful woman with a daughter who divorces her husband and finds life lonely. In time she meets a charming man and agrees to become his second wife. She is unable to reconcile her desires and self-identity with the role, however, and loses both her daughter and the attentions of her new husband. Her friend Opukuya is, likewise, a busy woman with family, husband, and career, but she makes more compromises with circumstances and juggles her role with a mixture of contentment, frustration, and exhaustion. Fusena, Esi's cowife, is a businesswoman of the traditional type, busily trading at a kiosk in the marketplace, having a life as full and exhausting as the more Westernized women. Various difficult choices are explored, made, and unmade throughout the novel, which ends ambivalently with Esi musing, "So what fashion of living was she ever going to consider adequate? She comforted herself that maybe her bone-blood-flesh self, not her unseen soul, would get answers to some of the big questions she was asking of life" (166). The novelist commented in an interview: "The title *Changes* addresses the issue of a woman's life, her loves, career and so on and how they change. It would be impossible within the pages of one novel to synthesize the different opinions that are circulating about women. Nonetheless the different voices represent different sorts of possibilities for different women in the society. . . . The way the novel ends means that the story is not finished, the issue is not resolved" (George, 302).

Commentary

George, Rosemary Marangoly, and Helen Scott. " 'A New Tail to an Old Tale': An
    Interview with Ama Ata Aidoo." *Novel* 26.3 (spring 1993): 297–308.

Chauvet, Marie. Born Marie Vieux in Port-au-Prince on September 16, 1916,
the daughter of an Antillean mother, Dilia Nones, from the Virgin Islands and
a Haitian senator and prominent politician, Constant Vieux. She began her career
in theater, as a playwright and actor, before writing her novel *Dance on the
Volcano.* She worked as a teacher for many years, was married three times, and
after going into exile when her book *Amour, colère et folie* was published and
banned in Haiti, she moved to New York, where she died of a brain tumor in
1973. Her daughter, Erma Saint-Gregoire, is also a writer. She was the author
of at least two plays, a short story, and seven novels, one of which has been
translated into English.

Work

*Dance on the Volcano. Translated by Salvator Attanasio. New York: W. Sloan, 1959.

Commentary

Dayan, Joan. "Reading Women in the Caribbean: Marie Chauvet's *Love, Anger, and
    Madness.*"*Displacements: Women, Tradition, Literatures in French.* Baltimore,
    MD: Johns Hopkins University, 1991. 228–253.
Dayan, Joan. "Erzulie: A Women's History of Haiti." *Research in African Literatures*
    25.2 (summer 1994): 5–31.
Rowell, Charles H. "Erma Saint-Gregoire" [interview with the daughter of Marie Chau-
    vet]. *Callaloo* 15.2 (spring 1992): 462–468.
Zimra, Clarisse. "Versions of Things Past in Contemporary Caribbean Women Writers."
    Explorations: Essays in Honor of Frank J. Jones. Washington, DC: American
    Press. 227–252.

Chedid, Andrée. Born on March 20, 1920, in Cairo of Egyptian parents with
Lebanese and Syrian antecedents. She spent most of her childhood in Egypt but
made frequent trips to France during the summer months. Her education began
in Egypt, but she attended French schools, completing her secondary schooling
in Paris. She then earned a journalism degree at the American University in
Cairo. At age twenty-two she married a medical student, Louis Chedid. They
lived in Lebanon from 1942 to 1946, then settled in Paris. She has had French
citizenship for many years and decided early in her writing career to adopt
French as her literary language. She has published a great many volumes of
poetry, ten novels, several collections of short stories (one of which was awarded
the Prix Goncourt in 1979), a number of plays, volumes of essays, and children's
books. Several of her works have been translated into English, including three
novels and a play. She is an important and versatile francophone writer, whose
works defy convenient labels.

Works

*From Sleep Unbound. Translated by Sharon Spencer. Athens, OH: Swallow, 1983.
Prose and Poetry of Andrée Chedid. Translated by Renée Linkhorn. Birmingham, AL: Summa Publications, 1990.
The Return to Beirut. Translated by Rose Schwartz. London, England: Serpent's Tail, 1989.
The Show-Man. Translated by Felicia Londre. New York: Ubu Repertory Theater, 1984.
*The Sixth Day. Translated by Isobel Strachey. London, England: Serpent's Tail, 1987.

Commentary

Accad, Evelyne. *Sexuality and War: Literary Masks of the Middle East.* New York: New York University, 1990.
Accad, Evelyne. "Sexuality, War, and Literature in Lebanon." *Feminist Issues* 11 (fall 1991): 27–42.
Knapp, Bettina. "An Interview with Andrée Chedid." *Drama and Theatre* 12.2 (1975): 121–124.
Knapp, Bettina. "Andrée Chedid" [interview]. *French Novelists Speak Out* Troy, NY: Whitston, 1976. 57–64.
Knapp, Bettina. *Andrée Chedid.* Amsterdam, Netherlands: Rodopi, 1984.

Ch'en Hsueh-Chao. Born on April 17, 1906, in the village of Chenjiadai on the north side of Hangzhou Bay, China, the daughter of a progressive school-teacher who provided an education for his daughter as well as his sons. She took advantage of his collection of classical literature, reading widely as a child. He died when she was seven and her mother was an invalid, so she was brought up by her nine elder brothers who often treated her harshly. She left home in 1919 to attend Shanghai Patriotic Girls' School, graduating in 1923, the same year in which she submitted an essay to a contest—on the subject of women's equality—and took second prize, after which it was published in a Shanghai newspaper. She was involved with the May 4th movement and was known as a nonconformist. She taught in Anhui and Shaoxing but within a few years was publishing regularly enough to live off her earnings as a writer, even financing a trip to France, where she studied from 1927 until 1935. There she supported herself by sending news dispatches to a newspaper at home and earning a doctorate from the University of Clermont. She married a Chinese physician in France, and they moved back to China. During World War II, working as a journalist, she met Communists fighting the Japanese, including Mao Zedong and Zhou Enlai, writing an account that was suppressed by the Kuomintang, who later detained her for nineteen days. She was divorced in 1941 and joined the Communists in 1942, becoming a writer of epic novels on land reform and other topics close to the Communist agenda. She suffered, like most intellectuals, during the Cultural Revolution and was rehabilitated in 1979, beginning to publish again after a twenty-year hiatus, publishing, among other things, her autobiography, which has been translated into English. She now lives in Hangzhou, China.

Work

Surviving the Storm: A Memoir. Translated by Ti Hua and Caroline Greene. Armonk, NY: M. E. Sharpe, 1991.

Chen Jo-hsi. A native of Taiwan, daughter of a carpenter. She witnessed the return of Taiwan to the control of the Nationalist Chinese government in the late 1940s, growing up in a time of turbulence and change. She joined a group of young writers at the National Taiwan University in the late 1950s and early 1960s where she studied foreign languages, specializing in English and American literature. Several of her stories were published in Chinese and in English translation. After graduating she went to the Iowa Writers' Workshop, left after a brief stay, and moved on to Mount Holyoke College and then Johns Hopkins University in 1963. There she met and married Tuan Shih-yao. Together they moved to Beijing in 1966, just at the start of the Cultural Revolution, eager to participate in what seemed a brave experiment. Seven years later they left to live in Hong Kong, having had two children in the intervening years, as well as chilling experiences that became the basis for many of her works. After a difficult year in Hong Kong, the family moved to North America, living in Canada and the United States. She is one of the most eloquent writers to tackle the subject of the Cultural Revolution.

Works

The Execution of Mayor Yin and Other Stories from the Great Proletarian Cultural Revolution. Translated by Howard Goldblatt. Bloomington: Indiana University, 1978.
The Old Man and Other Stories. Hong Kong: Renditions, 1986.
Short Stories of Chen Ruoxi, Translated from the Original Chinese. Lewiston, NY: E. Mellon, 1992.
Spirit-Calling: Tales About Taiwan. Taipei, Taiwan: Heritage. 1962.

Commentary

Duke, Michael S. ''Personae: Individual and Society in Three Novels by Chen Ruoxi.'' *Modern Chinese Women Writers: Critical Appraisals.* Armonk, NY: M. E. Sharpe, 1989. 53–77.
Hsin-sheng C. Kao, editor. *Nativism Overseas: Contemporary Chinese Women Writers.* Albany, NY: SUNY, 1993.
Kai-yu Hsu. ''A Sense of History: Reading Chen Jo-hsi's Stories.'' *Chinese Fiction from Taiwan: Critical Perspectives.* Bloomington: Indiana University, 1980. 206–233.

Chen Ruoxi. See **Chen Jo-hsi.**

Cheng Nien. Born on January 28, 1915, the eldest of five children in a prominent family. Her father was a rear admiral in the Chinese navy. She studied at Yenjing University (where she knew Han Suyin) and in 1953 went to study at the London School of Economics. She married and settled in Shanghai, where her husband was the general manager of the Shell International Petroleum Company Chinese office, living a life of unusual privilege and comfort. She took over his work when he died in 1957, but in 1966 she was caught up in the Cultural Revolution and was imprisoned for six and a half years. She moved to the United States in 1980 after her release. The story of her imprisonment, and the search she made for her murdered daughter, is the subject of her autobiography, which demonstrates her determination and intelligence in opposing her captors.

Work

Life and Death in Shanghai. New York: Grove, 1986.

Commentary

Ling, Amy. *Between Two Worlds: Women Writers of Chinese Ancestry.* New York: Pergamon, 1990.

Cheong, Fiona. A Singaporean writer, of Chinese heritage, currently living in Washington, D.C. She is the author of one novel thus far, an atmospheric rendering of family life in Singapore at a time of political intrigue and social unrest.

Work

*The Scent of the Gods. New York: Norton, 1991.

Child of the Dark: The Diary of Carolina Maria de Jesús by Carolina Maria de Jesús (New York: E. P. Dutton, 1962). Originally published in Portuguese in 1954, it was translated into many languages and was a best-seller in Brazil. The diary, edited by a journalist, recounts the life of an unemployed, uneducated mother of three illegitimate children in a *favela* of São Paulo. The author, a black woman, descended from slaves, uses colloquial language to describe her daily struggle to forage enough salvageable trash to feed her children, all the while offering blunt and incisive critiques of the economic and political institutions that created and maintain the *favelas.* Her social critique and depiction of the conditions in which she and her neighbors lived make this document one of the most telling of Latin American *testimonios.*

Commentary

Fox, Patricia D. "The Diary of Carolina Maria de Jesús: A Paradoxical Enunciation." *Proceedings of the Black Image in Latin American Culture.* Slippery Rock, AR: Slippery Rock University, 1990. 241–251.
Levine, Robert M. "The Cautionary Tale of Carolina Maria de Jesús." *Latin American Research Review* 29.1 (1994): 55–83.

Children's Literature. Many women writing in the third world write for children as well as for adults. Included among such writers are Buchi Emecheta, Efua Sutherland, Flora Nwapa, Opal Palmer Adisa, Ama Ata Aidoo, Jeni Couzyn, Anita Desai, Beryl Gilroy, Rosa Guy, Catherine Lim, Bette Bao Lord, Grace Nichols, Mabel Segun, and Charity Waciuma. Barbara Kimenye is primarily a writer for children, having created a series about the mischievous schoolboy Moses who gets in and out of various scrapes. Jean D'Costa has written some distinguished works for children using Jamaican Creole in order to provide children's books that speak to Jamaican children both in the Caribbean and in Britain. Works by Merle Hodge, Zee Edgell, and Marlene Nourbese Philip have a special appeal for young readers, having young heroines who negotiate the conflicting worlds of school and home with courage and resourcefulness. Other writers, such as Minfong Ho of Thailand, have written distinguished children's books that portray young people struggling to survive against the odds. For an excellent survey of children's literature, see *Against Borders*.

Works

*Bedford, Simi. *Yoruba Girl Dancing*. New York: Viking, 1992.
D'Costa, Jean. *Sprat Morrison*. Kingston, Jamaica: Collins, Sangster, 1979.
*Edgell, Zee. *Beka Lamb*. London, England: Heinemann, 1982.
Ho, Minfong. *Rice Without Rain*. New York: Lothrop, Lee and Shepard, 1990.
*Hodge, Merle. *Crick Crack, Monkey*. London, England: Heinemann, 1981.
*Hodge, Merle. *For the Life of Laetitia*. New York: Farrar, Straus, Giroux, 1993.
Kimenye, Barbara. *Moses in Trouble*. Nairobi, Kenya: Oxford University, 1968.
Kimenye, Barbara. *Moses*. Nairobi, Kenya: Oxford University, 1971.
*Philip, Marlene Nourbese. *Harriet's Daughter*. London, England: Heinemann, 1988.

Commentary

Children and Literature in Africa. Ibadan, Nigeria: Heinemann, 1992.
Rochman, Hazel, editor. *Against Borders: Promoting Books in a Multicultural World*.
    Chicago: American Library Association, 1993.
Schmidt, Nancy. "African Women Writers of Literature for Children." *World Literature Written in English* 17.1 (1978): 7–21.

Chin Ts'ai. Chinese-born actress and daughter of a classically trained actor who was persecuted during the Cultural Revolution, she made several popular films in the West and originated the role of Suzy Wong, a stereotypically exotic prostitute. Her memoirs recount her role as a stock Oriental in Western films while her father was experiencing persecution during the Cultural Revolution.

Work

Daughter of Shanghai. New York: St. Martin's, 1988.

A Chinese Winter's Tale: An Autobiographical Fragment by Yu Lo-chin (Hong Kong: Renditions, 1986). Retells the experiences of a woman whose brother was shot during the Cultural Revolution, who was sent to live a hard life in the Northern Wilderness and whose relationships with men were tainted by the poisoned political atmosphere. The paranoia and privations of the period are illuminated both in her depiction of personal relationships and in her account of arbitrary arrests and imprisonments. The novel employs contemporary adaptations in the Chinese language—Maospeak—which are effectively translated into English. A work that bears valuable witness to an important period in Chinese history.

Commentary

Nerlich, Jorg Michael. "In Search of the Ideal Man: Yu Luojin's Novel *A Winter's Tale.*" *Woman and Literature in China.* Bochum, Germany: Studienverlag, 1985. 454–472.

The Chosen Place, the Timeless People by Paule Marshall (New York: Harcourt, Brace and World, 1969). This novel follows the fortunes of a team of anthropologists who arrive on the fictional Bourne Island in order to start an ambitious development scheme. As their paths cross those of the islanders and of the mercurial Merle, their London-educated landlady, they begin to question their scheme and its assumptions, as well their own pasts. The island's history emerges as the characters begin to examine their own lives, and the community that the anthropologists set out to study not only evades their neat categories and theories but challenges them. This work charts many life stories in a texture that is as dense and eventful as a nineteenth-century novel and interweaves viewpoints to create a complex and engaging picture of a Caribbean island, its history, its people, and their effect on the Americans who seek to change it.

Commentary

Brathwaite, Edward. "West Indian History and Society in the Art of Paule Marshall's Novel." *Journal of Black Studies* 1 (1970): 225–238.
Christian, Barbara. "Sculpture and Space: The Interdependency of Character and Culture in the Novels of Paule Marshall." *Black Women Novelists: The Development of a Tradition, 1892–1976.* Westport, CT: Greenwood, 1980. 80–136.
Harris, Wilson. *The Womb of Space: The Cross-Cultural Imagination.* Westport, CT: Greenwood, 1983.
Nazareth, Peter. "Paule Marshall's Timeless People." *New Letters* 40 (autumn 1973): 116–131.
Pettis, Joyce. " 'Talk' as Defensive Artifice: Merle Kinbona in *The Chosen Place, the Timeless People.*" *African American Review* 26.1 (spring 1992): 109–118.
Rahming, Norman. "Towards a Caribbean Mythology: The Function of Africa in Paule Marshall's *The Chosen Place, the Timeless People.*" *Studies in the Literary Imagination* 26.2 (fall 1993): 77–88.
Spillers, Hortense. "Chosen Place, Timeless People: Some Figurations on the New World." *Conjuring: Black Women, Fiction, and Literary Tradition.* Bloomington: Indiana University, 1985. 151–175.
Stoelting, Winifred L. "Time Past and Time Present: The Search for Viable Links in *The Chosen Place, the Timeless People* by Paule Marshall." *CLA Journal* 16 (September 1972): 60–71.

Chronicles of the Hostile Sun by Dionne Brand (Toronto, Canada: Williams-Wallace, 1984). Highly political poetry, including a long sequence based

on the U.S. invasion of Grenada and "Anti-Poetry" in which the author challenges academic notions of poetry, questioning whether it is possible to describe
reality using "pretty words" and whether anything but pretty words will be
accepted as poetic. She invokes history and present politics not only to question
the power structures she addresses but to question the role of the poet and the
purpose of poetry.

Chua, Rebecca. Born in Singapore, Chua began writing as a child, often il-
lustrating her own stories and poetry. She earned a B.A. in English language
and literature (honors) from the University of Singapore in 1976 and an M.A.
in mass communications from the University of South Carolina. She has worked
as a journalist and as a magazine editor, has served as an adviser to the Young
Writers Circle at the National Library, and has taught both creative writing and
journalism for the Extra-Mural Department of the University of Singapore. She
is on the staff of the *Straights Times*. She has published short stories in many
magazines and anthologies, and some have been broadcast by the British Broadcasting Corporation (BBC).

Work

*The Newspaper Editor and Other Stories. Singapore: Heinemann Asia, 1981.

Chugtai, Ismat. See **Cughta'i, 'Ismat.**

Chungara, Domitila Barrios de. See **Barrios de Chungara, Domitila.**

Circling Song by Nawal Sa'dawi (London, England: Zed, 1989). An extraordinary experimental novel, the disjointed and nonlinear enigmatic tale of twins,
a boy and a girl, born of one embryo. The twins, Hamida and Hamido, are
doubles, linked and at times barely distinguishable from one another, yet op-
posites by virtue of gender roles in Arab society. The story concerns the darker
side of family relationships and the violence invoked in the name of family
honor. Hamida is raped, apparently by a relative, and becomes pregnant. Her
mother pushes her on a train bound for the city to hide her shame and protect
her from vengeance. Her father sends Hamido to kill her for dishonoring the
family. The twins pursue one another in a dark, confusing narrative full of
ambiguities and violent sexual imagery, both of them victims of destructive
gender roles. Sa'dawi uses both a dense, circular narrative structure and allusive
language to tell their story.

City of Kings by Rosario Castellanos (Pittsburgh, PA: Latin American Literary
Review, 1993). Translation of *Ciudad real*, first published in 1960. A collection
of stories set in the "City of Kings," now called San Cristobal de las Casas, in
Chiapas, Mexico. Some of the stories are about the Indians who are treated as
less than human and submissive to their dismal fates (as in "The Death of the

Tiger,'' in which the men of a tribe of Indians are shipped to the coast to work, unable to return to their home and their families) or about the Ladinos who become aware of the injustice but are ineffective when it comes to change (a nurse in ''The Wheel of Hunger'' is unable to help the Indians, her helplessness magnified in the person of the doctor who cynically decides to let a baby starve in order to impress the Indians with the need to pay for medicine so they will value his cures; an anthropologist in ''The Gift, Refused'' finds his offers of help misinterpreted, making him wonder what he did wrong, what it was that he failed to give). The last story is more optimistic. ''Arthur Smith Finds Salvation'' recounts the growing consciousness of an American missionary who gradually discovers that his organization is a Central Intelligence Agency (CIA) front, that the salvation he had hoped for will not come through missionary work, and in the end, he walks out to find a life among the Indians, with nothing left but hope and the wish that, in return for their help, he will be able to do something for them. First published years ago, this translation appeared ironically at the time of the quincentenary of Columbus's landing in the Americas and shortly before the Indians of Chiapas rose in revolt to briefly capture and hold the ''City of Kings'' before the intervention of Mexican troops.

Cixous, Hélène. An important literary critic, she was born in Oran, Algeria, in 1937. She is the founder of the Paris Centres des Recherches en Études Féminines and a professor of English literature at the University of Paris since 1968. Feminist critic, explorer of the concept of *écriture féminine*, which urges women to inscribe their own pleasures and defeat the patriarchal symbolic order; she suggests each writer has the capability of bisexuality, able to inscribe the repressed other. She has been instrumental in bringing the work of Brazilian writer Clarice Lispector to the attention of French- and English-speaking audiences.

Commentary

Cixous, Hélène. ''The Laugh of Medusa.'' *New French Feminisms*. New York: Schocken, 1981. 245–268.

Claiming an Identity They Taught Me to Despise by Michelle Cliff (Watertown, MA: Persephone Press, 1980). A book that refuses genres and claims its own identity. Short poetic essays are told like stories, broken into small pieces, defying the usual categories. Cliff explores the African roots that were hidden from her, and what that hidden history means. The very notion of identity is questioned in the course of the exploration. ''I am not what I seem to be'' (3), the narrator proclaims, and that is paradoxically the clue to her selfhood.

Clara: Thirteen Short Stories and a Novel by Luisa Valenzuela (New York: Harcourt Brace Jovanovich, 1976). A collection of mythical and magical short stories that portray sexual repression and occasional liberation. It includes the short novel "Clara," the story of a woman who goes from prostitution to playing a live severed head in a carnival; her head is, eventually, severed by her lover. They are ironic, mordantly humorous, and bizarre explorations of the magically real.

Clarise Cumberbatch Want to Go Home by Joan Cambridge (New York: Ticknor and Fields, 1987). The Guyanese heroine of this novel, Clarise Cumberbatch, arrives in New York, looking for her husband Harold, who has suddenly left her and her children, taking with him another woman. Her search, retold in a subjective, Creole narrative voice, is funny, touching, and sad. She stays with a friend and searches for a job using her friend's green card in order to pursue her search. Twinned with her desperate search is her desire to go home. Both get more frantic as a year passes, and she dreams about gold prospecting in the Guyanese bush while wandering the city, looking for work and for Harold. The wonders of New York quickly pale, and the beauty of her home grows in her memory. She ultimately turns herself in to immigration so she will be deported home, not a defeat but a triumphant gesture of escape.

Clear Light of Day by Anita Desai (New York: Harper and Row, 1980). The setting of the novel is a family gathering in Old Delhi, and the story is told by way of invoked memories and conversations between relatives. The narrative weaves back and forth through time, recalling childhood conspiracies and traumas. Partition, the major historical event of their lives, is glimpsed at a distance as a red glow and distant clamor, realized firsthand only through the sudden absence of Muslim neighbors and the political impossibility of the son to study Urdu at college. The moldering house in Old Delhi both protects and isolates its inhabitants, whose stories emerge as they remember the lives of their strangely distant parents and the warmth of the poor relation who mothers them, now a shambling alcoholic. Through conversation the roots of the estrangement between a brother and sister, once close, are uncovered and the ground for reconciliation cleared. Though India's experience since independence is part of the characters' lives, the focus of the book is on the personal experiences of four siblings as children and as adults, and their relationships, funny, touching, and sometimes bitter, form the subtle drama of the book.

Commentary

Chew, Shirley. "Searching Voices: Anita Desai's *Clear Light of Day* and Nayantara Sahgal's *Rich Like Us*." *Motherlands: Women's Writings from Africa, the Caribbean, and South Asia.* New Brunswick, NJ: Rutgers University, 1992. 43–63.
Huggan, Graham. "Philomela's Retold Story: Silence, Music, and the Post-Colonial Text." *Journal of Commonwealth Literature* 25.1 (August 1990): 12–23.

Cliff, Michelle. Born in Kingston, Jamaica, in 1946, a lighter-skinned child than her younger sister—a difference that is frequently touched on in her work.

She moved to New York as a child and graduated with a B.A. in European history from Wagner College. She then attended the Warburg Institute, London University, earning a master's degree in comparative historical studies of the Renaissance. She became involved in the feminist movement in the 1970s and is author of many articles, organizer of workshops, and lecturer on feminism and racism. She was coeditor (with Adrienne Rich) of the journal *Sinister Wisdom* (1981–1983) and has written several novels, autobiographical writings, poetry, and prose poems. A theme that surfaces in many of her works is that of finding an identity, both in terms of sexuality and in terms of race, and recovering history that has been erased from the books. "To write as a complete Caribbean woman, or man for that matter, demands of us retracing the African part of ourselves, reclaiming as our own, and as our subject, a history sunk under the sea, or scattered as potash in the canefields, or gone to bush, or trapped in a class system notable for its rigidity and absolute dependence on color stratification. On a past bleached from our minds. It means finding the art forms of these of our ancestors and speaking in the patois forbidden us. It means realizing our knowledge will always be wanting. It means also, I think, mixing in the forms taught us by the oppressor, undermining his language and co-opting his style, and turning it to our purpose" ("A Journey into Speech," 59).

Works

Abeng. Trumansburg, NY: Crossing Press, 1984.
Bodies of Water. London, England: Methuen, 1990.
Claiming an Identity They Taught Me to Despise. Watertown, MA: Persephone Press, 1980.
Free Enterprise. New York: Dutton, 1993.
The Land of Look Behind: Prose and Poetry. Ithaca, NY: Firebrand, 1985.
No Telephone to Heaven. New York: Dutton, 1987.

Commentary

Cliff, Michelle. "A Journey into Speech." *Graywolf Annual Five: Multi-Cultural Literacy*. St. Paul, MN: Graywolf, 1988. 57–62.
Cliff, Michelle. "Caliban's Daughter: The Tempest and the Teapot." *Frontiers* 12.2 (summer 1991): 36–51.
Davies, Carol Boyce. "Writing Home: Gender and Heritage in the Works of Afro/Caribbean/American Women Writers." *Out of the Kumbla: Women and Literature in the Caribbean*. Trenton, NJ: Africa World Press, 1990. 59–73.
Edmondson, Belinda. "Race, Privilege, and the Politics of (Re)Writing History: An Analysis of the Novels of Michelle Cliff." *Callaloo* 16.1 (winter 1993): 180–191.
Gikandi, Simon. "Narration at the Postcolonial Moment: History and Representation in *Abeng*." *Writing in Limbo: Modernism and Caribbean Literature*. Ithaca, NY: Cornell University, 1992. 231–251.
Johnson, Lemuel. "A-beng: (Re)calling the Body in(to) Question." *Out of the Kumbla: Women and Literature in the Caribbean*. Trenton, NJ: Africa World Press, 1990. 111–142.

Lima, Maria Helena. "Revolutionary Developments: Michelle Cliff's *No Telephone to Heaven* and Merle Collins's *Angel*." *Ariel* 24.1 (January 1993): 35–56.

Lionnet, Françoise. "Of Mangoes and Maroons: Language, History, and the Multicultural Subject of Michelle Cliff's *Abeng*." *De/Colonizing the Subject: The Politics of Gender in Women's Autobiography*. Minneapolis: University of Minnesota, 1992. 321–345.

Raiskin, Judith. "The Art of History: An Interview with Michelle Cliff." *Kenyon Review* 15.1 (1993): 57–61.

Schwartz, Meryl F. "An Interview with Michelle Cliff." *Contemporary Literature* 34.4 (winter 1993): 594–619.

Cofer, Judith Ortiz. See **Ortiz Cofer, Judith.**

The Coffer Dams by Kamala Markandaya (New York: John Day, 1969). The melodramatic story of an English engineering effort to build a dam in India. The engineers scorn Indian culture and the natural world that they are transforming, and their development scheme brings disaster, both to individuals and to the land they have set out to improve. The novel begins "It was a man's town . . ." and the masculine values that drive the development scheme forward are countered and criticized by the wife of the project leader, an Englishwoman who values India and respects both the natural world around them and the tribal people who have coexisted with its demands. The dam is ultimately destroyed through a combination of greed and poor execution and by the natural forces that are overwhelmingly more powerful than the schemes of Western engineers. An interesting, if somewhat melodramatic, examination of the assumptions that shape many development schemes and their disastrous implications.

The Collector of Treasures by Bessie Head (London, England: Heinemann, 1977). Tales here concern Botswanan life and history, including the migrations before colonial powers intervened. Head's style is, at times, documentary in nature, a kind of fictional re-creation of historical events drawing upon oral history sources. Some stories use a wide-angle focus; others are more concerned with the minutiae of family life. All are rendered with a narrative style that features dry detachment, cool and unemotional observation, with occasional biting satire or understated irony.

Commentary

Chetin, Sara. "Myth, Exile, and the Female Condition: Bessie Head's *The Collector of Treasures*." *Journal of Commonwealth Literature* 23.1 (1989): 114–137.

Katrak, Ketu H. "From Pauline to Dikeledi: The Philosophical and Political Vision of Bessie Head's Protagonists." *Ba Shiru* 12.2 (1985): 19–25.

Sample, Maxine. "Landscape and Spatial Metaphor in Bessie Head's *The Collector of Treasures*." *Studies in Short Fiction* 28 (summer 1991): 311–319.

Collins, Merle. Novelist, short story writer, and poet, born in Aruba in 1950 but raised in Grenada, where she worked as a teacher and researcher. She worked in the Ministry of Foreign Affairs during the Grenada Revolution and was a member of Grenada's National Women's Organization until 1983. She has studied at the University of the West Indies, Georgetown University, and the London School of Economics and teaches Caribbean Studies at the Polytechnic of North London. She has published poetry, a novel, and a collection of stories and performs her poetry with a fusion of verse and Afro-Caribbean music.

Works

*Angel. London, England: Women's Press, 1987.
Because the Dawn Breaks: Poems Dedicated to the Grenadian People. London, England: Karia, 1985.
*Rain Darling. London, England: Women's Press, 1990.
*Rotten Pomerack. London, England: Virago, 1992.

Commentary

Collins, Merle. "Themes and Trends in Caribbean Writing Today." *My Guy to Sci-Fi.* London, England: Pandora, 1989. 179–190.
Lima, Maria Helena. "Revolutionary Developments: Michelle Cliff's *No Telephone to Heaven* and Merle Collins's *Angel.*" *Ariel* 24.1 (January 1993): 35–56.
Wilson, Betty. "An Interview with Merle Collins." *Callaloo* 16.1 (winter 1993): 94–107.

A Compass for the Sunflower by Liyanah Badr (London, England: Women's Press, 1989). This nonlinear story fuses past and present, interweaving events in Palestinian history, the Arab-Israeli war of 1967, and the expulsion from Jordan in 1970 to a later hijacking and conflict in refugee camps just prior to the Lebanese civil war. The narrator says she is "embedded in the past"; this evocative and narratively daring novel explores that intersection of individual lives with history.

Condé, Maryse. Novelist, critic, and playwright. Born on February 11, 1937, in Pointe-à-Pitre, Guadeloupe, the youngest of eight children in a comfortably situated family. She began to write, and recognize the power of the written word, at an early age, writing a play at age seven or eight about her mother—and finding her mother dismayed at the portrait. She earned degrees in London and Paris, including a doctorate in comparative literature from the Sorbonne, where she taught West Indian literature for many years. A twelve-year stay in West Africa, the setting for several of her novels, led to her becoming disillusioned with her beliefs about Marxism, revolution, and race. She was married for a time to Mamadou Condé, of Guinea, in 1960, and left that country in 1964 for political reasons, taking her four children and a stepson with her to Ghana, where she taught at the Institute of Languages. She moved to Senegal in 1966, where she met and later married Richard Philcox, who has translated several of her novels into English. After her sojourn in Africa, she worked for the British Broadcasting Corporation (BBC) in England and then for *Présence Africaine* in Paris. She has since taught at several universities in France and the United States and resumed residence in Guadeloupe in 1986.

Works

The Children of Segu. Translated by Linda Coverdale. New York: Viking, 1989.
*Heremakhonon. Translated by Richard Philcox. Washington, DC: Three Continents, 1981.
The Hills of Massabielle. Translated by Richard Philcox. New York: Ubu Repertory Theater, 1991.
*I, Tituba, Black Witch of Salem. Translated by Richard Philcox. Charlottesville: University Press of Virginia, 1992.
A Season in Rihata. Translated by Richard Philcox. London, England: Heinemann, 1988.
Segu. Translated by Barbara Bray. New York: Viking, 1987.
*Tree of Life. Translated by Victoria Reiter. New York: Ballantine Books, 1992.

Commentary

Bruner, David K. "Maryse Condé, Creative Writer in a Political World." *Esprit Créateur* 17.2 (1977): 168–173.
Clark, Vévé. " 'I Have Made Peace with My Island': An Interview with Maryse Condé." *Callaloo* 12 (winter 1989): 86–133.
Clark, Vévé. "Developing Diaspora Literacy: Allusion in Maryse Condé's *Hérémakhonon*." *Out of the Kumbla: Women and Literature in the Caribbean.* Trenton, NJ: Africa World Press, 1990. 303–319.
Condé, Maryse. "Man, Women and Love in French Caribbean Writing." *Caribbean Quarterly* 27.4 (1981): 37–43.
Condé, Maryse. "Beyond Languages and Colors." *Discourse* 11 (spring-summer 1989): 110–113.
Condé, Maryse. "Order, Disorder, Freedom, and the West Indian Writer." *Yale French Studies* 83 (1993): 121–135.
Condé, Maryse. "The Role of the Writer." *World Literature Today* 67.4 (summer 1993): 697–699.
Dukats, Mara L. "A Narrative of Violated Maternity: *Moi, Tituba, sorcière . . . noire de Salem*." *World Literature Today* 67.4 (autumn 1993): 745–750.
King, Adele. "Two Caribbean Women Go to Africa: Maryse Condé's *Hérémakhonon* and Myriam Warner-Vieyra's *Juletane*." *College Literature* 18.3 (October 1991): 96–105.
Lionnet, Françoise. *Autobiographical Voices: Race, Gender, Self-Portraiture.* Ithaca, NY: Cornell University, 1989.
Mortimer, Mildred. "A Sense of Place and Space in Maryse Condé's *Les Dernières rois mages*." *World Literature Today* 67.4 (autumn 1993): 757–762.
Mudimbe-Boyi, Elisabeth. "Giving a Voice to Tituba: The Death of the Author?" *World Literature Today* 67.4 (autumn 1993): 751–756.
Ngate, Jonathan. "Maryse Condé and Africa: The Making of a Recalcitrant Daughter." *A Current Bibliography on African Affairs* 19.1 (1986–1987): 5–20.

"Return of a Native Daughter: An Interview with Paule Marshall and Maryse Condé." *Sage* 3.2 (fall 1986): 52–53.

Shelton, Marie-Denise. "Literature Extracted: A Poetic of Daily Life." *Callaloo* 15.1 (winter 1992): 167–178.

Shelton, Marie-Denise. "Condé: The Politics of Gender and Identity." *World Literature Today* 67.4 (autumn 1993): 717–722.

Wilson, Elizabeth. " *'Le Voyage et l'espace close'*—Island and Journey as Metaphor: Aspects of Women's Experience in the Works of Francophone Caribbean Women Writers." *Out of the Kumbla: Women and Literature in the Caribbean.* Trenton, NJ: Africa World Press, 1990. 45–58.

Zimra, Clarisse. "Negritude in the Feminine Mode: The Case of Martinique and Guadeloupe." *Journal of Ethnic Studies* 12.1 (1984): 53–77.

Considering Woman by Velma Pollard (London, England: Women's Press, 1989). A collection of short pieces, crafted carefully without any extraneous words or details, often making use of Jamaican Creole. There are "parables," "cages," in which men and women have broken relationships that look perfectly sound from the outside, and portraits of memorable women: a mother who never can get home from working in America until she comes home in an American coffin; a grandmother who holds the family together and has a wealth of experience behind her; a woman who commits suicide with her children, flying down to their deaths from a New York skyscraper; and another who flies to her life, escaping an arranged marriage to an important man living overseas. It forms a vivid album of sharply focused, well-composed snapshots of women's lives.

Couzyn, Jeni. Born in South Africa in 1942, she was educated at Natal University, Durban, and left for England in 1966. She has, in addition to publishing poetry, worked in film, appeared on radio and television, and was a founding member of the Poet's Conference and Poet's Union. She has recently been teaching in the Department of Creative Writing, University of Victoria, British Columbia.

Works

Bad Day. New York: Dutton, 1990.
Christmas in Africa. London, England: Heinemann, 1975.
Flying. London, England: Workshop Press, 1970.
The Happiness Bird. Victoria, British Columbia: Sono Nis Press, 1978.
House of Changes. London, England: Heinemann, 1978.
*Life by Drowning: Selected Poems. Toronto, Canada: Anansi, 1983.
Monkey's Wedding. London, England: Cape, 1972.
Singing Down the Bones. London, England: Women's Press, 1989.

Cracking India by Bapsi Sidhwa (Minneapolis, MN: Milkweed, 1991). Published in Great Britain under the title *Ice-Candy-Man.* A small child hearing about partition, about the "cracking" of India, wonders what that means and what it will be like. She is growing up in a Parsi family with a Hindu ayah who has an insistent Muslim admirer in Lahore. When India cracks, Lahore becomes a divided place, and the former lover becomes swept up in nationalistic frenzy, leading a violent gang to kidnap the ayah. The city goes up in flames, and the child narrator believes her mother is hoarding petrol in order to start fires; it turns out that she is using it to help find women in trouble and transport them to safety. Eventually, the kidnapped ayah is found, now working for the Muslim man in the city's red light district, and a young cousin, battered witness to horrible butchery, turns up to share his firsthand experience of partition. The witness to it all, a child and member of a sect that has remained outside the vortex of the violence, brings both a clarity and a simplicity to the violence and senselessness of partition that makes it poignantly personal and tangibly real.

Craig, Christine. Born in Kingston, Jamaica, in 1943, she was educated in Jamaica and then moved to London in 1964, where she helped to found the Caribbean Artists Movement. She started working as a journalist for the *Guardian* in 1967, married Karl Craig, and began to write books for children, which her husband illustrated. She became a full-time freelance writer in 1972 and soon after returned to Jamaica, where she worked with the Women's Bureau. In 1980 she earned a B.A. from the University of the West Indies, with a double major in communications and English. She wrote and produced a children's television series on Jamaican history before winning a fellowship to the International Writers' Program at the University of Iowa in 1989. In addition to her books for children, she has published poetry and short fiction in periodicals and anthologies, and has published poetry and short story collections.

Works

Emmanuel and His Parrot. London, England: Oxford University, 1970.
Emmanuel Goes to Market. London, England: Oxford University, 1971.
Mint Tea. Portsmouth, NH: Heinemann, 1993.
Quadrille for Tigers. Sebastopol, CA: Mina Press, 1984.

Commentary

Fido, Elaine Savory. "Textures of Third World Reality in the Poetry of Four African-
    Caribbean Women." *Out of the Kumbla: Women and Literature in the Caribbean.*
    Trenton, NJ: Africa World Press, 1990. 29–44.

Creider, Jane Tapsubei. Born and raised near Lake Nyanza, Kenya, she lived in Kisumu and Nairobi before emigrating to Canada, where she now lives in London, Ontario, with her two children and husband, the Africanist Chet A. Creider. She is a sculptor who has written several articles on the language and culture of her people, the Nandi, and has coauthored a grammar of the Nandi language with her husband. Her autobiography and the one novel she has published to date are based on the traditions and experiences of the Nandi people.

Works

The Shrunken Dream. Toronto, Canada: Women's Press, 1992.
*Two Lives: My Spirit and I. London, England: Women's Press, 1986.

Crick Crack, Monkey by Merle Hodge (London, England: Heinemann, 1981).
In this first-person *bildungsroman*, a young girl lives in two worlds—the lower-class, warm, generous, West Indian home where she was raised by an outspoken aunt, and the upper-class household of a social-climbing family that emulates British lifestyles and despises West Indian language and customs. She moves in with her wealthier relations to pursue her education and finally joins her long-absent father in England, advancing to greater opportunity while losing touch with her nourishing roots. She becomes a witness to, and a victim of, the post-colonial half-life of British culture in the Caribbean and the ways it devalues the culture in which she feels most at home.

Commentary

Gikandi, Simon. "Narration in the Post-Colonial Moment: Merle Hodge's *Crick Crack, Monkey." Past the Last Post: Theorizing Post-Colonialism and Post-Modernism.* Calgary, Canada: University of Calgary, 1990. 13–22.
Gikandi, Simon. "Writing After Colonialism: *Crick Crack, Monkey* and *Beka Lamb." Writing in Limbo: Modernism and Caribbean Literature.* Ithaca, NY: Cornell University, 1992. 197–230.
Thorpe, Marjorie. "The Problem of Cultural Identification in *Crick Crack, Monkey." Savacou* 13 (1977): 31–38.

Cughta'i, 'Ismat. Born on August 15, 1915, in Badayun, Uttar Pradesh, India, into a middle-class family, the youngest of six brothers and four sisters. Her father was a civil servant whose work took the family to Jodhpur; then, after his retirement, they moved to their ancestral home in Agra. She attended the local municipal school, refused to engage in typical feminine pastimes such as embroidery or playing with dolls, and distressed her family by playing with the servant's children. She was much influenced by her brother, Mirza Azim Beg Cughta'i, who was an established writer and who introduced her to literature. She struggled against parental disapproval to attend college, earning a B.A. and a B.T., and worked as principal of the Girls' College in Bareilly and later as Inspectress of Schools in Bombay. She married Shahid Latif, a filmmaker, in 1942, just after writing her story "Lihaaf" ("The Quilt"), which with its suggestion of lesbianism was considered so shocking she was charged with obscenity and was brought to trial in Lahore; after two years the charges were finally dropped because the material considered obscene is suggested rather than depicted directly. She is a prominent figure in Urdu literature, whose style is realistic and concerned with themes relevant to Uttar Pradesh Muslim women and their world. She published a number of story and essay collections, novels, and plays as well as one collection of stories in English translation and was involved with film, both writing and producing several films. She died in 1992.

Work

The Quilt and Other Stories. New Delhi, India: Kali for Women, 1990.

Cunha, Helena Parente. Born in 1929 in Salvador, Bahia, northeastern Brazil, she moved to Rio de Janeiro in 1958 and holds a teaching position at the Universidade Federal in Rio de Janeiro, where she formerly was dean and is now professor in the College of Letters, specializing in literary theory. Her first novel, *Woman Between Mirrors*, received much critical acclaim in Brazil; she also has published collections of short stories and poetry.

Work

*Woman Between Mirrors. Translated by Fred P. Ellison and Naomi Lindstrom. Austin: University of Texas, 1989.

Commentary

Tesser, Carmen Chaves. "Post-Structuralist Theory Mirrored in Helena Parente Cunha's *Woman Between Mirrors*." *Hispania* 74.3 (September 1991): 594–597.

Cuza Malé, Belkis. Born on June 15, 1942, in Guantanamo, Cuba, daughter of a cement factory worker. Her family was very encouraging about her early interest in writing and sent her to private schools that were mainly attended by children of professionals and bureaucrats, then to the Universidad del Oriente, where she earned a master's degree in Hispanic American and Cuban literature in 1964. After graduation she worked in Havana as a radio and television critic for the newspaper *Hoy*, then as the cultural editor of *Granma*, the official organ of the Communist Party. She began to publish poetry by 1963 and married the poet Heberto Padilla in 1966. In 1971, they both were jailed for subversive writing and for several years lived under threat of house arrest and censorship. Her book *Juego de damas*, in press at the time of their arrest, was shredded by the censors, as was one of her husband's books. In 1979, they left Cuba—she smuggled a bundle of her poems out—and they now live with their son in Princeton, New Jersey, where she continues to write novels and poetry and edits the literary magazine *Linden Lane*. A collection of her poetry, including the work shredded after her arrest, is available in a bilingual edition.

Work

*Woman on the Front Lines. Translated by Pamela Carmell. Greensboro, NC: Unicorn, 1987.

Commentary

Cuza Malé, Belkis. "A Woman and Her Poems." *Contemporary Women Authors of Latin America*. New York: Brooklyn College, 1983. 93–95.

D

d'Adesky, Anne-christine. Born in Michigan in 1958 to Haitian and French parents, she has spent much of her life in Haiti. She earned a master's degree from the Columbia School of Journalism in 1982 and has written editorial and news stories about Haiti for a number of newspapers and magazines. In her work as the Haiti stringer for the *San Francisco Examiner*, she covered military massacres during the 1987 presidential elections and was nominated for a Pulitzer Prize. She has written a novel set in Haiti dealing with political violence and repression.

Work

*Under the Bone. New York: Farrar, Straus, Giroux, 1994.

A Dakar Childhood by Nafissatou Diallo (Harlow, England: Longman, 1982). Translation of *De Tilène au plateau: Une enfance Dakaroise*, first published by Les Nouvelles Éditions Africaines in 1975. A memoir of the author's girlhood in Dakar that demonstrates the resilience of Senegalese culture in a metropolitan and francophone setting. She is strongly influenced by her father and her grandmother, who impart the values and traditions of her society, and receives a French-flavored education that makes her so at home with Western texts that she and her friends use nicknames for one of their circle based on Dumas's characters. Her motivation for telling her life story is in part to preserve the past, in part to celebrate her father. She says in the foreword: "I am not the heroine of a novel but an ordinary woman of this country, Senegal. . . . Perhaps it is worth reminding today's youngsters what we were like when we were their age.'' But in the end, her project is somewhat more ambitious: She will tell the world about her father and his way of life. ''I would tell this to his children, to his grandchildren; why should I not say to the world which lives with its eyes fixed on great men and women, that it is the unimportant, modest folk who support and carry the weight of the great? A just man has lived his life; he was modest and great'' (133). She succeeds in this and in creating a self-portrait that is just as meaningful and vibrant an image as that of her father.

Commentary

Lambrech, Regine. ''Three Black Women, Three Autobiographers.'' *Présence Africaine* 123 (1982): 136–143.

Dance on the Volcano by Marie Chauvet (New York: W. Sloan, 1959). Translation from French of *La Dance sur le volcan*, first published in 1957. A historical novel that focuses on the ambivalent position of the *afranchies*, free blacks, living in Haiti just before the French revolution and the independence of Haiti. Minette, a girl with a beautiful voice, becomes the diva of an opera house in Port-au-Prince, though not without controversy since she is a light-skinned mestiza. She is given a philosophical and political education by an idealistic young tutor and becomes more and more aware of the injustices of slavery. She falls in love with a slave-owning man of color who abuses his slaves even while sympathizing with revolutionary ideals. The presence of maroons living in the mountains provides an undercurrent of impending racial violence that finally erupts in the confusion following the revolution, as white plantation owners seek to consolidate their power and the maroons pour down the mountainsides into the city. The novel, while heavy on the costume-drama setting of theater and social soirées, and with characters who would be at home in romance novels, does engage complex questions of race and identity and depicts a turbulent moment in Haitian history.

Daneshvar, Simin. See **Danishvar, Simin.**

Daneshvar's Playhouse by Simin Danishvar (Washington, DC: Mage, 1989). A collection of stories about a disparate cast of characters. ''The Playhouse'' explores relations among players, one of whom is a young woman who desperately needs money for an abortion. In ''To Whom Can I Say Hello'' a lonely old woman, embittered by her experiences, finds herself surrounded by the kindness of strangers, who suddenly make her feel as if the population of the city are all her relatives. ''The Loss of Jalal'' is an autobiographical account of the death of the author's husband, the writer Jalal Al-e Ahmad. The collection offers a sampling of the Iranian writer's style and touches on the social and gender issues that she probes with a gentle touch.

Dangarembga, Tsitsi. Born on February 14, 1959, in Mtoko, eastern Zimbabwe (then called Rhodesia); her parents were among the first generation of highly educated Africans in Zimbabwe. She spent her early years, from two to six, in England where her parents were pursuing degrees. When the family returned in 1965, she was enrolled at the Marymount Mission school in Mutare, then attended the prestigious private and largely white Arundel School in Salisbury (now Harare). She worked briefly as a teacher. In 1977, she went to Cambridge to study for a medical degree, and there the "emotional trauma of leaving home, coupled inevitably with a small confrontation with England, released a mass of poetry" ("This Year, Next Year," 43); impatient with the racism and isolation she met in England, she decided to leave her studies and returned home in 1980, just before independence. After a brief tenure working in advertising, she enrolled in the psychology program at the University of Zimbabwe and joined the university's Drama Group, which performed three of her plays, *She No Longer Weeps, The Lost of the Soil*, and *The Third One*. In 1985, she finished her novel *Nervous Conditions*, but it took three years, and a number of disappointing contacts with Zimbabwean publishers, before it was accepted by the Women's Press of London and published in 1989, winning the Commonwealth Prize that year. Since then she has been living in Berlin, studying film and working on a sequel to her novel.

Works

*Nervous Conditions. Seattle, WA: Seal, 1989.
She No Longer Weeps. Harare: College Press Zimbabwe, 1987.

Commentary

Bardolph, Jacqueline. " 'The Tears of Childhood' of Tsitsi Dangarembga." *Commonwealth Essays and Studies* 13.1 (autumn 1990): 37–47.
Dangarembga, Tsitsi. "This Year, Next Year . . ." *Women's Review of Books* 8.10–11 (July 1991): 43–44.
Flockemann, Miki. " 'Not-Quite Insiders and Not-Quite Outsiders': The 'Process of Womanhood' in *Beka Lamb, Nervous Conditions* and *Daughters of the Twilight*." *Journal of Commonwealth Literature* 27.1 (1992): 37–47.
George, Rosemary Marangoly. "An Interview with Tsitsi Dangarembga." *Novel* 26.3 (spring 1993): 309–319.
McWilliams, Sally. "Tsitsi Dangarembga's *Nervous Conditions*: At the Crossroads of Feminism and Post-Colonialism." *World Literature Written in English* 31.1 (1991): 103–112.
Phillips, Maggi. "Engaging Dreams: Alternative Perspectives on Flora Nwapa, Buchi Emecheta, Ama Ata Aidoo, Bessie Head, and Tsitsi Dangarembga." *Research in African Literatures* 25.4 (winter 1994): 89–103.
Thomas, Sue. "Killing the Hysteric in the Colonized's House: Tsitsi Dangarembga's *Nervous Conditions*." *Journal of Commonwealth Literature* 27.1 (1992): 326–356.
Veit-Wild, Flora. "Women Write About Things that Move Them." *Matatu* 3.6 (1989): 101–108.

Veit-Wild, Flora. *Teachers, Preachers, Non-Believers: A Social History of Zimbabwean Literature*. London, England and Harare, Zimbabwe: Zell/Baobab, 1992.
Wilkinson, Jane, editor. *Talking With African Writers: Interviews with African Poets, Playwrights, and Novelists*. London, England: James Currey, 1991.

Danishvar, Simin. Born on April 28, 1921, in Shiraz, Iran, the third of six children. She moved to Teheran in 1942 to attend university there, where she studied Persian literature, receiving a doctorate in 1949. She met and married another writer, Jalal Al-e Ahmad, while a student. Two years later, she traveled to the United States on a Fulbright Fellowship to study creative writing at Stanford University. Returning to Iran, she taught at the Teheran Conservatory and then at Teheran University. She published several collections of stories and her novel *Savushun*, published when she was 48, became the most popular novel in modern Iran, having best-seller status for over a decade. She retired from the university in 1979 and wrote a second novel, *A Persian Requiem*. Though she involves herself in political life, she does so in a cautious, measured way. She was a founding member of the Writers' Association of Iran, which defended the rights of writers. She considers herself a voice for ordinary Iranian women, who have been idealized as beautiful and desirable objects in Iranian literature, having totemic rather than human status. Though very popular in Iran, her work has not received as much critical notice as might be expected for someone of her stature.

Works

Daneshvar's Playhouse. Translated by Maryam Mafi. Washington, DC: Mage, 1989.
A Persian Requiem: A Novel. Translated by Roxane Zand. New York: G. Braziller, 1992.
Savushun. Translated by M. R. Ghanooparvar. Washington, DC: Mage 1990.
Sutra and Other Stories. Translated by Hasan Javadi and Amin Neshati. Washington, DC: Mage, 1994.

Commentary

Milani, Farzaneh. *Veils and Words: The Emerging Voices of Iranian Women Writers*. Syracuse, NY: Syracuse University, 1992.

Danquah, Mabel Dove. Born in Ghana (then called the Gold Coast) in 1910, she was educated at local schools and then in England. She traveled in Europe and the United States before returning to Africa to edit the *Accra Evening News*. She served in Parliament in 1952, the first woman elected to an African legislative assembly. She and her husband, J. B. Danquah (who died in detention in 1965), worked together for independence. She is known as an activist and supporter of African cultural traditions. She wrote many columns for the *West African Times* under the pen name Marjorie Mensah, and her stories, particularly ''The Torn Veil,'' have appeared in several anthologies.

Work

The Torn Veil, and Other Stories. London, England: Evans Brothers, 1975.

Danticat, Edwidge. Born in Haiti in January 1969. Her parents left to find work in the United States when she was four, and she was cared for by an aunt and uncle until age twelve, when she and her brother moved to New York to be reunited with her parents and their two children born in America. She began writing at an early age, inspired by the tradition of storytelling first encountered in Haiti, where frequent power outages led to the elders in the family entertaining the rest of the family with stories. By age fourteen she was starting to publish stories, and she has since published over twenty stories and essays in a variety of periodicals and collections. She earned a B.A. in French literature from Barnard in 1980 and an M.F.A. from Brown University in 1993. She has recently been working with Jonathan Demme on a series of Haiti-related film projects while pursuing her work as a novelist. Her first novel, *Breath, Eyes, Memory,* was well received by critics as a lyrical and insightful, restrained, and understated coming of age story.

Work

*Breath, Eyes, Memory. New York: Soho, 1994.

Das, Kamala. Born in 1934 at Punnayurkulam, Malabar, India, Das is a prolific bilingual writer of poetry, essays, fiction, and autobiography, who writes in Malayalam and English. She is the daughter of a well-known woman poet, Balamaniyamma; her father was a car salesman. She was the only daughter in a family of five children. At age fifteen she was married by traditional arrangement to her maternal uncle, a banker, which proved to be an unhappy union. She has published a number of collections of poetry and has also published essays and autobiographical writing as well as serving for a time as editor of the *Illustrated Weekly of India.* She ran for a seat in Parliament as an independent candidate from Trivandrum in 1984 and, though defeated, earned the respect of many for her outspoken critique of political corruption. Her journalism is noted for its courage and outspokenness, her poetry for its frank exploration of sexuality and its bold critique of patriarchy.

Works

Alphabet of Lust. New Delhi, India: Orient Paperbacks, 1977.
The Best of Kamala Das. Kazhikade, India: Badhi, 1991.
Collected Poems. Trivandrum, India: Kamala Das, 1973.
The Descendants. Calcutta, India: Writers' Workshop, 1973.
A Doll for the Child Prostitute. New Delhi: India Paperbacks, 1977.
Kamala Das: A Collage. Delhi, India: D. K. Publishers, 1984.
Kamala Das: A Selection with Essays on Her Work. Adelaide, Australia: Centre for
    Research in the New Literatures in English, 1986.
My Story. New York: Quartet Books, 1978.

The Old Playhouse and Other Poems. London, England: Sangam, 1986.

Summer in Calcutta. New Delhi, India: R. Paul for Kamala Das, 1965.

Tonight, This Savage Rite: The Love Poems of Kamala Das and Pritish Nandy. New Delhi, India: Arnold-Heinemann, 1979.

Commentary

Ash, Ranjana. "The Search for Freedom in Indian Women's Writing." *Motherlands: Women's Writings from Africa, the Caribbean, and South Asia*. New Brunswick, NJ: Rutgers University, 1992. 152–174.

Daruwalla, Keki. "Confessional Poetry as Social Commentary: A View of English Poetry by Indian Women Poets." *Indian Horizons* 35.3–4 (1986): 15–24.

Dwivedi, A. N. *Kamala Das and Her Poetry*. Delhi, India: Doaba House, 1983.

Harrex, S. C. "The Strange Case of Matthew Arnold in a Sari or the Past as Prelude to Kamala Das." *The Writer's Sense of the Past: Essays on Southeast Asian and Australasian Literature*. Singapore: National University of Singapore, 1987. 55–64.

Ikabala, Kaura. *Untying and Retying the Text: An Analysis of Kamala Das's* My Story. New Delhi, India: Bahri, 1990.

Ikabala, Kaura. *Feminist Revolution and Kamala Das's* My Story. Patiala, India: Century Twentyone, 1992.

Lim, Shirley. "Terms of Empowerment in Kamala Das's *My Story*." *De/Colonizing the Subject: The Politics of Gender in Women's Autobiography*. Minneapolis: University of Minnesota, 1992. 346–369.

North, Marilla. "Watching Herself/Watching Herself: Kamala Das's Split Texts." *New Literatures Review* 21 (summer 1991): 42–57.

A Daughter of Han: The Autobiography of a Chinese Working Woman by Ning Lao T'ai-t'ai and Ida Pruitt (Stanford, CA: Stanford University, 1967). The life story of a woman from the north of China who describes a hardscrabble existence, covering the years from 1867 to 1937. A mother, a member of an extended family, and unhappily married to an opium addict, she worked incessantly to support her family. Even with her efforts, they often went hungry, and once, when she was away from home working, her husband sold one of their children to support his opium habit. The narrative, told in a blunt, straightforward manner, emphasizes the difficulties she has to endure and is a tribute to both the subject of the autobiography and the skill of Ida Pruitt, who recorded the life in a self-effacing and sensitive way.

Daughter of Persia: A Woman's Journey from Her Father's Harem Through the Islamic Revolution by Sattareh Farman-Farmaian and Dona Munker (New York: Anchor/Doubleday, 1993). The autobiography of a woman raised in a prominent and extremely wealthy Iranian household in Teheran. She left the world of strict tradition in which she was brought up and went to the United States to study social work in the early 1940s. She returned to Iran to found the Teheran School of Social Work. She was concerned about poverty and inequality in her country, and deplored the growing materialism of the culture under the shah, but was also dismayed by the increasingly fervent fundamentalism and anti-Western sentiments of the young intelligentsia. She witnessed the revolution firsthand, and through luck and her history of socially responsible activism, she narrowly escaped execution. An interesting insider's account of Iran before and during the revolution.

Daughter of Shanghai by Chin Ts'ai (New York: St. Martin's, 1988). Autobiography of a Chinese actress whose first major role was as Suzy Wong, a stereotyped prostitute. Her life in the West is intercut with news from China, where her father, a famous actor, has been caught up in and purged by the Cultural Revolution. Though the book tends to contain aspects of the show biz biography, with many names dropped and Hollywood roles discussed, there are interesting insights into Chinese drama and the representation of the Chinese woman in Western film, as well as information on the fate of an important actor during the Cultural Revolution.

Daughters by Paule Marshall (New York: Atheneum, 1991). A woman from the fictional island of Triunion refuses her father's request to return home to witness his reelection. She wrestles with her past, her problematic relationship with her father, who is a once-idealistic but now complacent politician, her relationship with her American-born and independent mother, and with her place as a black woman both in Triunion and in the United States. The central character notices many moments of past and present fusing together in "double exposures," when the resemblances between mother and daughter, between the island and the United States, become suddenly linked together. Both major and supporting characters are vividly realized in this novel, which treats political and social issues as fundamental aspects of the characters' self-definition.

Commentary

Dance, Daryl Cumber. "An Interview with Paule Marshall." *Southern Review* 28.1 (winter 1992): 1–20.
Jordan, Shirley M. "*Daughters*: The Unity That Binds Us." *American Visions* 6.5 (October 1991): 38–39.
Miller, Adam David. "Women and Power: The Confounding of Gender, Race, and Class." *Black Scholar* 22.4 (fall 1992): 48–52.
Pettis, Joyce. "Legacies of Community and History in Paule Marshall's *Daughters*." *Studies in the Literary Imagination* 26.2 (fall 1993): 89–99.

Daughters of the House by Indrani Aikath-Gyaltsen (New York: Ballantine, 1991). A group of women living in an old house in India are disturbed when the aunt and mother-figure marries. Her new husband disrupts their routines and does not share their love for the house. When the aunt becomes seriously ill with a disfiguring illness, Chchandra, the narrator, has an affair with her husband, a confused gesture of anger and resentment that results in a pregnancy.

When the aunt dies, she abruptly ends the affair and resolves to remain in the house, bringing another daughter into the house. The novel has a lyrical and introverted narration, in which the house is as much part of the family as the characters and in which the community of women has a unity that can't be shared with men.

Daughters of the Twilight by Farida Karodia (London, England: Women's Press, 1986). This story of a "coloured" family in South Africa relates their struggle to live normally in an abnormal world. The narrator's sister is raped by a vicious white Afrikaner and reluctantly bears the child. Unable to cope with mothering the baby, she runs away from home. The author interweaves political, personal, and moral threads in this sympathetic novel.

Commentary

Flockemann, Miki. " 'Not-Quite Insiders and Not-Quite Outsiders': The 'Process of Womanhood' in *Beka Lamb, Nervous Conditions* and *Daughters of the Twilight*." *Journal of Commonwealth Literature* 27.1 (1992): 37–47.

Days and Nights in Calcutta by Bharati Mukherjee and Clark Blaise (New York: Doubleday, 1977). A two-part invention by an Indian novelist and her Canadian husband, a dialogic narrative of a year spent in India. It includes analysis of Calcutta's upper-class lifestyle, particularly among the Brahmin women with whom Mukherjee grew up and went to school. Because of the double narration, gender differences are strongly brought out, while class issues are present but little analyzed.

D'Costa, Jean. Born in 1937 in St. Andrew, Jamaica, the daughter of two teachers. She grew up in the small farming community of St. James during the war years and then attended the University of the West Indies and University College, London. She did research on Jacobean drama at Oxford University and at Indiana University. Returning to Jamaica, she worked as a lecturer in English at the University of the West Indies and became a consultant to the government on English teaching, specializing in the study of Creole. In addition to her literary works, D'Costa has collaborated on two books on Jamaican Creole, *Voices in Exile* and *Language in Exile*, and has published criticism of the works of Roger Mais. She has written children's literature, using accurate dialects of Jamaica, and has been recently teaching at Hamilton College in Clinton, New York.

Works

Brother Man. Kingston, Jamaica: Longman Caribbean, 1978.
Escape to Last Man Peak. Kingston, Jamaica: Longman Caribbean, 1975.
Over Our Way. London, England: Longman, 1980.
Sprat Morrison. Kingston, Jamaica: Collins, Sangster, 1979.
Voice in the Wind. London, England: Longman Caribbean, 1978.

Commentary

D'Costa, Jean. "Expression and Communication: Literary Challenges to the Caribbean Polydialectal Writers." *Journal of Commonwealth Literature* 19.1 (1984): 123–141.

D'Costa, Jean, and Barbara Lalla, editors. *Voices in Exile: Jamaican Texts of the 18th and 19th Centuries.* Tuscaloosa: University of Alabama, 1989.

Lalla, Barbara, and Jean D'Costa. *Language in Exile: Three Hundred Years of Jamaican Creole.* Tuscaloosa: University of Alabama, 1990.

De la Parra, Teresa. See **Parra, Teresa de la.**

De Lima, Clara Rosa. Born in 1923 in Trinidad, of Spanish descent. She was educated at schools in Trinidad, Barbados, and Baltimore before attending Long Island University, where she began writing short stories. She has worked as a radio journalist as well as a writer of fiction and poetry.

Works

Countdown to Carnival. Ilfracombe, Devon: A. H. Stockwell, 1978.
Currents of the Yuna. Ilfracombe, Devon: A. H. Stockwell, 1978.
Dreams Non-Stop. Ilfracombe, Devon: A. H. Stockwell, 1974.
Kilometre Nineteen. Ilfracombe, Devon: A. H. Stockwell, 1980.
Not Bad, Just a Little Mad. Ilfracombe, Devon: A. H. Stockwell, 1975.
Reminiscing. Ilfracombe, Devon: A. H. Stockwell, 1975.
Thoughts and Dreams. Ilfracombe, Devon: A. H. Stockwell, 1973.
Tomorrow Will Always Come. New York: I. Obolensky, 1965.

The Dead Leaves by Barbara Jacobs (Willimantic, CT: Curbstone, 1993). A fond memoir of a father who is a gentle, reflective, quiet but politically involved man whose family were Maronite Christians who emigrated from Lebanon to the United States where his father disappeared and his mother took over business and family. He joins the Republicans during the Spanish American War and is horrified at the carnage he witnesses. He later serves in the U.S. forces during World War II, though not allowed to fight fascism because of his Communist beliefs, marries, and moves to Mexico, where he raises his family and spends much of his time reading. The narration is from the children's voice, collectively, first describing the Papa they know, then tracing his history, and finally his old age, when he wishes to simply lie down under a bridge and cover himself with dead leaves rather than contribute to "this death business." A tender and gentle family history.

Dear Diego by Elena Poniatowska (New York: Pantheon Books, 1986). This novel is an imaginary set of letters (based on real documents) written from Diego Rivera's wife, Angelina Beloff, to him after he left her. She lives to support him in his work and desperately wants to be needed by him, in the process failing to develop as an artist in her own right. There is a plaintive, anxious note to her correspondence: "I embrace you desperately across the ocean that separates us" (57). She never gains confidence in her own work. Her last words to him are: "what do you think of my engravings?" The author says in a postscript that she finally traveled to Mexico, but Diego Rivera passed her at a concert without recognizing her. The novel is a poignant exploration of the relations between a man and a woman, both artists but one crippled by her love for the other, told in the documentary style that Poniatowska has pioneered.

Commentary

Paul, Marcella L. "Letters and Desire: The Function of Marks on Paper in Elena Poniatowska's *Querido Diego, te abraza Quela.*" *Continental, Latin-American, and Francophone Women Writers.* Lanham, MD: University Press of America, 1990. 1–5.

Desai, Anita. Born on June 24, 1937, in Mussoorie, northern India, she grew up in Delhi, the daughter of a German mother and a Bengali father. She was raised trilingually, speaking German, English, and Hindi, learning to write in English before any other language. She was educated at Queen Mary's School and Miranda House, a women's college of Delhi University, earning a B.A. in English. She began publishing stories before marrying Ashvin Desai, with whom she has four children. She was a visiting professor at Girton College, Cambridge, in 1986. From 1987 to 1989 she taught at Smith College in the United States and then began to teach one semester a year at Mount Holyoke, though she lives most of the year in India and considers herself Indian, not a member of the Indian Diaspora. She resists reading criticism of her work or other criticism, preferring to think of writing as an instinctual process rather than one of analysis or interpretation. Her style, while not markedly innovative, is graceful and assured, with solid characterization and an undercurrent of gentle irony. She is one of the most critically acclaimed of Indian writers, receiving much praise in India and the West.

Works

Baumgartner's Bombay. New York: Knopf, 1989.
Bye-Bye Blackbird. Delhi, India: Vision Books, 1985.
Clear Light of Day. New York: Harper and Row, 1980.
Cry, the Peacock. Delhi, India: Orient Paperbacks, 1986.
Fire on the Mountain. Harmondsworth, England: Penguin, 1981.
Games at Twilight and Other Stories. Harmondsworth, England: Penguin, 1982.
In Custody. New York: Harper and Row, 1984.
The Peacock Garden. London, England: Heinemann, 1979.
The Village by the Sea: An Indian Family Story. London, England: Heinemann, 1982.
Voices in the City. Delhi, India: Orient Paperbacks, 1982.
Where Shall We Go This Summer? Delhi, India: Orient Paperbacks, 1982.

Commentary

Afzal-Khan, Fawzia. *Cultural Imperialism and the Indo-English Novel: Genre and Ideology in the Novels of R. K. Narayan, Anita Desai, Kamala Markandaya and Salman Rushdie.* University Park: Pennsylvania State University, 1993.

Ash, Ranjana. "The Search for Freedom in Indian Women's Writing." *Motherlands: Women's Writings from Africa, the Caribbean, and South Asia.* New Brunswick, NJ: Rutgers University, 1992. 152–174.

Bliss, Corinne Demas, editor. "Against the Current: A Conversation with Anita Desai." *The Massachusetts Review* 29.3 (autumn 1988): 521–537.

Chew, Shirley. "Searching Voices: Anita Desai's *Clear Light of Day* and Nayantara Sahgal's *Rich Like Us.*" *Motherlands: Women's Writings from Africa, the Caribbean, and South Asia.* New Brunswick, NJ: Rutgers University, 1992. 43–63.

Desai, Anita. "Indian Fiction Today." *Daedalus* 118.4 (fall 1989): 206–231.

Goel, Kunj Bala. *Language and Theme in Anita Desai's Fiction.* Jaipur, India: Classic, 1989.

Huggan, Graham. "Philomela's Retold Story: Silence, Music, and the Post-Colonial Text." *Journal of Commonwealth Literature* 25.1 (August 1990): 12–23.

Jain, Jasbir. *Stairs to the Attic: The Novels of Anita Desai.* Jaipur, India: Printwell, 1988.

Jussawalla, Feroza F., and Reed Way Dasenbrock. *Interviews with Writers of the Post-Colonial World.* Jackson: University Press of Mississippi, 1992.

Kanawar Asha. *Virginia Woolf and Anita Desai: A Comparative Study.* New Delhi, India: Prestige, 1989.

Kirpal, Viney. "An Image of India: A Study of Anita Desai's *In Custody.*" *Ariel* 17.4 (October 1986): 127–138.

Mann, Harveen Sachdeva. " 'Going in the Opposite Direction': Feminine Recusancy in Anita Desai's *Voices in the City.*" *Ariel* 23.4 (October 1992): 75–95.

Mukherjee, Bharati. "Mimicry and Reinvention." *The Commonwealth in Canada: Proceedings of the Second Triennial Conference of CACLALS, University of Winnipeg, 1-4 October, 1981.* Calcutta, India: Writers' Workshop, 1983. 147–157.

Pathania, Usha. *Human Bonds and Bondages: The Fiction of Anita Desai and Kamala Markandaya.* Delhi, India: Kanishka, 1992.

Ross, Robert L., editor. *International Literature in English: Essays on the Major Writers.* New York: Garland, 1991.

Seguet, Pascale. "An Interview with Anita Desai." *Commonwealth Essays and Studies* 10.2 (spring 1988): 43–50.

Sharma, Kajali. *Symbolism in Anita Desai's Novels.* New Delhi, India: Abhinav, 1991.

Solanki, Mrilani. *Anita Desai's Fiction: Patterns of Survival Strategies.* Delhi, India: Kanishka, 1992.

Deshpande, Gauri. Born in India in 1942. Her mother, Iravati Karve, was a well-known anthropologist and philosopher; her grandfather, D. K. Karve, founded the first women's university in Maharashtra. She writes poetry in English and fiction in Marathi, as well as working as a journalist in both languages. Some of her Marathi short fiction is available in English translations in anthologies.

Works

Between Births. Calcutta, India: Writers' Workshop, 1968.
Beyond the Slaughter House: Poems. Calcutta, India: Pritish Nandy, Dialogue, 1972.
Lost Love. Calcutta, India: Writers' Workshop, 1970.

Commentary

Varma, Monika. "Gauri Deshpande." *Commonwealth Quarterly* 3.9 (December 1978): 15–27.

Deshpande, Shashi. Born in Dharwad, India, daughter of a playwright and Sanskrit scholar Shriranga. She earned a degree in economics from Elphinstone College, Bombay, and won two medals for academic standing at Mysore University. After earning another degree in law, she married a pathologist, had two children, and then returned to studies, this time in journalism. She has worked on the staff of a magazine and written short stories, children's books, and several novels that examine issues of gender and patriarchy in India.

Works

The Binding Vine. London, England: Virago, 1993.
Come Up and Be Dead. New Delhi, India: Vikas, 1983.
The Dark Holds No Terrors. Sahibabad, Ghaziabad: Vikas, 1980.
The Legacy and Other Stories. Calcutta, India: Writers' Workshop, 1978.
The Narayanpur Incident. Bombay, India: IBH, 1982.
Roots and Shadows. Bombay, India: Sangam, 1983.
*That Long Silence. London, England: Virago, 1988.

Commentary

Ash, Ranjana. "The Search for Freedom in Indian Women's Writing." *Motherlands: Women's Writings from Africa, the Caribbean, and South Asia*. New Brunswick, NJ: Rutgers University, 1992. 152–174.
Sandhu, Sarbjit K. *The Image of Woman in the Novels of Shashi Deshpande*. New Delhi, India: Prestige, 1991.

Devi, Mahasweta. Born in 1926 in Dhaka to parents who were both successful writers. She graduated from Santiniketan in 1946, married the playwright Bijan Bhattacharya the next year, and worked briefly for the postal audit office before being sacked for her left-wing political beliefs. She worked at several jobs while beginning to write for a journal and in 1956 published her first book, *Jhansir Rani*, a biography of an Indian rani who fought the British after the Mutiny of 1857. In 1962, after a divorce, she married the writer Asit Gupta and earned a master's degree in English literature from Calcutta University and began to teach at Bijaygarh College, where she worked until 1984. Her writing has focused on the struggles of tribal peoples against the British in colonial times and against the Indian government in the 1960s and 1970s. She is the author of over a hundred books—novels, story collections, children's books, and plays—in Bengali, many of which have been translated into other Indian languages. She also is a columnist and editor of a quarterly publication by and about tribal and lower-caste Indians. She is a feminist who links patriarchal oppression to class and race issues, and a political activist on behalf of the poor. Her fiction uses a heteroglossia of Bengali dialects that are rarely used in "literary" writing. Some of her stories have been translated by distinguished literary critic Gayatri Chakravorty Spivak.

Work

Imaginary Maps. Translated by Gayatri Chakravorty Spivak. New York: Routledge, 1993.

Commentary

Spivak, Gayatri Chakravorty. *In Other Worlds: Essays in Cultural Politics.* New York: Methuen, 1987.

Dhingra, Leena. Born in India in 1942, she has lived abroad since childhood. Her family left at the time of the partition—they lived in the area that became Pakistan and lost their home. She moved frequently during her schooling, living in India, France, Switzerland, and England. She received a diploma in drama in 1962, worked for theaters for two years in both England and France, then worked as a public relations officer in Brussels, where she earned a certificate in film editing. Until 1990 she worked in the film industry in both the United Kingdom and India. She also studied for an education degree in London and taught for a time. She was a coordinator of the Asian Women Writers' Collective in London and has had writer residencies in schools and colleges around Britain. She is currently working on a master's degree in creative writing at East Anglia University. She has written television scripts, has published work in several anthologies, and has, to date, published one novel.

Work

*Amritvela. London, England: Women's Press, 1988.

Diallo, Nafissatou. Born in Senegal in 1941, she worked as a midwife and director of maternal and child health care at a center on the outskirts of Dakar before her death in 1982. Her first work was a memoir of her childhood, an eloquently written account of her life and the world she lived in, which won an award from the Association of French Language Speakers. She also wrote works for children.

Works

*A Dakar Childhood. Translated by Dorothy S. Blair. Harlow, England: Longman, 1982.
Fary, Princess of Tiali. Translated by Ann Woolcombe. Washington, DC: Three Continents Press, 1987.

Commentary

Lambrech, Regine. "Three Black Women, Three Autobiographers." *Présence Africaine*
    123 (1982): 136–143.
Stringer, Susan. "Nafissatou Diallo—A Pioneer in Black African Writing." *Continental,
    Latin-American, and Francophone Women Writers.* Lanham, MD: University
    Press of America, 1990. 165–171.

Dialogues in Paradise by Ts'an-hsueh (Evanston, IL: Northwestern University, 1989). Extraordinary stories that move out of realism into a fantastic realm—poetic, disturbing, dreamlike, puzzling. Some stories touch on the depredations of the Cultural Revolution, but for the most part, they defy categorization. Ts'an-hsueh's expression is remarkably free, perhaps uniquely in Chinese fiction. The landscapes that form the backdrop of these stories, when they can be recognized at all, are Chinese ones—for the most part rural, with the peasant class making up the cast of characters—but the author's focus is determinedly subjective, concerned with individual perception rather than a naturalistic social panorama.

The Diary of Maria Tholo by Maria Tholo (Johannesburg, South Africa: Ravan, 1979). This "diary" was compiled by its editor, Carol Hermer, based on a series of interviews held in 1976 with Maria Tholo. It covers a period of time when the townships were in upheaval following the Soweto riots, after a group of schoolchildren were fired on by police. Maria's statements provide eyewitness evidence of the historical events surrounding the riots and their after-effects in the townships near Cape Town. She braids that experience with the ordinary events of her life—her father's illness, her children's challenging of adult authority, and even such small matters as a Tupperware party she holds for a friend—filling out the political trauma of Soweto with a wealth of quotidian detail. Above all, she infuses her account of the riots with the ambivalence and complexity that history and hindsight sometimes erase.

Diaz Lozano, Argentina. Honduran novelist and short story writer, born in 1909 (some sources say 1912). She was a member of the Generation of 26, a literary movement that focused on social issues and national identity. She wrote numerous novels, including *Mayapan*, which attempts to reconstruct early encounters between indigenous peoples and the Spanish, and an autobiographical novel about a girl and her mother entitled *Enriqueta and I*. She won the National Prize in Literature in 1968.

Works

And We Have to Live. Palos Verdes, CA: Morgan Press, 1978.
Enriqueta and I. New York: Farrar and Rinehart, 1944.
Mayapan. Indian Hills, CO: Falcon's Wing, 1955.

Dike, Fatima. Born in Langa, near Cape Town, South Africa, on September 13, 1948, she attended school in Rustenburg and then joined the Space Theatre in Cape Town as a stage manager. Her first play was *The Sacrifice of Kreli* (1976), followed by *The First South African* (1979). She creates dramatic works in which the ambiguities of South African society become the source of dramatic tension. Her hybrid use of languages—English, Afrikaans, Xhosa—emphasizes the complex negotiations of culture that complicate South African reality.

Works

The First South African. Johannesburg, South Africa: Ravan, 1979.
The Sacrifice of Kreli. In *Theatre One: New South African Drama.* Johannesburg, South
    Africa: Ad. Donker, 1978. 33–79.

Dilemma of a Ghost by Ama Ata Aidoo (New York: Collier Books, 1971). A one-act play that explores dilemmas facing Africans: the waning authority of the traditionally important extended family, the complex differences between black Africans and African Americans, the distances imposed by the Diaspora, and the ways in which colonialism affected gender roles adversely. Written when Aidoo was a student and was working with the Drama Studio at the University of Ghana, the play employs elements of oral tradition and shows the influence of Efua Sutherland's notions of dramatic form and African theatrical traditions.

Commentary

Wilentz, Gay. *Binding Cultures: Black Women Writers in Africa and the Diaspora.* Bloo-
    mington: Indiana University, 1992.

Dinesen, Isak. Born Karen Dinesen in Rungstead, Denmark, in 1885, she wrote a number of works under various names, including Karen Blixen, which drew on her experiences in Africa. In 1914 she married her cousin, Baron Bror von Blixen-Finecke, and moved with him to Kenya—then British East Africa— where she managed a coffee plantation, staying on after her divorce in 1925 but giving up and returning to Denmark due to financial hardship in 1931. Her book *Out of Africa*, which elegantly creates an Africa that has a mythical preindustrial connection to nature, is her most famous work. She wrote her major works in English, then made Danish translations. She was a well-known and -respected public figure in Denmark and abroad until her death in 1962.

Works

Letters from Africa, 1914–1931. Translated by Anne Born. Chicago: University of Chi-
    cago, 1981.
Out of Africa. New York: Random House, 1938.
Shadows on the Grass. New York: Random House, 1961.

Commentary

Aiken, Susan Hardy. *Isak Dinesen and the Engendering of Narrative*. Chicago: University of Chicago, 1990.
Blackwell, Marilyn Johns. "The Transforming Gaze: Identity and Sexuality in the Works of Isak Dinesen." *Scandinavian Studies* 63.1 (winter 1991): 50–65.
JanMohamed, Abdul R. *Manichean Aesthetics: The Politics of Literature in Colonial Africa*. Amherst: University of Massachusetts, 1983.
Pelensky, Olga Anastasia, editor. *Isak Dinesen: Critical Views*. Athens: Ohio University, 1993.
Smith, Sidonie. "The Other Woman and the Radical Politics of Gender: Isak Dinesen and Beryl Markham." *De/Colonizing the Subject: The Politics of Gender in Women's Autobiography*. Minneapolis: University of Minnesota, 1992. 410–435.
Thurman, Judith. *Isak Dinesen: The Life of a Storyteller*. New York: St. Martin's, 1982.

Ding Ling. See **Ting Ling.**

Djebar, Assia. Born Fatima-Zohra Imalayen on June 30, 1936, in Cherchell, Algeria, daughter of a schoolteacher. Her early schooling was at a Koran school; later she entered a French boarding school in Blida and then went to France for higher education, where, in 1955, she was the first Algerian admitted to the École Normale Superior of Sèvres and the first colonial admitted on full scholarship. She joined other Algerian students in a strike at the end of her first year, in solidarity with the rebels fighting French colonial rule at home, and during this period wrote her first novel, *La Soif*, published in 1957 (*The Mischief*, 1958), which she completed in two months' time. Critics quickly hailed her as the "Françoise Sagan of Algeria," a title that now makes her wince. Her second book, *Les Impatients*, was somewhat of the same genre, and Algerian critics found fault with her for ignoring political themes; yet she was expelled from Sèvres by 1958 for her participation in political protest. Newly married, her husband wanted by the French police, they managed to get to Tunis, where she began to write for the revolutionary newspaper *El-Moudjahid*, edited by Franz Fanon, and where she completed an M.A. in history and her novel *Les enfants du nouveau monde*. She returned to Algiers on June 30, 1962, on the eve of independence, began to teach at the University of Algiers, and worked on a fourth novel, *Les alouettes naives*, in which she paired postcolonial politics and feminism, startling critics with its frank treatment of sexuality. She then ceased writing for a number of years, while she worked on adapting plays for her husband's theater, the Theatre de l'Arlequin in Paris, and then made the film *La Nouba des femmes de Mont Chenoua* in 1979. This film, made for Algerian state television, was controversial at home for its feminist slant but was awarded the International Critics' Prize. In 1980, she published *Les femmes d'Alger dans leur appartement* (*Women of Algiers in Their Apartment*, 1992) and then the novels *L'Amour, la fantasia* in 1985 (*Fantasia: An Algerian Cavalcade*, 1985), *Ombre sultane* two years later (*A Sister to Scheherazade*, 1987), and *Loin de*

Medine: filles d'Ismael in 1991. She continued filmmaking, bringing out *La Zerda et les chants de l'oublie* in 1982; she is currently at work on a film based on Fadhma Amrouche's autobiography. These later works are significantly different in style from her early works and weave together history and the present, a feminist perspective and political issues in a unique mixture of the documentary and the lyrical. She is the most prominent of North African women writers, widely read in both North Africa and France.

Works

Fantasia: An Algerian Cavalcade. Translated by Dorothy Blair. London, England: Quartet, 1985.
The Mischief. Translated by Frances Frenaye. New York: Simon and Schuster, 1958.
A Sister to Scheherazade. Translated by Dorothy S. Blair. London, England: Quartet, 1987.
Women of Algiers in Their Apartment. Translated by Marjolijn de Jager. Charlottesville: University of Virginia, 1992.

Commentary

Abdel-Jaouad, Hedi. "*L'Amour, la fantasia*: Autobiography as Fiction." *Celfan Review* 7.1–2 (1987/1988): 25–29.
Accad, Evelyne. *Veil of Shame: The Role of Women in the Contemporary Fiction of North Africa and the Arab World*. Sherbrooke, Quebec: Naaman, 1978.
Ghaussy, Soheila. "A Stepmother Tongue: 'Feminine Writing' in Assia Djebar's *Fantasia*." *World Literature Today* 68.3 (summer 1994): 457–462.
Green, Mary Jean. "Dismantling the Colonizing Text: Anne Hebert's *Kamouraska* and Assia Djebar's *L'Amour, la fantasia*." *French Review* 66.6 (May 1993): 959–966.
Marx-Scouras, Danielle. "Muffled Screams/Stifled Voices." *Yale French Studies* 82 (May 1993): 172–182.
Mortimer, Mildred. "The Feminine Image in the Algerian Novel of French Expression." *Ba Shiru* 8.2 (1977): 51–62.
Mortimer, Mildred. "The Evolution of Assia Djebar's Feminist Conscience." *Contemporary African Literature*. Washington, DC: Three Continents, 1983. 7–14.
Mortimer, Mildred. *Assia Djebar*. Philadelphia, PA: Celfan Editions, 1988.
Mortimer, Mildred. "Language and Space in the Fiction of Assia Djebar and Leïla Sebbar." *Research in African Literatures* 19 (fall 1988): 301–311.
Mortimer, Mildred. *Journeys Through the French African Novel*. Portsmouth, NH: Heinemann, 1990.
Murdoch, H. Adlai. "Rewriting Writing: Identity, Exile, and Renewal in Assia Djebar's *L'Amour, la fantasia*." *Yale French Studies* 83 (1993): 71–92.
Woodhull, Winifred. *Transfigurations of the Maghreb: Feminism, Decolonization, and Literatures*. Minneapolis: University of Minnesota, 1993.
Wylie, Hal, et al., editors. *Contemporary African Literature*. Washington, DC: Three Continents, 1983.
Zimra, Clarisse. "When the Past Answers Our Present: Assia Djebar Talks About *Loin de Medine*." *Callaloo* 16.1 (1993): 116–131.

Dogeaters by Jessica Hagedorn (London, England: Pandora, 1991). A complex and multifaceted novel about recent Philippine history. The polyphonic narration circles around the political setting in which a president and the "Madame" reign with the help of a refined and sadistic general over a country that is shot through with cultural ambivalence. The story shifts among various characters—a democratically inclined senator who opposes the ruling class and is assassinated, girls who are obsessed with American movies and movie stars, a mestizo boy prostitute, and his German filmmaker trick. They all live in a bricolage society that can achieve extremes of cruelty and banality at the same time, where illusion is everywhere on show and *tsismis*—gossip—is the tie that binds communities together. The author has said the novel is "a love letter to my motherland. It is a fact and a fiction born of rage, shame, pride, and my ongoing struggle and resistance to what I will simply refer to as white supremacy. . . . I wrote *Dogeaters* on my own terms, in the English I reclaim as a Filipino: the English mixed with Spanish and Tagalog. I did not want to use a glossary. I sought to subvert, exorcise, celebrate. Taking on the voices of characters from all levels of society, using fragments of overheard dialogue, newspaper clippings, found historical documents, soap opera plots, the script for a radio melodrama as foreground for the torture and rape of a young woman" (Hagedorn, 148). This fragmented and multivocal method lends itself to depicting a surreal and postmodern, postcolonial Philippines.

Commentary

Evangelista, Susan. "Jessica Hagedorn and Manila Magic." *Melus* 18.4 (winter 1993): 41–52.
Hagedorn, Jessica. [untitled essay]. *Critical Fictions: The Politics of Imaginative Writing.* Seattle, WA: Bay Press, 1991. 146–150.
San Juan, E. "Mapping the Boundaries: The Filipino Writer in the U.S.A." *Journal of Ethnic Studies* 19.1 (spring 1991): 117–131.

Don't Be Afraid, Gringo: A Honduran Woman Speaks from the Heart by Elvira Alvarado (San Francisco, CA: Institute for Food and Development, 1987). A *testimonio* of a woman who organizes the campesinos in Honduras, reclaiming land from landowners, helping peasants learn about their legal rights, and boosting their expectations. Her story is told in a blunt fashion—she characterizes herself, and her daughter, as "loudmouths"—and recounts both her personal life history, growing up poor, living on her own at thirteen, pregnant at fifteen, becoming socially active first in the church, and then more politically aware, and the story of the people she organizes, who lead a similar life and who face opposition from landowners, their government, and the United States. Her straightforward narrative does not invite pity or horror but simply urges action: "Whenever I start to cry, I put my hands into fists and say to myself, 'make your tears turn into anger, make your tears turn into strength' " (143). She even contrasts reading with action: "I hate to offend you, but we won't get anywhere by just writing and reading books . . . the important thing is for you to do something'' (146).

Dove Danquah, Mabel. See **Danquah, Mabel Dove.**

Dreaming in Cuban by Cristina Garcia (New York: Knopf, 1992). This novel tells the stories of the women of a Cuban family, scattered by revolution but still connected through a shared past. The narrative is a polyphony of several voices who, in turn, describe their world from their viewpoint. Characters include Lourdes, an anti-Castro exile who runs a chain of ''Yankee Doodle Bakeries,'' and Felicia, whose perceptions connect and blur the lines between insanity and *santeria*. Pilar, Lourdes's daughter and an aspiring punk artist, is determined to return to Cuba to reconnect with her grandmother and make her present life meaningful. She laments that history does not tell the important stories and longs to recover Cuba for herself: ''[T]here's only imagination where our history should be'' (138).

Du Plessis, Menan. Born in Cape Town in 1952, educated at the University of Cape Town, where she earned a degree in arts in 1981, with English and African literature as her major subjects. Her first novel, *A State of Fear* (1983), won the Olive Schreiner Prize. As her second novel was published, she was completing her doctoral degree in linguistics and was teaching at the University of Cape Town. Her novels deal with the personal price both black and white South Africans have paid for the institution of apartheid, tracing its effects on her characters' lives.

Works

Longlive. Cape Town, South Africa: D. Philip, 1989.
*A State of Fear. Cape Town, South Africa: D. Philip, 1983.

Commentary

Hunter, E. and C. MacKenzie, editors. *Between the Lines II: Interviews with Nadine Gordimer, Menan Du Plessis, Zöe Wicomb, Lauretta Ngcobo.* Grahamstown, South Africa: National English Literary Museum, 1993.

Dumba Nengue: Run for Your Life—Peasant Tales of Tragedy in Mozambique by Lina Magaia (Trenton, NJ: Africa World Press, 1988). Testimonial stories from the ''civil war'' in Mozambique. (The author questions labeling the conflict a ''civil war'' when she argues it was rather a case of thugs and bandits being trained and supported by South Africa to attack peaceful civilians in the countryside.) This short book is a series of vignettes retelling what has happened to various individuals who are victims of RENAMO (Mozambique National Resistance Party) terrorism, an album of verbal snapshots that illustrate in personal terms what the war has done to the people of Mozambique.

Duong, Thu Huong. A Vietnamese writer who was deeply involved in events in her country's history that have become her subject as a writer. Daughter of a tailor and a schoolteacher, she became a leader of a Communist youth brigade at age twenty, fighting at the front dividing North and South Vietnam. She was later the first woman to volunteer for the fighting at the northern frontier when China attacked Vietnam. In the 1980s she began to feel disillusioned with the party and became both a charismatic orator and an impassioned writer, criticizing corruption and human rights abuses. An immensely popular writer in her own country, Duong has spoken out eloquently against the mistakes made by Communist officials, with essays, poetry, and three novels. She was encouraged by a thaw in the official attitude toward literature started in 1987, but by 1989, the authorities were growing nervous about the democratic movements in eastern Europe and they cracked down on artists. Her second novel, *Paradise of the Blind*, was banned and withdrawn from circulation and she was expelled from the party. On April 13, 1991, she was arrested, to be released from prison in November of that year after objections by PEN and Amnesty International.

Work

Paradise of the Blind. Translated by Phan Huy Duong and Nina McPherson. New York: Morrow, 1993.

Commentary

Shenon, Philip. "In This Author's Book, Villains Are Vietnamese." *New York Times*, April 12, 1994, A4.

Duras, Marguerite. French novelist, filmmaker, and critic, born in 1914 and raised in Vietnam (then called French Indochina). She left for France at age nineteen to study law and wrote her first novel in 1943. Her early works are relatively conventional in style, while later ones have the spare and suggestive qualities that have become associated with *écriture féminine*. She became involved with film, writing the screenplay for Resnais's *Hiroshima mon Amour* in 1960 and many others since. Her 1950 novel *Un Barrage contre le Pacifique* (*The Sea Wall*, 1967) draws on her colonial childhood, as does the 1984 best-selling novel *L'Amant* (*The Lover*, 1985), which she amplified in 1991 after a dispute over the filming of the novel into *L'Amant de la Chine du nord* (*The North China Lover*, 1992). The colonial situation she grew up in and that is the setting for these novels introduces the power relations implicit in colonial discourse into the marginalization of both gender and race in a way that allows for a complex examination of those margins and their shifting boundaries.

Works

The Lover. Translated by Barbara Bray. New York: Pantheon, 1985.
The North China Lover. Translated by Leigh Hafrey. New York: New Press, 1992.
The Sea Wall. Translated by Herma Briffault. New York: Noonday, 1967.

Commentary

Chester, Suzanne. "Writing the Subject: Exoticism/Eroticism in Marguerite Duras's *The Lover* and *The Sea Wall." De/Colonizing the Subject: The Politics of Gender in Women's Autobiography*. Minneapolis: University of Minnesota, 1992. 436–457.

Ha, Marie-Paule. "Duras on the Margins." *Romanic Review* 84.3 (May 1993): 299–320.

Haskell, Molly. " 'You Saw Nothing in Indochina.' " *Film Comment* 29.1 (January-February 1993): 31–33.

Ramsay, Raylene. "Writing Power in Duras' *L'Amant de la Chine du nord." College Literature* 21.1 (February 1994): 46–61.

Dutt, Toru. Born in Calcutta, India, on March 4, 1856, the youngest of three daughters, to an Anglicized Bengali family of Christian converts. She and her sisters were taken by her father to France and England in 1869 when she was thirteen years old. They went to school in France, attended lectures for women at Cambridge, and then in 1873 returned to Bengal, where Dutt wrote in the family's home in Calcutta until her death of tuberculosis in 1877 at age 21. Her work was mostly published posthumously—a novel in French *(Le Journal de Mlle. d'Arvers*, Paris, 1879) and her verse translations from Sanskrit stories, which she undertook in her last two years of life. She was hailed as an exotic genius and prodigy and became very well known, though only after her death. Critic and poet Meena Alexander finds her situation one full of disjunctions. "While this might seem on the surface a life of literary fulfillment, Toru Dutt was haunted to the end of her short life by a sense of unreality, the double bind in which she found herself, a woman from the colonized world working in a language, which even as she refined it for poetry, was not truly hers" (Alexander, 15).

Works

Ancient Ballads and Legends of Hindustan. London, England: K. Paul, Trench and Co., 1882.

A Sheaf Gleaned in French Fields. London, England: C. K. Paul, 1880.

Commentary

Alexander, Meena. "Outcaste Power: Ritual Displacement and Virile Maternity in Indian Women Writers." *Journal of Commonwealth Literature* 23.1 (1989): 12–29.

Das, Harihar. *Life and Letters of Toru Dutt*. London, England: Oxford, 1921.

Harrex, S. C. "The Strange Case of Matthew Arnold in a Sari or the Past as Prelude to Kamala Das." *The Writer's Sense of the Past: Essays on Southeast Asian and Australasian Literature*. Singapore: National University of Singapore, 1987. 55–64.

Ramachandran Nair, K. R. *Three Indo-Anglian Poets: Henry Derozio, Toru Dutt, and Sarojini Naidu*. New Delhi, India: Sterling, 1987.

Ramamurti, K. S. *Rise of the Indian Novel in English*. New Delhi, India: Sterling, 1987.

E

Edgell, Zee. Born in 1940 in Belize, where she was raised. She became a reporter for the *Daily Gleaner* in Kingston, Jamaica, then taught at the St. Catherine Academy in Belize (1966–1968) and edited a newspaper in Belize City. After marriage, she traveled widely, living in Afghanistan, Nigeria, Bangladesh, and Britain. On return to Belize, she was appointed director of the Women's Bureau in Belize for the Belize government in 1981, then became director of the Department of Women's Affairs. She lectured at the University College of Belize in the academic year 1988–1989. She has published two novels to date, her first winning the 1982 Fawcett Society Book Prize; it had the distinction of being the first Belizean novel to reach an international audience.

Works

*Beka Lamb. London, England: Heinemann, 1982.
In Times Like These. London, England: Heinemann, 1991.

Commentary

Brown, Bev E. L. "Mansong and Matrix: A Radical Experiment." *A Double Colonization: Colonial and Post-Colonial Women's Writing.* Mundelstrup, Denmark: Dangaroo, 1986. 68–79.

Down, Lorna. "Singing Her Own Song: Women and Selfhood in Zee Edgell's *Beka Lamb.*" *Ariel* 18.4 (October 1987): 39–50.

Flockemann, Miki. " 'Not-Quite Insiders and Not-Quite Outsiders': The 'Process of Womanhood' in *Beka Lamb, Nervous Conditions* and *Daughters of the Twilight.*" *Journal of Commonwealth Literature* 27.1 (1992): 37–47.

Gikandi, Simon. "Writing after Colonialism: *Crick Crack, Monkey* and *Beka Lamb.*"

Writing in Limbo: Modernism and Caribbean Literature. Ithaca, NY: Cornell University, 1992. 197–230.

O'Callaghan, Evelyn. "Interior Schisms Dramatised: The Treatment of the 'Mad' Woman in the Work of Some Caribbean Novelists." *Out of the Kumbla: Women and Literature in the Caribbean.* Trenton, NJ: Africa World Press, 1990. 89–109.

Shea, Renee Hausmann. "Gilligan's 'Crisis of Connections': Contemporary Caribbean Women Writers." *English Journal* 81.4 (April 1992): 36–41.

Woodcock, Bruce. "Post-1975 Caribbean Fiction and the Challenge to English Literature." *Critical Quarterly* 28 (winter 1986): 79–95.

Efuru by Flora Nwapa (London, England: Heinemann, 1970). The first novel written by an African woman to be published and one that is now a set text in many African schools. Efuru is a woman who, though beautiful and well connected, is rejected by her society because she is unable to have children. The novel describes the social life of Efuru's village in detail, dwelling on traditional exchanges and on rituals connected with daily life, and is driven more by those cyclical social occasions than by linear plot. Ultimately, Efuru gives herself to the "woman of the lake," a spirit worshipped by women. The novel ends with a conundrum: "She never experienced the joy of motherhood. Why then did women worship her?" (221). Some critics, notably Nadine Gordimer, have faulted the novel for its repetitiveness and lack of dramatic tension. Others view the emphasis on ritual and repetition as a deliberate and successful use of oral traditions and the novel as a challenge to European notions of narration. The narrative technique, like the story it tells, both highlights tradition and challenges it.

Commentary

Andrade, Susan Z. "Rewriting History, Motherhood, and Rebellion: Naming an African Woman's Literary Tradition." *Research in African Literatures* 21.1 (spring 1990): 91–111.

Gordimer, Nadine. *The Black Interpreters: Notes on African Writing.* Braamfontein, South Africa: Spro-Cas/Ravan, 1973.

Holloway, Karla. *Moorings and Metaphors: Figures of Culture and Gender in Black Women's Literature.* New Brunswick, NJ: Rutgers University, 1992.

Nandakumar, Prema. "An Image of African Womanhood: A Study of Flora Nwapa's *Efuru.*" *African Quarterly* 11 (1971): 136–146.

Wilentz, Gay. *Binding Cultures: Black Women Writers in Africa and the Diaspora.* Bloomington: Indiana University, 1992.

Ellis, Zoila. Born in 1957, a resident of Belize. She studied at the University of the West Indies and Sussex University and works as a lawyer. She joins Zee Edgell as one of the few women from Belize to be published.

Work

On Heroes, Lizards and Passions. Belize: Cubola, 1988.

El-Saadawi, Nawal. See **Sa'dawi, Nawal.**

Emecheta, Buchi. An Igbo novelist, born in Nigeria in 1944 to working-class Ibuza parents, Alice Ogbanje and railroad laborer Jeremy Nwabudike. Her parents died when she was very young, and she was educated on scholarship at a Methodist girls' high school. On graduation she married, had her first child at age seventeen, and came to London with her husband in 1962, where he was to pursue a higher degree and where she bore four more children. She began writing at this time. Her husband, angered by her independence and her ambitions, burned the manuscript of *In the Ditch*, her first novel, an incident she replayed in her autobiographical novel *Second-Class Citizen*. She rewrote the novel, and while supporting her five young children, she also began studying for a B.Sc. in sociology at the London University. She worked for the British Library and for the Inner London Education Authority as a youth worker. She briefly returned to Nigeria to teach at the University of Calabar. With her sons she has founded the publishing house Ogwugwu Afor in London. She has written many novels, books for children, and an autobiography, *Head Above Water*. Her aim is to write simply in a style accessible to the average reader, rather than to create literature that is stylistically complex or linguistically playful. She told interviewers: "[M]y writing isn't English or African as much as more international, more universal" (Jussawalla and Dasenbrock, 85). Most of her work concerns Nigerian women, at home and in Britain, but a recent novel, *The Family* (titled *Gwendolyn* in the United Kingdom) focuses on a West Indian family in Britain. Her writing is noted for its critique of African patriarchy and colonial oppression as well as for its vivid depiction of racism in Britain.

Works

Adah's Story. London, England: Allison and Busby, 1983.
*The Bride Price. New York: Braziller, 1976.
Destination Biafra. London, England: Fontana/Collins, 1983.
Double Yoke. New York: Braziller, 1983.
*The Family. New York: Braziller, 1990.
Head Above Water. London, England: Ogwugwu Afor, 1986.
In the Ditch. London, England: Barrie and Jenkins, 1988.
*The Joys of Motherhood. New York: Braziller, 1979.
Kehinde. Portsmouth, NH: Heinemann, 1994.
The Moonlight Bride. New York: Braziller, 1983.
Naira Power. London, England: Macmillan, 1982.
Nowhere to Play. London, England: Allison and Busby, 1980.
*Second-Class Citizen. New York: Braziller, 1983.
The Slave Girl. New York: Braziller, 1977.
Titch the Cat. London, England: Allison and Busby, 1979.
The Wrestling Match. London, England Oxford, 1980.

Commentary

Andrade, Susan Z. "Rewriting History, Motherhood, and Rebellion: Naming an African Woman's Literary Tradition." *Research in African Literatures* 21.1 (spring 1990): 91–111.

Barthelemy, Anthony. "Western Time, African Lives: Time in the Novels of Buchi Emecheta." *Callaloo* 11 (1989): 539–574.

Bazin, Nancy Topping. "Feminist Perspectives in African Fiction: Bessie Head and Buchi Emecheta." *The Black Scholar* (March-April 1986): 34–40.

Bazin, Nancy Topping. "Feminism in the Literature of African Women." *The Black Scholar* 20.3–4 (summer-fall 1989): 8–17.

Brown, Lloyd W. *Women Writers in Black Africa.* Westport, CT: Greenwood, 1981.

Chukwuma, Helen. "Positivism and the Female Crisis: The Novels of Buchi Emecheta." *Nigerian Female Writers: A Critical Perspective.* Lagos, Nigeria: Malthouse, 1989. 2–16.

Coulon, Virginia. "Women at War: Nigerian Women Writers and the Civil War." *Commonwealth Essays and Studies* 13.1 (1990): 1–12.

Davies, Carole Boyce. "Motherhood in the Works of Male and Female Igbo Writers: Achebe, Emecheta, Nwapa and Nzekwu." *Ngambika: Studies of Women in African Literature.* Trenton, NJ: Africa World Press, 1986. 241–256.

Emecheta, Buchi. "Feminism with a Small 'f.' " *Criticism and Ideology: Second African Writers Conference, Stockholm 1986.* Uppsala, Sweden: Scandinavian Institute of African Studies, 1988. 173–185.

Fido, Elaine Savory. "Mother/Lands: Self and Separation in the Work of Buchi Emecheta, Bessie Head, and Jean Rhys." *Motherlands: Women's Writings from Africa, the Caribbean, and South Asia.* New Brunswick, NJ: Rutgers University, 1992. 330–349.

Flewellen, Elinor C. "Assertiveness vs. Submissiveness in Selected Works by African Women Writers." *Ba Shiru* 12.2 (1985): 3–18.

Frank, Katherine. "The Death of the Slave Girl: African Womanhood in the Novels of Buchi Emecheta." *World Literature Written in English* 21.3 (1982): 476–496.

Grandqvist, Raoul, and John Stotesbury, editors. *African Voices: Interviews with Thirteen African Writers.* Sydney, Australia: Dangaroo, 1990.

Haraway, Donna. "Reading Buchi Emecheta: Contests for Women's Experience in Women's Studies." *Inscriptions* 3–4 (1988): 107–124.

James, Adeola, editor. *In Their Own Voices: African Women Writers Talk.* London, England: James Currey, 1990.

Jussawalla, Feroza F., and Reed Way Dasenbrock. *Interviews with Writers of the Post-Colonial World.* Jackson: University Press of Mississippi, 1992.

Palmer, Eustace. "The Feminine Point of View: Buchi Emecheta's *The Joys of Motherhood.*" *African Literature Today* 13 (1983): 38–57.

Phillips, Maggi. "Engaging Dreams: Alternative Perspectives on Flora Nwapa, Buchi Emecheta, Ama Ata Aidoo, Bessie Head, and Tsitsi Dangarembga." *Research in African Literatures* 25.4 (winter 1994): 89–103.

Ravell-Pinto, Thelma. "Buchi Emecheta at Spelman College." *Sage* 2.1 (spring 1985): 50–51.

Ross, Robert L., editor. *International Literature in English: Essays on the Major Writers.* New York: Garland, 1991.

Stratton, Florence. "The Shallow Grave: Archetypes of Female Experience in African
    Fiction." *Research in African Literatures* 19.2 (1988): 143–169.
Umeh, Davidson, and Marie Umeh. "An Interview with Buchi Emecheta." *Ba Shiru*
    12.2: (1985) 19–25.
Umeh, Marie Linton. "Reintegration with the Lost Self: A Study of Buchi Emecheta's
    Double Yoke." *Ngambika: Studies of Women in African Literature*. Trenton, NJ:
    Africa World Press, 1986. 173–180.
Ward, Cynthia. "What They Told Buchi Emecheta: Oral Subjectivity and the Joys of
    'Otherhood.' " *PMLA* 105.1 (January 1990): 83–97.

Emily of Emerald Hill: A Monodrama by S. Kon (Singapore: Macmillan,
1989). A one-woman drama about a Straits-born Chinese matriarch that has been
performed in Singapore, Malaysia, Hawaii, and Edinburgh, at the Commonwealth Arts Festival and again at the Edinburgh Arts Festival Fringe. The character, Emily, talks on the phone, to friends, to children, and to the audience,
shifting in time from early in her marriage to her old age, alone in the big family
house of Emerald Hill. Bit by bit her story is revealed—her eldest son commits
suicide when she insists he leave a job at a riding school and become a lawyer,
her husband refuses to see her on his death bed, and finally the key piece of
information that she was abandoned by her mother in childhood and lived on
sufferance with relatives until her arranged marriage. "I learned that a woman
is nothing in this world that men have made, except in the role that men demand
of her. Your life is meaningless, you have no value, except as you are a wife
and mother: then be the very devil of a wife and mother. Look after your
husband and family, yes: do everything for them, wrap them, bind them in the
web of your providing, till they can't lift a finger to help themselves . . . so that
the whole world knows your worth—so that a screaming girl-child, long ago,
may be reassured that her life has some significance, that no-one is going to
throw her back into the gutter" (45). The character of Emily is modeled on the
author's own grandmother.

Escoffery, Gloria. Born in 1923 in Jamaica and educated at McGill University, Montreal, and the Slade School of Art, London. She is a painter, art critic,
and poet who has had a number of her poems anthologized in collections such
as *Caribbean Voices* and *The Penguin Book of Caribbean Verse* and who writes
a regular art column for the *Jamaica Journal*. Her poetry shows her artist's eye
and is full of telling visual moments, and she frequently writes about the business of painting. Other recurrent themes are early and unnecessary violent death,
interpersonal relations, and nature.

Works

Landscape in the Making: Poems. Kingston, Jamaica: The Herald, 1976.
*Loggerhead. Kingston, Jamaica: Sandberry, 1988.

Esquivel, Laura. Known primarily as a screenwriter, her screenplay *Chido Guan* was nominated for an award from the Mexican Academy of Motion Pictures. Her novel, *Like Water for Chocolate*, was at the top of the best-seller list in Mexico in 1990 and was popular in the United States. She wrote the screenplay for the film version.

Work

*Like Water for Chocolate. New York: Doubleday, 1992.

Commentary

Lawless, Cecelia. "Experimental Cooking in *Como agua para chocolate*." *Monographic Review: Revista Monografica* 8 (1992): 261–272.

L'Excisée by Evelyne Accad (Washington, DC: Three Continents, 1989). A novel about being a woman in a Muslim world, about female circumcision, and about the ways in which women are excised, one way and another, from existence. It is written in a style that mixes poetic and narrative prose, with resonances from holy texts. About the novel, the author says it "is the story of my adolescence trapped by a family whose religious system suffocates me, in a country where religion has no tolerance for the other.... *L'Excisée* is also a search in style, writing where the biblical and the Koranic mix, leaving space for song and poetry, voice in search of itself, in the stifling of a millennial condition, voice which becomes shriek" ("Writing to Explore," 184).

Commentary

Accad, Evelyne. "Writing to Explore (W)Human Experience." *Research in African Literatures* 23.1 (spring 1992): 179–185.

The Execution of Mayor Yin and Other Stories from the Great Proletarian Cultural Revolution by Chen Jo-hsi (Bloomington: Indiana University, 1978). Stories about the impact of the Cultural Revolution on families and communities. Rather than focus on atrocities, the author reveals the ways in which the fear generated by repeated reformulations of correct behavior undermines friendships and creates distrust and unhappiness on a very human scale. Skillfully wrought stories, especially in exploring the ways communication can be twisted under stress, employing the author's delicate use of irony.

Exile. Edward Said has said that exile is "strangely compelling to think about but terrible to experience. It is the unhealable rift forced between a human being and a native place, between the self and its true home: its essential sadness can never be surmounted." He argues that it is both a "potent, even enriching motif of modern culture" and the source of "a crippling sorrow of estrangement" (159). A common theme in postcolonial literature, the dislocated, decentered experience of exile is featured in many works by third world women. For some writers the experience is one of being divided or split between worlds, as Meena

Alexander describes in her memoir *Fault Lines*. In other works the experience is less of division or bisection as of loss. Kamala Markandaya's *Nowhere Man* is a character who finds he belongs nowhere, because the colonial India he left years ago no longer exists and the England he has adopted wants nothing to do with him. Bharati Mukherjee's characters are émigrés who sometimes find their way through sheer determination (as in *Jasmine*) or who are so dislocated by their experience they fall apart completely (as the title character in *Wife* does). Ken Bugul and Leïla Sebbar explore the world of women who have traveled from home to the metropole, while Assia Djebar probes the need of a woman who has left her culture to rejoin it. T'ao Yang and Cristina Garcia write about the experience of being second-generation exiles, a kind of double exile from home and from family. In *Baumgartner's Bombay*, Anita Desai explores exile in reverse—telling the story of a European Jew living in exile in the third world.

Ironically, many of these writers must themselves live in exile. Merle Hodge argues that "it's not really feasible to make writing a full-time career in developing countries. . . . The women from the Caribbean who have been able to produce prolifically live in metropolitan communities; they live outside" (Balutansky, 651). Others, like Cristina Peri Rossi, Griselda Gambaro, Isabel Allende, Mary Benson, Ruth First, Lauretta Ngcobo, and many others, have had to leave their homes for political reasons. Iranian feminist and exile Mahnaz Afkhami has collected the stories of women exiled for political reasons, including the stories of Marjorie Agosín and Alicia Partnoy, poets who have made a point of bearing witness for those whom they were forced to leave behind. Bessie Head is a writer whose isolation as an exile from South Africa was particularly acute. For many years she lived in Botswana as an officially stateless person. Her work is concerned with the quest for belonging, yet she lived largely separated from her reading public and outside of the shelter of a literary community.

Sara Suleri has commented on the effect of exile on rhetoric, on the "continually dislocated idiom of migrancy" that is the hallmark of much postcolonial discourse. For poet Abena Busia exile entails learning to speak in the "half-life, half-light of alien tongues" (9). Jessica Hagedorn sees it pragmatically: "When it comes down to it, it's all about finding shelter, finding your identity. I don't care whether you're an immigrant or native-born, you're discovering who and what and where you are all the time" (79). In spite of the loss exile betokens, it is an experience that allows for an enriching plurality of vision and gives rise to a complex literary voice that is, in the words of Said, "nomadic, decentred, contrapuntal" (172) and that carries an unsettling force.

Works

*Alexander, Meena. *Fault Lines: A Memoir*. New York: Feminist Press, 1992.

Bugul, Ken. *The Abandoned Baobab: The Autobiography of a Senegalese Woman*. Translated by Marjolijn de Jager. Brooklyn: Lawrence Hill, 1991.

*Busia, Abena P. A. *Testimonies of Exile*. Trenton, NJ: Africa World Press, 1990.

*Desai, Anita. *Baumgartner's Bombay*. New York: Knopf, 1989.
*Djebar, Assia. *A Sister to Scheherazade*. Translated by Dorothy S. Blair. London, England: Quartet, 1987.
*Garcia, Cristina. *Dreaming in Cuban*. New York: Knopf, 1992.
Hagedorn, Jessica. "Tenement Lover." *Between Worlds: Contemporary Asian-American Plays*. New York: Theatre Communications Group, 1990. 75–90.
*Markandaya, Kamala. *The Nowhere Man*. London, England: Allen Lane, 1973.
*Mukherjee, Bharati. *Jasmine*. New York: Grove Weidenfeld, 1989.
*Mukherjee, Bharati. *Wife*. Boston: Houghton Mifflin, 1975.
Sebbar, Leïla. *Sherazade: Missing: Aged 17, Dark Curly Hair, Green Eyes*. Translated by Dorothy Blair. London, England: Quartet, 1991.
*T'ao Yang. *Borrowed Tongue*. Hong Kong: Renditions, 1986.

Commentary

Afkhami, Mahnaz. *Women in Exile*. Charlottesville, VA: University of Virginia, 1994.
Balutansky, Kathleen M. "We Are All Activists: An Interview with Merle Hodge." *Callaloo* 12 (fall 1989): 651–662.
Chetin, Sara. "Myth, Exile, and the Female Condition: Bessie Head's *The Collector of Treasures*." *Journal of Commonwealth Literature* 23.1 (1989): 114–137.
Kaplan, Caren. "Deterritorializations: The Rewriting of Home and Exile in Western Feminist Discourse." *The Nature and Context of Minority Discourse*. New York: Oxford University, 1990. 357–368.
Lionnet, Françoise. "Inscriptions of Exile: The Body's Knowledge and the Myth of Authenticity." *Callaloo* 15.1 (winter 1992): 30–40.
Mudimbe-Boyi, Elisabeth. "The Poetics of Exile and Errancy in *Le Baobab Fou* by Ken Bugul and *Ti Jean L'Horizon* by Simone Schwarz-Bart." *Yale French Studies* 83 (June 1993): 196–212.
Murdoch, H. Adlai. "Rewriting Writing: Identity, Exile, and Renewal in Assia Djebar's *L'Amour, la fantasia*." *Yale French Studies* 83 (1993): 71–92.
Said, Edward. "Reflections on Exile." *Granta* 13 (autumn 1984): 159–172.
Salgado, Maria A. "Women Poets of the Cuban Diaspora: Exile and the Self." *Americas Review* 18 (fall-winter 1990): 227–234.
Sant-Wade, Arvindra, and Karen Marguerite Radell. "Refashioning the Self: Immigrant Women in Bharati Mukherjee's New World." *Studies in Short Fiction* 24.1 (winter 1992): 11–17.
Saunders, Rebecca. "Gender, Colonialism, and Exile: Flora Annie Steel and Sara Jeannette Duncan in India." *Women's Writing in Exile*. Chapel Hill: University of North Carolina, 1989. 303–324.
Suleri, Sara. *The Rhetoric of English India*. Chicago: University of Chicago, 1992.
Woodhull, Winifred. "Exile." *Yale French Studies* 82 (May 1993): 7–24.

The Expedition to the Baobab Tree by Wilma Stockenström (Boston, MA: Faber and Faber, 1983). Translation from Afrikaans of *Die Kumentartekspadisie*. A short, intense novel about a slave woman who is traded from hand to hand, finally belonging to a man who, with another trader known only as "the stranger," sets out on an expedition to map out an overland trade route. The members of the expedition die or run away, and she is finally left alone, helpless, in the veld, where bushmen leave food for her by the big baobab tree she has made her home. A war party arrives one day, and there is a slaughter, so that she is left alone once more, with a gift of poison to end her life. The story is an intensely subjective narration by a person who is denied status as a subject, a tale told in a voice that is almost bereft of identity, which was taken from her first when she was made a slave, then when her children were sold away from her, and finally when she is alone, unable to communicate with the "little people" who provide her with food but ignore her presence. The narrative style, which is not chronological and is obsessively without any viewpoint but the narrator's, is well suited to the tale. "Everything that has been in my life is always with me, simultaneously, and the events refuse to stand nicely one after the other in a row. They hook into each other, shift around, scatter, force themselves on me or try to slip out of my memory. I have difficulty with them in the necklace of my memory. I am not a carefree herder of time" (66). Slavery has deprived her of history and of a connection to time itself, and has stripped identity away, a point made not just by the poetic language of the text but also by its narrative practice that refuses simple chronology and straightforward narration.

Commentary

Brink, André. "Women and Language in Darkest Africa: The Quest for Articulation in Two Postcolonial Novels." *Literator* 13.1 (1992): 1–14.

Gray, Stephen. "Some Notes on Further Readings of Wilma Stockenström's Slave Narrative, *The Expedition to the Baobab Tree.*" *Literator* 12.1 (April 1991): 51–59.

Zeiss, Cecelia Scallan. "Myth and Metamorphosis: Landscape as Archetype in Quest Narratives by Samuel Beckett and Wilma Stockenström." *Irish University Review: A Review of Irish Studies* 21.1 (spring-summer 1991): 56–81.

F

Fagundes Telles, Lygia. See **Telles, Lygia Fagundes.**

Fall, Aminata Sow. Born in St. Louis, Senegal in 1941, she was educated in Dakar, earned a degree in French literature at the Sorbonne in 1967, and spent seven years in Paris before returning to Senegal. She was the first published black woman novelist from francophone black Africa. Her first novel grew out of a sense, on returning home from Paris, that Senegalese society had become too materialistic. She feels African writers should be concerned with their own self-discovery, not position themselves relative to others: "That's what the African novel should be; it should be a novel through which Africans discover themselves on their own" (Hawkins, 422). She is director of the Center of Civilization Studies at the Ministry of Culture, Dakar, and is known as a novelist of sharp, satiric wit and sophisticated narrative ability.

Work

The Beggars' Strike, or, The Dregs of Society. Harlow, England: Longman, 1986.

Commentary

Ajala, John D. *"The Beggars' Strike*: Aminata Sow Fall as a Spokeswoman for the Underprivileged." *CLA Journal* 34.2 (December 1990): 137–152.
Blair, Dorothy S. *Senegalese Literature: A Critical History.* Boston: Twayne, 1984.
Burness, Don, editor. *Wanasema: Conversations with African Writers.* Athens: Ohio University Center for International Studies, 1985.

Gadjigo, Samba. "Social Vision in Aminata Sow Fall's Literary Work." *World Literature Today* 63.3 (summer 1989): 411–415.

Hawkins, Peter. "An Interview with Aminata Sow Fall." *African Affairs* 87 (1988): 419–430.

Okeke-Ezigbo, Emeka. "Begging the Beggars: Restoration of the Dignity of Man in *The Beggars' Strike*." *Neohelicon* 19.1 (1992): 307–322.

Trinh T. Minh-ha. "Aminata Sow Fall and the Beggars' Gift." *When the Moon Waxes Red: Representation, Gender, and Cultural Politics*. New York: Routledge, 1991. 169–183.

The Fall of the Imam by Nawal Sa'dawi (London, England: Methuen, 1988). This novel is the strange and convoluted story of "Bint Allah," the Daughter of God—actually the daughter of a powerful imam. The narrative proceeds without chronology or a consistent narrative voice but rather shifts constantly in time and voice. Bint Allah's mother was stoned to death in accordance with Sharia law, and she herself is pursued and killed by the authorities working for the imam, who has all religious and civil authority in the novel's dark and frightening world. Like the author's *Circling Song*, the novel is a nightmarish tale of pursuit and violence, driven by male rage and absolute authority.

The Family by Buchi Emecheta (New York: Braziller, 1990). First published in the United Kingdom under the title *Gwendolyn*, this novel tells the story of a Jamaican girl who is left by her parents to live in poverty as they try to make a new start in Britain. She is molested as a child by her grandmother's friend, then again by her father after she moves to England. The relations between the West Indian family and their Nigerian neighbors draw out the differences between Africans and blacks of the Diaspora. The social problems of poverty, illiteracy, racism, and incest are all touched on in this book, though not in great depth. The novel raises many issues and sketches a number of interesting characters but fails to develop them in the depth attained by other novels she has written.

Family Album by Claribel Alegría (Willimantic, CT: Curbstone, 1991). Translation of *Pueblo de Dios y de Mandinga*, first published in 1986. Three novellas, very different in style and tone. One, "The Talisman," is a claustrophobic and psychologically complex story of a girl who fascinates her "spiritual advisor," a dour nun at her Catholic boarding school, with her unconventional life. The girl's experience of being abused by her mother's violent boyfriend helps her gain power over the nun, who was also sexually abused as a child. The girl consults regularly with her family and friends who appear to her in her room. The title story has a more familiar subject, the Sandinista movement and those involved in its struggle against Somoza: Ximena, who is living a housewife's life in Paris, and her cousin Armando, a political exile who plans to return to the struggle. Their shared family memories and their communal history intertwine as they watch the Sandinistas begin to gain control, and when Armando returns to Nicaragua, Ximena takes over the role of keeping the French press informed. He leaves her with the family album, in which the faces of the dead magically disappear—and where his face is suddenly missing. The last novella is a bizarre romp through the eccentric society of expatriates living on the island of Mallorca, including the poet Robert Graves who has helped a temporally displaced alchemist of the thirteenth century find his missing philosopher's stone. A physicist discovers it is actually a miniature black hole resident in the community, causing the eccentric behavior of the residents. When the black hole escapes and burrows into the center of the earth, they expect the end of the world to follow soon, but instead the village grows dull, no longer visited by mystics but by tourists. The three works are all touched by magic realism; their variety in tone and setting attests to the author's range.

Family Ties by Clarice Lispector (Austin: University of Texas, 1972). Thirteen short stories about moments of inner spiritual enlightenment or illumination within a setting of commonplace circumstances. In "Love," a woman who has "skillfully pacified life" (41) suddenly is swept with a feeling that life is meaningless. Her crisis deepens as she goes through the routine of her day, but she returns to complacency, passively taking her husband's hand to go to bed. "Before getting into bed, as if she were snuffing a candle, she blew out that day's tiny flame" (48). In "The Daydreams of a Drunk Woman" Lispector explores the thoughts of an alcoholic and in "The Mathematics Professor" examines the choices made by a "rational" man who maltreats a dog and calls it a crime "more astute than the Last Judgment." Lispector explores in these stories the intersection of existentialism and spiritual awakening.

The Family Tree: An Illustrated Novel by Margo Glantz (London, England: Serpent's Tail, 1990). An autobiographical novel, or novelistic autobiography, in which the Mexican writer traces her Ukrainian Jewish roots by interviewing her parents. She tackles the job with "archaeological enthusiasm" (183) and traces in anecdotes her parents' childhoods, emigration to Mexico, life in exile, and connections to friends and family members all around the world. The mosaic she constructs of all the pieces, including reflections on her own childhood and upbringing, is built up of much diversity, linked through coincidences and chance as much as through design. Throughout, as she deals with historic events and her family's part in them, she is self-deprecating: "[M]y family doesn't have any heroic episodes in its past, it just has a few hiccups, like what happened to my brother-in-law. . . ." (175). Yet she entwines these modest stories with her own and makes a funny and insightful family history that is also an exploration of being at home in two cultures.

Fantasia: An Algerian Cavalcade by Assia Djebar (London, England: Quartet, 1985). This novel weaves together two narratives, one autobiographical and the other historical. The autobiographical strand examines women's role in Algerian society and the difficulty of having a voice when the language of literature is that of a colonial oppressor. The historical strand focuses on the French conquest of the 1830s and the war for independence of 1954–1962, reconstructing the role of women in these battles, a role that has been deleted from official histories. There are inevitable parallels discovered between the French oppression of the Algerians and the oppression of women by men. For Djebar, speaking out not only liberates the individual but also resurrects "so many vanished sisters" lost to history (204). The novel is a fascinating merging of history and the individual voice.

Commentary

Ghaussy, Soheila. "A Stepmother Tongue: 'Feminine Writing' in Assia Djebar's *Fantasia*." *World Literature Today* 68.3 (summer 1994): 457–462.

Green, Mary Jean. "Dismantling the Colonizing Text: Anne Hebert's *Kamouraska* and Assia Djebar's *L'Amour, la fantasia*." *French Review* 66.6 (May 1993): 959–966.

Mortimer, Mildred. "Language and Space in the Fiction of Assia Djebar and Leïla Sebbar." *Research in African Literatures* 19 (fall 1988): 301–311.

Murdoch, H. Adlai. "Rewriting Writing: Identity, Exile, and Renewal in Assia Djebar's *L'Amour, la fantasia*." *Yale French Studies* 83 (1993): 71–92.

A Far Cry: The Making of a South African by Mary Benson (New York: Viking, 1989). The autobiography of journalist, activist, and novelist who led an adventurous life, fully chronicled in this work that is both of literary note and of historic importance. She left South Africa as a young woman to assist the Allied war effort, then worked in London and became aware for the first time of herself as a South African on reading Alan Paton's *Cry the Beloved Country*. Her life's work thereafter was to fight apartheid and oppression, in the process becoming intimately involved with African National Congress (ANC) members and with Bram Fischer, Athol Fugard, and others. Her memoirs constitute a compelling history of the movement and a personal account of a woman becoming a South African, most alive when in her own country, sharing all its troubles, but compelled to leave when it becomes clear she can only continue her work as an activist in exile.

Farewell My Concubine by Li Pi-hua (New York: Morrow, 1993). A novel set in the theatrical world of the Peking Opera, tracing the lives of two opera stars from their childhood training to their old age, and from the 1930s through the Japanese Occupation, the Cultural Revolution, and into the 1980s. In a sense, it also is about China's legendary past, as the two characters act out past glory in the role of a general and his concubine, roles that they adopt to an extent in their lives off stage, the man who plays the concubine falling in love with the one who plays the general. Their art is called into question after the revolution, and they are separated and forced into labor; one ends up moving

to Hong Kong and living in poverty, while the other in his old age is rehabilitated and celebrated again as an artist, though his voice is past its prime. The
novel provides an interesting glimpse of China's modern history that fuses its
self-representation in traditional art with the hard training, poverty, and pain that
went into making that illusory representation and contrasts it to the elements of
modern China that both reflect and reject the mythic China of Peking Opera.

Farman-Farmaian, Sattareh. Born to a wealthy family in Teheran, she grew
up in a traditional household in which women were, according to tradition,
secluded from public life. However, as a young adult, she traveled to America
to study social work. On her return, she founded the Teheran School of Social
Work and involved herself in social welfare programs and research. She was
dismayed by both growing materialism in her country and the countercurrent of
fundamentalism, and when the revolution began, her school was closed. She
eventually was arrested and seemed in danger of execution but was finally released through a happy coincidence, after which she took up an exile's life in
America.

Work

**Daughter of Persia: A Woman's Journey from Her Father's Harem Through the Islamic
Revolution.* With Dona Munker. New York: Anchor/Doubleday, 1993.

Farrokhzad, Forugh. See **Farrukhzad, Furugh.**

Farrukhzad, Furugh. Born in Teheran on January 5, 1935, the third of seven
children. She did not have an extensive formal education, being transferred after
ninth grade to a girls' school to study painting and sewing. At age sixteen she
was married, became a mother a year later, and was divorced at nineteen, losing
custody of her child in the process. She suffered a nervous breakdown and spent
a month in a psychiatric clinic. Before her divorce, she had begun to write
poetry, publishing her first volume at age twenty. It was considered controversial
because it was the first time an Iranian woman poet had addressed female sexuality from the stance of female subjectivity. Her rebellious analysis of women's
place in Iranian society was also grounds for a wider consideration of alienation
and the difficulty of communication. She published four volumes of poetry and
in 1962 became interested in film, making a documentary about a leper colony
that won several international awards. She was killed at age thirty-two in an
automobile accident, at the height of her creativity.

Works

*Another Birth: Selected Poems of Forugh Farrokhzad. Translated by Hasan Javadi and
Susan Sallee. Emeryville, CA: Albany, 1981.
Bride of Acacias: Selected Poems of Forugh Farrokhzad. Translated by Jascja Kessler
with Amin Berani. Delmar, NY: Caravan, 1982.
A Rebirth: Poems. Translated by David Martin. Lexington, KY: Mazda, 1985.

Commentary

Hillman, Michael C. "Forugh Farrokhzad: Modern Iranian Poet." *Middle Eastern Mus-
     lim Women Speak*. Austin: University of Texas, 1977. 291–317.
Hillman, Michael C. *A Lonely Woman: Forugh Farrokhzad and Her Poetry*. Washington,
     DC: Mage; Three Continents, 1987.
Hillman, Michael. "An Autobiographical Voice: Forugh Farrokhzad." *Women's Auto-
     biographies in Contemporary Iran*. Cambridge: Harvard University, 1990. 33–
     53.
Milani, Farzaneh. *Veils and Words: The Emerging Voices of Iranian Women Writers*.
     Syracuse, NY: Syracuse University, 1992.

Fault Lines: A Memoir by Meena Alexander (New York: Feminist Press,
1992). A memoir that moves not chronologically but, as memory works, through
connections. Alexander pieces her past together poetically, with its roots in her
grandparents' lives in Kerala, her life with her parents in Khartoum, where her
father served as a diplomat, her schooling in England and her adult life in New
York, teaching, writing, raising two children, and keeping up a long-distance
relationship with her husband, another academic working in Minnesota. Her life
is marked, fissured, with fault lines, places where the different parts of her past
shift, move apart, and disconnect. "In Manhattan I am a fissured thing, a body
crossed by fault lines. Where is my past?" (182). Her writing is an attempt to
explore those discontinuities, seek her history, and connect to it: "I think it is
the pain of no one knowing my name that drives me to write. That, and the
sense that I am living in a place where I have no history" (182). A well-
constructed autobiography and eloquent meditation on the state of cultural exile.

Feminism. *Feminism* is a term that carries many conflicting connotations in
the third world and is a concept to which writers respond very differently.
Though many texts written by women in the third world are undeniably feminist
in tone, their authors are frequently uncomfortable with that label. Buchi Emecheta, for example, calls herself a feminist with a small "f" in order to distance
herself from the movement in the West. Others prefer Alice Walker's term
"womanist," which she defines as "a black feminist or feminist of color. From
the black folk expression of mothers to female children 'You acting womanish,'
i.e. like a woman. Usually referring to outrageous, audacious, courageous or
willful behavior" (xi). Many writers perceive the feminist movement as being
dominated by white, Western women whose concerns and goals are not theirs.
The struggle for equality with men in a capitalist workplace, breaking the notorious glass ceiling, for example, seems a ludicrous goal to those who see
multinational capitalism as a threat. Many third world women resent their perceived objectification by Western feminists, who they may feel are either pa-
tronizing (as in, "Let us help you in your development toward a more just and
democratic society and, by the way, get rid of those oppressive traditions of
yours") or self-serving (as in, "Your experiences will be so enriching for us,

take a seat on this panel and tell us all about the third world''). Both approaches have disturbingly colonialist implications. There are problems with women being perceived as a single category, sharing a common oppression; the historical and economic factors involved in identity are reduced and dismissed when, in many cases, those appear more pressing issues than gender equity. Nadine Gordimer, for example, persistently dismissed the women's movement as irrelevant and divisive in the face of a more important issue, apartheid.

Cheryl Johnson-Odim argues: "Third World women can embrace the concept of gender identity, but must reject an ideology based solely on gender. Feminism, therefore, must be a comprehensive and inclusive ideology and movement that incorporates yet transcends gender-specificity. We must create a feminist movement which struggles against those things which can be clearly shown to oppress women, whether based on race, sex, or class or resulting from imperialism. Such a definition of feminism will allow us to isolate the gender-specific element in women's oppression while simultaneously relating it to broader issues, to the totality of what oppresses us as women. If the feminist movement does not address itself also to issues of race, class, and imperialism, it cannot be relevant to alleviating the oppression of most of the women of the world" (321–322). Trinh T. Minh-ha has said that "depending on how the work is carried out, the refocus on women of colour in white feminist discourse lately can be seen as a simultaneous form of appropriation and expropriation, or as an acknowledgment of intercultural enrichment and of interdependency in the fighting-learning process. The precarious line we walk on is one that allows us to challenge the West as authoritative subject of feminist knowledge, while also resisting the terms of a binarist discourse that would concede feminism to the West all over again" (Parmar, 67–68). For theoretical discussions of feminism and third world writers, see especially Trinh T. Minh-ha, Mohanty, and Lugones and Spelman.

Third world women's writings suggest that feminism is not—and never has been—defined in simple terms. Sor Juana Inés de la Cruz demonstrated that a Mexican woman could be both an intellectual and a poet. Other writers, such as Gertrudis Gómez de Avellaneda, Flora Annie Steel, Magdalena Jalandoni, and Adelaide Casely-Hayford, struggled against limits placed on them as women. Olive Schreiner contributed to the movement with her work *Women and Labour* as well as with her novels of ideas. Begum Rokeya wrote a remarkable feminist utopia one hundred years ago, and Sarojini Naidu and Huda Sha'rawi were tireless activists for women's rights as well as for nationalist causes. More recently, Buchi Emecheta, Assia Djebar, Nawal Sa'dawi, Chang Chieh, Rosario Castellanos, Maryse Condé, Shashi Deshpande, and countless others are contributing to the rewriting of feminism in their literary works.

Works

Castellanos, Rosario. *A Rosario Castellanos Reader*. Translated by Maureen Ahern and others. Austin: University of Texas, 1988.

*Chang Chieh. *Leaden Wings*. Translated by Gladys Yang. London, England: Virago, 1987.

*Condé, Maryse. *I, Tituba, Black Witch of Salem*. Translated by Richard Philcox. Charlottesville: University Press of Virginia, 1992.

*Deshpande, Shashi. *That Long Silence*. London, England: Virago, 1988.

*Djebar, Assia. *Women of Algiers in their Apartment*. Translated by Marjolijn de Jager. Charlottesville: University of Virginia, 1992.

*Emecheta, Buchi. *The Joys of Motherhood*. New York: Braziller, 1979.

Naidu, Sarojini. *Sarojini Naidu, Selected Poetry and Prose*. New Delhi, India: Indus, 1993.

*Rokeya, Begum. *Sultana's Dream and Selections from the Secluded Ones*. Translated by Roushan Jahan. New York: Feminist, 1988.

*Sa'dawi, Nawal. *Two Women in One*. Translated by Osman Nusairi and Jana Gough. Seattle, WA: Seal Press, 1986.

Schreiner, Olive. *Women and Labour*. London, England: Unwin, 1911.

Sha'rawi, Huda. *Harem Years: The Memoirs of an Egyptian Feminist*. Translated by Margot Badran. London, England: Virago, 1986.

Commentary

Ashcroft, W. D. "Intersecting Marginalities: Post-Colonialism and Feminism." *Kunapipi* 11.2 (1989): 23–35.

Bazin, Nancy Topping. "Feminism in the Literature of African Women." *The Black Scholar* 20.3–4 (May-July 1989): 8–17.

Castillo, Debra A. *Toward a Latin American Feminist Literary Criticism*. Ithaca, NY: Cornell University, 1992.

Davies, Carole Boyce. "Feminist Consciousness and African Literary Criticism." *Ngambika: Studies of Women in African Literature*. Trenton, NY: Africa World Press, 1986.

Emecheta, Buchi. "Feminism with a Small 'f.' " *Criticism and Ideology: Second African Writers' Conference, Stockholm 1986*. Uppsala, Sweden: Scandinavian Institute of African Studies, 1988. 173–185.

Feminist Readings on Spanish and Latin American Literature. Lewiston, NY: Mellen, 1991.

Gardiner, Judith Kegan. "On Female Identity and Writing by Women." *Critical Inquiry* 8.2 (winter 1982): 347–361.

Grewal, Inderpal, and Caren Kaplan. *Scattered Hegemonies: Postmodernity and Transnational Feminist Practice*. Minneapolis: University of Minnesota, 1994.

Jayawardena, Kumari. *Feminism and Nationalism in the Third World*. London, England: Zed, 1986.

Johnson-Odim, Cheryl. "Common Themes, Different Contexts: Third World Women and Feminism." *Third World Women and the Politics of Feminism*. Bloomington: Indiana University, 1991. 314–327.

Kaminsky, Amy. "Issues for an International Feminist Literary Criticism." *Signs* 19.1 (autumn 1993): 213–227.

Kaminsky, Amy K. *Reading the Body Politic: Feminist Criticism and Latin American Women Writers*. Minneapolis: University of Minnesota, 1993.

Lugones, Maria C., and Elizabeth V. Spelman. "Have We Got a Theory for You! Feminist Theory, Cultural Imperialism, and the Demand for the 'Woman's Voice.' " *Women's Studies International Forum* 6.6 (1983): 573–581.

Mitra, Indrani. "The Discourse of Liberal Feminism and Third World Women's Texts: Some Issues of Pedagogy." *College Literature* 18.3 (October 1991): 55–63.

Mohanty, Chandra Talpade, Ann Russo, and Lourdes Torres, editors. *Third World Women and the Politics of Feminism.* Bloomington: Indiana University, 1991.

Parmar, Pratibha. "*Woman, Native, Other*: Pratibha Parmar Interviews Trinh T. Minh-ha." *Feminist Review* 36 (autumn 1990): 65–74.

Trinh T. Minh-ha. *Woman, Native, Other: Writing Postcoloniality and Feminism.* Bloomington: Indiana University, 1989.

Walker, Alice. *In Search of Our Mothers' Gardens: Womanist Prose.* San Diego: Harcourt Brace Jovanovich, 1983.

Ferré, Rosario. Born in 1938 in Ponce on the southern coast of Puerto Rico to a politically active family; her father was the governor of Puerto Rico. She attended a convent school after spending first grade in a boys' school with her brother—a circumstance that she says was an early apprenticeship in rebellion. She married at nineteen and had two children in quick succession; after ten years her mother died, she inherited some money, divorced, and joined a circle of artists and writers. She studied English at Wellesley and Manhattanville College, earned a master's degree in Spanish and Latin American literature at the University of Puerto Rico, and received a doctorate from the University of Maryland in 1987. She began her writing career in 1970, founding and editing a Puerto Rican literary magazine, *Zona de carga y descarga,* and publishing fiction, poetry, and essays on literary and feminist topics, as well as fostering writing by new writers. She published a book of short stories, then contributed a literary criticism column to the newspaper *El Mundo* from 1977 to 1980. She has translated works from Spanish to English, including Lillian Hellman's *Scoundrel Time,* and has translated her own works into English, as well as writing short stories, a novel, and a number of critical works on Latin American writers. She has taught literature at several American universities and currently lives in Washington, D.C. She is the author of poetry, short stories, children's books, and a novel as well as literary criticism.

Works

Sweet Diamond Dust. New York: Ballantine, 1988.
The Youngest Doll. Lincoln: University of Nebraska, 1991.

Commentary

Ferré, Rosario. "The Writer's Kitchen." *Lives on the Line: The Testimony of Contemporary Latin American Authors.* Berkeley: University of California, 1988. 214–227.

Gazarian-Gautier, Marie Lise. "Rosario Ferré." *Interviews with Latin American Writers.* Elmwood, IL: Dalkey Archives, 1989. 81–92.

Hintz, Suzanne. "An Annotated Bibliography of Works By and About Rosario Ferré: The First Twenty Years, 1970–1990." *Revista Interamericana de Bibliographía.* 41.4 (1991): 643–654.

Olmos, Margarite Fernandez. "From a Woman's Perspective: The Short Stories of Rosario Ferré and Ana Lydia Vega." *Contemporary Women Authors of Latin America*. New York: Brooklyn College, 1983. 78–90.

Olmos, Margarite Fernandez. "Constructing Heroines: Rosario Ferré's *Cuentos infantiles* and Feminine Instruments of Change." *Lion and the Unicorn* 10 (1986): 83–94.

Perry, Donna. "Rosario Ferré" [interview]. *Backtalk: Women Writers Speak Out*. New Brunswick, NJ: Rutgers University, 1993. 83–103.

Pinto, Magdalena Garcia. *Women Writers of Latin America: Intimate Histories*. Austin: University of Texas, 1991.

Fido, Elaine Savory. See **Savory, Elaine.**

The Field of Life and Death and Tales of Hulan River by Hsiao Hung (Bloomington: Indiana University, 1979). Two novels by a noted Chinese writer. The first, written when the author was only twenty-three, portrays the peasant population of a poor village in China, contrasting the physical beauty of the landscape with the brutishness and difficulty of the people's lives. The second is an autobiographical novel about the author's childhood in a small town. She says of it: "The tales I have written here are not beautiful ones, but since my childhood memories are filled with them, I cannot forget them—they remain with me—and so I have recorded them here" (275). She planned to write a sequel but died at the age of thirty before she could carry it out.

Commentary

Liu, Lydia. "The Female Body and Nationalist Discourse: *The Field of Life and Death* Revisited." *Scattered Hegemonies: Postmodernity and Transnational Feminist Practices*. Minneapolis: University of Minnesota, 1994. 37–62.

Film. A surprising number of third world women writers have been involved, one way and another, in filmmaking. Ruth Prawer Jhabvala has written many award-winning film scripts, working with the team of James Ivory and Ismail Merchant on film versions of E. M. Forster's novels, her own works, and others. Laura Esquival, author of the novel *Like Water for Chocolate* and its film script, is better known as a film script writer than as a novelist. Other writers who have turned their hands to script writing are María Luisa Bombal, 'Ismat Cughta'i, Li Pi-hua, C. S. Lakshmi, and Leena Dhingra. Edla van Steen and Ellen Kuzwayo have both acted in films. Trinh T. Minh-ha, an important theorist, has also made several critically acclaimed films, including *Surname Viet, Given Name Nam* and *Réassemblage*. Furugh Farrukhzad made a critically acclaimed documentary before her untimely death. Marguerite Duras is a filmmaker as well as a novelist; her revision of *The Lover*, entitled *The North China Lover*, written after collaborating unsuccessfully on a film version of it, includes notes about film shots as part of the novel. Assia Djebar has interspersed novel writing with filmmaking, making *La Nouba des femmes de Mont Chenoua* in 1979 and *La Zerda et les chants d'oublie* in 1982. She found the experience liberating and necessary to her writing: "In order to put [*La Nouba*] together, I had lengthy, unending private conversations with the women of my own tribe. There, I realized that the chain of solidarity was gradually reforming, tightening itself; that, in fact, its links had never been broken. These women rooted me back into myself all over again'' (Zimra, 124).

Recently, a number of film versions of third world women's works have been made, including *Farewell My Concubine* (with a script by the author), *Heaven and Earth* (based on Le Ly Hayslip's *When Heaven and Earth Changed Places*, adapted for the big screen by Oliver Stone), a lush and star-studded production of Isabel Allende's *The House of the Spirits*, and a disastrous version of Jean Rhys's *Wide Sargasso Sea*, films that betray a growing interest in the third world but are perhaps more revealing about Western representations of the other than they are about the third world. Cinematic representation has been the subject of some writers' work. Michelle Cliff's novel *No Telephone to Heaven* ends with a bizarre film shoot that becomes mixed up with actual shooting on a Caribbean island, an ironic critique of Hollywood depictions of the third world that makes for an interesting corrective reading.

Works

Ivory, James. *Autobiography of a Princess: Also Being the Adventures of an American Film Director in the Land of the Maharajas*. London, England: Murray, 1975. Includes script of the film *Autobiography of a Princess*, written by Ruth Prawer Jhabvala.

Trinh T. Minh-ha. *Framer Framed*. New York: Routledge, 1992. Includes scripts for three of her films as well as stills and interviews.

Commentary

Bhabha, Homi K. "The Other Question . . . Homi K. Bhabha Reconsiders the Stereotype and Colonial Discourse." *Screen* 24.6 (November-December 1983): 18–36.

Cham, Mbye. "African Women and Cinema: A Conversation with Anne Mungai." *Research in African Literatures* 25.3 (fall 1994): 93–104.

Gooneratne, Yasmine. "Film into Fiction: The Influence upon Ruth Prawer Jhabvala's Fiction of Her Work for Cinema, 1960–1976." *World Literature Written in English* 18 (1979): 368–386.

Mayne, Judith. "From a Hybrid Place: An Interview with Trinh T. Minh-ha." *Afterimage* 18 (December 1990): 6–9.

Pines, Jim, and Paul Willemen, editors. *Questions of Third Cinema*. London, England: BFI, 1989.

Shohat, Ella. "Gender and Culture of Empire: Toward a Feminist Ethnography of the Cinema." *Quarterly Review of Film and Video* 13.1–3 (May-October 1991): 45–84.

Trinh T. Minh-ha. "Documentary Is/Not a Name." *October* 52 (spring 1990): 76–98.

"Women and African Cinema" [special issue]. *Matatu*, forthcoming, spring 1996.

Zimra, Clarisse. " 'When the Past Answers Our Present:' Assia Djebar Talks about *Loin de Médine*." *Callaloo* 16.1 (1993): 116–131.

First, Ruth. Born in Johannesburg, South Africa, in 1925, the daughter of radical socialist parents. She studied at the University of Witwatersrand and then worked for a time for the Social Welfare Department of the Johannesburg City Council before resigning in protest over political affairs. She edited a series of newspapers on social issues, all of which were banned, and was a member of the African National Congress when it was an outlawed organization. In the 1950s she was arrested and tried for treason, and in 1963, she was detained under the Preventive Detention Act, which allowed for holding political prisoners without trial, and was in solitary confinement for 117 days, an experience described in her prison memoir, *117 Days*. After her release she moved with her family to London. She was married to political activist and Communist Party leader Joe Slovo. All three of their daughters became writers. Some years later, she moved to Mozambique, where she worked at the Centre for African Studies. She wrote, in addition to her prison memoir, a number of studies of southern African affairs and a distinguished literary biography, with Ann Scott, of Olive Schreiner. In 1982 she was killed by a letter bomb in Mozambique. The film, *A World Apart*, with script by her daughter Shawn Slovo, is a fictionalized account of her life and relationship with her daughter.

Work

117 Days. New York: Stein and Day, 1965.

Commentary

Harlow, Barbara. *Barred: Women, Writing, and Political Detention*. Middletown, CT: Wesleyan University, 1992.

The First South African by Fatima Dike (Johannesburg, South Africa: Ravan, 1979). A play, first produced in 1977, at Space Theatre in Cape Town. It concerns a township woman who has a white son, the product of a liaison with a white man in Namibia. She is now married to a black man who accepts the situation. The boy's identity is constantly questioned and becomes the subject of bureaucratic snarls. He is initiated into adulthood in the traditional African way, but he is unable to become a man according to his parents' definition. His father's way of life seems a dead end. He gets into various kinds of trouble— getting a girl pregnant but refusing to pay the bride price, getting into fights, having an affair with a white woman. He ends up divided, dialogically speaking in two roles, white *baas* and black boy, carrying on an abusive dialogue while beating himself. Written in a mixture of English, Afrikaans, and Xhosa, the play demonstrates the divisions and the many tongues in which a conflicted, multiracial South African must speak.

Flame Tree Time by Elaine Savory (Kingston, Jamaica: Sandberry, 1993). A collection of poetry by a Barbadian author who sees in the flame trees and other natural aspects of the Caribbean landscape a reflection of the Caribbean experience. The flamboyance of the flame trees is akin to the persistence of beauty and expressiveness, of the courage to rise. There are intertextual references throughout the poems to Bessie Head, Phyllis Shand Allfrey, Jean Rhys, and Isak Dinesen, markers that the author, who is also a literary critic, uses to trace common themes through their work and her experience. There are also poems about being a woman, about giving birth, creating a balance "between shell and centre" (11) and the domestic work of poetry being written in the kitchen, set to rise beside a warm stove.

Flowers from the Volcano by Claribel Alegría (Pittsburgh, PA: University of Pittsburgh, 1982). These poems are loaded with political meaning, exploring Central America's agony in poetic form. They include "Sorrow," which eulogizes political deaths, telling a "rosary of names" while expressing the loneliness and frustration of the exile. In the title poem, Alegría evokes the violent past, and the plundering greed of the conquistadors is equated with the hegemony of the Yanqui. Ultimately, peasants who live in the volcanic craters, raising flowers, flow over the mountains like lava, modern-day avatars of an ancient Mayan god.

For the Life of Laetitia by Merle Hodge (New York: Farrar, Straus, Giroux, 1993). A novel about coming of age and coming to terms with a society that fails to value its own culture. Laetitia belongs to a warm, extended family but moves to the city to live with her father and stepmother so that she can attend high school. There she meets teachers who are kind and teachers who despise the culture of the country. In one comic scene, she is taught that the nuclear family is a happy family; "broken" families are unhappy—the opposite of her own situation, in which the nuclear family she lives with is more broken than her extended one, but she has the confidence and resources to hold on to what she knows is true. She befriends an Indian girl whose family opposes her attending school and who despairs of finishing successfully and escaping the life of unrelieved toil her mother leads. Laetitia's problem is more tractable; she wants to live with her extended family rather than with her father but has to come to terms with the situation if she is to continue schooling. Like the author's *Crick Crack, Monkey*, this novel is a multilayered and convincing depiction of a strong young girl coping with the injustices, conundrums, and opportunities of life in Trinidad.

Fornés, Maria Irene. Born in Havana on May 14, 1930, the youngest of six children, Fornés was raised and schooled in Cuba. Her father did not believe in formal education and taught his children at home—she attended school only for grades three through six. In 1945, she migrated to the United States with her mother and sisters. She worked as a waitress and at a factory and began to paint and at age nineteen went to Europe to study art. In Paris she was strongly impressed by *Waiting for Godot*, and shortly after returning to the United States, she began to write. For a time, she shared an apartment with critic Susan Sontag, with whom she exchanged ideas for writing. She began to write plays, having had no formal training and having only read one play, Ibsen's *Hedda Gabler*, but she soon was having works produced in New York and elsewhere. She is a noted playwright, having contributed to INTAR (International Arts Relations, New York's Spanish theater) and having won six Obie awards. She has also adapted the works of Garcia Lorca, Calderón, and Chekhov. Her work is multifaceted, inventive, and theatrical and combines in collagelike vignettes both violent and slapstick comedy scenes in order to explore themes that are feminist and political.

Works

Fefu and Her Friends: A Play. New York: PAJ Publications, 1990.
Lovers and Keepers: A Musical Play. New York: Theatre Communications, 1987.
Plays: Mud, the Danube, the Conduct of Life, Sarita. New York: PAJ Publications, 1986.
Promenade and Other Plays. New York: Winter House, 1971.

Commentary

Geis, Deborah R. "Wordscapes of the Body: Performative Language as Gestus in Maria
      Irene Fornés's Plays." *Theatre Journal* 42.3 (October 1990): 291–307.
Keyssar, Helene. "Drama and the Dialogic Imagination: *The Heidi Chronicles* and *Fefu
      and Her Friends.*" *Modern Drama* 34.1 (March 1991): 88–106.
Marranca, Bonnie. "The State of Grace: Maria Irene Fornés at Sixty-two." *Performing
      Arts Journal* 41 (May 1992): 24–31.

Frangipani House by Beryl Gilroy (London, England: Heinemann, 1986). A novel that protests the existence of institutions that isolate and deny respect and responsibility for the old and weak. It relates the story of the infirm but intrepid Mama King at the rest home Frangipani House and how she escaped to the dangerous world of the poor, joining a band of beggars to regain a sense of self. Finally, she is able to reweave her family ties and find a place in life when she is taken in by a granddaughter and helps to deliver her first baby.

Free Enterprise by Michelle Cliff (New York: Dutton, 1993). A remarkable reweaving of history that brings new patterns to light. A woman, living on the banks of the Mississippi, a voluntary companion to the residents of an isolated leper colony, remembers her past attempts to end slavery and her involvement with the raid on Harper's Ferry. Tying together African origins, Jamaican slave revolts, women's unrecorded contributions to the raid on Harper's Ferry, and the cataclysm of the San Francisco earthquake, Cliff makes the composing of history itself, and the erasures it commits, her subject in a complex, lyrical, and narratively daring novel.

Freed, Lynn. Born in Durban, South Africa, she was educated at a girls' boarding school and went to America in 1963 as an American Field Service exchange scholar. She returned to South Africa, earned a B.A. at the University of Witwatersrand, and then moved to New York to marry and work on an M.A. and

Ph.D. in literature at Columbia University. She has lived in New York, Boston, Montreal, and San Francisco and currently lives in Sonoma, California. She is the recipient of fellowships from the Guggenheim and Rockefeller Foundations and from the National Endowment for the Arts. Thus far, she is the author of three novels and has published short stories in several American, British, and South African literary periodicals.

Works

The Bungalow. New York: Poseidon, 1993.
Heart Change. New York: New American Library, 1982.
Home Ground. New York: Summit, 1986.

Commentary

Freed, Lynn. "Sex with the Servants: Or, Autobiography and Fiction." *The Confidence Woman: 26 Women Writers at Work*. Atlanta, GA: Longstreet, 1991. 101–109.

From Eve's Rib by Gioconda Belli (Willimantic, CT: Curbstone Press, 1989). A bilingual poetry collection, originally entitled *De la costilla de Eva*. Poems that are sometimes political, sometimes erotic, often both. Belli was involved with the overthrow of the Somoza regime and worked for the Sandinista government. Her background in advertising and as a publicist at times shows in those poems that have an unabashedly public, celebratory function.

From Sleep Unbound by Andrée Chedid (Athens, OH: Swallow, 1983). This novel portrays the life of an Arab woman who rebels against the place women have been given in Muslim society. She is considered a failure because she has not conceived after eight years of marriage, and when she finally has a child, it is, disappointingly, a girl. She is delighted with her daughter, but when the child dies, she becomes paralyzed, apparently as a willful act of rebellion. Her final act of defiance is the murder of her husband. The original title, *Le Sommeil délivré*, suggests deliverance both in the sense of childbirth and in the sense of liberation. The narrative, which alternates between first and third person and shifts in time, suggests a situation that, though recognizably set in Egypt, could exist in any place or time.

Fugard, Sheila. Born in Birmingham in 1932 of an Irish mother and an Afrikaner father, a physician who had studied in Dublin, where he met and married her mother. When she was eight years old and World War II was beginning, they moved to South Africa, to live on a family farm in the Eastern Cape. Her mother was uncomfortable with the rural Afrikaner milieu, and her parents eventually divorced. Fugard spent the rest of her childhood in Johannesburg and Cape Town, then studied drama at the University of Cape Town, became an actress, and met and married the playwright Athol Fugard. She directed and acted in his first play, *The Cell* (1956), in an amateur theater they founded.

Together they have worked in theater that has received critical acclaim and caused official displeasure; they have also shared house arrest, police searches, and social ostracism. They moved to England briefly in 1959—she supporting his work by typing—but in the next year, the massacre at Sharpeville compelled them to return to South Africa to participate in the struggle for change. Later, in India for the filming of *Gandhi* (Athol Fugard played the role of Smuts), Sheila Fugard became deeply interested in Indian history and philosophy, which came into play in her novel *A Revolutionary Woman*, which parallels the Indian caste system with apartheid. She is the author of several novels and volumes of poetry with themes of racism, colonialism, feminism, and the search for a spiritual regeneration.

Works

The Castaways. London, England: Macmillan, 1972.
Mythic Things. Johannesburg, South Africa: Donker, 1981.
A Revolutionary Woman. New York: Braziller, 1985.
Rite of Passage. Johannesburg, South Africa: Donker, 1976.
Threshold. Johannesburg, South Africa: Donker, 1975.

Commentary

Fugard, Sheila. "A Castaway in Africa." *Momentum: On Recent South African Writing*. Pietermaritzburg, South Africa: University of Natal, 1984. 29–31.
Gray, Rosemary. "Sheila Fugard's *The Castaways*: Myth and Psychic Survival." *Commonwealth Essays and Studies* 10.1 (1987): 41–48.

G

Gambaro, Griselda. Argentinean playwright and novelist, born in 1928. She published her first book in 1963. Her plays written in the 1960s were part of the "theatre of crisis"; in the 1970s, she focused primarily on the drama of the missing of her country, those "disappeared" by the military regime, an issue addressed in her powerful and innovative play *Information for Foreigners*. She stayed in Argentina as long as she could during the "dirty war," burying or burning books and magazines that could have led to her own disappearance if they had been found. She fled the country at last when one of her books was expressly banned by the leader, Jorge Rafael Videla, a gesture that suggested she was being targeted by the ruling junta. She lived in Barcelona until the junta's power ebbed in 1980 and she could safely return. Since then, she has resumed writing plays, including *Antigona furiosa*, which parallels classical tragedy and contemporary politics. She is one of the most renowned playwrights in Latin America and is frequently produced in Europe, though she is less well known in North America.

Works

The Camp. In *Voices of Change in Spanish American Theater*. Translated by William Oliver. Austin: University of Texas, 1971. 49–103.
*The Impenetrable Madam X. Translated by Evelyn Picón Garfield. Detroit, MI: Wayne State University, 1991.
*Information for Foreigners: Three Plays. Translated by Marguerite Feitlowitz. Evanston, IL: Northwestern University, 1992.

Commentary

Boyle, Catherine. "Griselda Gambaro and the Female Dramatist: The Audacious Trespasser." *Knives and Angels: Women Writers in Latin America*. London, England: Zed, 1990. 145–157.

Taylor, Diana. "Theater and Terrorism: Griselda Gambaro's *Information for Foreigners*." *Theatre Journal* 42.2 (May 1990): 165–182.

Taylor, Diana. *Theatre of Crisis: Drama and Politics in Latin America*. Lexington: University of Kentucky, 1991.

Waldman, Gloria Feiman. "Three Female Playwrights Explore Contemporary Latin American Reality: Myrna Casas, Griselda Gambaro, Luisa Josefina Hernandez." *Latin American Women Writers: Yesterday and Today*. Pittsburgh, PA: Latin American Literary Review, 1977. 75–84.

Ganesan, Indira. Born on November 5, 1960, in Srirangam, India, she moved with her family to the United States when she was starting school. She earned a degree from Vassar, worked at the Writers' Workshop at the University of Iowa, and has since worked at the MacDowell Colony and the Fine Arts Work Center in Provincetown, Massachusetts. Her one novel published to date, *The Journey*, deals with an emigrant returning to visit India, something she herself does frequently.

Work

The Journey. New York: Knopf, 1990.

Garcia, Cristina. Born in 1958 in Havana, Cuba. At an early age she moved with her family to New York City, where she grew up. She attended Barnard College there and then the Johns Hopkins School of Advanced International Studies, preparatory to working as a correspondent for *Time* magazine. Her first novel, *Dreaming in Cuban*, explores the interrelated lives of women separated by the Cuban revolution, and the necessity of remembering the past in order to make connections.

Work

Dreaming in Cuban. New York: Knopf, 1992.

Garro, Elena. Born in Puebla, Mexico, on December 15, 1920. Much of her childhood was spent in Iguala, Guerrero, the setting of her novel *Recollections of Things to Come*. She attended the National Autonomous University, where she choreographed dance for the University Theatre and earned a degree in philosophy. She married the writer Octavio Paz, with whom she had a daughter. They divorced and she moved to Europe, spending time in both Spain and France. She started her writing career as a journalist and a playwright, though she has also written stories, essays, and a novel, which won the Xavier Villaurrutia Prize in 1963. Her style is tinged with the fantastic, and she is known for her unconventional handling of psychological characterization and narrative.

Works

The Dogs. Translated by Beth Miller. In *Latin American Literary Review* 8.15 (1979): 68–85.

The Lady on her Balcony. Translated by Beth Miller. In *Shantih* 3.3 (1976): 36–44.

*Recollections of Things to Come. Translated by Ruth L. C. Simms. Austin: University of Texas, 1969.

A Solid Home. In *Selected Latin American One-Act Plays.* Translated by Francesca Colecchia and Julio Matas. Pittsburgh, PA: University of Pittsburgh, 1973.

Commentary

Anderson, Robert K. "Myth and Archetype in *Recollections of Things to Come.*" *Studies in Twentieth Century Literature* 9.2 (1985): 213–227.

Balderston, Daniel. "The New Historical Novel: History and Fantasy in *Los recuerdos del porvenir.*" *Bulletin of Hispanic Studies* 66.1 (January 1989): 41–46.

Boling, Becky. "Tracking the Feminine Subject in Elena Garro's *El Rastro.*" *Continental, Latin-American, and Francophone Women Writers.* Vol. 2. Lanham, MD: University Press of America, 1990. 7–14.

Cypress, Sandra Messinger. "Visual and Verbal Distances in the Mexican Theatre: The Plays of Elena Garro." *Woman as Myth and Metaphor in Latin American Literature.* Columbia: University of Missouri, 1985. 44–62.

Fox-Lockert, Lucía. *Women Novelists in Spain and Spanish America.* Metuchen, NJ: Scarecrow Press, 1979.

Kaminsky, Amy K. *Reading the Body Politic: Feminist Criticism and Latin American Women Writers.* Minneapolis: University of Minnesota, 1993.

Larson, Catherine. "Recollections of Plays to Come: Time in the Theatre of Elena Garro." *Latin American Theatre Review* 22.2 (spring 1989): 5–17.

Mora, Gabriela. "A Thematic Exploration of the Works of Elena Garro." *Latin American Women Writers: Yesterday and Today.* Pittsburgh, PA: Latin American Literary Review, 1977. 91–97.

Stoll, Anita K. "Elena Garro's Lope de Vega's *La dama boba*: Seventeenth-Century Inspiration for a Twentieth-Century Dramatist." *Latin American Theatre Review* 23.2 (spring 1990): 21–31.

Stoll, Anita K., editor. *A Different Reality: Studies on the Works of Elena Garro.* Lewisburg, PA: Bucknell University, 1990.

Taylor, Kathy. *The New Narrative of Mexico: Sub-versions of History in Mexican Fiction.* Lewisburg, PA: Bucknell University, 1994.

Gilroy, Beryl. Born in Berbice, Guyana, in 1924, where she grew up and was educated for the teaching profession. She worked for UNICEF for a time before moving to the United Kingdom in the 1950s, where she worked in a shop and as a maid before becoming a teacher in a primary school in 1954. A teacher for forty years, she also was the first black headmistress in her North London borough. She completed a Ph.D. in child psychology in the 1980s and became a child psychotherapist and multicultural researcher at London University's Institute of Education. She has written a series of children's books as well as several novels, one of which, *Frangipani House*, won the Greater London Council Black Literature Prize in 1986.

Works

Arthur Small. London, England: Macmillan, 1979.
Black Teacher. London, England: Cassell, 1976.
*The Boy Sandwich. London, England: Heinemann, 1989.
Bubu's Street. London, England: Macmillan, 1977.
Echoes and Voices (Open-Hearted Poetry). New York: Vantage, 1991.
*Frangipani House. London, England: Heinemann, 1986.
Grandpa's Footsteps; Auntie Olive's Wedding; Elvira. London, England: Macmillan, 1978.
In Bed. London, England: Macmillan, 1977.
In for a Penny. London, England: Cassell, 1980.
Knock at Mrs. Herbs'. London, England: Macmillan, 1973.
New People at Twenty Four. London, England: Macmillan, 1973.
New Shoes. London, England: Macmillan, 1976.
No More Pets. London, England: Macmillan, 1975.
Once upon a Time. London, England: Macmillan, 1977.
Outings for Everyone. London, England: Macmillan, 1975.
The Paper Bag. London, England: Macmillan, 1975.
The Present. London, England: Macmillan, 1975.
Rice and Peas. London, England: Macmillan, 1975.
Stedman and Joanna: A Love in Bondage. New York: Vantage, 1993.
A Visitor from Home. London, England: Macmillan, 1973.

A Girl Like Me and Other Stories by Hsi Hsi (Hong Kong: Renditions, 1986). These stories are characterized by a sense of isolation and loneliness. Many of them are imaginative scenes from distant places, as diverse as the Belgian Congo and Kazakhstan. One story, ''The Cold,'' describes an unhappy arranged marriage, interweaving its history with lines of classical poetry, ending on a note of liberation. The title story in this collection won a prize for fiction from the *United Daily News*.

Githae Mugo, Micere. See **Mugo, Micere Githae.**

Glantz, Margo. Born in Mexico City in 1930, the daughter of Ukrainian Jews who emigrated to Mexico in 1925. Her father had several occupations, ranging from selling shoes to dentistry, but he also was interested in literature and was among those who founded the first Jewish newspaper in Mexico. She earned a doctorate at the Sorbonne and became a professor of literature at the University of Mexico. She has also taught in the United States and has served as a member of the Mexican diplomatic corps in England. She has written over a dozen books of fiction and literary criticism, tending to blur the boundaries between the two in her work. Her autobiography, *The Family Tree*, is the work that has received the most attention of her books.

Work

*The Family Tree: An Illustrated Novel. Translated by Susan Bassnett. London, England: Serpent's Tail, 1990.

Commentary

Pinto, Magdalena Garcia. *Women Writers of Latin America: Intimate Histories.* Austin: University of Texas, 1991.

Gloria, Angela Manalang. Born in the Philippines in 1907, the daughter of a building contractor, she published her first book of poetry in 1940. Her work has been popular and well received enough to be taught in the schools, though the schoolbook versions have been censored because her work is considered to deal too frankly with themes of passion and sexuality by the school officials.

Works

Poems. Manila, Philippines: n.p., 1950.
Poems by Angela Manalang Gloria. Manila, Philippines: n.p., 1940.

Commentary

Manlapaz, Edna Z., and Stella Pagsanghan. ''A Feminist Reading of the Poetry of Angela Manalang Gloria.'' *Philippine Studies* 37.4 (1989): 389-411.
Manlapaz, Edan Z., and Stella Pagsanghan. ''A Feminist Reading of the Poetry of Angela Manalang Gloria.'' *Women Reading . . . Feminist Perspectives on Philippine Literary Texts.* Quezon City: University of the Philippines, 1992. 187–212.
Pagsanghan, Stella. ''Angela Manalang Gloria: The Writer and Her Milieu.'' *Philippine Studies* 39.3 (1991): 303–320.

Gómez de Avellaneda, Gertrudis. Born on March 23, 1814, in Puerto Principe, central Cuba, daughter of the wealthy and well-connected Creole Dona Francisca de Arteaga y Betancourt and a Spanish naval officer, Don Manuel Gómez de Avellaneda y Gil de Taboada. When she was young, her father died, and her first poems were written in his memory. Her mother quickly remarried. She was educated by tutors and by the age of twelve was writing odes and directing plays for her friends and even wrote a novel. One of her tutors was the poet José Maria Heredia, who influenced her writing significantly. In 1836 her stepfather, nervous about the slave uprisings in Haiti and a rebellion in Puerto Principe itself, sold off his wife's property and slaves, and the family moved to Spain, after a stay in France. There her first published novel, *Sab*, was a popular success, quickly followed by other novels, plays, and poetry. Her first two novels were banned in Cuba; *Sab* was considered subversive and immoral. Her personal life was dramatic: She had an affair with a poet that resulted in her bearing a child out of wedlock who died in infancy; she married a friend in 1846 who died within months of cancer; and she married again in 1855. Her writing career flourished, and there was a campaign to gain her a chair in the Royal Spanish Academy, which failed because the majority would not consider admitting a woman. In 1859 she returned to Cuba, where she received a golden crown of laurels on her induction into the Havana Lyceum. She completed a number of novels, plays, and folk legends and started a short-lived women's magazine. She returned to Spain in 1864 and spent the last years of her life compiling and editing her works. She died of diabetes on February 1, 1873, at age fifty-six. Her works are relatively unknown in the English-speaking world, but her autobiography and the abolitionist novel *Sab* are of interest for the ways they explore feminist and racial themes.

Works

Baltasar: A Biblical Drama in Four Acts and in Verse. New York: American Book Co., 1908.
Love Letters. Havana, Cuba: Tall. Graf de J. F. Burgos, 1956.
Sab; and, Autobiography. Translated by Nina M. Scott. Austin: University of Texas, 1993.

Commentary

Fox-Lockert, Lucía. *Women Novelists in Spain and Spanish America.* Metuchen, NJ: Scarecrow, 1979.
Gold, Janet. "The Feminine Bond: Victimization and Beyond in the Novels of Gertrudis Gómez de Avellaneda." *Letras femeninas* 15 (1989): 83–89.
Harter, Hugh A. *Gertrudis Gómez de Avellaneda.* Boston: Twayne, 1981.
Miller, Beth. "Avellaneda, Nineteenth-Century Feminist." *Revista Interamericana* 4 (1974): 131–135.
Miller, Beth. "Gertrude the Great: Avellaneda, Nineteenth-Century Feminist." *Women in Hispanic Literature: Icons and Fallen Idols.* Berkeley: University of California, 1983. 201–214.
Schlau, Stacey. "Stranger in a Strange Land: The Discourse of Alienation in Gómez de Avellaneda's Abolitionist Novel *Sab*." *Hispania* 69 (1986): 495–503.
Williams, Edwin Bucher. *The Life and Dramatic Works of Gertrudis Gómez de Avellaneda.* Philadelphia, PA: n.p., 1924.

Goodison, Lorna. Artist and writer, born in Kingston, Jamaica, in 1947, she studied at the Jamaica School of Art and the Art Student League of New York. She has worked as art teacher, copywriter, scriptwriter, and writer. Her paintings have been exhibited in Jamaica and Guyana, and she has illustrated books, including Mervyn Morris's *On Holy Week.* She has been appointed writer in residence at the University of the West Indies and Radcliffe College and has given public readings of her works in London. Her short stories and poetry examine the bruises of Diaspora, explore the difficult relations between men and women, and celebrate memory, both personal and that of the community.

Works

*Baby Mother and the King of Swords: Short Stories. Harlow, England: Longman, 1990.
Heartease. London, England: New Beacon, 1988.
*I Am Becoming My Mother. London, England: New Beacon, 1986.

Selected Poems. Ann Arbor: University of Michigan, 1992.
Tamarind Season. Kingston: Institute of Jamaica, 1980.

Commentary

Chang, V., editor. *Three Caribbean Poets on Their Work: E. Kamau Brathwaite, Mervyn Morris, Lorna Goodison.* Kingston, Jamaica: University of the West Indies Institute of Caribbean Studies, 1993.
DeCaires Narain, Denise. "Interview with Lorna Goodison." *Wasafiri* 8–9.11 (1989): 20–24.
Mordecai, Pamela. "Wooing with Words: Some Comments on the Poetry of Lorna Goodison." *Jamaica Journal* 14 (1981): 35–40.
Pollard, Velma. "Mothertongue Voices in the Writing of Olive Senior and Lorna Goodison." *Motherlands: Women's Writings from Africa, the Caribbean, and South Asia.* New Brunswick, NJ: Rutgers University, 1992. 238–253.
Pollard, Velma. "Overlapping Systems: Language in the Poetry of Lorna Goodison." *Carib* (1989): 33–47.

Gooneratne, Yasmine. Born in Colombo, Sri Lanka, in 1935, she earned an honors degree in English from the University of Ceylon and pursued postgraduate studies at Girton College. She earned a Ph.D. in English from Cambridge, writing her dissertation on nineteenth-century Sri Lankan literature. She taught at her home university in Peradeniya, then moved with her husband and two children to Australia in 1972, where she teaches at Macquairie University in New South Wales. That institution granted her an honorary Litt.D. in 1981. She has published poetry, criticism, and a memoir of her distinguished and prominent family. She has also been active in fostering new writers, as a cofounder and editor of *New Sri Lankan Writing* and the compiler of anthologies of Sri Lankan literature.

Works

A Change of Skies. Sydney, Australia: Picador Australia, 1991.
*Relative Merits: A Personal Memoir of the Bandaranaike Family of Sri Lanka. New York: St. Martin's, 1986.
6,000 Ft. Death Dive. Colombo, Sri Lanka: Swadeshi, 1981.
Word, Bird, Motif. Kandy, Sri Lanka: T.B.S. Godamunne and Sons, 1971.

Commentary

Gooneratne, Yasmine. *Diverse Inheritance: A Personal Perspective on Commonwealth Literature.* Adelaide, Australia: Center for Research in the New Literatures in English, 1980.
Gooneratne, Yasmine. "Biographical Writing: Personal and Private." *A Sense of Exile: Essays in the Literature of the Asia-Pacific Region.* Nedlands, Australia: CSAL, 1988. 197–210.
Gooneratne, Yasmine. "Writing a Family History." *Journal of Indian Writing in English* 16.2 (1988): 126–135.

Gordimer, Nadine. Born in 1923 in Springs, South Africa, a mining town in the Witwatersrand (a town that she has described as one of the few parts of South Africa that is not beautiful), the daughter of Nan Meyer and Isidore Gordimer, a watchmaker and jeweler. She began her education at a convent school but left at age ten under the pretext of a heart ailment, something that she later felt her mother had engineered to keep her home. She had tutors until age fifteen or sixteen and spent a year at the University of Witwatersrand when she was twenty-one. Her writing career is long—having published her first story in 1937 at age fifteen. She characterizes herself as a "natural writer," not one driven by considerations of audience or of political necessity, though her novels are markedly political and often deal not only with the personal decisions that need to be made (as in *The Late Bourgeois World*) but with the actual business of doing politics (as in *A Guest of Honour* and *Burger's Daughter*). She is as accomplished in short fiction as in the novel and has written many essays, though she cautions that her nonfiction can't possibly be as true as her fiction. She has been active in supporting both political change and the development of writers and literature in her country. She was awarded a Nobel Prize for literature in 1991.

Works

Burger's Daughter. New York: Viking, 1979.
The Conservationist. New York: Viking, 1975.
Crimes of Conscience. Portsmouth, NH: Heinemann, 1991.
Face to Face: Short Stories. Johannesburg, South Africa: Silver Leaf, 1949.
*A Guest of Honour. New York: Viking, 1970.
*July's People. New York: Viking, 1981.
Jump and Other Stories. New York: Farrar, Straus, Giroux, 1991.
*The Late Bourgeois World. New York: Viking, 1966.
Livingstone's Companions. New York: Viking, 1971.
The Lying Days. New York: Simon and Schuster, 1953.
My Son's Story. New York: Farrar, Straus, Giroux, 1990.
None to Accompany Me. New York: Farrar, Straus, Giroux, 1994.
Not for Publication and Other Stories. New York: Viking, 1965.
Occasion for Loving. New York: Viking, 1963.
Selected Stories. New York: Viking, 1976.
Six Feet of the Country. New York: Simon and Schuster, 1956.
A Soldier's Embrace. New York: Viking, 1980.
Some Monday for Sure. London, England: Heinemann, 1976.
Something Out There. New York: Viking, 1984.
*A Sport of Nature. New York: Knopf, 1987.
Why Haven't You Written? Selected Stories 1950–1972. New York: Penguin, 1993.
A World of Strangers. New York: Simon and Schuster, 1958.

Commentary

Bazin, Nancy Topping. "Madness, Mysticism, and Fantasy: Shifting Perspectives in the Novels of Doris Lessing, Bessie Head, and Nadine Gordimer." *Extrapolation* 33.1 (1992): 73–87.

Bodenheimer, Rosemarie. "The Interregnum of Ownership in *July's People.*" *The Later Fiction of Nadine Gordimer.* New York: St. Martin's, 1993. 108–120.

Boyers, Robert, et al. "A Conversation with Nadine Gordimer." *Salmagundi* 62 (winter 1984): 3–31.

Clingman, Stephen. "Writing in a Fractured Society: The Case of Nadine Gordimer." *Literature and Society in South Africa.* Harlow, England: Longman, 1984. 161–174.

Clingman, Stephen. *The Novels of Nadine Gordimer: History from the Inside.* London: Allen and Unwin, 1986.

Clingman, Stephen. "*A Sport of Nature* and the Boundaries of Fiction." *The Later Fiction of Nadine Gordimer.* New York: St. Martin's, 1993. 173–190.

Cooke, John. *The Novels of Nadine Gordimer: Private Lives/Public Landscapes.* Baton Rouge: Louisiana State University, 1985.

Cooper, Brenda. "New Criteria for 'Abnormal Mutation'? An Evaluation of Gordimer's *A Sport of Nature.*" *Rendering Things Visible: Essays on South African Literary Culture.* Athens: Ohio University, 1990. 68–93.

Donaghy, Mary. "Double Exposure: Narrative Perspective in Gordimer's *A Guest of Honor.*" *Ariel* 19.4 (1988): 19–32.

Driver, Dorothy, editor. *Nadine Gordimer: A Bibliography of Primary and Secondary Sources.* London, England: H. Zell, 1994.

Ettin, Andrew Vogel. *Betrayals of the Body Politic: The Literary Commitments of Nadine Gordimer.* Charlottesville: University Press of Virginia, 1992.

Fido, Elaine. "*A Guest of Honour*: A Feminine View of Masculinity." *World Literature Written in English* 17.1 (1978): 30–37.

Gardiner, Susan. " 'A Story for This Place and Time': An Interview with Nadine Gordimer about *Burger's Daughter.*" *Kunapipi* 3.2 (1981): 99–112.

Gordimer, Nadine. "English-Language Literature and Politics in South Africa." *Aspects of South African Literature.* London, England: Heinemann, 1976. 99–120.

Gordimer, Nadine. *The Essential Gesture: Writing, Politics, and Places.* New York: Knopf, 1988.

Gordimer, Nadine. *Conversations with Nadine Gordimer.* Jackson: University Press of Mississippi, 1990.

Gordon, Jennifer. "Dreams of a Common Language: Nadine Gordimer's *July's People.*" *African Literature Today* 15 (1987): 102–108.

Gray, Rosemary. "Text and Context: A Reading of Elizabeth Charlotte Webster's *Ceremony of Innocence* and Nadine Gordimer's *The Conservationist.*" *Commonwealth Essays and Studies* 13.1 (1990): 55–67.

Gray, Stephen. "Gordimer's *A World of Strangers* as Memory." *Ariel* 19.4 (October 1988): 11–16.

Green, Robert. "From *The Lying Days* to *July's People*: The Novels of Nadine Gordimer." *Journal of Modern Literature* 14.4 (spring 1988): 543–563.

Greenstein, Susan M. "Miranda's Story: Nadine Gordimer and the Literature of Empire." *Novel: A Forum on Fiction* 18.3 (spring 1985): 227–242.

Greenstein, Susan M. "*My Son's Story*: Drenching the Censors—the Dilemma of White Writing." *The Later Fiction of Nadine Gordimer.* New York: St. Martin's, 1993. 191–209.

Huggan, Graham. "Echoes from Elsewhere: Gordimer's Short Fiction as Social Critique." *Research in African Literatures* 25.1 (spring 1994): 61–73.

Hunter, E., and C. MacKenzie, editors. *Between the Lines II: Interviews with Nadine Gordimer, Menan Du Plessis, Zöe Wicomb, Lauretta Ngcobo*. Grahamstown, South Africa: National English Literary Museum, 1993.

Ingersoll, Earl, and Stan Sanvel Rubin. "A Voice from a Troubled Land: A Conversation with Nadine Gordimer." *Ontario Review* 26 (spring-summer 1987): 5–14.

Jacobs, J. U. "Living Space and Narrative Space in Nadine Gordimer's 'Something Out There.' " *English in Africa* 14.2 (October 1987): 31–43.

JanMohamed, Abdul R. "The Economy of Manichean Allegory: The Function of Racial Difference in Colonialist Literature." *Critical Inquiry* 12.1 (autumn 1985): 59–87.

King, Bruce, editor. *The Later Fiction of Nadine Gordimer*. New York: St. Martins, 1993.

Louvel, Liliane. "Nadine Gordimer's *My Son's Story* or the Experience of Fragmentation." *Commonwealth Essays and Studies* 14.2 (spring 1992): 28–33.

Martin, Richard G. "Narrative, History, Ideology: A Study of *Waiting for the Barbarians* and *Burger's Daughter*." *Ariel* 17.3 (July 1986): 3–21.

Mazurek, Raymond A. "Gordimer's *Something Out There* and Ndebele's *Fools and Other Stories*: The Politics of Literary Form." *Studies in Short Fiction* 26.1 (1989): 71–79.

Meese, Elizabeth A. "The Political Is the Personal: The Construction of Identity in Nadine Gordimer's *Burger's Daughter*." *Feminism and Institutions: Dialogues on Feminist Theory*. Oxford, England: Blackwell, 1989. 253–275.

Newman, Judie. "Prospero's Complex: Race and Sex in Nadine Gordimer's *Burger's Daughter*." *Journal of Commonwealth Literature* 20.1 (1985): 81–99.

Petersen, Kirsten Holst. "The Search for a Role for White Women in a Liberated South Africa: A Thematic Approach to the Novels of Nadine Gordimer." *Kunapipi* 13.1–2 (1991): 170–177.

Read, Daphne. "The Politics of Place in *Burger's Daughter*." *The Later Fiction of Nadine Gordimer*. New York: St. Martin's, 1993. 121–139.

Roberts, Sheila. "South African Post-Revolutionary Fiction." *The Commonwealth in Canada: Proceedings of the Second Triennial Conference of CACLALS, University of Winnipeg, 1–4 October, 1981*. Calcutta, India: Writers' Workshop, 1983. 203–215.

Roberts, Sheila. "Sites of Paranoia and Taboo: Lessing's *The Grass Is Singing* and Gordimer's *July's People*." *Research in African Literatures* 24 (fall 1993): 73–85.

Ross, Robert L., editor. *International Literature in English: Essays on the Major Writers*. New York: Garland, 1991.

Smyer, Richard I. "Risk, Frontier, and Interregnum in the Fiction of Nadine Gordimer." *Journal of Commonwealth Literature* 20.1 (1985): 168–180.

Sonza, Jorshinelle. " 'My Turn Now': Debunking the Gordimer 'Mystique' in *My Son's Story*." *Research in African Literatures* 25.4 (winter 1994): 105–116.

Visel, Robin. "A Half-Colonization: The Problem of the White Colonial Woman Writer." *Kunapipi* 10.3 (1988): 39–45.

Visel, Robin. "Othering the Self: Nadine Gordimer's Colonial Heroines." *Ariel* 19.4 (1988): 33–42.

Wade, Michael. "*A Sport of Nature*: Identity and Repression of the Jewish Subject." *The Later Fiction of Nadine Gordimer*. New York: St. Martin's, 1993. 155–172.

Wagner, Kathrin M. *Rereading Nadine Gordimer*. Bloomington: Indiana University, 1994.

Weinhouse, Linda. "The Deconstruction of Victory: Gordimer's *A Sport of Nature*." *Research in African Literatures* 21.2 (summer 1990): 91–100.

What Happened to Burger's Daughter *or How South African Censorship Works*. Emmarentia, South Africa: Taurus, 1980.

White, Landeg, and Tim Couzens, editors. *Literature and Society in South Africa*. Harlow, England: Longman, 1984.

Winnett, Susan. "Making Metaphors/Moving On: *Burger's Daughter* and *A Sport of Nature*." *The Later Fiction of Nadine Gordimer*. New York: St. Martin's, 1993. 140–154.

Yelin, Louise. "Problems of Gordimer's Poetics: Dialogue in *Burger's Daughter*." *Feminism, Bakhtin, and the Dialogic*. Albany, NY: SUNY, 1991. 219–238.

Yelin, Louise. "Decolonizing the Novel: Nadine Gordimer's *A Sport of Nature* and British Literary Traditions." *Decolonizing Tradition: New Views of Twentieth-Century "British" Literary Canons*. Urbana: University of Illinois, 1992. 191–211.

A Guest of Honour by Nadine Gordimer (New York: Viking, 1970). The story of Evelyn James Bray, a British colonial district commissioner who was thrown out of the fictional central African country where he worked because he sympathized with those who were fighting colonial rule. He returns at the president's request when the country gains independence. He quickly learns that two old comrades are now fighting one another and that the new government is not much different than the old, that corruption, injustice, and exploitation by multinational corporations are still the norm. Bray idealistically throws in his lot with the opposition, first urging them to work within the parliamentary system, then reluctantly agreeing to raise money for the resistance forces. As he awakens to the complexities of political reality and the futility of liberal responses, he also is awakening to love in the person of Rebecca, a young mother who has been thrown haphazardly into his path. Eventually, as the political situation grows unstable—and even British troops are called in to quell the rebellion—Bray is killed, mistakenly, by a gang of angry workers who take him for a mine owner's security chief. His life is brutally interrupted, his work ironically co-opted by the corrupt government, which posthumously publishes the "Bray Report" on education. Rebecca goes to England, where she is a stranger; her life is no less interrupted by the tragedy. The novel is rich with sensual imagery, well-rounded characters, political intrigue, a text that is dense with detail and laced with irony. The novel is the first in which Gordimer tackled the workings of politics as a subject and employed a complex narrative structure. It was awarded the James Tait Black Memorial prize.

Commentary

Donaghy, Mary. "Double Exposure: Narrative Perspective in Gordimer's *A Guest of Honour*." *Ariel* 19.4 (1988): 19–32.

Fido, Elaine. "*A Guest of Honour*: A Feminine View of Masculinity." *World Literature Written in English* 17.1 (1978): 30–37.

Guppy, Shusha. Born in Iran, she grew up in a wealthy family in Teheran and was sent in her teens to study in Paris. She married naturalist Nicholas Guppy (now divorced) and moved with him to London in the early 1960s, where she still lives. She is the London editor of the *Paris Review* and is a singer and songwriter, having made a number of recordings of Persian folk songs and contemporary compositions of her own and other songwriters. Her memoir *The Blindfold Horse* is a nostalgic celebration of a vanished world.

Works

*The Blindfold Horse: Memories of a Persian Girlhood. London, England: Heinemann, 1988.
A Girl in Paris. London, England: Heinemann, 1991.

Guy, Rosa. Born in Trinidad in 1925, she moved with her family to Harlem, New York, at age seven. She was orphaned by age fourteen and left school to work in a factory, where she became involved in union activities and then in civil rights issues. She joined the American Negro Theatre and held several jobs while going to school to study acting. In the 1950s she helped black writers found the Harlem Writers' Guild and became its president. In 1954 one of her plays was produced off Broadway, but only much later was she recognized as a writer for both adults and children. In 1941 she married Warner Guy, and they divorced in 1950; after his death in 1962, she spent time living in Haiti, where she worked on her first novel. She has also written a number of works for children and was an editor of *Children of Longing,* a collection of interviews with young African Americans shortly after the assassination of Martin Luther King.

Works

And I Heard a Bird Sing. New York: Delacorte, 1987.
Billy the Great. New York: Delacorte, 1992.
Bird at My Window. Philadelphia, PA: Lippincott, 1966.
Children of Longing. New York: Holt, Rinehart, Winston, 1970.
The Disappearance. New York: Delacorte, 1979.
Edith Jackson. New York: Holt, Rinehart, Winston, 1978.
The Friends. New York: Holt, Rinehart, Winston, 1973.
A Measure of Time. New York: Holt, Rinehart, Winston, 1983.
Mirror of Her Own. New York: Delacorte, 1981.
The Music of Summer. New York: Delacorte, 1992.
My Love, My Love or the Peasant Girl. New York: Holt, Rinehart, Winston, 1985.
New Guys Around the Block. New York: Delacorte, 1983.
Paris, Pee Wee, and Big Dog. New York: Delacorte, 1984.
Ruby. New York: Viking, 1976.
The Ups and Downs of Carl Davis III. New York: Delacorte, 1989.

Commentary

Chamberlain, Mary, editor. *Writing Lives: Conversations Between Women Writers*. London, England: Virago, 1988.

Norris, Jerrie. *Presenting Rosa Guy*. Boston: Twayne, 1988.

Gyaltsen, Indrani Aikath. See **Aikath-Gyaltsen, Indrani.**

H

Hagedorn, Jessica. Born in Manila, of Filipino, Spanish, Scotch-American, and Chinese heritage, she grew up in a privileged, Catholic, progressive, Westernized household. She was considered fortunate in her mestizo background, though she was told her nose was "too Filipino." Her grandfather was a writer, and she began writing in early childhood, compiling "little novels" that she illustrated herself. She moved to California when she was a teenager and spent her twenties in San Francisco, writing poetry and performing music with her band, the West Coast Gangster Choir, for which she was lyricist and leader. She worked theatrical bits into their performances in between songs. Later she moved to New York, where she now lives, performing her poetry at the Public Theater and appearing with both theater and dance groups, including the group Thought Music. She contributes to *Crossroads*, a weekly newsmagazine on public radio, and has published poetry, drama, and novels. Her work refuses to settle into specific genres and cultures: "I think there is a multicultural aesthetic, in the sense that you can draw from many different cultures that have similar experiences. For example, black music really influenced the way I write poetry. Certain rhythms go along with certain forms of jazz and R&B I listen to. But it gets kind of sticky when you try to define things. I don't want limitations imposed on me" (introduction to "Tenement Lover," 78).

Works

Danger and Beauty. New York: Penguin, 1993.
*Dogeaters. London, England: Pandora, 1991.
Pet Food and Tropical Apparitions. San Francisco: Momo's Press, 1981.

Teeny Town. In *Out from Under: Texts by Women Performance Artists.* New York: Theatre Communications Group, 1990. 90–117.

Tenement Lover. In *Between Worlds: Contemporary Asian-American Plays.* New York: Theatre Communications Group, 1990. 75–90.

Travels in the Combat Zone. New York: D. Chase, 1982.

Commentary

DeManuel, Maria Teresa. "Jessica Hagedorn's *Dogeaters*: A Feminist Reading." *Likha* 12.2 (1990–1991): 10–32.

Evangelista, Susan. "Jessica Hagedorn: Pinay Poet." *Philippine Studies* 35.4 (1987): 475–487.

Evangelista, Susan. "Jessica Hagedorn and Manila Magic." *Melus* 18.4 (winter 1993): 41–52.

Hagedorn, Jessica. "The Exile Within/The Question of Identity." *The State of Asian America: Activism and Resistance in the 1990s.* Boston: South End Press, 1994. 173–182.

Hagedorn, Jessica [untitled essay]. *Critical Fictions: The Politics of Imaginative Writing.* Seattle, WA: Bay Press, 1991. 146–150.

Hagedorn, Jessica. "On Theater and Performance." *Melus* 16.3 (fall 1989–1990): 13–15.

San Juan, E. "Mapping the Boundaries: The Filipino Writer in the U.S.A." *Journal of Ethnic Studies* 19.1 (spring 1991): 117–131.

Halimi, Gisèle. Born in Tunisia in 1927, the second child of a poor orthodox Jewish family. Her father, a law clerk, was so disappointed she wasn't a boy he delayed announcing her birth for two weeks. Her mother had married at age fifteen and had her first child at sixteen. Gisèle's education was not a priority for the family, but she learned when she was ten years old that she could sit for a scholarship examination, and she did so well she earned a place at a lycée. She was determined to be a lawyer, and in order to earn money for university, she tutored a lawyer's son. She went to France after finishing at the lycée and there became disillusioned with French culture and law, encountering racism she had not expected. She earned a law degree, practiced for a time in Tunisia, and there began to take on and win political cases. Later, in France, she became notorious for defending women's right to abortion. (She herself had undergone an illegal abortion at age nineteen.) Her career as a lawyer handling sensitive political and feminist cases is recounted in her memoir *Milk for the Orange Tree*, which is structured around the death of her father, an event around which she focuses her memories of the past; typically, she refused to sit in the women's section of the synagogue at his funeral.

Work

Milk for the Orange Tree. Translated by Dorothy S. Blair. London, England: Quartet, 1990.

Han Suyin. Born in China in 1917, one of eight children of a Belgian mother and a Chinese father. Because of her mixed heritage, she experienced racism at an early age, having it directed at her from both the Western and Chinese communities. She was educated at a Catholic convent school and Yenjing University, then traveled to visit her grandfather in Belgium and attended the Université Libre of Brussels. She is a prolific writer and has written many volumes of fiction, nonfiction, and autobiography.

Works

. . . *And the Rain My Drink*. Boston: Little, Brown, 1956.
Birdless Summer. New York: Putnam, 1968.
The Crippled Tree. New York: Putnam, 1965.
Destination Chungking. London, England: Jonathan Cape, 1942.
The Enchantress. New York: Bantam, 1985.
The Four Faces. New York: Putnam, 1963.
A Many Splendored Thing. Boston: Little, Brown, 1952.
A Mortal Flower. New York: Putnam, 1966.
The Mountain Is Young. New York: Putnam, 1958.
My House Has Two Doors. New York: Putnam, 1980.
Till Morning Comes. New York: Bantam, 1982.
Two Loves. New York: Putnam, 1962.

Commentary

Ling, Amy. *Between Two Worlds: Women Writers of Chinese Ancestry*. New York: Pergamon, 1990.

Harem Years: The Memoirs of an Egyptian Feminist by Huda Sha'rawi (London, England: Virago, 1986). A memoir written by a woman who was brought up in seclusion according to traditional ways, was married very young, and became a feminist. She was very involved in both the nationalist movement and in seeking rights for women. Her memoir, amply illustrated with photographs and with an informative introduction that puts her life in context, is both a description of the experiences of being a woman in Egypt at the time and a documentation of the movement for independence, both for Egypt and Egyptian women.

Harriet's Daughter by Marlene Nourbese Philip (London, England: Heinemann, 1988). A novel that follows the friendship and adventures of two young girls in Toronto; one is a second-generation West Indian immigrant and the other has only recently arrived from Tobago, leaving behind a dearly loved grandmother to settle into an uneasy relationship with her stepfather and mother. While Margaret plots to get enough money to take her friend home, her friend gives her lessons in "Tobago talk." According to Margaret, "her talk had all these hills and valleys—nothing like my flat, old, boring Canadian talk" (10). Learning to speak like a Tobagonian is part of her quest for selfhood, as is her increasing respect for her Jamaican mother's ways. This novel written for young readers is a thoughtful and acute exploration of the generational and cultural differences facing children in émigré families.

Have You Seen Zandile? by Gcina Mhlophe (Portsmouth, NH: Heinemann, 1990). A play based on the author's childhood, concerning a little girl whose mother and father were not married to each other and who lives with her beloved grandmother. She is kidnapped by her mother's people and taken to their rural home in the Transkei, where she keeps writing letters to her grandmother that she cannot send. Grown up, she finally, through a friend, reestablishes contact with her father's family and learns the grandmother has died. The final scene shows her unpacking the suitcase full of treasures that, like Zandile's unsent letters, were stored up over the years by her grandmother in the hope of being reunited. Urban and rural life are contrasted in the play, girls' experiences in school and in adolescence are explored, and the language reflects the usage of South African blacks, mingling Zulu, Xhosa, and English. The play was first presented in Johannesburg at the Market Theatre. It went to the Edinburgh Festival, where the play won the Fringefirst Award and where Gcina Mhlophe won the Sony Award for best actress. It has also been performed in Switzerland and the United States.

Head, Bessie. Born in Pietermaritzburg, South Africa, in 1937, daughter of a Zulu stablehand and Bessie Emery, a white daughter of a wealthy Natal racing family. This union led to her mother being certified insane and being committed to a mental hospital until her death in 1943, an autobiographical situation replayed in the novels *Maru* and *A Question of Power*. She was given to a couple for adoption, but they soon returned her because she was too dark skinned. She was then raised in a foster home by coloured parents and at age thirteen was sent to live at an Anglican mission school in Durban. She trained as a teacher, taught for four years, and then worked as a journalist for the *Golden City Post*, writing a column for teens. She was briefly married and then applied for a teaching post in Botswana, migrating there with her young son in 1964. On leaving South Africa, she was given only an exit visa, which did not allow reentry. For many years she was stateless, being refused citizenship in Botswana until 1979. She worked in Botswana as a teacher and market gardener, a novelist, and an historian. She struggled with mental illness, beginning in 1969 with sporadic attacks over the next few years, which no doubt accounts for the persuasiveness and vividness of the heroine's experiences in *A Question of Power*. She died suddenly of hepatitis in 1986 and is buried in Serowe. Agnes Sam asserts that by living in a village Head avoided the isolation of the writer living in exile, forced to live apart from the African experience. Yet, ironically, Head felt isolated in the village in part because her audience was so distant and the rewards of writing so scant that she couldn't afford books and magazines, travel, or memberships in writers' organizations. Her work is characterized by a twin search for personal identity and a commitment to recovering and celebrating Africa's precolonial past.

Works

A Bewitched Crossroad. New York: Paragon House, 1986.
The Cardinals, With Meditations and Short Stories. Cape Town, South Africa: D. Philip, 1993.
The Collector of Treasures. London, England: Heinemann, 1977.
Letters from Bessie Head, 1965–1979. London, England: SA Writers, 1991.
Maru. London, England: Heinemann, 1987.
A Question of Power. London, England: Heinemann, 1974.
Serowe: The Village of the Rain-Wind. London, England: Heinemann, 1981.
Tales of Tenderness and Power. Portsmouth, NH: Heinemann, 1990.
When Rain Clouds Gather. New York: Simon and Schuster, 1969.
A Woman Alone: Autobiographical Writings. Portsmouth, NH: Heinemann, 1990.

Commentary

Abrahams, Cecil A. "The Tyranny of Place: The Context of Bessie Head's Fiction." *World Literature Written in English* 17 (1978): 22–29.
Abrahams, Cecil, editor. *The Tragic Life: Bessie Head and Literature in South Africa.* Trenton, NJ: Africa World Press, 1990.
Bazin, Nancy Topping. "Feminist Perspectives in African Fiction: Bessie Head and Buchi Emecheta." *The Black Scholar* (March-April 1986): 34–40.
Bazin, Nancy Topping. "Feminism in the Literature of African Women." *The Black Scholar* 20.3–4 (summer-fall 1989): 8–17.
Bazin, Nancy Topping. "Madness, Mysticism, and Fantasy: Shifting Perspectives in the Novels of Doris Lessing, Bessie Head, and Nadine Gordimer." *Extrapolation* 33.1 (1992): 73–87.
Beard, Linda Susan. "Bessie Head in Gaborone, Botswana: An Interview." *Sage* 3.2 (fall 1986): 44–47.
Beard, Linda Susan. "Bessie Head's Syncretic Fictions: The Reconceptualization of Power and the Recovery of the Ordinary." *Modern Fiction Studies* 37.3 (autumn 1991): 575–589.
Brown, Lloyd W. *Women Writers in Black Africa.* Westport, CT: Greenwood, 1981.
Bruner, Charlotte. "Been-To or Has-Been: A Dilemma for Today's African Woman." *Ba Shiru* 8.2 (1977): 21–30.
Bruner, Charlotte. "Child Africa as Depicted by Bessie Head and Ama Ata Aidoo." *Studies in the Humanities* 7.2 (1979): 5–11.
Bryce-Okunlola, Jane. "Motherhood as a Metaphor for Creativity in Three African Women's Novels: Flora Nwapa, Rebeka Njau, and Bessie Head." *Motherlands: Women's Writings from Africa, the Caribbean, and South Asia.* New Brunswick, NJ: Rutgers University, 1992. 200–218.
Chetin, Sara. "Myth, Exile, and the Female Condition: Bessie Head's *The Collector of Treasures.*" *Journal of Commonwealth Literature* 23.1 (1989): 114–137.
Clayton, Cherry. " 'A World Elsewhere': Bessie Head as Historian." *English in Africa* 15.1 (May 1988): 55–69.
Eke, Ebele. "Beyond the Myth of Confrontation: A Comparative Study of African and African-American Female Protagonists." *Ariel* 17.4 (1986): 139–152.

Fido, Elaine Savory. "Mother/Lands: Self and Separation in the Work of Buchi Emecheta, Bessie Head, and Jean Rhys." *Motherlands: Women's Writings from Africa, the Caribbean, and South Asia*. New Brunswick, NJ: Rutgers University,
1992. 330–349.

Flewellen, Elinor C. "Assertiveness vs. Submissiveness in Selected Works by African
Women Writers." *Ba Shiru* 12.2 (1985): 3–18.

Gardner, Susan. " 'Don't Ask for the True Story': A Memoir of Bessie Head." *Hecate*
12.1–2 (1986): 110–129.

Gardner, Susan, and Patricia E. Scott. *Bessie Head: A Bibliography*. Grahamstown, South
Africa: National English Literary Museum, 1986.

Geurtz, Kathryn. "Personal Politics in the Novels of Bessie Head." *Présence Africaine*
140 (1986): 47–74.

Grant, Jane. "Bessie Head: An Appreciation." *Bananas* 22 (August 1980): 25–26.

Ibrahim, Huma. "The Autobiographical Content in the Works of South African Women
Writers: The Personal and the Political." *Biography East and West: Selected
Conference Papers*. Honolulu: University of Hawaii, 1989. 122–126.

Johnson, J. "Bessie Head and the Oral Tradition: The Structure of *Maru*." *Wasafiri* 3
(1985): 5–8.

Johnson, Joyce. "Structures of Meaning in the Novels of Bessie Head." *Kunapipi* 8.1
(1986): 56–69.

Katrak, Ketu H. "From Pauline to Dikeledi: The Philosophical and Political Vision of
Bessie Head's Protagonists." *Ba Shiru* 12.2 (1985): 19–25.

Kibera, Valerie. "Adopted Motherlands: The Novels of Marjorie Macgoye and Bessie
Head." *Motherlands: Women's Writings from Africa, the Caribbean, and South
Asia*. New Brunswick, NJ: Rutgers University, 1992. 310–329.

Lionnet, Françoise. "Geographies of Pain: Captive Bodies and Violent Acts in the Fictions of Myriam Warner-Vieyra, Gayl Jones, and Bessie Head." *Callaloo* 16.1
(winter 1993): 132–152.

Lorenz, Paul. "Colonization and the Feminine in Bessie Head's *A Question of Power*."
Modern Fiction Studies 37.3 (autumn 1991): 591–605.

MacKenzie, Craig, and Cherry Clayton. *Between the Lines: Interviews with Bessie Head,
Sheila Roberts, Ellen Kuzwayo, Miriam Tlali*. Grahamstown, South Africa: National English Literary Museum, 1989.

Marquand, Jean. "Bessie Head: Exile and Community in Southern Africa." *London
Magazine* 18.9–10 (December 1978–January 1979): 48–61.

Nichols, Lee, editor. *Conversations with African Writers*. Washington, DC: Voice of
America, 1981.

Ogungbesan, Kolawole. "The Cape Gooseberry Also Grows in Botswana: Alienation
and Commitment in the Writings of Bessie Head." *Présence Africaine* 109
(1979): 92–106.

Ola, Virginia U. "Women's Role in Bessie Head's Ideal World." *Ariel* 17.4 (October
1986): 39–47.

Olaogun, Modupe O. "Irony and Schizophrenia in Bessie Head's *Maru*." *Research in
African Literatures* 25.4 (winter 1994): 69–87.

Pearse, Adetokunbo. "Apartheid and Madness: Bessie Head's *A Question of Power*."
Kunapipi 5.2 (1983): 81–93.

Peek, Andrew. "Interview with Bessie Head." *New Literatures Review* 14 (1985): 5–
13.

Phillips, Maggi. "Engaging Dreams: Alternative Perspectives on Flora Nwapa, Buchi Emecheta, Ama Ata Aidoo, Bessie Head, and Tsitsi Dangarembga." *Research in African Literatures* 25.4 (winter 1994): 89–103.

Ravenscroft, Arthur. "The Novels of Bessie Head." *Aspects of South African Literature.* London, England: Heinemann, 1976. 174–186.

Rooney, Carolyn. " 'Dangerous Knowledge' and the Poetics of Survival: A Reading of *Our Sister Killjoy* and *A Question of Power.*" *Motherlands: Women's Writings from Africa, the Caribbean, and South Asia.* New Brunswick, NJ: Rutgers University, 1992. 99–126.

Rose, Jacqueline. "On the 'Universality' of Madness: Bessie Head's *A Question of Power.*" *Critical Inquiry* 20.3 (spring 1994): 401–418.

Ross, Robert L., editor. *International Literature in English: Essays on the Major Writers.* New York: Garland, 1991.

Sam, Agnes. "Bessie Head: A Tribute." *Kunapipi* 8.1 (1986): 53–56.

Sample, Maxine. "Landscape and Spatial Metaphor in Bessie Head's *The Collector of Treasures.*" *Studies in Short Fiction* 28 (summer 1991): 311–319.

Visel, Robin. " 'We Bear the World and We Make It': Bessie Head and Olive Schreiner." *Research in African Literatures* 21.3 (fall 1990): 115–124.

Hecker, Liliana. Born in 1943, an Argentinean writer, she was a cofounder of the literary magazine *El Ornitorrinco*, which was started in a brief hiatus of political repression and continued during the military dictatorship in spite of threats. She was awarded the Casa de las Américas Prize for a volume of short stories, published when she was only twenty-three. Altogether she has published three collections of short stories, a novella, and a novel. One collection of stories, taken from all periods of her work, has been translated into English. They demonstrate her interest in philosophical themes (as in the story "Bishop Berkeley, or Mariana of the Universe" in which an older sister terrorizes a little girl with Berkeley's theories, and she feels responsible for all the things she imagines, including her mother and the color red, a terrible burden) and the compromising situations imposed by society, as in "The Stolen Party," in which a servant's child, invited to a birthday party, holds out her hand for a party favor and, her gesture misinterpreted, is offered a tip instead.

Work

The Stolen Party. Translated by Alberto Manguel. Toronto, Canada: Coach House, 1994.

Heremakhonon by Maryse Condé (Washington, DC: Three Continents, 1981). This novel skillfully explores the divided consciousness of a Caribbean woman who has returned to West Africa to uncover her tangled roots. She has ambivalent feelings about her origins, wanting to connect to her African heritage, yet angry that Africans once played a part in the slave trade. She becomes involved in the murky politics of a fictional nation through men whose political leanings exemplify the different possibilities the young nation faces. Her intensely personal meditations on her involvement with the African nation reflect the continuing human cost of the African Diaspora.

Commentary

Clark, Vévé. "Developing Diaspora Literacy: Allusion in Maryse Condé's *Hérémak-honon.*" *Out of the Kumbla: Women and Literature in the Caribbean.* Trenton, NJ: Africa World Press, 1990. 303–319.

King, Adele. "Two Caribbean Women Go to Africa: Maryse Condé's *Hérémakhonon* and Myriam Warner-Vieyra's *Juletane.*" *College Literature* 18.3 (October 1991): 96–105.

Lionnet, Françoise. *Autobiographical Voices: Race, Gender, Self-Portraiture.* Ithaca, NY: Cornell University 1989.

The Hills of Hebron by Sylvia Wynter (New York: Simon and Schuster, 1962). A man named Moses leads a group of Jamaicans into the hills to create a new religion and a new way of life, one that will set them free. As with all utopian communities, human nature intrudes and the members of the community of Hebron fall out with one another. Moses tries to meet God directly by crucifying himself; his last words, heard by one of his followers, are, "God is white after all." The community struggles over a successor to the prophet, and nearly breaks apart, but the ending is optimistic, suggesting that with a less utopian outlook and with a focus on the well-being of their children the community can survive and retain their freedom, if not living out the original vision of their prophet.

Commentary

Liddell, Janice Lee. "The Narrow Enclosure of Motherdom/Martyrdom: A Study of Gatha Randall Barton in *The Hills of Hebron.*" *Out of the Kumbla: Women and Literature in the Caribbean.* Trenton, NJ: Africa World Press, 1990. 321–330.

History. Many third world women have chosen history as the subject of their work. In many instances the reclamation of history—both women's history and the history of the colonial subject—is a major literary project. Such reclamation may be simply telling stories that are left out of standard histories. Assia Djebar recovers the role played by women in the Algerian revolution in her novel *Fantasia*; Lauretta Ngcobo does the same for the part rural women have played, often without celebration, in opposing apartheid in her novel *And They Didn't Die*. Bessie Head is as much local historian as novelist in many of her works, particularly in *Serowe: Village of the Rain-Wind* and *A Bewitched Crossroad*. Maryse Condé reconstructs precolonial African history in *Segu* and *The Children of Segu*. Linda Ty-Casper recovers untold Filipino history in her many historical novels by examining events that are left out of textbooks. Other writers have taken cataclysmic events that have played a role in the formation of their nation and retold it from a fresh point of view. The partition of India and Pakistan is a major event that finds interpretation in the works of Bapsi Sidhwa and Anita

Desai. The Mexican Revolution is the subject of Argentina Diaz Lozano's *May-apan* and Nellie Campobello's *Cartucho*. Many contemporary writers of China have dealt with the Cultural Revolution in their work, including Chen Jo-hsi, Zhai Zhenhua, Jung Chang, Li Pi-hua, and Tai Hou-ying. Frequently, these formative national events are seen from a woman's point of view.

In other cases, writers reclaim history that has been falsified in standard historical treatments. Michelle Cliff, Paule Marshall, and others have told alternate histories of the Middle Passage and its effects on contemporary race relations (see also **African Diaspora**). In Cliff's *Abeng*, for example, the questing heroine returns to an overgrown country house in the Caribbean and unearths fragments of her family's past, excavating and reassembling fragments of glass and pottery while reassembling her fractured identity. Soraya Antonius and Manny Shirazi tackle historical events from a point of view often inaccessible to Western eyes, exploring how colonial and neocolonial powers have manipulated political life in their countries. Others have chosen to treat history as a fictive text, one subject to multiple revisionings. Early in the twentieth century, Flora Annie Steel imagined how a woman would have fared in the Indian Mutiny, placing a heroine with feminist ideals in a carefully researched historical setting, using details gleaned from firsthand accounts to lend color and life to her narrative. In Bharati Mukherjee's novel *The Holder of the World*, history is re-created through a virtual reality game, witnessed anew through imaginatively fitting together known data and building out of facts a fully realized experience. In *I, Tituba, Black Witch of Salem*, Maryse Condé views the Salem witch trials from the point of view of a black slave woman, basing her reconstruction on both historical documentation and literary representations—even placing Hester Prynne with Tituba in a prison scene. Michelle Cliff uses the raid on Harper's Ferry in *Free Enterprise* to reexamine women's role in slave revolts, imaginatively tying together disparate events to study their possible connections. Elena Garro explores the very concept of linear time in her novel of the Mexican Revolution and how it is experienced by a small town, challenging the concept of time even in her title, *Recollections of Things to Come*. For these writers, history is a text still being written, and it provides a discursive ground full of echoes and possibilities.

Many critics of postcolonial literature have also addressed questions of historiography and find that writers exploring the past often use elements of oral tradition, collective memory, and myth in ways that challenge Western concepts of time and the past. See, in particular, Holloway, Sharpe, Slemon, and Tiffin for searching analyses of history as viewed by postcolonial writers.

Works

*Antonius, Soraya. *The Lord*. New York: Henry Holt, 1986.
*Belgrave, Valerie. *Ti Marie*. London, England: Heinemann, 1988.
*Campobello, Nellie. *Cartucho; and, My Mother's Hands*. Translated by Doris Meyer
    and Irene Matthews. Austin: University of Texas, 1988.

*Castellanos, Rosario. *The Nine Guardians*. Translated by Irene Nicholson. London, England: Faber and Faber, 1959.

*Chauvet, Marie. *Dance on the Volcano*. Translated by Salvator Attanasio. New York: W. Sloan, 1959.

*Chen Jo-hsi. *The Execution of Mayor Yin and Other Stories from the Great Proletarian Cultural Revolution*. Translated by Howard Goldblatt. Bloomington: Indiana University, 1978.

*Cliff, Michelle. *Abeng*. Trumansburg, NY: Crossing Press, 1984.

*Cliff, Michelle. *Free Enterprise*. New York: Dutton, 1993.

Condé, Maryse. *Segu*. Translated by Barbara Bray. New York: Viking, 1987.

Condé, Maryse. *The Children of Segu*. Translated by Linda Coverdale. New York: Viking, 1989.

*Condé, Maryse. *I, Tituba, Black Witch of Salem*. Translated by Richard Philcox. Charlottesville: University Press of Virginia, 1992.

Diaz Lozano, Argentina. *Mayapan*. Indian Hills, CO: Falcon's Wing, 1955.

*Djebar, Assia. *Fantasia: An Algerian Cavalcade*. Translated by Dorothy Blair. London, England: Quartet, 1985.

*Garro, Elena. *Recollections of Things to Come*. Translated by Ruth L. C. Simms. Austin: University of Texas, 1969.

Head, Bessie. *Serowe: The Village of the Rain-Wind*. London, England: Heinemann, 1981.

*Head, Bessie. *A Bewitched Crossroad*. New York: Paragon House, 1986.

*Jung Chang. *Wild Swans: Three Daughters of China*. London, England: HarperCollins, 1992.

*Li Pi-hua. *Farewell My Concubine*. Translated by Andrea Lingen Felter. New York: Morrow, 1993.

*Marks, Shula. *"Not Either an Experimental Doll"*: *The Separate Worlds of Three South African Women*. Bloomington: Indiana University, 1987.

*Mukherjee, Bharati. *The Holder of the World*. New York: Knopf, 1993.

*Ngcobo, Lauretta. *And They Didn't Die*. New York: Braziller, 1991.

*Nichols, Grace. *Whole of a Morning Sky*. London, England: Virago, 1986.

*Shirazi, Manny. *Javady Alley*. London, England: Women's Press, 1984.

*Sidhwa, Bapsi. *Cracking India*. Minneapolis: Milkweed, 1991.

*Steel, Flora Annie. *On the Face of the Waters*. New York: Macmillan, 1911.

Ty-Casper, Linda. *Dread Empire*. Exeter, England: Heinemann, 1982.

*Zhai Zhenhua. *Red Flower of China*. New York: Soho, 1993.

Commentary

Andrade, Susan Z. "Rewriting History, Motherhood, and Rebellion: Naming an African Woman's Literary Tradition." *Research in African Literatures* 21.1 (spring 1990): 91–111.

Balderston, Daniel. "The New Historical Novel: History and Fantasy in *Los recuerdos del porvenir*." *Bulletin of Hispanic Studies* 66.1 (January 1989): 41–46.

Clayton, Cherry. " 'A World Elsewhere:' Bessie Head as Historian." *English in Africa* 15.1 (May 1988): 55–69.

Clingman, Stephen. *The Novels of Nadine Gordimer: History from the Inside*. London, England: Allen and Unwin, 1986.

Edmondson, Belinda. "Race, Privilege, and the Politics of (Re)Writing History: An Analysis of the Novels of Michelle Cliff." *Callaloo* 16.1 (winter 1993): 180–191.

Gikandi, Simon. "Narration at the Postcolonial Moment: History and Representation in *Abeng*." *Writing in Limbo: Modernism and Caribbean Literature*. Ithaca, NY: Cornell University, 1992. 231–251.

Holloway, Karla. *Moorings and Metaphors: Figures of Culture and Gender in Black Women's Literature*. New Brunswick, NJ: Rutgers University, 1992.

Lionnet, Françoise. "Of Mangoes and Maroons: Language, History, and the Multicultural Subject of Michelle Cliff's *Abeng*." *De/Colonizing the Subject: The Politics of Gender in Women's Autobiography*. Minneapolis: University of Minnesota, 1992. 321–345.

Menton, Seymour. *Latin America's New Historical Novel*. Austin: University of Texas, 1993.

Murdoch, H. Adlai. "Rewriting Writing: Identity, Exile, and Renewal in Assia Djebar's *L'Amour, la fantasia*." *Yale French Studies* 83 (1993): 71–92.

Sandiford, Keith A. "Paule Marshall's *Praisesong for the Widow*: The Reluctant Heiress, or Whose Life Is It Anyway?" *Black American Literature Forum* 20.4 (winter 1986): 371–392.

Sangari, Kumkum, and Sudesh Vaid, editors. *Recasting Women: Essays in Indian Colonial History*. New Brunswick, NY: Rutgers University, 1990.

Sharpe, Jenny. *Allegories of Empire: The Figure of the Woman in the Colonial Text*. Minneapolis: University of Minnesota, 1993.

Slemon, Stephen. "Post-Colonial Allegory and the Transformation of History." *Journal of Commonwealth Literature* 23.1 (1988): 157–168.

Tapping, Craig. "Children and History in the Caribbean Novel: George Lamming's *In the Castle of My Skin* and Jamaica Kincaid's *Annie John*." *Kunapipi* 11.2 (1989): 51–59.

Tiffin, Helen. "Post-Colonialism, Post-Modernism, and the Rehabilitation of Post-Colonial History." *Journal of Commonwealth Literature* 23.1 (1988): 169–181.

Ho, Minfong. A Thai writer, born in 1951 in Rangoon, Burma (now Myanmar), she attended Tunghai University and earned a B.A. from Cornell University in 1973. She has worked as a journalist, writing for the *Straights Times* and the Singapore *Sunday Times* and has lectured at Chiengmai University, Thailand, in the department of mass transportation. Earlier jobs ranged from factory work to agricultural labor, and she served for a time as a trade union representative. She began to write fiction while studying in the United States, out of a sense of homesickness. Her first book was awarded a prize by the Council for Interracial Books for Children in 1973. She has written several novels for young readers in a style that is realistic and complex, focusing on life in contemporary Thailand.

Works

Brother Rabbit. With Saphon Ros. New York: Lothrop, Lee and Shepard, 1994.
The Clay Marble. New York: Farrar, Straus, Giroux, 1991.
Rice Without Rain. New York: Lothrop, Lee and Shepard, 1990.

Sing to the Dawn. New York: Lothrop, Lee and Shepard, 1975.
The Two Brothers. With Saphon Ros. New York: Lothrop, Lee and Shepard, 1994.

Hodge, Merle. Born in 1944 in Curepe, Trinidad, she earned a scholarship and left home nine days after independence in 1962 to study French at London University, where she earned B.A. honors in 1965 and a Master of Philosophy in French, focusing on francophone Caribbean and African writers. She traveled in Europe and lived for a time in Senegal and Gambia, then worked in a children's home in Denmark before returning to Trinidad and Tobago in the 1970s. There she taught French, English, and West Indian literature at a Port of Spain high school and later became a lecturer at the University of the West Indies in French Caribbean and French African literature. In 1979 she moved to Grenada to work for the government of Prime Minister Maurice Bishop as director of Curriculum Development but left after his assassination and the U.S. invasion. She now lives in St. Augustine, Trinidad, where she teaches in the Language and Linguistics Department of the University of the West Indies. She is a social activist and writer, and in her concern for giving Caribbean children a literary landscape that is recognizably theirs, rather than a colonial import, she has written two novels that are about children gaining an identity while gaining an understanding of their own culture.

Works

*Crick Crack, Monkey. London, England: Heinemann, 1981.
*For the Life of Laetitia. New York: Farrar, Straus, Giroux, 1993.
"*Is Freedom We Making*": *The New Democracy in Grenada.* St. George's, Grenada: Government Information Service, 1981.

Commentary

Balutansky, Kathleen M. "We Are All Activists: An Interview with Merle Hodge." *Callaloo* 12 (fall 1989): 651–662.
Gikandi, Simon. "Narration in the Post-Colonial Moment: Merle Hodge's *Crick Crack, Monkey.*" *Past the Last Post: Theorizing Post-Colonialism and Post-Modernism.* Calgary, Canada: University of Calgary, 1990. 13–22.
Gikandi, Simon. "Writing After Colonialism: *Crick Crack, Monkey* and *Beka Lamb.*" *Writing in Limbo: Modernism and Caribbean Literature.* Ithaca, NY: Cornell University, 1992. 197–230.
Hodge, Merle. "The Shadow of the Whip: A Comment on Male-Female Relations in the Caribbean." *Is Massa Day Dead? Black Moods in the Caribbean.* Garden City, NY: Anchor, 1974. 111–118.
Thorpe, Marjorie. "The Problem of Cultural Identification in *Crick Crack, Monkey.*" *Savacou* 13 (1977): 31–38.

The Holder of the World by Bharati Mukherjee (New York: Knopf, 1993). Mukherjee weaves together her fascination for Moghul miniatures and for the insights provided by the point of view of the immigrant in this novel. An American woman, an "assets researcher," is on the trail of a fabulous jewel that once belonged to the Salem Bibi, an American puritan who ended an adventurous life at the court of the emperor of India. She is engaged, in her research, in a kind of time travel. The narrative weaves between times as she reconstructs the Bibi's life through her research; at the same time, her husband, an Indian computer scientist working on creating a virtual past based on manipulating historical data, creates a moment in time that she enters to find out what finally happened. An elegant, engaging, and thoughtful novel.

Home Ground by Lynn Freed (New York: Summit, 1986). A *bildungsroman* about a young girl in a South African Jewish theatrical family. She has nightmarish sisters—one who docilely marries a brutal and business-savvy man in order to escape her family home, and another who is both cruel toward others and self-destructive. Ruth, the heroine, is known as a rebel in her family, but she herself is unclear as to what she wants, until she discovers that it is escape. A wise English actress helps her realize her own desires by prompting her to plan her departure, from a country that is growing more and more unwelcoming and from a family that is increasingly strange. In the end, she is free, leaving on a plane for England with an Indian friend—but even then she bitterly mourns parting with her family and finds she must wait until the plane leaves South Africa to sit with her "coloured" friend—signs that her freedom is still potential, not entirely realized. The sequel, *The Bungalow*, tells of the heroine's return in adulthood to family and to South Africa.

Hosain, Attia. Born in Lucknow, Uttar Pradesh, India, in 1913, the daughter of a Cambridge-educated man who died when she was eleven years old and a mother who had been educated in the Urdu tradition, one of a family of intellectuals. There were five children in the family, which her mother headed after her father's death, unusual for that time and place. She had English governesses and then attended the Martiniere School for Girls and the Isabella Thoburn College; at her insistence, she attended the University of Lucknow, graduating in 1933, though she resented the fact that she was not allowed to attend Cambridge like her brothers. She married a cousin against her mother's wishes and became involved in a more progressive form of politics than that engaged in by her family. Inspired by Sarojini Naidu, she attended the All India Women's Conference in Calcutta in 1933, and she began to write for newspapers, first *The Pioneer* and then *The Statesman*. At the time of partition, she moved to England in 1947 with her husband and two children, where she worked as a journalist and broadcaster as well as a writer of fiction and a stage and television actress. She also had her own British Broadcasting Corporation (BBC) Eastern Service radio program, aimed at a female audience. She has published one novel and a volume of short stories, recently reissued in paperback.

Works

Phoenix Fled and Other Stories. London, England: Chatto and Windus, 1953.
*Sunlight on a Broken Column. London, England: Chatto and Windus, 1961.

Hossain, Rokeya Sakhawat. See **Rokeya, Begum.**

The House of the Spirits by Isabel Allende (New York: Knopf, 1985). A novel in the form of a family chronicle, set in a house where the magical and the mundane coexist, where unearthly characters and incidents rub shoulders with their down-to-earth relatives. It is mainly a woman's tale constructed from the diaries of the character Clara, family stories that help to reclaim the past and overcome terrors faced in the present. Generations of women experience the historical events shaping Chile's society while giving those events a magical twist.

Commentary

Allende, Isabel. ''The World Is Full of Stories.'' *Review: Latin American Literature and Arts* 34 (January-June 1985): 18–20.

Boschetto, Sandra M. ''Threads, Connections, and the Fairy Tale: Reading the Writing in Isabel Allende's *La casa de los espíritus.*'' *Continental, Latin-American, and Francophone Women Writers.* Lanham, MD: University Press of America, 1990. 51–63.

Levine, Linda Gould. ''A Passage to Androgyny: Isabel Allende's *La casa de los espíritus.*'' *In the Feminine Mode: Essays on Hispanic Women Writers.* Lewisburg, PA: Bucknell University, 1990. 164–176.

Magnarelli, Sharon. ''Framing Power in Luisa Valenzuela's *Cola de lagartija* [*The Lizard's Tail*] and Isabel Allende's *Casa de los espíritus* [*The House of the Spirits*].'' *Splintering Darkness: Latin American Women Writers in Search of Themselves.* Pittsburgh, PA: Latin American Literary Review, 1990. 43–62.

How I Became a Holy Mother, and Other Stories by Ruth Prawer Jhabvala (New York: Harper and Row, 1976). These fine stories reveal India from two perspectives: that of the Indian and that of the British sojourner who is besotted with India. The author seems equally at home in both worlds. ''Bombay'' is the story of an elderly Indian man's relationship with his daughter and her extended family of in-laws. ''Two More Under the Indian Sun'' is the story of two Englishwomen in India, one married to an Indian and the other married to the idea of India. ''How I Became a Holy Mother'' is the tale of a young model who leaves the rat race of a materialistic life only to become a performer of sorts, representing the ''mother principle'' for an Indian guru on tour. Jhabvala excels at ironically contrasting India and the Western idea of India, using irony to highlight the paradoxes that arise out of juxtaposing variant images of the country.

Hsi Hsi. Pseudonym of Zhang Yan. Born in China, she moved from Shanghai to Hong Kong in 1950, where she worked as a teacher. Her stories are imaginative and wide ranging in style and setting and have more than a touch of magic realism about them.

Works

A Girl Like Me and Other Stories. Hong Kong: Renditions, 1986.
My City: A Hong Kong Story. Translated by Eva Hung. Hong Kong: Renditions, 1993.

Hsiao Hung. Born in Hulan, in the rural Heilongjiang province, northern China, on June 2, 1911, into a petty landowning family. Her mother died when she was nine, and she did not get along well with her father. She attended the First Municipal Girls' Middle School in Harbin until her father took her out of school and told her he had arranged her marriage to the son of a local warlord. At this point she left home and moved in with an intellectual who took her to Beijing and soon abandoned her. She returned to Harbin, pregnant and without any money, in 1931. After a gruesome time living in abject poverty, she moved in with the writer Xiao Jun, after the birth and adoption of her child. Their difficult life together is the subject of her autobiographical novel *Market Street.* The Japanese occupation began at around the same time, and they eventually made their way to Shanghai, where both she and her husband became well-known writers against the Japanese occupation. After their breakup, she was married to Duanmu Hongliang for the last four years of her life. She died in Hong Kong on January 22, 1941, at age thirty. Her work, strongly autobiographical in content, depicts the hardships of life in China, both for rural peasants and in the city during the Japanese occupation, using a style that emphasizes the blunt truths she tells.

Works

The Field of Life and Death and Tales of Hulan River. Translated by Howard Goldblatt
        and Ellen Young. Bloomington: Indiana University, 1979.
Market Street: A Chinese Woman in Harbin. Translated and with an introduction by
        Howard Goldblatt. Seattle: University of Washington, 1986.
Selected Stories of Xiao Hong. Translated by Howard Goldblatt. Beijing, China: Panda,
        1982.

Commentary

Goldblatt, Howard. *Hsiao Hung.* Boston: Twayne, 1976.
Goldblatt, Howard. "Life as Art: Xiao Hong and Autobiography." *Woman and Litera-
        ture in China.* Bochum, Germany: Studienverlag, 1985. 345–363.
Liu, Lydia. "The Female Body and Nationalist Discourse: *The Field of Life and Death*
        Revisited." *Scattered Hegemonies: Postmodernity and Transnational Feminist
        Practices.* Minneapolis: University of Minnesota, 1994. 37–62.

Hsieh Ping-ying. Born in 1906 (some sources say 1903) in Shanghai, she grew up in tumultuous times. She was born early enough that her mother felt compelled to bind her feet at age ten, though she did it halfheartedly; she didn't go so far as to break the foot bones, as she had done with her elder daughter. As a child, she was an avid reader of both Chinese works and European classics in Chinese translation. Her father was a classical scholar, but she needed to fight to have a chance to attend school with her brothers. She joined the revolutionary army in 1926; on her discharge she was imprisoned by her mother when she refused an arranged marriage, finally rejoining her revolutionary comrades after a long confinement in her home, where her mother tried to make her adopt the more traditional woman's ways and accept an arranged marriage. She was arrested for a time, bore a child out of wedlock, and fought with the Communist forces against the Japanese occupation. Her autobiography, including selections from journalistic pieces entitled *New War Diary*, was translated into English twice, for British and American audiences, at the beginning of World War II in part to demonstrate the courage of Chinese resistance to the Japanese to the American public. After the war, she continued to write and work as an editor in Taiwan. Her work is revealing not only as a document of Chinese political history but as a highly personal and touching polemic on the situation for women in a time of change.

Works

*The Autobiography of a Chinese Girl. Translated by Tsui Chi. London, England: Pandora, 1986.
Girl Rebel: The Autobiography of Hsieh Pingying with Extracts from Her New War Diary. Translated by Adet Lin and Anor Lin. New York: John Day, 1940.

Commentary

Knapp, Bettina. "The New Era for Women Writers in China." *World Literature Today* 65 (summer 1991): 432–439.
Ling, Amy. *Between Two Worlds: Women Writers of Chinese Ancestry*. New York: Pergamon, 1990.

Huberman, Angelina Muniz. See **Muniz-Huberman, Angelina.**

Huxley, Elspeth Joscelin (Grant). Born in London in 1907, daughter of Eleanor Lillian Grosvenor and Major Joscelin Grant. At age five she moved with her parents to Kenya, where she grew up in a rural and free environment. She was educated at a European school in Nairobi, then attended both Reading University and Cornell in the 1920s. While an assistant press officer for the Empire Marketing Board in London, she met and married Gervais Huxley and continued to travel widely. She served as a member of the Monkton Advisory Commission on Central Africa in 1959 and on the British Broadcasting Corporation (BBC) Advisory Council. Her best-known work is her autobiography, *The Flame Trees of Thika*, a fond memoir of her childhood in the hills of Kenya. She is also known as a novelist, travel writer, biographer, and detective fiction writer.

Works

The African Poison Murders. New York: Harper, 1940.
Back Street, New Worlds: A Look at Immigrants in Britain. New York: Morrow, 1965.

The Flame Trees of Thika. New York: Morrow, 1959.
Murder on Safari. New York: Harper, 1938.
On the Edge of the Rift: Memories of Kenya. New York: Morrow, 1962.
The Red Rock Wilderness. New York: Morrow, 1957.
Red Strangers. New York: Harper, 1939.
A Thing to Love. London, England: Chatto and Windus, 1954.
The Walled City. Philadelphia, PA: J. B. Lippincott, 1949.

I Am Becoming My Mother by Lorna Goodison (London, England: New Beacon, 1986). A collection of accomplished poetry that includes "Lullaby for Jean Rhys," a tender and insightful eulogy, and "Guinea Woman," in which the poet traces her lineage back to Africa through her great-grandmother. An interest in history and the connections that tie the poet to her African and Caribbean past is also reflected in "Nanny," a poem about the legendary Maroon leader of rebellious Africans in Jamaica, in which she recounts how she was trained and sent to lead her people to freedom.

I Is a Long Memoried Woman by Grace Nichols (London, England: Karnak House, 1983). The memories referred to in the title are the shared experience of the African Diaspora. The author, like so many writers of African descent, is engaged in a project of retracing her roots, from Europe to the Caribbean to Africa, attempting to restring her life, gathering it together "like scattered beads" (20). The epilogue ends with hope that memories and the past are recoverable despite the violence that tried to erase them, a new tongue springing from the roots of one that, through slavery, had been severed.

I Myself Am a Woman: Selected Writings of Ding Ling by Ting Ling (Boston, MA: Beacon, 1989). This collection includes a lengthy introduction by Tani E. Barlow, placing Ting Ling's work in the broader context of contemporary Chinese literature. Selections include "Miss Sophie's Diary," an exploration of a young woman's feelings in diary form that drew on *Madame Bovary* as a model and that was innovative in its frankness about sexual matters; "When

I Was in Xia Village,'' a story narrated by a party functionary about a young woman who was sent by the party to gather intelligence from the Japanese, who raped her and infected her with venereal disease; and ''Thoughts on March 8,'' an essay on the occasion of International Women's Day in which she articulates her interpretation of the role of women in the party. A representative anthology of the works of a writer who was both loyal to the Communist Party and persecuted by it.

I, Rigoberta Menchu: An Indian Woman in Guatemala by Rigoberta Menchu (London, England: Verso, 1984). ''This is my testimony. I didn't learn it from a book and I didn't learn it alone. I'd like to stress that it's not only my life, it's also the testimony of my people.'' This narrative, the product of extensive interviews by the editor, contains both political testimony, based on the author's experiences in political struggle, and much ethnographic material, which gives testimony to the daily concerns, rituals, and knowledge of her people. She contrasts the Ladino culture and Indian cultures and records those aspects of her people's traditions that would otherwise go unrecorded. She combines a lively mixture of feminist, socialist, and Christian beliefs.

Commentary

Sommer, Doris. ''Not Just a Personal Story: Women's *Testimonios* and the Plural Self.'' *Life/Lines: Theorizing Women's Autobiography*. Ithaca, NY: Cornell University, 1988. 107–130.
Sommer, Doris. ''No Secrets: Rigoberta's Guarded Truth.'' *Women's Studies* 20 (1991): 51–72.

I, Tituba, Black Witch of Salem by Maryse Condé (Charlottesville: University Press of Virginia, 1992). Translation of *Moi, Tituba, sorcière . . . Noire de Salem*. Condé creates the first-person account of Tituba, whose story is only glancingly alluded to in the records of the Salem witchcraft trials. She is the child of an African woman raped by a sailor as she is taken to be a slave in Barbados. After her mother is hanged for defending herself from her owner, Tituba is raised by an old woman who teaches her herbal medicine. Ultimately, she is taken by a dour preacher to Puritan New England where she becomes a player in the witchcraft hysteria, imprisoned for a time with a feminist and outspoken Hester Prynne. Finally, she returns to Barbados, is caught up in a maroon uprising, and is hanged, living on as a spirit and in folk song. A picaresque, postmodernist mock-epic.

Commentary

Dukats, Mara L. ''A Narrative of Violated Maternity: *Moi, Tituba, sorcière . . . Noire de Salem*.'' *World Literature Today* 67.4 (autumn 1993): 745–750.
Mudimbe-Boyi, Elisabeth. ''Giving a Voice to Tituba: The Death of the Author?'' *World Literature Today* 67.4 (autumn 1993): 751–756.

The Impenetrable Madam X by Griselda Gambaro (Detroit, MI: Wayne State University, 1991). Translation of *Lo Impenitrable*. An "erotic novel" about erotic novels, making fun of the genre by telling a plot that is like a schoolboy's joke. A man is overwhelmingly and disastrously aroused; a woman, Madam X, enjoys the arousal but not the climax, so only participates in the former. It ends with "Instructions for Writing an Erotic Novel."

In White Ink by Mimi Khalvati (Manchester, England: Carcanet, 1992). The title of this poetry collection is taken from Cixous's *Laugh of the Medusa*: "A woman is never far from mother. . . . There is always within her at least a little of that good mother's milk. She writes in white ink." These poems take memories, things seen out of the corner of the eye, airplane travels, visits to the hospital, the bricolage of a woman's life as poetry. There is something metaphysical in even the smallest parts of life, and the poet strives to interpret their meaning, as in the poem "Plant Care:" "I strain to catch the nub of what is" (73).

Incantations and Other Stories by Anjana Appachana (London, England: Virago, 1991). An accomplished collection of stories, some lighthearted ("When Anklets Tinkle," a gently ironic love story), others angry ("Bahu," about a woman who comes to realize her marriage situation is impossible), and some tragic ("The Prophecy," about a pregnant schoolgirl seeking an abortion). Two of the stories feature the rascally Sharma, who avoids work at his office and "composes" poetry entirely cribbed from other sources. The title story concerns a young bride who is repeatedly raped by her brother-in-law and takes her revenge before her suicide, and the effect her story has on her young sister. The lack of sexual knowledge before marriage, the silence on the part of mothers, is contrasted with their willingness to tell their daughters to submit to their husbands—who hear "during the act, like incantations, the distant refrain of their mothers' voices, chanting, do what your husband tells you to, accept, endure" (92). This combination of silence and incantation is contrasted with the bride's obsessive need to tell the details of her trauma to her horrified sister, whose life is filled with the stories she reads, *Jane Eyre*, the *Ramayana*, the *Mahabharata*. The tragedy is a tale whose meaning she ponders for the rest of her life.

Indian Diaspora. South Asians of Indian descent have settled around the world, one wave of immigrants traveling their own middle passages in the wake of Africans when they were exported to Africa and the Caribbean as workers following the abolition of the slave trade. Another population settled in Britain and North America following the end of colonial rule. The condition of exile, generational differences, and the Diasporic Indian's relationship to home are themes frequently addressed by writers of the Indian Diaspora. Bharati Mukherjee paints a grim picture of personal disintegration of an émigré in her novel

Wife but in *Jasmine* offers a heroine who is a strong survivor. Characters in her short stories, many of whom are immigrants from other parts of the world, reinscribe America with their own mark. Leena Dhingra's heroine in *Amritvela* is questing for a sense of place, divided between England and India, learning how to belong to both. Jayapraga Reddy and Agnes Sam reflect a hybrid sensibility in their stories, offering the reader a view of South Africa that is not drawn in only black and white. For general discussion of writers of the Indian Diaspora, see Nelson; for the Caribbean in particular, see Poynting.

Works

*Dhingra, Leena. *Amritvela*. London, England: Women's Press, 1988.

Ladha, Yasmin. *Lion's Granddaughter and Other Stories*. Edmonton, Canada: NeWest, 1992.

*Mukherjee, Bharati. *Wife*. Boston: Houghton Mifflin, 1975.

Mukherjee, Bharati. *Darkness*. New York: Penguin, 1985.

Mukherjee, Bharati. *The Middleman and Other Stories*. New York: Grove, 1988.

*Mukherjee, Bharati. *Jasmine*. New York: Grove Weidenfeld, 1989.

Namjoshi, Suniti. *Because of India: Selected Poems and Fables*. London, England: Onlywoman Press, 1989.

*Narayan, Kirin. *Love, Stars, and All That*. New York: Pocket Books, 1993.

*Randhawa, Ravinder. *A Wicked Old Woman*. London, England: Women's Press, 1987.

*Reddy, Jayapraga. *On the Fringe of Dreamtime and Other Stories*. Johannesburg, South Africa: Skotaville, 1987.

Sam, Agnes. *Jesus Is Indian and Other Stories*. London, England: Women's Press, 1989.

Shan, Sharan-Jeet. *In My Own Name*. London, England: Women's Press, 1985.

Commentary

Nelson, Emmanuel S. *Reworlding: The Literature of the Indian Diaspora*. Westport, CT: Greenwood, 1992.

Nelson, Emmanuel S. *Writers of the Indian Diaspora: A Bio-Bibliographical Critical Sourcebook*. Westport, CT: Greenwood, 1993.

Paranjape, Makarand. ''Distinguishing Themselves: New Fiction by Expatriate Indian Women.'' *World Literature Today* 65.1 (winter 1991): 72–74.

Poynting, Jeremy. *East Indians in the Caribbean: A Bibliography of Imaginative Literature in English (1894–1984)*. St. Augustine, Trinidad: University of the West Indies, 1985.

Poynting, Jeremy. ''East Indian Women in the Caribbean: Experience, Image, and Voice.'' *Journal of East Asian Literature* 1 (winter-spring 1986): 8–18.

Information for Foreigners: Three Plays by Griselda Gambaro (Evanston, IL: Northwestern University, 1992). Includes *The Walls*, written in 1963, *Information for Foreigners*, written 1971–1973, and *Antigona Furiosa*, which premiered in 1986. These are all powerful political plays that address the conditions in Argentina differently. The first play concerns an abduction, in which a man is placed in a comfortable prison, tastefully appointed, but gradually the walls close in on him; it questions the ways in which art can alert us to social malaise or can mask our perceptions. The second is a tour de force, written as a samizdat text, smuggled out of the country and finally published in 1987; it has not been performed in Argentina. The audience is taken by guides around a large, labyrinthine house in which rooms contain scenes of torture, indignity, repression, and deliberate, calculated cruelty. A key scene deals with the Milgram experiment, in which experimental subjects, told they were helping in an experiment, were found to willingly inflict pain and even death if ordered to do so. The play juxtaposes bizarre humor, children's games, scenes from *Othello*, graphic violence, and badly acted histrionics, demonstrating the ways in which state violence before and during the "dirty war" was hidden in plain view, denied while completely obvious. The final play, "Antigona Furiosa," continues the theme by focusing on the complicity of people who respond to state terror passively, without resistance. Just as Antigone made the moral decision to bury her brother, the mothers of the Plaza de Mayo made the moral commitment of finding and burying their children, those disappeared, taken by the military government. Her plays are powerful, disturbing, theatrical, and though they draw on and investigate the experiences of modern Argentina, they are eloquent in universal terms about repression, collaboration, cruelty, and its disguises.

Commentary

Taylor, Diana. "Theater and Terrorism: Griselda Gambaro's *Information for Foreigners.*" *Theatre Journal* 42.2 (May 1990): 165–182.

Iremonger, Lucille. Born in 1919 (some sources say 1915) near Port Royal, Jamaica, descended from slave-owning planters on both sides. She was educated at Wolmer's Girls' School and then went to England to study at St. Hugh's College, Oxford, where she earned a B.A. in English. She married in England and began to broadcast for the British Broadcasting Corporation (BBC). She was the author of several novels, an autobiography, a collection of Ananse stories, and several biographical works on the lives of prime ministers, their wives, and the British royal family. She died in 1989.

Works

And His Charming Lady. London, England: Secker and Warburg, 1961.
The Cannibals, a Novel. London, England: Hammond, 1952.
Creole. New York: Hutchinson, 1950.
The Ghosts of Versailles. London, England: Faber and Faber, 1957.
How Do I Love Thee. London, England: Sphere, 1977.
It's a Bigger Life. New York: Hutchinson, 1948.
Love and Princesses. New York: Crowell, 1960.
My Sister, My Love. New York: Morrow, 1981.
Orphans of the Heart. London, England: Secker and Warburg, 1984.

West Indian Folk-Tales. London, England: G. G. Harrop, 1956.
Yes, My Darling Daughter. London, England: Secker and Warburg, 1964.
The Young Traveller in the South Seas. London, England: Phoenix House, 1952.
The Young Traveller in the West Indies. London, England: Phoenix House, 1955.

Jabavu, Noni. Born in Cape Province, South Africa, in 1921 into a Xhosa family of intellectuals—the daughter of Professor D. D. T. Jabavu and granddaughter of journalist, teacher, and editor John Tengo Jabavu. At age fourteen she went to England to study, remaining until 1939 to pursue studies at the Royal Academy of Music. She was planning a career in film when the war broke out, and changed course to work as an engineer and welder in a bomber engines factory. After the war, she worked in television and married an English film director, after which she was unable to return to South Africa since her marriage to a white man was in violation of South African miscegenation laws. She has traveled and lived in Mozambique, Uganda, and Zimbabwe.

Works

Drawn in Colour: African Contrasts. New York: St. Martin's, 1962.
The Ochre People: Scenes from a South African Life. New York: St. Martin's, 1963.

Commentary

Deck, Alice A. "Autoethnography: Zora Neale Hurston, Noni Jabavu, and Cross-Disciplinary Discourse." *Black American Literature Forum* 24.2 (summer 1990): 237–256.

Jacobs, Barbara. A Mexican writer whose memoir of her father and his picaresque travels from his homeland in Lebanon to the United States and finally to Mexico is a charming family history.

Work

*The Dead Leaves. Willimantic, CT: Curbstone, 1993.

Jalandoni, Magdalena G. Born in Jaro, Iloilo, Philippines, in 1891, she was a poet, composing in the Hiligaynon language from an early age. An early performance of her work was her delivery of a poem she had composed at her grandmother's funeral. She was the first woman novelist of her country. Her family did not encourage her writing. Her mother felt her writing, public speaking, and excellence at school dangerously unfeminine traits and beat her to make her stop, but she nevertheless completed her first novel at the age of fifteen. At first she published under a pseudonym, then under her own name, often addressing subjects considered taboo for women writers. She supported women demonstrating for the right to vote and remained single because she said she wanted to find a man with the soul of an artist, who could write a good novel; failing that, she remained alone. Her novels are characterized by romantic plots and heroic characters, but they also have a realistic side, portraying aspects of middle-class Filipino life and culture with sensitivity to class differences. She died in 1978.

Work

The Lady in the Market. Translated by Edward D. Defensor. Iloilo: University of the Philippines, 1976.

Jane and Louisa Will Soon Come Home by Erna Brodber (London, England: New Beacon Books, 1980). A novel told in fragments, mysterious and cryptic, somewhat in the style of Kincaid's *At the Bottom of the River.* The protagonist Nellie returns home to the islands after education abroad and is alienated from a sense of home. The fragments of the stories she hears, oral accounts of her family's past that include distortions of female identity and childhood misconceptions about sexuality, are pieces of the puzzle that she needs to assemble—and that the reader assembles with her—to recover a sense of belonging through understanding her ancestry. An interesting novel for its use of Creole, its mix of oral and scribal forms, and its poetic imagery.

Commentary

Cooper, Carolyn. "The Fertility of the Gardens of Women." *New Beacon Review* 2–3 (1986): 139–147.
Cooper, Carolyn. "Afro-Jamaican Folk Elements in Brodber's *Jane and Louisa Will Soon come Home." Out of the Kumbla: Women and Literature in the Caribbean.* Trenton, NJ: Africa World Press, 1990. 279–288.
O'Callaghan, Evelyn. "Rediscovering the Natives of My Person." *Jamaica Journal* 16.3 (1984): 61–64.
Walker-Johnson, Joyce. "Autobiography, History and the Novel: Erna Brodber's *Jane and Louisa Will Soon Come Home." Journal of West Indian Literature* 3.1 (January 1989): 47–59.

Woodcock, Bruce. "Post-1975 Caribbean Fiction and the Challenge to English Literature." *Critical Quarterly* 28 (winter 1986): 79–95.

Jasmine by Bharati Mukherjee (New York: Grove Weidenfeld, 1989). This well-woven story shifts between present and past, between various narrative selves, between India, New York, and Iowa. Jasmine is an illegal immigrant to New York City, caring for a city couple's child and fascinated by the way in which she can shut out her past—and evade the destiny foretold by an Indian village astrologer. Jasmine's story is told in a series of memories, and the reader reconstructs her life—her lives—piecing together the clues given by the narrator that relate her husband's assassination by Sikh terrorists, her illegal and disastrous entry to America, her eventual settling in Iowa with a small-town banker. It is a novel about a woman composing her own life, even to the choice she makes at the end of the book, defying the patterns her life, and traditional narration, might be expected to follow.

Javady Alley by Manny Shirazi (London, England: Women's Press, 1984). A child's eye view of politics in Iran in the 1950s. Seven-year-old Homa lives in Javady Alley in a closely circumscribed family circle, but the world of grownups invades as Prime Minister Mosadegh attempts to nationalize the oil industry, taking it from the control of the British. Personal and political worlds intersect as the girl learns about power, gender, and what those two abstractions mean for her own identity.

Jesús, Carolina Maria de. Born in Sacramento, Minas Gerais state, Brazil, in 1914, a black woman, she moved at age twenty-three to São Paolo, where she lived in a shantytown, feeding her three children by scavenging for scrap paper and foraging in garbage. She took up writing to unburden herself and escape into storytelling. With the help of a reporter, Audálio Dantas, she published her autobiography in 1960, which was an enormous success, selling out its first edition of 10,000 copies in three days. It remained on the best-seller list for two years, selling more than any other Brazilian book in history, but she died in poverty on February 13, 1977. Currently, her work is not well known in her own country, though it is considered an important work of testimonial literature elsewhere.

Work

Child of the Dark: The Diary of Carolina Maria de Jesús. New York: E. P. Dutton, 1962.

Commentary

Fox, Patricia D. "The Diary of Carolina Maria de Jesús: A Paradoxical Enunciation." *Proceedings of the Black Image in Latin American Culture.* Slippery Rock, AR: Slippery Rock University, 1990. 241–251.

Levine, Robert M. "The Cautionary Tale of Carolina Maria de Jesús." *Latin American Research Review* 29.1 (1994): 55–83.
Platt, Kamala. "Race and Gender Representations in Clarice Lispector's 'A menor mulher do mundo' and Carolina Maria de Jesús' 'Quarto de despejo.' " *Afro-Hispanic Review* 11.1–3 (1992): 51–57.

Jhabvala, Ruth Prawer. Born on May 7, 1927, in Cologne, Germany, the younger child of a Polish Jewish lawyer, Marcus Prawer, and Leonora Cohn Prawer. The family emigrated to England in 1939 when the writer was twelve years old; most of their extended family and many friends were killed in the Holocaust. She took a degree at the University of London and wrote an M.A. thesis on the short story in England, 1700–1750. She married Cyrus Jhabvala, a Parsi architect, in 1951 and moved with him to India. There she wrote a number of novels and collections of short stories and, in the early 1960s, began to collaborate with James Ivory and Ismail Merchant on films, beginning with a cinematic version of her own novel *The Householder*, released in 1963. In 1975 she moved to New York, the same year in which she received the Booker Prize for *Heat and Dust*, and has continued to write novels, short stories, and highly acclaimed film scripts. She has received numerous awards and honors including several honorary degrees and a MacArthur Fellowship.

Works

Amrita. New York: Norton, 1956.
A Backward Place. London, England: J. Murray, 1965.
Esmond in India. New York: Norton, 1958.
An Experience of India. New York: Norton, 1972.
Get Ready for Battle. New York: Norton, 1963.
Heat and Dust. New York: Harper and Row, 1976.
The Householder. New York: Norton, 1960.
How I Became a Holy Mother, and Other Stories. New York: Harper and Row, 1976.
In Search of Love and Beauty. New York: Morrow, 1983.
Like Birds, Like Fishes, and Other Stories. New York: Norton, 1964.
The Nature of Passion. New York: Norton, 1957.
The New Dominion. London, England: Panther, 1983.
Out of India: Selected Stories. New York: Morrow, 1986.
Poet and Dancer. New York: Doubleday, 1993.
A Stronger Climate. New York: Norton, 1968.
Three Continents. New York: Morrow, 1987.
Travelers. New York: Harper and Row, 1977.

Commentary

Bawer, Bruce. "Passage to India: The Career of Ruth Prawer Jhabvala." *New Criterion* (December 1987): 5–19.
Chadha, Ramesh. *Cross-Cultural Interaction in Indian English Fiction: An Analysis of the Novels of Ruth Jhabvala and Kamala Markandaya.* New Delhi, India: National Book Organisation, 1988.

Crane, Ralph J. *Ruth Prawer Jhabvala*. Boston: Twayne, 1992.

Dudt, Charmazel. "Jhabvala's Fiction: The Passage from India." *Faith of a (Woman) Writer*. New York: Greenwood, 1988. 159–164.

Gooneratne, Yasmine. " 'Traditional' Elements in the Fiction of Kamala Markandaya, R. K. Narayan, and Ruth Prawer Jhabvala." *World Literature Written in English* 15 (1976): 121–134.

Gooneratne, Yasmine. "Film into Fiction: The Influence upon Ruth Prawer Jhabvala's Fiction of Her Work for Cinema, 1960–1976." *World Literature Written in English* 18 (1979): 368–386.

Gooneratne, Yasmine. *Silence, Exile and Cunning*. Hyderabad, India: Orient Longman, 1983.

Gooneratne, Yasmine. "The Expatriate Experience: The Novels of Ruth Prawer Jhabvala and Paul Scott." *The British and Irish Novel Since 1960*. New York: St. Martin's, 1991. 48–61.

Ivory, James. *Autobiography of a Princess: Also Being the Adventures of an American Film Director in the Land of the Maharajas*. London, England: Murray, 1975.

Jha, Rekha. *The Novels of Kamala Markandaya and Ruth Jhabvala: A Study in East-West Encounter*. New Delhi, India: Prestige, 1990.

Ross, Robert L., editor. *International Literature in English: Essays on the Major Writers*. New York: Garland, 1991.

Shahane, Vasant Anant. *Ruth Prawer Jhabvala*. New Delhi, India: Arnold-Heinemann, 1976.

Sucher, Laurie. *The Fiction of Ruth Prawer Jhabvala: The Politics of Passion*. New York: St. Martin's, 1989.

Summerfield, H. "Holy Women and Unholy Men: Ruth Prawer Jhabvala Confronts the Non-rational." *Ariel* 77.3 (July 1986): 85–101.

Johannesburg Requiem: A Novel by Sheila Roberts (New York: Taplinger, 1980). A South African novel that is only indirectly about apartheid but focuses its attention on the relations between white men and women. One young woman, an indifferent teacher, befriends a hopelessly asocial and clumsy young man who has returned to South Africa after an English education in order to reform things. He ends up in jail, and she is fired from her job and placed under surveillance for her ties to him. In a separate plot line, her brother's girlfriend goes on a camping trip with a gang of young men who are celebrating their virility and power by indiscriminate boozing, drunken sex, and a violent feud between two brothers, which ends in one being hurt so badly he later dies. The author uses a light touch, with plenty of irony and understatement, in describing lives that are cramped, desperate, and brutal.

Johnson, Amryl. Born in Tunapuna, Trinidad, she was brought up by her grandmother to age eleven and then joined her parents in England. She earned a degree in African and Caribbean studies at the University of Kent, then returned to Trinidad in 1982 and traveled widely in the Caribbean; these travels became the basis of her book *Sequins for a Ragged Hem*. She is also the author of a volume of poetry and contributor to several anthologies and teaches creative writing.

Works

*Long Road to Nowhere. London, England: Virago, 1988.
Sequins for a Ragged Hem. London, England: Virago, 1988.

Jones, Marion Patrick. See **O'Callaghan, Marion.**

Joseph, Helen. Born on April 8, 1905, in Midhurst, Sussex, she graduated from the University of London in 1927, taught in India for three years, and then moved to South Africa in 1946, where she became a social worker in Johannesburg and in Cape Town. An activist in South African politics, she opposed apartheid for over forty years and was one of the founders of the Congress of Democrats, the white wing of the African National Congress. She was detained and put under house arrest in 1962, confined to her house at night and on weekends and forbidden to have visitors for nine years. Her impressive credentials as a thorn in the side of the South African government include her being secretary of the Federation of South African Women, a listed Communist, and a defendant in the Treason Trial. She died Christmas Day in 1992. Her memoirs are important documents of South African history and moving evidence of a life devoted to activism.

Works

Side by Side. London, England: Zed, 1986.
Tomorrow's Sun: A Smuggled Journal from South Africa. New York: John Day, 1966.

Commentary

Akhalwaya, Ameen. "The Mother of the Struggle." *Africa Report* 33.3 (May-June 1988): 60–62.

Joubert, Elsa. An Afrikaner, born in Paarl, to a conservative family. She had what she calls a "rather late-Victorian Cape upbringing and homelife" (*Momentum*, 58). She studied at Stellenbosch University. Her political consciousness was raised at the time of the massacre at Sharpeville in 1960 (which her husband, a journalist, witnessed). It gave her the strong sense that she should use her writing efforts to "bear witness." She wrote the novel *To Die at Sunset* in 1963 as a way of exploring in words her sense of disquiet and awareness of cruelty and suffering in her country. She wrote other works in Afrikaans based on her travels in Angola, Mozambique, and Madagascar, and in 1973 she took a magazine assignment to write on the refugees leaving Angola, an experience that made her want to concentrate her writing on current conditions in South Africa. She began to research her own country and in 1976 found a subject to write about. She met the woman whose story she tells in *Poppie Nongena*, a book that she claims in the introduction to be a true story, without embellishment, based on the taped account the woman gave her of her life when, on the day after Christmas 1976 (the year of the Soweto uprising), she came to Elsa Joubert's house in a state of despair and poured out her story. It was a best-seller and literary event in South Africa, being widely read in both English and Afrikaans, often being praised by both right- and left-wing readers for different reasons.

Works

The Last Sunday. Bergvlei, South Africa: Southern Book Publishers, 1989.
Poppie Nongena. Translated by Elsa Joubert. New York: Norton, 1985.
To Die at Sunset. Translated by Klaus Steytler. London, England: Hodder and Stoughton, 1982.

Commentary

Carlean, Kevin. "The Narrative Functions of Elsa Joubert's *Poppie Nongena.*" *English in Africa* 16.2 (1989): 49–59.
Davies, Carole Boyce. "Collaboration and the Ordering Imperative in Life Story Pro-duction." *De/Colonizing the Subject: The Politics of Gender in Women's Auto-biography*. Minneapolis: University of Minnesota, 1992. 3–19.
Joubert, Elsa. [untitled autobiographical sketch]. *Momentum: On Recent South African Writing*. Pietermaritzburg, South Africa: University of Natal, 1984. 58–61.
Lenta, Margaret. "A Break in the Silence: *The Long Journey of Poppie Nongena.*" *Momentum: On Recent South African Writing*. Pietermaritzburg, South Africa: University of Natal, 1984. 147–158.
Lenta, Margaret. "Independence as the Creative Choice in Two South African Fictions." *Ariel* 17.1 (January 1986): 35–52.
Schalwyk, David. "The Flight from Politics: An Analysis of the South African Reception of *Poppie Nongena.*" *Journal of South African Studies* 12.2 (April 1986): 183–195.

The Journey by Indira Ganesan (New York: Knopf, 1990). The novel's setting is on a mythical island called Pi, off the coast of India. There, two sisters, born in America, journey to the island for a cousin's funeral. Of the two sisters, one is independent and able to construct her own identity; the other is tied to tra-dition and the past. She is particularly entwined with her dead cousin, who is referred to as her twin, and is nearly driven to commit *sati*, to sacrifice herself and join him in death, but finally she chooses to go on living. This first novel is an ambitious exploration of character, family, myth, and India and its repre-sentation.

The Joys of Motherhood by Buchi Emecheta (New York: Braziller, 1979). Based on the life of Emecheta's own mother-in-law, this is the story of an unfulfilled woman who struggled all her life and could never understand why the supposed "joys of motherhood" did not fulfill her. It traces her life through two marriages, one traditional and one more modern, both dependent upon the wife's duty to produce and sustain children. Though her children do, in fact, bring the heroine much joy, that joy is more due to a woman's growing sense of self-worth—as a woman who cares for and provides for her children despite all odds—rather than as a traditional role as a mother. The ironic title comes from the novel *Efuru* by Flora Nwapa, which refers to the joys of motherhood in its closing lines.

Commentary

Andrade, Susan Z. "Rewriting History, Motherhood, and Rebellion: Naming an African Woman's Literary Tradition." *Research in African Literatures* 21.1 (spring 1990): 91–111.

Flewellen, Elinor C. "Assertiveness vs. Submissiveness in Selected Works by African Women Writers." *Ba Shiru* 12.2 (1985): 3–18.

Palmer, Eustace. "The Feminine Point of View: Buchi Emecheta's *The Joys of Motherhood.*" *African Literature Today* 13 (1983): 38–57.

Stratton, Florence. "The Shallow Grave: Archetypes of Female Experience in African Fiction." *Research in African Literatures* 19.2 (1988): 143–169.

Ward, Cynthia. "What They Told Buchi Emecheta: Oral Subjectivity and the Joys of 'Otherhood.' " *PMLA* 105.1 (January 1990): 83–97.

Juana Inés de la Cruz. Born Juana Ramírez y Asbaje in 1648 (though she later recorded her birth date as 1651) in Nepantla, not far from Mexico City. Her mother, an illiterate Mexican woman, managed a farm and had six children, though apparently she was never married to either of the two men who fathered them. Juana, a self-educated omnivorous intellect, benefited by her learned grandfather's large library. Before the age of fourteen she wrote her first poem, and she taught herself Latin in very short order. In her teens she was interviewed by a group of some forty scholars from the University in Mexico City and convinced them of her extensive knowledge. She entered holy orders in 1668, in a time and place when a convent was the most logical venue for a woman who wanted to devote herself to a life of solitary learning. She built up her own library of over 4,000 volumes, possibly the largest in the Americas at the time. Her erudition did not go without challenge, and while she had powerful friends at court, she also had determined enemies in the church. She wrote love poetry and designed a triumphal arch to welcome the viceregal couple to Mexico, an elaborate concoction with mythological emblems, inscriptions, and narrative poetry that became a public emblem of her abilities. Her poems were published in Spain in 1689, going into several editions and spreading her fame throughout all of the Spanish world. Her position was questioned most strongly when she wrote a letter to the Bishop of Puebla challenging a theological tract written some forty years earlier; he published it, with a critique composed by a pseudonymous "Sor Filotea." She countered with her important autobiographical and philosophical work *Repuesta a Sor Filotea de la Cruz* [*Answer to Sor Filotea de la Cruz*] in which she defended herself as a woman and an intellectual. In 1692 she sold her library and donated the proceeds to charity. In 1694 she renewed her vows, signing a statement of self-condemnation, and took up a life of penance and self-sacrifice, dying a year later (1695) when caring for her sisters during a typhus epidemic. She was an important writer as a Mexican who identified herself with the new world, a feminist, and an ardent defender of intellectual curiosity.

Works

The Answer: La Repuesta. Translated by Electa Arenal and Amanda Powell. New York: Feminist, 1994.

Selected Sonnets. Translated by Sandra Sider. Saskatoon, Saskatchewan, Canada: Peregrina, 1987.

A Sor Juana Anthology. Translated by Alan S. Trueblood. Cambridge, MA: Harvard University, 1988.

Sor Juana Inés de la Cruz: Poems. Translated by Margaret Sayers Peden. Binghamton, NY: Bilingual Press/Editorial Bilingue, 1985.

Sor Juana's Dream. Translated by Luis Harss. New York: Lumen, 1986.

A Woman of Genius: The Intellectual Autobiography of Sor Juana Inés de la Cruz. Translated by Margaret Sayers Peden. Salisbury, CT: Lime Rock Press, 1982.

Commentary

Arenal, Electa. "This Life Within Me Won't Keep Still." *Reinventing the Americas: Comparative Studies of Literature of the United States and Spanish America.* Cambridge: Cambridge University, 1986. 158–202.

Arenal, Electa, and Amanda Powell. "A Life Without and Within: Juana Ramírez/Sor Juana Inés de la Cruz (1648/51–1695)." *Women's Studies Quarterly* 21.1–2 (spring-summer 1993): 67–80.

Flynn, Gerard. *Sor Juana Inés de la Cruz*. New York: Twayne, 1971.

Franco, Jean. *Plotting Women: Gender and Representation in Mexico*. New York: Columbia University, 1989.

Johnson, Julie Greer. *Satire in Colonial Spanish America: Turning the New World Upside Down*. Austin: University of Texas, 1993.

Kaminsky, Amy Katz. "Nearly New Clarions: Sor Juana Inés de la Cruz Pays Homage to a Swedish Poet." *In the Feminine Mode: Essays on Hispanic Women Writers.* Lewisburg, PA: Bucknell University, 1990. 31–53.

Merrim, Stephanie, editor. *Feminist Perspectives on Sor Juana Inés de la Cruz*. Detroit, MI: Wayne State University, 1991.

Paz, Octavio. *Sor Juana, or, the Traps of Faith*. Cambridge, MA: Belknap, 1988.

Tavard, George H. *Juana Inés de la Cruz and the Theology of Beauty: The First Mexican Theology*. Notre Dame, IN: University of Notre Dame, 1991.

Juletane by Myriam Warner-Vieyra (London, England: Heinemann, 1987). Hélène is preparing pragmatically for a marriage of convenience when she finds the diary of a West Indian woman, Juletane, who wrote about her lonely childhood in France, her move to Africa with her new African husband, and her struggle to deal with the change of culture, a polygamous marriage, and growing madness. This short novel, in which journal entries are interleaved with an account of its reading by Hélène, contrasts two figures who turn out to have something in common. Juletane says in her diary, "Thanks to my diary I discover that my life is not in pieces, that it had only been coiled deep down inside of me and now comes back in huge raging waves'' (30). Both writing the diary and reading it are acts of making meaning, seeking self, as well as creating a connection between black women separated by the Diaspora.

Commentary

King, Adele. "Two Caribbean Women Go to Africa: Maryse Condé's *Heremakhonon* and Myriam Warner-Vieyra's *Juletane.*" *College Literature* 18.3 (October 1991): 96–105.

Lionnet, Françoise. "Inscriptions of Exile: The Body's Knowledge and the Myth of Authenticity." *Callaloo* 15.1 (winter 1992): 30–40.

Ngate, Jonathan. "Reading Warner-Vieyra's *Juletane.*" *Callaloo* 9.4 (fall 1986): 553–564.

July's People by Nadine Gordimer (New York: Viking, 1981). A novel set in a hypothetical near future when blacks and whites are in open warfare. A family escapes Johannesburg through the agency of their black servant July. Living in July's village, they become "July's people" while at the same time becoming acquainted with his people for the first time. They become aware of the intimate details of his life, which were never connected with his city identity, and gain a new awareness of the country they have always called home and never really known. The breaking down of barriers between them leads to a disturbing re-working of their relationship, tangled political relations playing out in complex human terms. The ambiguous ending appropriately resists conventional closure.

Commentary

Bodenheimer, Rosemarie. "The Interregnum of Ownership in *July's People.*" *The Later Fiction of Nadine Gordimer.* New York: St. Martin's, 1993. 108–120.

Gordon, Jennifer. "Dreams of a Common Language: Nadine Gordimer's *July's People.*" *African Literature Today* 15 (1987): 102–108.

Greenstein, Susan M. "Miranda's Story: Nadine Gordimer and the Literature of Empire." *Novel* 18.3 (spring 1985): 227–242.

Roberts, Sheila. "South African Post-Revolutionary Fiction." *The Commonwealth in Canada: Proceedings of the Second Triennial Conference of CACLALS, University of Winnipeg, 1–4 October, 1981.* Calcutta, India: Writers' Workshop, 1983. 203–215.

Roberts, Sheila. "Sites of Paranoia and Taboo: Lessing's *The Grass Is Singing* and Gordimer's *July's People.*" *Research in African Literatures* 24 (fall 1993): 73–85.

Jung Chang. See **Chang, Jung.**

K

Kabbani, Rana. Born in Damascus, Syria, a poet, translator, and cultural critic. She earned a B.A., M.A., and Ph.D. in English literature at Georgetown University, the American University of Beirut, and Jesus College, Cambridge. She has translated poetry from the Arabic, publishing a collection of works by Mahmud Darwish, as well as her own poetry and an analysis of Western representations of the Middle East, particularly the white male fascination with the idea of the harem.

Work

The Road to You. Damascus, Syria: n.p., 1974.

Commentary

Kabbani, Rana. *Europe's Myths of the Orient.* London, England: Macmillan, 1986.
Kabbani, Rana. "Pride and Prejudice." *New Statesman and Society* 2.72 (October 20, 1989): 36–39.

Karodia, Farida. Born in Aliwal North, South Africa, in 1942, daughter of Mary and Ebrahim K. Basie. She taught in Johannesburg for four years, married, and left South Africa in 1966, shortly after divorce. After teaching in Zambia and Swaziland, she moved to Canada in 1969 with a small child. She wrote radio plays for the Canadian Broadcasting Corporation (CBC) while upgrading her teaching certificate at the University of Calgary. She taught for a few years before taking up writing full-time, writing both for publication and radio. Her novel and short stories have provided a unique and insightful view on a part of

South African life and culture often left unexamined, that of the "coloured" population.

Works

Coming Home and Other Stories. London, NH: Heinemann, 1988.
*Daughters of the Twilight. London, England: Women's Press, 1986.
A Shattering of Silence. Portsmouth, NH: Heinemann, 1993.

Commentary

Flockemann, Miki. " 'Not-Quite Insiders and Not-Quite Outsiders': The 'Process of Womanhood' in *Beka Lamb, Nervous Conditions* and *Daughters of the Twilight." Journal of Commonwealth Literature* 27.1 (1992): 37–47.

Khaing, Mi Mi. See **Mi Mi Khaing.**

Khalifeh, Sahar. Born in Nablus, Palestine, in 1941. She entered into a traditional, arranged marriage when she was eighteen, and after having two daughters, she divorced and began to write while supporting herself with teaching at Bir Zeit University and the University of Iowa. The manuscript of her first novel was confiscated by Israeli authorities. Her second was published in Cairo in Arabic. Her third, *Wild Thorns*, a meditation on the costs of living under occupation, has been translated into English, Hebrew, and French.

Work

*Wild Thorns. Translated by Trevor LeGassich and Elizabeth Fernea. London, England: Al Saqui, 1985.

Khalvati, Mimi. Born in Teheran on April 28, 1944, she was educated at the University of Neuchâtel, Switzerland, and the Drama Centre, London. She worked for a time in Teheran, as an actress and director at the Theatre Workshop and as a translator and playwright. She has since cofounded the Theatre in Exile Group in England, worked on children's literature, and is a member of the Blue Nose Poets, publishing poetry in many journals and anthologies, winning awards for her poems "Persian Miniatures" and "Amanuensis."

Work

*In White Ink. Manchester, England: Carcanet, 1992.

Kimenye, Barbara. Born around 1940 in Uganda, where she worked for the government before becoming a writer. She worked as a journalist for the *Uganda Nation*, then moved to Kenya and joined the staff of the Nairobi *Daily Nation*. She is the author of satiric short stories and a series of children's books about Moses, an adventurous Ugandan schoolboy.

Works

The Gemstone Affair. Sunbury-on-Thames, England: Nelson, 1978.
Kalasanda. London, England: Oxford, 1965.
Kalasanda Revisited. London, England: Oxford, 1966.
Moses. Nairobi, Kenya: Oxford, 1971.
Moses and Mildred. Nairobi, Kenya: Oxford, 1967.
Moses and the Ghost. Nairobi, Kenya: Oxford, 1971.
Moses and the Kidnappers. Nairobi, Kenya: Oxford, 1968.
Moses and the Penpal. Nairobi, Kenya: Oxford, 1973.
Moses in a Mess. Nairobi, Kenya: Oxford, 1991.
Moses in a Muddle. Nairobi, Kenya: Oxford, 1970.
Moses in Trouble. Nairobi, Kenya: Oxford, 1968.
Moses on the Move. Nairobi, Kenya: Oxford, 1972.
Moses, the Camper. Nairobi, Kenya: Oxford, 1973.
Paulo's Strange Adventure. Nairobi, Kenya: Oxford, 1971.
The Runaways. Nairobi, Kenya: Oxford, 1973.
The Scoop. Sunbury-on-Thames, England: Nelson, 1978.
The Smugglers. London, England: Nelson, 1966.
The Winged Adventure. Nairobi, Kenya: Oxford, 1969.

Kincaid, Jamaica. Born in 1949 in St. John's, Antigua, daughter of Annie Richardson of Dominica. She attended a local girl's school and was apprenticed to a seamstress. At the age of sixteen she left her family and moved to the United States, where she worked as an au pair, a receptionist, and a magazine writer. She attended Franconia College in New Hampshire for a year, studied photography at the New School for Social Research, and began to write seriously in 1973. She became a staff writer for the *New Yorker* in 1976, after George S. Trow wrote a number of "Talk of the Town" pieces about her and she became a protégée of editor William Shawn; many of her stories were published there, as well as in the *Paris Review.* She married his son, Allen Shawn, a composer and college professor, and they now live in North Bennington, Vermont. Her works deal mainly with the world of childhood, with the strong figure of the mother and the child's need to break away and become independent. There is also a strong current of anger at the damage done by colonization, expressed particularly in her book about Antigua, *A Small Place*, as well as in her fiction.

Works

Annie, Gwen, Lilly, Pam, and Tulip. New York: Library Fellows, Whitney, 1986.
*Annie John. New York: Farrar, Straus, Giroux, 1985.
At the Bottom of the River. New York: Vintage Books, 1985.
Lucy. New York: Farrar, Straus, Giroux, 1990.
*A Small Place. New York: Farrar, Straus, Giroux, 1988.

Commentary

Covi, Giovanna. "Jamaica Kincaid and the Resistance to Canons." *Out of the Kumbla: Women and Literature in the Caribbean.* Trenton, NY: Africa World Press, 1990. 345–354.

Davies, Carol Boyce. "Writing Home: Gender and Heritage in the Works of Afro/Caribbean/American Women Writers." *Out of the Kumbla: Women and Literature in the Caribbean*. Trenton, NY: Africa World Press, 1990. 59–73.

de Abruna, Laura Niesen. "Family Connections: Mother and Mother Country in the Fiction of Jean Rhys and Jamaica Kincaid." *Motherlands: Women's Writings from Africa, the Caribbean, and South Asia*. New Brunswick, NJ: Rutgers University, 1992. 257–289.

Ferguson, Moira. *Jamaica Kincaid: Where the Land Meets the Body*. Charlottesville: University of Virginia, 1994.

Ferguson, Moira. "A Lot of Memory." *Kenyon Review* 16.1 (winter 1994): 163–188.

Ismond, Patricia. "Jamaica Kincaid: 'First They Must Be Children.' " *World Literature Written in English* 28.2 (1988): 336–341.

Kincaid, Jamaica. [untitled essay]. *Critical Fictions: The Politics of Imaginative Writing*. Seattle, WA: Bay Press, 1991. 223–229.

Perry, Donna. "An Interview with Jamaica Kincaid." *Reading Black, Reading Feminist: A Critical Anthology*. New York: Meridian, 1990. 492–509.

Simmons, Diane. "The Rhythm of Reality in the Works of Jamaica Kincaid." *World Literature Today* 68.3 (summer 1994): 466–472.

Tapping, Craig. "Children and History in the Caribbean Novel: George Lamming's *In the Castle of My Skin* and Jamaica Kincaid's *Annie John*." *Kunapipi* 11.2 (1989): 51–59.

Tiffin, Helen. "Cold Hearts and (Foreign) Tongues: Recitation and the Reclamation of the Female Body in the Works of Erna Brodber and Jamaica Kincaid." *Callaloo* 16.4 (fall 1993): 909–921.

A Kindness to the Children by Joan Riley (London, England: Women's Press, 1993). A novel about three women, one going to Jamaica to heal after her Jamaican husband's death, another going there with her children when her marriage is falling apart and her alcoholism and a repressed childhood rape are driving her mad, and a third who learns how to assert her own identity in the face of a disapproving and unhelpful husband. Jamaica is not glamorized in the novel, with its extremes of poverty, sexism, and corruption depicted along with its beauty and the closeness of the people. The problems the women have are not neatly resolved, and in the end, there is the likelihood that one has been murdered while another tries to distance herself from the necessity of caring. The only one of the three who seems to have gained ground is the Jamaican woman, who has earned a degree of independence and strength by the end of the novel.

Kociancich, Vlady. Born in Argentina in 1941, she became the first member of her family to attend the university, where she made the acquaintance of Jorge Luis Borges. She has written three novels, well received at home and in Spain, and also works as a journalist and literary critic. She won a Spanish literary award, the Gonzalo Torrent Ballester Prize, for a collection of short stories. She currently lives in Buenos Aires.

Work

The Last Days of William Shakespeare. Translated by Margaret Jull Costa. New York: William Morrow, 1991.

Kon, S. Born in Edinburgh, Scotland, but grew up and was educated in Singapore, where she obtained a degree from the University of Singapore. Her parents were Chinese Singaporeans whose families lived in Singapore and Malaysia for many generations. She has lived both in Singapore and Ipoh, Malaysia, and is the author of a novel, short stories, and numerous plays that have been successfully performed both in Singapore and abroad.

Works

Emily of Emerald Hill: A Monodrama. Singapore: Macmillan, 1989.
Emporium and Other Plays. Singapore: Heinemann, 1977.
The Scholar and the Dragon. Singapore: Federal Publications, 1986.

Kuo, Helena. Born in 1911 on the island of Macao, the fourth of eight children. She studied at a Portuguese convent school and with tutors, then attended the Lingnan University, Canton, and Shanghai University. She wanted to be involved in the war against Japan, so she abandoned her studies and began to write for the *China Times*, later becoming the editor of the women's page in the *China Evening News*. She wrote a column for the *London Daily Mail*, broadcast on the British Broadcasting Corporation (BBC), and went to America, where she caused a media stir, meeting many celebrities and even having a personal interview with Eleanor Roosevelt. She settled in America and married artist Dong Kingman; they live in New York. In addition to an autobiography and a novel, she has written a collection of essays, a children's book, and a commentary on her husband's paintings.

Works

I've Come a Long Way. New York: Appleton-Century, 1942.
Peach Path. London, England: Methuen, 1940.
Westward to Chungking. New York: Appleton-Century, 1944.

Commentary

Ling, Amy. *Between Two Worlds: Women Writers of Chinese Ancestry.* New York: Pergamon, 1990.

Kuzwayo, Ellen. Born on June 29, 1914, in South Africa, the only child of Phillip Serasengwe and Emma Mutsi Merafe; her parents divorced and she was raised by her grandparents on their farm, where she lived until 1927. She trained as a teacher and taught for some years and then attended the University of Witwatersrand, where she earned a degree in social work. She has been a teacher, social worker, an actress in the film version of *Cry, the Beloved Country*, a general secretary of the YWCA, and a member of the Soweto Committee of Ten, a group of moderate black leaders with whom she was detained in 1977 for five months. She first became a published writer in her sixties, with the publication of her autobiography, *Call Me Woman*. As well as writing, she has worked on films (*Awake from Mourning* and *Tsiamelo: A Place of Goodness*) and continues to be a social activist.

Works

Call Me Woman. Johannesburg, South Africa: Ravan, 1985.
Sit Down and Listen: Stories from South Africa. Cape Town, South Africa: David Philip; London: Women's Press, 1990.

Commentary

Ibrahim, Huma. "The Autobiographical Content in the Works of South African Women Writers: The Personal and the Political." *Biography East and West: Selected Conference Papers*. Honolulu: University of Hawaii, 1989. 122–126.
James, Adeola, editor. *In Their Own Voices: African Women Writers Talk*. London, England: James Currey, 1990.
MacKenzie, Craig, and Cherry Clayton. *Between the Lines: Interviews with Bessie Head, Sheila Roberts, Ellen Kuzwayo, Miriam Tlali*. Grahamstown, South Africa: National English Literary Museum, 1989.

L

Ladha, Yasmin. Born in Mwanza, Tanzania, in 1958 of Muslim Indian heritage. Though she grew up in Africa, she frequently visited family members in India. She emigrated to Canada at age twenty and attended the University of Calgary. Several of her stories have been anthologized, and she has published a collection of her own. Her stories explore the experiences of the Indian Diaspora and the relationship between the reader (whom she addresses familiarly as "readerji") and writer of "Other literature," making interesting experiments in narration as she questions the idea of third world literature.

Work

Lion's Granddaughter and Other Stories. Edmonton, Canada: NeWest, 1992.

Lakshmi, C. S. Born in 1944 into a large middle-class Tamil family living in Bangalore, India. She was influenced by her grandmother, a self-taught Tamil literary scholar, and her mother, a musician, and began to write at an early age. At nineteen she left home to study in Madras, earned a master's degree, and worked for a time as a schoolteacher before embarking on a Ph.D. program in political science. She has published stories and novels in Tamil (using the pseudonym Ambai) as well as criticism of Tamil women's literature and works on film scripts in association with her filmmaker husband, Vishnu Mathur, with whom she lives and works in Bombay.

Work

A Purple Sea. Translated by Lakshmi Holstrom. London, England: Virago, 1993.

Commentary

Lakshmi, C. S. *The Face Behind the Mask: Women in Tamil Literature.* New Delhi, India: Vikas, 1984.

Language. All language is politically charged and potent with multiple meanings; this is especially true in postcolonial literature. For the colonial writer the choice of which language in which to write is itself a crisis, since often the language used in "standard" literary discourse is the language of colonial power. English is termed by Marlene Nourbese Philip a "foreign anguish" (58), an expression of estrangement and pain echoed by many other writers. For Jamaica Kincaid, the English language is inevitably tied to the crimes of colonialism: "What I see is the millions of people, of whom I am just one, made orphans: no motherland, no fatherland, no gods, no mound of earth for holy ground, no excess of love which might lead to the things that an excess of love sometimes brings, and the worst and most painful of all, no tongue. For isn't it odd that the only language I have in which to speak of this crime is the language of the criminal who committed this crime?" (226–227). For Maryse Condé, each word of French that she uses "hearkens back to the historic defeat of my ancestors, their collective rage and loss of identity in the Middle Passage" (110); and in the words of Assia Djebar, "[M]y writing is ... caught in the snare of the old war between two peoples. . . . I journey through myself at the whim of the former enemy, the enemy whose language I have stolen" (216). Not only is English or French the language of former enemies; it is charged with class values; Jessica Hagedorn recalls, "We learned Tagalog, our native language, as if it were a foreign language. It was also the language used to address servants" (147).

Responses to the crisis of language vary. The most famous solution is that of Ngugi wa Thiong'o, who has chosen to write only in Gikuyu, and expresses his reasoning in *Decolonising the Mind.* Other writers object that only someone as famous as Ngugi, with an already-established market for translations, could afford the luxury of writing in a language with such a small publishing market. (For a good survey of the language question in African literature, see David Westley.) On another note, Gayatri Spivak has remarked, in her acerbic way, that humanities scholarship has not paid adequate attention to language study: "[T]he Army, the Foreign Service, the multi-nationals themselves, and intelligence and counter-intelligence take the necessity of language-learning with the utmost seriousness. We have something to learn from our enemies" (228).

Other writers have deliberately chosen to write in a colonialist language for political and economic reasons. In South Africa, where the Bantu Education Act attempted to force the Afrikaans language on the African majority, writing in English has been, according to Miriam Tlali, "a political statement ... we all speak it and in a sense it unites us" (Lee, 41). Shirley Lim argues that English is an excellent choice for an adaptable literary language in a multicultural environment such as that of Singapore. Buchi Emecheta considers Igbo her emotional language, yet she writes in English, a language she didn't learn until adolescence, because it is only in English that she can reach an audience; she finds the African publishing scene discouraging to women writers (Jussawalla, 98).

Another solution is to use a new formulation of a language, one evolved apart from Europe and its linguistic traditions. Nelida Piñon describes Brazilian Portuguese as a "porous" language adapting and changing in response to the Brazilian experience (200). Creole dialects are frequently used to enrich standard English by writers such as Louise Bennett, Merle Collins, Joan Cambridge, and others. Creole is not only useful for communicating with Creole speakers; it is a mark of the rich possibilities inherent in language. According to Jean D'Costa, it is "a language capable of irony, satire, praise, lamentation, abuse, endearment, consolation, and, indeed, capable of expanding itself to any range which its users might desire. The making of this language mirrors a singular human achievement: the forging of meaning out of chaos, of communication out of isolation, of creativity and action out of silent dismemberment" (*Voices in Exile*, 8). Indeed, multiple versions and variations on a European language can subtly enrich and oppose it, opening the possibility of using various languages to create a dialogic echo-chamber effect. Many South African writers, for example, use elements of Afrikaans, Xhosa, and Zulu, making the heteroglossia of South African society a new literary language. Poet Agueda Pizarro creates neologisms of fused Spanish and English words to convey a dual consciousness. In an article on *Lionheart Gal*, critic Carolyn Cooper takes a dialogic approach to a dialogic book. The first half of her analysis is an authoritative, scholarly discussion of oral literature and mediation, seeing in *Lionheart Gal* a curiously divided book that, on the one hand, gives women a chance to speak in their own voice yet, on the other, depends on the written word to validate it by publishing it rather than producing oral theater from it. She then subverts the "authority of English as our exclusive voice of scholarship" (52) by completing the second half of the analysis in Creole.

Many writers chose to use European languages in an oppositional way. bell hooks locates language as a place of struggle, as a place where the margins create a counterlanguage, not entirely apart from the colonizer's language but a transformation of it. Marlene Nourbese Philip argues language "has to be dislocated and acted upon—even destroyed—so that it begins to serve our purposes. . . . [The challenge] is to use the language in such a way that the historical realities are not erased or obliterated. So that English is revealed as the tainted tongue it truly is" (19). For Condé, "[w]hat is paramount . . . is the rediscovery of the power of words of our people. Metropolitan French, English, Spanish— all languages of colonization to be colonized in turn" (111). The subversive possibilities of language are acutely observed by Kwame Anthony Appiah, who at the same time recognizes the difficulty of embracing the language of colonial powers: "European languages and European disciplines have been 'turned,' like double agents, from the projects of the metropole to the intellectual work of postcolonial cultural life. But though officially in the service of new masters, these tools remain, like all double agents, perpetually under suspicion'' (156). Whatever approach is taken to the question of language choice, postcolonial discourse is the site of extraordinary and rich linguistic experimentation, opposition, and invention.

Works

Bennett, Louise. *Jamaica Labrish*. Kingston, Jamaica: Sangsters, 1966.

*Cambridge, Joan. *Clarise Cumberbatch Want to Go Home*. New York: Ticknor and Fields, 1987.

*Collins, Merle. *Angel*. London, England: Women's Press, 1987.

*Djebar, Assia. *Fantasia: An Algerian Cavalcade*. Translated by Dorothy Blair. London, England: Quartet, 1985.

*Philip, Marlene Nourbese. *She Tries Her Tongue, Her Silence Softly Breaks*. Charlottetown, Canada: Ragweed, 1989.

*Pizarro, Agueda. *Shadowinnower*. New York: Columbia University, 1979.

Commentary

Adelugba, Dapo. "Language and Drama: Ama Ata Aidoo." *African Literature Today* 8 (1976): 72–84.

Appiah, Kwame Anthony. "Out of Africa: Typologies of Nativism." *Yale Journal of Criticism* 2.1 (fall 1988): 153–178.

Barlow, Tani. "Theorizing Women: *Funu, Guojia, Jiating* [Chinese Women, Chinese State, Chinese Family]." *Genders* 10 (spring 1991): 132–160.

Brink, André. "Women and Language in Darkest Africa: The Quest for Articulation in Two Postcolonial Novels." *Literator* 13.1 (1992): 1–14.

Cameron, Deborah. "What Is the Nature of Women's Oppression in Language?" *Oxford Literary Review* 8 (1986): 79–87.

Coetzee, J. M. "Simple Language, Simple People: Smith, Paton, Mikro." *White Writing: On the Culture of Letters in South Africa*. New Haven, CT: Yale University, 1988. 115–135.

Condé, Maryse. "Beyond Languages and Colors." *Discourse* 11 (spring-summer 1989): 110–113.

Cooper, Carolyn. "Writing Oral History: Sistren Theatre Collective's *Lionheart Gal*." *Kunapipi* 7.1 (1989): 49–57.

D'Costa, Jean. "Expression and Communication: Literary Challenges to the Caribbean Polydialectal Writers." *Journal of Commonwealth Literature* 19.1(1984): 123–141.

D'Costa, Jean, and Barbara Lalla, editors. *Voices in Exile: Jamaican Texts of the 18th and 19th Centuries*. Tuscaloosa: University of Alabama, 1989.

Devonish, Hubert. *Language and Liberation: Creole Language Politics in the Caribbean*. London, England: Karia, 1986.

Flockemann, Miki. "Language and Self in Opal Palmer Adisa's *Bake-Face and Other Guava Stories*." *Ariel* 24.1 (January 1993): 59–73.

Gordimer, Nadine. "English-Language Literature and Politics in South Africa." *Aspects of South African Literature*. London, England: Heinemann, 1976. 99–120.

Gordon, Jennifer. "Dreams of a Common Language: Nadine Gordimer's *July's People*." *African Literature Today* 15 (1987): 102–108.

Hagedorn, Jessica. [untitled essay]. *Critical Fictions: The Politics of Imaginative Writing.* Seattle, WA: Bay Press, 1991. 146–150.

hooks, bell. "Choosing the Margin as a Space of Radical Openness." *Framework* 36 (1989): 15–23.

Jussawalla, Feroza F., and Reed Way Dasenbrock. *Interviews with Writers of the Post-Colonial World.* Jackson: University Press of Mississippi, 1992.

Kantaris, Elia Geoffrey. "The Silent Zone: Marta Traba." *Modern Language Review* 87.1 (January 1992): 86–101.

Kincaid, Jamaica. [untitled essay]. *Critical Fictions: The Politics of Imaginative Writing.* Seattle, WA: Bay Press, 1991. 223–229.

Lee, Sonia. "Conversation with Miriam Tlali." *African Literature Association Bulletin* 17.3 (summer 1991): 40–42.

Lim, Shirley. "Voices from the Hinterland: Plurality and Identity in the National Literatures in English from Malaysia and Singapore." *World Literature Written in English* 28.1(1988): 145–153.

Lionnet, Françoise. "Of Mangoes and Maroons: Language, History, and the Multicultural Subject of Michelle Cliff's *Abeng*." *De/Colonizing the Subject: The Politics of Gender in Women's Autobiography.* Minneapolis: University of Minnesota, 1992. 321–345.

Nelson, Cecil L. "New Englishes, New Discourses: New Speech Acts." *World Englishes* 10.3 (1991): 317–323.

Ngugi wa Thiong'o. *Decolonising the Mind: The Politics of Language in African Literature.* London, England: James Currey, 1986.

Owomoyela, Oyekan. "The Question of Language in African Literatures." *A History of Twentieth-Century African Literatures.* Lincoln: University of Nebraska, 1993. 347–368.

Piñon, Nelida. "The Myth of Creation." *Lives on the Line: The Testimony of Contemporary Latin American Authors.* Berkeley: University of California, 1988. 198–204.

Pollard, Velma. "Overlapping Systems: Language in the Poetry of Lorna Goodison." *Carib* (1989): 33–47.

Pollard, Velma. "Mothertongue Voices in the Writing of Olive Senior and Lorna Goodison." *Motherlands: Women's Writings from Africa, the Caribbean, and South Asia.* New Brunswick, NJ: Rutgers University, 1992. 238–253.

Spivak, Gayatri Chakravorty. "The Political Economy of Women as Seen by a Literary Critic." *Coming to Terms: Feminism, Theory, Politics.* New York: Routledge, 1989. 218–229.

Suleri, Sara. *The Rhetoric of English India.* Chicago: University of Chicago, 1992.

Westley, David. "Choice of Language and African Literature: A Bibliographic Essay." *Research in African Literatures* 23.1 (spring 1992): 159–171.

Wilentz, Gay. " 'English Is a Foreign Anguish': Caribbean Writers and the Disruption of the Colonial Canon." *Decolonizing Tradition: New Views of Twentieth-Century "British" Literary Canons.* Urbana: University of Illinois, 1992. 261–278.

The Women and Language Debate: A Sourcebook. New Brunswick, NJ: Rutgers University, 1994.

The Last Days of William Shakespeare by Vlady Kociancich (New York: William Morrow, 1991). "All the world's a stage" is taken literally in this surreal novel. The reputation of an unnamed Latin American country is besmirched when a foreign journalist, writing in a small town newspaper in Ohio, reports that the glorious National Theater is hard to find, the government that supports it does not know of its existence, and the only play ever performed there is *Hamlet*, continually played by the same ancient actor since 1920. The government rises to the occasion by appointing a committee to refurbish the theater, commission plays that will reflect national glory, and redeem national honor. A famous writer is called in to help. However, the government moves in mysterious ways and its actions take on sinister significance, gestures and words begin to carry multifaceted meaning, and the politics of national honor make the entire country a violent stage for a brutal spectacle. Greengrocers are bundled away in black cars shouting, "Long live Shakespeare!" and a young aspiring writer, whose journal and letters accompany the reader through the hall of mirrors plot, is gradually beaten down by the workings of the baffling and elliptical government officials. The entire story comes as a flashback from the theater when *Hamlet* is once again being performed, after a "happy ending" in which those who have disappeared are forgotten and art is once again tamed and at the service of the state. A funny and horrifying novel about the theater of politics.

The Late Bourgeois World by Nadine Gordimer (New York: Viking, 1966). A short novel, told from the point of view of a woman whose ex-husband, a white activist against apartheid in South Africa, has just committed suicide. His earnest gestures of rebellion have been immature, futile, and he has driven his car off a pier in Cape Town to drown with a backseat full of politically sensitive papers. The narrator has a more sophisticated, cool approach to the politics around her, and she distances herself from action until, at the end of the novel, she is approached by a black friend who asks her to launder money for their cause through a bank account she controls; the novel ends with her wondering if she will, in fact, enter politics again and what the costs will be. The inevitable personal fallout from political commitment and the trade-offs made are explored within the dynamics of a woman's relations with her family.

The Latin Deli by Judith Ortiz Cofer (Athens: University of Georgia, 1993). A collection of prose pieces and poetry that deal with childhood, adolescence, the growing identity of a writer, and her feelings of marginalization, being a Puerto Rican in the United States. "I was born a white girl in Puerto Rico, but became a brown girl when I came to live in the United States" (135). Much of her work deals with forging an identity as a member of a minority; a related theme is that of finding a role as a woman writer.

Leaden Wings by Chang Chieh (London, England: Virago, 1987). A novel with a large cast of characters—workers, hairdressers, officials, and journalists— whose experiences and psychological insights combine to yield a picture of China after the Cultural Revolution. The problems attendant on industrial modernization and economic change, countered by bureaucratic stagnation and ideological exhaustion, are portrayed on a large canvas.

Lee, Lillian. See **Li Pi-hua.**

Legacies: A Chinese Mosaic by Bette Bao Lord (New York: Knopf, 1990). A combination of a memoir and a documentary. Lord, who was born in China but left at an early age, traveled back to China with her American husband, who had been appointed ambassador. They were there for several years and left just as the student prodemocracy movement was seemingly beginning to cool; shortly after her return to the United States, the military moved in to suppress the demonstrations in Tiananmen Square. Her memoir tells of her life, the lives of her family members, about family she met in China, and recounts the stories of people she met there, those who were purged back in the 1950s, those who were victims of the Cultural Revolution, and, at the end, one who was facing similar fears after the Tiananmen Square violence. The book is a mingling of personal and political, of past and present existing simultaneously.

Leopoldina's Dream by Silvina Ocampo (New York: Penguin Books, 1988). These well-crafted stories are, for the most part, very short and often involve a gothic twist of fate or a satirical surprise for the reader. In the title story the narrator is revealed to be a dog who wrote the story during one of the dreams discussed in the story. In ''The House of Sugar,'' a woman who is constantly mistaken for someone else is accused by a madwoman of stealing her life; she eventually becomes the woman whose life she has inadvertently stolen. And in the charming and delicate story ''Thus Were Their Faces'' a class of deaf-mute children who are obsessed with drawing wings fly out of a plane, seraphim in a celestial vision.

Lessing, Doris. Born in 1919 of British parents in Iran, where her father worked for the Imperial Bank of Persia. In 1925, he attended the Empire Exhibition in London and was taken with the idea of settling in southern Rhodesia (now Zimbabwe) to farm. He took his family there in 1925 and bought 3,000 acres of land, on which they made a meager living. The children were brought up on this remote and isolated farm and for their education were sent to boarding schools—for Doris, a Catholic convent school in Salisbury (now Harare) followed by a year in a state school. She left at age fourteen to become an au pair, to do clerical work for a law office and to serve as a Hansard secretary for the Rhodesian Parliament. She married at nineteen, then left her husband and their two children a few years later. With a new interest in politics, she joined a

Marxist circle where she met Gottfried Lessing, a German Jewish exile whom she married in 1945. They moved to England in 1949 with their son and soon divorced. Her first book, *The Grass Is Singing*, a novel about Africa, was immediately accepted by the first publisher she approached and was well received by critics. Her next books also dealt with Africa, culminating in the *Children of Violence* series of novels, which follows the life of Martha Quest who, like Lessing, migrates from a southern African colony (called "Zambesia") to England. The series is a meditation on the individual consciousness in relation to society and explores various collective responses to the human condition— Marxist, feminist, metaphysical. Her more recent books are characterized by a more speculative, mystical style, one that began to show itself in the *Children of Violence* series. All of her work demonstrates an interest in using the novel to explore ideas. She has also written some works under the name Jane Somers, in part to see if her writing would be acceptable to a publisher and the reading public under an unknown name.

Works

African Laughter: Four Visits to Zimbabwe. New York: HarperCollins, 1992.
African Stories. New York: Simon and Schuster, 1965.
Briefing for a Descent into Hell. New York: Knopf, 1971.
Collected Stories. London, England: J. Cape, 1978.
The Diary of a Good Neighbor. New York: Knopf, 1983.
Documents Relating to the Sentimental Agents of the Volyen Empire. London, England: Cape, 1983.
The Doris Lessing Reader. New York: Knopf, 1988.
The Four-Gated City. London, England: MacGibben and Key, 1969.
Going Home. London, England: M. Joseph, 1957.
The Golden Notebook. London, England: J. Cape, 1962.
The Good Terrorist. New York: Knopf, 1985.
The Grass Is Singing. New York: Crowell, 1950.
The Habit of Loving. New York: Crowell, 1957.
If the Old Could. New York: Knopf, 1984.
Landlocked. New York: New American Library, 1970.
The Making of the Representative from Planet 8. London, England: Cape, 1982.
A Man and Two Women. New York: Simon and Schuster, 1963.
The Marriages Between Zones Three, Four, and Five. New York: Knopf, 1980.
Martha Quest. London, England: M. Joseph, 1952.
Memoirs of a Survivor. New York: Knopf, 1974.
No Witchcraft for Sale. Moscow, Russia: Foreign Languages, 1956.
Particularly Cats. New York: Simon and Schuster, 1967.
Play with a Tiger. London, England: Davis-Poynter, 1972.
A Proper Marriage. New York: New American Library, 1970.
The Real Thing: Stories and Sketches. New York: HarperCollins, 1992.
A Ripple from the Storm. New York: New American Library, 1970.
Shikasta. New York: Knopf, 1979.
The Sirian Experiments. New York: Knopf, 1981.

A Small Personal Voice: Essays, Reviews, Interviews. New York: Knopf, 1974.

Stories. New York: Knopf, 1978.

The Story of a Non-Marrying Man and Other Stories. London, England: Cape, 1972.

The Summer Before Dark. New York: Knopf, 1973.

The Temptation of Jack Orkney and Other Stories. New York: Knopf, 1972.

This Was the Old Chief's Country. London, England: M. Joseph, 1952.

To Room Nineteen. London, England: J. Cape, 1978.

Under My Skin: Volume One of My Autobiography, to 1949. New York: HarperCollins, 1994.

The Wind Blows Away Our Words and Other Documents Relating to the Afghan Resistance. New York: Vintage, 1987.

Commentary

Bazin, Nancy Topping. "Madness, Mysticism, and Fantasy: Shifting Perspectives in the Novels of Doris Lessing, Bessie Head, and Nadine Gordimer." *Extrapolation* 33.1 (1992): 73–87.

Beck, Antony. "Doris Lessing and the Colonial Experience." *Journal of Commonwealth Literature* 19.1 (1984): 64–73.

Bertelsen, Eve. "The Quest and the Quotidian: Doris Lessing in South Africa." *In Pursuit of Doris Lessing: Nine Nations Reading.* New York: St. Martin's, 1990. 41–60.

Bertelsen, Eve. "Veldtanschauung: Doris Lessing's Savage Africa." *Modern Fiction Studies* 37.4 (winter 1991): 647–658.

Chennells, Anthony. "Reading Doris Lessing's Rhodesian Stories in Zimbabwe." *In Pursuit of Doris Lessing: Nine Nations Reading.* New York: St. Martin's, 1990. 17–40.

Daymond, M. J. "Areas of the Mind: *The Memoirs of a Survivor* and Doris Lessing's African Stories." *Ariel* 7.3 (July 1986): 65–82.

Fishburn, Katherine. *Doris Lessing: Life, Work, and Criticism.* Fredericton, News Brunswick, Canada: York, 1987.

Fishburn, Katherine. "The Manichean Allegories of Doris Lessing's *The Grass Is Singing.*" *Research in African Literatures* 25.4 (winter 1994): 1–15.

Gardiner, Judith Kegan. *Rhys, Stead, Lessing, and the Politics of Empathy.* Bloomington: Indiana University, 1989.

Hunter, Eva. "Tracking Through the Tangles: The Reader's Task in Doris Lessing's *The Grass Is Singing.*" *Kunapipi* 8.3 (1986): 121–135.

Magarey, Kevin. "The Sense of Place in Doris Lessing and Jean Rhys." *A Sense of Place in the New Literatures in English.* St. Lucia: University of Queensland, 1986. 47–60.

Manion, Eileen. " 'Not About the Colour Problem': Doris Lessing's Portrayal of the Colonial Order." *World Literature Written in English* 21 (1982): 435–455.

Peel, Ellen. "The Self Is Always an Other: Going the Long Way Home to Autobiography." *Twentieth Century Literature* 35.1 (1989): 1–16.

Pickering, Jean. *Understanding Doris Lessing.* Columbia: University of South Carolina, 1990.

Roberts, Sheila. "Sites of Paranoia and Taboo: Lessing's *The Grass Is Singing* and Gordimer's *July's People.*" *Research in African Literatures* 24 (fall 1993): 73–85.

Robinson, Sally. "Repetition and Resistance in Doris Lessing's *Children of Violence*." *Engendering the Subject: Gender and Self-Representation in Contemporary Women's Fiction.* Albany, NY: SUNY, 1991. 29–75.

Ross, Robert L., editor. *International Literature in English: Essays on the Major Writers.* New York: Garland, 1991.

Seligman, Dee. *Doris Lessing: An Annotated Bibliography of Criticism.* Westport, CT: Greenwood, 1981.

Showalter, Elaine. *A Literature of Their Own: British Women Novelists from Brontë to Lessing.* Princeton, NJ: Princeton University, 1977.

Taylor, Jennie, editor. *Notebooks/Memoirs/Archives: Reading and Rereading Doris Lessing.* London, England: Routledge & Kegan Paul, 1982.

Thorpe, Michael. *Doris Lessing's Africa.* London, England: Evans Brothers, 1978.

Visel, Robin. "A Half-Colonization: The Problem of the White Colonial Woman Writer." *Kunapipi* 10.3 (1988): 39–45.

Whitaker, Ruth. *Doris Lessing.* New York: St. Martin's, 1988.

Let Me Speak! Testimony of Domitila, A Woman of the Bolivian Mines by Domitila Barrios de Chungara with Moema Viezzer (London, England: Monthly Review, 1978). The *testimonio* of a woman who has experienced the oppression of the mine workers in Bolivia and the ways in which the wives and children of the mine workers are drawn into the system of exploitation, and who has attempted to present a report on and analysis of her people's situation. This work is based on interviews held with her after her testimony at the International Women's Year Tribunal, organized by the United Nations and held in Mexico in 1975. In insisting on speaking out, bearing witness to injustice, and presenting the claims of the Bolivian poor, she assumes a collective identity, making her witness a political act and a critique. "I don't want anyone at any moment to interpret the story I'm about to tell as something that is only personal. Because I think that my life is related to my people. What happened to me could have happened to hundreds of people in my country" (15).

Li Ang. Born Shi Shuduan in Lugang, Taiwan, on April 4, 1952, she is the youngest of three sisters, all of whom are engaged in literary occupations, one as a critic and the other as a novelist. She began her literary career at age sixteen when she published a short story. In 1970 she moved from a small town to attend college in Taipei, where she studied philosophy. At this time, she published some stories and began to write about the topic of sexual taboos and their effects on gender issues, which made her reputation as a powerful writer or a notoriously immoral one, depending on one's point of view. She left for graduate studies in 1975, earning a master's degree in theater from the University of Oregon, and returned to Taiwan in 1978, where she began to teach at the College of Chinese Culture in Taipei. Her novel, *The Butcher's Wife*, was awarded the annual fiction prize given by the *United Daily News* and earned much criticism at the same time for its violence and explicit sexual scenes.

Work

*The Butcher's Wife. Translated by Howard Goldblatt and Ellen Yeung. San Francisco, CA: North Point, 1986.

Commentary

Chien, Ying-ying. "From Utopian to Dystopian World: Two Faces of Feminism in Contemporary Taiwanese Women's Fiction." *World Literature Today* (winter 1994): 35–42.

Goldblatt, Howard. "Sex and Society: The Fiction of Li Ang." *Worlds Apart: Recent Chinese Writing and Its Audiences.* Armonk, NY: M. E. Sharpe, 1990. 150–165.

Liu, Joyce C. H. "From Loo Port to Taipei: The World of Women in Lee Ang's Works." *Fu Jen Studies* 19 (1986): 65–85.

Martin, Melmont, editor. *Modern Chinese Writers: Self Portrayals.* Armonk, NY: M. E. Sharpe, 1992.

Yeh, Michael. "Shapes of Darkness: Symbols in Li Ang's Dark Night." *Modern Chinese Women Writers: Critical Appraisals.* Armonk, NY: M. E. Sharpe, 1989. 78–95.

Li Pi-hua. Born in Hong Kong, Li is the author of many popular novels that generally become instant best-sellers in Hong Kong as soon as they are published. She is also a filmmaker and has adapted her novels for film, including the well-received *Farewell My Concubine*, awarded the Palme d'Or at the Cannes Film Festival.

Works

*Farewell My Concubine. Translated by Andrea Lingen Felter. New York: Morrow, 1993.

The Last Princess of Manchuria. Translated by Andrea Kelly. New York: Morrow, 1992.

Life by Drowning: Selected Poems by Jeni Couzyn (Toronto, Canada: Anansi, 1983). A substantial collection of poetry that includes the series "Christmas in Africa" in which a struggle between a mother and daughter over her lack of femininity is battled out, a girl drowns in the sea, and the threat of poisonous snakes drives the family away from their home for good. Natural and biological imagery, suggesting an organic connectedness of things, is frequently used in her poems, as in "The Cell Attempts to Communicate with the Giant," in which the poet is an alert cell in the body of the pained world, the human race a cancer threatening the Giant. A series of poems on pregnancy and childbirth ends the collection.

Like Water for Chocolate by Laura Esquivel (New York: Doubleday, 1992). Subtitled *A Novel in Monthly Installments with Recipes, Romances, and Home Remedies*, this magic realist novel focuses on the life of Tita, a woman born in the kitchen and destined to remain there. Her oppressive mother insists she remain unmarried to take care of her in her old age. Her lover, when he asks for her hand, is persuaded to marry her sister instead. Tita's cooking, for the wedding and afterward, has a remarkable effect on those who eat it, since it carries the cook's emotion with it. Interspersed with the events of the novel, there are recipes given for food, for home items, and other lore of the household, mixing the domestic with romance and the bizarre.

Commentary

Lawless, Cecelia. "Experimental Cooking in *Como agua para chocolate.*" *Monographic Review: Revista Monografica* 8 (1992): 261–272.

Lim, Catherine. Born in 1942 (some sources say 1943) in Kulim, Malaysia. She was educated at an English-language convent school. There she developed a love of reading and a familiarity with the British literary canon, first reading the novels of Enid Blyton and, later, Dickens and Maugham. She continued her education at the University of Malaya in Kuala Lumpur, earning a B.A. (honors) degree in English in 1964 and then a diploma in education. She taught secondary school in Malaysia for a time, then in Singapore, where she received a scholarship in 1978 to complete a master's degree in applied linguistics at the Regional Language Centre, after which she left teaching for work in developing local curriculum materials for Singapore's school system. She later earned a Ph.D. in linguistics, studying the status of English in Singapore. She has published a novel and a number of collections of short stories as well as works for children. The conflict between colonial and local cultures has been a recurrent theme in her work.

Works

The Choom-Choom-Tokkee. Singapore: Educational Publications, 1978.
Deadline for Love and Other Stories. Singapore: Heinemann Asia, 1992.
The Girl from Sarawak. Singapore: Educational Publications, 1979.
Little Ironies: Stories of Singapore. Singapore: Heinemann Asia, 1982.
Love's Lonely Impulses. Singapore: Heinemann Asia, 1992.
The Man Who Rode a Tiger and Other Stories. London: Target, 1985.
O Singapore: Stories in Celebration. Singapore: Times Books International, 1989.
Or Else, the Lighting God and Other Stories. Singapore: Heinemann Asia, 1980.
The Serpent's Tooth. Singapore: Time Books International, 1982.
The Shadow of a Dream: Love Stories of Singapore. Singapore: Heinemann Asia, 1987.
They Do Return. Singapore: Times Books International, 1983.

Lim, Janet. Born in China in 1923, she was sold by her mother to a family in Singapore to do domestic work, a common practice at the time. Her memoirs recount her childhood and her internment by the Japanese occupying Singapore during World War II.

Work

Sold for Silver. Cleveland, OH: World, 1958.

Commentary

Lim, Shirley. "Up Against the Nationalist Canon: Women's War Memoirs from Malaysia
    and Singapore." *Journal of Commonwealth Literature* 29.1 (August 1993): 47–
    64.

Lim, Shirley. Born on December 27, 1944, in Malacca, Malaysia, to a Chinese-
Malayan father and a Singaporean mother, one of ten children. At home, English
and Hokkien, a dialect of Chinese, were the languages spoken, though once she
went to school, she stopped speaking and learning Chinese. She earned a B.A.
(honors) in English from the University of Malaya, Kuala Lumpur, in 1967,
after which she worked as a part-time lecturer and teaching assistant there. She
then was a teaching assistant at Brandeis University and Queens College, New
York. She received a Ph.D. in English and American literature from Brandeis
in 1973 and for several years was assistant professor at Hostos Community
College before taking her current position at Westchester Community College.
She has received support from the National Endowment for the Humanities and
had Mellon and Fulbright fellowships. Her collection *Crossing the Peninsula*
won the Commonwealth Prize in 1980. She has published short stories and
poetry as well as literary criticism.

Works

Another Country and Other Stories. Singapore: Times Books International, 1982.
Crossing the Peninsula and Other Poems. Kuala Lumpur, Malaysia: Heinemann, 1980.
Modern Secrets. Sydney, Australia: Dangaroo, 1989.
No More Grove. Singapore: National University, 1985.

Commentary

Lim, Shirley. "Voices from the Hinterland: Plurality and Identity in the National Liter-
    atures in English from Malaysia and Singapore." *World Literature Written in
    English* 28.1 (1988): 145–153.
Lim, Shirley. "Semiotics, Experience, and the Material Self: An Inquiry into the Subject
    of the Contemporary Asian Woman Writer." *Women's Studies* 18 (1990): 153–
    175.

Lin, Adet. Born on May 6, 1923, in Amoy, China, the eldest daughter of writer
Lin Yutang. The family moved to the United States when she was thirteen, and
she collaborated on a humorous book about her family with her sisters before
going to study at Columbia University. During the war years, she returned to
China, serving in a unit of the Chinese Medical Service from 1943 to 1946
while working for the Chinese Blood Bank. She then returned to the United
States and worked for the U.S. Information Service and the Voice of America
as well as publishing several books using the pseudonym Tan Yun. She died in
1971.

Works

Dawn over Chungking. New York: John Day, 1941.
Flame from the Rock. New York: John Day, 1943.
The Milky Way and Other Chinese Folk Tales. New York: Harcourt, Brace, 1961.
Our Family. With Anor Lin. New York: John Day, 1939.

Commentary

Ling, Amy. *Between Two Worlds: Women Writers of Chinese Ancestry.* New York: Pergamon, 1990.

Lin, Tai-yi. Born on April 1, 1926, in Beijing, the second daughter of the writer Lin Yutang. She attended Columbia University from 1946 to 1949, taught Chinese at Yale for a year, and married R. Ming Lai, moving with him to Hong Kong. She wrote for various magazines and edited the *Chinese Reader's Digest* in Hong Kong. By age twenty she had already written two novels and had, with her sister, translated *Girl Rebel*, the autobiography of Hsieh Ping-ying. She now lives in Washington, D.C.

Works

The Eavesdropper. Cleveland, OH: World, 1959.
The Golden Coin. New York: John Day, 1946.
Kampoon Street. Cleveland, OH: World, 1964.
The Lilacs Overgrown. Cleveland, OH: World, 1960.
War Tide. New York: John Day, 1943.

Commentary

Ling, Amy. *Between Two Worlds: Women Writers of Chinese Ancestry.* New York: Pergamon, 1990.

Ling, Ding. See **Ting Ling.**

Lionheart Gal: Life Stories of Jamaican Women by the Sistren Theatre Collective (London, England: Women's Press, 1986). A wonderful collection of stories from the women in the Sistren Collective, an artistic and educational group in Jamaica, who reminisce about their childhoods, their working lives, and their family relationships. They illustrate both the difficulty of their lives and their own creative responses to those challenges. The use of patois in their stories allows for their voices to shape and enrich our reading of their lives. The sensitive editorial decisions made by Honor Ford Smith, the compiler of the book, and the variety of experiences and voices make for a rich and multilayered ensemble of women's life stories.

Commentary

Carr, Robert. "Crossing the First World/Third World Divides: Testimonial, Transnational Feminisms, and the Postmodern Condition." *Scattered Hegemonies: Postmod-*

ernity and Transnational Feminist Practices. Minneapolis: University of Minnesota, 1994. 153–172.

Cooper, Carolyn. "Writing Oral History: Sistren Theatre Collective's *Lionheart Gal.*" *Kunapipi* 7.1 (1989): 49–57.

Davies, Carole Boyce. "Collaboration and the Ordering Imperative in Life Story Production." *De/Colonizing the Subject: The Politics of Gender in Women's Autobiography.* Minneapolis: University of Minnesota, 1992. 3–19.

Katrak, Ketu H. "Decolonizing Culture: Toward a Theory for Postcolonial Women's Texts." *Modern Fiction Studies* 35.1 (spring 1989): 157–179.

Lispector, Clarice. Born in 1925 of Ukrainian Jews who emigrated to Brazil when she was two months old. She lived in poverty in the northeastern capitals of Maceio and later Recife. Her mother died in 1934. Three years later, the family moved to Rio de Janeiro, and she began to think of herself as a writer. She published her first story while in secondary school, and it was impressive enough that she was accused of copying it out of a book. She attended law school in the 1940s and worked as an editor for a press agency and as a reporter for a Rio daily. In 1943 she married a fellow law student and finished her law degree the same year she published her first novel, *Near to the Wild Heart* (1944). For the next fifteen years she traveled with her husband, who had become a diplomat, living in Italy, Switzerland, England, and the United States. The marriage ended in 1959, and she returned to Rio with her two children. She published *Family Ties* a year later and then, in the following year, *The Apple in the Dark*, which established her as a writer of importance. She supported herself and her children with her writing and suffered from insomnia, financial difficulties, and her elder son's mental illness. She was diagnosed with cancer in 1976 and died a year later. She was recognized as a writer of significance within her lifetime, but because of the difficult nature of her work, it did not lend itself to the popular market. Her reputation gained new international attention when French critic Hélène Cixous wrote about her in the late 1970s.

Works

The Apple in the Dark. Translated by Gregory Rabassa. Austin: University of Texas, 1986.

An Apprenticeship, or the Book of Delights. Translated by Richard A. Mazzara and Lori A. Parris. Austin: University of Texas, 1986.

Discovering the World. Translated by Giovanni Pontiero. Manchester, England: Carcanet, 1992.

Family Ties. Translated by Giovanni Pontiero. Austin: University of Texas, 1972.

The Foreign Legion: Stories and Chronicles. Translated by Giovanni Pontiero. Manchester, England: Carcanet, 1986.

The Hour of the Star. Translated by Giovanni Pontiero. Manchester, England: Carcanet, 1986.

Near to the Wild Heart. Translated by Giovanni Pontiero. Manchester, England: Carcanet, 1990.

The Passion According to G. H. Translated by Ronald W. Sousa. Minneapolis: University of Minnesota, 1988.

Soulstorm. Translated by Alexis Levitin. New York: New Directions, 1989.

The Stream of Life. Translated by Elizabeth Lowe and Earl Fitz. Minneapolis: University of Minnesota, 1989.

Commentary

Brower, Keith H. "The Naratee in Clarice Lispector's *Agua Viva.*" *Romance Notes* 32.2 (winter 1991): 111–118.

Cixous, Hélène. "Reaching the Point of Wheat, or a Portrait of the Artist as a Maturing Woman." *New Literary History* 19 (1987): 1–21.

Cixous, Hélène. *Reading with Clarice Lispector.* Minneapolis: University of Minnesota, 1990.

Cixous, Hélène. *Readings: The Poetics of Blanchot, Joyce, Kafka, Kleist, Lispector, and Tsvetayeva.* Minneapolis: University of Minnesota, 1991.

Fitz, Earl E. *Clarice Lispector.* Boston, MA: Twayne, 1985.

Fitz, Earl E. "A Discourse of Silence: The Postmodernism of Clarice Lispector." *Contemporary Literature* 28.4 (1989): 421–436.

Lindstrom, Naomi. *Women's Voice in Latin America.* Washington, DC: Three Continents, 1989.

Lispector, Clarice. "Since One Feels Obliged to Write . . ." *Lives on the Line: The Testimony of Contemporary Latin American Authors.* Berkeley: University of California, 1988. 33–36.

Marting, Diane E., editor. *Clarice Lispector: A Bio-Bibliography.* Westport, CT: Greenwood, 1993.

Mathie, Barbara. "Feminism, Language or Existentialism: The Search for the Self in the Works of Clarice Lispector." *Subjectivity and Literature from the Romantics to the Present Day.* London, England: Pinter, 1991. 121–134.

Peixoto, Marta. *Passionate Fictions: Gender, Narrative, and Violence in Clarice Lispector.* Minneapolis: University of Minnesota, 1994.

Platt, Kamala. "Race and Gender Representations in Clarice Lispector's 'A menor mulher do mundo' and Carolina Maria de Jesús' 'Quarto de despejo.' " *Afro-Hispanic Review* 11.1–3 (1992): 51–57.

Pontiero, Giovanni. "Clarice Lispector: An Intuitive Approach to Fiction." *Knives and Angels: Women Writers in Latin America.* London, England: Zed, 1990. 74–85.

Literary Canon. Third world women writers have often been taught the British (or French) literary canon in school and in some cases have had it as their only literary model. Aminata Sow Fall, for example, studied French literature and only encountered African writers after the end of her formal schooling. In many instances, the educational establishment in third world countries has been more reluctant to let go of the traditional canon than have schools in the West. Some works by third world women have achieved canonical status; *Efuru* by Flora Nwapa is taught widely as a set text in African schools, for example. In the United States, there have been instances in which a reformulated canon has included third world women—as in Rigoberta Menchu's autobiography being included in Stanford's controversial reading list. However, there are ironies involved in the notion of canon for third world women writers. It is easy to add one or two titles to a "core" of literary works to somehow stand in for the third world, thus practicing a reductivist strategy toward the third world without challenging the notion of canon itself. It has even been argued convincingly by Gauri Viswanathan that the study of English literature as a field of scholarship (and, one might extend the notion, the idea of a canon of essential works) was invented for the colonies to support the imperialist mission. It can also be argued that feminist and postcolonial texts offer a challenge to the idea of a literary canon both by offering alternative texts and by prompting alternate readings to canonical works. Jean Rhys's *Wide Sargasso Sea* is an obvious challenge or rewriting of a canonical text, Brontë's *Jane Eyre*. However problematic the notion of a canon of worthy or seminal texts may be, many critics don't argue for the excision of heretofore canonical texts from the curriculum as much as to challenge their supremacy and to historicize and problematize the notion of canonicity itself. As Nadine Gordimer has pointed out, cultures have hybrid roots and continue to borrow from one another. "There is a commonwealth of literature and it belongs to all of us." (Boyers et al., 30).

Commentary

Boyers, Robert, et al. "A Conversation with Nadine Gordimer." *Salmagundi* 62 (winter 1984): 3–31.

Juneja, Renu. "Pedagogy of Difference: Using Post-Colonial Literature in the Undergraduate Curriculum." *College Teaching* 41.2 (spring 1993): 64–69.

Lawrence, Karen R. *Decolonizing Tradition: New Views of Twentieth-Century "British" Literary Canon*. Urbana: University of Illinois, 1992.

Owusu, Kofi. "Canons Under Siege: Blackness, Femaleness, and Ama Ata Aidoo's *Our Sister Killjoy*." *Callaloo* 13.2 (spring 1990): 341–363.

Sullivan, Constance A. "Re-Reading the Hispanic Literary Canon: The Question of Gender." *Ideologies and Literature* 16 (1983): 93–101.

Tawake, Sandra Kiser. "Multi-Ethnic Literature in the Classroom: Whose Standards?" *World Englishes* 10.3 (winter 1991): 335–340.

Viswanathan, Gauri. *Masks of Conquest: Literary Study and British Rule in India*. New York: Columbia University, 1989.

Little Things by Prajaub Thirabutana. (Sydney, Australia: Collins, 1971). Vignettes of village life in Thailand told in a straightforward, unadorned style by a woman who claims in the preface, "[M]y English is poor" (viii) but who nevertheless is able to convey much of the tenor of rural life, her early childhood games, her experiences going to school, her father's absence as he is driven to find work in the city, and finally her work as a teacher and her marriage to another teacher. The title is as deprecating as the narrative sometimes is, not claiming great significance for itself, yet documenting in some detail one woman's life and the life of her village.

The Lizard's Tail by Luisa Valenzuela (New York: Farrar, Straus, Giroux, 1983). Translation of *Cola de lagartija*. This fantastic tale of magic and power is a fictional biography based on the life of Peron's minister of social well-being. In this novel, the sorcerer is a man born with a third testicle that he believes to be Estrella, his sister. Together they conceive, so that he is in one act becoming a parent to himself. The novel has several narrators, sometimes the sorcerer, sometimes an omniscient, detached voice, sometimes Valenzuela herself who claims the story is being taken over by the sorcerer. This exploration of political power and of the writer's role in shaping the world—and of their responsibilities—makes for an intriguing, funny, disturbing book.

Commentary

Hicks, D. Emily. *Border Writing: The Multidimensional Text*. Minneapolis: University of Minnesota, 1991.

Magnarelli, Sharon. "*The Lizard's Tail*: Discourse Denatured." *Review of Contemporary Fiction* 6.3 (1986): 97–104.

Magnarelli, Sharon. "Framing Power in Luisa Valenzuela's *Cola de lagartija [The Lizard's Tail]* and Isabel Allende's *Casa de los espíritus [The House of the Spirits]*." *Splintering Darkness: Latin American Women Writers in Search of Themselves*. Pittsburgh, PA: Latin American Literary Review, 1990. 43–62.

Loggerhead by Gloria Escoffery (Kingston, Jamaica: Sandberry, 1988). Poems about nature, about the Caribbean, about being a poet and an artist. Escoffery uses painterly descriptions for concepts that are not notably visual in nature, as in "the caged, carmine bud of lust" (35). Dreams fly after knowledge like loggerhead birds snapping at insects in the air, waiting for just the right moment to strike. Escoffery writes in a style that is both traditional (even mimicking Shakespeare in "On Not Being Shakespeare") and very much her own.

Long Road to Nowhere by Amryl Johnson (London, England: Virago, 1988). A collection of poems that deal with experiences and encounters in Trinidad and in Britain. "A Far Cry" finds remnants of slavery embedded in the present; "The Wheel" evokes the days of the large sugar plantations through a huge rusting wheel overtaken by nature in a Trinidad field, lying in a rut where history itself flows. Several poems deal with carnival in Trinidad and one, "Granny," brings to life a character arguing with market stall owners in a vivid and sassy Creole voice. Johnson uses both Caribbean history and Creole in interesting and effective ways.

The Lord by Soraya Antonius (New York: Henry Holt, 1986). A historical novel that re-creates the tangled allegiances and emotions of both colonizers and the colonized in Palestine after World War I until the founding of the state of Israel. The narrator interviews an elderly British schoolteacher who taught and befriended Tareq, a child of ordinary gifts until, as an adult, he begins to work miracles. He travels around Palestine and Lebanon, crossing British and French borders, inciting rebellion through his conjuring tricks, which range from the regular fare of the conjurer to revealing the British governor naked to an Arab audience at the Government House Christmas party. He heals the broken ribs of a reporter, and in a reverse of the miracle at Cana, he changes his flask of spirits into mulberry juice. His miraculous powers are subtly presented in a narrative that is dense with detail that evokes the sounds and smells of the Levant, the story carried forward by a rich cast of characters who reveal the complexities and the sordid colonial desires that set the stage for later conflicts.

Lord, Bette Bao. Born in Shanghai in 1938, she moved to the United States at the age of eight. Her husband, Winston Lord, was named ambassador to China, where they stayed from 1985 through mid-April 1989, during which time she served as a consultant for CBS News during the Tiananmen Square pro-democracy demonstrations, leaving China just before their suppression. She has written a novel based on her younger sister's life in China, and a well-received book for children as well as her account of her stay in China and her encounters with relatives there.

Works

In The Year of the Boar and Jackie Robinson. New York: Harper and Row, 1984.
*Legacies: A Chinese Mosaic. New York: Knopf, 1990.
Spring Moon. New York: Harper and Row, 1981.

Commentary

Fox, Mary Virginia. *Bette Bao Lord: Novelist and Chinese Voice for Change.* Chicago, IL: Children's Press, 1993.

Love, Stars, and All That by Kirin Narayan (New York: Pocket Books, 1993). A charming love story wrapped inside a lampoon of academia. Gita, a young and innocent student from India, knows she can expect to meet her mate in March 1984 because of a horoscope her aunt had drawn up. She is mistaken about which one of the men she meets is her intended, however, and first falls for a pallid poet, then marries a renowned and ridiculous literary critic. The marriage fails and she takes up a job in New England, still looking for the right man. She contemplates an arranged marriage with another expatriate Indian but luckily recovers her wits and at last recognizes her good friend Firoze is her best choice. Scenes alternate between India and America, with the point of view often reflecting Gita's innocence in a way that particularly succeeds at making the world she has landed in strange. The pretensions, ambitions, languages, and obsessions of American academia are hilariously sent up all the while.

The Lover by Marguerite Duras (New York: Pantheon, 1985). An autobiographical work based on the author's childhood in Indochina, focusing on a love affair with a Chinese man and ambivalent relations with a dominating family. This book, a best-seller in France, raises questions about sexuality and power, exoticism and desire, gender and colonialism, conundrums embedded in a seemingly spare and simple story. Recently, a film version of the book was the subject of a dispute between Duras and its director, and she published a reworking of the story told in *The Lover*, covering the same scenes and same material but expanding on them. Traces of envisioning the work as film are in the *North China Lover* (New York: New Press, 1992), which ends with a series of ''insert shots'' or cinematic images that could be used to punctuate the story.

Commentary

Chester, Suzanne. ''Writing the Subject: Exoticism/Eroticism in Marguerite Duras's *The Lover* and *The Sea Wall*.'' *De/Colonizing the Subject: The Politics of Gender in Women's Autobiography*. Minneapolis: University of Minnesota, 1992. 436–457.

Haskell, Molly. '' 'You Saw Nothing in Indochina.' '' *Film Comment* 29.1 (January–February 1993): 31–33.

Ramsay, Raylene. ''Writing Power in Duras' *L'Amant de la Chine du nord*.'' *College Literature* 21.1 (February 1994): 46–61.

Lozano, Argentina Diaz. See **Diaz Lozano, Argentina.**

Luft, Lya Fett. Born in 1938 in the small town of Santa Cruz do Sul in the state of Rio Grande do Sul in the extreme south of Brazil, a community of German settlers, where she grew up speaking mainly German. Her father, a lawyer, had a large library, and as a child she was an avid reader. As she grew up she became aware for the first time that she was Brazilian and struggled to shape for herself a national identity, a process that has influenced her work. She began to write at age forty and has published several novels. Her works emphasize the difficulty of communicating, and the persistence of secrets among family members. She frequently uses a stream of consciousness technique that is similar to Virginia Woolf's, a writer whose works she has translated.

Works

The Island of the Dead. Translated by Carmen Chaves McClendon and Betty Jean Craig. Athens: University of Georgia, 1986.

The Red House. Translated by Giovanni Pontiero. Manchester, England: Carcanet, 1994.

Commentary

Payne, Judith A. ''Lya Luft: Fiction and the Possible Selves.'' *Brasil/Brazil: Revisita de Literatura Brasileira* 5.4 (1991): 104–114.

Quinlan, Susan Canty. *The Female Voice in Contemporary Brazilian Narrative*. New York: P. Lang, 1991.

Luisa in Realityland by Claribel Alegría (Willimantic, CT: Curbstone, 1987). This ''novel'' is half prose, half poetry, snippets of images and events from the life of Luisa, evoking both her traditional village life and modern political oppression. Virtually plotless and sewn together with recurrent images and characters, the novel uses many of the same metaphors as the author's *Flowers from the Volcano*—the population of the dead living side-by-side with the living, the volcanoes, the Mayan gods. The final piece, ''The Cartography of Memory,'' maps the tortured terrain of Central America, anticipating a return, a new growth of dormant seeds of independence and justice.

M

Macgoye, Marjorie Oludhe. Born in England in 1928, she moved to Kenya to work as a lay missionary in 1954. There she married a Kenyan national and settled permanently, working in the book trade. She has published a book for children, a collection of poetry, and two history books as well as novels.

Works

Coming to Birth. Nairobi: Heinemann Kenya, 1986.
The Present Moment. Nairobi: Heinemann Kenya, 1987.
Song of Nyarloka and Other Poems. Nairobi, Kenya: Oxford, 1977.

Commentary

Kibera, Valerie. ''Adopted Motherlands: The Novels of Marjorie Macgoye and Bessie Head.'' *Motherlands: Women's Writings from Africa, the Caribbean, and South Asia.* New Brunswick, NJ: Rutgers University, 1992. 310–329.

Magaia, Lina. Born in Maputo, Mozambique, she joined the Mozambican Liberation Front (FRELIMO) while she was still in school and was jailed for three months for political activities. She earned a B.Sc. in economics from the University of Lisbon before going to Tanzania for military training and becoming a member of the liberation army in 1975. She has written one book that is a documentary account of life in a southern Mozambican area dominated by the South African–supported Mozambique National Resistance Party (RENAMO).

Work

*Dumba Nengue: Run for your Life—Peasant Tales of Tragedy in Mozambique. Translated by Michael Wolfers. Trenton, NJ: Africa World Press, 1988.

Makdisi, Jean Said. Born in Egypt to a Palestinian family, she was educated in English and American schools. She married Samir Makdisi, a Lebanese academic, and they lived in America for many years before moving to Beirut in 1972, where her husband had accepted a teaching position at the American University. They remained in Beirut throughout the war years, which she wrote about eloquently and angrily in her memoir.

Work

Beirut Fragments: A War Memoir. New York: Persea, 1990.

Makhalisa, Barbara C. Born in Zimbabwe (then Rhodesia) in 1949. Her first novel, written in Ndebele in 1969, is *Qilindini*, composed when she was a student at Gweru Teacher's College, where she majored in English. She has written all her work in Ndebele, except for *The Underdog* and a collection of stories. She has worked as a teacher and in 1981 became an editor at Longman Zimbabwe. In the 1970s, she published two Ndebele novels and one play, winning awards for all three. She wrote another novel in Ndebele in 1983 and in 1984 published a collection of stories in English. Her work is both strongly moralistic and critical of the victimization of women.

Work

The Underdog and Other Stories. Gweru, Zimbabwe: Mambo, 1984.

Malé, Belkis Cuza. See **Cuza Malé, Belkis.**

Manley, Edna. Born in Cornwall in 1900, daughter of a Yorkshire clergyman and a Jamaican mother. She studied art in London before marrying her cousin, Norman Manley, a Jamaican who would later become instrumental in Jamaica's independence. She moved to Jamaica with him and their infant son Douglas in 1921, where Norman practiced law and she became involved in the arts. Norman, as head of the People's National Party, became the leader of the newly independent country, and their son Michael later entered politics and eventually became prime minister, having a stormy and innovative tenure. Edna Manley continued working as an artist, particularly in sculpture, and fostering the arts and political action. Her diary, a fascinating record of Jamaican politics and society, was published posthumously.

Work

The Diaries. London, England: André Deutsch, 1989.

Commentary

Springfield, Consuelo Lopez. "Edna Manley's *The Diaries*: Cultural Politics and the
Discourse of Self." *Explorations in Ethnic Studies* 15.1 (January 1992): 33–46.

Markandaya, Kamala. Born in 1924 into a Brahmin family in south India,
she was educated at Madras University—though her interest in travel and in
writing got in the way of her completing a history degree—and she began her
writing career as a journalist for *The Hindu*, a daily paper in Madras. She left
India for England when she married an Englishman in 1948, and she hasn't
returned since the 1960s; yet her work is well received in India and her novels
are on school reading lists. Her first novel, *Nectar in a Sieve*, is a portrayal of
the lives of poor Indian villagers, taking up themes that appear in many of her
novels of the strength of determined women and the clash between traditional
ways and the technological changes wrought by Western notions of modernization that have disastrous effects on the environment and reinforce class distinctions. Her work has received much critical attention both in India and abroad.

Works

*The Coffer Dams. New York: John Day, 1969.
The Golden Honeycomb. New York: Crowell, 1977.
A Handful of Rice. New York: John Day, 1966.
Nectar in a Sieve. New York: John Day, 1954.
*The Nowhere Man. London, England: Allen Lane, 1973.
Pleasure City. London, England: Chatto and Windus, 1982. Published in the United
States under the title *Shalimar*.
*Possession. New York: John Day, 1963.
A Silence of Desire. New York: John Day, 1960.
Some Inner Fury. New York: New American Library, 1956.
Two Virgins. New York: John Day, 1973.

Commentary

Afzal-Khan, Fawzia. *Cultural Imperialism and the Indo-English Novel: Genre and Ide-
ology in the Novels of R. K. Narayan, Anita Desai, Kamala Markandaya and
Salman Rushdie*. University Park: Pennsylvania State University, 1993.
Ahmad, Hena. "Kamala Markandaya and the Immigrant Experience in Britain." *Re-
worlding: The Literature of the Indian Diaspora*. Westport, CT: Greenwood,
1992. 141–148.
Barbato, Louis R. "The Arrow in the Circle: Time and Reconciliation of Cultures in
Kamala Markandaya's *Nectar in a Sieve*." *Ariel* 22.4 (October 1991): 7–15.
Chadha, Ramesh. *Cross-Cultural Interaction in Indian English Fiction: An Analysis of
the Novels of Ruth Jhabvala and Kamala Markandaya*. New Delhi, India: Na-
tional Book Organisation, 1988.
Drum, Alice. "Kamala Markandaya's Modern Quest Tale." *World Literature Written in
English* 22.2 (autumn 1983): 323–332.
Geetha, P. "Images and Archetypes in Kamala Markandaya's Novels: A Study in Cul-
tural Ambivalence." *Journal of Commonwealth Literature* 26.1 (1991): 169–178.

Gooneratne, Yasmine. " 'Traditional' Elements in the Fiction of Kamala Markandaya, R. K. Narayan, and Ruth Prawer Jhabvala." *World Literature Written in English* 15 (1976): 121–134.

Jha, Rekha. *The Novels of Kamala Markandaya and Ruth Jhabvala: A Study in East-West Encounter.* New Delhi, India: Prestige, 1990.

Joseph, Margaret P. *Kamala Markandaya.* New Delhi, India: Heinemann, 1980.

Kumar, Prem. "Conflict and Resolution in the Novels of Kamala Markandaya." *World Literature Today* 60.1 (winter 1986): 22–27.

Pathania, Usha. *Human Bonds and Bondages: The Fiction of Anita Desai and Kamala Markandaya.* Delhi, India: Kanishka, 1992.

Ross, Robert L., editor. *International Literature in English: Essays on the Major Writers.* New York: Garland, 1991.

Rustomji-Kerns, Roshni. "Expatriates, Immigrants, and Literature: Three South Asian Women Writers." *Massachusetts Review* 29.4 (1988): 655–665.

Sethuraman, Ramchandran. "Writing Across Cultures: Sexual/Racial 'Othering' in Kamala Markandaya's *Possession.*" *Ariel* 23.3 (July 1992): 101–120.

Wali, S. K. *Kamala Markandaya: Nectar in a Sieve, a Stylistic Study.* Jaipur, India: Printwell, 1987.

Market Street: A Chinese Woman in Harbin by Hsiao Hung (Seattle: University of Washington, 1986). This novel is a thinly fictionalized autobiography of a Chinese woman who lived in Harbin, Manchuria, from 1932 to 1934 in dire poverty, eking out a living with a man who made ends meet with tutoring and odd jobs. The couple are self-absorbed, and the only impression one gets of the city is very much through the narrator's limited viewpoint, but the writer's alienation fits in with the fractured and dysfunctional society she lives in. Harbin, dominated by disenfranchised white Russian émigrés and recently fallen under Japanese occupation, is a city in a state of collapse, a city as unsure of its place on the map as the narrator is of her place in society. The nonlinear, discontinuous style of the work is in keeping with its subject.

Commentary

Goldblatt, Howard. "Life as Art: Xiao Hong and Autobiography." *Woman and Literature in China.* Bochum, Germany: Studienverlag, 1985. 345–363.

Markham, Beryl. Born in England on October 26, 1902; when she was three years old, she and her mother joined her father in British East Africa, where he had emigrated to farm. Within eighteen months her parents separated, her mother returning to England with the eldest child, Richard, leaving Beryl with her father. She grew up at their farm at Njoro, where she became an expert rider. Her father taught her to read and later appointed a series of unwelcome governesses to see to her education. She was eventually sent to Nairobi to school but was expelled within three years for inciting fellow pupils to revolt. On her return to the farm, aged sixteen, she married a neighboring farmer twice her age. Her father went bankrupt and left the country; her marriage soon disintegrated and she took up horse training, a career in which she quickly made her mark: When she was only twenty-three years old a horse she trained won the prestigious Kenya St. Leger. After another brief marriage, she took up flying and in 1936 was the first woman to fly the Atlantic, the first of either sex to fly from England to North America. She lived in America for some time; after her third marriage failed, she returned to Africa and to horse training with notable success. She wrote stories for magazines and her autobiography, which was well received, reaching best-seller status, but it faded into obscurity until it was republished forty years later. At that point, her third husband, Raoul Schumacher, whom she had divorced in 1948, claimed he had written the book, an assertion she contested. She died on August 3, 1986. The controversy over authorship continues, rekindled in the most recent biography by Errol Trzebinski.

Works

The Splendid Outcast: Beryl Markham's African Stories. San Francisco: North Point, 1987.
West with the Night. Boston: Houghton Mifflin, 1942.

Commentary

Lovell, Mary S. *Straight on Till Morning: The Biography of Beryl Markham.* New York: St. Martin's, 1987.
Smith, Sidonie. "The Other Woman and the Radical Politics of Gender: Isak Dinesen and Beryl Markham." *De/Colonizing the Subject: The Politics of Gender in Women's Autobiography.* Minneapolis: University of Minnesota, 1992. 410–435.
Trzebinski, Errol. *The Lives of Beryl Markham.* New York: Norton, 1993.

Married to a Stranger by Nahid Rachlin (New York: Dutton, 1983). A novel about Iran just before the revolution and about the stifling atmosphere for women in prerevolutionary, industrialized Iran. It opens as Minou is preparing for her wedding. She is happy that her husband is a teacher she found attractive in high school and looks forward to having her own life ahead of her, to escaping her claustrophobic family home. However, living with her new husband in a town where options for her are limited, at a time when the modernization of the shah and the Westernizing influences on women are looked on with suspicion, Minou finds her choices circumscribed and the man she married a mystery. He is deeply involved in putting out a politically outspoken newspaper and, she finds out, involved with another woman. She tries to publish a journal for women's writing and is unable to find an audience and decides at last to leave her husband and try to make a new life in America. In prerevolutionary Iran, Minou does not have the support of an extended family of the traditional household, nor does she have the freedom a Western woman might have to work and circulate in society. The novel pairs political turmoil with the personal turmoil of a woman whose identity is defined by society in limited terms and whose society has merged with Western culture, gaining the worst of both worlds.

Marshall, Paule. Born in Brooklyn in 1929 to Barbadian parents who emigrated to New York after World War I. Though born in the United States, her family always considered it "this country" while "home" meant Barbados. Her first visit to the island was when she was nine years old. (Her mother was urged by her father to spend the money on buying a brownstone rather than on the trip home, but her mother's wish to go home prevailed.) She earned a B.A. at Brooklyn College, where she was elected to Phi Beta Kappa, and did graduate work at Hunter. After graduating from college, she worked at a magazine, *Our World*, which was in competition with *Ebony* at the time, and in the evenings, she worked on her first novel, *Brown Girl, Brownstones*. It came out in 1959 and, after being long out of print, was reissued by Feminist Press in 1983, selling well ever since. Her second novel, *The Chosen Place, the Timeless People* (1969), was one she worked on over a long period of time, doing much research on slavery, the sugar industry, and Caribbean history and society. Two other novels, *Praisesong for the Widow* and *Daughters*, continue her concern with weaving together the cultural strands of the African Diaspora. She was awarded a MacArthur Fellowship in 1992.

Works

Brown Girl, Brownstones. New York: Random House, 1959.
The Chosen Place, the Timeless People. New York: Harcourt, Brace and World, 1969.
Daughters. New York: Atheneum, 1991.
Praisesong for the Widow. New York: Dutton, 1984.
Reena and Other Stories. Old Westbury, NY: Feminist Press, 1983.
Soul Clap Hands and Sing. Washington, DC: Howard University Press, 1988.

Commentary

Brathwaite, Edward. "West Indian History and Society in the Art of Paule Marshall's Novel." *Journal of Black Studies* 1 (1970): 225–238.
Busia, Abena P. A. "Words Whispered over Voids: A Context for Black Women's Rebellious Voices in the Novel of the African Diaspora." *Black Feminist Criticism and Critical Theory*. Greenwood, FL: Penkevill, 1988. 1–41.
Busia, Abena P. A. "What Is Your Nation? Reconnecting Africa and Her Diaspora Through Paule Marshall's *Praisesong for the Widow.*" *Changing Our Own Words: Essays on Criticism, Theory, and Writing by Black Women*. New Brunswick, NJ: Rutgers University, 1989. 196–211.
Chamberlain, Mary, editor. *Writing Lives: Conversations Between Women Writers*. London, England: Virago, 1988.
Christian, Barbara. "Sculpture and Space: The Interdependency of Character and Culture in the Novels of Paule Marshall." *Black Women Novelists: The Development of a Tradition, 1892–1976*. Westport, CT: Greenwood, 1980. 80–136.
Christian, Barbara. "Ritualistic Process and the Structure of Paule Marshall's *Praisesong for the Widow.*" *Callaloo* 6.2 (1983): 31–45.
Dance, Daryl Cumber. "An Interview with Paule Marshall." *Southern Review* 28.1 (winter 1992): 1–20.
Davies, Carol Boyce. "Writing Home: Gender and Heritage in the Works of Afro/Car-

ibbean/American Women Writers." *Out of the Kumbla: Women and Literature in the Caribbean.* Trenton, NJ: Africa World Press, 1990. 59–73.

Denniston, Dorothy L. "Early Short Fiction by Paule Marshall." *Callaloo* 6.2 (1983): 31–45.

Eke, Ebele. "Beyond the Myth of Confrontation: A Comparative Study of African and African-American Female Protagonists." *Ariel* 17.4 (1986): 139–152.

Evans, Mari, editor. *Black Women Writers (1950–1980): A Critical Evaluation.* Garden City, NY: Anchor/Doubleday 1984.

Gikandi, Simon. "Modernism and the Masks of History: The Novels of Paule Marshall." *Writing in Limbo: Modernism and Caribbean Literature.* Ithaca, NY: Cornell University, 1992. 168–196.

Harris, Wilson. *The Womb of Space: The Cross-Cultural Imagination.* Westport, CT: Greenwood, 1983.

Jordan, Shirley M. "*Daughters*: The Unity That Binds Us." *American Visions* 6.5 (October 1991): 38–39.

Kapai, Leela. "Dominant Themes and Technique in Paule Marshall's Fiction." *CLA Journal* 16 (September 1972): 49–59.

Kulkarni, Harihar. "Paule Marshall: A Bibliography." *Callaloo* 16.1 (winter 1993): 243–267.

Marshall, Paule. "Shaping the World of My Art." *New Letters* 40 (1973): 97–112.

Miller, Adam David. "Women and Power: The Confounding of Gender, Race, and Class." *Black Scholar* 22.4 (fall 1992): 48–52.

Nazareth, Peter. "Paule Marshall's Timeless People." *New Letters* 40 (autumn 1973): 116–131.

Pettis, Joyce. "A Melus Interview: Paule Marshall." *Melus* 17.4 (winter 1991–1992): 117–129.

Pettis, Joyce. "'Talk' as Defensive Artifice: Merle Kinbona in *The Chosen Place, the Timeless People.*" *African American Review* 26.1 (spring 1992): 109–118.

Pettis, Joyce. "Legacies of Community and History in Paule Marshall's *Daughters.*" *Studies in the Literary Imagination* 26.2 (fall 1993): 89–99.

Pettis, Joyce. "Ritualistic Process and the Structure of Paule Marshall's *Praisesong for the Widow.*" *Studies in the Literary Imagination* 26.6 (fall 1993): 89–100.

Pollard, Velma. "Cultural Connections in Paule Marshall's *Praisesong for the Widow.*" *World Literature Written in English* 25.2 (1985): 285–298.

Rahming, Norman. "Towards a Caribbean Mythology: The Function of Africa in Paule Marshall's *The Chosen Place, the Timeless People.*" *Studies in the Literary Imagination* 26.2 (fall 1993): 77–88.

"Return of a Native Daughter: An Interview with Paule Marshall and Maryse Condé." *Sage* 3.2 (fall 1986): 52–53.

Sandiford, Keith A. "Paule Marshall's *Praisesong for the Widow*: The Reluctant Heiress, or, Whose Life Is It Anyway?" *Black American Literature Forum* 20.4 (winter 1986): 371–392.

Schneider, Deborah. "A Feminine Search for Selfhood: Paule Marshall's *Brown Girl, Brownstones.*" *The Afro-American Novel Since 1960.* Amsterdam, Netherlands: Gruner, 1982. 53–74.

Spillers, Hortense. "Chosen Place, Timeless People: Some Figurations on the New World." *Conjuring: Black Women, Fiction, and Literary Tradition.* Bloomington: Indiana University, 1985. 151–175.

Stoelting, Winifred L. "Time Past and Time Present: The Search for Viable Links in
    The Chosen Place, the Timeless People by Paule Marshall." *CLA Journal* 16
    (September 1972): 60–71.
Wilentz, Gay. *Binding Cultures: Black Women Writers in Africa and the Diaspora*. Bloo-
    mington: Indiana University, 1992.

Marson, Una. Jamaican poet, activist, and journalist, born in St. Elizabeth in
1905. She attended the Hampton School for girls but was forced to drop out
when her parents died. She began to work for *The Gleaner* in the 1920s. In
1928, she founded and edited *The Cosmopolitan*, a publication of the Jamaica
Stenographer's Association and the first women's publication of Jamaica. Her
first book of poetry came out in 1930, and in the same year, she was awarded
the Musgrave Medal of the Institute of Jamaica for her poetry. She moved to
England where, between 1932 and 1935, she worked as the secretary for the
League of Coloured People, after which she served as Haile Selassie's secretary
during his exile from Ethiopia. She wrote a play with Horace Vaz in 1932, *At
What Price*, which was said to be the first play written and performed by black
colonials in London. Returning to Jamaica in 1936, she worked as a social
worker and helped to found the progressive paper *Public Opinion* and the journal
Jamaica Standard. During World War II she worked for the British Broadcasting Corporation (BBC) World Service in England and, returning home after the
war, resumed her social work and journalistic activities. She published poetry
throughout the 1930s and 1940s that charts a growing sense of resistance to the
dominant representation of blackness, an increasing interest in using West Indian
language in her work, and a critique of the treatment of women. Her poetry is
characterized by its musical style and its use of Creole, which had a major
impact on the work of later women poets in Jamaica. She died in 1965.

Works

Heights and Depths. Kingston, Jamaica: Gleaner, 1931.
The Moth and the Star. Kingston, Jamaica: Gleaner, 1937.
Towards the Stars: Poems. Bickley, Kent: University of London, 1945.

Commentary

Smilowitz, Erika Sollish. " 'Weary of Life and All My Heart's Dull Pain': The Poetry
    of Una Marson." *Critical Issues in West Indian Literature*. Parkersburg, IA: Car-
    ibbean Books, 1984. 19–32.

Matto de Turner, Clorinda. Born in Peru in 1852, she married an English
businessman at the age of seventeen and moved from her hometown of Cuzco
to a small village in the Andes, Tinta, which became the setting for her most
famous novel, *Birds Without a Nest*, an *indigenista* saga of oppression and
endurance. She founded a weekly newspaper for women, *El Recreo*, in 1876
and in 1887 founded another publication, the weekly *El Peru Ilustrado*, in which
she continued her defense of Andean Indians. She also wrote essays, lectures,

a chronicle of the 1894 revolution in Peru, books on Indian legends and traditions, and other novels sympathetic to the Indian way of life. She died in Buenos Aires in 1909.

Work

Birds Without a Nest: A Story of Indian Life and Priestly Oppression in Peru. London, England: C. J. Thynne, 1904.

Commentary

Fox-Lockert, Lucía. *Women Novelists in Spain and Spanish America.* Metuchen, NJ: Scarecrow Press, 1979.

Miller, John C. "Clorinda Matto de Turner and Mercedes Cabello de Carbonera: Societal Criticism and Morality." *Latin American Women Writers: Yesterday and Today.* Pittsburgh, PA: Latin American Literary Review, 1977. 25–32.

Mean Woman by Alicia Borinsky (Lincoln: University of Nebraska, 1993). Translation of *Mina cruel*, first published in Spanish in 1989. A broken mirror image of Argentina's past, a fragmentary series of vignettes that link the disintegration of society to the representation and spectacle of womanhood. There is no story told, as such; rather, there are several fantastic stories that don't quite cohere, and all of them deal one way or another with the manipulation of spectacle, the strange power of simulation and theatricalization. Women take on their symbolic roles as a means to power: "In this world the bed is a passport to power. I am going to eat men with knife and fork, very slowly, licking my lips" (78)—yet power can be an illusion, too. Cristina, image of female power, is plotting her luxurious life in exile, but the Europe she retreats to is an underground simulation of Europe, built under the surface of Argentina, ultimately collapsing in upon the unsuspecting prisoners. People disappear, murders are committed for small slights, and witnesses turn away in a "shame of silence": "They lived like a Byzantine mosaic, each one trying to keep to its own color and occupation without knowing the pattern of the whole" (129). And interrogators lose track of the point of their questions and keep asking and recording the minutiae of their victims' lives: "What color suit was uncle Antonio wearing the day of your confirmation; why didn't your aunt Elena come to the party and who was the guy who gave you the receipt and bill for the sandwiches for the reception in the courtyard? How is it possible you don't remember? Communist son of a bitch" (127). The arbitrary cruelty and meaninglessness of the regime lend a curiously carnivalistic, feverishly funny air to the proceedings; there is no tragic dignity presented here, only farce with a mean streak.

Meatless Days by Sara Suleri (Chicago, IL: University of Chicago, 1989). A series of interlocking meditations on being between cultures, about family, about the languages, customs, and habits that pattern our lives. Suleri chooses a focus for each piece—food, friends, family members, daylight savings time—and family history begins to grow around the focus like barnacles. Her father, a Pakistani nationalist, journalist, and sometime political prisoner, has a habit when elderly of writing absentmindedly on the air with one finger; her Welsh mother is accidentally knocked down and killed by a rickshaw driver, whom her university students nearly kill in their rage; her sister is murdered, apparently for political reasons, though guilt is never established. And the author, writing in America, speaks of London with as much familiarity as Lahore, with the legacy of a mother who "could not do without Jane Austen." She is at home in several cultures but not firmly grounded in any one place. An elegant, lyrical, witty, and unsentimental family history.

Commentary

Warley, Linda. "Assembling Ingredients: Subjectivity in *Meatless Days*." *A/B: Auto/ Biography Studies* 7.1 (spring 1991): 107–123.

Mehta, Gita. Born in Delhi into a wealthy family. She was educated at the University of Bombay and at Cambridge and has lived in London, New York, and India with her husband and son. She has worked on films for television and has written commentary on popular culture and the representation of India as well as fiction.

Works

Karma Cola: Marketing the Mystic East. New York: Simon and Schuster, 1979.
Raj: A Novel. New York: Simon and Schuster, 1989.
*A River Sutra. New York: Doubleday, 1993.

Meireles, Cecilia. Born in Rio de Janeiro in 1901, she was raised by her grandmother after her parents' death. She was a poet that while not allied with any particular literary movement was often associated with Catholic poets and spiritualists. Her recurrent theme is mutability and mortality, though her work is not morbid; rather, her interest is in the transcendence of the spirit over being and mortality. She also was an expert on Brazilian folklore, particularly on Afro-Brazilian traditions. She died in 1964.

Works

Batuque, Samba, and Macumba: Drawings of Gestures and Rhythm, 1926–1934. Rio de Janeiro, Brazil: Funarte, 1983.
Poems in Translation. Washington, DC: Brazilian-American Cultura, 1977.

Commentary

Jentsch-Grooms, Lynda. *Exile and the Process of Individuation: A Jungian Analysis of Marine Symbolism in the Poetry of Rafael Alberti, Pablo Neruda, and C. Meireles.* Valencia, Spain: Albatross, 1986.
Sadlier, Darlene J. *Imagery and Theme in the Poetry of Cecilia Meireles: A Study of Mar absoluto.* Madrid, Spain: J. Porrua Turanzas, 1989.

Menchu, Rigoberta. Born in Chimel, San Miguel de Uspantan, in rural Guatemala on January 9, 1959, Menchu became an outspoken and determined political organizer for her people, the Quiché peasants. Members of her family were affected by the brutal conditions under which they lived; several brothers and sisters died of malnutrition, and her parents and a brother were killed in the political struggle for Indian rights. Though without formal schooling, she learned Spanish in order to effect change and devoted herself to political activism. Her autobiography/*testimonio I, Rigoberta Menchu* details both her life as an activist and the life of her people. She was awarded the Nobel Peace Prize in 1992.

Work

*I, Rigoberta Menchu: An Indian Woman in Guatemala. Translated by Ann Wright. London, England: Verso, 1984.

Commentary

''The Quincentenary, a Question of Class, Not Race: An Interview with Rigoberta Menchu.'' *Latin American Perspectives* 19.3 (summer 1992): 96–100.
McConahay, Mary Jo. ''Rigoberta Menchu'' [interview]. *Progressive* 57.1 (January 1993): 28–31.
Sommer, Doris. ''Not Just a Personal Story: Women's *Testimonios* and the Plural Self.'' *Life/Lines: Theorizing Women's Autobiography.* Ithaca, NY: Cornell University, 1988. 107–130.
Sommer, Doris. ''No Secrets: Rigoberta's Guarded Truth.'' *Women's Studies* 20 (1991): 51–72.

Mhlophe, Gcina. Actor, dramatist, storyteller, and poet. Born in Durban, South Africa, in 1959, the youngest of a large family, she began writing stories and poems in Xhosa when in school, only later in English after moving to Johannesburg. She worked for a time as a journalist in print and on radio. She is an actress, frequently performing with the Market Theatre in Johannesburg (where she was resident director in 1989–1990) as well as at the Edinburgh Festival and on tour in the United States and Europe. She won an award in England for her performance in her own play, *Have You Seen Zandile?* She is a feminist who fuses elements of African women's performance traditions with Western forms of theater.

Works

*Have You Seen Zandile? Portsmouth, NH: Heinemann, 1990.
Queen of the Tortoises. Braamfontein, South Africa: Skotaville, 1990.

Mi Mi Khaing. Born in 1916 in Burma, now Myanmar. She is an academic and a social scientist who has described the lives of Burmese women in two works. She is also the author of a cookbook on Burmese cuisine.

Works

*Burmese Family. London, England: Longmans, Green, 1946.
The World of Burmese Women. London, England: Zed, 1984.

Millin, Sarah Gertrude. Born in 1888 in Lithuania to a Russian Jewish family; she was taken to South Africa in infancy. Her childhood was spent in the diamond mining region of the Vaal River, near Kimberley. She married and moved to Johannesburg, where began her career as a prolific writer, publishing some thirty novels in her lifetime as well as biographies of Cecil Rhodes and General Smuts, autobiographical works, and newspaper articles. Her books were popular abroad as well as at home; *God's Stepchildren* was a best-seller in the United States. She wrote in a realist style that served to embroider and justify the white supremacist politics that she supported and that dominated her period of history. South African colonialist history, the dangers of miscegenation, and racial decay are common themes in her work, and she employed sociological and social-Darwinist theories to drive her overheated plots. She died in 1968.

Works

Adam's Rest. New York: H. Liveright, 1930.
An Artist in the Family. New York: Boni and Liveright, 1928.
The Burning Man. New York: Putnam, 1952.
The Coming of the Lord. New York: H. Liveright, 1928.
The Dark Gods. New York: Harper, 1941.
The Dark River. London, England: Collins, 1919.
The Fiddler. New York: H. Liveright, 1929.
Fire Out of Heaven. London, England: Faber and Faber, 1947.
God's Stepchildren. New York: Boni and Liveright, 1924.
Goodbye, Dear England. London, England: Heinemann, 1965.
The Herr Witchdoctor. London, England: Heinemann, 1941.
The Jordans. New York: Boni and Liveright, 1923.
King of the Bastards. New York: Harper, 1949.
Mary Glenn. Chicago, IL: Academy Chicago, 1982.
The Measure of My Days. New York: Abeland-Schuman, 1955.
Men on a Voyage. London, England: Constable, 1930.
Middle-Class. London, England: W. Collins, 1921.
The Night Is Long. London, England: Faber and Faber, 1941.
The Pit of the Abyss. London, England: Faber and Faber, 1946.
The Reeling Earth. London, England: Faber and Faber, 1945.
The Seven Thunders. London, England: Faber and Faber, 1948.
The Sons of Mrs. Aab. New York: H. Liveright, 1931.
The Sound of the Trumpet. London, England: Faber and Faber, 1947.
Three Men Die: A Novel. New York: Harper, 1934.
Two Bucks Without Hair and Other Stories. London, England: Faber and Faber, 1957.
What Hath a Man? New York: Harper, 1938.
The Wizard Bird. Johannesburg, South Africa: Central News Agency, 1962.
World Blackout. London, England: Faber and Faber, 1944.

Commentary

Coetzee, J. M. "Blood, Taint, Flaw, Degeneration: The Novels of Sarah Gertrude Millin." *White Writing: On the Culture of Letters in South Africa*. New Haven, CT: Yale University, 1988. 136–162.

De Reuck, J. A. "Humour and Betrayal: Reading the 'Alita' Short Stories of Sarah Gertrude Millin." *English Studies in Africa* 30.2 (1987): 83–90.

Levy, Fanelle, compiler. *The Works of Sarah Gertrude Millin 1952–1968; a Bibliography*. Johannesburg, South Africa: University of Witwatersrand, 1969.

Rubin, Martin. *Sarah Gertrude Millin: A South African Life*. Johannesburg, South Africa: Ad. Donker, 1977.

Minh-ha, Trinh T. See **Trinh T. Minh-ha.**

Mistral, Gabriela. Born Lucila Godoy Alcayaga, in a small town in Chile in 1889, where she grew up among Indian peasants whose culture she continued to admire and draw on through her life. She was an elementary school teacher, and her interest in children and childhood is a common theme in her poetry. She launched her career as a poet in 1914 when, at a tournament in Santiago, she was awarded first prize for her poem "Sonnets of Death." She was a highly acclaimed poet both at home and internationally, and in 1945, she became the first Latin American writer to receive the Nobel Prize for literature. She was active in civic life, being influential in educational reform, serving as Chile's representative to the Institute for Intellectual Cooperation of the League of Nations and working as a Chilean consul in Naples, Madrid, Lisbon, Nice, Rio de Janeiro, and Los Angeles. She also taught in the United States as a visiting professor for several years. She died on January 10, 1957, in New York.

Works

Crickets and Frogs. Translated and adapted by Doris Dana; illustrated by A. Frasconi. New York: Atheneum, 1972.

The Elephant and His Secret: Based on a Fable by Gabriela Mistral. Translated and adapted by Doris Dana. New York: Atheneum, 1974.

A Gabriela Mistral Reader. Translated by Maria Giachetti. Fredonia, NY: White Pine, 1993.

Selected Poems of Gabriela Mistral. Translated by Doris Dana. Bloomington: Indiana University Press, 1957.

Commentary

Alegría, Fernando. "Notes Toward a Definition of Gabriela Mistral's Ideology." *Women in Hispanic Literature: Icons and Fallen Idols*. Berkeley: University of California, 1983. 215–226.

Caimano, Rose Aquin. *Mysticism in Gabriela Mistral*. New York: Pageant, 1969.

Gazarian-Gautier, Marie-Lise. *Gabriela Mistral, the Teacher from the Valley of Elqui*. Chicago, IL: Franciscan Herald, 1975.

Horan, Elizabeth. *Gabriela Mistral: An Artist and Her People*. Washington, DC: Organization of American States, 1994.

Taylor, Martin C. *Gabriela Mistral's Religious Sensibility*. Berkeley: University of California, 1968.

Vazquez, Margot Arce de. *Gabriela Mistral: The Poet and Her Work*. New York: New York University, 1964.

Virgillo, Carmelo. "Woman as Metaphorical System: An Analysis of Gabriela Mistral's Poem, 'Fruta.' " *Woman as Myth and Metaphor in Latin American Literature*. Columbia: University of Missouri, 1985. 137–150.

Modern Secrets by Shirley Lim (Sydney, Australia: Dangaroo, 1989). Poetry that explores the pain of exile and the mixed feelings of crossing cultures. "I have been faithful to you, my language" the poet says of English in the poem "Lament," even though it is not her native tongue (30). In the title poem, she plays with the ability to communicate across cultures, in various languages. Over an American breakfast, she describes a dream she had in Chinese to a friend in English, who answers in monosyllables, and all of these communications are understandable.

Molloy, Sylvia. Born and raised in Buenos Aires, Argentina, her mother was from a French family and her father was British. Spanish was spoken at home, but she attended a British school and spoke English with her father. She left for France at age twenty, where she studied for four years and where she met Alejandra Pizarnik. On her return to Argentina, she taught at the Alliance Française and began to write for *Sur*. In 1967 she returned to Paris with a scholarship to finish her dissertation, and passing through the United States on the way home, she decided to stay. She has taught at both Princeton and Yale University. She is the author of many works of criticism and has written short stories and a novel.

Work

Certificate of Absence. Translated by Daniel Balderston with the author. Austin: University of Texas, 1989.

Commentary

Kaminsky, Amy K. *Reading the Body Politic: Feminist Criticism and Latin American Women Writers*. Minneapolis: University of Minnesota, 1993.

Masiello, Francine. "Subversions of Authority: Feminist Literary Culture in the River Plate Region." *Chasqui: Revista de Literatura Latinoamericana* 21.1 (May 1992): 39–48.

Pinto, Magdalena Garcia. *Women Writers of Latin America: Intimate Histories*. Austin: University of Texas, 1991.

Mordecai, Pamela. Born in Jamaica in 1943, she was educated at the University of the West Indies and in the United States. She taught English in schools and at Mico Teachers' College, has worked as a journalist and radio and television broadcaster, and is publications officer of the University of the West

Indies School of Education, editing the *Caribbean Journal of Education*. She was an editor of the well-received anthology *Her True-True Name* and has published poetry.

Work

Journey Poem. Kingston, Jamaica: Sandberry, 1989.

Morejón, Nancy. Born in 1944 in Havana, Cuba. She had an early interest in writing, fostered by a teacher who read parts of her diary and found poetry in them. She studied French language and literature at Havana University. She is the author of many volumes of poetry, which have been translated into a number of languages, and works of criticism, as well as translations for a government publishing house. She is the director of the Centro de Estudios del Caribe de las Américas/Casa de las Américas in Havana.

Works

Grenada Notebook (Cuaderno de Grenada). Translated by Lisa Davis. New York: Circulo de Cultura Cubana, 1984.
Ours Is the Earth. Translated by J. R. Pereira. Mona, Jamaica: University of the West Indies, 1990.
Where the Island Sleeps Like a Wing: Selected Poetry. Translated by Kathleen Weaver. San Francisco: Black Scholar, 1985.

Commentary

Captain-Hidalgo, Yvonne. "The Poetics of the Quotidian in the Works of Nancy Morejón." *Callaloo* 10 (1987): 596–604.
Fido, Elaine Savory. "A Womanist Vision of the Caribbean: An Interview [with Nancy Morejón]." *Out of the Kumbla: Women and Literature in the Caribbean*. Trenton, NJ: Africa World Press, 1990. 265–269.

Mother and Daughter: Memoirs and Poems by Adelaide and Gladys Casely-Hayford (Freetown: Sierra Leone University, 1983). Includes the memoirs of Adelaide Casely-Hayford, written some time after her retirement in the 1940s, and a sketch of her daughter, Gladys, in which her ambivalence toward her shows through with statements such as "she had no sense of values and never could discriminate in any way, either with human beings or commodities. Then, too, she utterly lacked determination and perseverance" (68). She ends expressing her surprise at how deeply the affections of the community were expressed at Gladys's funeral. The second half of the book contains Gladys's poems, some in Krio. She expresses ambivalent feelings for her mother in the poem "Twenty-one" in which she is interrupted in her search for identity by her mother's apparent disapproval: "[T]he truth of my mother's eyes renders me humble" (90).

Motherhood. Mothers, daughters, and motherhood are thematically central to many works of literature by third world women, and—it has been argued by Carole Boyce Davies and others—these themes are treated differently by women than by men, women dealing with motherhood as a complex and multilayered part of women's experience, rather than as a simplified mythic or nationalistic symbol of origin. Infertility, and its social implications, is an issue in a great many novels, ranging from Flora Nwapa's seminal *Efuru* and Buchi Emecheta's ironically titled *The Joys of Motherhood* to Andrée Chedid's *From Sleep Unbound*. Conflicts between mothers and daughters form the focus of many works. Meena Alexander's poetry sequence *Night-Scene, the Garden* draws its drama from the pull and separation between a mother and her child, a conflict explored by T'ao Yang, Marie Cardinal, Marguerite Duras, Cristina Garcia, and others. Perhaps the most painful mother-daughter relationship is found in novels by Jamaica Kincaid, in which a girl is torn between clinging to her mother and resenting the way she pushes her into adulthood, setting up resentment so deep that once she is grown and living on her own, she refuses to open letters from her mother. In *Annie John* and *Lucy* the mother is endowed with a kind of colonizing power that the daughter must both love and resist to have an identity of her own. In other works, motherhood is a source of almost superhuman strength. The mother in Chedid's *The Sixth Day* endures and sacrifices for her son's sake; Nellie Campobello remembers her mother in a lyrical and tender memoir, *My Mother's Hands*.

Matriarchal ancestry can also be a site of connectedness and power. In Paule Marshall's *Praisesong for the Widow*, Avatara connects to her past through the knowledge passed on to her through her grandmother. The women of Isabel Allende's *House of the Spirits* bear a community and a tradition that is unavailable to the men in the novel. These women become storytellers to their daughters and granddaughters and, as bearers of tradition, transmit culture through generations, making literature itself a form of motherhood, of giving birth to and sustaining language and history.

Works

*Alexander, Meena. *Night-Scene, the Garden*. New York: Red Dust, 1992.

*Allende, Isabel. *The House of the Spirits*. Translated by Magda Bogin. New York: Knopf, 1985.

*Campobello, Nellie. *Cartucho; and, My Mother's Hands*. Translated by Doris Meyer and Irene Matthews. Austin: University of Texas, 1988.

*Cardinal, Marie. *The Words to Say It*. Translated by Pat Goodheart. Cambridge, MA: Van Vector and Goodheart, 1983.

*Chedid, Andrée. *From Sleep Unbound*. Translated by Sharon Spencer. Athens, OH: Swallow, 1983.

*Chedid, Andrée. *The Sixth Day*. Translated by Isobel Strachey. London, England: Serpent's Tail, 1987.

*Duras, Marguerite. *The Lover*. Translated by Barbara Bray. New York: Pantheon, 1985.

*Emecheta, Buchi. *The Joys of Motherhood*. New York: G. Braziller, 1979.

*Garcia, Cristina. *Dreaming in Cuban.* New York: Knopf, 1992.
*Kincaid, Jamaica. *Annie John.* New York: Farrar, Straus, Giroux, 1985.
Kincaid, Jamaica. *Lucy.* New York: Farrar, Straus, Giroux, 1990.
*Marshall, Paule. *Praisesong for the Widow.* New York: Dutton, 1984.
*Nwapa, Flora. *Efuru.* London, England: Heinemann Educational, 1970.
*T'ao Yang. *Borrowed Tongue.* Hong Kong: Renditions, 1986.

Commentary

Andrade, Susan Z. "Rewriting History, Motherhood, and Rebellion: Naming an African
    Woman's Literary Tradition." *Research in African Literatures* 21.1 (spring
    1990): 91–111.
Andrist, Debra D. "Non-traditional Concepts of Motherhood: Hispanic Women Poets of
    the Twentieth Century." *Letras Femeninas* 25.1–2 (1989): 100–104.
Cummings, Kate. "Reclaiming the Mother('s) Tongue: *Beloved, Ceremony, Mothers and
    Shadows.*" *College English* 52.5 (September 1990): 552–569.
Davies, Carole Boyce. "Motherhood in the Works of Male and Female Igbo Writers:
    Achebe, Emecheta, Nwapa and Nzekwu." *Ngambika: Studies of Women in Af-
    rican Literature.* Trenton, NJ: Africa World Press, 1986. 241–256.
Dukats, Mara L. "A Narrative of Violated Maternity: *Moi, Tituba, sorcière . . . noire de
    Salem.*" *World Literature Today* 67.4 (autumn 1993): 745–750.
Lewis, Desiree. "Myths of Motherhood and Power: The Construction of 'Black Women'
    in Literature." *English in Africa* 19.1 (May 1992): 35–51.
Motherlands: Women's Writings from Africa, the Caribbean, and South Asia. New
    Brunswick, NJ: Rutgers University, 1992.
Ngcobo, Lauretta. "African Motherhood—Myth and Reality." *Criticism and Ideology:
    Second African Writers Conference, Stockholm 1986.* Uppsala, Sweden: Scandi-
    navian Institute of African Studies, 1988. 141–154.
Stratton, Florence. "The Shallow Grave: Archetypes of Female Experience in African
    Fiction." *Research in African Literatures* 19.2 (1988): 143–169.
Ward, Cynthia. "What They Told Buchi Emecheta: Oral Subjectivity and the Joys of
    'Otherhood.' " *PMLA* 105.1 (January 1990): 83–97.

Mothers and Shadows by Marta Traba (New York: Readers International,
1989). Translation of *Conversación al sur.* An engrossing and deeply disturbing
novel about life under siege. Two women of different generations, with different
experiences and sets of values, come together to deal with the disappearance of
loved ones, caught up in violent repression in Latin America's southern cone.
Set in Montevideo, and depicting Uruguay's agony during a violent military
dictatorship, it also has scenes set in the Plaza de Mayo in Argentina. The
women's experiences and memories amount to a human approach to the inhu-
man madness of political violence.

Commentary

Cummings, Kate. "Reclaiming the Mother('s) Tongue: *Beloved, Ceremony, Mothers and
    Shadows.*" *College English* 52.5 (September 1990): 552–569.

Mugo, Micere Githae. Born in 1942 in Baricho, Kirinyaga District, Kenya, one of ten children. Her parents were both teachers, active in the struggle for Kenyan independence and both determined that all of their children get an education, regardless of their gender. She had a relatively privileged childhood, acting in school plays at the Kangaru Girls' School and studying drama under Rebecca Njau at the Alliance Girls' High School. She also attended Limuru Girls' School, the first black student to be admitted into an all-white high school in Kenyan colonial history, where she was ostracized by the other students. She retreated into books, discovering African and African-American literature, and gained strength and pride in her Africanness. She earned a B.A. (honors) in literature and philosophy from Makerere University in 1966, where she won an award for best actress at the Uganda Drama Festival held at the university. She earned a postgraduate degree in education from the University of Nairobi, after which she worked as headmistress of a girls' school. She then earned a master's and Ph.D. in literature from the University of New Brunswick, Canada. She worked as senior lecturer in the department of English at the University of Nairobi and served as dean of the Faculty of Arts before being expelled from Kenya in 1982 for her political views and Marxist philosophy. She taught literature at the University of St. Lawrence (United States) for two years, then at the University of Zimbabwe, where she currently teaches. She is the author of several works of criticism, poetry, and plays, including one written with Ngugi wa Thiong'o. She views writing as a political act: "My call to African women writers is to find ways and means of reaching the majority of our people, who are women, to speak for them" (James, 98).

Works

Daughter of My People, Sing! Nairobi, Kenya: East African Literature Bureau, 1976.
The Long Illness of Ex-Chief Kiti. Nairobi, Kenya: East African Literature Bureau, 1976.
The Trial of Dedan Kimathi. With Ngugi wa Thiong'o. Nairobi, Kenya: Heinemann, 1976.

Commentary

James, Adeola, editor. *In Their Own Voices: African Women Writers Talk.* London, England: James Currey, 1990.
Wilkinson, Jane, editor. *Talking with African Writers: Interviews with African Poets, Playwrights, and Novelists.* London, England: James Currey, 1991.

Mukherjee, Bharati. Born on July 27, 1940, in Calcutta, India, into an upper-middle-class Brahmin family, the second of three girls. She attended schools in Switzerland and England when her father took the family abroad and then, on their return to Calcutta, attended the prestigious Loreto Convent Girls' High School and graduated with honors from Calcutta University in 1959, with a degree in English. She earned an M.A. from Baroda University in 1961 and then went to the United States for postgraduate work. She joined the Writers' Workshop at the University of Iowa, where she met and married Clark Blaise in September 1963. Finishing a master's, then a doctorate at Iowa, she taught briefly in Wisconsin and then accepted a teaching position at McGill University in Montreal. She and her writer husband scrambled to make ends meet and to find time to write. She also found Canada a discouraging place for a South Asian to live, experiencing racism and intolerance. They moved to the United States in 1978, and she has taught at several colleges and universities since. She has written short stories and novels, and she has collaborated with her husband on books about a return visit to India and the Air India bombing of 1985. She has received a number of awards as a writer and has received a Guggenheim Foundation grant. She is now an American citizen and sees rewriting America as her task. "In the Moghul miniature of my life, there would be women investigating their bodies with mirrors, but they would be doing it on a distant balcony under fans wielded by bored serving girls; there would be a small girl listening to a bent old woman; there would be a white man eating popcorn and watching a baseball game; there would be cocktail parties and cornfields and a village set among rice paddies and skyscrapers. . . . I will be writing, in the Moghul style, till I get it right" ("A Four-Hundred-Year-Old Woman," 28.)

Works

Darkness. New York: Penguin, 1985.
*Days and Nights in Calcutta. With Clark Blaise. New York: Doubleday, 1977.
*The Holder of the World. New York: Knopf, 1993.
*Jasmine. New York: Grove Weidenfeld, 1989.
The Middleman and Other Stories. New York: Grove, 1988.
The Tiger's Daughter. Markham, Ontario: Penguin Books Canada, 1982.
*Wife. Boston, MA: Houghton Mifflin, 1975.

Commentary

Carb, Alison B. "An Interview with Bharati Mukherjee." *Massachusetts Review* 28 (winter 1988): 645–654.
Chua, C. L. "Passages from India: Migrating to America in the Fiction of V. S. Naipaul and Bharati Mukherjee." *Reworlding: The Literature of the Indian Diaspora.* Westport, CT: Greenwood, 1992. 51–61.
Hancock, Geoff. "An Interview with Bharati Mukherjee." *Canadian Fiction Magazine* 59 (1987): 30–44.
"An Interview with Bharati Mukherjee." *Iowa Review* 20.3 (1990): 7–32.
Mukherjee, Bharati. "Mimicry and Reinvention." *The Commonwealth in Canada: Proceedings of the Second Triennial Conference of CACLALS, University of Winnipeg, 1-4 October, 1981.* Calcutta, India: Writers' Workshop, 1983. 147–157.
Mukherjee, Bharati. "A Four-Hundred-Year-Old Woman." *Critical Fictions: The Politics of Imaginative Writing.* Seattle, WA: Bay Press, 1991. 24–28.
Nelson, Cecil L. "New Englishes, New Discourses: New Speech Acts." *World Englishes* 10.3 (1991): 317–323.
Nelson, Emmanuel S., editor. *Bharati Mukherjee: Critical Perspectives.* New York: Garland, 1993.

Ross, Robert L., editor. *International Literature in English: Essays on the Major Writers.* New York: Garland, 1991.

Rustomji-Kerns, Roshni. "Expatriates, Immigrants, and Literature: Three South Asian Women Writers." *Massachusetts Review* 29.4 (1988): 655–665.

Sant-Wade, Arvindra, and Karen Marguerite Radell. "Refashioning the Self: Immigrant Women in Bharati Mukherjee's New World." *Studies in Short Fiction* 24.1 (winter 1992): 11–17.

Sicherman, Carol. " 'Transport Me . . . into the Hearts of Men': Bharati Mukherjee's *Darkness*." *Kunapipi* 14.3 (1992): 83–98.

Mulberry and Peach: Two Women of China by Nieh Hua-ling (London, England: Women's Press, 1986). A woman leaves her own identity—"Mulberry"—behind in order to cope with her shattered past and chaotic life on the run from the U.S. Immigration Service. The novel consists of a series of letters posted to an immigration official by "Peach" who is traveling America, evading capture. With her letters she includes portions of Mulberry's diary beginning with entries from 1945, through her stay in besieged Beijing, to a period of hiding in Taiwan, and finally to her arrival in the United States and her flight from the authorities. The narrative posted by a dislocated, free-floating Peach, who defies both government and social convention, contrasts with the narrative of her earlier self as it disintegrates into insanity. A powerful and inventive work that questions the construction of identity and views both China and America from an unusual vantage point. It was first published in China in 1976 and has been translated into several languages.

Muñiz-Huberman, Angelina. Born in France in 1937 where her Jewish Spanish parents had taken refuge during the civil war. They moved from there to Cuba, where they lived briefly, and then to Mexico City, where she has lived ever since. She writes regularly for the Mexican periodicals *Vuilta* and *Uno mas uno* and is a professor of Spanish and comparative literature at the National Autonomous University of Mexico. She has published novels, poetry, and stories; one collection has been translated into English. Her themes are influenced by Renaissance Spanish literature and often modern issues are transformed into medieval scenes—the Spanish Civil War being fought by knights; unicorns and minstrels appearing in magic realist settings. Her work is also influenced by her status as an exile, and though she has lived in Mexico most of her life, she is still very much between cultures. Her fiction shows a sense of displacement both in time and space.

Work

Enclosed Garden. Translated by Lois Parkinson Zamora. Pittsburgh, PA: Latin American Literary Review, 1988.

Commentary

Menton, Seymour. *Latin America's New Historical Novel.* Austin: University of Texas, 1993.

Muriel at Metropolitan by Miriam Tlali (Harlow, England: Longman, 1987). This book was banned immediately in South Africa and not published there until six years after its writing. It is only barely fictional, paralleling to a large extent the author's own experiences, and tells of a black accountant and her job at Metropolitan, an electric appliance and furniture store. The apartheid system is clearly depicted, demonstrating the ambivalent and frustrating feelings it causes in a small community. Muriel copes admirably within the system but ultimately chooses to leave her job, unwilling to continue to be part of the "web that has been woven to entangle a people whom I love and am part of" (190). The novel portrays the quotidian stresses of living under apartheid and portrays them with understated power.

Commentary

Ibrahim, Huma. "The Autobiographical Content in the Works of South African Women Writers: The Personal and the Political." *Biography East and West: Selected Conference Papers*. Honolulu: University of Hawaii, 1989. 122–126.

Mvungi, Martha. Born in Kidugala, Njombe, southern Tanzania. She was educated at the University of Edinburgh and the University of Dar es Salaam. After a career teaching at several levels, she joined the Department of Education at the University of Dar es Salaam. She is the author of a collection of traditional stories based on those she learned as a child growing up among the Bena and Hene peoples and has also published a novel in Swahili.

Work

*Three Solid Stones. London, England: Heinemann, 1985.

My Barren Song by Grace Akello (Dar es Salaam, Tanzania: Eastern African Publications, 1979). A collection of poems, including a long title poem in the voice of a childless woman, facing the sea, contemplating suicide. It relates her life story and the crucial impact infertility has played. Other poems discuss love, old age, and the contrast between the natural beauty of Uganda and its human history.

My Country, Africa: Autobiography of the Black Pasionaria by Andrée Blouin with Jean MacKellar (New York: Praeger, 1983). Autobiography of a woman who played an active part in the independence movement of the Congo. It begins with her childhood in an orphanage in Brazzaville, a "prison" she was sentenced to for being born of an African mother and a European father. There, in a grim life marked with beatings and near starvation, she became a rebel and came to recognize the racism underlying colonial power. As an adult, she married first an abusive racist, then a kind and loving Frenchman with whom she spent several idyllic years. Her involvement in politics led to their being exiled from the country. As an émigré activist, she presented the case of Congolese independence under the leadership of Lumumba to the world. Her relationship to Lumumba, his tragic end and the impact of neocolonialist exploitation of Africa, and her loving relationship with her African mother are recounted in the book.

My Life Story: The Autobiography of a Berber Woman by Fadhma Amrouche (New Brunswick, NJ: Rutgers University, 1988). This autobiography is the detailed account of the daily life of a Kabyle Berber, observed from a detached stance due to the author's status as an outsider in her own society. She recounts without ceremony, but with great directness, her childhood, marriage, childbirth experiences, and day-to-day existence in a culture that has been seldom described in the voice of one of its own. Though in a sense an exile within her society, she is in a position to view it clearly and without exotic trappings. Assia Djebar is reportedly working on a film of her life.

Naidu, Sarojini. Born in 1879 in Hyderabad, India, the eldest of eight children born to poet Varada Sundari and educator Aghorenath Chattopadhyay, founder of the Nizam's College, Hyderabad. After childhood in a household that was a crossroads of the Hindu, Muslim, and Western cultures and a meeting place for artists, politicians, and intellectuals, she set off to England on scholarship at the age of fifteen—a move her parents hoped would cause her to forget her love for a Dr. Naidu, unsuitable material for marriage because he was of the wrong caste and much older than she was. Her first book of poetry was published in England, with an introduction by Arthur Symonds, and it has both the diction of English decadent poetry and many of its world-weary themes. She married Dr. Naidu, had four children with him, and became involved in politics, beginning to practice her oratory as early as 1903 when she traveled India speaking on national independence. By 1917 she had stopped writing poetry and became a noted activist. She helped found the All India Women's Conference and demanded full franchise for women as early as 1917. In 1925 she was the first woman elected president of the National Congress. She joined Gandhi's Salt March in 1930, in which thousands defied the British monopoly on salt, after which Gandhi was arrested and the leadership of the nonviolent movement rested with her. She continued the resistance to the salt laws and soon was arrested herself. After compiling a record of three arrests, and when India achieved independence, she was appointed governor of Uttar Pradesh, the largest state in India. She died in 1949, and her poetry, in spite of its reputation for sentimentality and a romanticized representation of her country, is still popular in India.

Works

The Bird of Time. New York: John Lane, 1912.
The Broken Wing: Songs of Love, Death and Destiny. New York: John Lane, 1917.
The Feather of the Dawn. New York: Asia Publishing House, 1962.
The Golden Threshold. New York: John Lane, 1905.
India's Future. New York: Foreign Policy Association, 1929.
Sarojini Naidu, Selected Poetry and Prose. New Delhi, India: Indus, 1993.
The Sceptered Flute: Songs of India. New York: Dodd and Mead, 1928.

Commentary

Alexander, Meena. "Sarojini Naidu: 'Romanticism and Resistance.' " *Ariel* 17.4 (October 1986): 49–61.
Alexander, Meena. "Outcaste Power: Ritual Displacement and Virile Maternity in Indian Women Writers." *Journal of Commonwealth Literature* 23.1 (1989): 12–29.
Nageswara Rao, G. *Hidden Eternity: A Study of the Poetry of Sarojini Naidu.* Tirupati, India: Sri Venkateswara University, 1986.
Prasad, Deobrata. *Sarojini Naidu and Her Art of Poetry.* Delhi, India: Capital, 1988.
Ramachandran Nair, K. R. *Three Indo-Anglian Poets: Henry Derozio, Toru Dutt, and Sarojini Naidu.* New Delhi, India: Sterling, 1987.
Sengupta, Padmini (Sathianadhan). *Sarojini Naidu: A Biography.* London, England: Asia Publishing House, 1966.
Sharma, K. K., editor. *Perspectives on Sarojini Naidu.* Ghaziabad, India: Vimal Prakashan, 1989.

Namjoshi, Suniti. Born in Bombay, India, in 1941, she began her working career in the Indian Administrative Service in 1964 but found it dull work. Taking a leave of absence, she studied public administration at the University of Missouri, earning a master's degree, then resigned from the service to work on a Ph.D. in literature at McGill, which she completed in 1972 with a dissertation on Ezra Pound. She then taught at Scarborough College, University of Toronto. She spent the 1978–1979 academic year in England, where she became more politically aware and active and began to explore feminist and lesbian issues. She moved to Devon, England, in 1987, in order to write full-time. She is an experimental writer who has published volumes of poetry, fables, and children's stories as well as literary criticism, using sharp irony and fabulist structures to examine questions of gender, identity, and power.

Works

Aditi and the One-Eyed Monkey. Boston, MA: Beacon, 1989.
The Authentic Lie. Fredericton, New Brunswick: Fiddlehead, 1982.
Because of India: Selected Poems and Fables. London, England: Onlywoman Press, 1989.
Blue Donkey Fables. London, England: Women's Press, 1988.
The Conversations of Cow. London, England: Women's Press, 1985.
Cyclone in Pakistan. Calcutta, India: Writers' Workshop, 1971.
Feminist Fables. London, England: Sheba Feminist, 1981.

From the Bedside Book of Nightmares. Fredericton, New Brunswick: Fiddlehead, 1984.
More Poems. Calcutta, India: Writers' Workshop, 1971.
The Mothers of Maya Diip. London, England: Women's Press, 1989.
Poems. Calcutta, India: Writers' Workshop, 1967.

Narayan, Kirin. Novelist and ethnographer, she was born and raised in India, the daughter of an Indian father and an American mother. She earned her degrees at universities in the United States and has published a well-received study of Hindu folk narrative and a novel about an Indian academic in America.

Works

Love, Stars, and All That. New York: Pocket Books, 1993.
Storytellers, Saints, and Scoundrels: Folk Narrative in Hindu Religious Teaching. Philadelphia: University of Pennsylvania, 1989.

Nash, Thirza. Born in the 1800s in South Africa not far from the border with South West Africa (now Namibia), Nash was the author of autobiography, travelogues, ethnological articles, and four novels, the most successful of which was *The Ex-Gentleman.* Though she referred to herself in one newspaper profile as "every inch a Johannesburger," she also spent ten years in South West Africa with her husband, a mining geologist, and portrayed herself there as a frontierswoman, relaying her impressions to the South African press. She argued for votes for women but did not, evidently, expect suffrage to extend to nonwhites, and her novels reflect colonialist attitudes toward the indigenous population. Though she was an observer of the local landscape, she remained chiefly silent about the lives of its black inhabitants.

Works

The Ex-Gentleman. London, England: Jarrolds, 1925.
For Passion Is Darkness. London, England: Cassell, 1951.
The Geyer Brood. London, England: Cassell, 1946.
Witchweed. London, England: Cassell, 1947.

Commentary

Haarhoff, Dorian. "Emeralds, Ex-Gentlemen, Escom and Iscor: Frontier Literature in Namibia Circa 1925." *English Studies in Africa* 31 (1988): 1–18.

Nasrallah, Emily. Born in 1938 in Kfeir, South Lebanon. She left when she was nine years old to attend boarding school. She later attended the American University of Beirut and Beirut College for Women, after which she taught at the prestigious Ahliya School while writing for the Beirut press. She refused to leave Beirut during the civil war there, even though she was in danger; her house, at one point, was burned along with thirty years' worth of manuscripts. The war is a theme in her work, as is the disjunction between rural and urban life in Lebanon. She has published several novels and many short stories and essays.

Work

Flight Against Time. Charlottetown, Canada: Ragweed, 1987.

Commentary

Cooke, Miriam. *War's Other Voices: Women Writers on the Lebanese Civil War, 1975–82.* Cambridge, England: Cambridge University, 1988.

Nervous Conditions by Tsitsi Dangarembga (Seattle, WA: Seal, 1989). This novel relates the education of a young woman who gets her chance to go to school because of two things: Her uncle is an educated and powerful local figure, headmaster of a school himself; and her brother, who was the first choice for the opportunity, dies. That death, and the opportunity to receive an education, provides her with the means of escape from poverty. She goes to live with her relatives, and her rebellious cousin, Nyasha, shows her how even those who lead a privileged life have problems. She begins to understand, for the first time, how unequal are the relationships between rich and poor blacks and between black men and women. This *bildungsroman* ends with her dawning strength and skepticism. The title was drawn from Sartre's introduction to Fanon's *The Wretched of the Earth*—describing the condition of the native as a nervous one. It was first published by Women's Press in London after being neglected by a Zimbabwean publishing house (though on its success, it was published a year later in Zimbabwe) and received the Commonwealth Prize.

Commentary

Flockemann, Miki. " 'Not-Quite Insiders and Not-Quite Outsiders': The 'Process of Womanhood' in *Beka Lamb, Nervous Conditions* and *Daughters of the Twilight.*" *Journal of Commonwealth Literature* 27.1 (1992): 7–47.

McWilliams, Sally. "Tsitsi Dangarembga's *Nervous Conditions*: At the Crossroads of Feminism and Post-Colonialism." *World Literature Written in English* 31.1 (1991): 103–112.

Veit-Wild, Flora. "Women Write About Things that Move Them." *Matatu* 3.6 (1989): 101–108.

New Islands and Other Stories by María Luisa Bombal (New York: Farrar, Straus, Giroux, 1982). These stories are charged with strangeness, their images and events loaded with mysterious significance. In one much-anthologized story, "The Final Mist," images of sexuality and death and a claustrophobic atmosphere create a fevered and disturbingly unfamiliar world. "New Islands" has the same heavy atmosphere but is balanced with a less melodramatic narration. It deals with mysterious new islands that surface overnight in a lake, only to disappear by the end of the story without their mystery being resolved. The imagery is rich, loaded with references to evolution and primal regeneration, creating a strange but compelling landscape.

The Newspaper Editor and Other Stories by Rebecca Chua (Singapore: Heinemann Asia, 1981). Stories dealing with women's role changing in the modern world; materialism crowding out values, generational differences between older people and the young who have grown up wealthy, the sense of loss when cultures are too easily mingled and watered down. Chua tells some stories in a fairly straightforward narrative, while others, such as "Vertices," experiment with stream of consciousness passages inserted into a more conventional text.

Next Year Will Be Better by Hylda M. Richards (Lincoln: University of Nebraska, 1985). A frontier story of an English family's life in Rhodesia, having emigrated there hoping to make good after failing miserably at farming in England. The narrator, who tells their modest adventures in a self-deprecating voice, exhibits unconscious racism at times but also feels obviously silly in the role of the grande dame, which being a colonial landowner with black workers invites. A combination of a pioneer memoir with the hapless-urban-farmer genre that illustrates colonialist assumptions in an unusual framework.

Ngcobo, Lauretta. Born in Ixopo, Natal, South Africa, in 1931, the first of four children. She was influenced by her great-grandmother's poetry and traditional storytelling; her grandfather was also an influence, composing a poem for each child in the family at their birth. When she was seven years old, her father died, and her mother, Rosa Fisekile Cele, became the sole support of the family. She began writing at an early age. She was educated at Webbstown, Nazweja, and Dunusa Schools and Inanda Seminary and was one of the few women attending Fort Hare University, where she earned a B.A. in education. She went into exile with her husband and three of her children after the upheaval of the 1960s, living in Swaziland, Tanzania, and Zambia, then settling in Britain in the early 1970s, where she worked as a teacher. She edited *Let It Be Told*, a collection of essays by black women in Britain, and is the author of two novels. In spite of her strong sense of her family and community's ties to poetry, she has felt mutilated by the conflict between cultures, and her life of exile has called for sacrifices; though she wrote constantly, she often was forced to destroy her manuscripts when she had to move from place to place. Her two novels are strongly plotted, historically based explorations of the effects of apartheid not only on her characters but on the whole of African culture.

Works

And They Didn't Die. New York: Braziller, 1991.
Cross of Gold. London, England: Longman, 1981.

Commentary

Farred, Grant. " 'Not Like Women at All': Black Female Subjectivity in Lauretta Ngcobo's *And They Didn't Die*." *Genders* 16 (spring 1993): 94–112.

Grandqvist, Raoul, and John Stotesbury, editors. *African Voices: Interviews with Thirteen African Writers.* Sydney, Australia: Dangaroo, 1990.

Hunter, E., and C. MacKenzie, editors. *Between the Lines II: Interviews with Nadine Gordimer, Menan Du Plessis, Zöe Wicomb, Lauretta Ngcobo.* Grahamstown, South Africa: National English Literary Museum, 1993.

Ngcobo, Lauretta. "My Life and My Writing." *Kunapipi* 7.2–3 (1985): 83–86.

Ngcobo, Lauretta. "The African Woman Writer." *A Double Colonization: Colonial and Post-Colonial Women's Writing.* Mundelstrup, Denmark: Dangaroo, 1986. 81–82.

Ngcobo, Lauretta. "African Motherhood—Myth and Reality." *Criticism and Ideology: Second African Writers Conference, Stockholm 1986.* Uppsala, Sweden: Scandinavian Institute of African Studies, 1988. 141–154.

Nichols, Grace. Born in Georgetown, Guyana, in 1950, she earned a diploma in communications from the University of Guyana, taught for several years, and worked as a reporter and in the government information service before moving to Britain in 1977. She now lives in Lewes, East Sussex, with poet John Agard and her daughters. She is author of several volumes of poetry, a novel, and books for children.

Works

Baby Fish and Other Stories from Village to Rain Forest. London, England: Nanny Books, 1983.

Come on into My Tropical Garden: Poems for Children. London, England: A. C. Black, 1988.

The Fat Black Woman's Poems. London, England: Virago, 1985.

*I Is a Long Memoried Woman. London, England Karnak House, 1983.

Lazy Thoughts of a Lazy Woman. London, England: Virago, 1989.

Leslyn in London. London, England: Hodder, 1984.

Poetry Jump Up. Harmondsworth, England: Penguin, 1989.

Trust You Wriggly. London, England: Hodder, 1980.

*Whole of a Morning Sky. London, England: Virago, 1986.

Commentary

Green, Veronica. *The Rhythm of Our Days.* Cambridge, England: Cambridge University, 1991.

Nieh Hua-Ling. Born in 1925 in Hubei, China, she was a cofounder and director of the International Writing Program at the University of Iowa. She is the author of several novels and has published collections of short stories and essays. She has written about the effect of exile on identity and has explored the cross-cultural divide using a subjective style that is innovative and effective.

Work

*Mulberry and Peach: Two Women of China. Translated by Jane Parish Yang with Linda Lappin. London, England: Women's Press, 1986.

Night-Scene, the Garden by Meena Alexander (New York: Red Dust, 1992). A series of interlinked poems in two voices—a daughter and her mother (and perhaps a third, that of "the poet broken loose, speaking against silence") and their shared past in a family home in Kerala, their losses through death and change. They are separate but seeking some parallels in their lives, sensing the "confusions of our blood" (15). Many of the images and incidents alluded to in this work are discussed in the author's memoir *Fault Lines*.

The Nine Guardians by Rosario Castellanos (London, England: Faber and Faber, 1959). Translation of *Balun-Canan,* first published in 1957. A novel set in Chiapas in the times of the presidency of Cardenas, who put into motion land reform started by the Mexican Revolution. The Arguellos family of landowners, confident in the remote fastness of their landholdings, are used to Indians serving as subhuman beasts of burden. The coming of land reform upsets the balance of power and unsettles the family. The beginning and end of the novel are told by the young daughter of the house, whose deepest connection is to her Indian nanny. In between are the stories of Ernesto, an illegitimate mestizo son of the family, recruited to serve as an inadequate teacher for the Indians, required by law, but resisted by the landowners; of Maltilde, who carries another illegitimate child; of the young Mario who wastes away after a curse is put on him. Early in the novel one character warns that one must take care not to touch "trees and orchids and birds one ought to respect. The Indians have singled them out specially to appease the guardians' mouths. Don't touch them or they'll bring bad luck" (28); without possessing the knowledge of the indigenous people, one can blunder into danger. Though the novel focuses on the wealthy ladinos and their experiences, there is a rich undertone of the story that goes untold, of the Indians' point of view only suggested through the insights of uncorrupted people like the child narrator. It is telling that much of the drama of the plot is sprung over the building of the school—resisted by the landowner, fought for by the Indians, who realize that language is the ground for a crucial battle for power.

Commentary

Castillo, Debra A. "Rosario Castellanos: 'Ashes Without a Face.' " *De/Colonizing the Subject: The Politics of Gender in Women's Autobiography*. Minneapolis: University of Minnesota, 1992. 242–269.
Cypess, Sandra Messinger. "*Balun-Canan*: A Model Demonstration of Discourse as Power." *Revista de Estudios Hispánicos* 19 (1985): 1–15.

Ning Lao T'ai-t'ai. Born in 1867 in northern China, she lived under harsh and punishing circumstances. Her husband was an opium addict, and she struggled to support her family and her husband's addiction. Her life story was recorded by Ida Pruitt and is published as *A Daughter of Han*. She died in 1937.

Work

A Daughter of Han: The Autobiography of a Chinese Working Woman. With Ida Pruitt. Stanford, CA: Stanford University, 1967.

Commentary

Knapp, Bettina. "The New Era for Women Writers in China." *World Literature Today* 65 (summer 1991): 432–439.

Nisa. Anthropologist Marjorie Shostak interviewed Nisa in 1971 and published her story ten years later. Nisa, born in 1921, lived, at the time she was interviewed, on the northern edge of the Kalahari Desert. She was married at the age of twelve, bore four children, none of whom survived, was married five times, divorced, and widowed. Her life story, and the story of her community told from her viewpoint, provides a life history of a woman belonging to a hunting and gathering community using a distinctive voice.

Work

Nisa: The Life and Words of a !Kung Woman by Marjorie Shostak. New Haven, CT: Harvard University, 1981.

Commentary

Bernick, Susan E. "Toward a Value-Laden Theory: Feminism and Social Science." *Hypatia* 6.2 (summer 1991): 118–136.

Davies, Carole Boyce. "Collaboration and the Ordering Imperative in Life Story Production." *De/Colonizing the Subject: The Politics of Gender in Women's Autobiography.* Minneapolis: University of Minnesota, 1992. 3–19.

Shostak, Marjorie. " 'What the Wind Won't Take Away': The Genesis of *Nisa: The Life and Words of a !Kung Woman.*" *Interpreting Women's Lives: Feminist Theory and Personal Narratives.* Bloomington: Indiana University, 1989. 228–240.

Njau, Rebeka. Born in Kanyariri, Kenya, in 1932, one of twelve children. She was raised by a strong mother who treated her sons and daughters equally. She attended Alliance Girls' High School and Makerere University College. She wanted to be an actress when she was young but settled on a teaching career and taught for many years, becoming headmistress of the Nairobi Girl's Secondary School in 1964. She later went to work as a researcher for the Kenyan Council of Churches in Nairobi—partly so she could find more time to write— after which she wrote her novel *Ripples in the Pool* and began to experiment with textile design. Her first experience as a writer was as a playwright, author of the unpublished *The Round Chain* (performed in 1964) and *The Scar* (a prize-winning one-act drama published in 1965). Her first novel was awarded the East African Writing Committee Prize. More recently, she is the author of *Kenyan Women Heroes and Their Mystical Power*, an exploration of the unwritten history of women and their impact on Kenyan society, for which she drew on interviews and colonial records in the national archives. Her writing reflects her concern that traditional African values deserve respect and remembrance.

Works

The Hypocrite. Nairobi, Kenya: Uzima Press, 1977.
Kenyan Women Heroes and Their Mystical Power. Nairobi, Kenya: Risk, 1984.
**Ripples in the Pool.* London, England: Heinemann, 1978.
The Scar: A Tragedy in One Act. Moshi, Tanzania: Kibo Art Gallery, 1965.

Commentary

Bryce-Okunlola, Jane. "Motherhood as a Metaphor for Creativity in Three African Women's Novels: Flora Nwapa, Rebeka Njau, and Bessie Head." *Motherlands: Women's Writings from Africa, the Caribbean, and South Asia.* New Brunswick, NY: Rutgers University, 1992. 200–218.
James, Adeola, editor. *In Their Own Voices: African Women Writers Talk.* London, England: James Currey, 1990.

No Sweetness Here by Ama Ata Aidoo (Garden City, NY: Doubleday, 1972). This collection of short stories has vivid vignettes of West African life, rendered in a language that is lively and colloquial. Stories tend to portray moments in life when old and new, tradition and change, rural and urban ways, are juxtaposed, using irony without the sting of sarcasm. The most notable aspect of the stories is their use of language, both in terms of narration and in terms of dialogue. Aidoo achieves an unforced, genuine tone, very much as if the characters are speaking in their own voices. The author said in a recent interview that these stories are "part of the many discourses about culture in the 'postcolonial' context, that are about what has been lost in the process of colonization, and what is being lost in the process of 'Westernization' " (George, 302).

Commentary

George, Rosemary Marangoly, and Helen Scott. " 'A New Tail to an Old Tale': An Interview with Ama Ata Aidoo." *Novel* 26.3 (spring 1993): 297–308.
Kilson, Marion. "Women and African Literature." *Journal of African Studies* 4.2 (1977): 161–166.
Nwankwo, Chimalum. "The Feminist Impulse and Social Realism in Ama Ata Aidoo's *No Sweetness Here* and *Our Sister Killjoy.*" *Ngambika: Studies of Women in African Literature.* Trenton, NJ: Africa World Press, 1986. 151–159.

No Telephone to Heaven by Michelle Cliff (New York: Dutton, 1987). The journey of Clare, a light-skinned, deeply divided Jamaican woman, to the sources of her matriarchal past and, through her recovery of the past, herself. She is uprooted from Jamaica and moves to New York as a child, though her mother, yearning for her home, eventually returns to Jamaica with her darker-skinned sister. She spends years in England, playing an academic game with distinction but without conviction. She then makes a mad pilgrimage through Europe with a lover who has never recovered from his experiences in Vietnam and at last returns to a Jamaica that is close to rupturing its tourist postcard surface in social turmoil. There she excavates her grandmother's past under an overgrown house on a piece of ground claimed by the bush, which has become the site of a revolutionary group planning revolutionary action. The novel ends in a bizarre scene in which an absurd film shoot and real shooting blend. The narrative weaves past and present, Jamaica and its colonizers, in the form of a personal quest for identity.

Commentary

Cliff, Michelle. "Caliban's Daughter: The Tempest and the Teapot." *Frontiers* 12.2 (summer 1991): 36–51.

"Not Either an Experimental Doll": The Separate Worlds of Three South African Women by Shula Marks (Bloomington: Indiana University, 1987). While doing historical research, Shula Marks found a collection of letters among three women, Lily Moya, a Xhosa girl, a Zulu social worker, and a white Fabian socialist, concerning the education of the girl. She was brought to a boarding school, the first of several, under the white woman's patronage, where she did not prosper. Eventually, she left school, expressing bitterness and pain in her letters. After leaving the school, she suffered a breakdown, was diagnosed as schizophrenic, and spent time in mental institutions, which she likened to the schools she had attended, her hospital stay one more transfer of many. This book is a history based on the letters and subsequent interviews with the Xhosa girl in adulthood.

Commentary

Marks, Shula. "The Context of Personal Narrative: Reflections on *'Not Either an Experimental Doll': The Separate Worlds of Three South African Women.'"* *Interpreting Women's Worlds: Feminist Theory and Personal Narratives.* Bloomington: Indiana University, 1989. 39–58.

Nourbese Philip, Marlene. See **Philip, Marlene Nourbese.**

The Nowhere Man by Kamala Markandaya (London, England: Allen Lane, 1973). A novel about an elderly Indian man who has lived for fifty years in England, arriving at the end of World War I and now hospitalized with the exotic disease of leprosy. He remembers in flashback his days in India, nostalgically if imperfectly remembered—his leaving for England to escape charges of subversion, his marriage and his widowhood, and the growing savage racism he encounters in England. He is a citizen of a colonial power that no longer exists, and a colonial citizen of a country that does not want him, so is effectively erased as a person—a "nowhere man."

Commentary

Ahmad, Hena. "Kamala Markandaya and the Immigrant Experience in Britain." *Reworlding: The Literature of the Indian Diaspora*. Westport, CT: Greenwood, 1992. 141–148.

Nwapa, Flora. The first African woman writer to publish a novel. Born in 1931, in Oguta, eastern Nigeria, where her parents were both teachers, she attended school in Ibadan, earning a B.A. from University College, and then went to Scotland, where she attended Edinburgh University and earned a degree in education. She worked as a teacher first in Calabar, then at Queen's College, Enugu, and in that time she wrote her first two novels. After the civil war she began to work in public service, taking a post in the Ministry of Health and Social Welfare for the East-Central State (1970–1975), during which period she chiefly wrote short stories. She founded the Tana and the Flora Nwapa publishing houses to publish both adult and children's books. She is notable for almost ethnographic detail in her earliest and most effective novels, *Efuru* and *Idu*, both of which make rich use of Igbo oral tradition. In her later work, she took on more of an instructive role in her writing, trying to address contemporary problems of birth control, the civil war's effects, the impact of modernization on Nigeria, and the relations between men and women. She died in October 1993 in Enugu.

Works

Cassava Song and Rice Song. Enugu, Nigeria: Tana, 1986.
*Efuru. London, England: Heinemann, 1970.
Emeka, Driver's Guard. London, England: University of London, 1972.
Idu. London, England: Heinemann, 1970.
Journey into Space. Enugu, Nigeria: Flora Nwapa, 1980.
Mammywater. Enugu, Nigeria: Flora Nwapa, 1984.
The Miracle Kittens. Enugu, Nigeria: Flora Nwapa, 1980.
Never Again. Enugu, Nigeria: Tana, 1986.
One Is Enough. Enugu, Nigeria: Tana, 1984.
This Is Lagos and Other Stories. Enugu, Nigeria: Tana, 1986.
Wives at War and Other Stories. Enugu, Nigeria: Tana, 1984.
Women Are Different. Enugu, Nigeria: Tana, 1986.

Commentary

Agetua, John, editor. *Interviews with Six Nigerian Writers*. Benin City, Nigeria: Bendel Newspapers, 1976.
Andrade, Susan Z. "Rewriting History, Motherhood, and Rebellion: Naming an African Woman's Literary Tradition." *Research in African Literatures* 21.1 (spring 1990): 91–111.
Bazin, Nancy Topping. "Feminism in the Literature of African Women." *The Black Scholar* 20.3–4 (summer-fall 1989): 8–17.
Boehmer, Elleke. "Stories of Women and Mothers: Gender and Nationalism in the Early

Fiction of Flora Nwapa." *Motherlands: Women's Writings from Africa, the Caribbean, and South Asia*. New Brunswick, NJ: Rutgers University, 1992. 3–23.

Brown, Lloyd W. *Women Writers in Black Africa*. Westport, CT: Greenwood, 1981.

Bruner, Charlotte. "Been-To or Has-Been: A Dilemma for Today's African Woman." *Ba Shiru* 8.2 (1977): 21–30.

Bryce-Okunlola, Jane. "Motherhood as a Metaphor for Creativity in Three African Women's Novels: Flora Nwapa, Rebeka Njau, and Bessie Head." *Motherlands: Women's Writings from Africa, the Caribbean, and South Asia*. New Brunswick, NJ: Rutgers University, 1992. 200–218.

Condé, Maryse. "Three Female Writers in Modern Africa: Flora Nwapa, Ama Ata Aidoo and Grace Ogot." *Présence Africaine* 82 (1972): 132–144.

Coulon, Virginia. "Women at War: Nigerian Women Writers and the Civil War." *Commonwealth Essays and Studies* 13.1 (1990): 1–12.

Davies, Carole Boyce. "Motherhood in the Works of Male and Female Igbo Writers: Achebe, Emecheta, Nwapa and Nzekwu." *Ngambika: Studies of Women in African Literature*. Trenton, NJ: Africa World Press, 1986. 241–256.

Emenyonu, Ernest N. "Who Does Flora Nwapa Write For?" *African Literature Today* 7 (1975): 27–33.

Gordimer, Nadine. *The Black Interpreters: Notes on African Writing*. Braamfontein, South Africa: Spro-Cas/Ravan, 1973.

Holloway, Karla. *Moorings and Metaphors: Figures of Culture and Gender in Black Women's Literature*. New Brunswick, NJ: Rutgers University, 1992.

James, Adeola, editor. *In Their Own Voices: African Women Writers Talk*. London, England: James Currey, 1990.

Mojola, Yemi I. "The Works of Flora Nwapa." *Nigerian Female Writers: A Critical Perspective*. Lagos, Nigeria: Malthouse, 1989. 19–29.

Nandakumar, Prema. "An Image of African Womanhood: A Study of Flora Nwapa's *Efuru*." *African Quarterly* 11 (1971): 136–146.

Phillips, Maggi. "Engaging Dreams: Alternative Perspectives on Flora Nwapa, Buchi Emecheta, Ama Ata Aidoo, Bessie Head, and Tsitsi Dangarembga." *Research in African Literatures* 25.4 (winter 1994): 89–103.

Wilentz, Gay. *Binding Cultures: Black Women Writers in Africa and the Diaspora*. Bloomington: Indiana University, 1992.

O

O'Callaghan, Marion. Born in Trinidad in 1934, she graduated from St. Joseph's Convent, Port of Spain, was a winner of the Girls' Open Island Scholarship in 1950, and attended the Imperial College of Tropical Agriculture. She worked in the United States for one year before taking a position at the public library in Trinidad. She earned a diploma in library science in 1959 and did graduate work in social anthropology at University College, London, in 1962. In the early 1970s, she went to work for UNESCO in Paris. She is the author of two novels (published under her maiden name, Marion Patrick Jones) that explore the various options facing Trinidadians who must make choices and sometimes compromises as they grow up and raise their own children. She has also written nonfiction works on Africa under her married name of Marion O'Callaghan.

Works

J'ouvert Morning. Port of Spain, Trinidad: Columbus Publishers, 1976.
Pan Beat. Port of Spain, Trinidad: Columbus Publishers, 1973.

Ocampo, Silvina. Born in Buenos Aires in 1903, she was the youngest of six daughters born to a wealthy and prominent family. She was educated by English and French governesses and was fluent in three languages. The family enjoyed annual trips to Europe. She set out to become a painter and studied in Paris with de Chirico and Leger, but she became discouraged in spite of having some success in the art world and decided to devote herself to writing, a family occupation; her sister, Victoria, was a leading figure in the fertile world of

Argentine literature of the time. She married writer Adolfo Bioy Casares, with whom she has written a detective novel, and has edited several anthologies with him and with Jorge Luis Borges.

Work

Leopoldina's Dream. Translated by Daniel Balderston. New York: Penguin Books, 1988.

Commentary

Klingenberg, Patricia N. "A Portrait of the Writer as Artist: Silvina Ocampo." *Perspectives on Contemporary Literature* 13 (1987): 58–64.
Klingenberg, Patricia N. "The Mad Double in the Stories of Silvina Ocampo." *Latin American Literary Review* 16.22 (July-August 1988): 29–40.

Ocampo, Victoria. Born in 1890, the eldest of six daughters born to a wealthy Buenos Aires family. She was educated in the European tradition, traveled with her family annually to Europe, and used her position in society to create a focus for Argentinean literary activity. She was married briefly, in order to escape the stifling atmosphere of her father's house, but found her marriage equally oppressive, and so ended it. She reveled in independence and was the first woman of her class to drive her own car and smoke a cigarette in public. She lived for a time in Paris, from 1928 to 1931, where she entered into the most prestigious circles of literature and art, and became acquainted with Jose Ortega y Gasset and Igor Stravinsky, among many others. She began to write essays, biographical profiles, translations, and criticism. In 1931 she founded the important literary journal *Sur* and a couple of years later began a publishing house of the same name. She gathered a salon of young writers around her, including Borges, Adolfo Bioy Casares, and others. Known as a feminist (she corresponded with Virginia Woolf on women's issues) and as a champion of liberalism and the arts, she represented an enlightened, metropolitan, and sophisticated Argentina. *Sur* came under fire during the Peronist years, and Ocampo herself spent a short time in jail on unspecified charges, but the action taken against her and her literary efforts was more a case of serious harassment than overt suppression, and the journal continued to publish until 1970. In 1977 she was the first woman to be elected to the Argentine Academy of Letters. Though some criticized Ocampo and her efforts as being elitist, too enamored of European models, and out of touch with political and social reality, Victoria Ocampo's contribution to letters in Latin America is enormous. She died in 1979.

Commentary

Christ, Roland. "Figuring Literarily: An Interview with Victoria Ocampo." *Review (Center for Inter-American Relations)* 7 (1972): 5–13.
Falcoff, Mark. "Victoria Ocampo's *Sur.*" *New Creation* 7 (1988): 27–37.
Hausman, Bernice L. "Words Between Women: Victoria Ocampo and Virginia Woolf."

In the Feminine Mode: Essays on Hispanic Women Writers. Lewisburg, PA: Bucknell University, 1990. 201–226.

King, John. Sur: *A Study of the Argentine Literary Journal and Its Role in the Development of a Culture, 1931–1970*. Cambridge, England: Cambridge University, 1988.

King, John. "Victoria Ocampo (1890–1979): Precursor." *Knives and Angels: Women Writers in Latin America*. London, England: Zed, 1990. 9–25.

Masiello, Francine. *Between Civilization and Barbarism: Women, Nation, and Literary Culture in Modern Argentina*. Lincoln: University of Nebraska, 1992.

Meyer, Doris. " 'Feminine' Testimony in the Works of Teresa de la Parra, María Luisa Bombal, and Victoria Ocampo." *Contemporary Women Authors of Latin America*. New York: Brooklyn College, 1983. 3–15.

Meyer, Doris. *Victoria Ocampo: Against the Wind and the Tide*. Austin: University of Texas, 1989.

Meyer, Doris. "Letters and Lines of Correspondence in the Essays of Victoria Ocampo." *Revista Interamericana de Bibliographía*. 42.2 (1992): 233–240.

Molloy, Sylvia. *At Face Value: Autobiographical Writing in Spanish America*. New York: Cambridge, 1991.

Ocampo, Victoria. "Woman's Past and Present." *Lives on the Line: The Testimony of Contemporary Latin American Authors*. Berkeley: University of California, 1988. 51–58.

Of Love and Shadows by Isabel Allende (New York: Knopf, 1987). "Here, write it, or it will be erased by the wind." This novel is the love story of a man and woman whose romance is entangled with Chilean politics, specifically their efforts to uncover the fates of the "disappeared." This novel has few of the magic realism features of Allende's other novels, though one character is literally a miracle worker. It contains a graphic and strongly felt scene in which the young lovers discover a cave full of bodies. They eventually are forced to go underground and escape, in the end, over the mountain passes in a scene reminiscent of Adam and Eve's exit from a mountain-bound Eden. The novel is a curious mix of political thriller and romance, with sometimes an uneasy resonance between them.

Ogot, Grace. Born in the Central Nyanza District of Kenya in 1930, daughter of a schoolteacher and granddaughter of a renowned storyteller. She attended Butere High School, then studied nursing and midwifery in Uganda and England. In 1959 she married historian Bethwell Ogot, who encouraged her to begin writing. She has worked as a nurse, midwife, tutor, radio broadcaster, newspaper columnist, and politician—elected as a Minister of Parliament (MP) in 1985 and serving as a delegate to the United Nations and UNESCO—as well as working for an airlines and managing several clothing stores. She was the founding chair of the Writer's Association of Kenya. Her writing is concerned with depicting the social milieu of Kenya and with questions of nationhood; she has most recently focused on exploring the precolonial past.

Works

The Graduate. Nairobi, Kenya: Uzima, 1980.
The Island of Tears. Nairobi, Kenya: Uzima, 1980.
Land Without Thunder. Nairobi, Kenya: East African Publishing House, 1968.
The Other Woman and Other Stories. Nairobi, Kenya: Transafrica, 1976.
The Promised Land. Nairobi, Kenya: East Africa, 1966.
The Strange Bride. Translated by Okoth Okombo. Nairobi, Kenya: Heinemann Kenya, 1989.

Commentary

Achufusi, Ify. "Problems of Nationhood in Grace Ogot's Fiction." *Journal of Commonwealth Literature* 26.1 (August 1991): 178–187.
Bruner, Charlotte. "Been-To or Has-Been: A Dilemma for Today's African Woman." *Ba Shiru* 8.2 (1977): 21–30.
Burness, Don, editor. *Wanasema: Conversations with African Writers.* Athens: Ohio University Center for International Studies, 1985.
Condé, Maryse. "Three Female Writers in Modern Africa: Flora Nwapa, Ama Ata Aidoo and Grace Ogot." *Présence Africaine* 82 (1972): 132–144.
Kilson, Marion. "Women and African Literature." *Journal of African Studies* 4.2 (1977): 161–166.
Lindfors, Bernth. "Interview with Grace Ogot." *World Literature Written in English* 18.1 (1979): 58–68.
Lindfors, Bernth, editor. *Mazungumzo: Interviews with East African Writers, Publishers, Editors, and Scholars.* Athens: Ohio University, 1980.
Nichols, Lee, editor. *Conversations with African Writers.* Washington, DC: Voice of America, 1981.

Ogundipe-Leslie, Molara. A Yoruba woman from western Nigeria, born in 1949. She started writing as a child, writing stories and even comic books in secondary school, poetry in her college years. She was educated at Queen's School, Ede, and University College, Ibadan, where she earned a B.A. (honors) degree in English in 1977. Since then she has taught English and African literature at universities in Nigeria and the United States. A Marxist and feminist literary critic, she is particularly known for her exploration of the concept of African aesthetics. She has written articles for both academic and general publications, is a member of the Nigerian Federal Directorate for Social Mobilization, and serves as chair of its Ogun State branch. For a time she was a member of the editorial board of the newspaper *The Guardian* in Lagos. More recently, she was made head of the Department of English at Ogun State University. She has published a volume of poetry in addition to her works of literary criticism.

Work

Sew the Old Days and Other Poems. Ibadan, Nigeria: Evans Brothers, 1985.

Commentary

James, Adeola, editor. *In Their Own Voices: African Women Writers Talk.* London, England: James Currey, 1990.
Maduakor, Obi. "Female Voices in Poetry: Catherine Acholonu and Omolara Ogundipe-Leslie as Poets." *Nigerian Female Writers: A Critical Perspective.* Lagos, Nigeria: Malthouse, 1989. 75–91.
Ogundipe-Leslie, Molara. "The Female Writer and Her Commitment." *African Literature Today* 15 (1987): 5–13.
Ogundipe-Leslie, Molara. *Recreating Ourselves: African Women and Critical Transformations.* Trenton, NJ: Africa World Press, 1994.

Okoye, Ifeoma. Born and raised in Nigeria, she attended Saint Monica's College, Ogbunike, where she earned a teacher's certificate in 1959. She earned a B.A. in English from the University of Nigeria, Nsukka, in 1977. She taught at several levels in schools and married novelist Mokugo Okoye, with whom she has five children. She teaches mass communications at the Institute of Management and Technology, Enugu. Primarily known as a writer of children's literature, she has also written a couple of novels for adult readers.

Works

Behind the Clouds. Harlow, England: Longman, 1982.
Men Without Ears. Harlow, England: Longman, 1984.
Only Bread for Eze. Enugu, Nigeria: Fourth Dimension, 1980.

Commentary

James, Adeola, editor. *In Their Own Voices: African Women Writers Talk.* London, England: James Currey, 1990.
Nolim, Charles. "The Writings of Ifeoma Okoye." *Nigerian Female Writers: A Critical Perspective.* Lagos, Nigeria: Malthouse, 1989. 30–36.

The Old Man and Other Stories by Chen Jo-hsi (Hong Kong: Renditions, 1986). Stories about the Cultural Revolution and the April Fifth movement that brought it to an end. The stories are tinged with a gentle irony and are peopled with fully realized individuals. The drama, such as it is, is kept on a very human scale, so that the horrors of the time are all the more moving. The final story contrasts ironically the machinations of American academics trying to gain influence with Chinese visitors so that they can travel to China—while at the same time the Chinese visitors are vying to establish a means for their relatives to come to America.

Old Wives' Tales: Life-Stories from Ibibioland collected by Iris Andreski (New York: Schocken, 1970). A collection of life stories related by elderly women from the Ibibio people of Nigeria. They are stories of their birth, their marriage, and family circumstances and often reveal something about their belief system, frequently reflecting some conflict between Christianity and indigenous beliefs. The tales are brief, and the tellers often are diffident about the lack of excitement in their lives. There is a certain repetitiveness in the structure of the tales due to the way in which they were collected and the questions that prompted the stories, but they create a layered impact, reflecting oral traditions and contemporary life experiences.

On the Face of the Waters by Flora Annie Steel (New York: Macmillan, 1911). A novel based on the Indian Mutiny of 1857 that focuses on a woman who remains in Delhi after it is taken by the rebels, disguised as a Persian woman, able to escape to the English side just before the siege. Her resistance leads to the growth of self-reliance, survival skills, and courageous independence. This was perhaps the most popular of all fiction based on the mutiny, carefully researched by the author to achieve historical accuracy, though it reflects the judgments and interpretations of the author's times.

Commentary

Sharpe, Jenny. *Allegories of Empire: The Figure of the Woman in the Colonial Text.* Minneapolis: University of Minnesota, 1993.

On the Fringe of Dreamtime and Other Stories by Jayapraga Reddy (Johannesburg, South Africa: Skotaville, 1987). Stories that give brief snapshots of diverse South African lives. The title story is about an elderly Indian who returns to the place that was once his land, now inhabited by callous whites; he sees his past through their present as if in double exposure. "The Love Beads" tells of a rickshaw driver who is hurt in an accident and, in the hospital, is attracted to a nurse. She recalls him back to his wife by looking at the love beads his wife gave him to remind her of her faithfulness and affection, in the face of apartheid laws that force them to live apart. "Snatch the Wind and Run" is about a boy who, in a passion to protect some money he won in a lottery, knifes a man and is jailed; a social worker helps him recover his freedom and money, as well as the dream he had seen fade of a better life. "The Slumbering Spirit" tells of a coloured boy who begins to do favors for an elderly white woman in the neighborhood in spite of warnings that white people will take advantage of him. When she dies, she leaves him her ancient dog and some sense that communication and caring are possible. The stories are gentle, optimistic, and unassuming dramas that sample the rich diversity of traditions in South African society. Several of these stories were broadcast on the BBC.

Onwubiko, Pauline. Born at Uvuru in Imo State, Nigeria, she attended the Owerri Girls' Secondary School and earned a B.A. in literature from the University of Port Harcourt in 1982 and a master's degree in English and literary studies from the University of Calabar. She now is an assistant lecturer in the Department of English, Calabar. She is the author of one autobiographical work, a child's-eye view of the Nigerian civil war.

Work

*Running for Cover. Owerri, Nigeria: KayBeeCee, 1988.

Onwueme, Tess. Born on September 8, 1955, at Ogwashi-uku, Bendel State, Nigeria. She attended Mary Mount College in Agbor for her secondary education, then earned a B.A. in education and English and an M.A. in literature from the University of Ife. She currently lectures at the University of Technology, Owerri. She has produced some of her plays at the university, with student actors, and has toured in Nigeria and abroad. Her play *The Desert Encroaches* won the Association of Nigerian Authors prize for drama.

Works

Ban Empty Barn. Owerri, Nigeria: Totan, 1986.
The Broken Calabash. Owerri, Nigeria: Totan, 1984.
The Children's Way. Owerri, Nigeria: Totan, 1982.
The Desert Encroaches. Ibadan, Nigeria: Heinemann, 1988.
Go Tell It to Women: An Epic Drama for Women. Newark, NJ: African Heritage, 1992.
Legacies: A Play. Ibadan, Nigeria: Heinemann, 1989.
Let's Play Together. Owerri, Nigeria: Totan, 1982.
Mirror for Campus. Owerri, Nigeria: Headway Communications, 1987.
The Reign of Wazobia: A Play. Ibadan, Nigeria: Heinemann, 1988.
Three Plays. Detroit, MI: Wayne State University, 1993.

Commentary

Amuta, Chidi. "The Nigerian Woman as Dramatist: The Instance of Tess Onwueme." *Nigerian Female Writers: A Critical Perspective.* Lagos, Nigeria: Malthouse, 1989. 53–59.
Dunton, Chris. *Make Man Talk True: Nigerian Drama in English Since 1970.* London: Hans Zell, 1992.
Nwachukwu-Agbada, J. O. J. "Tess Onwueme: Dramatist in Quest of Change." *World Literature Today* 66.3 (summer 1992): 464–467.

Open Door by Luisa Valenzuela (San Francisco, CA: North Point Press, 1988). This collection includes stories from *The Heretics,* first published in 1967, *Strange Things Happen Here,* 1975, and *Up Among the Eagles,* 1983. Many of the stories are ironic explorations of the political climate of Argentina, such as in "The Censors," in which a man schemes to become a censor in order to intercept a questionable letter he has posted, only to become so involved in the system that he denounces himself. In the story "Strange Things Happen Here," two men find a jacket and briefcase and spend hours speculating about it, only to wake up in the night having—perhaps—heard an explosion of a bomb that might have been in the briefcase. In turns ironic, bitter, surreal, and sympathetic, these stories are innovative explorations of the ambiguities and disjunctions of the political and social climate of Argentina.

Oral Literature. Critic Trinh T. Minh-ha has pointed out that "[t]he world's earliest archives or libraries were the memories of women" (121). Women have played a critical role in creating and sustaining oral literature, though their contributions are sometimes ignored—*griots* receiving the attentions of Western male anthropologists, for example, while the work of *griottes* goes largely unrecorded. In Mali, slave women traditionally performed oral works and preserved the nation's history (Diawara). Women in the Philippines served as priestesses in precolonial times, chanting and performing forms of possession as well as being the community's healers and preservers of both natural and social knowledge. With colonization, women were denied a public voice, and it was late in the nineteenth century before they reemerged as poets. Though in many parts of the world women remain active performers of oral literature, their work is often devalued and lost, ignored in favor of the printed word. In modern-day Nigeria, Hausa poets play an active role in women's affairs, broadcasting oral literature that has both a didactic function and a defining role in Hausa women's self-representation (Mack). Somali women are accomplished poets, though their poetry is not generally recorded in print (Jama). A recent special issue of *Research in African Literatures* devoted to women and the oral tradition suggests that more scholarly attention is being paid to women's oral literature than in the past.

Many writers of printed literature acknowledge a debt to women's oral traditions. Paule Marshall became aware of literature early in her life, taught the value of literature by the "poets in the kitchen," the mothers gathered for coffee and talk who "taught me my first lessons in the narrative art. They trained my ear. They set a standard of excellence. This is why the best of my work must be attributed to them: it stands as a testimony to the rich legacy of language and culture they so freely passed on to me in the wordshop of the kitchen" (35). Isabel Allende, who incorporates storytelling techniques in her novels, has said, "I come from a family of storytellers, and that helps a lot. As women, we were kept silent in public, but we had a private voice" (Gautier, 14). Many writers incorporate traditions of oral literature in their work. Performance poets such as Jean Binta Breeze, Louise Bennett, and Jessica Hagedorn carry on the tradition of fusing texts with public presentation. Efua Sutherland has designed theatrical works and performance spaces that make use of traditional African performance practices (Asagba). Ama Ata Aidoo employs aspects of oral literary practice into her novel *Our Sister Killjoy* (Elder). And both Assia Djebar and Leïla Sebbar have paid homage to the storyteller Scheherazade, who told stories as a means of survival. For many novelists and poets whose works are known only on the printed page, their work remains connected to the oral tradition, because it is through their storytelling they reclaim the past, connect to a tradition of women's literature, and resist efforts to silence women's voices.

Works

*Andreski, Iris. *Old Wives' Tales: Life-Stories from Ibibioland.* New York: Schocken, 1970.

*Djebar, Assia. *A Sister to Scheherazade.* Translated by Dorothy S. Blair. London, England: Quartet, 1987.

*Scheub, Harold. *The Xhosa Ntsomi.* Oxford, England: Clarendon, 1975.

Sebbar, Leila. *Sherazade: Missing: Aged 17, Dark Curly Hair, Green Eyes.* Translated by Dorothy Blair. London, England: Quartet, 1991.

Commentary

Asagba, Austin Ovigueraye. "Roots of African Drama: Critical Approaches and Elements of Continuity." *Kunapipi* 8.3 (1986): 84–99.

Barber, Karin. *I Could Speak Until Tomorrow: Oriki, Women, and the Past in a Yoruba Town.* Washington, DC: Smithsonian, 1991.

Busia, Abena P. A. "Words Whispered Over Voids: A Context for Black Women's Rebellious Voices in the Novel of the African Diaspora." *Black Feminist Criticism and Critical Theory.* Greenwood, FL: Penkevill, 1988. 1–41.

Davies, Carole Boyce. " 'Woman Is a Nation . . .': Women in Caribbean Oral Literature." *Out of the Kumbla: Women and Literature in the Caribbean.* Trenton, NJ: Africa World Press, 1990. 165–193.

Diawara, Mamadou. "Women, Servitude and History: The Oral Historical Traditions of Women of Servile Condition in the Kingdom of Jaara (Mali) from the Fifteenth to the Mid-nineteenth Century." *Discourse and Its Disguises: The Interpretation of African Oral Texts.* Birmingham, AL: Birmingham University, 1989. 109–137.

Elder, Arlene. "Ama Ata Aidoo and the Oral Tradition: A Paradox of Form and Substance." *African Literature Today* 15 (1985): 109–118.

Gautier, Marie-Lise Gazarian. *Interviews with Latin American Writers.* Elmwood Park, IL: Dalkey Archive, 1989.

Gleason, Judith. "My Year Reached, We Heard Ourselves Singing: Dawn Songs of Girls Becoming Women in Ogbogbo, Okrika, Rivers State, Nigeria, January 1990." *Research in African Literatures* 22.3 (fall 1991): 135–149.

Gunner, Elizabeth. "Songs of Innocence and Experience: Women as Composers and Performers of *Izibongo*, Zulu Praise Poetry." *Research in African Literatures* 10.2 (fall 1979): 239–267.

Jama, Zainab Mohamed. "Fighting to Be Heard: Somali Women's Poetry." *African Languages and Cultures* 4.1 (1991): 43–53.

Mack, Beverly B. " 'Waka Daya Ba Ta Kare Nike': One Song Will Not Finish the Grinding: Hausa Women's Oral Literature." *Contemporary African Literature.* Washington, DC: Three Continents, 1983. 15–48.

Mack, Beverly B. "Hausa Women Poets: Ghost Writers." *Ba Shiru* 12.2 (1985): 36–50.

Mack, Beverly B. "Songs from Silence: Hausa Women's Poetry." *Ngambika: Studies of Women in African Literature.* Trenton, NJ: Africa World Press, 1986. 181–190.

Marshall, Paule. "From the Poets in the Kitchen." *New York Times Book Review* (January 9, 1983): 3, 34–35.

Nnaemeka, Obioma. "From Orality to Writing: The (Re)Inscription of Womanhood." *Research in African Literatures* 25.4 (winter 1994): 137–157.

Pike, Charles. "Women Narrative Performers in Six Luiya Tsingano." *Ba Shiru* 12.2 (1985): 51–57.

Trinh T. Minh-ha. *Woman, Native, Other: Writing Postcoloniality and Feminism.* Bloomington: Indiana University, 1989.

"Women as Oral Artists" [special issue]. *Research in African Literatures* 25.3 (fall 1994).

The Orchid House by Phyllis Shand Allfrey (London, England: Constable, 1953). In this novel, narrated by a black nurse, a "house of women" is portrayed. Three sisters return to their home in the lush, beautiful, decaying hills of Dominica. They have each left to marry but have returned and conspire to take care of the hapless men in their lives by removing their tubercular cousin and their emotionally crippled and drug-dependent father from the island. One of the sisters, a political activist with a young son, chooses to remain on the island to raise her son there. The narrator predicts that the child will "outstay us all, living here perhaps to repair some of our mistakes" (235). This well-crafted, atmospheric novel is reminiscent of the novels of Jean Rhys.

Commentary

"Neglected West Indian Writers, No. 1: Phyllis Allfrey's *The Orchid House*. London: Constable, 1953." *World Literature Written in English* 11.1 (1972): 81–83.
Wylie, Herb. "Narrator/Narrated: The Position of Lally in *The Orchid House*." *World Literature Written in English* 31.1 (spring 1991): 21–33.

Orphée, Elvira. Born on May 22, 1929 (some sources say 1930), in Tucuman, a province in northern Argentina. Her father, a chemist, was from a Greek family; her mother was a teacher. She was frequently an invalid in childhood and learned to read at an early age. She attended a convent school when her health permitted and then left for Buenos Aires at age sixteen, after her mother died. She studied philosophy there, then traveled for further studies to Spain and France. She married an Argentinean painter in Paris, Miguel Ocampo, the nephew of Victoria Ocampo. They returned to Argentina, where she began to publish in Ocampo's influential literary journal *Sur*. She traveled with her husband on diplomatic assignment to Italy and spent considerable time in Venezuela. She has published several novels, though most of her work has been censored in her own country.

Work

El Angel's Last Conquest. Translated by Magda Bogin. New York: Available Press, 1985.

Commentary

Pinto, Magdalena Garcia. *Women Writers of Latin America: Intimate Histories.* Austin: University of Texas, 1991.

Ortiz Cofer, Judith. Born in Hormigueros, Puerto Rico in 1952, she moved to Patterson, New Jersey, as a child when her father was transferred by the army. The family moved frequently, and she attended high school and college in Georgia. She earned an M.A. from Florida Atlantic University, attended Oxford University on a scholarship in 1977, and has since been awarded many writing fellowships. She is the author of novels, stories, and poetry and has edited a collection of Chicano, Puerto-Rican, and Cuban-American poetry. She currently teaches in the English Department of the University of Georgia.

Works

*The Latin Deli. Athens: University of Georgia, 1993.
The Line of the Sun: A Novel. Athens: University of Georgia, 1989.
Peregrina. Golden, CO: Riverstone, 1986.
Silent Dancing: A Partial Remembrance of a Puerto Rican Childhood. Houston, TX: Arte Público, 1990.
Terms of Survival: Poems. Houston, TX: Arte Público, 1987.

Özdamar, Emine Sevgi. Born in Malatya, Turkey, in 1946, she is a writer and actor. She had her first role, in *Le Bourgeois Gentilhomme*, at the Bursa National Theatre at age twelve. She went to Germany to work in a factory in 1965 and, after a two-year stay, returned to Turkey to attend theater school in Istanbul, followed by graduate studies in Paris. She has had roles in many plays and films in Turkey, Germany, and France. Her first play, *Karagoz in Alemania*, was written in 1986 and was based on the letter written in broken German and ill-remembered Turkish, sent to her by a fellow Turk who felt "home is where you have a job." She published a novel, *Das Leben ist eine Karawanserei*, in 1992, which was awarded the prestigious Ingeborg Bachmann prize. A collection of short stories has been recently translated into English. Her stories are inventive and dreamlike, focused on the experience of Turks living in Germany and the ways in which the negotiations of language mirror the trade-offs and dislocations of the economically and culturally displaced.

Work

Mother Tongue. Translated by Craig Thomas. Toronto, Canada: Coach House, 1994.

P

Pan, Lynn. Born in Shanghai, China, she has lived in North Borneo and England and worked in several capitals in Europe and Asia as a journalist. She has written several works of travel literature and Chinese history as well as a memoir, *Tracing It Home*.

Works

China's Sorrow: Journeys Around the Yellow River. London, England: Century, 1985.
Into China's Heart: An Émigré's Journey Along the Yellow River. New York: Weatherhill, 1985.
*Tracing It Home: Journeys Around a Chinese Family. Tokyo, Japan: Kodansha, 1993.

Pande, Mrnala. Born in 1946 in India, the daughter of the popular novelist Shivani. She earned a B.A. at the University of Allahabad, studying English and Sanskrit literature, history, and archeology, and trained in music and the visual arts. Writing in Hindi, she has published stories and novels and has written musical drama and plays, winning awards for her work. As a journalist she writes on literature, the arts, and women's issues and serves as the editor of the magazine *Vama*. One of her novels is available in English translation.

Work

Daughter's Daughter. London, England: Mantra, 1993.

Parente Cunha, Helena. See **Cunha, Helena Parente.**

Parra, Teresa de la. Born in Paris in 1890, her real name Ana Parra Sanojo, she was brought to the family's sugar plantation near Caracas, where she spent her early childhood. She was sent to study at a convent school in Spain, returning to Venezuela at age eighteen. Parra was a writer who addressed the ways in which women are excluded from public and civic life in her first novel *Iphigenia* (1924) and depicted childhood on a sugar plantation in *Mama Blanca's Memoirs* (1929). She achieved some fame during her lifetime and her work is now being reexamined from a feminist perspective. She died in 1936.

Works

Iphigenia: The Diary of a Young Lady Who Wrote Because She Was Bored. Translated by Bertie Acker. Austin: University of Texas, 1993.
Mama Blanca's Memoirs. Translated by Harriet de Onis. Pittsburgh, PA: University of Pittsburgh, 1993.

Commentary

Fox-Lockert, Lucía. *Women Novelists in Spain and Spanish America.* Metuchen, NJ: Scarecrow Press, 1979.
Gambarini, Elsa Krieger. "The Male Critic and the Woman Writer: Reading Teresa de la Parra's Critics." *In the Feminine Mode: Essays on Hispanic Women Writers.* Lewisburg, PA: Bucknell University, 1990. 177–194.
Lemaitre, Louis Antoine. *Between Flight and Longing: The Journey of Teresa de la Parra.* New York: Vantage, 1986.
Meyer, Doris. " 'Feminine' Testimony in the Works of Teresa de la Parra, María Luisa Bombal, and Victoria Ocampo." *Contemporary Women Authors of Latin America.* New York: Brooklyn College, 1983. 3–15.
Sommer, Doris. "Jumbled Mirrors." *Transition: An International Review* 53 (1991): 159–162.
Stillman, Ronni Gordon. "Teresa de la Parra, Venezuelan Novelist and Feminist." *Latin American Women Writers: Yesterday and Today.* Pittsburgh, PA: Latin American Literary Review, 1977. 42–48.

Partnoy, Alicia. Born in Argentina in 1955, she was among the "disappeared" after the coup in 1976. She spent years in detention as a political prisoner. Her stories and poems were smuggled out and published anonymously in human rights journals. She was expelled from the country in December 1979, escorted directly from the prison to the airport. In 1984 she returned to Argentina to testify before the Commission for the Investigation of the Disappearances, but her testimony was dismissed because corroborating witnesses were too frightened to speak up. She has also testified before the United Nations and the Organization of American States on the cases of political killings in Argentina. She currently lives in Washington with her husband and two daughters and is a member of the board of directors of Amnesty International. She is, in addition to being an activist, a poet and teacher.

Works

The Little School: Tales of Disappearance and Survival in Argentina. Translated by
    Alicia Partnoy with Lois Athey and Sandra Braunstein. Pittsburgh, PA: Cleis,
    1986.
Revenge of the Apple/Venganza de la manzana. Translated by Richard Schaaf and others.
    Pittsburgh, PA: Cleis, 1992.

Commentary

Kaminsky, Amy K. *Reading the Body Politic: Feminist Criticism and Latin American
    Women Writers.* Minneapolis: University of Minnesota, 1993.
Manzor-Coats, Lillian. "The Reconstructed Subject: Women's Testimonials as Voices
    of Resistance." *Splintering Darkness: Latin American Women Writers in Search
    of Themselves.* Pittsburgh, PA: Latin American Literary Review, 1990. 157–171.

The Passion According to G. H. by Clarice Lispector (Minneapolis: University of Minnesota, 1988). This is a woman's "Notes from Underground,"
an introverted first-person narrative of a woman who is unpeeling reality in a
quest for self-discovery. As does Dostoevsky's Underground Man, the narrator
chooses self-abasement as a route to selfhood. She performs the "lowest of all
acts"—eating a cockroach—in order to arrive at a state of being "baptized by
the world." "Finally, finally, my husk had really broken, and I was, without
limit. By not being, I was" (172). The word *passion* refers both to her quest
for self-respect and the route she chooses to arrive at self-respect, one reminiscent of Christ's passion and sacrifice, linking the existentialist quest with the
aestheticism of Latin American Christianity.

Perera, Padma. Born and raised in India, she moved to the United States for
graduate study at the University of Michigan, where she won the Hopgood
Award for Fiction. She has since taught seminars and given readings at Vassar,
Columbia University, and the Rhode Island School of Design and has taught at
the University of Colorado at Boulder. She has published essays and stories in
several magazines, including *The New Yorker, The Saturday Evening Post,* and
The Iowa Review, and has published criticism and several collections of short
stories.

Works

Birthday, Deathday and Other Stories. London, England: Women's Press, 1985.
Coigns of Vantage. Calcutta, India: Writers' Workshop, 1972.
Dr. Salaam and Other Stories of India. Santa Barbara, CA: Capra, 1978.

Peri Rossi, Cristina. Born in 1941 in Montevideo, Uruguay, she earned a
degree in humanities and has worked as a journalist as well as a writer of fiction.
She went into exile in 1972, in the wake of a brutal coup, having to flee with
only ten dollars in her pocket and without luggage. She has lived ever since in
Spain, where she writes for *Diario 16, El Periódico,* and *Agencia Efe.* Her

essays, fiction, and poetry have been translated into many languages. Her works are ironic, philosophical, sometimes humorous in a mordant way, and present a Kafkaesque vision of the absurdity of the state and its political power.

Works

A Forbidden Passion. Pittsburgh, PA: Cleis, 1993.
*The Ship of Fools. Translated by Psiche Hughes. London, England: Readers International, 1989.

Commentary

Chanady, Amaryll B. "Cristina Peri Rossi and the Other Side of Reality." *Antigonish Review* 54 (1983): 44–48.
Kaminsky, Amy K. *Reading the Body Politic: Feminist Criticism and Latin American Women Writers.* Minneapolis: University of Minnesota, 1993.
Mora, Gabriela. "Enigmas and Subversions in Cristina Peri Rossi's *La nave de los locos* [Ship of Fools]." *Splintering Darkness: Latin American Women Writers in Search of Themselves.* Pittsburgh, PA: Latin American Literary Review, 1990. 19–30.

Philip, Marlene Nourbese. Born in 1947 in Tobago and raised there, she was the daughter of a school headmaster. Though she had filled notebooks with stories and poetry as a child, she was slow to think of herself as a writer. She attended the University of the West Indies, earning a first in economics, then earning a master's in political science at the University of Western Ontario, Canada, where she moved in 1968. She studied law and was admitted to the bar in 1975. After practicing law for seven years, she turned to writing full-time. She has published a novel and several volumes of poetry, one of which, *She Tries Her Tongue, Her Silence Softly Breaks*, won the Casa de las Américas Prize in 1988 in manuscript form—it had not yet found a publisher. She was a Guggenheim Fellow in poetry for 1990–1991. Her work explores the conundrum of language in a postcolonial context, the erasures of history, and the experience of exile and uprooting.

Works

*Harriet's Daughter. London, England: Heinemann, 1988.
Salmon Courage. Toronto, Canada: Williams Wallace, 1983.
*She Tries Her Tongue, Her Silence Softly Breaks. Charlottetown, Canada: Ragweed, 1989.
Thorns. Toronto, Canada: Williams Wallace, 1980.

Commentary

Hunter, Lynette. "After Modernism: Alternative Voices in the Writings of Dionne Brand, Claire Harris and Marlene Philip." *University of Toronto Quarterly* 62.2 (winter 1992): 256–280.
Philip, Marlene Nourbese. "The Absence of Writing, or, How I Almost Became a Spy." *Out of the Kumbla: Women and Literature in the Caribbean.* Trenton, NJ: Africa World Press, 1990. 271–278.

Thomas, H. Nigel. "Caliban's Voice: Marlene Nourbese Philip's Poetic Response to Western Hegemonic Discourse." *Studies in the Literary Imagination* 26.2 (fall 1993): 63–76.

Piñon, Nelida. Born in Brazil in 1936, she graduated from the Catholic University of Rio de Janeiro, after which she worked as a journalist for the newspaper *O Globo* and the magazine *Cadernos Brasileiros*. She has published a number of novels and short story collections and has taught writing in workshops and at a number of institutions, including Columbia, Johns Hopkins, and the University of Miami, where she is the Stanford Professor of Humanities. In 1989 she was the fourth woman elected to the Brazilian Academy of Letters. She is considered among the foremost writers in Brazil today. Her style is existentialist, following the lead of Clarice Lispector, but is also lyrical, and at times her novels take on epic dimensions without becoming heavy-handed. She has been an outspoken critic of dictatorship, and her works reflect concern that national history and family memory be rediscovered.

Works

Caetana's Sweet Song. Translated by Helen Lane. New York: Knopf 1992.
The Republic of Dreams: A Novel. Translated by Helen Lane. New York: Knopf, 1989.

Commentary

Piñon, Nelida. "The Myth of Creation." *Lives on the Line: The Testimony of Contemporary Latin American Authors*. Berkeley: University of California, 1988. 198–204.
Pontiero, Giovanni. "Notes on the Fiction of Nelida Piñon." *Review (Center for Interamerican Relations)* 17 (1976): 67–71.

Pizarnik, Alejandra. Born in Buenos Aires, Argentina, on April 29, 1936, to a White Russian family in exile, she studied philosophy and letters at the University of Buenos Aires and later studied art under Juan Planas. She traveled in 1960 to Paris, where she lived for four years, writing poetry and criticism for Spanish and French periodicals and translating poetry from French to Spanish as well as working on the staff of the journal *Cuardernos*. She also took courses at the Sorbonne on the history of religion and contemporary French literature. She met Octavio Paz in Paris, and he became a close friend. She published her first collection of poetry in 1955, the first volume of a trilogy much influenced by French poets, and in 1965, her book, *Los trabajos y las noches*, was named the best book of poetry by the Argentine Foundation of Arts. She received a Guggenheim Fellowship in 1969 and in 1971 a Fulbright Scholarship. On September 25, 1972, at the age of thirty-six, she committed suicide in Buenos Aires. Her work explores the limits of language and the nature of death. A selection of poems, excerpts from her journals, prose pieces, and comments by other writers can be found in *Alejandra Pizarnik: A Profile*.

Work

Alejandra Pizarnik: A Profile. Durango, CO: Logbridge-Rhodes, 1987.

Commentary

Bassnett, Susan. "Speaking with Many Voices: The Poems of Alejandra Pizarnik."
    Knives and Angels: Women Writers in Latin America. London, England: Zed,
    1990. 36–51.
Running, Thorpe. "The Poetry of Alejandra Pizarnik." *Chasqui* 14.2–3 (1985): 45–55.

Pizarro, Agueda. Born in 1941 in the United States to Colombian parents of
Rumanian and Spanish heritage, she is a poet and teacher at Barnard College.
She writes poetry in Spanish that explores the themes of exile and language,
creating neologisms in her work to express the exile's fused identity.

Work

Shadowinnower. New York: Columbia University, 1979.

Commentary

Pizarro, Agueda. "The Arc of Paradox." *Contemporary Women Authors of Latin Amer-
    ica.* New York: Brooklyn College, 1983. 98–101.

A Place Where the Sea Remembers by Sandra Benitez (Minneapolis, MN:
Coffee House, 1993). A novel built of short glimpses of interrelated lives, tied
together by the characters' dependence on Remedios, the woman they go to for
counsel and healing, who understands the events that link their lives together.
Remedios is the one who remembers the past and knows the future, and she
believes "it is stories that save us" (103). A promising first novel.

Plans for Departure by Nayantara Sahgal (New York: Norton, 1985). Set in
the 1920s, this novel focuses on the experiences of Europeans leaving India,
wrestling with the implications of their status as colonizers. The Danish heroine
provides a narrative viewpoint from which to examine the terrain—the mountainous physical setting and the shifting social landscape. A different vantage
point is provided through the views of modern grandchildren who reflect on
their mixed Indian/European heritage.

Politics. An inevitable theme of third world women's literature is politics and
the politically charged choices facing women. Many works of literature tackle
political questions in terms that are often personal, oppositional, and many-sided,
acknowledging the complex intersections formed between racism, sexism, and
colonial and neocolonial oppression. Indeed, because of their positioning at these
intersections, many third world women have a unique perspective. According
to critic Chandra Mohanty, "[T]he challenge of third world feminisms has been
precisely this inescapable link between feminist and political liberation move-

ments'' (10), a challenge surely faced by the writer whose literary landscape is necessarily complicated by that link.

Political events have made their mark on women's literature. Many Latin American writers, notably Claribel Alegría, Marjorie Agosín, Marta Traba, and Isabel Allende, have written about the ''disappeared'' victims of state violence. Chinese writers—Chen Jo-hsi and Tai Hou-ying among them—have found the Cultural Revolution an inescapably formative political movement that demands literary exploration. For South African writers, apartheid has proven an equally compelling subject—Nadine Gordimer, in particular, treating it as not only a political crisis but a personal one. Colonial rule, independence movements, and the persistence of imperialism in the postcolonial era have also formed the plots of many works. *Testimonios* and autobiographies of women involved in politics offer firsthand accounts of the political life.

Political culture has also provided unusually rich ground for grotesque explorations of the human condition. The novels of Vlady Kociancich, Alicia Borinsky, Aminata Sow Fall, and Jessica Hagedorn have taken political situations and treated them with high black humor. Griselda Gambaro has provided as chilling a picture of Argentinean politics in her play *Information for Foreigners* as any *testimonio* or documentary has achieved. In general, political issues are both an unavoidable ingredient of third world women's literature and a particularly powerful theme in the hands of many writers.

Works

Agosín, Marjorie. *Circles of Madness: Circulos de locura: Mothers of the Plaza de Mayo: Madres de la Plaza de Mayo.* Translated by Celeste Kostopulos-Cooperman. Fredonia, NY: White Pine, 1992.

*Alegría, Claribel. *Flowers from the Volcano.* Translated by Carolyn Forche. Pittsburgh: University of Pittsburgh, 1982.

*Alegría, Claribel. *Luisa in Realityland.* Translated by Darwin J. Flakoll. Willimantic, CT: Curbstone, 1987.

*Allende, Isabel. *Of Love and Shadows.* Translated by Margaret Sayers Peden. New York: Knopf, 1987.

*Badr, Liyanah. *A Compass for the Sunflower.* Translated by Catherine Cobham. London, England: Women's Press, 1989.

*Belli, Gioconda. *From Eve's Rib.* Willimantic, CT: Curbstone Press, 1989.

*Blouin, Andrée, with Jean MacKellar. *My Country, Africa: Autobiography of the Black Pasionaria.* New York: Praeger, 1983.

*Chen Jo-hsi. *The Execution of Mayor Yin and Other Stories from the Great Proletarian Cultural Revolution.* Translated by Howard Goldblatt. Bloomington: Indiana University, 1978.

*Collins, Merle. *Angel.* London, England: Women's Press, 1987.

Condé, Maryse. *A Season in Rihata.* Translated by Richard Philcox. London, England: Heinemann, 1988.

*Fall, Aminata Sow. *The Beggars' Strike, or, the Dregs of Society.* Harlow, England: Longman, 1986.

*Gambaro, Griselda. *Information for Foreigners: Three Plays*. Translated by Marguerite
    Feitlowitz. Evanston, IL: Northwestern University, 1992.
*Gordimer, Nadine. *A Guest of Honour*. New York: Viking, 1970.
*Gordimer, Nadine. *Burger's Daughter*. New York: Viking, 1979.
*Gordimer, Nadine. *A Sport of Nature*. New York: Knopf, 1987.
*Hagedorn, Jessica. *Dogeaters*. London, England: Pandora, 1991.
Joseph, Helen. *Side by Side*. London, England: Zed, 1986.
Khaled, Leila, with George Hajjar. *My People Shall Live: The Autobiography of a Rev-
    olutionary*. London, England: Hodder and Stoughton, 1973.
*Kociancich, Vlady. *The Last Days of William Shakespeare*. Translated by Margaret Jull
    Costa. New York: William Morrow, 1991.
*Mugo, Micere Githae, and Ngugi wa Thiong'o. *The Trial of Dedan Kimathi*. Nairobi,
    Kenya: Heinemann, 1976.
*Sahgal, Nayantara. *Rich Like Us*. New York: New Directions Publishing, 1988.
Suzman, Helen. *In No Uncertain Terms: A South African Memoir*. New York: Knopf,
    1993.
*Tai Hou-ying. *Stones of the Wall*. Translated by Frances Wood. New York: St. Martin's,
    1986.
*Traba, Marta. *Mothers and Shadows*. Translated by Jo Labanyi. New York: Readers
    International, 1989.

Commentary

Dawes, Greg. *Aesthetics and Revolution: Nicaraguan Poetry, 1979–1990*. Minneapolis:
    University of Minnesota, 1993.
Ettin, Andrew Vogel. *Betrayals of the Body Politic: The Literary Commitments of Nadine
    Gordimer*. Charlottesville: University Press of Virginia, 1992.
Geurtz, Kathryn. "Personal Politics in the Novels of Bessie Head." *Présence Africaine*
    140 (1986): 47–74.
Gordimer, Nadine. "English-Language Literature and Politics in South Africa." *Aspects
    of South African Literature*. London, England: Heinemann, 1976. 99–120.
Gordimer, Nadine. *The Essential Gesture: Writing, Politics, and Places*. New York:
    Knopf, 1988.
Gunn, Janet Varner. "A Politics of Experience: Leila Khaled's *My People Shall Live:
    The Autobiography of a Revolutionary*." *De/Colonizing the Subject: The Politics
    of Gender in Women's Autobiography*. Minneapolis: University of Minnesota,
    1992. 65–80.
Harlow, Barbara. *Resistance Literature*. New York: Methuen, 1987.
Harlow, Barbara. *Barred: Women, Writing, and Political Detention*. Middletown, CT:
    Wesleyan University, 1992.
Kintz, Linda. *The Subject's Tragedy: Political Poetics, Feminist Theory, and Drama*.
    Ann Arbor: University of Michigan, 1992.
Lima, Maria Helena. "Revolutionary Developments: Michelle Cliff's *No Telephone to
    Heaven* and Merle Collins's *Angel*." *Ariel* 24.1 (January 1993): 35–56.
Miaz, Magdalena, and Luis H. Pena. "Between Lines: Constructing the Political Self."
    A/B: Auto/Biography Studies 3.4 (summer 1988): 23–36.
Mohanty, Chandra Talpade. "Cartographies of Struggle: Third World Women and the
    Politics of Feminism." *Third World Women and the Politics of Feminism*. Bloo-
    mington: Indiana University, 1991. 1–47.

Mohanty, S. P. "Us and Them: On the Philosophical Bases of Political Criticism." *Yale Journal of Criticism* 2.2 (spring 1989): 1–31.

Monsman, Gerald. "Olive Schreiner: Literature and the Politics of Power." *Texas Studies in Literature and Language* 30.4 (winter 1988): 583–610.

Seely, Clinton B., editor. *Women, Politics, and Literature in Bengal.* East Lansing: Michigan State University, 1981.

Smith, Sidonie, and Julia Watson, editors. *De/Colonizing the Subject: The Politics of Gender in Women's Autobiography.* Minneapolis: University of Minnesota, 1992.

Tahon, Marie-Blanche. "Women Novelists and Women in the Struggle for Algeria's National Liberation (1957–1980)." *Research in African Literatures* 23.2 (summer 1992): 39–50.

Trinh T. Minh-ha. *When the Moon Waxes Red: Representation, Gender, and Cultural Politics.* New York: Routledge, 1991.

Pollard, Velma. Sister of Erna Brodber, born in rural Jamaica in 1937 to a schoolteacher and a farmer and grew up in Woodside, St. Mary. She holds a Ph.D. in language education, has taught in Montreal, New York, Guyana, and Trinidad, and is now lecturer in education at the University of the West Indies, specializing in teaching English in a Creole-speaking environment, language in Caribbean literature, and language of the Rastafari. She also writes fiction, poetry, and criticism.

Works

*Considering Woman. London, England: Women's Press, 1989.
Crown Point and Other Poems. Leeds, England: Peepal Tree, 1988.
Karl and Other Stories. Harlow, England: Longman, 1993.
Shame Trees Don't Grow Here. Leeds, England: Peepal Tree, 1991.

Poniatowska, Elena. Born in Paris, on May 19, 1933, of Polish-Mexican ancestry. On her father's side, she is the descendant of Prince Poniatowski, marshal of France under Napoleon, and Stanislaw August, the last king of Poland. Her mother came from a family of reactionary Mexican landowners, though she herself was born in Paris. In 1942 her family left occupied France for Mexico. Since 1954 she has worked as a journalist, serving on the staff of *Excelsior* and, later, *Novedades.* She is particularly noted for her interviews of prominent artists and intellectuals. Her literary career started at the same time as her journalistic one, with her first novel seeing publication in 1954. She combines her journalism with novelistic techniques, mingling interviews, eyewitness accounts, and fictional narration. She is considered one of the most prominent Mexican women of letters today.

Works

*Dear Diego. Translated by Katherine Silver. New York: Pantheon Books, 1986.
Massacre in Mexico. Translated by Helen Lane. New York: Viking, 1975.

Commentary

Bruce-Novoa, Juan. "Elena Poniatowska: The Feminist Origins of Commitment." *Women's Studies International Forum* 6.5 (1983): 509–516.

Bruce-Novoa, Juan. "Subverting the Dominant Text: Elena Poniatowska's *Querido Diego*." *Knives and Angels: Women Writers in Latin America*. London, England: Zed, 1990. 115–131.

Chevigny, Bell Gale. "The Transformation of Privilege in the Work of Elena Poniatowska." *Latin American Literary Review* 13 (July-December 1985): 49–62.

Conde, Susana. "*Belles Lettres* Interview: Elena Poniatowska." *Belles Lettres* 7.2 (winter 1992): 41–44.

Davis, Lisa. "An Invitation to Understanding Among Poor Women of the Americas: *The Color Purple* and *Hasta no verte, Jesús mío*." *Reinventing the Americas: Comparative Studies of Literature of the United States and Spanish America*. Cambridge, England: Cambridge University, 1986. 224–241.

Fox-Lockert, Lucía. *Women Novelists in Spain and Spanish America*. Metuchen, NJ: Scarecrow Press, 1979.

Gautier, Marie-Lise Gazarian. *Interviews with Latin American Writers*. Elmwood Park, IL: Dalkey Archive, 1989.

Gold, Janet. "Feminine Space and the Discourse of Silence: Yolanda Oreamuno, Elena Poniatowska, and Luisa Valenzuela." *In the Feminine Mode: Essays on Hispanic Women Writers*. Lewisburg, PA: Bucknell University, 1990. 195–203.

González, Aníbal. *Journalism and the Development of Spanish-American Narrative*. Cambridge, England: Cambridge University, 1993.

Hancock, Joel. "Elena Poniatowska's *Hasta no verte, Jesús mío*: The Remaking of the Image of Woman." *Hispania* 66.3 (1983): 353–359.

Jörgensen, Beth E. "Framing Questions: The Role of the Editor in Elena Poniatowska's *La noche de Tlatelolco*." *Latin American Perspectives* 18.3 (summer 1991): 80–90.

Jörgensen, Beth E. *The Writings of Elena Poniatowska: Engaging Dialogues*. Austin: University of Texas, 1994.

Kerr, Lucille. "Gestures of Authorship: Lying to Tell the Truth in Elena Poniatowska's *Hasta no verte, Jesús mío*." *MLN* 106 (1991): 371–394.

Miller, Beth. "Interview with Elena Poniatowska." *Latin American Literary Review* 4.7 (1975): 73–78.

Paul, Marcella L. "Letters and Desire: The Function of Marks on Paper in Elena Poniatowska's *Querido Diego, te abraza Quela*." *Continental, Latin-American, and Francophone Women Writers*. Lanham, MD: University Press of America, 1990. 1–5.

Pinto, Magdalena Garcia. *Women Writers of Latin America: Intimate Histories*. Austin: University of Texas, 1991.

Price, Greg, editor. *Latin America: The Writer's Journey*. London, England: Hamish Hamilton, 1990.

Starcevic, Elizabeth. "Elena Poniatowska: Witness for the People." *Contemporary Women Authors of Latin America*. New York: Brooklyn College, 1983. 72–77.

Tatum, Charles M. "Elena Poniatowska's *Hasta no verte, Jesús mío* [*Until I See You, Dear Jesus*]." *Latin American Women Writers: Yesterday and Today*. Pittsburgh, PA: Latin American Literary Review, 1977. 49–58.

Taylor, Cathy. *The New Narrative of Mexico: Sub-versions of History in Mexican Fiction.* Lewisburg, PA: Bucknell University, 1994.

Possession by Kamala Markandaya (New York: John Day, 1963). A novel about an Englishwoman who carries off an Indian goatherd with artistic talent to become her exotic pet artist at home in England. She struggles for his soul with his elderly swami and eventually loses, as the man returns to India and to the swami's mystical understanding of the world. The "possession" of the title refers not only to the desire of the woman to own the man but to his state of being "possessed" by Western values, filled with and taken over by a foreign identity.

Commentary

Sethuraman, Ramchandran. "Writing Across Cultures: Sexual/Racial 'Othering' in Kamala Markandaya's *Possession.*" *Ariel* 23.3 (July 1992): 101–120.

Prado, Adélia. Brazilian poet, born in 1935 in Divinopolis, Mina Gerais state. Her family were laborers on the railroad, and her mother and grandmother both died in childbirth. She was the first member of her family to attend the university and earned degrees in philosophy and religious education; she taught religion in public schools until 1979. She currently works as cultural liaison for the city of Divinopolis, where she still lives. She began to write poetry at an early age but did not show it to anyone and only published for the first time in her forties. She has since published eight books of poetry that have been well received; a theatrical production based on her work was very popular in Rio and on tour in 1987. She has been a member of literary delegations to Cuba and to Portugal but does not participate much in literary or academic circles.

Work

The Alphabet in the Park: Selected Poems of Adélia Prado. Translated by Ellen Watson. Middletown, CT: Wesleyan University, 1990.

Commentary

Bolton, Betsy. "Adélia Prado: Romanticism Revisited." *Luso-Brazilian Review* 29 (1992): 45–48.

Praisesong for the Widow by Paule Marshall (New York: Dutton, 1984). The story of a woman's recovery of her past and her connectedness to her community. While on a Caribbean cruise, Avey Johnson, a well-to-do black widow from White Plains, is driven by dreams and unexpected feelings to leave the cruise ship at Grenada and return home. She does, indeed, return home, but in a spiritual sense as she relives her life in flashbacks, remembering how her grandmother told her stories of the slaves landing at the offshore island, where her people lived, and how they turned around and walked across the water back to Africa. She is persuaded by an old islander, Lebert Joseph, to go with a group of people to the little island of Carriacou, where they will celebrate their roots in an annual festival, and there she participates in a Pardon Dance, and then in the dances of the nations of Africa, remembered from the time they were brought over as slaves. She recovers a memory of her ancestry and resolves to relive the storytelling with her grandchildren so that the threads of connection will not be broken again.

Commentary

Busia, Abena P. A. "What Is Your Nation? Reconnecting Africa and Her Diaspora Through Paule Marshall's *Praisesong for the Widow." Changing Our Own Words: Essays on Criticism, Theory, and Writing by Black Women.* New Brunswick, NJ: Rutgers University, 1989. 196–211.

Christian, Barbara. "Ritualistic Process and the Structure of Paule Marshall's *Praisesong for the Widow." Callaloo* 6.2 (1983): 31–45.

Pollard, Velma. "Cultural Connections in Paule Marshall's *Praisesong for the Widow." World Literature Written in English* 25.2 (1985): 285–298.

Sandiford, Keith A. "Paule Marshall's *Praisesong for the Widow*: The Reluctant Heiress, or Whose Life Is It Anyway?" *Black American Literature Forum* 20.4 (winter 1986): 371–392.

Wilentz, Gay. *Binding Cultures: Black Women Writers in Africa and the Diaspora.* Bloomington: Indiana University, 1992.

Prajaub Thirabutana. A Thai woman who, in the course of studying the English language, began to record her observations of village life. Encouraged by her teacher to publish them, she wrote an unassuming memoir that covers her childhood, her family's life, her schooling, and her work as a teacher.

Work

Little Things. Sydney, Australia: Collins, 1971.

Prince, Mary. Born a slave in Bermuda in 1788, she was the first black British woman to escape from slavery and publish an autobiography. As a child, she worked as a houseworker and child minder and later was sent to the salt ponds on Turk's Island where slaves collected salt standing in water most of the day, getting huge boils on their legs and feet. After working there for around ten years, she again became a house slave and worked around the grounds, gardening and taking care of livestock. She was sold and moved to Antigua in 1814, and when her owners went to England, they took her with them, separating her from her husband, a free black carpenter in Antigua. In London her owners threw her out after she became too sick to do their washing, and in 1828 she went to the offices of the Anti-Slavery Society and petitioned for their help in gaining her freedom. She became a campaigner against slavery, contributing her memoirs, with their graphic witness of the brutality of slavery, to the cause. She died in 1833.

Work

The History of Mary Prince, a West Indian Slave, Related by Herself. London, England: Pandora, 1987.

Commentary

Paquet, Sandra Pouchet. "The Heartbeat of a West Indian Slave: *The History of Mary Prince." African American Review* 26.1 (spring 1992): 131–146.

Publishing. Publishing has always been problematic for women writers, a difficulty compounded for third world women. The first world dominates the publishing industry, and so its perceptions of market forces drive the choice of what is to be published. A third world writer often faces the choice of writing for a first world market as a representative of the third world or writing for a third world audience with little hope of reaching them. Ama Ata Aidoo finds the publishing industry tainted with neocolonialism. "It has to do with the limitations of publishing opportunities and also the straightjacket to be a 'third world woman.' . . . Maybe with us the pressures are heavier because there are fewer publishing possibilities for 'third world' writers. Someone can declare that your manuscript doesn't read like a manuscript from a third world person" (George, 305). In many cases, women writers have faced the additional problem of not being taken seriously because they are women. Both Buchi Emecheta and Tsitsi Dangarembga were unable to find African publishers until their reputations were established in the British publishing world. Finally, women writers in the third world have difficulty establishing the necessary "room of one's own" and independent income to afford to write at all. Merle Hodge has said of the situation that "it's not really feasible to make writing a full-time career in developing countries. . . . I don't think that any of us find it possible to withdraw and be writers in the political and economic situation in which we live. . . . [Also, women writers] don't have the time and the space and all of the other things that male writers seem to have that allow them just to write books" (Balutansky, 651–652).

Some women have founded publishing houses to gain more control over the situation. Victoria Ocampo's publishing house and literary journal *Sur* had enormous influence on Latin American letters. More recently, Flora Nwapa and Buchi Emecheta started their own publishing houses, but financial backing is difficult to come by, particularly in a volatile African publishing market. The Indian journal *Manushi* has proven a venue for many feminist writers. Several first world feminist publishers, notably the Women's Press, have created opportunities for many third world writers, as have third world publishing ventures such as Skotaville Press of South Africa, the Calcutta-based Writers' Workshop, and the South African journal *Staffrider.* See Appendix III for a selective list of journals and publishing houses which have been involved with third world women's literature.

Commentary

Altbach, Philip G. *Publishing and Development in the Third World*. London, England: Hans Zell, 1992.

Balutansky, Kathleen M. "We Are All Activists: An Interview with Merle Hodge." *Callaloo* 12 (fall 1989): 651–662.

Falcoff, Mark. "Victoria Ocampo's 'Sur.' " *New Creation* 7 (1988): 27–37.

George, Rosemary Marangoly and Helen Scott. " 'A New Tail to an Old Tale': An Interview with Ama Ata Aidoo." *Novel* 26.3 (spring 1993): 297–308.

Hahner, June S. "The Nineteenth-Century Feminist Press and Women's Rights in Brazil." *Latin American Women: Historical Perspectives*. Westport, CT: Greenwood, 1978. 254–285.

King, John. Sur: *A Study of the Argentine Literary Journal and Its Role in the Development of a Culture, 1931–1970*. Cambridge, England: Cambridge University, 1988.

Kirkwood, Mike. "*Staffrider*: An Informal Discussion." *English in Africa* 7.2 (September 1980): 22–31.

Mutloatse, Mothobi. "Indigenous Publishing in South Africa: The Case of Skotaville Publishers." *Publishing and Development in the Third World*. London, England: Hans Zell, 1992. 211–222.

Vaughan, Michael. "*Staffrider* and Directions Within Contemporary South African Literature." *Literature and Society in South Africa*. Harlow, England: Longman, 1984. 196–212.

Yeager, Gertrude M. "Women and the Intellectual Life of Nineteenth Century Lima." *Revista Interamericana de Bibliografía* 40.4 (1990): 361–393.

Zell, Hans M. "Publishing in Africa: The Crisis and the Challenge." *A History of Twentieth-Century African Literatures*. Lincoln: University of Nebraska, 1993. 369–387.

Q

Queiroz, Rachel de. Born in Ceara, Brazil, in 1910, she wrote her first novel at the age of twenty. She has written several novels, plays, and short stories, particularly focused on the lives of women in the northeastern region of Brazil. She was the first woman to become a member of the Brazilian Academy of Letters and was a major figure both among northeastern regional writers and the social novelists of the 1930s. Her style is neonaturalist, and her stories are often about women who are searching for a role in society. *As tres Marias* (1939; *The Three Marias*, translated 1963) follows the lives of three women who chafe under the boundaries of provincial patriarchal society; her later novel, *Dora Doralina* (1975; translated 1984), is a first-person account of a woman who recounts a similar life but who breaks through and achieves a strong, independent identity. Queiroz has also written short stories and plays as well as works on northeastern folklore.

Works

Dora, Doralina. Translated by Dorothy Scott Loos. New York: Avon Books, 1984.
*The Three Marias. Austin: University of Texas, 1963.

Commentary

Courteau, Joanna. ''The Problematic Heroines in the Novels of Rachel de Queiroz.''
    Luso-Brazilian Review 22.2 (1985): 123–144.
Elison, Fred P. *Brazil's New Novel.* Berkeley: University of California, 1954.
Woodbridge, Benjamin. ''The Art of Rachel de Queiroz.'' *Hispania* 40 (May 1957):
    144–148.

A Question of Power by Bessie Head (London, England: Heinemann, 1974). This extraordinary narrative is the journey of a mentally ill woman through madness, a madness that takes the form of a power struggle between two male figures who manipulate her in their struggle for power. In between bouts of insanity, she works on a model gardening development scheme and tends her young son. She, like the heroine of *Maru*, is a product of two cultures, born of an unhappy union between a white woman and her black servant. The power struggle within subtly mirrors the political and personal struggle, and in the conclusion, there is some hope that the woman is regaining control of her self-hood. Head said of this book in an interview that it was "totally autobiographical" (MacKenzie and Clayton, 24). While the struggle isn't settled entirely, there is a sense that there are alternatives to power in an ethic of caring and of community implicit in the closing passages: "As she fell asleep, she placed one soft hand over her land. It was a gesture of belonging" (206). The journal *Black Scholar* named this one of the "most influential books for the decade" (March-April 1981, 521).

Commentary

Abrahams, Cecil A. "The Tyranny of Place: The Context of Bessie Head's Fiction." *World Literature Written in English* 17 (1978): 22–29.

Berger, Roger A. "The Politics of Madness in Bessie Head." *The Tragic Life: Bessie Head and Literature in Southern Africa*. Trenton, NJ: Africa World Press, 1990. 31–43.

Bryce-Okunlola, Jane. "Motherhood as a Metaphor for Creativity in Three African Women's Novels: Flora Nwapa, Rebeka Njau, and Bessie Head." *Motherlands: Women's Writings from Africa, the Caribbean, and South Asia*. New Brunswick, NJ: Rutgers University, 1992. 200–218.

Davison, Carol Margaret. "A Method in the Madness." *The Tragic Life: Bessie Head and Literature in Southern Africa*. Trenton, NJ: Africa World Press, 1990. 19–29.

Geurtz, Kathryn. "Personal Politics in the Novels of Bessie Head." *Présence Africaine* 140 (1986): 47–74.

Ibrahim, Huma. "The Autobiographical Content in the Works of South African Women Writers: The Personal and the Political." *Biography East and West: Selected Conference Papers*. Honolulu: University of Hawaii, 1989. 122–126.

Lorenz, Paul. "Colonization and the Feminine in Bessie Head's *A Question of Power*." *Modern Fiction Studies* 37.3 (autumn 1991): 591–605.

MacKenzie, Craig, and Cherry Clayton. *Between the Lines: Interviews with Bessie Head, Sheila Roberts, Ellen Kuzwayo, Miriam Tlali*. Grahamstown, South Africa: National English Literary Museum, 1989.

Pearse, Adetokunbo. "Apartheid and Madness: Bessie Head's *A Question of Power*." *Kunapipi* 5.2 (1983): 81–93.

Ravenscroft, Arthur. "The Novels of Bessie Head." *Aspects of South African Literature*. London, England: Heinemann, 1976. 174–186.

Rooney, Carolyn. " 'Dangerous Knowledge' and the Poetics of Survival: A Reading of *Our Sister Killjoy* and *A Question of Power*." *Motherlands: Women's Writings from Africa, the Caribbean, and South Asia.* New Brunswick, NJ: Rutgers University, 1992. 99–126.

Rose, Jacqueline. ''On the 'Universality' of Madness: Bessie Head's *A Question of Power.*'' *Critical Inquiry* 20.3 (spring 1994): 401–418.

R

Rachlin, Nahid. Iranian novelist and short story writer, she spent her early childhood with a childless aunt in a traditional household; she rejoined her parents at age ten, and she found herself in a family that was influenced by the presence of foreign oil company workers. Her father, who opposed her ambitions to write, grudgingly allowed her to travel to the United States to study. She began to write in earnest, winning the Bennet Cerf Award at Columbia while a student there. She has held a Doubleday-Columbia Fellowship, a Wallace Stegner Fellowship at Stanford University, and was awarded a grant from the National Endowment for the Arts. She lives in New York, where she teaches creative writing at New York University. She has published short stories in numerous periodicals, including the *Minnesota Review, Ararat*, and *Shenandoah*, as well as a collection of stories and two novels.

Works

The Foreigner. New York: Norton, 1978.
*Married to a Stranger. New York: Dutton, 1983.
Veils: Short Stories. San Francisco: City Lights, 1992.

Commentary

Rachlin, Nahid. "Would I Have Become a Writer Without My Sister?" *The Confidence Woman: 26 Women Writers at Work.* Atlanta, GA: Longstreet, 1991. 183–192.

Rain Darling by Merle Collins (London, England: Women's Press, 1990). Short stories about families, about relations between mothers and daughters, and about women's relationship to the girls they once were. The title story tells of a woman whose "father" believes her to be someone else's daughter; she grows up rejected and resented, which takes its toll. Her story is told in flashback from her adulthood in a hospital. In "Gran" a child gets to know the details of her grandmother's life only at her grand funeral. In "The Visit," a woman goes to stay with her children in England for a time and can't wait to get home to the Caribbean. Each story is narrated by a compelling voice, exploring the traumas of family relationships and the heritage of colonialism.

Rama Rau, Santha. Born on January 24, 1923, in Madras, India. Her father was a noted diplomat, instrumental in Indian independence, and her mother was a pioneer in family planning issues and health care. Because they spoke different languages, they settled on English as a *lingua franca* for their home. Rau spent her early childhood in India, but at age six, her father received a diplomatic assignment in England. The family later moved to South Africa, where her father was the Indian high commissioner and where she came face to face with the racist heritage of colonialism. She spent the war years back in India, in her grandmother's highly traditional household, and then attended Wellesley College in the United States, majoring in English. She wrote *Home to India* soon after graduation and began to write for a magazine, later moving to postwar Japan with her father who had been appointed ambassador. She began to travel in the Far East and then Europe, basing travel writings on her adventures, and married an American writer, Faubion Bowers, whom she later divorced. She wrote for numerous magazines and published several travel accounts and the novels *Remember the House* and *The Adventurers* as well as autobiographical works and a dramatization of *A Passage to India* by E. M. Forster, whom she knew personally. She married again in 1970, to Gordon Wallace Wattles, and lives in Amenia, New York.

Works

The Adventurers. New York: Harper and Row, 1970.
East of Home. New York: Harper and Row, 1950.
Gifts of Passage. New York: Harper and Row, 1961.
Home to India. New York: Harper and Brothers, 1945.
My Russian Journey. New York: Harper and Row, 1959.
A Passage to India. New York: Harcourt, Brace and World, 1961.
A Princess Remembers: The Memoirs of the Maharani of Jaipur. With Gayatri Devi.
          London, England: Century, 1976.
Remember the House. New York: Harper and Row, 1956.
This Is India. New York: Harper and Row, 1954.
View to the Southeast. New York: Harper and Row, 1956.

Commentary

Desai, S. K. *Santha Rama Rau.* New Delhi, India: Arnold-Heinemann, 1976.

Randhawa, Ravinder. Born in India, she moved to England with her parents when she was only seven years old. She is the author of a novel that depicts the lives of several Indian women living in Britain, linked through the observations of a determinedly eccentric "wicked old woman." She is a founding member of the Asian Women Writers' Collective, has worked with an organization that sets up refuges and resource centers for Asian women, and has been involved in antiracist campaigns.

Work

*A Wicked Old Woman. London, England: Women's Press, 1987.

Rau, Santha Rama. See **Rama Rau, Santha.**

Recollections of Things to Come by Elena Garro (Austin: University of Texas, 1969). A novel about the Mexican Revolution that mixes history and the fantastic and challenges not only the notion of history as a set of facts but the notion of time itself. The narrator is a collective one, the residents of the town of Ixtepec, through which the military players of the revolution battle while the inhabitants watch the spectacle. History as a concept is explored in the process— memory of the past, the representation of events, is subject to interpretation, so the history of the war is an act of narrative interpretation. In the same way, time is curiously nonlinear. The war proceeds in chronology, but the town itself seems locked in timelessness; it is possible, in this suspended world, to remember things to come, to see death and life as concomitant events, to find in past and future little separation. An interesting mix of historical events and historicism, of magic and realism.

Commentary

Anderson, Robert K. "Myth and Archetype in *Recollections of Things to Come.*" *Studies in Twentieth Century Literature* 9.2 (1985): 213–227.

Red Flower of China by Zhai Zhenhua (New York: Soho, 1993). The autobiography of a woman who grew up in China after the revolution and became one of the young "Red Guards," who were the first wave of the Cultural Revolution. She recounts the events and pressures that made teens turn on their teachers and elders and the self-consuming nature of the beast that for ten years caused citizens to lead attacks and then become the victims of other attackers themselves. She makes clear both the extraordinary nervousness and fear of being incorrect that drove students to extreme behavior, and the obsessively symbolic meanings that gestures, images, and ordinary objects accrued in the heated and demanding atmosphere. She herself was purged soon after being on the leading edge of the revolution and spent years as a peasant, a factory laborer, and finally a propagandist before the end of the period. She was finally rehabilitated and allowed to attend a university and, finally, to study abroad. The author uses a naive and unembellished tone that makes it possible to understand how a child could be sucked into the destructive energies unleashed in 1966.

Red Ivy, Green Earth Mother by Ai Bei (Salt Lake City, UT: Peregrine Smith Books, 1990). These stories are unusual explorations of selfhood, intense and dreamlike, in which reality and dream are inextricable. The first story deals with a young woman trying to find a mythical China, finding every place she visits corrupted until she comes to a strange mountain village. Her life story is interleaved with her pilgrimage, her past merging strangely with the curious landscape in which she finds herself. The author has a style that is highly unusual and experimental, practicing a sort of magic realism in which the magic gets the upper hand.

Reddy, Jayapraga. A South African writer of Indian heritage who has had her stories dramatized on the British Broadcasting Corporation (BBC), published in *Staffrider* magazine, and collected in one published volume. She takes her ideas from news stories or anecdotes she encounters in life and tells them in spare, understated narratives that demonstrate her belief that there is no "typical" South African way of life.

Work

On the Fringe of Dreamtime and Other Stories. Johannesburg, South Africa: Skotaville, 1987.

Relative Merits: A Personal Memoir of the Bandaranaike Family of Sri Lanka by Yasmine Gooneratne (New York: St. Martin's, 1986). This family portrait of several generations of an influential high-caste Singhalese family, one that included two prime ministers, has a curiously Edwardian flavor, demonstrating the ways in which British and Sri Lankan cultures fuse and oppose one another. The author has also fused family memories with their public history, enriching her own understanding of her family and at the same time enlarging the public's knowledge of an important dynasty.

Commentary

Gooneratne, Yasmine. "Writing a Family History." *Journal of Indian Writing in English* 16.2 (1988): 126–135.

Reports by May Wong (New York: Harcourt, Brace, 1972). Powerful poetry told in haunting images and sounds. The opening poem, "First," has in it the image of Persephone going underground, as underground water, hell a place where man is the climate, woman the country. Another poem, "East Bengal," describes children dying, the first victims of human conflict. A wide-ranging and substantial collection.

The Republic of Dreams: A Novel by Nelida Piñon (New York: Knopf, 1989). This book, vast in its scope, traces the formation of Brazil as a "republic of dreams," as a landscape and a nation composed by a family's shared memory, tenaciously preserved and handed down. The family's history, arriving from Spain and tenaciously hanging on to Galician culture, is also the history of the nation of Brazil, where indigenous cultures absorb and counter the traditions of the conquerors. At the end of the novel, its own story is born as a young woman determines to write the book of family dreams, the tale of the arrival of her family and the shared memory that constitutes their landscape.

A Revolutionary Woman by Sheila Fugard (New York: Braziller, 1985). A historical novel about a South African woman living in the Karoo District in the 1920s who is a follower of Gandhi but ambivalent about the submissive role assumed by Gandhi's wife. The plot revolves around the seduction of a retarded Boer girl by a colored man and the violence that follows. The narrative is spare and stark, mythic rather than naturalistic in tone. Parallels are drawn between the Indian caste system and apartheid, while the narration explores the psychology of Afrikaner culture, scarred by the Boer War, and the role of women in political resistance.

Rhys, Jean. Born in 1890 (some sources say 1894) in Dominica, daughter of a Welsh physician and a Creole mother, descendant of a family of planters and slave owners. When she was seventeen she left the island for England and Paris, returning only briefly in 1936. She studied drama at the Royal Academy of Dramatic Arts but had to leave when her father died and the family could no longer afford her schooling. She joined the chorus of a show touring Britain. Later, she moved to Paris where she met Ford Madox Ford, who promoted her work until a quarrel broke up their problematic relationship. She was married three times, her first marriage a disastrous union with a Dutchman who was arrested and imprisoned for financial misdoings. She established a modest literary reputation beginning in 1927 with the publication of *The Left Bank*, followed by four novels. She stopped writing for thirty years and was virtually forgotten until the British Broadcasting Corporation (BBC) did a radio adaptation of her novel *Good Morning Midnight* and she published her masterpiece, *Wide Sargasso Sea*. It was not until the publication of this novel in 1966 that she was identified as a Caribbean writer, even though many of her works reflect the sense of alienation, loss, and exile that she herself felt as a Creole, belonging to neither white nor black worlds. She was working on an autobiography at the time of her death in 1979, which was published posthumously as *Smile, Please*.

Works

After Leaving Mr. MacKenzie. New York: Harper and Row, 1972.
The Collected Short Stories. New York: Norton, 1987.
Good Morning Midnight. New York: Vintage, 1974.

Jean Rhys: The Complete Novels. New York: Norton, 1985.
Left Bank, and Other Stories. Freeport, NY: Books for Libraries, 1970.
My Day; Three Pieces. New York: F. Hallman, 1975.
Quartet. New York: Harper and Row, 1981.
Sleep It Off, Lady: Stories. New York: Harper and Row, 1976.
Smile Please: An Unfinished Autobiography. New York: Harper and Row, 1979.
Tales of the Wide Caribbean. London, England: Heinemann, 1985.
Tigers Are Better-Looking. New York: Popular Library, 1976.
Voyage in the Dark. New York: Popular Library, 1966.
*Wide Sargasso Sea. New York: Norton, 1967.

Commentary

Brandmark, Wendy. "The Power of the Victim: A Study of *Quartet, After Leaving Mr. MacKenzie,* and *Voyage in the Dark* by Jean Rhys." *Kunapipi* 8.2 (1986): 21–29.

Brown, Bev E. L. "Mansong and Matrix: A Radical Experiment." *A Double Colonization: Colonial and Post-Colonial Women's Writing.* Mundelstrup, Denmark: Dangaroo, 1986. 68–79.

Cliff, Michelle. "Caliban's Daughter: The Tempest and the Teapot." *Frontiers* 12.2 (summer 1991): 36–51.

Davison, Carol Margaret. "A Method in the Madness." *The Tragic Life: Bessie Head and Literature in Southern Africa.* Trenton, NJ: Africa World Press, 1990. 19–29.

de Abruna, Laura Niesen. "Family Connections: Mother and Mother Country in the Fiction of Jean Rhys and Jamaica Kincaid." *Motherlands: Women's Writings from Africa, the Caribbean, and South Asia.* New Brunswick, NJ: Rutgers University, 1992. 257–289.

Emery, Mary Lou. *Jean Rhys at "World's End": Novels of Colonial and Sexual Exile.* Austin: University of Texas, 1990.

Erwin, Lee. " 'Like in a Looking-Glass': History and Narrative in *Wide Sargasso Sea.*" *Novel* 22.2 (winter 1989): 143–158.

Fayad, Mona. "Unquiet Ghosts: The Struggle for Representation in Jean Rhys's *Wide Sargasso Sea.*" *Modern Fiction Studies* 34.3 (autumn 1988): 437–452.

Fido, Elaine Savory. "Mother/Lands: Self and Separation in the Work of Buchi Emecheta, Bessie Head, and Jean Rhys." *Motherlands: Women's Writings from Africa, the Caribbean, and South Asia.* New Brunswick, NJ: Rutgers University, 1992. 330–349.

Frickey, Pierrette, editor. *Critical Perspectives on Jean Rhys.* Washington, DC: Three Continents, 1991.

Gardiner, Judith Kegan. *Rhys, Stead, Lessing, and the Politics of Empathy.* Bloomington: Indiana University, 1989.

Harris, Wilson. *The Womb of Space: The Cross-cultural Imagination.* Westport, CT: Greenwood, 1983.

Harris, Wilson. "Jean Rhys's Tree of Life." *Review of Contemporary Fiction* 5.2 (summer 1985): 114–117.

Harrison, Nancy R. *Jean Rhys and the Novel as Women's Text.* Chapel Hill: University of North Carolina, 1988.

Hawthorne, Evelyn. "Ethnic Contrasts in Historical Perspective: A Study of V. S. Naipaul and Jean Rhys." *Commonwealth Novel in English* 3.2 (fall 1990): 177–185.

Huggan, Graham. "A Tale of Two Parrots: Walcott, Rhys, and the Uses of Colonial Mimicry." *Contemporary Literature* 35.4 (winter 1994): 643–652.

Kendrik, Robert. "Edward Rochester and the Margins of Masculinity in *Jane Eyre* and *Wide Sargasso Sea.*" *Papers on Language and Literature* 30.3 (summer 1994): 235–257.

Kloepfer, Deborah Kelly. "*Voyage in the Dark*: Jean Rhys's Masquerade for the Mother." *Contemporary Literature* 26.4 (winter 1985): 443–459.

Lalla, Barbara. "Discourse of Dispossession: Ex-Centric Journeys of the Un-Living in *Wide Sargasso Sea* and the Old English 'The Wife's Lament.' " *Ariel* 24.3 (July 1993): 55–72.

Leigh, Nancy J. "Mirror, Mirror: The Development of Female Identity in Jean Rhys's Fiction." *World Literature Written in English* 25.2 (1985): 270–285.

Magarey, Kevin. "The Sense of Place in Doris Lessing and Jean Rhys." *A Sense of Place in the New Literatures in English*. St. Lucia: University of Queensland, 1986. 47–60.

Nuñez-Harrell, Elizabeth. "The Paradoxes of Belonging: The White West Indian Woman in Fiction." *Modern Fiction Studies* 31.2 (summer 1985): 281–293.

O'Callaghan, Evelyn. "Interior Schisms Dramatised: The Treatment of the 'Mad' Woman in the Work of Some Caribbean Novelists." *Out of the Kumbla: Women and Literature in the Caribbean*. Trenton, NJ: Africa World Press, 1990. 89–109.

Ochshorn, Kathleen. "Of Woodlice and White Cockroaches: The West Indian Girlhood of Jean Rhys." *Frontiers* 12.2 (summer 1991): 25–33.

O'Connor, Teresa F. *Jean Rhys: The West Indian Novels*. New York: Columbia University, 1986.

Plante, David. "Jean Rhys: A Remembrance." *Paris Review* 76 (fall 1979): 238–284.

Raiskin, Judith. "Jean Rhys: Creole Writing and the Strategies of Reading." *Ariel* 22.4 (October 1991): 51–67.

Ross, Robert L., editor. *International Literature in English: Essays on the Major Writers*. New York: Garland, 1991.

Scharfman, Ronnie. "Mirroring and Mothering in Simone Schwarz-Bart's *Pluie et vent sur Telumée Miracle* and Jean Rhys's *Wide Sargasso Sea.*" *Yale French Studies* 62 (1981): 88–106.

Smilowitz, Erika. "Childlike Women and Paternal Men: Colonialism in Jean Rhys's Fiction." *Ariel* 17.4 (October 1986): 93–103.

Tiffin, Helen. "Post-Colonial Literatures and Counter-Discourse." *Kunapipi* 9.3 (1987): 17–34.

Visel, Robin. "A Half-Colonization: The Problem of the White Colonial Woman Writer." *Kunapipi* 10.3 (1988): 39–45.

Vreeland, Elizabeth. "Jean Rhys: The Art of Fiction LXIV" [interview]. *Paris Review* 76 (fall 1979): 219–237.

Williamson, Karina. *Voyages in the Dark: Jean Rhys and Phyllis Shand Allfrey*. Warwick, England: University of Warwick, 1987.

Rich Like Us by Nayantara Sahgal (New York: New Directions, 1988). This novel traces the fortunes of two women living in India during the Emergency of 1976–1977. One, an Indian civil servant, confronts corruption and loses her job in the hiatus of democracy. The other, a transplanted Cockney who has adapted to Indian life, also loses out in the changes wrought by the Emergency. Human relationships entangle with political change in this acerbic portrait of a traumatic point in Indian history.

Commentary

Chew, Shirley. "Searching Voices: Anita Desai's *Clear Light of Day* and Nayantara Sahgal's *Rich Like Us.*" *Motherlands: Women's Writings from Africa, the Caribbean, and South Asia.* New Brunswick, NJ: Rutgers University, 1992. 43–63.
Mathur, O. P. "The Nausea of Totalitarianism: A Note on Nayantara Sahgal's *Rich Like Us.*" *World Literature Today* 65.1 (winter 1991): 68–71.

Richards, Hylda M. Born in England in 1898, she emigrated with her husband to Rhodesia (now Zimbabwe) to homestead; their not entirely successful efforts at farming are described in a memoir that is tinged with a frontier flavor.

Work

*Next Year Will Be Better. Lincoln: University of Nebraska, 1985.

Rifʻat, Alifa. Pseudonym of Fatma Abdallah, born in Cairo on June 5, 1930, daughter of an architect. She wrote her first short story at age nine, but her writing was discouraged first by her father and then by her husband, a cousin to whom her marriage was arranged. In 1955 she published her first story, drawing complaints from her husband, causing her to begin to write under a pseudonym to avoid angering him. When he found out in 1960 that she was still publishing her stories, he threatened to divorce her unless she stopped. She remained unpublished for fifteen years but continued to write in the secrecy of her bathroom. Her work demonstrates both a keen eye for the details of contemporary women's lives in Egypt and a critical look at the restrictions on their freedom. She has published several volumes of stories in Arabic, one of which is available in English translation, and a number of her stories have been broadcast by the British Broadcasting Corporation (BBC) and the Egyptian Broadcasting Service.

Work

Distant View of a Minaret and Other Stories. London, England: Heinemann, 1987.

Commentary

Nwachukwu-Agbada, J. O. J. "The Lifted Veil: Protest in Alifa Rifaat's Short Stories." *International Fiction Review* 17.2 (1990): 108–110.

Riley, Joan. Born in 1959 in St. Mary, Jamaica, the youngest of eight children. She studied at the University of Sussex, earning a B.A. in 1979, and the University of London, earning an M.A. in communications in 1984. She lives with her daughter and son in London, teaching culture and black history in literacy programs. She has written several novels, all of which deal one way or another with the experiences of Jamaicans in Britain, or British blacks in Jamaica. Her books have had a mixed reception in Jamaica because they are critical of government corruption and depict racism and class distinctions not only in Britain but in the West Indies.

Works

A Kindness to the Children. London, England: Women's Press, 1993.
Romance. London, England: Women's Press, 1988.
The Unbelonging. London, England: Women's Press, 1985.
Waiting in the Twilight. London, England: Women's Press, 1987.

Commentary

Perry, Donna. "Joan Riley" [interview]. *Backtalk: Women Writers Speak Out*. New Brunswick, NJ: Rutgers University, 1993. 261–286.
Suarez, Isabel Carrera. "Absent Mother(Land)s: Joan Riley's Fiction." *Motherlands: Women's Writings from Africa, the Caribbean, and South Asia*. New Brunswick, NJ: Rutgers University, 1992. 290–309.

Ripples in the Pool by Rebeka Njau (London, England: Heinemann, 1978). This unusual novel sets traditional magic and spirituality against modern greed and corruption. Tragedy and mysterious misfortune link the lives of several residents of a village. One is a hospital assistant who wants to start a clinic; he is thwarted by the actions of a corrupt politician and by his own wife. Traditional ways are articulated by an old man and his assistant, a goatherd. They live outside the village near a mysterious pool of water that holds a secret that is never fully revealed. The old man abandons his healing powers because he thinks people have lost their ability to comprehend the spiritual in their quest for material possessions. Magic, witchcraft, and mystery all play a role in this novel.

Commentary

Bryce-Okunlola, Jane. "Motherhood as a Metaphor for Creativity in Three African Women's Novels: Flora Nwapa, Rebeka Njau, and Bessie Head." *Motherlands: Women's Writings from Africa, the Caribbean, and South Asia*. New Brunswick, NJ: Rutgers University, 1992. 200–218.

A River Sutra by Gita Mehta (New York: Doubleday, 1993). A man retreats to a guest house by a holy river, keeping it ready for pilgrims and passers-by while escaping the burdens of his own life. The novel is a series of the stories he hears—some occult, some dreamlike, others romantic or dramatic. Ultimately, a holy man turned anthropologist convinces the narrator to think about reentering life. While the guest house host learns about the lives of his pilgrim visitors, the anthropological team excavates the stories of humans inhabiting the shores of the river since prehistoric times. *Sutra* means literally "thread" or "string," appropriate for both the shape of the river and of its human history as well as of the intertwined stories told by those who visit the holy site.

Riverbed of Memory by Daisy Zamora (San Francisco, CA: City Lights, 1988). A bilingual collection of poems political and personal, ranging from short, tender poems for a child who died in infancy to poems that include chants from protesters and the headlines in the newspapers called out by a newsboy. Zamora mixes autobiographical elements with *testimonio* in her work.

Roberts, Sheila. Born in Johannesburg, South Africa, in 1937, she was educated at the Universities of South Africa and Pretoria and has worked as a typist, a teacher, and a lecturer as well as being a novelist and short story writer. She left South Africa to teach creative writing at Michigan State University in June 1977. She has written acclaimed short stories and novels that tend to deal with the lives of ordinary white women in South Africa, depicting a more complex class structure among South African whites than most writers acknowledge. She takes a satirical and feminist, and often pessimistic, view of the isolation and restrictiveness of working-class white women's lives in South Africa. She now lives in exile, teaching in the United States, and describes her ambivalent position as a white South African writer in an autobiographical sketch in *Momentum*, in which she recounts how having a novel banned in South Africa while she was teaching in America changed her status as a writer, making her an instantly attractive literary property, even aiding in her retaining her green card.

Works

Dialogues and Divertimenti. Johannesburg, South Africa: Donker, 1985.
Jacks in Corners. Craighall, South Africa: Donker, 1987.
*Johannesburg Requiem: A Novel. New York: Taplinger, 1980.
Outside Life's Feast. Johannesburg, South Africa: Donker, 1975.
This Time of Year. Johannesburg, South Africa: Donker, 1983.
The Weekenders. Johannesburg, South Africa: Bateleur, 1981.

Commentary

Kearney, J. A. "Sheila Roberts's Concern with Stereotypes in her Short Stories." *Momentum: On Recent South African Writing*. Pietermaritzburg, South Africa: University of Natal, 1984. 182–197.
Lenta, Margaret. "Two Women and Their Territories: Sheila Roberts and Miriam Tlali." *Tulsa Studies in Women's Literature* 11.1 (spring 1992): 103–111.
MacKenzie, Craig, and Cherry Clayton. *Between the Lines: Interviews with Bessie Head, Sheila Roberts, Ellen Kuzwayo, Miriam Tlali*. Grahamstown, South Africa: National English Literary Museum, 1989.
Roberts, Sheila. "South African Post-Revolutionary Fiction." *The Commonwealth in Canada: Proceedings of the Second Triennial Conference of CACLALS, University of Winnipeg, 1–4 October, 1981*. Calcutta, India: Writers' Workshop, 1983. 203–215.

Roberts, Sheila. [untitled autobiographical sketch]. *Momentum: On Recent South African Writing*. Pietermaritzburg, South Africa: University of Natal, 1984. 305–306.

Roberts, Sheila. " 'Why Don't You Write a Nice Story?' " *The Confidence Woman: 26 Women Writers at Work*. Atlanta, GA: Longstreet, 1991. 243–252.

Rojas, Marta. Born in 1931, a black Cuban journalist, the only writer present when Castro was tried after the 1953 attack on the Mondada army barracks in Santiago, which she dealt with in her book *El Juicio del Mondada*. She has written several books based on her experience as a war correspondent, one of which won the Casa de las Américas Prize in 1978.

Works

Dead Man's Cave. Translated by Margaret Zimmerman. Havana, Cuba: José Marti, 1988.
Tania, the Unforgettable Guerrilla. New York: Random House, 1974.

Rokeya, Begum. Born in 1880 in Pairaband, Rangpur, in a part of India that later became Bangladesh. Rokeya Sakhawat Hossain's mother was one of several wives of a conservative and wealthy landowner. He was learned and knew several languages including Urdu, Arabic, English, Hindi, and Bangla. He saw to his son's education but, in keeping with custom, did not consider his daughters needing an education. The eldest of the girls, Karimunnessa, learned to read with a brother's help, and she taught Rokeya before being married off at age fifteen. Her brother then took over her education and secretly taught her both Bangla and English. He also vetted her future husband for her, and even though it was a traditionally arranged marriage, her husband was sympathetic and supportive of both her writing efforts and her radical views on women's rights. She began to publish essays on women's role in 1903, and two years later her utopian fantasy, *Sultana's Dream*, was published in a Calcutta magazine. They had two daughters who died in infancy, and then her husband, too, died in 1909, leaving her an inheritance (unusual at the time) and a fund for women's education. Moving to Calcutta, Rokeya opened a school for girls in 1911, which started with only eight students but quickly grew so that by 1930 it had classes for ten grades, through high school. In 1916 she founded the Muslim Women's Association and worked toward literacy for women in all classes. She began to publish *The Secluded Ones* in the *Monthly Mohammadi* as short vignettes documenting the nature of purdah from women's point of view. She continued to work for women's rights as a journalist, teacher, and organizer until her sudden death of heart failure in 1932.

Works

Inside Seclusion. Dacca, Bangladesh: Women for Women, 1981.
*Sultana's Dream and Selections from the Secluded Ones. Translated by Roushan Jahan. New York: Feminist, 1988.

Commentary

Joarder, Hasima, and Safiuddin Joarder. *Begum Rokeya, the Emancipator.* Dacca, Bang-
    ladesh: Nari Kalyan Sangstha, 1980.

Rosca, Ninotchka. Born in Caloocan, the Philippines, in 1946, the daughter
of a businessman. She was educated in public schools and at the state university.
She founded and was kicked out of several student progressive organizations,
starting a "love-hate relationship" with the radical Left. She has experienced
both detention and exile for political reasons. An activist during student days
during the 1960s at the University of the Philippines, she was arrested and
detained when martial law was declared in 1972. Currently, she lives in New
York. Her work is concerned with exploring the history of her country and
uncovering those aspects of it that are left out of the history books.

Works

The Monsoon Collection. St. Lucia: University of Queensland, 1983.
State of War. New York: Norton, 1988.
Twice Blessed. New York: Norton, 1992.

Commentary

Mestrovic, Marta. "Ninotchka Rosca." *Publishers Weekly* 233.18 (May 6, 1988): 90–
    91.

Rossi, Cristina Peri. See **Peri Rossi, Cristina.**

Rotten Pomerack by Merle Collins (London, England: Virago, 1992). Poetry
that deals with themes of history, storytelling, racism, and exile. Many of the
poems deal with the life of Caribbean people living in Britain—the isolation,
the racism, and the coldness of the neighbors and the landscape; the problems
of children growing up as permanent outsiders; and the exclusion of black readers from the white canons of literature and history that they were taught instead
of their own past and traditions. The poem "Rotten Pomerack" refers to the
traditional opening of stories—"crick crack, money break he back on a rotten
pomerack"—and the way in which British stories of greatness don't start with
the signal that they are, after all, just stories. Another poem, "Seduction,"
speaks of the "cold confinement" of England and the "seductive dying" (14)
that silences blacks and moves them further and further from the possibility of
going home. "Nabel-String" tells of the tenacious connection to home, the
umbilical cord buried by a grandmother under a palm tree, pulling the adult
child back. Other poems (such as "Where the Scattering Began") take the
search for home back to African shores, the collection as a whole weaving and
reweaving the broken strands of the Diaspora.

Rudet, Jacqueline. Born in 1962 in East London to émigré parents, she was sent to Dominica at the age of two to live for several years with her grandparents. Returning to Britain for secondary education, she took a drama course and began a career as an actress with Cast Theatre Company and Belt and Braces. She formed the Imani-Faith group in 1983 to perform plays by and for black women. Her plays have been performed at the Royal Court Theatre Upstairs and on British Broadcasting Corporation (BBC) Radio and have been published in anthologies. They are concerned with being female and being black, having a West Indian heritage in a racist society and not having enough money, but she argues they are not ''just'' about blacks, but about human relationships.

Works

Basin. In *Black Plays.* London, England: Methuen, 1987.
Money to Live. In *Plays by Women: Volume Five.* London, England: Methuen, 1986.
    145–181.

Rungano, Kristina. Born into a Catholic Zimbabwean family in 1963, she attended Martindale Primary School, St. John's High School, and Kutama in Zvimba, where her father had a small business. After high school she went to Britain, where she earned a diploma in computer science. She returned to Zimbabwe in 1979 to work at the Scientific Computing Centre in Harare. She has published one collection of poetry written before she was twenty-one years old.

Work

A Storm Is Brewing. Harare: Zimbabwe Publishing House, 1984.

Commentary

Wild, Flora. ''Interview with Kristina Rungano.'' *Patterns of Poetry in Zimbabwe.*
    Gweru, Zimbabwe: Mambo, 1988. 105–121.

Running for Cover by Pauline Onwubiko (Owerri, Nigeria: KayBeeCee, 1988). A short novel about the Nigerian civil war, told from the point of view of a girl living in Biafra. The war front is at first distant from their home, then moves closer and closer. As her mother is expecting a baby, the family has to flee to the east. Eventually, the war is over, their side defeated, and they return home in time for the baby's arrival. Told very much without the interpolation of an adult viewpoint, the narrative is less concerned with the political situation than with the impact of war on the child and the ways in which the experiences are part of the game playing, celebrating, and observation of peculiar adult behavior that are her more immediate concerns.

Ruoxi, Chen. See **Chen Jo-hsi.**

S

Sa'dawi, Nawal. Born in 1931 in the Nile Delta village of Kafr Tahla, she trained and practiced as a physician and psychiatrist. She served as Egypt's director of public health from 1966 to 1972 and editor of *Health* magazine, losing both positions when she published her outspoken study *Women and Sex*. She then served as deputy general of the Egyptian Medical Syndicate as well as being a consultant to the United Nations on women and development from 1978 to 1980. In 1981 she was arrested along with over a thousand other people for allegedly stirring up sectarian strife. She spent eighty days and nights in prison, the same prison in which she had earlier interviewed Firdaus, the subject of *Woman at Point Zero*, finally being released by Hosni Mubarak a few weeks after President Sadat was assassinated. In 1987 her book *The Fall of the Imam* was declared heretical by some religious authorities, and she lived under armed protection for eighteen months. She is not only innovative and daring in her social beliefs; she has stretched the novel as a genre in extraordinary ways, at times mingling journalistic aspects with fiction (as in *Woman at Point Zero*) and at times creating nonlinear and complex narrative structures (as in *Circling Song* and *The Fall of the Imam*). Criticized by religious conservatives and attacked by some Middle Eastern women for her outspoken critique of traditional Muslim practices, she has a strong and unique voice.

Works

Circling Song. London, England: Zed, 1989.
Death of an Ex-Minister. Translated by Shirley Eber. London, England: Methuen, 1987.
The Fall of the Imam. Translated by Sherif Hetata. London, England: Methuen, 1988.

God Dies by the Nile. Translated by Sherif Hetata. London, England: Zed, 1985.

The Innocence of the Devil. Translated by Sherif Hetata. Berkeley: University of California, 1994.

Memoirs from the Women's Prison. Translated by Marilyn Booth. Berkeley: University of California, 1994.

Memoirs of a Woman Doctor. Translated by Catherine Cobham. San Francisco: City Lights, 1989.

My Travels Around the World. Translated by Shirley Eber. London, England: Methuen, 1991.

Searching. Translated by Shirley Eber. London, England: Zed, 1991.

She Has No Place in Paradise. Translated by Shirley Eber. London, England: Methuen, 1987.

*Two Women in One. Translated by Osman Nusairi and Jana Gough. Seattle, WA: Seal Press, 1986.

The Well of Life; the Thread. Translated by Sherif Hetata. London, England: Lime Tree, 1993.

*Woman at Point Zero. Translated by Sherif Hetata. London, England: Zed Press, 1983.

Commentary

Busia, Abena P. A. "Rebellious Women: Fictional Biographies—Nawal el Sa'adawi's *Woman at Point Zero* and Mariama Bâ's *So Long a Letter*." *Motherlands: Women's Writings from Africa, the Caribbean, and South Asia*. New Brunswick, NJ: Rutgers University, 1992. 88–98.

Clunie, Rosemary. "Writing Is Power." *West Africa* 18 (August 1986): 1735–1736.

Harlow, Barbara. *Barred: Women, Writing, and Political Detention*. Middletown, CT: Wesleyan University, 1992.

Hitchcock, Peter. *Dialogics of the Oppressed*. Minnesota: University of Minnesota, 1993.

Johnson, Angela. "Speaking at Point Zero: *oob* Talks with Nawal El-Saadawi." *Off Our Backs* 22.3 (March 1992): 1–3.

Malti-Douglas, Fedwa, and Allen Douglas. "Reflections of a Feminist [interview with Nawal Sa'dawi]." *Opening the Gates: A Century of Arab Feminist Writing*. Bloomington: Indiana University, 1990. 395–404.

Payne, Kenneth. "*Woman at Point Zero*: Nawal el Saadawi's Feminist Picaresque." *Southern Humanities Review* 26.1 (winter 1992): 11–18.

Sa'dawi, Nawal. [untitled essay]. *Critical Fictions: The Politics of Imaginative Writing*. Seattle, WA: Bay Press, 1991. 155–156.

Sahgal, Nayantara. Born in Allahabad, India, in 1927, she was the child of prominent parents, Vijaya Lakshmi Nehru Pandit and Ranjit Sitaram Pandit, activists in the struggle for independence. Her mother served as the ambassador to the Soviet Union and the United States. She was educated at a school run by U.S. missionaries, then earned a B.A. at Wellesley College in 1947. She married soon after graduation and divorced after three children and five years of marriage. She is the author of many novels, all with feminist and/or political themes, and has been critical in both fiction and nonfiction works of corruption and injustice in the Indian political and social system.

Works

The Day in Shadow. New York: Norton, 1971.
From Fear Set Free. New York: Norton, 1963.
Mistaken Identity. New York: New Directions, 1988.
*Plans for Departure. New York: Norton, 1985.
Prison and Chocolate Cake. New York: Knopf, 1954.
*Rich Like Us. New York: New Directions, 1988.
A Situation in New Delhi. London, England: London Magazine Editions, 1977.
Storm in Chandigarh. New York: Norton, 1969.
This Time of Morning. New York: Norton, 1966.
A Time to Be Happy. New York: Knopf, 1958.

Commentary

Ash, Ranjana. "The Search for Freedom in Indian Women's Writing." *Motherlands: Women's Writings from Africa, the Caribbean, and South Asia.* New Brunswick, NJ: Rutgers University, 1992. 152–174.

Bhatnagar, Manmohan Krishna. *Political Consciousness in Indian English Writing: A Study of Manohar Malgonkar, Naintara Sahgal, and Bhabani Bhattacharya.* New Delhi, India: Bahri, 1991.

Chew, Shirley. "Searching Voices: Anita Desai's *Clear Light of Day* and Nayantara Sahgal's *Rich Like Us.*" *Motherlands: Women's Writings from Africa, the Caribbean, and South Asia.* New Brunswick, NJ: Rutgers University, 1992. 43–63.

Jain, Jasbir. *Nayantara Sahgal.* New Delhi, India: Arnold-Heinemann, 1978.

Mathur, O. P. "The Nausea of Totalitarianism: A Note on Nayantara Sahgal's *Rich Like Us.*" *World Literature Today* 65.1 (winter 1991): 68–71.

Ross, Robert L., editor. *International Literature in English: Essays on the Major Writers.* New York: Garland, 1991.

Sahgal, Nayantara. "The Schizophrenic Imagination." *Wasafiri* 11 (1990): 20–22.

Sahgal, Nayantara. "Some Thoughts on the Puzzle of Identity." *Journal of Commonwealth Literature* 29.1 (August 1993): 3–16.

Sales-Pontes, A. Hilda. *Nayantara Sahgal.* New Delhi, India: Concept, 1985.

Sam, Agnes. Born in Port Elizabeth, South Africa, of Indian heritage. Her grandfather was brought to South Africa as an indentured laborer in 1860, remaining indentured for fifty-three years in a form of virtual slavery that provided labor for South African landowners once slavery became illegal. (One of the works in her collection *Jesus Is Indian*, "The Story Teller" recounts the family version of how he was kidnapped by British sailors and taken to Africa.) She studied in Lesotho and Zimbabwe before taking up a teaching position in Zambia. She wrote for children under the pen name "Dominique" in the *Sunday Times* of Zambia. She earned a degree in English at the University of York and has written a novel (as yet unpublished), short stories, poetry, and essays. She is concerned with the struggle to retain history, language, and identity in the face of migration and exile; her stories, like the family story passed down the generations, are an attempt to hang on to an experience that is marginalized by the dominant culture.

Work

Jesus Is Indian and Other Stories. London, England: Women's Press, 1989.

Commentary

Peterson, Kirsten Holst, and Anna Rutherford, editors. *A Double Colonization: Colonial and Post-Colonial Women's Writing*. Mundelstrup, Denmark: Dangaroo, 1986.
Sam, Agnes. "South Africa: Guest of Honour Amongst the Uninvited Newcomers to England's Great Tradition." *Kunapipi* 7.2–3 (1985): 92–96.

Sans Souci and Other Stories by Dionne Brand (Ithaca, NY: Firebrand, 1989). A collection of stories dealing with Caribbean lives and the experiences of West Indians in Canada. The title story relates the life of a woman raped and made pregnant at age thirteen, caring, without much hope, for her many children, and finally having an abortion rather than bear yet another child. The man who visits her from time to time talks of a piece of land he'd like to have, Sans Souci, but his notion of being "without cares" is different from hers. She has so many cares—her ability to care for her children and for herself is being drained out of her. Another story tells of a common racist comment made to a black woman in a train station and what its effect is: anger, shame, and humiliation combined. She must apologize to her past for not responding more violently. "I Used to Love the Dallas Cowboys" is an ironic, funny, and frightening story about the way American culture colonizes the minds of young blacks. The narrator tells how she responded, as an adolescent, to American football and how she feels about it as she weathers an American invasion of her adopted Caribbean home, where she has gone to add her "puny little woman self to an upheaval" (126). She has changed her mind: "[T]he day I look outside to see who is trying to kill me, to tell them that I surrender, I see the Dallas Cowboys coming down my hot tropical street, among the bougainvillea and the mimosa, crouching, pointing their M16 weapons, laden with grenade launchers. . . . Their faces are painted and there's that smell, like fresh blood and human grease, on them. And I hate them" (129). Brand tells sharply focused, pointed stories, using vivid natural imagery and a repertoire of varied and inventive narrative strategies.

Savory, Elaine. Critic, poet, and playwright, she has taught literature at the University of Ghana, the University of Ibadan, and the University of the West Indies, Cave Hill. She is a longtime resident of Barbados and currently spends her time writing, dividing her time between Barbados and New York. Her work is strongly feminist and deeply concerned with the history and culture of the Caribbean.

Work

*Flame Tree Time. Kingston, Jamaica: Sandberry, 1993.

Savushun by Simin Danishvar (Washington, DC: Mage, 1990). The most popular work of literature in modern Iran. The novel encompasses recent Iranian history in an epic sense yet focuses on smaller details of the experiences of a family living in the city of Shiraz in southern Iran. The action takes place mainly between 1941 and 1945, when the Allies occupied Iran to control its strategic position and to draw on its resources for their war effort. Hardship, famine, epidemics, and humiliation result from the occupation; the pride and decency of the Iranians are exemplified in the heroic figure of Yusof. The narrative viewpoint, however, is chiefly that of his wife Zari, an ideal spouse and mother who fulfills those roles while evolving her own sense of strength and identity.

Scarlet Song by Mariama Bâ (Harlow, England: Longman, 1986). An ill-fated love match between a white French woman and a black Senegalese man provides the grounds of an inquiry into the subtleties of race relations and the colonial legacy. Mireille, daughter of a French diplomat, falls in love with Ousmane, a fellow student in Senegal. Their union is opposed by both families, and that difficulty, coupled with their inability to compromise in finding common ground for their different backgrounds and values, leads to estrangement. Ousmane takes a second wife in order to reclaim his roots, and Mireille, driven mad, ends their relationship in violence and tragedy. Their tortured relationship, begun in love, illustrates the cultural and psychological depth charges deeply implanted in the postcolonial experience.

Commentary

d'Almeida, Irene Assiba. "The Concept of Choice in Mariama Bâ's Fiction." *Ngambika: Studies of Women in African Literature*. Trenton, NJ: Africa World Press, 1986. 161–171.

Makward, Edris. "Marriage, Tradition and Woman's Pursuit of Happiness in the Novels of Mariama Bâ." *Ngambika: Studies of Women in African Literature*. Trenton, NJ: Africa World Press, 1986. 271–281.

Nwachukwu-Agbada, J. O. J. " 'One Wife for One Man': Mariama Bâ's Doctrine for Matrimony." *Modern Fiction Studies* 37.3 (autumn 1991): 561–573.

The Scent of the Gods by Fiona Cheong (New York: Norton, 1991). A child's-eye view of shadowy political events in Singapore and their implications for her family. The young narrator and her cousins live in a comfortable house in Singapore, with a loving extended family, but their parents have disappeared, apparently in connection with their work for the government. Her eldest cousin joins a young paramilitary organization, something his grandmother, a fiercely loyal Chinese, opposes. He argues that he is now a Singaporean and must be prepared to defend his country. He is killed in a shadowy and secretive confrontation with Communists. In the end, the narrator is about to be sent away to a Catholic boarding school, forced to leave behind her childhood, feeling the same sense of loss and exile that her grandmother did on leaving China. The closeness of siblings is well represented in this book, in which children try to piece together an understanding of the mysterious political and social events that threaten them.

Schreiner, Olive. Born in 1855 on the border of Basutoland, the ninth child of Rebecca Lyndall Schreiner, an Englishwoman, and Gottlob Schreiner, a German missionary. She spent her early years there at an isolated mission station, where her mother imposed strict rules of behavior, even beating her for using an Afrikaans word. When she was six the family moved to the Eastern Cape, where her father was to run a training institute; his work there was a failure, and in dire financial straits, the family was scattered. Schreiner spent the next years of her life traveling from one place to another, living with older family members and friends. Her education was equally unconventional—she was essentially self-educated, without the formal schooling that her brothers received. She went to work as a governess at age fifteen, a way of making a living that she engaged in for over ten years, while writing her novels *Undine* and *The Story of an African Farm*. She had already become an atheist and free thinker and suffered from bouts of asthma that lasted all her life. In 1881 she left for England, where she intended to study medicine, but the success of *The Story of an African Farm* encouraged her to settle on a literary career. She had been fortunate that her publisher's reader for the novel had been George Meredith; she also counted Havelock Ellis, George Moore, and Arthur Symons among her circle. In 1889 she returned to South Africa, settling in Matjesfontein for her health, and a few years later married Samuel Con Cronwright. They had a daughter who died at birth. As a couple, they became involved in political resistance to the racist policies of South African leaders; her novel *Trooper Peter Halket of Mashonaland* was a passionate criticism of Cecil Rhodes' racist policies. She labored for nearly forty years on the never-quite-finished novel *From Man to Man*, and nearly as long on another book, a political essay on feminism and pacifism, *Women and Labour*, published in 1911. It was very influential, considered by Vera Britten and others the Bible of the women's movement. Schreiner spent the war years in England, separated from her husband, and returned to South Africa to die on December 10, 1920. She is known best for her progressive feminist and political beliefs, which are worked out in *Women and Labour* and explored allegorically in her novels.

Works

Dream Life and Real Life. London, England: Unwin, 1893.

Dreams. London, England: Unwin, 1890.

From Man to Man; or, Perhaps Only . . . London, England: Unwin, 1926.

"My Other Self": The Letters of Olive Schreiner and Havelock Ellis. New York: Peter Lang, 1993.

Olive Schreiner Letters. Vol. 1–. New York: Oxford, 1988–.

The Story of an African Farm. London, England: Chapman and Hall, 1883.

Thoughts on South Africa. London, England: Unwin, 1923.
Trooper Peter Halket of Mashonaland. London, England: Unwin, 1897.
Undine. London, England: Harper, 1929.
Women and Labour. London: Unwin, 1911.

Commentary

Barash, Carol L. "Virile Womanhood: Olive Schreiner's Narratives of a Master Race." *Speaking of Gender.* New York: Routledge, 1989. 269–281.

Beckman, Joyce Avrech. *The Healing Imagination of Olive Schreiner: Beyond South African Colonialism.* Amherst: University of Massachusetts, 1989.

Clayton, Cherry. "Forms of Dependence and Control in Olive Schreiner's Fiction." *Olive Schreiner and After.* Cape Town, South Africa: David Phillip, 1983. 20–29.

Clayton, Cherry. "Olive Schreiner and Katherine Mansfield: Artistic Transformations of the Outcast Figure by Two Colonial Woman Writers in Exile." *English Studies* 32.2 (1989): 109–119.

Coetzee, J. M. "Farm Novel and *Plaasroman* in South Africa." *English in Africa* 13.2 (October 1986): 1–19.

First, Ruth, and Ann Scott. *Olive Schreiner.* New York: Schocken, 1980.

Gray, Stephen. "An Approach to Schreiner's Realism in *The Story of an African Farm.*" *Standpunte* 31 (1978): 38–49.

Gray, Stephen. "Schreiner and the Novel Tradition." *Southern African Literature: An Introduction.* Cape Town, South Africa: David Phillip, 1979. 133–159.

Green, Robert. "Stability and Flux: The Allotropic Narrative of an African Farm." *Olive Schreiner.* Johannesburg, South Africa: McGraw-Hill, 1983. 157–169.

Holloway, Miles. "Thematic and Structural Organization in Olive Schreiner's *The Story of an African Farm.*" *English in Africa* 16.2 (October 1989): 77–89.

Lareldo, Ursula. "Olive Schreiner." *Journal of Commonwealth Literature* 8 (1969): 107–124.

Lenta, Margaret. "Independence as the Creative Choice in Two South African Fictions." *Ariel* 17.1 (January 1986): 35–52.

Marcus, Jane. "Olive Schreiner: Cartographer of the Spirit: A Review Article." *Minnesota Review* 17.5 (1979): 58–66.

Marquard, Jean. "Hagar's Child: A Reading of *The Story of an African Farm.*" *Standpunte* 29 (1976): 35–47.

Monsman, Gerald. "The Idea of 'Story' in Olive Schreiner's *Story of an African Farm.*" *Texas Studies in Literature and Language* 27.3 (fall 1985): 249–269.

Monsman, Gerald. "Olive Schreiner: Literature and the Politics of Power." *Texas Studies in Literature and Language* 30.4 (winter 1988): 583–610.

Monsman, Gerald Cornelius. *Olive Schreiner's Fiction: Landscape and Power.* New Brunswick, NJ: Rutgers University, 1991.

Pechey, Graham. "*The Story of an African Farm*: Colonial History and the Discontinuous Text." *Critical Arts: A Journal of Media Studies* 3 (1983): 65–68.

Ross, Robert L., editor. *International Literature in English: Essays on the Major Writers.* New York: Garland, 1991.

Showalter, Elaine. *A Literature of Their Own: British Women Novelists from Brontë to Lessing.* Princeton, NJ: Princeton University, 1977.

Smith, Malvern Van Wyck, and Don MacLennan, editors. *Olive Schreiner and After:*

Essays on South African Literature in Honour of Guy Butler. Cape Town, South Africa: David Phillip, 1983.

Visel, Robin. " 'We Bear the World and We Make It': Bessie Head and Olive Schreiner." *Research in African Literatures* 21.3 (fall 1990): 115–124.

Vivan, Itala, editor. *The Flawed Diamond: Essays on Olive Schreiner.* Sydney, Australia: Dangaroo, 1991.

Wilkinson, Jane. "Dust and Dew: Moonlight and Utopia—Natural Imagery in the First South African Novel." *Commonwealth Essays and Studies* 14.2 (spring 1992): 34–43.

Wilson, Elaine. "Pervasive Symbolism in *The Story of an African Farm.*" *English Studies in Africa* 14 (1971): 179–186.

Schwarz-Bart, Simone. Born in France in 1938 to Guadeloupean parents, who returned to Guadeloupe when she was three years old. She studied in Paris and then later lived for a time in Dakar, Senegal. She now lives in Guadeloupe and Lausanne, Switzerland, with her husband, novelist André Schwarz-Bart, whom she married in 1959 and with whom she collaborated on her first published work of fiction, *Un Plat de porc aux bananes vertes.* She is the author of several novels that are poetic, mythic, and lyrical in style. She has recently compiled a six-volume work, *Homage à la femme noire,* published in 1989, which gathers together the history and culture of black women.

Work

*Between Two Worlds. Translated by Barbara Bray. New York: Harper, 1981.
*The Bridge of Beyond. Translated by Barbara Bray. New York: Atheneum, 1974.
Your Handsome Captain. Translated by Jessica Harris and Catherine Temerson. In *Plays by Women: An International Anthology.* New York: Ubu Repertory Theater, 1988. 231–249.

Commentary

Busia, Abena P. A. "Words Whispered over Voids: A Context for Black Women's Rebellious Voices in the Novel of the African Diaspora." *Black Feminist Criticism and Critical Theory.* Greenwood, FL: Penkevill, 1988. 1–41.

Mudimbe-Boyi, Elisabeth. "The Poetics of Exile and Errancy in *Le Baobab Fou* by Ken Bugul and *Ti Jean L'Horizon* by Simone Schwarz-Bart." *Yale French Studies* 83 (June 1993): 196–212.

Omerod, Beverley. "The Boat and the Tree: Simone Schwarz-Bart's *The Bridge of Beyond.*" *An Introduction to the French Caribbean Novel.* London, England: Heinemann, 1985. 108–131.

Scarboro, Ann Armstrong. "A Shift Toward the Inner Voice and Créolité in the French Caribbean Novel." *Callaloo* 15.1 (winter 1992): 12–29.

Scharfman, Ronnie. "Mirroring and Mothering in Simone Schwarz-Bart's *Pluie et vent sur Télumée Miracle* and Jean Rhys's *Wide Sargasso Sea.*" *Yale French Studies* 62 (1981): 88–106.

Shelton, Marie-Denise. "Literature Extracted: A Poetic of Daily Life." *Callaloo* 15.1 (winter 1992): 167–178.

Wilson, Elizabeth. " '*Le Voyage et l'espace close*'—Island and Journey as Metaphor:

Aspects of Women's Experience in the Works of Francophone Caribbean Women
Writers.'' *Out of the Kumbla: Women and Literature in the Caribbean.* Trenton,
NJ: Africa World Press, 1990. 45–58.

Wilson, Elizabeth Betty. ''History and Memory in *Un Plat de porc aux bananes vertes*
and *Pluie et vent sur Télumée Miracle.*'' *Callaloo* 15.1 (winter 1992): 179–189.

Zimra, Clarisse. ''Negritude in the Feminine Mode: The Case of Martinique and Guadeloupe.'' *Journal of Ethnic Studies* 12.1 (1984): 53–77.

The Sea Wall by Marguerite Duras (New York: Noonday, 1967). A novel of
ideas that indicts the French colonial administration of Indochina, including its
collusion with banks and speculators, its indifference to poverty, and its corruption. Twinned with this theme is a plot line in which a young daughter is used
by a family trying to arrange a profitable marriage, the exchange value of women
being paralleled with the colonial enterprise.

Commentary

Chester, Suzanne. ''Writing the Subject: Exoticism/Eroticism in Marguerite Duras's *The
Lover* and *The Sea Wall.*'' *De/Colonizing the Subject: The Politics of Gender in
Women's Autobiography.* Minneapolis: University of Minnesota, 1992. 436–457.

Seacole, Mary. Born in Jamaica in 1805 to a free black woman and a Scottish
army officer. She was briefly married to the godson of Viscount Nelson but
lived most of her colorful life a single woman. She was an intrepid traveler who
was a gold prospector, a writer, and a nurse in the Crimean War, where her
contribution was in many ways as notable as that of Florence Nightingale. Her
autobiography was enormously popular when it was published in 1857, and she
became an exotic celebrity in London's high society. She died in 1881.

Work

The Wonderful Adventures of Mrs. Seacole in Many Lands. London, England: Oxford
University, 1988.

Commentary

Paquet, Sandra Pouchet. ''The Enigma of Arrival: *The Wonderful Adventures of Mrs.
Seacole in Many Lands.*'' *African American Review* 26.4 (winter 1992): 651–663.

Sebbar, Leïla. Born in Aflou, Algeria, in 1941, the daughter of a French
mother and an Algerian father, she grew up in Algeria and left for Paris at age
seventeen. She writes for several magazines and has published a number of
novels. Her writing shows special concern for the conditions of life for *beurs*—
second-generation Algerians living in France.

Work

Sherazade: Missing: Aged 17, Dark Curly Hair, Green Eyes. Translated by Dorothy
Blair. London, England: Quartet, 1991.

Commentary

du Plessis, Nancy. "Leïla Sebbar, Voice of Exile." *World Literature Today* 63.3 (summer 1989): 415–417.

Mortimer, Mildred. "Language and Space in the Fiction of Assia Djebar and Leïla Sebbar." *Research in African Literatures* 19 (fall 1988): 301–311.

Mortimer, Mildred. *Journeys Through the French African Novel.* Portsmouth, NH: Heinemann, 1990.

Mortimer, Mildred. "On the Road: Leïla Sebbar's Fugitive Heroines." *Research in African Literatures* 23.2 (summer 1992): 195–201.

Woodhull, Winifred. "Exile." *Yale French Studies* 82 (May 1993): 7–24.

Woodhull, Winifred. *Transfigurations of the Maghreb: Feminism, Decolonization, and Literatures.* Minneapolis: University of Minnesota, 1993.

Second-Class Citizen by Buchi Emecheta (New York: Braziller, 1983). A fictionalized autobiography about the author's childhood and life after her marriage to a hypocritically traditional Nigerian man. The heroine marries initially because she must marry to accomplish her goals; but it turns out to be a serious mistake when, settled in London, her husband fails to pass his exams and relies on her to provide for a rapidly growing family. The novel chronicles the increasing difficulty and indignity faced by a woman forced to cope with both the demands of a traditional African marriage and the racism and poverty she encounters in London.

Segun, Mabel. Born on February 18, 1930, in Ondo, Nigeria, she attended school in Lagos, graduating from University College, Ibadan, in 1953 with a degree in English, Latin, and history. She has been a teacher at a number of schools in Nigeria, school administrator, advertising copywriter and editor, and an award-winning radio broadcaster for the Federal Ministry of Education, a delegate to UNESCO, and a champion table tennis star. She founded and served as president of the Children's Literature Association of Nigeria and has been active in children's affairs, in publishing, and in the arts. She is a senior research fellow at the Institute of African Studies, University of Ibadan.

Works

Conflict and Other Poems. Ibadan, Nigeria: New Horn Press, 1986.

Friends, Nigerians, Countrymen. Ibadan, Nigeria: Oxford University Press, 1977.

My Father's Daughter. Lagos, Nigeria: African University Press, 1977.

Olu and the Broken Statue. Ibadan, Nigeria: New Horn Press, 1985.

Under the Mango Tree: Songs and Poems for Primary Schools. Harlow, England: Longman, 1980.

Youth Day Parade. Ibadan, Nigeria: Daystar, 1984.

Commentary

Aiyejina, Funso. "Mabel Segun: A Critical Review." *Nigerian Female Writers: A Critical Perspective.* Lagos, Nigeria: Malthouse, 1989. 132–140.

Senior, Olive. Born in 1943 in a poor Jamaican village, where there was no mass media form of entertainment; she attributes her interest in writing to the influence of the oral traditions of storytelling, preaching, and conversation that made drama out of the villagers' everyday lives. Senior distinguished herself at the Montego Bay High School for Girls, where she earned the role of "head girl" and where she started a school magazine to publish the students' literary efforts. She also wrote for *The Daily Gleaner* after school and during vacations, being trained into the profession of journalism by its editor. She attended Carleton University in Ottawa, Canada, earning a degree in print journalism in 1967; there she also began to write short stories. She has worked as a journalist and a researcher and in publishing and public relations. She has served as editor of two important publications, the *Journal of Social and Economic Studies* of the University of the West Indies and the *Jamaica Journal*. She is also managing director of the Institute of Jamaica Publishing Company. Her collection of short stories, *Summer Lightning*, won the Commonwealth Writers Award.

Works

A-Z of Jamaican Heritage. Kingston, Jamaica: Heinemann/Gleaner, 1983.
*Arrival of the Snake Woman and Other Stories. Harlow, England: Longman, 1989.
The Message Is Change. Kingston, Jamaica: Kingston Publishers, 1972.
Summer Lightning and Other Stories. Harlow, England: Longman, 1986.
Talking of Trees. Kingston, Jamaica: Calabash, 1985.
Working Miracles: Lives of Caribbean Women. London, England: James Currey, 1991.

Commentary

Patteson, Richard F. "The Fiction of Olive Senior: Traditional Society and the Wider World." *Ariel* 24.1 (January 1993): 13–33.
Pollard, Velma. "Mothertongue Voices in the Writing of Olive Senior and Lorna Goodison." *Motherlands: Women's Writings from Africa, the Caribbean, and South Asia.* New Brunswick, NJ: Rutgers University, 1992. 238–253.
Pollard, Velma. "Olive Senior: Journalist, Researcher, Poet, Fiction Writer." *Callaloo* 11.3 (summer 1988): 479–490.

Shadowinnower by Agueda Pizarro (New York: Columbia University, 1979). A bilingual edition of poems that explore womanhood, language, literature, and the natural landscape. Images are surrealistic, and words are fused to create resonant neologisms. According to the introduction, the poems "are based on the composite word, which seems to me to be the most perfect trope. . . . The double word is not, in this book, a verbal game, but a symbol of my life, amalgam of cultures and tongues simultaneously seeking to take root and to be free. . . . The composite word is a crossbreed taking strength as much from the tension between its parts as its unity" (xi–xii).

Shan, Sharan-Jeet. Born in 1945 to a Sikh family in Dhootkalan, Punjab, India. She was educated in New Delhi, where her father, an army officer, was stationed, and started medical school; however, there she met and fell in love with a Muslim student, and her family, who strongly opposed the liaison, removed her from school and forced her to marry a Sikh who was resident in England and home for a visit. At age twenty, she traveled to England with her husband, obtained a teacher's certificate from Newland Park College of Education, and began to teach. She divorced in 1985 and earned a master's degree in social science from Birmingham University in 1990. She has coauthored books on race and the teaching of science and math and is best known for her autobiography in which she tells in compelling and spare prose the story of her childhood and forced marriage. This book has been chosen as a recommended textbook for high school students in England for its straightforward treatment of patriarchy, racism, and the immigrant experience in Britain.

Work

In My Own Name. London, England: Women's Press, 1985.

Shand Allfrey, Phyllis. See **Allfrey, Phyllis Shand.**

Sha'rawi, Huda. Born in Minya, Egypt, in 1879, the daughter of a wealthy provincial administrator from upper Egypt and a Circassian mother from Turkey. She grew up in Cairo in traditional seclusion, one of the last upper-class women to live in the segregation of the harem. She was married at age thirteen to a much older cousin, an arranged liaison she opposed, and after a year, she was separated from him for seven years, during which time she became a feminist. She became an activist in the nationalist struggle and for the liberation of women, leading the first women's nationalist demonstration in 1919 and causing scandal when she unveiled at a railway station in 1923 on her return from an international women's meeting in Rome. Her photo in the newspaper was one of the first to be published of an unveiled woman in Egypt. She founded the publications *L'Egyptienne* in 1925 and *al-Misriyya* in 1937. In addition, she was the founder of the Egyptian Feminist Union, fighting for a minimum marriage age, education for women, and better working conditions for women employed in textile factories. She was president of the union from 1923 until her death in 1947. Her memoirs are a valuable document of harem life and of the nationalist and feminist struggles in Egypt.

Work

*Harem Years: The Memoirs of An Egyptian Feminist. Translated by Margot Badran. London, England: Virago, 1986.

Commentary

Ahmed, Leila. "Between Two Worlds: The Formation of a Turn-of-the-Century Egyptian Feminist." *Life/Lines: Theorizing Women's Autobiography.* Ithaca, NY: Cornell University, 1988. 154–174.

Shaykh, Hanan. Born in 1945 in Lebanon, she grew up in Beirut in Ras al-Naba, a conservative area of town. Her father was a strict and devout Muslim. She attended a local Muslim girls' primary school, then persuaded her father to send her to the Ahliya School, a more modern and fashionable school. She finished her education in Cairo, where she wrote her first novel, then returned to Beirut where she worked for a major Arabic-language paper, *Al-Nahar*, before moving to Saudi Arabia for a time, then to London, where she now lives. She has published short stories and two novels.

Works

*The Story of Zahra. Translated by the author and Peter Ford. New York: Anchor/ Doubleday, 1994.
Women of Sand and Myrrh. Translated by Catherine Cobham. London, England: Quartet, 1989.

Commentary

Accad, Evelyne. *Sexuality and War: Literary Masks of the Middle East.* New York: New York University, 1990.
Accad, Evelyne. ''Sexuality, War, and Literature in Lebanon.'' *Feminist Issues* 11 (fall 1991): 27–42.
Cooke, Miriam. *War's Other Voices: Women Writers on the Lebanese Civil War, 1975–82.* Cambridge, England: Cambridge University, 1988.
Larson, Charles R. ''The Fiction of Hanan al-Shaykh, Reluctant Feminist.'' *World Literature Today* 65.1 (winter 1991): 14–17.
Sunderman, Paula W. ''An Interview with Hanan al-Shaykh.'' *Michigan Quarterly Review* 31.4 (fall 1992): 625–636.

She Has Reddish Hair and Her Name Is Sabina by Julieta Campos (Athens: University of Georgia, 1993). Translation of *Tiene los cabellos rojizos y se llama Sabina*, first published in 1974. A novel about novels, told in a single long paragraph in which the narrator obsessively explores the act of narration. The text is full of meditations on identity and the search for form. It is also a reflection on literature and resonates with intertextual references that examine the relationship between subject and object and the acts of witness and formulation that link them. In the end, though, the reader still knows little that is concrete about the woman, other than that she has reddish hair and her name is Sabina.

She Tries Her Tongue, Her Silence Softly Breaks by Marlene Nourbese Philip (Charlottetown, Canada: Ragweed, 1989). A collection of distinguished and innovative poems that won the Casa de las Américas Prize in 1988 while it was still in manuscript form. It contains an essay on writing, language, and image (or ''i-mage'' as she puts it) entitled ''The Absence of Writing or How I Almost Became a Spy'' and a number of poems that explore the problematics of language in the case of women of the African Diaspora. ''Discourse on the

Logic of Language'' arranges texts in three parts of the page, one being a description of a mother cleaning a baby of afterbirth and touching its tongue, breathing life into it, blowing words into it. Another is a poetic exploration of English as a mother tongue, a father tongue, and a ''foreign anguish.'' The third part is a discussion of the parts of the brain and a mock multiple-choice test on the nature and purpose of the tongue. A funny, complex, angry, and multivoiced collection.

Shih Shu-ch'ing. Born in 1945 in Taiwan, she grew up in the port city of Lu Kang. She attended Tamkang College, graduating in 1969, and then traveled to the United States with her husband, Robert Silin, an American scholar. She studied drama at Hunter College in New York and earned an M.A. in 1973. She returned to Taiwan that year and has since taught drama at Chengchi University, Taipei. She has published several works including biography and literary history; a collection of her stories and plays is available in English translation. Her themes are typically isolation, meaninglessness in contemporary life, intercultural misunderstandings, and communication problems in marriage.

Work

The Barren Years and Other Short Stories and Plays. Translated by John M. McLellan. San Francisco, CA: Chinese Materials Center, 1975.

The Ship of Fools by Cristina Peri Rossi (London, England: Readers International, 1989). First published in 1984 in Spain, this surreal novel recounts the voyages of a traveler named Eck. The title refers to the Bosch painting. The work is composed of fragments of stories and clippings from various fictional sources, along with references to a tapestry of creation. The role and nature of art and fiction are probed in this unusual and challenging novel.

Commentary

Mora, Gabriela. ''Enigmas and Subversions in Cristina Peri Rossi's *La nave de los locos* [*Ship of Fools*].'' *Splintering Darkness: Latin American Women Writers in Search of Themselves.* Pittsburgh, PA: Latin American Literary Review, 1990. 19–30.

Shirazi, Manny. Born in Iran in 1946 into a working-class family. She was educated and worked there as a teacher for five years while writing short fiction. Her first story was published when she was only twelve. She moved to Britain, where she is a writer and a photographer, having held an exhibit of photographs of women in Iran at the Women's Arts Alliance in 1979. She writes in both Farsi and English, composing poetry and short fiction in Farsi and her first novel in English. Her themes are strongly feminist and politically charged.

Work

Javady Alley. London, England: Women's Press, 1984.

Sibal, Nina. An Indian short story writer and novelist. She earned a B.A. and M.A. in English from Delhi University and now works as a diplomat in the Indian Administrative Service. Her diplomatic duties have taken her to Cairo, Egypt, where she has lived for some time. She has published short fiction and a novel, a historical work with a large canvas and cast of characters.

Works

The Secret Life of Gujjar Mal and Other Stories. New Delhi, India: Rupa, 1993.
Yatra: The Journey. London, England: Women's Press, 1987.

Sidhwa, Bapsi. Born in Karachi, Pakistan, into a Parsi family. Her mother tongue is Gujarati, but she also speaks Urdu and writes in English. When she was a child, her family moved to Lahore, where she was raised. She is a social worker as well as being an accomplished novelist, and she served as a representative from Pakistan to the Asian Women's Congress in 1975. She received the prestigious Sitara-I-Imtiaz Award, the highest honor bestowed on civilians by the state of Pakistan in 1991 and in 1994 was granted a Lila Wallace–Reader's Digest Fund award to promote literature. She lived and taught in Houston, Texas, for a time and was a Buntin Fellow at Radcliffe. As the first novelist to depict Parsi life, she was the object of a certain amount of resentment from members of her community, one that does not embrace publicity. One of the themes she has tackled from a Parsi viewpoint is the trauma of the partition.

Works

*An American Brat. Minneapolis, MN: Milkweed, 1993.
The Bride. New York: St. Martin's, 1983.
*Cracking India. Minneapolis, MN: Milkweed, 1991.
The Crow Eaters. New York: St. Martin's Press, 1981.

Commentary

Jussawalla, Feroza F., and Reed Way Dasenbrock. *Interviews with Writers of the Post-Colonial World.* Jackson: University Press of Mississippi, 1992.
Montenegro, David. "Bapsi Sidhwa: An Interview." *Massachusetts Review* 31 (winter 1990): 513–533.
Ross, Robert L., editor. *International Literature in English: Essays on the Major Writers.* New York: Garland, 1991.

Sikakane, Joyce. Born in South Africa in 1943, she grew up in the Orlando District of Soweto. She worked as a reporter for *The World*, then became the first black woman employed by the *Rand Daily Mail.* She became engaged to a Scottish doctor and planned to leave the country to marry him (an illegal act at the time because of miscegenation laws) but was arrested first and detained for seventeen months before she could leave. They finally married and went to live in Scotland. She later moved to Zimbabwe, where she remained an anti-

apartheid activist and member of the African National Congress. She is the
author of an autobiography.

Work

A Window on Soweto. London, England: International Defense and Aid Fund for South
Africa, 1977.

A Sister to Scheherazade by Assia Djebar (London, England: Quartet,
1987). Two women, one traditional, veiled but struggling to establish her own
identity, and the other, Westernized, free, trying to recover her past, are the
subjects of two converging story lines. As the stories merge, the one woman
succeeds in shedding her veil and the other returns home to rediscover the
company of women in a traditional North African setting. The reader comes to
understand that these women were married to the same man and are intimately
connected, though their lives run along different plots. The central motif is of
Scheherazade the storyteller and her sister, who wakes her and urges her to tell
her stories—and how central to women are those who tell the stories and the
silent ones who insist that they be told.

Commentary

Mortimer, Mildred. "Language and Space in the Fiction of Assia Djebar and Leïla Sebbar." *Research in African Literatures* 19 (fall 1988): 301–311.

Sistren. Formed in 1977 in Jamaica and originally funded by the Emergency
Employment Programme of the People's National Party (PNP) government, the
Sistren Theatre Collective produces plays, educational materials, research on
women's history in Jamaica, and publications in an unusually collaborative environment. The first play produced by the group, *Downpression Get a Blow*,
was put together by ten working-class women with the assistance of dramatist
Honor Ford Smith. It dealt with the subject of women sewing for an American
company in Jamaica and was based on the women's concerns, drawing on personal experiences. The group decided to continue work and trained for a time
with the Jamaica School of Drama. They went on to produce more plays, including *Bellywoman Bangarang*, about four pregnant women and dealing with
domestic violence, rape, women's work, and poverty, and *Nana Yah*, about the
legendary Maroon leader, focusing on women's role in the resistance to European colonization. After 1980 the group branched out, trying to connect wom-
en's personal histories with the broader social history of Jamaica. Research on
women's work in the sugar industry and women in labor organizations was
conducted, a newsletter started, and workshops that used theater to generate
discussion and learning were taken to community centers and schools. *Lionheart
Gal*, a book of life stories told by collective members, was published in 1986,
receiving much critical attention. The group remains an active producer of
drama, making use of Jamaican women's experiences, language, and concerns,

and has proven in its collective approach to cultural production a model of community-based creativity. Like Efua Sutherland's theater in Ghana, Sistren incorporates traditional storytelling and dramatic practices, using spaces that are not bound by European stage conventions, directing its dramatic productions to a local audience based on the local audience's own interests and concerns.

Works

Lionheart Gal: Life Stories of Jamaican Women. London, England: Women's Press, 1986.

Wid Dis Ring. Toronto, Canada: Sister Vision, 1987.

Commentary

Carr, Robert. "Crossing the First World/Third World Divides: Testimonial, Transnational Feminisms, and the Postmodern Condition." *Scattered Hegemonies: Postmodernity and Transnational Feminist Practices.* Minneapolis: University of Minnesota, 1994. 153–172.

Cobham, Rhonda. " 'A Wha Kind a Pen Dis?': The Function of Ritual Frameworks in Sistren's *Bellywoman Bangarang.*" *Theatre Research International* 15.3 (autumn 1990): 233–242.

Cooper, Carolyn. "Writing Oral History: Sistren Theatre Collective's *Lionheart Gal.*" *Kunapipi* 7.1 (1989): 49–57.

Davies, Carole Boyce. "Collaboration and the Ordering Imperative in Life Story Production." *De/Colonizing the Subject: The Politics of Gender in Women's Autobiography.* Minneapolis: University of Minnesota, 1992. 3–19.

Di Cenzo, Maria, and Susan Bennett. "Women, Popular Theatre, and Social Action: Interviews with Cynthia Grant and the Sistren Collective." *Ariel* 23.1 (January 1992): 73–94.

Ford Smith, Honor. "Sistren: Jamaican Women's Theatre." *Cultures in Contention.* Seattle, WA: Real Comet, 1985.

Ford Smith, Honor. "Sistren: Exploring Women's Problems Through Drama." *Jamaica Journal* 19.1 (February-April 1986): 2–12.

Ford Smith, Honor. "Sistren Women's Theatre, Organising and Conscientization." *Women of the Caribbean.* London, England: Zed, 1986. 122–128.

Ford Smith, Honor. "Sistren at Work." *Carib* 4 (1987): 55–61.

Ford Smith, Honor. *Ring Ding in a Tight Corner: A Case Study of Funding and Organizational Democracy in Sistren, 1977–1988.* Toronto, Canada: Women's Program, ICAE, 1989.

Katrak, Ketu H. "Decolonizing Culture: Toward a Theory for Postcolonial Women's Texts." *Modern Fiction Studies* 35.1 (spring 1989): 157–179.

Sitt Marie Rose by Etel Adnan (Sausalito, CA: Post-Apollo, 1982). A short, poetic novel that views the last days of a woman's life from various viewpoints. Marie-Rose, a Lebanese Christian teaching in a school for the deaf, is captured by an old friend, a Christian militiaman who objects to her activism on the behalf of Palestinian refugees. Their relationship from the past, their debate as the militiamen hold her prisoner, and her final execution before the children she teaches are told in short passages from a variety of viewpoints that reveal both the brutality of the militiamen and their beliefs and the intimate link between the values of the men fighting a senseless war and their oppression of women.

Commentary

Accad, Evelyne. "Sexuality, War, and Literature in Lebanon." *Feminist Issues* 11 (fall 1991): 27–42.
Fernea, Elizabeth. "The Case of *Sitt Marie Rose*: An Ethnographic Novel from the Modern Middle East." *Literature and Anthropology*. Lubbock: Texas Tech, 1989. 153–164.

The Sixth Day by Andrée Chedid (London, England: Serpent's Tail, 1987). There is something mythic and timeless about this novel, which concerns an Egyptian mother's struggle to conceal her child from the authorities and nurse him through cholera. She joins forces with a street musician, wise and ironical, generous and often cruel, and he becomes her reluctant companion on a boat in which she takes her son down the Nile to the sea, a journey that takes on the dimensions of the journey undertaken by the dying in ancient Egyptian mythology. When they finally reach the sea, the street musician has become her ally, and he assures her, as she collapses, that her dead son has been given her last breath and will live. Though melodramatic, the story succeeds by operating on a large, mythic stage.

Slavery. Mamadou Diawara has established the role of African slave women in creating and maintaining an oral literary tradition. Early printed works by third world women relating to slavery include the poetry of Phillis Wheatley, who was a slave when her prodigious talents became celebrated, and slave narratives, such as *The History of Mary Prince,* which was an instrumental document in British abolitionist efforts. A modern variation on the slave narrative can be found in Wilma Stockenström's novel *The Expedition to the Baobab Tree*, originally published in Afrikaans, which is a meditation on the effects of ownership on self-representation. Another unusual account of a former slave can be found in the memoir of the Chinese writer Janet Lim, who was sold as a slave by her mother in childhood. Agnes Sam, a South African writer of Indian heritage, connects slavery with the experiences of Indian indentured workers, whose labor replaced that of Africans when slavery was abolished.

The importance of remembering and recounting the experience of slavery and its lingering effects is a theme taken up by many contemporary writers. Works include Maryse Condé's *Heremakhonon* and *I, Tituba, Black Witch of Salem*, Simone Schwarz-Bart's *Bridge of Beyond*, and Paule Marshall's *Praisesong for the Widow*. Buchi Emecheta's *The Slave Girl* links slavery and the subject position of women in marriage, and in *The Bride Price*, she explores the ways in which slave ancestry imposes a lingering burden on the descendants of slaves. Valerie Belgrave has treated the subject of slavery within the context of conventional historical romances in an effort to make a form of popular literature relevant to the Caribbean experience. The Maroon rebel leader, Nanny, appears as a woman warrior in many Caribbean writers' works, including the novels of Michelle Cliff and the poetry of Lorna Goodison, signifying resistance, female strength, and a close connection to African ancestry.

Works

*Belgrave, Valerie. *Ti Marie.* London, England: Heinemann, 1988.

*Cliff, Michelle. *Abeng.* Trumansburg, NY: Crossing Press, 1984.

*Cliff, Michelle. *Free Enterprise.* New York: Dutton, 1993.

*Condé, Maryse. *Heremakhonon.* Translated by Richard Philcox. Washington, DC: Three Continents, 1981.

*Condé, Maryse. *I, Tituba, Black Witch of Salem.* Translated by Richard Philcox. Charlottesville: University Press of Virginia, 1992.

*Emecheta, Buchi. *The Bride Price.* New York: G. Braziller, 1976.

Emecheta, Buchi. *The Slave Girl.* New York: G. Braziller, 1977.

*Goodison, Lorna. *I Am Becoming My Mother.* London, England: New Beacon, 1986.

*Lim, Janet. *Sold for Silver.* Cleveland, OH: World, 1958.

*Marshall, Paule. *Praisesong for the Widow.* New York: Dutton, 1984.

Prince, Mary. *The History of Mary Prince, a West Indian Slave, Related by Herself.* London, England: Pandora, 1987.

Sam, Agnes. *Jesus Is Indian and Other Stories.* London, England: Women's Press, 1989.

*Schwarz-Bart, Simone. *The Bridge of Beyond.* Translated by Barbara Bray. New York: Atheneum, 1974.

*Stockenström, Wilma. *The Expedition to the Baobab Tree.* Translated by J. M. Coetzee. Boston, MA: Faber and Faber, 1983.

Wheatley, Phillis. *The Collected Works of Phillis Wheatley.* New York: Oxford University, 1988.

Commentary

Diawara, Mamadou. "Women, Servitude and History: The Oral Historical Traditions of Women of Servile Condition in the Kingdom of Jaara (Mali) from the Fifteenth to the Mid-nineteenth Century." *Discourse and Its Disguises: The Interpretation of African Oral Texts.* Birmingham, AL: Birmingham University, 1989. 109–137.

A Small Place by Jamaica Kincaid (New York: Farrar, Straus, Giroux, 1988). A long essay on Antigua, the "small place" of the title, highly critical of the British colonial past and the corruption of the postcolonial government, describing the place and its past with concise, ironic, and vivid language. Though many of Kincaid's novels were first published in *The New Yorker*, this work was rejected as being too political. It makes an interesting companion piece for her less overtly political novels *Annie John* and *At the Bottom of the River*.

A Smell of Onions by Peggy Appiah (Harlow, England: Longman, 1979). Gentle interwoven stories about village life seen through the eyes of the observant Kwaku Hoampam, an old farmer and shopkeeper who, like the smell of onions, is everywhere at once. The tales revolve around some small village conflict, all of which are settled in an easygoing fashion, the most dramatic being a crime that, when it comes to trial, becomes theater for the entire village. It ends with the comment: "Writing a story is like the weaving of a mat. At the finish the ends need tidying off, but in reality they are only cut short" (84). The village, she suggests, is common to many places, the tale one that has no particular beginning or end. In folktale style, these stories are based more on tradition and continuity than on conflict or drama.

Smith, Pauline. Born in 1882 in the "Little Karoo" region of the Cape Colony, South Africa, to an English physician and a Scotswoman from Aberdeen. She was educated by governesses until age twelve, when the family went to Britain and she was enrolled at a boarding school in Scotland. Her earliest published writings appeared in Scottish newspapers, the first having a Scottish setting and theme; she then began to draw on her memories of the Karoo for inspiration, and thereafter most of her fiction concerned South Africa, which she visited frequently in adulthood. Arnold Bennett became one of her champions; she also was a friend of Frank Swinnerton. She published short fiction, novels, a travel memoir, and a play. She died in 1959.

Works

The Beadle. New York: Doran, 1927.
Hold Yourself Dear. New York: J. Messner, 1965.
The Little Karoo. New York: Vanguard, 1952.
Platkop's Children. London, England: Cape, 1935.

Commentary

Coetzee, J. M. "Simple Language, Simple People: Smith, Paton, Mikro." *White Writing: On the Culture of Letters in South Africa.* New Haven, CT: Yale University, 1988. 115–135.
Coetzee, J. M. "Farm Novel and *Plaasroman* in South Africa." *English in Africa* 13.2 (October 1986): 1–19.
Driver, Dorothy, editor. *Pauline Smith.* New York: McGraw-Hill, 1983.
Haresnape, Geoffrey. *Pauline Smith.* New York: Twayne, 1969.

So Long a Letter by Mariama Bâ (London, England: Heinemann, 1981). A critically acclaimed novel in the form of a letter from the recently widowed Ramatoulaye to her old friend Aissatou, in which Ramatoulaye recounts her emotional battle after her husband's decision to take a second wife, the best friend of their young daughter. The long letter is a rumination on both social issues and the narrator's search for a new way of life, a middle ground between traditional male-dominated Senegalese culture and modern life, dominated by Western values. The shape of her future is unclear, but she is looking forward to refashioning her life. In this novel, Bâ addresses questions of marriage and identity in terms that are both feminist and respectful of Islamic traditions.

Commentary

Busia, Abena P. A. "Rebellious Women: Fictional Biographies—Nawal el Sa'adawi's *Woman at Point Zero* and Mariama Bâ's *So Long a Letter*." *Motherlands: Women's Writings from Africa, the Caribbean, and South Asia.* New Brunswick, NJ: Rutgers University, 1992. 88–98.

d'Almeida, Irene Assiba. "The Concept of Choice in Mariama Bâ's Fiction." *Ngambika: Studies of Women in African Literature.* Trenton, NJ: Africa World Press, 1986. 161–171.

Harrell-Bond, Barbara. "Mariama Bâ, Winner of the First Noma Award for Publishing in Africa for Her Novel *Une si longue lettre*." *African Book Publishing Record* 6.3–4 (1980): 209–214.

Makward, Edris. "Marriage, Tradition and Woman's Pursuit of Happiness in the Novels of Mariama Bâ." *Ngambika: Studies of Women in African Literature.* Trenton, NJ: Africa World Press, 1986. 271–281.

McElaney-Johnson, Ann. "The Place of the Woman or the Woman Displaced in Mariama Bâ's *Une si longue lettre*." *CLA Journal* 37.1 (September 1993): 19–28.

Miller, Christopher L. *Theories of Africans: Francophone Literature and Anthropology in Africa.* Chicago, IL: University of Chicago, 1990.

Nwachukwu-Agbada, J. O. J. " 'One Wife for One Man': Mariama Bâ's Doctrine for Matrimony." *Modern Fiction Studies* 37.3 (autumn 1991): 561–573.

Ojo-Ade, Femi. "Still a Victim? Mariama Bâ's *Une si longue lettre*." *African Literature Today* 12 (1987): 71–87.

Schipper, Mineke. " 'Who Am I?' Fact and Fiction in African First-Person Narrative." *Research in African Literatures* 16.1 (spring 1985): 53–79.

Stratton, Florence. "The Shallow Grave: Archetypes of Female Experience in African Fiction." *Research in African Literatures* 19.2 (1988): 143–169.

Sofola, 'Zulu. A playwright, born in 1931 in Issele-Uke, Bendel State, Nigeria, to Igbo parents. She went to the United States as an adolescent, attending the Southern Baptist Seminary in Nashville, earning a B.A. in English from Virginia Union University (graduating cum laude) and an M.A. in drama from Catholic University of America in 1965, where she focused her thesis on dramatic features of Igbo ritual. During her stay in the United States, she met and married her Yoruba husband, with whom she has five children. She returned to Nigeria in 1966 to lecture in the Theatre Arts Department of the University of Ibadan and to earn a Ph.D. in drama. She is now head of the Department of Performing Arts at the University of Ilorin. She has written and directed many plays both for stage and for television. As a playwright she finds no contradiction between being feminist and respecting African traditional culture. She attributes many of the repressive tendencies of African society toward women to the heritage of colonialism and feels that traditions need to be remembered and revered: "Many people are beginning to realize that without the traditional base they just don't have any voice at all. . . . [T]he only way that the African woman of today, with her European orientation which we call education, can be liberated, is to study the traditional system and the place of the woman as defined by it. There was no area of human endeavour in the traditional system where the woman did not have a role to play'' (James, 147–151).

Works

The Disturbed Peace of Christmas. Ibadan, Nigeria: Daystar, 1971.
King Emene. London, England: Heinemann, 1974.
Old Wines Are Tasty. Ibadan, Nigeria: University Press, 1981.
Song of a Maiden: A Play. Ibadan, Nigeria: University Press, 1991.
The Sweet Trap. Ibadan, Nigeria: Oxford University Press, 1977.
The Wedlock of the Gods. Ibadan, Nigeria: Evans Brothers, 1973.
The Wizard of Law. London, England: Evans Brothers, 1975.

Commentary

Akinwale, Ayo. "Zulu Sofola: Her Writings and Their Undermeanings." *Nigerian Female Writers: A Critical Perspective.* Lagos, Nigeria: Malthouse, 1989. 68–73.
Asagba, Austin Ovigueraye. "Roots of African Drama: Critical Approaches and Elements of Continuity." *Kunapipi* 8.3 (1986): 84–99.
Dunton, Chris. *Make Man Talk True: Nigerian Drama in English Since 1970.* London: Hans Zell, 1992.
Fido, Elaine Savory. "A Question of Realities: Zulu Sofola's *The Sweet Trap.*" *Ariel* 18.4 (1987): 53–66.
James, Adeola, editor. *In Their Own Voices: African Women Writers Talk.* London, England: James Currey, 1990.
Nichols, Lee, editor. *Conversations with African Writers.* Washington, DC: Voice of America, 1981.
Obafemi, Olu. "Zulu Sofola's Theatre." *Nigerian Female Writers: A Critical Perspective.* Lagos, Nigeria: Malthouse, 1989. 60–67.

Sold for Silver by Janet Lim (Cleveland, OH: World, 1958). The autobiography of a Chinese woman whose father died when she was young and whose mother, unable by law to inherit his estate, was left in dire poverty. When she remarried, Janet was unwanted and was sold to a family in Singapore to serve as a *mui-tsai*, a household worker. She escaped and was raised in a Christian orphanage, then became a nurse, hoping to serve during the war. She was bombed and set adrift from a ship, captured by the Japanese, interned for a time, imprisoned when resisting the attentions of the head of the local military police, and eventually, at the close of the war, was able to return to Singapore. She survived with a combination of resourcefulness, toughness, and naïveté, all reflected in the style of her unassuming and interesting life story.

Commentary

Lim, Shirley, "Up Against the Nationalist Canon: Women's War Memoirs from Malaysia and Singapore." *Journal of Commonwealth Literature* 29.1 (August 1993): 47–64.

Sommers, Jane. See **Lessing, Doris.**

Sor Juana Inéz de la Cruz. See **Juana Inés de la Cruz.**

Sorabji, Cornelia. Born in India in 1866, the daughter of Sorabji Kharsedji, a Christianized Parsi. She was raised in a household that was English in language and culture. She attended Deccan College in Poona and was the first woman to graduate from Bombay University, after which she taught at a men's college at Gujarat for a period of time. She later went to England to study at Oxford, earning the friendship and support of Benjamin Jowett, master of Balliol College, and became trained as a lawyer, the first woman to read for the B.C.L. (bachelor of canon law). She moved in high circles, meeting the Toynbees, calling on Tennyson, and being presented to Queen Victoria. Returning to India, she took up as her first case a woman accused of murder; later she often represented women in purdah who were wards of the British courts. She returned to England more than once for further study and medical care and in India rose to prominence as a government officer and a member of the bar, before her death in 1954. She was politically conservative and was not in favor of independence for India, nor was she a feminist in her beliefs, though in her life she frequently broke barriers and behaved in ways considered unusually forthright for a woman. She wrote a number of stories, essays, and articles, as well as two autobiographies.

Works

Between the Twilights: Being Studies of Indian Women by One of Themselves. New York: Harper and Brothers, 1908.
India Calling; The Memories of Cornelia Sorabji. London, England: Nisbet, 1935.
India Recalled. London, England: Nisbet, 1936.
Indian Tales of the Great Ones Among Men, Women, and Bird-People. Bombay, India: Blackie and Son, 1916.
Love and Life Behind the Purdah. London, England: Freemantle, 1901.
The Purdahnashin. Calcutta, India: Thacker, Spink, 1917.
Queen Mary's Book for India. London, England: Harrap, 1943.
Sun-Babies. Bombay, India: Blackie and Son, 1918.

Commentary

Ramamurti, K. S. *Rise of the Indian Novel in English.* New Delhi, India: Sterling, 1987.

Soueif, Ahdaf. Born in Egypt in 1950, she was educated at the University of Cairo, where she received a B.A. in English. She later earned a Ph.D. from the University of Lancaster, after which she lectured on English literature at the universities of Cairo and Riyadh. She is the author of two works of fiction thus far, the latest one an ambitious and complex novel with a wide variety of historical settings and a large cast of characters.

Works

Aisha. London, England: Cape, 1983.
In the Eye of the Sun. New York: Pantheon, 1993.

Commentary

Said, Edward. "The Anglo-Arab Encounter." *TLS* (June 19, 1992): 19.

Spivak, Gayatri Chakravorty. Distinguished critic and translator. Born in India in 1941, she earned a B.A. from the University of Calcutta in 1959 and then attended Cambridge and Cornell, where she earned a Ph.D. in 1967. She is a professor of literature at the University of Pittsburgh and an influential critic, first known for her translation of Derrida's *Of Grammatology* (1967) and later for her criticism of cultural politics, which blends deconstruction, Marxism, and feminism. Her collection *In Other Worlds* includes many of her most important essays.

Works

"The Burden of English." *Orientalism and the Postcolonial Predicament: Perspectives on South Asia*. Philadelphia: University of Pennsylvania, 1993. 134–157.
"Can the Subaltern Speak?" *Marxism and the Interpretation of Culture*. Urbana: University of Illinois, 1988. 271–313.
In Other Worlds: Essays in Cultural Politics. New York: Methuen, 1987.
Outside in the Teaching Machine. New York: Routledge, 1993.
The Post-Colonial Critic: Interviews, Strategies, Dialogues. New York: Routledge, 1989.
"Responsibility." *boundary 2* 21.3 (1994): 19–64.

Commentary

Danius, Sara. "An Interview with Gayatri Chakravorty Spivak." *boundary 2* 20.2 (summer 1993): 24–50.

A Sport of Nature by Nadine Gordimer (New York: Knopf, 1987). Portrays the life of a woman who is an active revolutionary through an elusive, shifting narrative focus. Though Hillela is successful in her political activities and the novel ends with a glowing futuristic vision of an independence celebration in a liberated Cape Town, there is some question whether there can be a real change in the hierarchical or patriarchal norms. Hillela, the self-serving, sensual, and revolutionary heroine, is made purposely an out-of-focus character as if to emphasize the ambiguity of the political situation and the variety of ways in which evidence can be appropriated for political uses and variously interpreted. Her union with the black revolution—and her ability to transcend colonial history and her people's racist past—only underscores how unlikely, how difficult, how fraught with contradictions it is for whites in South Africa to participate fully in making its future. The novel met with conflicting critical assessment, many critics feeling it missed its mark or failed to live up to Gordimer's earlier work; in any assessment, it must be recognized as a daringly innovative novel.

Commentary

Clingman, Stephen. *"A Sport of Nature* and the Boundaries of Fiction." *The Later Fiction of Nadine Gordimer.* New York: St. Martin's, 1993. 173–190.

Cooper, Brenda. "New Criteria for 'Abnormal Mutation'? An Evaluation of Gordimer's *A Sport of Nature." Rendering Things Visible: Essays on South African Literary Culture.* Athens: Ohio University, 1990. 68–93.

Visel, Robin. "Othering the Self: Nadine Gordimer's Colonial Heroines." *Ariel* 19.4 (1988): 33–42.

Wade, Michael. *"A Sport of Nature:* Identity and Repression of the Jewish Subject." *The Later Fiction of Nadine Gordimer.* New York: St. Martin's, 1993. 155–172.

Weinhouse, Linda. "The Deconstruction of Victory: Gordimer's *A Sport of Nature." Research in African Literatures* 21.2 (summer 1990): 91–100.

Winnett, Susan. "Making Metaphors/ Moving On: *Burger's Daughter* and *A Sport of Nature." The Later Fiction of Nadine Gordimer.* New York: St. Martin's, 1993. 140–154.

Yelin, Louise. "Decolonizing the Novel: Nadine Gordimer's *A Sport of Nature* and British Literary Traditions." *Decolonizing Tradition: New Views of Twentieth-Century "British" Literary Canons.* Urbana: University of Illinois, 1992. 191–211.

Spring Cleaning by Jean Binta Breeze (London, England: Virago, 1992). Poems, some of which are "dub" (including her famous "Riddym Ravings") and others that are more conventional in their poetics. They often deal with the sense of exile and the memory of West Indian landscapes. In "Testament" a mother tells her daughter, embarrassed by her origins, of the losses she has sustained for her future: She compares herself to an old, rough-barked tree, and her daughter to a newly sprouting seed. She reassures her that "dere's more to you dan skin" (9). She recalls the girl's grandmother, "mountain strong," connecting the girl to her foremothers. Another poem, "Ilands," charts the islands of the Caribbean and her connectedness to them. The final poem is about coming to poetry through connections, through her reading of the world around her, her poems containing all of the people and the experiences she has had.

Springer, Eintou Pearl. Born in Santa Cruz, Trinidad, she works as a librarian and has been involved in theater most of her life. She is a poet and playwright; some of her poetry was written for a young audience.

Works

Godchild. London, England: Karia, 1987.
Out of the Shadows. London, England: Karia, 1986.

A State of Fear by Menan Du Plessis (Cape Town, South Africa: D. Philip, 1983). An accomplished novel about a teacher whose students are calling South African policies and values into question, forcing her to confront her own moral dilemmas. She harbors two fugitive students while the school is on strike, as they go about their mysterious nighttime business. In a violent confrontation, one that reminds her of a demonstration turned vicious in her own past, one of the students is apparently arrested and the other barely escapes. The narrator ponders her actions and the future of her country, raising questions that bring out her family's past and the unknown fate of her brother, who walked out one day into the desert, heading toward Botswana, in search of the wisdom of the bushmen who live at one with their natural world, in search of a wholeness he cannot find in South African society. The twinned questions—What has happened to the student? to her brother? Are they still alive?—become the foreground to a general anxious, uncertain state of fear that is the current of her life. A remarkable novel, rich in the sound of South African conversations, many shifting between English and Afrikaans, and redolent with the particulars of its natural landscape, so dear to the heart of the narrator's missing brother.

Steel, Flora Annie. Born in 1847 in England, Steel married a civil servant and moved with him to his assignment in India in 1868. He rapidly advanced up the civil service ladder, and she learned to read and write several languages, assumed the post of inspectress of mission schools, and was vice president of the Victoria Female Orphan Asylum. For a year she lived apart from her husband in order to carry on her work when his assignment took him to a different part of India, evidence of independence that earned her criticism. She returned to Britain in 1890 and was active in the suffragist movement. She was an independent and forward-looking woman, but at the same time she exhibited many of the characteristics of the colonialist mentality, not questioning the superiority of the ruling races so long as they ruled intelligently. She wrote a number of novels, some set in India and others in Scotland or elsewhere. She also published an autobiography, *The Garden of Fidelity,* collected folktales in India, and published an Indian cookbook. Her novel *On the Face of the Waters* was the most popular fictional account of the Indian Mutiny, and she labored at painstaking research to give it an accurate historical flavor. She died in 1929.

Works

The Flower of Forgiveness and Other Stories. London, England: Macmillan, 1894.
The Garden of Fidelity. London, England: Macmillan, 1929.
Indian Scene: Collected Short Stories of Flora Annie Steel. Freeport, NY: Books for Libraries, 1971.
Miss Stuart's Legacy. New York: Macmillan, 1893.
Mistress of Men. New York: Frederick Stokes, 1917.
*On the Face of the Waters. New York: Macmillan, 1911.

Commentary

Cowasjee, Saros. ''The Memsahib at the Writing Table: Women Writers of the Raj.'' *Encounter* 75.1 (July-August 1990): 53–56.
Paxton, Nancy L. ''Feminism Under the Raj: Complicity and Resistance in the Writings

of Flora Annie Steel and Annie Besant.'' *Women's Studies International Forum* 13 (spring 1990): 333–346.

Powell, Violet. *Flora Annie Steel: Novelist of India.* London, England: Heinemann, 1981.

Saunders, Rebecca. ''Gender, Colonialism, and Exile: Flora Annie Steel and Sara Jeannette Duncan in India.'' *Women's Writing in Exile.* Chapel Hill: University of North Carolina, 1989. 303–324.

Sharpe, Jenny. *Allegories of Empire: The Figure of the Woman in the Colonial Text.* Minneapolis: University of Minnesota, 1993.

Steen, Edla van. Born on July 12, 1936, in the southern Brazilian state of Santa Catarina. Her mother was of German ancestry and her father was a Belgian. She studied at a Catholic boarding school until age fifteen, when she began to work as a radio broadcaster, later becoming a journalist in Curitiba, Parana State, Brazil. She starred in a film, *Garganta do Diabo*, in 1958 and won an award as best actress in Brazil, and at the same time, still working as a journalist, she began to write short stories. She has written stories, novels, plays, translations, and criticism and compiled collections of interviews and literary anthologies. She has been active in promoting literature in Brazil through publishing efforts, festivals, and book fairs.

Works

A Bag of Stories. Translated by David George. Pittsburgh, PA: Latin American Literary Review, 1991.

Love Stories: A Brazilian Collection. Translated by Elizabeth Lowe. São Paulo, Brazil: Grafica Editora Hamburg, 1978.

Village of the Ghost Bells. Translated by David George. Austin: University of Texas, 1991.

The Stillborn by Zaynab Alkali (Harlow, England: Longman, 1989). The story of a woman struggling for a place of her own in society. As an adolescent, she is characterized as stubborn and impatient. She questions woman's place in a traditional society and resists the ''stillborn'' fate of women's dreams and abilities. The novel is a funny and thoughtful exploration of contemporary problems in a northern Nigerian family, beset by issues brought on by urbanization, Westernization, and broken marriages.

Commentary

Koroye, Seiyifa. ''The Ascetic Feminist Vision of Zaynab Alkali.'' *Nigerian Female Writers: A Critical Perspective.* Lagos, Nigeria: Malthouse, 1989. 47–51.

Stockenström, Wilma. Actress and writer, born in Napier, Cape Province, South Africa, in 1933 to a family of Dutch and Scandinavian ancestry. She was educated at the University of Stellenbosch, where she received a B.A. in stagecraft. She has published five volumes of poetry, a novel, and three novellas in Afrikaans. One, a postmodern slave narrative, has been translated into English by the distinguished novelist J.M. Coetzee. She has received a number of literary prizes for her poetry and the Super Primio Grinzane Cavour Prize for an Italian translation of her novel *The Expedition to the Baobab Tree.*

Work

*The Expedition to the Baobab Tree. Translated by J.M. Coetzee. Boston, MA: Faber and Faber, 1983.

Commentary

Brink, André. "Women and Language in Darkest Africa: The Quest for Articulation in Two Postcolonial Novels." *Literator* 13.1 (1992): 1–14.
du Plessis, Michael. "Bodies and Signs: Inscriptions of Femininity in John Coetzee and Wilma Stockenström." *Journal of Literary Studies/Tydsrif Vir Literaturweten- skap* 4.1 (March 1988): 118–128.
Gray, Stephen. "Some Notes on Further Readings of Wilma Stockenström's Slave Nar- rative, *The Expedition to the Baobab Tree.*" *Literator* 12.1 (April 1991): 51–59.
Zeiss, Cecelia Scallan. "Myth and Metamorphosis: Landscape as Archetype in Quest Narratives by Samuel Beckett and Wilma Stockenström." *Irish University Review* 21.1 (spring-summer 1991): 56–81.

Stones of the Wall by Tai Hou-ying (New York: St. Martin's, 1986). A novel about the psychological and spiritual aftermath of the Cultural Revolution. A group of friends from student days, now all teachers and writers, reflect one by one on their past and the things they endured for twenty years, experiences that were handled differently in each case. Each chapter is narrated in the voice of one of the friends, and the variation of responses builds up a multilayered collage of the personal costs of the Cultural Revolution.

Storni, Alfonsina. Born in Switzerland in 1892, she was raised in Argentina. She worked as a teacher while writing as a journalist and as a poet, publishing novellas, stories, plays, and literary criticism. She was an outspoken feminist who was welcomed into the literary circles of Buenos Aires. In 1938, on learning that she had inoperable cancer, she committed suicide by walking into the sea at Mar del Plata, Argentina.

Works

Alfonsina Storni: Argentina's Feminist Poet. Los Cerrillos, NM: San Marcos, 1975.
Alfonsina Storni: Poemas de amor and Other Selections. Mexico City, Mexico: B. Costa- Amic, 1974.
Selected Poems. Fredonia, NY: White Pine Press, 1987.

Commentary

Fishburn, Evelyn. "Alfonsina Storni: A Feminist Reading of Her Poetry." *Feminist Readings on Spanish and Latin American Literature.* Lewiston, NY: Mellen, 1991. 121–136.
Jones, Sonia. *Alfonsina Storni.* Boston, MA: Twayne, 1979.

Masiello, Francine. *Between Civilization and Barbarism: Women, Nation, and Literary Culture in Modern Argentina.* Lincoln: University of Nebraska, 1992.

Phillips, Rachel. *Alfonsina Storni: From Poetess to Poet.* London, England: Tamesis, 1975.

The Story of Zahra by Hanan Shaykh (New York: Anchor/Doubleday, 1994). Translation of *Hikayat Zahrah,* first published in English by Quartet Books, London, 1986. The novel is the interior narrative of a woman who lets herself be used by men repeatedly—her uncle makes advances, a married man casually uses her for sex while she endures abortions alone, and she is married off to a man who doesn't even know her. She ends up living in Beirut in the midst of war, going voluntarily to visit a sniper on a roof, who might shoot her but who instead has sex with her day after day. When she finds herself pregnant and a doctor tells her she is too far advanced to have an abortion, the sniper says he will marry her, but on her way home in the street, he shoots her from his rooftop. The novel is an intense and frightening portrait of a woman who is filled with self-loathing and for whom sexuality, violence, and power are grotesquely entwined.

Commentary

Accad, Evelyne. "Sexuality, War, and Literature in Lebanon." *Feminist Issues* 11 (fall 1991): 27–42.

Suleri, Sara. Born in Pakistan to a wealthy family, daughter of a Pakistani father who was a journalist, nationalist, and politically committed activist who was from time to time detained for his political writings and a Welsh mother who was a professor of English literature at Punjab University. She grew up between cultures, living sometimes in London and sometimes in Lahore, attending Kinnaird College for Women and Punjab University, before going to the United States for further education. She now lives in New Haven, Connecticut, where she teaches at Yale University. She has published criticism and her autobiography, which is a sharp, intelligent meditation on her family, her country, and her status as a citizen of multiple cultures.

Work

Meatless Days. Chicago, IL: University of Chicago, 1989.

Commentary

Suleri, Sara. "Karachi, 1990." *Raritan* 11.4 (spring 1992): 50–71.

Suleri, Sara. *The Rhetoric of English India.* Chicago, IL: University of Chicago, 1992.

Warley, Linda. "Assembling Ingredients: Subjectivity in *Meatless Days.*" *A/B: Auto/Biography Studies* 7.1 (spring 1991): 107–123.

Sultana's Dream and Selections from the Secluded Ones by Begum Rokeya (New York: Feminist, 1988). Two works by a Muslim woman who knew very well the life of seclusion led by traditional Muslim women in Bangladesh and who wrote eloquent protests against the practice. *Sultana's Dream* is a utopian vision of a world in which women are free and men, too dangerous and warlike to be loose, are secluded. The enlightened reign of women leads to a peaceful, intelligent, scientifically advanced garden of a state. The short dream points out through reversal not only how cruel purdah is but how stupidly men run the affairs of the world. The selections from *The Secluded Ones* are brief anecdotes about seclusion that dramatize pointedly the effects of the custom taken to extremes, as in the case of the woman who, entangled in her enveloping *burqa*, falls on a railway line and is killed by an oncoming train because her maid can't get her up and won't let any men assist her. These short pieces are accompanied by helpful biographical and historical information.

Sunlight on a Broken Column by Attia Hosain (London, England: Chatto and Windus, 1961). A wealthy Muslim family in old Lucknow is the locus of this novel, with a title taken from Eliot's "Hollow Men." Conflict between generations arises over privileges assumed by the older members of the family, raised with wealth and power. Political turmoil, independence, the trauma of partition are all backdrops to the complex web of family relations and the narrator's struggle to maintain integrity and identity against the effacement of women that is an assumed condition of her life. This novel has been recently reprinted by Virago.

Sutherland, Efua. Born and raised in Cape Coast, Ghana, in 1924. She attended Saint Monica's School, Mampong, earned a B.A. at Homerton College, Cambridge University, and studied at the School of Oriental and African Studies, London University. She returned to Ghana in 1951 to teach, first at a secondary school and a teacher's college, then becoming a lecturer at the University of Ghana. She married William Sutherland, and African-American official working with an international aid organization, with whom she has three children. In 1958, she founded the Experimental Theatre Group, which performed plays in both Twi and English, drawing on local folklore and dances. She founded the Ghana Drama Studio in Accra and in 1960 built a theater using traditional performance area concepts. She also founded the Ghana Society of Writers, which evolved into the Writers' Workshop of the Institute of African Studies, University of Ghana, Legon, and helped to found the magazine *Okyeame* as an outlet for Ghanaian emerging writers. The earliest Ghanaian playwright-director and popular broadcaster, involved in both radio and television, she also writes for children in both Fanti and English. She has been vastly influential in African theater and has been a noted proponent of African dramatic forms and the rediscovery of indigenous theatrical and oral traditions.

Works

Edufa. Washington, DC: Three Continents, 1979.

Foriwa. Accra, Ghana: Ghana Publishing, 1967.

The Marriage of Anansewa. Harlow, England: Longman, 1987.
Odasani. Accra, Ghana: Anowuo Educational, 1967.
The Original Bob. Accra, Ghana: Anowuo Educational, 1969.
Playtime in Africa. New York: Atheneum, 1962.
The Roadmakers. Accra, Ghana: Information Services, 1961.
The Voice in the Forest: A Tale from Ghana. New York: Philomel Books, 1983.
Vulture! Vulture! and Tahina: Two Rhythm Plays. Accra, Ghana: Ghana Publishing House, 1968.

Commentary

Akyea, E. Ofori. "The Atwia-Ekumfi Kodzidan—An Experimental African Theatre." *Okyeame* 4.1 (1970): 82–84.
Brown, Lloyd W. *Women Writers in Black Africa.* Westport, CT: Greenwood, 1981.
Duerden, Dennis, and Cosmo Pieterse. *African Writers Talking.* London, England: Heinemann, 1972.
Holloway, Karla. *Moorings and Metaphors: Figures of Culture and Gender in Black Women's Literature.* New Brunswick, NJ: Rutgers University, 1992.
Nichols, Lee, editor. *Conversations with African Writers.* Washington, DC: Voice of America, 1981.
Park, Christine, and Caroline Heaton, editors. *Close Company: Stories of Mothers and Daughters.* London, England: Virago, 1987.
Pearce, Adetokunbo. "The Didactic Essence of Efua Sutherland's Plays." *African Literature Today* 15 (1985): 71–81.
Sutherland, Efua. *Story-Telling Drama in Ghana.* Accra, Ghana: Afram, 1975.
Wilentz, Gay. *Binding Cultures: Black Women Writers in Africa and the Diaspora.* Bloomington: Indiana University, 1992.

Suzman, Helen. Liberal politician, born in South Africa in 1917 to Jewish parents who had emigrated from Lithuania. She entered politics as a party worker for the United Party of Jan Smuts and won a seat in South Africa's all-white Parliament representing Johannesburg in 1952. In 1959 she was a founding member of the Democratic Party. She served for thirty-six years in Parliament, often the only member of her party holding a seat. She cleverly manipulated parliamentary privilege to publicize abuses of power and was a frequent visitor to Nelson Mandela and other political prisoners held at Robben Island. Her politics have been and remain liberal in a country where liberalism had few supporters among the Right or the Left; young black leaders would have little to do with her after the Soweto uprising of 1976. Her memoir is an insider's view of the political process in South Africa from the 1950s to the present.

Work

In No Uncertain Terms: A South African Memoir. New York: Knopf, 1993.

T

Tai Hou-ying. Born in Anhui, central China, in 1938. Her father, a store manager, was criticized as a rightist for objecting to economic policies; her mother worked as a seamstress. She earned a degree from the Normal School of the University of Shanghai and then was assigned to the Association of Writers, married, and had a child. After divorce, and during the Cultural Revolution, she met the writer Wen Jie. He was called before a committee of which she was a member on charges of ideological incorrectness. He was found guilty and sent to prison, and his wife committed suicide. Soon after, Tai Hou-ying found herself in similar circumstances, as she, in turn, was accused and sent to work on a farm, where she reencountered Wen Jie. They fell in love but were refused permission to marry, and when more charges were leveled against Wen Jie, he, too, committed suicide. Years later she wrote a memorial to him, in which she said that out of his death was born a writer—herself. When the Gang of Four fell from grace in 1976, she resigned from the Association of Writers and began to teach literature at the University of Shanghai; since then she has written many books, including one on Wen Jie, and several novels, many of which have been translated into French. One novel is available in English translation.

Work

Stones of the Wall. Translated by Frances Wood. New York: St. Martin's, 1986.

Commentary

Duke, Michael S. "Chinese Marxist Humanism: Dai Houying's Novel *Ren a, ren!*" *Blooming and Contending: Chinese Literature in the Post-Mao Era.* Bloomington: Indiana University, 1985. 152–185.

Knapp, Bettina. "The New Era for Women Writers in China." *World Literature Today* 65 (summer 1991): 432–439.

Pruyn, Carolyn S. "Humanism in Post-Mao Mainland Chinese Literature: The Case of *Jen A Jen!* by Tai Hou-ying." *Asian Cultural Quarterly* (autumn 1985): 15–34.

Pruyn, Carolyn S. *Humanism in Modern Chinese Literature: The Case of Dai Houying.* Bochum, Germany: Studienverlag, 1988.

T'ao Yang. A Chinese writer, living in Taiwan. Her exploration of her roots, severed from China by political and personal events, and her long-term estrangement from her mother, is the subject of an unusual and moving autobiographical novel.

Work

*Borrowed Tongue. Hong Kong: Renditions, 1986.

Tapsubei Creider, Jane. See **Creider, Jane Tapsubei.**

Tawil, Raymonda Hawa. Born in 1940 to Christian Arab parents living in Palestine. The family suffered from the political turmoil of 1948 and became separated. In 1957 she finally was able to join her brothers in Jordan and became a political activist, organizing both on behalf of Palestinians but also for the rights of women. She was placed under house arrest after the 1967 war and continued to agitate for Palestinian rights, though her activities sometimes came under fire from other Palestinians who felt she was too accommodating with Israelis and too concerned with feminist issues. Her memoir is a valuable account of war, repression, and resistance.

Work

My Home, My Prison. New York: Holt, 1980.

Commentary

Manganaro, Elise Salem. "The Politics of Public Disclosure: Race and Gender in Raymonda Tawil's *My Home, My Prison.*" *Biography East and West: Selected Conference Papers.* Honolulu: University of Hawaii, 1989. 127–133.

Tekin, Latife. Born in 1957 in a village near the town of Bünyan, Turkey, one of eight children, she moved with her family to Istanbul when she was nine years old. There her father and three brothers worked as laborers, and they lived in poverty. She was able to finish school and began to write, her first novel, *Sevgili Arsiz Ölüm,* being well received both by critics and by the public. Another novel, one that focuses on a community formed on the hills of an urban waste dump, has been translated into English. She is noted for her use of magic realism, her focus on the gap between rich and poor, and her use of a lively provincial dialect of Turkish.

Work

Berji Kristin: Tales from the Garbage Hills. Translated by Ruth Christie and Saliha
  Paker. New York: Marion Boyars, 1993.

Commentary

Gün, Güneli. "The Woman in the Darkroom: Contemporary Women Writers in Turkey."
  World Literature Today 60.2 (spring 1986): 275–279.

Telles, Lygia Fagundes. Born in São Paulo, Brazil, in 1923, she moved frequently as a child because her father, a public official, was often transferred,
giving her a penchant for the nomadic life. She began to write in high school,
composing poems and stories for a school magazine, and then publishing a book
of her stories, paying for it herself at a printer's shop across the street from her
school. Her first commercially published book came out while she was studying
law. She has been elected to the Brazilian Academy of Letters and was vice
president of the Brazilian Writers' Union and president of the Brazilian Cine-
matique. Her books are popular in Brazil, and several have been translated into
English. Her mood is generally psychologically probing, fantastic, and claustrophobic, with frustratingly narrow family settings that imprison the female protagonists. Her most famous novel is *As Meninas*, published in Portuguese in
1973 (*The Girl in the Photograph*, 1982), which uses multiple narrators and
shifting viewpoints to explore the psyches of three girls who live in a board-
inghouse, delving into both feminist concerns for identity and political criticism
of dictatorship.

Works

The Girl in the Photograph. Translated by Margaret A. Neves. New York: Avon Books,
  1982.
Marble Dance. Translated by Margaret A. Neves. New York: Avon Books, 1986.
Tigrela and Other Stories. Translated by Margaret A. Neves. New York: Avon Books,
  1986.

Commentary

Brown, Richard L. "Lygia Fagundes Telles: Equalizer of the Sexes." *Romance Notes*
  32.2 (winter 1991): 157–161.
Mautner Wasserman, Renata R. "The Guerrilla in the Bathtub: Telles's *As Meninas* and
  the Irruption of Politics." *Modern Language Studies* 19.1 (1989): 50–65.
Price, Greg, editor. *Latin America: The Writer's Journey.* London, England: Hamish
  Hamilton, 1990.
Telles, Lygia Fagundes. "The Truth of Invention." *Lives on the Line: The Testimony of
  Contemporary Latin American Authors.* Berkeley: University of California, 1988.
  267–271.

Testimonies of Exile by Abena P. A. Busia (Trenton, NJ: Africa World Press,
1990). Poems about exile, about recovery of the past, and about personal relationships. Includes one that is in Twi and English, using ideas from her mother's

people, the Ga of southern Ghana, and the language spoken by her father's people, the Asante. The poem "Migrations" captures the loss and the strength of the exile, gathering together a past through reliving the past and unraveling memories in "the half-life, half-light of alien tongues" (9).

Testimonios. Works that can be described as *testimonios* are personal narratives that represent a collective memory of a people in crisis told through the voice of a witness. *Testimonios* are often blunt and sincere in tone, rather than literary in style. Perhaps the most familiar *testimonio* for European and North American readers is that of Rigoberta Menchu, Nobel Peace Prize–winning activist on behalf of the Quiché Indians of Guatemala. It is a genre particularly identified with Latin American literature, though it is by no means limited to it. Though related to autobiography and life story production, *testimonios* are distinguished by emphasizing the collective experience of a politically and economically oppressed group, with a narrative voice that is intentional but not concerned with exploring subjectivity so much as with bringing a people's story urgently to the world's attention. As a genre the *testimonio* has frequently been discounted among literary critics, particularly under the influence of new criticism, which discounted both the social construction of texts and the intentionality of the author, but more recently, they have been examined by literary critics as legitimate objects of study; see, particularly, the work of John Beverly and Doris Sommer.

Works

*Alegría, Claribel, and D. J. Flakoll. *They Won't Take Me Alive*. Translated by Amanda Hopkinson. London, England: Women's Press, 1986.
*Alvarado, Elvira. *Don't Be Afraid, Gringo: A Honduran Woman Speaks from the Heart*. Translated and edited by Medea Benjamin. San Francisco, CA: Institute for Food and Development, 1987.
*Barrios de Chungara, Domitila. *Let Me Speak! Testimony of Domitila, a Woman of the Bolivian Mines*. London, England: Monthly Review, 1978.
Hammond, Jenny. *Sweeter Than Honey: Ethiopian Women and Revolution: Testimonies of Tigrayan Women*. Trenton, NJ: Red Sea Press, 1990.
*Jesús, Carolina Maria de. *Child of the Dark: The Diary of Carolina Maria de Jesús*. New York: E. P. Dutton, 1962.
*Magaia, Lina. *Dumba Nengue: Run for Your Life—Peasant Tales of Tragedy in Mozambique*. Translated by Michael Wolfers. Trenton, NJ: Africa World Press, 1988.
*Menchu, Rigoberta. Edited by Elizabeth Burgos-Debray. *I, Rigoberta Menchu: An Indian Woman in Guatemala*. Translated by Ann Wright. London, England: Verso, 1984.
Partnoy, Alicia. *The Little School: Tales of Disappearance and Survival in Argentina*. Translated by Alicia Partnoy with Lois Athey and Sandra Braunstein. Pittsburgh, PA: Cleis, 1986.
"*We Were Making History*": *Life Stories of Women in the Telangana People's Struggle*. London, England: Zed, 1989.

Commentary

Beverly, John. "Through All Things Modern: Second Thoughts on *Testimonio*." *boundary 2* 18.2 (1991): 1–21

Beverly, John. "The Margin at the Center: On *Testimonio* (Testimonial Narrative)." *De/Colonizing the Subject: The Politics of Gender in Women's Autobiography.* Minneapolis: University of Minnesota, 1992. 91–110.

Carr, Robert. "Crossing the First World/Third World Divides: Testimonial, Transnational Feminisms, and the Postmodern Condition." *Scattered Hegemonies: Postmodernity and Transnational Feminist Practices.* Minneapolis: University of Minnesota, 1944. 153–172.

Harlow, Barbara. *Resistance Literature.* New York: Methuen, 1987.

Levine, Robert M. "The Cautionary Tale of Carolina Maria de Jesús." *Latin American Research Review* 29.1 (1994): 55–83.

Manzor-Coats, Lillian. "The Reconstructed Subject: Women's Testimonials as Voices of Resistance." *Splintering Darkness: Latin American Women Writers in Search of Themselves.* Pittsburgh, PA: Latin American Literary Review, 1990. 157–171.

Moody, Michael. "Isabel Allende and the Testimonial Novel." *Confluencia* 2.1 (fall 1986): 39–43.

Rice-Sayre, Laura P. "Witnessing History: Diplomacy Versus Testimony." *Testimonio y literatura.* Edina, MN: Society for the Study of Contemporary Hispanic and Lusophone Revolutionary Literatures, 1986. 48–72.

Sommer, Doris. "Not Just a Personal Story: Women's *Testimonios* and the Plural Self." *Life/Lines: Theorizing Women's Autobiography.* Ithaca, NY: Cornell University, 1988. 107–130.

Sommer, Doris. "No Secrets: Rigoberta's Guarded Truth." *Women's Studies* 20 (1991): 51–72.

That Long Silence by Shashi Deshpande (London, England: Virago, 1988). A long-married woman must go into hiding with her husband, who is in trouble over a case of government corruption. Their marriage suffers from the strain, and he eventually leaves her. When she reflects on her marriage, she discovers that she has been living a fiction, and it is in her own fiction—the writing that her husband always despised and that she, herself, discounted—that she is able to recover herself. The novel uses a backdrop of family affairs to explore the institution of marriage and the need for selfhood and self-respect.

Theater. Third world women have long been active in theater, arguably from the time when oral literature and storytelling were the primary means of verbal cultural production. Playwrights such as Ama Ata Aidoo and Efua Sutherland employ traditional African spaces and rituals in their drama, building on indigenous traditions. Other women use theater as a chance to explore communal responses to shared issues, as in the work of the Sistren Theatre Collective and the projects of Penina Muhando Mlama, who has linked theater with locally controlled development projects. Some playwrights have achieved some fame in the first world. Both Stella Kon of Singapore and Gcina Mhlope of South

Africa have taken plays to the Edinburgh Fringe Festival, receiving awards. Maria Irene Fornés, born in Cuba, has won six Obies for both writing and directing her plays. Her work is daring and experimental, as are Jessica Hagedorn's performance pieces and the highly political and absurdist plays of Griselda Gambaro, who creates in her nightmarish dramas a picture of Argentinean life that is as disturbing as any news story or commentary on political terror. Theater provides a medium particularly adaptable to various cultural projects in the third world, whether it is continuing and building on indigenous traditions, performing a didactic function, or taking on critical questions in society that a dramatic treatment can publicly explore.

Works

Acholonu, Catherine Obianuju. *Trial of the Beautiful Ones: A Play in One Act.* Owerri, Nigeria: Totan, 1985.

*Aidoo, Ama Ata. *Dilemma of a Ghost.* New York: Collier, 1971.

Chedid, Andrée. *The Show-Man.* Translated by Felicia Londre. New York: Ubu Repertory Theater, 1984.

*Dike, Fatima. *The First South African.* Johannesburg, South Africa: Ravan, 1979.

Fornés, Maria Irene. *Fefu and Her Friends: A Play.* New York: PAJ, 1990.

*Gambaro, Griselda. *Information for Foreigners: Three Plays.* Translated by Marguerite Feitlowitz. Evanston, IL: Northwestern University, 1992.

Garro, Elena. *A Solid Home.* In *Selected Latin American One-Act Plays.* Translated by Francesca Colecchia and Julio Matas. Pittsburgh, PA: Pittsburgh University, 1973.

Hagedorn, Jessica, Laurie Carlos, and Robbie McCauley. *Teeny Town.* In *Out from Under: Texts by Women Performance Artists.* New York: Theatre Communications Group, 1990. 90–117.

*Kon, S. *Emily of Emerald Hill: A Monodrama.* Singapore: Macmillan, 1989.

*Mhlophe, Gcina. *Have You Seen Zandile?* Portsmouth, NH: Heinemann, 1990.

*Mugo, Micere Githae, and Ngugi wa Thiong'o. *The Trial of Dedan Kimathi.* Nairobi, Kenya: Heinemann, 1976.

Onwueme, Tess. *Three Plays.* Detroit, MI: Wayne State University, 1993.

Pai Feng-hsi. *Three Women Trilogy.* Translated by Gua Yuehua. Beijing, China: Chinese Literature Press, 1991.

Schwarz-Bart, Simone. *Your Handsome Captain.* Translated by Jessica Harris and Catherine Temerson. In *Plays by Women: An International Anthology.* New York: Ubu Repertory Theater, 1988. 231–249.

Sofola, 'Zulu. *The Sweet Trap.* Ibadan, Nigeria: Oxford University Press, 1977.

Sutherland, Efua. *Edufa.* Washington, DC: Three Continents Press, 1979.

Commentary

Akyea, E. Ofori. "The Atwia-Ekumfi Kodzidan—An Experimental African Theatre." *Okyeame* 4.1 (1970): 82–84.

Amuta, Chidi. "The Nigerian Woman as Dramatist: The Instance of Tess Onwueme." *Nigerian Female Writers: A Critical Perspective.* Lagos, Nigeria: Malthouse, 1989. 53–59.

Asagba, Austin Ovigueraye. "Roots of African Drama: Critical Approaches and Elements of Continuity." *Kunapipi* 8.3 (1986): 84–99.

Boyle, Catherine. "Griselda Gambaro and the Female Dramatist: The Audacious Tres-
    passer." *Knives and Angels: Women Writers in Latin America*. London, England:
    Zed, 1990. 145–157.
Cobham, Rhonda. " 'A Wha Kind a Pen Dis?': The Function of Ritual Frameworks in
    Sistren's *Bellywoman Bangarang*." *Theatre Research International* 15.3 (autumn
    1990): 233–242.
Cypress, Sandra Messinger. "Visual and Verbal Distances in the Mexican Theatre: The
    Plays of Elena Garro." *Woman as Myth and Metaphor in Latin American Lit-
    erature*. Columbia: University of Missouri, 1985. 44–62.
Fido, Elaine. "Radical Woman: Woman and Theatre in the Anglophone Caribbean."
    Critical Issues in West Indian Literature. Parkersburg, IA: Caribbean Books,
    1984. 33–45.
Fido, Elaine Savory. "Finding a Way to Tell It: Methodology and Commitment in The-
    atre About Women in Barbados and Jamaica." *Out of the Kumbla: Women and
    Literature in the Caribbean*. Trenton, NJ: Africa World Press, 1990. 331–343.
Gray, Stephen. "Women in South African Theatre." *South African Theatre Journal* 4.1
    (May 1990): 75–87.
King, Bruce, editor. *Post-Colonial English Drama: Commonwealth Drama Since 1960*.
    New York: St. Martin's, 1992.
Larson, Catherine. "Playwrights of Passage: Women and Game-Playing on the Stage."
    Latin American Literary Review 19.38 (July–December 1991): 78–89.
Laughlin, Miriam. "Mayan Women Playwrights." *Belles Lettres* 7 (winter 1991–1992):
    45–47.
Mlama, Penina Muhando. *Culture and Development: The Popular Theatre Approach in
    Africa*. Uppsala, Sweden: Nordiska Afrikainstitut, 1991.
Obafemi, Olu. "Zulu Sofola's Theatre." *Nigerian Female Writers: A Critical Perspec-
    tive*. Lagos, Nigeria: Malthouse, 1989. 60–67.
Pearce, Adetokunbo. "The Didactic Essence of Efua Sutherland's Plays." *African Lit-
    erature Today* 15 (1985): 71–81.
Sutherland, Efua. *Story-Telling Drama in Ghana*. Accra, Ghana: Afram, 1975.
Taylor, Diana. *Theatre of Crisis: Drama and Politics in Latin America*. Lexington: Uni-
    versity Press of Kentucky, 1991.
Waldman, Gloria Feiman. "Three Female Playwrights Explore Contemporary Latin
    American Reality: Myrna Casas, Griselda Gambaro, Luisa Josefina Hernandez."
    Latin American Women Writers: Yesterday and Today. Pittsburgh, PA: Latin
    American Literary Review, 1977. 75–84.

They Won't Take Me Alive by Claribel Alegría and D. J. Flakoll (London,
England: Women's Press, 1986). Translation of *No me agarran viva*, first published in 1983. A reconstruction, using narrative techniques that are at once
documentary and novelistic, of the life of Commander Eugenia of the Salva-
dorean guerrilla forces. The material is based on interviews with her family and
her comrades at arms, with their comments reproduced in the text, as well as
some of Eugenia's letters. It is careful to couch the testimonies in a historical
framework while making a compelling story of the narrative. The heroic woman
at the center does not speak for herself. (It makes an interesting companion to
a novel that also depicts a larger-than-life woman activist, *A Sport of Nature* by

Nadine Gordimer, in which the periphery contains the detail, creating a legendary and curiously absent center through the various views brought to bear on
it from the margins.) It is both a portrayal of a woman's growing commitment
and the history of political resistance in El Salvador.

Commentary

Shea, Maureen. "Latin American Women and the Oral Tradition: Giving Voice to the
    Voiceless." *Critique* 34.3 (spring 1993): 139–153.

Thirabutana, Prajaub. See **Prajaub Thirabutana.**

Tholo, Maria. South African resident of Soweto who was interviewed in 1976
by a researcher; these interviews became the basis of her "diary" when the
material was reworked into chronological order. In it she not only bears witness
to the events of the Soweto Uprising but provides the point of view of a woman
who is ambivalent about the children's crusade and the violence it sparks.

Work

The Diary of Maria Tholo. Johannesburg, South Africa: Ravan, 1979.

Thomas, Elean. Born in St. Catherine, Jamaica, in 1947, she studied political
science and history at the University of the West Indies and did postgraduate
work in communications at Goldsmiths College, London. She is an activist in
feminist, nationalist, and social movements. She was a founder of the Workers
Party of Jamaica and served as its international secretary. She has written poetry
(which she calls "word rhythms") stories, a novel, and numerous articles. She
currently lives in Jamaica after having spent several years in London.

Works

Before They Can Speak of Flowers: Word Rhythms. London, England: Karia, 1988.
The Last Room. London, England: Virago, 1991.
Word Rhythms from the Life of a Woman. London, England: Karia, 1986.

Three Continents by Ruth Prawer Jhabvala (New York: Morrow, 1987). This
disturbing novel traces the lives of twins who are drawn into the influence of
an Eastern spiritualist and his sinister sidekicks. The novel moves from America
to London to India, where it ends grimly with the murder of one twin, which
the other twin, the narrator, refuses to acknowledge as murder. Jhabvala is mas-
terful in her treatment of emotional domination, first of one twin by the other,
then by the spiritualists who insinuate themselves into their lives, a theme of
religious figures assuming power over vulnerable people that is common in her
works.

The Three Marias by Rachel de Queiroz (Austin: University of Texas, 1963).
A story that demonstrates how Brazilian society limits the life and career pos-

sibilities of three young girls in boarding school. This traditional novel follows the lives of three young women, schoolmates in a convent school, after they graduate and go their separate ways. Social criticism and a feminist consciousness are gently brought to bear on the narrative without engaging in polemicism.

Three Solid Stones by Martha Mvungi (London, England: Heinemann, 1985). A collection of twelve stories drawing from the Bena and Hene folklore of southern Tanzania; Mvungi herself is a Bena and spent her early childhood among the Hene people. These traditional stories, originally passed on orally, are cast in the format of Western folktales rather than attempting to reproduce the tone of the African oral tradition. According to the author's introduction, writing the stories down deprives them of the important social nature of the oral tradition, yet serves as a record of a people's culture. There are many overtones of magic in these stories, as well as a number of strong women protagonists who undertake heroic tasks on behalf of their children.

Ti Marie by Valerie Belgrave (London, England: Heinemann, 1988). A romance set in Trinidad at the end of the eighteenth century in which a handsome regency rake—the sort of character encountered in a typical costume romance—leaves England after a duel to take refuge in Barbados. He (and the novel) are redeemed by his grandmother who instilled liberal traditions in him and the character of Elena, nicknamed Ti Marie, a mixed-race Creole woman, daughter of an Amerindian woman and a French republican refugee. The action is driven by historical events—the European land grab and struggle for dominion, the increase in the slave trade, and the growing restrictions on nonwhite residents—yielding an entertaining, unpretentious historical romance. The author's intention, to provide in a genre popular with her intended audience a historical novel based on the Caribbean past, is carried out successfully.

Commentary

Tanifeani, William. "Interview with Valerie Belgrave, Novelist, Visual Artist." *Wasafiri* 11 (1990): 24–25.

Tiempo, Edith Lopez. Poet and novelist and a teacher of writing, she earned a B.A., magna cum laude, from Silliman University in the Philippines (where she later became chair of the English Department), an M.A. from the State University of Iowa, and a Ph.D. in literature from the University of Denver. She has published several novels and volumes of poetry and short fiction.

Works

Abide, Joshua, and Other Stories. Manila, Philippines: A. S. Florentino, 1964.
The Alien Corn: A Novel. Quezon City, Philippines: New Day, 1992.
A Blade of Fern. Hong Kong: Heinemann, 1978.
The Charmer's Box: Poetry. Manila, Philippines: De La Salle University, 1993.

His Native Coast. Quezon City, Philippines: New Day, 1979.
The Tracks of Babylon, and Other Poems. Denver, CO: A. Swallow, 1966.

Commentary

Chow, Maria Elena Barretto. "Edith Tiempo and the Problem of Language in Philippine Poetry." *Philippine Studies* 38.3 (1990): 388–397.
Chow, Maria Elena Barretto. "Edith Tiempo's Definition of Poetry: 1950–86." *Philippine Studies* 37.3 (1989): 255–282.
Grow, L. M. "The Architecture of the Interior: Angst and *Nada* in the Fiction of Edith Tiempo." *University of Windsor Review* 22.2 (1989): 78–94.

Ting Ling. Pseudonym of Jiang Bingzhi. She was born in 1904 in Linli, Hunan, China. She began her literary career in the twenties and won a wide readership with stories that examined questions of identity and sexuality—most particularly with the bold themes expressed in *Miss Sophie's Diary*, published in 1928—works that would later be held against her. In 1930 she joined the League of Left-Wing Writers and then the Communist Party in 1932. She was detained by the Kuomintang from 1933 to 1936, when she escaped to Yan'an, where she continued writing, though with an increasing interest in depicting social movements and using reportage in her fiction. In 1949 she wrote *The Sun Shines over the Sanggan River*, an attempt at socialist realism that was awarded the Stalin Prize. In 1957 she was labeled a rightist, in part because of her early, sexually frank writings, and was imprisoned. In 1979 she was finally rehabilitated and was made vice president of the Chinese Writers' Association. In spite of her long persecution, she remained loyal to the Communist Party in her old age and earned the ire of many younger writers by indulging in propagandism and attacking them in ideological battles. She died in 1986.

Works

*I Myself Am a Woman: Selected Writings of Ding Ling. Boston, MA: Beacon, 1989.
The Sun Shines over the Sanggan River. Translated by Yang Xianyi and Gladys Yang. Beijing, China: Foreign Languages Press, 1984.

Commentary

Barlow, Tani E. "Gender and Identity in Ding Ling's *Mother*." *Modern Chinese Women Writers: Critical Appraisals.* Armonk, NY: M. E. Sharpe, 1989. 1–24.
Feuerwerker, Yi-tsi Mei. *Ding Ling's Fiction: Ideology and Narrative in Modern Chinese Literature.* Cambridge, MA: Harvard University, 1982.
Larson, Wendy. "The End of 'Funu Wenxue': Women's Literature from 1925 to 1935." *Modern Chinese Literature* 4.1–2 (spring-autumn 1988): 39–54.
Liu, Lydia H. "The Female Tradition in Modern Chinese Literature: Negotiating Feminisms Across East/West Boundaries." *Genders* 12 (winter 1991): 22–44.
Ting Ling. "Foolish Dreams: Like a Blind Person Going Fishing." *Modern Chinese Writers: Self-Portrayals.* Armonk, NY: M. E. Sharpe, 1992. 303–306.

Tlali, Miriam. Born in 1933 in Doornfontein, Johannesburg, South Africa, to a father who was a teacher and a mother who encouraged her writing. Her father died when she was young, leaving her his collection of books. She attended Witwatersrand University for two years until it was closed to blacks, then studied medicine in Lesotho until she could no longer afford to. She then went to secretarial school and became a clerk, an experience she drew upon in her novel *Muriel at Metropolitan*, which was banned in South Africa, as was her second novel, *Amandla*. She has contributed to many South African publications, including the *Rand Daily Mail* and *Staffrider*, for which she wrote a series of interviews entitled "Soweto Speaking." She has traveled abroad, participating in the International Writing Program at the University of Iowa in 1979 and a PEN conference in Canada and living for six months in the Netherlands. During an academic year (1989–1990) spent at Yale University, her play *Crimen Injuria* was staged. She works on encouraging emerging writers in South Africa and fostering political change.

Works

Amandla. Johannesburg, South Africa: Raven, 1980.
Footprints in the Quag: Stories and Dialogues from Soweto. Cape Town, South Africa: David Philip, 1989.
Mihloti. Johannesburg, South Africa: Skotaville, 1989.
*Muriel at Metropolitan. Harlow, England: Longman, 1987.
Soweto Stories. London, England: Pandora, 1989.

Commentary

Alvarez-Pereyre, Jacques. "Images of Power in the South African Novel: The Novels of Miriam Tlali." *Matatu: Journal for African Culture and Society* 2.3–4 (1988): 111–124.
Grandqvist, Raoul, and John Stotesbury, editors. *African Voices: Interviews with Thirteen African Writers.* Sydney, Australia: Dangaroo, 1990.
Ibrahim, Huma. "The Autobiographical Content in the Works of South African Women Writers: The Personal and the Political." *Biography East and West: Selected Conference Papers.* Honolulu: University of Hawaii, 1989. 122–126.
Lee, Sonia. "Conversation with Miriam Tlali." *African Literature Association Bulletin* 17.3 (summer 1991): 40–42.
Lenta, Margaret. "Two Women and Their Territories: Sheila Roberts and Miriam Tlali." *Tulsa Studies in Women's Literature* 11.1 (spring 1992): 103–111.
Locket, Cecily. "The Fabric of Experience: A Critical Perspective on the Writing of Miriam Tlali." *Women and Writing in South Africa: A Critical Anthology.* Marshalltown, South Africa: Heinemann, 1989. 275–285.
MacKenzie, Craig, and Cherry Clayton. *Between the Lines: Interviews With Bessie Head, Sheila Roberts, Ellen Kuzwayo, Miriam Tlali.* Grahamstown, South Africa: National English Literary Museum, 1989.
Rive, Richard. "Miriam Tlali." *Index on Censorship* 13.6 (December 1984): 23.
Sole, Kelwyn. "The Days of Power: Depictions of Politics and Community in Four Recent South African Novels." *Research in African Literatures* 19.1 (spring 1988): 65–88.

Tlali, Miriam. ''Remove the Chains: South African Censorship and the Black Writer.''
    Index on Censorship 13.6 (December 1984): 22–26.
Tlali, Miriam. ''The Dominant Tone of Black South African Writing.'' *Criticism and
    Ideology: Second African Writers Conference, Stockholm 1986.* Uppsala, Sweden:
    Scandinavian Institute of African Studies, 1988. 198–204.

Traba, Marta. Born in Buenos Aires, Argentina, in 1930, the daughter of a
bohemian journalist. The family moved often, sometimes being evicted for non-
payment of rent. She was a voracious reader as a child. She studied art and is
known best for her works of art criticism. She moved to Columbia in the early
1950s, where she was involved in teaching, television production, museum management, publication of an arts magazine, and writing. She taught at several
Latin American universities, was founder and director of the Museum of Modern
Art in Bogotá, Colombia, and published many books and articles on the plastic
arts. She published her first literary work, a collection of poems, in 1951 and
then wrote several novels. She died in November 1983.

Work

*Mothers and Shadows. Translated by Jo Labanyi. New York: Readers International,
    1989.

Commentary

Cummings, Kate. ''Reclaiming the Mother('s) Tongue: *Beloved, Ceremony, Mothers and
    Shadows.*'' *College English* 52.5 (September 1990): 552–569.
Kantaris, Elia Geoffrey. ''The Silent Zone: Marta Traba.'' *Modern Language Review*
    87.1 (January 1992): 86–101.
Masiello, Francine. ''Subversions of Authority: Feminist Literary Culture in the River
    Plate Region.'' *Chasqui: Revista de Literatura Latinoamericana* 21.1 (May
    1992): 39–48.
Pinto, Magdalena Garcia. *Women Writers of Latin America: Intimate Histories.* Austin:
    University of Texas, 1991.

Tracing It Home: Journeys Around a Chinese Family by Lynn Pan
(Tokyo, Japan: Kodansha, 1993). A cool, somewhat distanced family narrative
by a Chinese woman whose family left China at the time of the revolution. Her
memories of revolutionary China—where she stayed as a small child while her
parents sought a new home—are confused, filled in with meaning only in adulthood. She travels to China to recover the family's past, a project that takes her
around the country. Her grandfather, a wealthy businessman, left imposing
buildings all over Shanghai that have withstood the stresses of time; ironically,
the wealthy family suffered far less from the revolution than a devoted family
servant who, because he would not incriminate them, spent twenty years in
forced labor under horrific conditions. It is his story that takes center stage by
the end of the memoir.

Tree of Life by Maryse Condé (New York: Ballantine Books, 1992). A wide-ranging family saga that deftly interweaves the lives of generations of a Guadeloupean family, shifting from the island of Guadeloupe to Panama (where the patriarch of the family helps build the canal), San Francisco, Paris, Brittany, London, and New York. The patriarch strives to escape a life of bondage and drudgery in the sugar cane fields and manages to give his children and grandchildren many options, but their conflicts and ambitions tend to drive them apart. The story is narrated by a young woman who has grown up disconnected to family and her island heritage but who painstakingly reconstructs it by rediscovering the intertwined lives of her forebears—an attempt to locate history in the lives of people, not in events. Though this novel has received less critical attention than others by Condé, it is an accomplished, thoughtful, and entertaining novel.

Trial by Terror: Sri Lankan Poems by Jean Arasanayagam (Hamilton, New Zealand: Rimu, 1987). A collection of poetry that provides a shocking view of the terrorism, chaos, and conflict of the civil war that tore apart Sri Lanka. The sequence begins in the early 1980s and is based on the author's experiences in a refugee camp. They draw attention away from the nationalistic and religious differences that drive the secessionist movement and focus on the experiences of noncombatants caught in the crossfire.

The Trial of Dedan Kimathi by Micere Githae Mugo and Ngugi wa Thiong'o (Nairobi, Kenya: Heinemann, 1976). A play based on the life and career of Dedan Kimathi, a revolutionary hero of the Mau Mau uprising. The authors, who met while university students and who kept in touch until they both had teaching positions at the University of Nairobi, wanted to recover history that was misrepresented elsewhere and do it in a manner that reflected the way that Kenyans remember Kimathi, as a powerful leader who never died. The didactic and antiimperialist tone is deliberate: Ngugi argues in the introduction that writers who fail to take the side of the people are on the side of imperialism. ''We agreed that the most important thing was for us to reconstruct imaginatively our history, envisioning the world of the Mau Mau and Kimathi in terms of the peasants' and workers' struggle before and after constitutional independence.'' To do this, historical events are collapsed together and characters are made larger than life and given political speeches that address all of Kenyan history. The play was first performed in Nairobi, meeting with great popular success; the audience participated in the final triumphal dance, following the actors into the streets.

Trinh T. Minh-ha. A writer, filmmaker, composer, and critic born in Vietnam in 1952. She studied music and comparative literature for a year at the University of Saigon before moving to the United States at age seventeen. She earned degrees in ethnomusicology, music composition, and French literature at institutions in the United States and Paris. She has performed and composed music, using piano, organ, percussion instruments, and Vietnamese zither. She taught for three years in Senegal at the National Conservatory of Music in Dakar, while carrying out ethnographic fieldwork, serving as codirector of a five-month research expedition for the Research Expedition Program of the University of California, Berkeley. She is an associate professor of cinema at San Francisco State University. She has made several films—*Réassemblage* (1982), *Naked Spaces: Living Is Round* (1985), and *Surname Viet, Given Name Nam* (1989)— and has contributed to the theory of film documentary, a genre that she argues does not exist as such. She has written two books in French, one of criticism (*Un Art sans oeuvre*, 1981, on contemporary Western conceptions of art and their relationship to Eastern philosophies) and one of poetry (*En Miniscules*, 1987. She coauthored a work on African architecture with Jean-Paul Bourdier. Her book *Woman, Native, Other* (1989) is a groundbreaking work of criticism that explores questions of identity and representation for third world women. Interestingly, this much-cited text was submitted to thirty-three publishers, trade, academic, and small presses before being accepted because it is unconventionally poetic and personal and resists standard marketing niches. She pointed out in an interview, "I am always working at the borderlines of several shifting categories. . . . For academics, 'scholarly' is a normative territory that they own all for themselves, hence theory is not theory if it is not dispensed in a way recognizable to and validated by them" (Mayne, 6).

Works

Framer Framed [includes film scripts and stills from her films]. London, England: Routledge, 1992.

When the Moon Waxes Red: Representation, Gender, and Cultural Politics. New York: Routledge, 1991.

Woman, Native, Other: Writing Postcoloniality and Feminism. Bloomington: Indiana University, 1989.

Commentary

Mayne, Judith. "From a Hybrid Place: An Interview with Trinh T. Minh-ha." *Afterimage* 18 (December 1990): 6–9.

Parmar, Pratibha. "Woman, Native, Other: Pratibha Parmar Interviews Trinh T. Minh-ha." *Feminist Review* 36 (autumn 1990): 65–74.

Penley, Constance, and Andrew Ross. "Interview with Trinh T. Minh-ha." *Camera Obscura* 13–14 (1985): 86–103.

Trinh T. Minh-ha. "Introduction: (Un)Naming Cultures" [theme issue]. *Discourse* 11.2 (spring-summer 1989): 5–17.

Trinh T. Minh-ha. "Outside In Inside Out." *Questions of Third Cinema*. London, England: BFI, 1989. 133–149.

Trinh T. Minh-ha. "Documentary Is/Not a Name." *October* 52 (spring 1990): 76–98.

Ts'an-hsueh. Born on May 30, 1953, in Changsha, Hunan; her real name is Deng Xiao-hua. Her mother and father were both revolutionaries who, during the war against Japan, walked from Hunan to Manchuria to join the resistance. When she was born, her father was serving as chief editor of the *Hunan News*, but in 1957, he was declared an ultra-rightist and both parents were sent to the country for labor reform. In 1959 the family moved to the outskirts of Changsha. When she was finishing elementary school, her parents were again caught up in political strife, this time victims of the Cultural Revolution. Her father was imprisoned, and her mother was sent to a cadre's reform school. Beginning in 1970, Ts'an-hsueh worked in a factory, a job she held for ten years. She and her husband, Lu Yong, were unable to find the kind of working conditions they wanted, and both became tailors, setting up their own business. She began to write in 1983 and was published for the first time in 1985, becoming well known in China within a year. She has a style that is remarkably individual, dreamlike, and subjective. A collection of short stories and a novel are available in English translation.

Works

*Dialogues in Paradise. Translated by Ronald R. Janssen and Jian Zhang. Evanston, IL: Northwestern University, 1989.
Old Floating Cloud. Translated by Ronald R. Janssen and Jian Zhang. Evanston, IL: Northwestern University, 1991.

Tuqan, Fadwa. Born in 1917 in Nablus on the West Bank of the Jordan, one of ten children in an influential and fairly wealthy family. The year of her birth, her father was banished to Egypt by the British occupying forces for his activism on behalf of Arab nationalism. She was introduced to poetry by her brother, Ibrahim Tuqan, himself a noted poet. She has published many volumes of poetry in Arabic, about love and about refugees and the status of Palestine. She has also published an autobiography, available in English translation in a volume that also includes a selection of her poems.

Work

A Mountainous Journey: A Poet's Autobiography. Translated by Olive Kenny and Naomi Shihab Nye. St. Paul, MN: Graywolf, 1990.

Turner, Clorinda Matto de. See **Matto de Turner, Clorinda.**

Two Lives: My Spirit and I by Jane Tapsubei Creider (London, England: Women's Press. 1986). The autobiography of a Nandi woman who grew up in rural Kenya, lived a ruggedly independent life, and met and married an American Africanist, finally settling with him in Canada. She also relates the story of a woman who died eighty years earlier who, according to Nandi traditional beliefs, was herself in an earlier incarnation. She includes in both her story and that of her earlier namesake many details about Nandi culture and values in a straightforward voice that avoids any traces of exoticism. Her adaptability and independence in both lives are notable, and while she does not oppose or contradict her people's traditions, she demonstrates that they can embrace many perspectives; indeed, Tapsubei seems to have lived not two lives but many more in her passage from her homeland to urban Kenya to life in Canada.

Two Women in One by Nawal Sa'dawi (Seattle, WA: Seal Press, 1986). A novel that deals with a woman's reaction and relationship to a patriarchal society. It relates the story of a young woman who has been raised in a Westernized household, liberated from the veil, yet denied a sexual identity. As a student she becomes involved in a strike that is brutally suppressed; after her parents bail her out of prison, they pull her out of the university and marry her off. Her struggle to resist social limits, to become whole, brings her to life.

Ty-Casper, Linda. Born on September 17, 1931, in Manila, Philippines, the daughter of a civil engineer and a writer. She trained as a lawyer, earning degrees from the University of the Philippines and Harvard. She turned to writing, wanting to shed light on aspects of Filipino history that have been misrepresented or are simply absent in the history books. She has been a writer-in-residence at the University of the Philippines and a fellow at Silliman University and Radcliffe College. She has written several novels, short stories, and articles, most with historical themes.

Works

Awaiting Trespass: A Pasión. New York: Readers International, 1985.
Common Continent: Selected Stories. Manila, Philippines: Arteneo de Manila University, 1991.
Dread Empire. Exeter, England: Heinemann, 1982.
Fortress in the Plaza. Quezon City, Philippines: New Day, 1985.
The Hazards of Distance. Quezon City, Philippines: New Day, 1981.
The Peninsulars. Manila, Philippines: Bookmark, 1964.
The Secret Runner and Other Stories. Manila, Philippines: A. S. Florentino, 1974.
A Small Party in a Garden. Quezon City, Philippines: New Day, 1988.
Ten Thousand Seeds. Manila, Philippines: Ateneo de Manila University, 1987.
The Three-Cornered Sun: A Historical Novel. Quezon City, Philippines: New Day, 1979.
Wings of Stone. Columbia, LA: Readers International, 1986.

U

Ulasi, Adaora Lily. Born in Aba, eastern Nigeria, in 1932. The daughter of an Igbo chief of the house of Nnewi, she attended St. Michael's Primary School in Aba, then several schools in Lagos, after which she traveled to the United States, where she attended Pepperdine and the University of California, receiving a B.A. in journalism in 1954, the first African woman to earn a journalism degree. In the 1960s she worked as women's page editor of the *Daily Times* and the *Sunday Times* of Nigeria. She married, moved to England, and had three children. In 1972 she divorced and spent four years in Nigeria before returning to Britain, where she currently lives. She has worked on radio broadcasts for the Voice of America and writes for the *Nigerian Daily Star*. Her use of pidgin in her first novel was controversial at the time—some faulting it for inaccuracy and for making Nigerian characters seem buffoons. She was the first Nigerian to write detective fiction in English, using historical settings and elements of magic in her plots.

Works

The Man from Sagamu. New York: Macmillan, 1978.
Many Thing Begin for Change. London, England: Fontana, 1975.
Many Thing You No Understand. London, England: Collins, 1973.
The Night Harry Died. Lagos, Nigeria: Educational Research Institute, 1974.
Who Is Jonah? Ibadan, Nigeria: Onibonoje, 1978.

Commentary

Mojola, Yemi I. "The Novels of Adaora Ulasi." *Nigerian Female Writers: A Critical Perspective.* Lagos, Nigeria: Malthouse, 1989. 37–46.

The Umbrella Tree by Rose Zwi (New York: Penguin, 1990). A novel set just after the start of the Soweto uprising. Two women, one the mother of a white political prisoner and the other his wife, visit the family of a servant in the countryside, where a boy who was involved in the uprising is in hiding. The novel chooses this moment of meeting under an umbrella tree in the South African countryside to explore the different responses to the crisis of the white women and the black family, all disenfranchised and embittered, but in ways that make it hard for them to work together to end apartheid. Yet the novel ends on a hopeful note, that somehow there is still time to repair the divisions and build something better.

Under the Bone by Anne-christine d'Adesky (New York: Farrar, Straus, Giroux, 1994). This novel opens with a woman in Haiti finding the body of a peasant activist dumped in a forest. She becomes a pawn in a political coverup, and an American journalist works to uncover the real murderers of the "disappeared" activist. The story, a mixture of journalistic observation of the Haitian political scene, social commentary, and political thriller, is told in a rich mixture of narrative styles and is enlivened with dialogue in Creole. The author, a journalist herself who uncovered military massacres during the 1987 Haitian presidential election, brings a strong sense of place and the historical moment to her novel.

V

Valenzuela, Luisa. Born in Buenos Aires, Argentina, in 1938, the daughter of Luisa Mercedes Levinson, a noted writer, and Pablo Valenzuela, a physician. She began to work as a writer at age fifteen, when she became a journalist. She wrote for *La Nación* and other publications and for a time worked under Jorge Luis Borges at the National Library. From 1958 to 1961 she lived in Paris, writing short stories and contributing to *La Nación*'s literary supplement. In 1969 she went to the United States with a Fulbright grant to take part in a writing workshop at the University of Iowa. In 1979 she was invited to be a writer-in-residence at Columbia University, and she has lived in New York ever since, with frequent stays in Mexico and Argentina. She became writer-in-residence for the Center for Inter-American Relations and has conducted writing workshops and lectured at institutions throughout Canada and the United States, as well as in the Hispanic communities of New York. She was awarded a Guggenheim Fellowship in 1983 and is active in PEN. She has published many collections of stories and several novels. Her style is marked by irony, hyperbolic humor, the fantastic, and narrative daring, particularly in her novel *The Lizard's Tail*.

Works

Black Novel with Argentines. Translated by Toby Talbot. New York: Simon and Schuster, 1992.
The Censors. Translated by Hortense Carpentier and others. Willimantic, CT: Curbstone, 1992.

Clara: Thirteen Short Stories and a Novel. Translated by Hortense Carpentier and J. Jorge Castello. New York: Harcourt Brace Jovanovich, 1976.

He Who Searches. Elmwood Park, IL: Dalkey Archive, 1977.

The Lizard's Tail. Translated by Gregory Rabassa. New York: Farrar, Straus, Giroux, 1983.

Open Door. Translated by Hortense Carpentier and others. San Francisco, CA: North Point Press, 1988.

Other Weapons. Translated by Deborah Bonner. Hanover, NH: Ediciones del Norte, 1985.

Strange Things Happen Here. Translated by Helen Lane. New York: Harcourt Brace Jovanovich, 1979.

Commentary

Case, Barbara. "On Writing, Magic, and Eva Peron: An Interview with Argentina's Luisa Valenzuela." *Ms.* 12.4 (1983): 12–20.

Garfield, Evelyn Picón. "Interview with Luisa Valenzuela." *Review of Contemporary Fiction.* 6.3 (fall 1986): 25–30.

Gautier, Marie-Lise Gazarian. *Interviews with Latin American Writers.* Elmwood Park, IL: Dalkey Archive, 1989.

Gold, Janet. "Feminine Space and the Discourse of Silence: Yolanda Oreamuno, Elena Poniatowska, and Luisa Valenzuela." *In the Feminine Mode: Essays on Hispanic Women Writers.* Lewisburg, PA: Bucknell University, 1990. 195–203.

Hicks, D. Emily. *Border Writing: The Multidimensional Text.* Minneapolis: University of Minnesota, 1991.

Magnarelli, Sharon. "Censorship and the Female Writer: An Interview-Dialogue with Luisa Valenzuela." *Letras Femeninas* 10.1 (1984): 55–64.

Magnarelli, Sharon. "*The Lizard's Tail*: Discourse Denatured." *Review of Contemporary Fiction* 6.3 (1986): 97–104.

Magnarelli, Sharon. *Reflections/Refractions: Reading Luisa Valenzuela.* New York: P. Lang, 1988.

Magnarelli, Sharon. "Framing Power in Luisa Valenzuela's *Cola de lagartija* [*The Lizard's Tail*] and Isabel Allende's *Casa de los espiritus* [*The House of the Spirits*]. *Splintering Darkness: Latin American Women Writers in Search of Themselves.* Pittsburgh, PA: Latin American Literary Review, 1990. 43–62.

Payne, Johnny. *Conquest of the New World: Experimental Fiction and Translation in the Americas.* Austin: University of Texas, 1993.

Pinto, Magdalena Garcia. *Women Writers of Latin America: Intimate Histories.* Austin: University of Texas, 1991.

Price, Greg, editor. *Latin America: The Writer's Journey.* London, England: Hamish Hamilton, 1990.

Valenzuela, Luisa. "The Word, That Milk Cow." *Contemporary Women Authors of Latin America.* New York: Brooklyn College, 1983. 96–97.

Valenzuela, Luisa. "The Other Face of the Phallus." *Reinventing the Americas: Comparative Studies of Literature of the United States and Spanish America.* Cambridge, England: Cambridge University, 1986. 242–248.

van Steen, Edla. See **Steen, Edla van.**

A Very Angry Letter in January by Ama Ata Aidoo (Sydney, Australia: Dangaroo, 1992). Poems written while abroad at women's conferences or while working as a visiting professor in America or at her home-in-exile, Harare. They concern Africa's future, Africa's neocolonial repetition of its past, and the latent prejudices left from colonial times as well as more personal subjects, such as the growing up of the author's daughter (''A Young Woman's Voice Doesn't Break. It Gets Firmer''). Particularly effective are poems such as ''Loving the Black Angel,'' which was dedicated ''to fallen heroes'' one week after an activist was hanged. In it she declares, ''I just love Lucifer,'' challenging Western religious imagery by describing the ''first rebel'' as rough and hairy and pitch black (47). Her poems combine humor, irony, political outrage, and a lively, observant voice.

Vicens, Josephina. Born on November 23, 1911, in Villahermosa, Tabasco, Mexico. Her mother was Mexican and her father Spanish, from the Balearic Islands. Together they had five daughters. Vicens left high school to learn secretarial skills at a professional school, taking her first job at age fifteen with the Mexico-Puebla Transport Company, the first of many administrative jobs. She started to work in the film industry and eventually became an influential figure in the 1960s and 1970s. She wrote two novels, *El libro vacío* in 1958 (*The Empty Book,* 1992), an influential novel that started a trend of metaphysical literature and that received the Xavier Villaurrutia Prize, and *Años falsos* in 1982 (*The False Years,* 1989), a scathing critique of Mexican politics and of traditional gender roles. She died in Mexico City in 1988 on her seventy-seventh birthday.

Works

The Empty Book. Translated by David Lauer. Austin: University of Texas, 1992.
The False Years. Translated by Peter G. Earl. Pittsburgh, PA: Latin American Literary
     Review, 1989.

W

Waciuma, Charity. A Gikuyu woman, born sometime in the 1930s; she grew up in Fort Hall in the Central Province of Kenya, the daughter of a couple who were Christians and who also believed in traditional Gikuyu values. Her father, who had been trained in medicine at a missionary school, worked with both Western medical practices and traditional healing customs. Her grandfather was a storyteller and an encyclopedia of clan lore. The rift between Western ways and Gikuyu tradition grew wider with the movement of independent schools that challenged missionary schooling, and Waciuma, as a Christian enrolled at an independent school, felt the conflict personally. She followed her family's beliefs and did not participate in the traditional initiation rite of circumcision, which led to her becoming the object of mockery. She was sympathetic with the Mau Mau movement but as a Christian remained outside it. Her family life was threatened by the government, which forcibly placed Gikuyus in patrolled compounds, and her father, arrested by the Home Guard, died under suspicious circumstances. She explored the conflicts she experienced and her commitment to independence and the retention of Gikuyu tradition in her autobiographical account of her adolescence during the Mau Mau emergency, *Daughter of Mumbi*. She has also written for children, using Gikuyu folklore as material.

Works

Daughter of Mumbi. Nairobi, Kenya: East African Publishing House, 1974.
The Golden Feather. Nairobi, Kenya: East African Publishing House, 1966.
Merry-Making. Nairobi, Kenya: East African Publishing House, 1972.

Mweru, the Ostrich Girl. Nairobi, Kenya: East African Publishing House, 1966.
Who's Calling? Nairobi, Kenya: East African Publishing House, 1972.

Commentary

Neubauer, C. E. "Tradition and Change in Charity Waciuma's Autobiography *Daughter of Mumbi.*" *World Literature Written in English* 25.2 (1985): 211–221.

Wang An-i. Born in 1954 in Nanjing, the daughter of a man who was proclaimed a rightist when she was very young and a mother who was a celebrated writer and Communist Party member. She grew up in Shanghai, in a relatively privileged household, but was sent down to rural Anhui at age fifteen during the Cultural Revolution. She achieved recognition in the post-Mao era writing about her generation, its experiences during the hiatus of the Cultural Revolution, and the frustrations of readjusting to urban life afterward. She traveled with her mother, the writer Ru Zhijuan, to the Iowa International Writing Program in 1983 and has had her novels translated into English and German. Her themes of marriage, love, and sexuality and the detached, cool narrative in which she delivers stories that concern subjects often left unexpressed in China have caused some Chinese critics to find fault with her writing.

Works

*Baotown. Translated by Martha Avery. New York: W. W. Norton, 1989.
Brocade Valley. Translated by Bonnie S. McDougall and Chen Maiping. New York: New Directions, 1992.
Lapse of Time. Beijing, China: Chinese Literature Press, 1988.
Love in a Small Town. Translated by Eva Hung. Hong Kong: Renditions, 1988.

Commentary

Liu, Lydia H. "The Female Tradition in Modern Chinese Literature: Negotiating Feminisms Across East/West Boundaries." *Genders* 12 (winter 1991): 22–24.
Wang An-i. "Needed: A Spirit of Courageous Self-Examination." *Modern Chinese Writers: Self-Portrayals.* Armonk, NY: M. E. Sharpe, 1992.
Zheng, Wang. "Three Interviews: Wang Anyi, Zhu Lin, Dai Qing." *Modern Chinese Literature* 4 (1988): 99–148.

Ward, Harriet. South African colonialist novelist, born in Norfolk, England, in 1808. She moved to the Eastern Cape, South Africa, in the early 1840s, returning to England in 1847. Her first book, a memoir, also included information for emigrants. She used her experiences, reworking them into fiction in the first novel to be written by a South African colonial, *Jasper Lyle*, a romantic and melodramatic work. She died in 1873.

Works

Five Years in Kaffirland. London, England: H. Colburn, 1848.
Jasper Lyle: A Tale of Kaffirland. London, England: B. Routledge, 1851.

Warner-Vieyra, Myriam. Born in Pointe-à-Pitre, Guadeloupe, she left for France at age twelve, though she frequently returned during vacations. At age twenty-two, after marrying an African, she moved to Senegal, where she works as a librarian and researcher for the University of Dakar. She is the author of two novels (both available in English translation) and a volume of short stories.

Works

*As the Sorcerer Said. Harlow, England: Longman, 1982.
*Juletane. London, England: Heinemann, 1987.

Commentary

King, Adele. "Two Caribbean Women Go to Africa: Maryse Condé's *Hérémakhonon* and Myriam Warner-Vieyra's *Juletane.*" *College Literature* 18.3 (October 1991): 96–105.
Lionnet, Françoise. "Inscriptions of Exile: The Body's Knowledge and the Myth of Authenticity." *Callaloo* 15.1 (winter 1992): 30–40.
Lionnet, Françoise. "Geographies of Pain: Captive Bodies and Violent Acts in the Fictions of Myriam Warner-Vieyra, Gayl Jones, and Bessie Head." *Callaloo* 16.1 (winter 1993): 132–152.
Mortimer, Mildred. "An Interview with Myriam Warner-Vieyra. *Callaloo* 16.1 (winter 1993): 108–115.
Ngate, Jonathan. "Reading Warner-Vieyra's *Juletane.*" *Callaloo* 9.4 (fall 1986): 553–564.
O'Callaghan, Evelyn. "Interior Schisms Dramatised: The Treatment of the 'Mad' Woman in the Work of Some Caribbean Novelists." *Out of the Kumbla: Women and Literature in the Caribbean.* Trenton, NJ: Africa World Press, 1990. 89–109.
Wilson, Elizabeth. " '*Le Voyage et l'espace close*'—Island and Journey as Metaphor: Aspects of Women's Experience in the Works of Francophone Caribbean Women Writers." *Out of the Kumbla: Women and Literature in the Caribbean.* Trenton, NJ: Africa World Press, 1990. 45–58.

Wheatley, Phillis. Noted poet, born in Senegal in 1753 and taken as a slave to America at the age of seven. In 1761, Susannah Wheatley bought her and taught her to read and write. Phillis quickly showed her talents and was able to read the Bible in sixteen months, learning Latin as well as English. She began to write poetry at the age of thirteen and became a celebrity, being asked to perform her prodigious feats of knowledge and erudition before groups of white spectators. She was the first black to publish a book of poetry in the United States. In spite of her fame, she died at the age of thirty in poverty, after burying her three children. She died in 1784.

Works

The Collected Works of Phillis Wheatley. New York: Oxford University, 1988.
The Poems of Phillis Wheatley. Chapel Hill: University of North Carolina, 1989.

Commentary

Flanzbaum, Hilene. "Unprecedented Liberties: Re-reading Phillis Wheatley." *Melus* 18.3 (fall 1993): 71–81.

Kendrick, Robert L. "Snatching a Laurel, Wearing a Mask: Phillis Wheatley's Literary Nationalism and the Problem of Style." *Style* 27.2 (summer 1993): 222–251.

Nott, Walt. "From 'Uncultivated Barbarian' to 'Poetical Genius': The Public Presence of Phillis Wheatley." *Melus* 18.3 (fall 1993): 21–32.

Robinson, William Henry. *Phillis Wheatley: A Bio-bibliography.* Boston, MA: G. K. Hall, 1981.

Robinson, William Henry. *Phillis Wheatley and Her Writings.* New York: Garland, 1984.

Where the Jinn Consult by Soraya Antonius (London, England: Hamish Hamilton, 1987). Sequel to *The Lord*, the novel opens with unrest after the execution of Tareq, a miracle-working young Palestinian who has incited feelings of rebellion and whose body is now mysteriously missing. A complex plot involves the shady dealings of the British police, the Irgun, and the opportunists who are willing to buy, sell, and when necessary, manufacture information. The characters are for the most part fictional, but historical events—the Deir Yassin massacre, the bombing of the King David Hotel, and the partition of Palestine—are framed in a novel that is ironic, sophisticated, and angry.

Whole of a Morning Sky by Grace Nichols (London, England: Virago, 1986). A novel that, alternating a child's viewpoint with a more omniscient narration, describes the progress of a Guyanese family from a small town to urban life, the upheaval of a political struggle as the country moves toward independence, and the attendant economic and racial strife it unleashes. The book conveys a vivid sense of place and history.

A Wicked Old Woman by Ravinder Randhawa (London, England: Women's Press, 1987). Khuli, an Indian living in England, assumes the identity of a lame, eccentric bag lady as a form of protest and as a way of evading labeling. She goes about with her cane ("Stick-leg-shuffle-leg-shuffle" opens many of the chapters) visiting friends and children, whose stories interweave with hers and with that of a runaway girl who killed a man while defending herself from rape. The women of the novel are building a culture distinct from that of Britain or India, with bricolage elements of both, but one of their own making and with their own stamp. A funny, at times elliptical, novel.

Wicomb, Zöe. Born in Cape Province, South Africa, in 1948. She completed an arts degree at the University for Cape Coloureds, Western Cape. In 1970 she went to England and studied English literature at Reading University. She now lives in Nottingham, where she teaches English, specializing in black literature and women's studies. She is author of many articles and an accomplished collection of stories.

Work

You Can't Get Lost in Cape Town. New York: Pantheon, 1987.

Commentary

Hunter, E., and C. MacKenzie, editors. *Between the Lines II: Interviews with Nadine Gordimer, Menan Du Plessis, Zöe Wicomb, Lauretta Ngcobo.* Grahamstown, South Africa: National English Literary Museum, 1993.

Wicomb, Zöe. "An Author's Agenda." *Critical Fictions: The Politics of Imaginative Writing.* Seattle, WA: Bay Press, 1991. 13–16.

Wicomb, Zöe. "Tracing the Path from National to Official Culture." *Critical Fictions: The Politics of Imaginative Writing.* Seattle, WA: Bay Press, 1991. 242–250.

Wide Sargasso Sea by Jean Rhys (New York: Norton, 1967). This novel retells *Jane Eyre* from the viewpoint of the madwoman in the attic. It is a first-person account of a Creole woman, the daughter of a ruined plantation family, who enters into an unhappy arranged marriage. She is divided between the black and West Indian world (where she feels most at home but where she is rejected as a member of a disenfranchised, slave-owning ruling class) and the foreign world of England, a world she only knows through images of the lush, green south, a world very different from her husband's brooding Yorkshire. The dissonance of cultures and her isolation contribute to her growing madness, which is harrowingly depicted in the final passages of the novel. This novel led to Rhys's rediscovery and the recognition that she is a Caribbean novelist whose themes of isolation, self-disgust, and displacement reflect not only modernist disenchantment but the postcolonial experience.

Commentary

Cliff, Michelle. "Caliban's Daughter: The Tempest and the Teapot." *Frontiers* 12.2 (summer 1991): 36–51.

Erwin, Lee. " 'Like in a Looking-Glass': History and Narrative in *Wide Sargasso Sea.*" *Novel* 22.2 (winter 1989): 143–158.

Fayad, Mona. "Unquiet Ghosts: The Struggle for Representation in Jean Rhys's *Wide Sargasso Sea.*" *Modern Fiction Studies* 34.3 (autumn 1988): 437–452.

Harris, Wilson. *The Womb of Space: The Cross-Cultural Imagination.* Westport, CT: Greenwood, 1983.

Harris, Wilson. "Jean Rhys's Tree of Life." *Review of Contemporary Fiction* 5.2 (summer 1985): 114–117.

Lalla, Barbara. "Discourse of Dispossession: Ex-Centric Journeys of the Un-Living in *Wide Sargasso Sea* and the Old English 'The Wife's Lament.' " *Ariel* 24.3 (July 1993): 55–72.

O'Callaghan, Evelyn. "Interior Schisms Dramatised: The Treatment of the 'Mad' Woman in the Work of Some Caribbean Novelists." *Out of the Kumbla: Women and Literature in the Caribbean.* Trenton, NJ: Africa World Press, 1990. 89–109.

Scharfman, Ronnie. "Mirroring and Mothering in Simone Schwarz-Bart's *Pluie et vent sur Télumée Miracle* and Jean Rhys's *Wide Sargasso Sea.*" *Yale French Studies* 62 (1981): 88–106.

Tiffin, Helen. "Post-Colonial Literatures and Counter-Discourse." *Kunapipi* 9.3 (1987): 17–34.

Wife by Bharati Mukherjee (Boston, MA: Houghton Mifflin, 1975). A dark and searing book about a woman who, after a traditional arranged marriage, emigrates with her husband from India to America. She wavers between the expatriate Indian community and a more American lifestyle, assuming Americanness as she spends time house-sitting an apartment for an absent neighbor. Gradually, her grasp of reality disintegrates and the violent climax is both shocking and yet inevitable. The portrait of the stresses of emigration and its effects on identity is powerful and disturbing.

Wijenaike, Punyakante. Born in 1935, she was raised and educated in Sri Lanka. She writes in English and has been published in journals and newspapers in her home country, as well as having published books of short stories. Some of her stories have been translated into Russian and Sinhala. She is considered by some critics one of the most accomplished of Sri Lankan writers.

Works

Giraya. Colombo, Sri Lanka: Lake House Investments, 1971.
The Rebel. Colombo, Sri Lanka: Lake House Investments, 1979.
The Third Woman and Other Stories. Maharagama, Sri Lanka: Saman, 1963.
The Waiting Earth. Colombo, Sri Lanka: Colombo Apothecaries, 1966.
A Way of Life. Nugegoda, Sri Lanka: Deepanee, 1987.
Yukthi and Other Stories. Kelaniya, Sri Lanka: New Kelanai Printers, 1991.

Wild Swans: Three Daughters of China by Jung Chang (London, England: HarperCollins, 1992). A fascinating family history covering the lives of three women: the author, her mother, and her grandmother. Her grandmother was born when foot binding was still practiced. She became a concubine for a war lord at age fifteen. Her daughter, the author's mother, became a revolutionary, living through the Japanese occupation, marrying a man whose devotion to the party was paramount, and fighting in the Civil War. The author grew up as a privileged member of the governing class, secure in a cocoon of safety until the Cultural Revolution, in which her family was scattered in different directions, forced to work on the land or into camps. She spent time working in a remote rural area as a "barefoot doctor" and as an untrained electrician at a factory. She eventually moved to England after the death of Mao, and ten years later, when her mother visited her there, she learned the details of the lives she recounts in this remarkable book.

Wild Thorns by Sahar Khalifeh (London, England: Al Saqui, 1985). This novel presents a scathing picture of life in occupied Palestine and follows the experiences of a Palestinian worker returning from contract work in the Gulf.

He sees more clearly than those accustomed to it the complacency and submissiveness of his people forced to buy Israeli goods and work in Israeli factories. It is an angry and bitter book in which freedom is bartered for material culture, and in which dignity and national identity are eroded by economic pressures more deeply than by military measures.

The Wiles of Men and Other Stories by Salwa Bakr (London, England: Quartet, 1992). Vignettes of Egyptian women's lives, told with a rich variety of narrative voices. In the title story, cowives plot the murder of their husband when he announces that he plans to marry a third time. In ''Thirty One Beautiful Trees'' the vanishing of nature in the city is mourned by a woman who has been institutionalized after cutting out her own tongue. The longest story, ''The Shrine of Atia,'' explores the ways a woman can be represented by others—as a saint or as an eccentric—and appropriated as a symbol for various purposes.

Woman at Point Zero by Nawal Sa'dawi (London, England: Zed Press, 1983). The story of Firdaus, a prisoner awaiting execution, and of her lifetime struggle for independence, selfhood, and love, a victim of incest, a prostitute, and eventually, a murderer. The novel is based on interviews conducted during the course of the author's study of women and neuroses. The narration is in the voice of Firdaus, a woman under sentence of death for murdering her pimp, and it eloquently portrays a strong and honest woman who has refused to exist within the social system that makes women commodities to be bought and sold, either as prostitutes or as law-abiding wives and mothers. Her story is a testimonial that sheds light on the lives of women living in desperate straits—a compelling life story told in a vibrant and unsilenceable voice.

Commentary

Hitchcock, Peter. *Dialogics of the Oppressed.* Minneapolis: University of Minnesota, 1993.
Payne, Kenneth. ''*Woman at Point Zero*: Nawal el Saadawi's Feminist Picaresque.'' *Southern Humanities Review* 26.1 winter 1992): 11–18.

Woman Between Mirrors by Helena Parente Cunha (Austin: University of Texas, 1989). Translation of *Mulher no espelho*, first published in Brazil in 1983. A novel about finding one's identity through words, through images, and through memory. A woman stands before a three-paneled mirror and debates her identity and the very act of self-representation with the woman who writes her and the woman who reads her. She extends her exploration to the ways in which women are represented by society. Through the self-involved narrative, pieces of a family tragedy surface; her son comes to her room with a gun in order to defend her honor, and after she refuses to let him in, he is killed in a gun battle with police. The multilayered and often hidden African aspects of Brazilian culture are also reflected in the woman's narrative in which she remembers and explores what she knows of Xango (Shango), the Yoruba god who strikes at mirrors with bolts of lightning. Her struggle to forge an identity is a work of reconciling and recognizing her mixed-race background, her mixed cultural heritage, and her own sexual and intellectual needs apart from the socially accepted representation of woman that has so far defined her.

Commentary

Tesser, Carmen Chaves. "Post-Structuralist Theory Mirrored in Helena Parente Cunha's *Woman Between Mirrors.*" *Hispania* 74.3 (September 1991): 594–597.

Woman on the Front Lines by Belkis Cuza Malé (Greensboro, NC: Unicorn, 1987). A bilingual collection of poems, many of them dealing with poets and poetry ("And Here Are the Poets in Their Sad Portraits," "Oh, My Rimbaud," "I, Virginia Woolf, Rushing Headlong Toward Death"). Others are focused on women and their representation. "Women don't die on the front lines," she says in one poem, and describes how women are treated as ahistorical and passive, yet when they give birth, they create history and then sleep off their exhaustion like soldiers on leave from the front lines (31).

Women of Algiers in Their Apartment by Assia Djebar (Charlottesville: University of Virginia, 1992). An important collection of stories and an essay, "Forbidden Gaze, Severed Sound," in which Djebar explores the barriers keeping women severed and silent, those that are orientalist gazes, looking on the women of Algiers as Delacroix did, as silent, exotic, and incarcerated, and those imposed by Arab men, who are threatened by strong and vociferous women. The stories recall the women of the past, recounting their strength, their role in resisting the French, their community. Djebar attempts to find a space for women's voices and women's history within their tradition without allowing a current male definition of tradition to silence them. It includes an interview and helpful afterword by Clarisse Zimra.

Women of Smoke by Marjorie Agosín (Pittsburgh, PA: Latin American Literary Review, 1988). Poems that aren't centered in a particular place or point in history but that probe women's experience across time. Women from history, myth, even fairy tales are the subject of poems that explore sexuality, social expectations, and the representation of women. The poem "Women of Smoke" describes a wind that binds the poet with narrations made by women who have been turned to smoke, later returning to the image in "Salem" in which the narrator becomes a "tangled skein of smoke" (74).

The Wonderful Adventures of Mrs. Seacole in Many Lands by Mary Seacole (London, England: Oxford University, 1988). The picaresque adventures of a Jamaican woman, daughter of a Scots soldier and a free black boarding-house keeper, who disposes of her husband in the first pages of her memoir and proceeds to relate her experiences as an entrepreneur and a nurse, first in Central America and then in the Crimea. She engages in business in the boom-town atmosphere in Panama as prospectors flock toward California and later, after some resistance from the authorities, joins the British military forces in the Crimea in order to help with provisioning and nursing the wounded. Her style is arch and conversational, and she portrays the racism she encounters subtly, though it is clear that her contributions to the war effort are reluctantly accepted.

Commentary

Paquet, Sandra Pouchet. "The Enigma of Arrival: *The Wonderful Adventures of Mrs. Seacole in Many Lands.*" *African American Review* 26.4 (winter 1992): 651–663.

Wong, May. Poet, born in 1944 in Chungking, China. She moved as a young child to Singapore, where she published her first poems in various Singaporean literary journals. She emigrated to the United States, where all of her collections of poetry have been published.

Works

A Bad Girl's Book of Animals. New York: Harcourt, Brace, 1968.
*Reports. New York: Harcourt, Brace, 1972.
Superstitions. New York: Harcourt, Brace, 1978.

The Words to Say It by Marie Cardinal (Cambridge, MA: VanVactor and Goodheart, 1983). Translation of *Les Mots pour le dire*. An autobiographical novel by a French writer who was born in Algiers and spent her childhood there and at a country estate. It follows the course of her mental illness, psychoanal-ysis, and recovery. Much of the book concerns her early life in Algeria, her mother's role there and crippling sense of loss on leaving, and the tortured relationship between the mother and daughter. The book won an award as the best medical arts book of 1976 in France, but beyond being a document about psychoanalysis, it explores the psychology of colonialism, the ways in which the narrator becomes gradually aware of Algeria and its agony of revolution: "I'd looked upon the Algerian war as a sentimental matter, a sad story of a family worthy of the Greeks. And why was that? Because I had no role to play in the society where I was born and had gone crazy. No role, that is, other than to produce sons to carry on wars and found governments, and daughters who, in their turn, would produce sons. Thirty-seven years of absolute submission. Thirty-seven years of accepting the inequality and the injustice, without flinch-ing, without even being aware of it!" (264). Her recovery is a braiding of a new feminist consciousness, an awakening political awareness, and a discovery of herself as a writer, as she begins to narrate her own life.

Commentary

Lionnet, Françoise. *Autobiographical Voices: Race, Gender, Self-Portraiture.* Ithaca, NY: Cornell University, 1989.

Wynter, Sylvia. Born in 1928 to Jamaican parents in Cuba. She returned with them to Jamaica at age two. In 1946 she was awarded a scholarship that took her to King's College, London University, where she read Spanish. After earning a B.A., she worked as a writer for television and radio. She won a scholarship to study in Spain and earned an M.A. with a thesis on Spanish drama of the seventeenth century. She married Jan Carew, a novelist. In addition to writing a number of plays and a novel, she has taught at the University of the West Indies and at universities in Michigan and California and in 1977 went to Stanford to teach African and Afro-American studies and comparative literature. She has published widely as a literary critic and feminist.

Works

The Hills of Hebron. New York: Simon and Schuster, 1962.
Jamaica Is the High of Bolivia. New York: Vantage Press, 1979.

X

The Xhosa Ntsomi compiled by Harold Scheub (Oxford, England: Clarendon, 1975). Scheub collected and transcribed thousands of *ntsomi*, a performing art that takes a core cliché and develops it before a group of family members or friends. The performers are women, and every woman in the society is a potential practitioner. The compiler, who gathered the *ntsomi* by traveling, on foot, some 1,500 miles around the Transkei and KwaZulu, taping thousands of performances given by over 2,000 artists, provides an analysis of the genre in the first half of the book; the second half consists of transcriptions of the Xhosa texts and English translations.

Xi Xi. See **Hsi Hsi.**

Xiao Hong. See **Hsiao Hung.**

Xue, Can. See **Ts'an-hsueh.**

Y

Yang, Belle. Born in Taipei, Taiwan, in 1960, she moved with her parents to the United States when she was seven years old. After growing up hearing her father's stories of life in China, she studied at the Academy of Traditional Chinese Painting in Beijing from 1985 to 1989, when the crackdown on the pro-democracy movement prompted her return to the United States. She has written an illustrated history of her father's life in Manchuria before and during the Japanese occupation.

Work

Baba: A Return to China upon My Father's Shoulders. New York: Harcourt Brace, 1994.

Yang, T'ao. See **T'ao Yang.**

Year of the Elephant: A Moroccan Woman's Journey Toward Independence by Leila Abouzeid (Austin, TX: Center for Middle Eastern Studies, 1989). The title novella relates the history of a woman who has been divorced and left with nothing to her name but a small apartment in her home village. She goes through a period of depression and recounts her life story, her involvement in the independence movement, her marriage to a young man who becomes seduced by materialism, her growing feeling that the colonization that held Morocco in a powerless position is not over, that it has simply been replaced by ambitious and greedy Moroccans wielding power over the disenfranchised—the poor and women. She relates her story to a holy man and finds some peace and self-identity in Islamic beliefs. The remaining stories are short vignettes, character studies marked with irony.

Yoruba Girl Dancing by Simi Bedford (New York: Viking, 1992). A *bildungsroman* in which a Nigerian girl, part of a wealthy and influential extended family with rich traditions of its own, is sent at a very early age to study in England. There she encounters bitter cold and gray skies, dreadful food, loneliness, extraordinary perceptions of Africa based entirely on Tarzan films, and in short, a way of life that is ignorant and impoverished compared to her African experiences. Nevertheless, her father insists that an English education is the road to finer things. She adapts to her strange surroundings, becomes almost as English as her schoolmates, and seems to recover her connections to her homeland when, as a young woman in London, she becomes friends with an assortment of émigrés and, for the first time since early childhood, she is surrounded by faces that look like hers. The upbeat ending promises, in the words of her Nigerian boyfriend, that "we have survived, and soon we are going home" (185). The book offers young readers an engaging and level-headed narrator, humorous comments on Western assumptions, and a vivid contrast between African family life and the rigors of an English boarding school.

You Can't Get Lost in Cape Town by Zöe Wicomb (New York: Pantheon, 1987). A series of interrelated stories about a young woman who grows up on the veld with parents who are adamant about her learning English in order to better herself. She goes off to school, enduring embarrassment on the train platform, and gains a minor victory when she has sharp words for a sassy white boy. One story deals with a relationship she has with a young white man who, when he learns she is pregnant, wants them to go away to England, a mixed-race union being unthinkable in South Africa, but she decides to have an abortion instead. In the final story, she is returning from England for her father's funeral, coming to terms with her mother who finds her published stories something to be ashamed of. She finds herself thinking about staying in Cape Town. An accomplished, touching, and insightful collection of stories.

Yu Lo-chin. Born in China on May 31, 1946; her father was an engineer who had studied in Japan, her mother an owner of a small factory that she later handed over to the state. She had a happy childhood until her eleventh year, when her parents were targeted in the Anti-Voice Campaign of 1957 and among other difficulties her father lost his job. Her schooling was at a Beijing high school, followed by art school, from which she graduated in 1965. She started an apprenticeship in the carpentry shop of a toy factory and became a designer there. In 1966, during the early days of the Cultural Revolution, she was detained in connection with the diaries she and her brother kept and was sent for three years of labor cure at the Lingxiang Camp south of Beijing and then at the Qinghe Camp near the Gulf of Bohai. The pay she received for her labor there was barely enough to sustain herself. Her brother met with a more dire sentence: He was guilty of writing articles criticizing the concept of family lineage as a determinant of political consciousness and was executed on March 5, 1970. Her father was subjected to forced labor, and her mother had her head shaved and was the object of a public meeting of criticism. In the same year, Yu Lo-chin was sent to the remote and impoverished area of Linxi in the southern Hebei Province, then transferred to the wilder but less poverty-stricken province of Heilongjiang, also known as the Great Northern Wilderness. There she married Wang Shijun, another urban exile, from whom she was divorced four years later. Their relationship is the subject of *A Chinese Winter's Tale*, which she drafted in 1974. By 1976 she returned to Beijing, found employment as a nurse, and married a second time, to an electrician, Cai Zhongpei. In 1979 she was officially rehabilitated. She sought a divorce from her second husband in 1980, and the resulting scandal—her name was connected to that of the literary editor of a major national daily—and the banning of her second autobiographical book, *Spring Tale*, made her a celebrity among the literati. In 1981 she married for the third time, to Wu Fanjun, a teacher at the Beijing Institute of Metallurgy. In late 1985 she made a privately sponsored visit to Germany, where she applied for political asylum. The first of her autobiographical novels has been translated into English.

Work

A Chinese Winter's Tale: An Autobiographical Fragment. Translated by Rachel May and Zhu Zhiyu. Hong Kong: Renditions, 1986.

Commentary

Nerlich, Jorg Michael. "In Search of the Ideal Man: Yu Luojin's Novel *A Winter's Tale*." *Woman and Literature in China*. Bochum, Germany: Studienverlag, 1985. 454–472.

Z

Zamora, Daisy. Born to a well-to-do upper-middle-class family in Nicaragua. Her father was arrested when she was four years old for involvement in an attempted coup against the dictator Somoza. She was raised by her great-aunt and grandfather and was educated in convent schools. When she started her college education at the University of Managua in 1967, she became involved hesitantly with the political Left but felt constrained by her class background. She married Dionisio Marenco and moved to Chinandega, where her husband had taken a job as a sugar mill engineer. There she taught in a school for the workers' children and became more aware of issues of social justice. In 1972 she returned to Managua to nurse her dying grandfather, and he persuaded her to become more active in the political movement. She and her husband joined the Sandinistas and eventually had to go into exile in Honduras and Costa Rica, where she worked as an announcer and program director for Radio Sandino. In 1979 she served as vice minister of culture for the Sandinista Party and headed publishing at a research institute. She then became a professor at the Universidad Centroamericana in Managua, teaching seventeenth-century literature, including a course on Sor Juana Inés de la Cruz. She has published poetry on themes that are both political and personal.

Works

Clean Slate: New and Selected Poems. Translated by Margaret Randall and Elinor Randall. Willimantic, CT: Curbstone, 1993.

*Riverbed of Memory. Translated by Barbara Paschke. San Francisco, CA: City Lights, 1988.

Commentary

Dawes, Greg. *Aesthetics and Revolution: Nicaraguan Poetry, 1979–1990*. Minneapolis: University of Minnesota, 1993.

Randall, Margaret. *Risking a Somersault in the Air: Conversations with Nicaraguan Writers*. San Francisco, CA: Solidarity, 1984.

Zhai Zhenhua. Born in China in 1951, she became a member of the Red Guard and was one of the impassioned young activists who attacked the old ways at the start of the Cultural Revolution. She was herself purged, was re-habilitated after working on the land and in a factory, and eventually emigrated to Canada, where she wrote her autobiography.

Work

*Red Flower of China. New York: Soho, 1993.

Zhang Zhie. See **Chang Chieh.**

Zones of Pain: Las zonas del dolor by Marjorie Agosín (Fredonia, NY: White Pine, 1988). Memories preserved of the "disappeared" victims of state terror in Chile in an effort to oppose the oppression of silence. In the poem "Disappeared Woman I," she pleads against forgetting and oblivion: "Tear down the silence" (28). The poem "Torture" graphically, horrifically probes the pain that enforces silence. Her exploration of the experiences suffered during the political repression after Allende's death are a chilling witness to history and oppose the desire to erase the painful memories.

Zwi, Rose. Born in Mexico, she lived for a time in London and Israel but was for the most part raised in South Africa. She has written several novels, winning prizes in South Africa for her writing. Since 1988 she has lived in Sydney, Australia.

Works

Another Year in Africa. Johannesburg, South Africa: Bateleur, 1980.
Exiles. Craighall, South Africa: Ad. Donker, 1984.
The Inverted Pyramid. Johannesburg, South Africa: Ravan, 1981.
*The Umbrella Tree. New York: Penguin, 1990.

Appendix I
List of Authors by Region and Country

This list is intended to help the interested reader identify writers geographically. In the case of some writers, many of whom have lived in several countries, it is no simple matter to identify nationality; in these cases, writers are listed under the country with which they are most commonly identified or, in the case of European writers who have a third world connection, under the country with which they are connected. (Isak Dinesen, for example, is listed under Kenya, though she was a Danish writer.)

AFRICA SOUTH OF THE SAHARA

Botswana

Head, Bessie
Nisa

Congo

Blouin, Andrée

Ghana

Aidoo, Ama Ata
Appiah, Peggy
Busia, Abena P. A.
Danquah, Mabel Dove

Sutherland, Efua

Kenya

Creider, Jane Tapsubei
Dinesen, Isak
Huxley, Elspeth Joscelin (Grant)
Macgoye, Marjorie Oludhe
Markham, Beryl
Mugo, Micere Githae
Njau, Rebeka
Ogot, Grace
Waciuma, Charity

Mozambique

Magaia, Lina

Nigeria

Acholonu, Catherine Obianuju
Ali, Hauwa
Alkali, Zaynab
Bedford, Simi
Emecheta, Buchi
Nwapa, Flora
Ogundipe-Leslie, Molara
Okoye, Ifeoma
Onwubiko, Pauline
Onwueme, Tess
Segun, Mabel
Sofola, 'Zulu
Ulasi, Adaora Lily

Senegal

Bâ, Mariama
Bugul, Ken
Diallo, Nafissatou
Fall, Aminata Sow
Wheatley, Phillis

Sierra Leone

Casely-Hayford, Adelaide
Casely-Hayford, Gladys May

South Africa

Benson, Mary
Couzyn, Jeni
Dike, Fatima
Du Plessis, Menan
First, Ruth
Freed, Lynn
Fugard, Sheila
Gordimer, Nadine
Jabavu, Noni

Joseph, Helen
Joubert, Elsa
Karodia, Farida
Kuzwayo, Ellen
Mhlophe, Gcina
Millin, Sarah Gertrude
Nash, Thirza
Ngcobo, Lauretta
Reddy, Jayapraga
Roberts, Sheila
Sam, Agnes
Schreiner, Olive
Sikakane, Joyce
Smith, Pauline
Stockenström, Wilma
Suzman, Helen
Tholo, Maria
Tlali, Miriam
Ward, Harriet
Wicomb, Zöe
Zwi, Rose

Tanzania

Ladha, Yasmin
Mvungi, Martha

Uganda

Akello, Grace
Kimenye, Barbara

Zimbabwe

Dangarembga, Tsitsi
Lessing, Doris
Makhalisa, Barbara C.
Richards, Hylda M.
Rungano, Kristina

ASIA AND SOUTHEAST ASIA
China

Bei, Ai
Chang, Ai-ling
Chang Chieh
Chang, Jung
Ch'en Hsueh-Chao
Chen Jo-hsi
Cheng Nien
Chin Ts'ai
Han Suyin
Hsi Hsi
Hsiao Hung
Hsieh Ping-ying
Kuo, Helena
Li Pi-hua
Lin, Adet
Lin, Tai-yi
Lord, Bette Bao
Nieh Hua-ling
Ning Lao T'ai-t'ai
Pan, Lynn
Tai Hou-ying
Ting Ling
Ts'an-hsueh
Wang An-i
Wong, May
Yu Lo-chin
Zhai Zhenhua

Malaysia

Lim, Shirley

Myanmar

Mi Mi Khaing

Philippines

Alfon, Estrella
Gloria, Angela Manalang
Hagedorn, Jessica
Jalandoni, Magdalena G.
Rosca, Ninotchka
Tiempo, Edith Lopez
Ty-Casper, Linda

Singapore

Cheong, Fiona
Chua, Rebecca
Kon, S.
Lim, Catherine
Lim, Janet

Taiwan

Li Ang
Shih Shu-ch'ing
T'ao Yang
Yang, Belle

Thailand

Ho, Minfong
Prajaub Thirabutana

Vietnam

Duong, Thu Huong
Duras, Marguerite
Trinh T. Minh-ha

CARIBBEAN
Antigua

Kincaid, Jamaica

Barbados

Marshall, Paule
Savory, Elaine

Belize

Edgell, Zee
Ellis, Zoila

Bermuda

Prince, Mary

Cuba

Cuza Malé, Belkis
Fornés, Maria Irene
Garcia, Cristina
Gómez de Avellaneda, Gertrudis
Morejón, Nancy
Rojas, Marta

Dominica

Allfrey, Phyllis Shand
Rhys, Jean
Rudet, Jacqueline

Grenada

Collins, Merle

Guadeloupe

Condé, Maryse
Schwarz-Bart, Simone
Warner-Vieyra, Myriam

Guyana

Cambridge, Joan
Gilroy, Beryl
Nichols, Grace

Haiti

Chauvet, Marie
d'Adesky, Anne-christine
Danticat, Edwidge

Jamaica

Adisa, Opal Palmer
Bennett, Louise
Bloom, Valerie
Breeze, Jean Binta
Brodber, Erna
Cliff, Michelle
Craig, Christine
D'Costa, Jean
Escoffery, Gloria
Goodison, Lorna
Iremonger, Lucille
Manley, Edna
Marson, Una
Mordecai, Pamela
Pollard, Velma
Riley, Joan
Seacole, Mary
Senior, Olive
Sistren [Theatre Collective]
Thomas, Elean
Wynter, Sylvia

Puerto Rico

Benitez, Sandra
Ferré, Rosario
Ortiz Cofer, Judith

Trinidad and Tobago

Belgrave, Valerie
Brand, Dionne

De Lima, Clara Rosa
Guy, Rosa
Hodge, Merle
Johnson, Amryl
O'Callaghan, Marion
Philip, Marlene Nourbese
Springer, Eintou Pearl

LATIN AMERICA
Argentina

Borinsky, Alicia
Gambaro, Griselda
Hecker, Liliana
Kociancich, Vlady
Molloy, Sylvia
Ocampo, Silvina
Ocampo, Victoria
Orphée, Elvira
Partnoy, Alicia
Pizarnik, Alejandra
Storni, Alfonsina
Traba, Marta
Valenzuela, Luisa

Bolivia

Barrios de Chungara, Domitila

Brazil

Cunha, Helena Parente
Jesús, Carolina Maria de
Lispector, Clarice
Luft, Lya Fett
Meireles, Cecilia
Piñon, Nelida
Prado, Adélia
Queiroz, Rachel de

Steen, Edla van
Telles, Lygia Fagundes

Chile

Agosín, Marjorie
Allende, Isabel
Bombal, María Luisa
Mistral, Gabriela

Colombia

Pizarro, Agueda

El Salvador

Alegría, Claribel

Guatemala

Menchu, Rigoberta

Honduras

Alvarado, Elvira
Diaz Lozano, Argentina

Mexico

Campobello, Nellie
Campos, Julieta
Castellanos, Rosario
Esquivel, Laura
Garro, Elena
Glantz, Margo
Jacobs, Barbara
Juana Inés de la Cruz
Muñiz-Huberman, Angelina
Poniatowska, Elena
Vicens, Josephina

Nicaragua

Belli, Gioconda

Zamora, Daisy

Peru

Matto de Turner, Clorinda

Uruguay

Peri Rossi, Cristina

Venezuela

Parra, Teresa de la

**MIDDLE EAST AND
NORTH AFRICA**

Algeria

Amrouche, Fadhma

Cardinal, Marie

Cixous, Hélène

Djebar, Assia

Sebbar, Leïla

Egypt

Bakr, Salwa

Chedid, Andrée

Rif'at, Alifa

Sa'dawi, Nawal

Sha'rawi, Huda

Soueif, Ahdaf

Iran

Danishvar, Simin

Farman-Farmaian, Sattareh

Farrukhzad, Furugh

Guppy, Shusha

Khalvati, Mimi

Rachlin, Nahid

Shirazi, Manny

Lebanon

Accad, Evelyne

Adnan, Etel

Alamuddin, Rima

Makdisi, Jean Said

Nasrallah, Emily

Shaykh, Hanan

Morocco

Abouzeid, Leila

Palestine

Antonius, Soraya

Badr, Liyanah

Khalifeh, Sahar

Tawil, Raymonda Hawa

Tuqan, Fadwa

Syria

Kabbani, Rana

Tunisia

Halimi, Gisèle

Turkey

Özdamar, Emine Sevgi

Tekin, Latife

SOUTH ASIA

Bangladesh

Rokeya, Begum

India

Aikath-Gyaltsen, Indrani
Alexander, Meena
Amrita Pritam
Appachana, Anjana
Cughta'i, 'Ismat
Das, Kamala
Desai, Anita
Deshpande, Gauri
Deshpande, Shashi
Devi, Mahasweta
Dhingra, Leena
Dutt, Toru
Ganesan, Indira
Hosain, Attia
Jhabvala, Ruth Prawer
Lakshmi, C. S.
Markandaya, Kamala
Mehta, Gita
Mukherjee, Bharati
Naidu, Sarojini
Namjoshi, Suniti
Narayan, Kirin
Pande, Mrnala
Perera, Padma
Rama Rau, Santha
Randhawa, Ravinder
Sahgal, Nayantara
Shan, Sharan-Jeet
Sibal, Nina
Sorabji, Cornelia
Spivak, Gayatri Chakravorty
Steel, Flora Annie

Pakistan

Sidhwa, Bapsi
Suleri, Sara

Sri Lanka

Arasanayagam, Jean
Gooneratne, Yasmine
Wijenaike, Punyakante

Chronological List of Authors

This list organizes by birth date those authors discussed in the dictionary for whom dates are available. Those for whom dates are unknown are listed at the end of the list, by century. In some instances, the year of birth is in dispute, in which case what seems to be the most likely date is given here.

SEVENTEENTH CENTURY

Juana Inés de la Cruz. 1648–1695

EIGHTEENTH CENTURY

Wheatley, Phillis. 1753–1784

Prince, Mary. 1788–1833

NINETEENTH CENTURY

Seacole, Mary. 1805–1881

Ward, Harriet. 1808–1860

Gómez de Avellaneda, Gertrudis. 1814–1873

Steel, Flora Annie. 1847–1929

Matto de Turner, Clorinda. 1852–1909

Schreiner, Olive. 1855–1920

Dutt, Toru. 1856–1877

Sorabji, Cornelia. 1866–1954

Ning Lao T'ai-t'ai. 1867–1937

Casely-Hayford, Adelaide. 1868–1959

Naidu, Sarojini. 1879–1949

Sha'rawi, Huda. 1879–1947

Rokeya, Begum. 1880–1932

Amrouche, Fadhma. 1882–1967

Smith, Pauline. 1882–1959

Dinesen, Isak. 1885–1962

Millin, Sarah Gertrude. 1888–1968

Mistral, Gabriela. 1889–1957

Ocampo, Victoria. 1890–1979

Parra, Teresa de la. 1890–1936

Rhys, Jean. 1890–1979

Jalandoni, Magdalena G. 1891–1978

Storni, Alfonsina. 1892–1938
Richards, Hylda M. 1898–

TWENTIETH CENTURY

Manley, Edna. 1900–
Meireles, Cecilia. 1901–1964
Markham, Beryl. 1902–1986
Ocampo, Silvina. 1903–
Casely-Hayford, Gladys May. 1904–1950
Ting Ling. 1904–1986
Joseph, Helen. 1905–1992
Marson, Una. 1905–1965
Ch'en Hsueh-Chao. 1906–
Hsieh Ping-ying. 1906–
Gloria, Angela Manalang. 1907–
Huxley, Elspeth Joscelin (Grant). 1907–
Bombal, María Luisa. 1909–1980
Campobello, Nellie. 1909–
Diaz Lozano, Argentina. 1909–
Danquah, Mabel Dove. 1910–
Queiroz, Rachel de. 1910–
Hsiao Hung. 1911–
Kuo, Helena. 1911–
Vicens, Josephina. 1911–1988
Hosain, Attia. 1913–
Duras, Marguerite. 1914–
Jesús, Carolina Maria de. 1914–1977
Kuzwayo, Ellen. 1914–
Allfrey, Phyllis Shand. 1915–
Cheng Nien. 1915–
Cughta'i, 'Ismat. 1915–1992
Chauvet, Marie. 1916–1973
Mi Mi Khaing. 1916–
Alfon, Estrella. 1917–1982
Han Suyin. 1917–
Suzman, Helen. 1917–
Tuqan, Fadwa. 1917–

Amrita Pritam. 1919–
Bennett, Louise. 1919–
Benson, Mary. 1919–
Iremonger, Lucille. 1919–1989
Lessing, Doris. 1919–
Chedid, Andrée. 1920–
Garro, Elena. 1920–
Blouin, Andrée. 1921–
Chang, Ai-ling. 1921–
Danishvar, Simin. 1921–
Jabavu, Noni. 1921–
Nisa. 1921–
De Lima, Clara Rosa. 1923–
Escoffery, Gloria. 1923–
Gordimer, Nadine. 1923–
Lim, Janet. 1923–
Lin, Adet. 1923–
Rama Rao, Santha. 1923–
Telles, Lygia Fagundes. 1923–
Alegría, Claribel. 1924–
Castellanos, Rosario. 1924–1974
Gilroy, Beryl. 1924–
Markandaya, Kamala. 1924–
Sutherland, Efua. 1924–
Adnan, Etel. 1925–
First, Ruth. 1925–1982
Guy, Rosa. 1925–
Lispector, Clarice. 1925–
Nieh Hua-ling. 1925–
Devi, Mahasweta. 1926–
Lin, Tai-yi. 1926–
Halimi, Gisèle. 1927–
Jhabvala, Ruth Prawer. 1927–
Sahgal, Nayantara. 1927–
Gambaro, Griselda. 1928–
Macgoye, Marjorie Oludhe. 1928–
Wynter, Sylvia. 1928–

Bâ, Mariama. 1929–1981

Cardinal, Marie. 1929–

Cunha, Helena Parente. 1929–

Marshall, Paule. 1929–

Orphée, Elvira. 1929–

Fornés, Maria Irene. 1930–

Glantz, Margo. 1930–

Ogot, Grace. 1930–

Rif'at, Alifa. 1930–

Segun, Mabel. 1930–

Traba, Marta. 1930–1983

Ngcobo, Lauretta. 1931–

Nwapa, Flora. 1931–1993

Rojas, Marta. 1931–

Sa'dawi, Nawal. 1931–

Sofola, 'Zulu. 1931–

Ty-Casper, Linda. 1931–

Campos, Julieta. 1932–

Fugard, Sheila. 1932–

Njau, Rebeka. 1932–

Ulasi, Adaora Lily. 1932–

Poniatowska, Elena. 1933–

Stockenström, Wilma. 1933–

Tlali, Miriam. 1933–

Arasanayagam, Jean. 1934–

Das, Kamala. 1934–

O'Callaghan, Marion. 1934–

Farrukhzad, Furugh. 1935–

Gooneratne, Yasmine. 1935–

Prado, Adélia. 1935–

Wijenaike, Punyakante. 1935–

Djebar, Assia. 1936–

Piñon, Nelida. 1936–

Pizarnik, Alejandra. 1936–1972

Steen, Edla van. 1936–

Barrios de Chungara, Domitila. 1937–

Chang Chieh. 1937–

Cixous, Hélène. 1937–

Condé, Maryse. 1937–

D'Costa, Jean. 1937–

Desai, Anita. 1937–

Head, Bessie. 1937–1986

Muñiz-Huberman, Angelina. 1937–

Pollard, Velma. 1937–

Roberts, Sheila. 1937–

Ferré, Rosario. 1938–

Lord, Bette Bao. 1938–

Luft, Lya Fett. 1938–

Nasrallah, Emily. 1938–

Schwarz-Bart, Simone. 1938–

Tai Hou-ying. 1938–

Valenzuela, Luisa. 1938–

Brodber, Erna. 1940–

Edgell, Zee. 1940–

Mukherjee, Bharati. 1940–

Tawil, Raymonda Hawa. 1940–

Alamuddin, Rima. 1941–1963

Diallo, Nafissatou. 1941–

Fall, Aminata Sow. 1941–

Khalifeh, Sahar. 1941–

Kociancich, Vlady. 1941–

Namjoshi, Suniti. 1941–

Peri Rossi, Cristina. 1941–

Pizarro, Agueda. 1941–

Sebbar, Leïla. 1941–

Spivak, Gayatri Chakravorty. 1941–

Aidoo, Ama Ata. 1942–

Allende, Isabel. 1942–

Couzyn, Jeni. 1942–

Cuza Malé, Belkis. 1942–

Deshpande, Gauri. 1942–

Dhingra, Leena. 1942–

Karodia, Farida. 1942–

Lim, Catherine. 1942–

Mugo, Micere Githae. 1942–

Craig, Christine. 1943–

Hecker, Liliana. 1943–

Mordecai, Pamela. 1943–

Senior, Olive. 1943–

Sikakane, Joyce. 1943–

Emecheta, Buchi. 1944–

Hodge, Merle. 1944–

Khalvati, Mimi. 1944–

Lakshmi, C. S. 1944–

Lim, Shirley. 1944–

Morejón, Nancy. 1944–

Wong, May. 1944–

Shan, Sharan-Jeet. 1945–

Shaykh, Hanan. 1945–

Shih Shu-ch'ing. 1945–

Cliff, Michelle. 1946–

Özdamar, Emine Sevgi. 1946–

Pande, Mrnala. 1946–

Rosca, Ninotchka. 1946–

Shirazi, Manny. 1946–

Yu Lo-chin. 1946–

Philip, Marlene Nourbese. 1947–

Goodison, Lorna. 1947–

Thomas, Elean. 1947–

Belli, Gioconda. 1948–

Bugul, Ken. 1948–

Dike, Fatima. 1948–

Wicomb, Zöe. 1948–

Kincaid, Jamaica. 1949–

Makhalisa, Barbara C. 1949–

Ogundipe-Leslie, Molara. 1949–

Abouzeid, Leila. 1950–

Alkali, Zaynab. 1950–

Collins, Merle. 1950–

Nichols, Grace. 1950–

Soueif, Ahdaf. 1950–

Acholonu, Catherine Obianuju. 1951–

Alexander, Meena. 1951–

Ho, Minfong. 1951–

Zhai Zhenhua. 1951–

Aikath-Gyaltsen, Indrani. 1952–1993

Chang, Jung. 1952–

Du Plessis, Menan. 1952–

Li Ang. 1952–

Ortiz Cofer, Judith. 1952–

Trinh T. Minh-ha. 1952–

Brand, Dionne. 1953–

Busia, Abena P. A. 1953–

Ts'an-hsueh. 1953–

Adisa, Opal Palmer. 1954–

Wang An-i. 1954–

Agosín, Marjorie. 1955–

Onwueme, Tess. 1955–

Partnoy, Alicia. 1955–

Bloom, Valerie. 1956–

Breeze, Jean Binta. 1956–

Ellis, Zoila. 1957–

Tekin, Latife. 1957–

d'Adesky, Anne-christine. 1958–

Garcia, Cristina. 1958–

Ladha, Yasmin. 1958–

Dangarembga, Tsitsi. 1959–

Menchu, Rigoberta. 1959–

Mhlophe, Gcina. 1959–

Riley, Joan. 1959–

Ganesan, Indira. 1960–

Yang, Belle. 1960–

Rudet, Jacqueline. 1962–

Rungano, Kristina. 1963–

Danticat, Edwidge. 1969–

NINETEENTH-CENTURY WRITER—DATES UNKNOWN

Nash, Thirza

TWENTIETH-CENTURY WRITERS—DATES UNKNOWN

Accad, Evelyne
Akello, Grace
Ali, Hauwa
Alvarado, Elvira
Antonius, Soraya
Appachana, Anjana
Appiah, Peggy
Badr, Liyanah
Bakr, Salwa
Bedford, Simi
Bei, Ai
Belgrave, Valerie
Benitez, Sandra
Borinsky, Alicia
Cambridge, Joan
Chen Jo-hsi
Cheong, Fiona
Chin Ts'ai
Chua, Rebecca
Creider, Jane Tapsubei
Deshpande, Shashi
Duong, Thu Huong
Esquivel, Laura
Farman-Farmaian, Sattareh
Freed, Lynn
Guppy, Shusha

Hagedorn, Jessica
Hsi Hsi
Jacobs, Barbara
Johnson, Amryl
Joubert, Elsa
Kabbani, Rana
Kimenye, Barbara
Kon, S.
Li Pi-hua
Magaia, Lina
Makdisi, Jean Said
Mehta, Gita
Molloy, Sylvia
Mvungi, Martha
Narayan, Kirin
Okoye, Ifeoma
Onwubiko, Pauline
Pan, Lynn
Perera, Padma
Prajaub Thirabutana
Rachlin, Nahid
Randhawa, Ravinder
Reddy, Jayapraga
Sam, Agnes
Savory, Elaine
Sibal, Nina
Sidhwa, Bapsi
Springer, Eintou Pearl
Suleri, Sara
T'ao Yang
Tholo, Maria
Tiempo, Edith Lopez
Waciuma, Charity
Warner-Vieyra, Myriam
Zamora, Daisy
Zwi, Rose

Resources for Research

REFERENCE BOOKS

The following list is a sampling of works available in many reference sections of libraries that aid in research on third world women writers. It is a fast-growing area in publishing, so the researcher is well advised to check with a librarian for current and locally available reference materials.

Acosta-Belen, Edna, and Christine E. Bose, editors. *Researching Women in Latin America and the Caribbean*. Boulder, CO: Westview, 1993.

Benson, Eugene and L. W. Conolly, editors. *Encyclopedia of Post-Colonial Literatures in English*. New York: Routledge, 1994.

Blain, Virginia, Patricia Clements, and Isobel Grundy, editors. *The Feminist Companion to Literature in English: Women Writers from the Middle Ages to the Present*. New Haven, CT: Yale University, 1990. Particularly good for colonial and Commonwealth writers.

Buck, Claire, editor. *The Bloomsbury Guide to Women's Literature*. New York: Prentice-Hall, 1992. Includes excellent regional surveys as well as inclusive entries for authors and works.

Cortes, Eladio. *Dictionary of Mexican Literature*. Westport, CT: Greenwood, 1992.

Cumber-Dance, Daryl, editor. *Fifty Caribbean Writers*. New York: Greenwood, 1986.

Kanellos, Nicolas. *Biographical Dictionary of Hispanic Literature in the United States: The Literature of Puerto Ricans, Cuban Americans, and Other Hispanic Writers*. New York: Greenwood, 1989.

Krstovic, Jelena, editor. *Hispanic Literature Criticism*. Detroit: Gale, 1994.

Lindfors, Bernth, and Reinhard Sander. *Twentieth-Century Caribbean and Black African Writers*. Detroit, MI: Gale, 1992.

Nelson, Emmanuel S. *Writers of the Indian Diaspora: A Bio-Bibliographical Critical Sourcebook.* Westport, CT: Greenwood, 1993.

Simms, Norman. *Writers from the South Pacific: A Bio-Bibliographical Critical Encyclopedia.* Washington, DC: Three Continents, 1991.

Sole, Carlos A., editor. *Latin American Writers.* New York: Scribner's, 1989.

Stern, Irwin, editor. *Dictionary of Brazilian Literature.* New York: Greenwood, 1988.

BIBLIOGRAPHIES

"Annual Bibliography of Commonwealth Literature." *Journal of Commonwealth Literature* annual, usually in issue no. 2.

Berrian, Brenda F. *Bibliography of African Women Writers and Journalists (Ancient Egypt—1984).* Washington, DC: Three Continents, 1985.

Berrian, Brenda F. "An Update: Bibliography of Twelve African Women Writers." *Research in African Literatures* 19 (1988): 206–231.

Berrian, Brenda F., and Aart Broek. *Bibliography of Women Writers from the Caribbean (1831–1986).* Washington, DC: Three Continents, 1989.

Contemporary Literary Criticism. Detroit, MI: Gale, 1973–. Includes useful geographical index.

Cypess, Sandra Messinger, David R. Kohut, and Rachelle Moore. *Women Authors of Modern Hispanic South America: A Bibliography of Literary Criticism and Interpretation.* Metuchen, NJ: Scarecrow, 1989.

Guptara, Prabhu, editor. *Black British Literature: An Annotated Bibliography.* Mundelstrup, Denmark: Dangaroo, 1986.

House, Ameleia. *Black Women Writers from South Africa: A Preliminary Checklist.* Evanston, IL: Northwestern University Women's Program, 1980.

Lindfors, Bernth, editor. *Black African Literature in English: A Guide to Information Sources.* Detroit, MI: Gale, 1979.

Marting, Diane E., editor. *Women Writers of Spanish America: An Annotated Bio-Bibliographic Guide.* Westport, CT: Greenwood, 1987.

"The New Literatures in English." *The Year's Work in English Studies.* London, England: The English Association, 1919/1920–. A highly useful chapter in this annual collection of evaluative bibliographic essays.

Paravisini-Gebert, Lizabeth. *Caribbean Women Novelists: An Annotated Bibliography.* Westport, CT: Greenwood, 1993.

Poynting, Jeremy. *East Indians in the Caribbean: A Bibliography of Imaginative Literature in English (1894–1984).* St. Augustine, Trinidad: University of the West Indies, 1985.

Resnick, Margery, and Isabelle de Courtivron, editors. *Women Writers in Translation: An Annotated Bibliography, 1945–1982.* New York: Garland, 1984.

Rochman, Hazel, editor. *Against Borders: Promoting Books in a Multicultural World.* Chicago, IL: American Library Association, 1993.

Sonntag-Grigera, María Gabriela. "Lesser-Known Latin American Women Authors: A Bibliography." *Revista Interamericana de Bibliographía.* 42.3 (1992): 463–488.

JOURNALS

This list is a selection of journals that frequently have articles on third world women's literature. While by no means complete, it does suggest avenues for current awareness of scholarship, news, and reviews.

African Literature Today. London, England: Heinemann; New York: Africana, 1968–.
Ariel. Calgary, Canada: University of Calgary, 1970–. Supersedes: *Review of English Literature.*
Belles Lettres. Arlington, VA, 1985–.
boundary 2. Durham, NC: Duke University, 1972–.
Callaloo. Baton Rouge, LA, 1976–.
Commonwealth Essays and Studies. Mont Saint-Aignon: Société française d'études du Commonwealth, 1974–. Continues *Commonwealth Miscellanies.*
Critical Inquiry. Chicago, IL: University of Chicago, 1974–.
Current Bibliography on African Affairs. Farmingdale, NY: Baywood, 1962–.
English in Africa. Grahamstown, South Africa: Institute for the Study of English in Africa, Rhodes University, 1974–.
Feminist Review. London, England, 1979–.
Frontiers. Boulder: University of Colorado, Women Studies Program, 1975–.
Hispania. Wichita, KS: American Association of Teachers of Spanish and Portuguese, 1918–.
Jamaica Journal. Kingston: Institute of Jamaica, 1967–.
Journal of Commonwealth and Postcolonial Studies. Statesboro, GA: Department of English and Philosophy, Georgia Southern University, 1993–.
Journal of Commonwealth Literature. Oxford, England: Hans Zell, 1965–.
Journal of South Asian Literature. East Lansing: Asian Studies Center, Michigan State University, 1973–.
Kunapipi. Aarhus, Denmark: Dangaroo, 1979–.
Latin American Literary Review. Pittsburgh, PA: Department of Modern Languages, Carnegie-Mellon University, 1972–.
Latin American Perspectives. Newbury Park, CA: Sage, 1974–.
Latin American Research Review. Austin, TX: Latin American Studies Association, 1965–.
Letras Femeninas. Boulder, CO: Asociación de Literatura Femenina Hispanica, 1975–.
Luso-Brazilian Review. Madison: University of Wisconsin, 1964–.
Manushi. Delhi, India: Everest, 1978–.
Matatu: Journal for African Culture and Society. Amsterdam, Netherlands: Rodopi, 1987–.
Modern Chinese Literature. San Francisco, CA: San Francisco State University Center for the Study of Modern Chinese Literature, 1984–.
Modern Fiction Studies. West Lafayette, IN: Department of English, Purdue University, 1955–.
Présence Africaine. Paris, France: Editions du Seuil, 1967–.
Research in African Literatures. Austin: African and Afro-American Research Institute, University of Texas at Austin, 1970–.
Review: Latin American Literature and Arts. New York: Americas Society, 1987–. Continues: *Review (Center for Inter-American Relations).*

Revista Interamericana de Bibliographía. Washington, DC: Biblioteca Conmemorativa
    de Colon, Departamento de Asuntos Culturales, Union Panamericano, 1951–.
Sage. Atlanta, GA: Sage Women's Educational Press, 1984–.
Savacou. Kingston, Jamaica: Caribbean Artists Movement, 1970–.
Staffrider. Braamfontein, South Africa: Ravan, 1978–.
Studies in the Literary Imagination. Atlanta: Department of English, Georgia State Uni-
    versity, 1968–.
Wasafiri. London, England: Instructa, 1984–.
Women's Review of Books. Wellesley, MA: Wellesley College Center for Research on
    Women, 1983–.
Women's Studies. New York: Gordon and Breach, 1972–.
World Literature Today. Norman: University of Oklahoma, 1977–. Continues: *Books
    Abroad.*
World Literature Written in English. Arlington: University of Texas at Arlington,
    1971–.
Yale French Studies. New Haven, CT: Yale French Studies, 1948–.

PUBLISHERS

Many publishers, from the largest trade publishers to the smallest of literary presses,
publish works by women of the third world. This list is a gathering of addresses for
publishers that consistently publish such works and that may not be as well known—or
have titles as often reviewed—as more mainstream presses.

Ad. Donker
111 Central Street
Houghton, Johannesburg 2192
South Africa
*Founded in 1975 by Adriaan Donker; includes important South African writers in his
list.*

Africa World Press
556 Bellevue Avenue
POB 1892
Trenton NJ 08607
*Affiliated with the Red Sea Press, publisher of works by writers of Africa and the African
Diaspora.*

Bilingual Press
Hispanic Research Center
Arizona State University
Tempe, AZ 85287–2702
Publisher of bilingual Spanish-English editions.

Cleis Press
PO Box 8933
Pittsburgh, PA 15221
Includes experimental, lesbian, and Latin American titles in its unusual list.

The College Press
PO 3041 Harare
Zimbabwe
Important Zimbabwean publisher; includes many literary works in its list.

Curbstone
321 Jackson Street
Willimantic, CT 06226
A nonprofit literary arts organization that publishes many works in translation or bilingual Spanish-English editions.

Feminist Press
City University of New York
311 East 94th Street
New York, NY 10128
A nonprofit publisher of women's literature, works on feminism, and women's studies materials.

Graywolf
PO Box 75006
St. Paul, MN 55175
A small press that has had several award-winning titles and publishes an annual anthology, often on multicultural themes.

Heinemann
70 Court Street
Portsmouth, NH 03801
Important publisher for Commonwealth publications, particularly significant for its African Writers and Caribbean Writers Series.

Interlink
99 Seventh Avenue
Brooklyn, New York 11215
Publisher and distributor of books from and about the third world.

James Currey
54 Thornhill Square
Islington, London, England N1 1BE
Founded in 1985; specializes in eastern and southern Africa, the Caribbean, third world.

Karnak
300 Westbourne Park Road
London, England WE11 1EH
Specializes in the culture of Africa and the African Diaspora.

Latin American Literary Review Press
2300 Palmer Street
Pittsburgh, PA 15218
An important publisher of quality translations of Latin American literature; also publishes a scholarly journal.

Longman
Burnt Mill, Harlow, Essex
United Kingdom CM20 2JE
Founded in 1724; now has an extensive list of works by third world writers; often publishes for a third world market.

New Day
Quezon City, Philippines
Distributed in the United States by Cellar Bookstore.
18090 Wyoming
Detroit, MI 48221
An important publisher of contemporary Filipino literature.

Persea
60 Madison Avenue
New York, NY 10010
Includes many Middle Eastern authors in its list.

Quartet Books
London
Distributed by Charles River Books
Thompson Square
PO Box 65
Boston, MA 02129
Notable for a strong list of Middle Eastern titles.

Ravan
POB 31134
Braamfontein, Johannesburg 2017
South Africa
An oppositional press, with a strong list including two Noma award-winning titles.

Readers International
PO Box 959
Columbia, LA 71418
Publishes solely fiction by non-Western writers, usually in translation for the first time.

Red Sea
556 Bellevue Avenue
Trenton, NJ 08618
Affiliated with Africa World Press.

Renditions
Research Centre for Translation
Chinese University of Hong Kong
Shatin, NT
Hong Kong
Publisher of a translation magazine and paperback series.

Seal Press
3131 Western Avenue, Suite 410
Seattle, WA 98121–1028
Feminist publisher of women's writing.

Serpent's Tail
401 West Broadway #1
New York, NY 10012
Publishes literary and experimental work in paperback.

Sheba
PO Box 59637
Potomac, MD 20889–9633
A feminist publishing house.

Sister Vision Press
PO Box 217
Station E
Toronto, Ontario M6H 4E2
Canada
Feminist publisher focusing on books by third world women of color in Canada.

Skotaville
307 Hampstead House
46 Biccard Street
PO Box 32483
Braamfontein, Johannesburg 2017
South Africa
A wholly black-owned publishing collective established in 1982 and named after Mweli Skota, secretary general of the African National Congress (ANC) in the 1930s and a writer and editor; set up by the African Writers Association; Miriam Tlali is on the board of directors.

Three Continents
PO Box 38009
Colorado Springs, CO 80937–8009
Specializes in humanities works from the non-Western world.

Virago
20–23 Mandela Street
London NW1 OHQ
England
Feminist publisher that includes many rediscoveries of previously published work in its list.

Women in Translation
3131 Western Avenue
Seattle, WA 98121–1028
Nonprofit publisher of works in English translation.

Women's Press
United Kingdom and Canada
Distributed by Inland Book Company
PO Box 120261
East Haven, CT 06512
Innovative feminist publisher with a strong list, including many emerging third world writers.

Zed
London
Distributed by Humanities Press International
165 First Avenue
Atlantic Highlands, NJ 07716–1289
Specializes in third world issues and literature, particularly in Africa and the Middle East.

Anthologies

Many fine anthologies of works by third world women have been published that provide both selections of literature and, often, biographical and critical commentary. This bibliography is arranged geographically with general collections listed first.

GENERAL WORKS

Arkin, Marion, and Barbara Schollar, editors. *The Longman Anthology of World Literature by Women*. New York: Longman, 1989.

Bankier, Joanna, and Deirdre Lashgari, editors. *Women Poets of the World*. New York: Macmillan, 1983.

Busby, Margaret, editor. *Daughters of Africa: An International Anthology of Words and Writings by Women of African Descent from the Ancient Egyptians to the Present*. New York: Pantheon, 1992.

Charting the Journey: Writings by Black and Third World Women. London, England: Sheba Feminist, 1988.

Chew, Shirley, and Anna Rutherford, editors. *Unbecoming Daughters of the Empire*. Aarhus, Denmark: Dangaroo, 1993.

Cobham, Rhonda, and Merle Collins, editors. *Watchers and Seekers: Creative Writing by Black Women in Britain*. London, England: Women's Press, 1987.

AFRICA SOUTH OF THE SAHARA

Brown, Susan, Isabel Hofmeyr, and Susan Rosenberg, editors. *Lip: From Southern African Women*. Johannesburg, South Africa: Ravan, 1983.

Bruner, Charlotte H., editor. *Unwinding Threads: Writing by Women in Africa*. Exeter, England: Heinemann, 1983.

Bruner, Charlotte, editor. *The Heinemann Book of African Women's Writing*. Portsmouth, NH: Heinemann, 1993.

Kabira, W.M. et al., editors. *Our Secret Lives: An Anthology of Poems and Short Stories by Kenyan Women Writers*. Nairobi, Kenya: Phoenix, 1991.

Lockett, Cecily, editor. *Breaking the Silence: A Century of South African Women's Poetry*. Johannesburg, South Africa: Ad. Donker, 1990.

Mabuza, Lindiwe, editor. *One Never Knows: An Anthology of Black South African Women Writers in Exile*. Braamfontein, South Africa: Skotaville, 1989.

Mizra, Sarah, and Margaret Strobel, editors. *Three Swahili Women: Life Histories from Mombasa, Kenya*. Bloomington: Indiana University, 1989.

Oosthuizen, Ann, editor. *Sometimes When It Rains: Writings by South African Women*. London, England: Pandora, 1987.

Schreiner, B., editor. *A Snake with Ice Water: Prison Writings by South African Women*. Johannesburg, South Africa: COSAW, 1992.

Tsikang, Segang, and Diana Lefkane, editors. *Women in South Africa: From the Heart—An Anthology of Stories by a New Generation of Writers*. Johannesburg, South Africa: Seriti sa Sechaba, 1988.

van Niekerk, Annemarie, editor. *Raising the Blinds: A Century of Women's Stories*. Parklands, South Africa: Ad. Donker, 1990.

ASIA AND SOUTHEAST ASIA

Carver, Ann C., and Sung-sheng Yvonne Chang, editors. *Bamboo Shoots After the Rain: Contemporary Stories by Women Writers of Taiwan*. New York: Feminist Press, 1991.

Chinese Women Writers: A Collection of Short Stories by Chinese Women. Translated by Jennifer Anderson and Theresa Munford. Hong Kong: Joint, 1985.

Contemporary Women Writers. (*Renditions* Special Issue, vols. 27 and 28.) Hong Kong: China University, 1987.

Garcia, Mila Astorga, Marra Pl. Lanot, and Lalia Quindoza Santiago, editors. *Filipina I: Poetry, Drama, Fiction by Women Writers in Media Now*. Quezon City, Philippines: New Day, 1984.

Heng, Geraldine, editor. *The Sun in Her Eyes: Stories*. Singapore: Woodrose, 1976.

Hung, Eva, editor. *Contemporary Women Writers: Hong Kong and Taiwan*. Hong Kong: Renditions, 1990.

Lanot, Marra Pl., editor. *Filipina II: An Anthology of Contemporary Women Writers in the Philippines: Essays*. Quezon City, Philippines: New Day, 1985.

Li Yu-Ning, editor. *Chinese Women Through Chinese Eyes*. Armonk, NY: M. E. Sharpe, 1992.

The Muse of China: A Collection of Prose and Short Stories. Taipei, China: Chinese Women Writers Association, 1974.

The Muse of China, Vol. II: A Collection of Prose and Short Stories. Taipei, China: Chinese Women Writers Association, 1978.

Nieh, Hwa-ling, editor. *Eight Stories by Chinese Women*. Taipei, China: Heritage, 1962.

One Half of the Sky: Stories from Contemporary Women Writers of China. Translated by R. A. Roberts and Angela Knox. London, England: Heinemann, 1987.

Rexroth, Kenneth, and Ling Chung, editors. *The Orchid Boat: Women Poets of China.* New York: McGraw-Hill, 1972.

The Rose Colored Dinner: New Works by Contemporary Chinese Women Writers. Translated by Neinling Liu. Hong Kong: Joint, 1988.

Seven Contemporary Chinese Women Writers. Beijing, China: Chinese Literature, 1982.

Sokkyong, Kang, editor. *Words of Farewell: Stories by Korean Women Writers.* Translated by Bruce Fulton and Ju-Chan Fulton. Seattle, WA: Seal, 1989.

CARIBBEAN

Espinet, Ramabai, editor. *Creation Fire: A Cafra Anthology of Caribbean Women's Poetry.* Toronto, Canada: Sister Vision and Cafra, 1990.

Esteves, Carmen C., and Elizabeth Paravisini-Gebert, editors. *Green Cane and Juicy Flotsam: Short Stories by Caribbean Women.* New Brunswick, NJ: Rutgers University, 1991.

Mordecai, Pamela, and Mervyn Morris, editors. *Jamaica Woman: An Anthology of Poems.* Exeter, England: Heinemann, 1982.

Mordecai, Pamela, and Betty Wilson, editors. *Her True-True Name: An Anthology of Women's Writing from the Caribbean.* Portsmouth, England: Heinemann, 1989.

Randall, Margaret, editor. *Breaking the Silences: An Anthology of 20th-Century Poetry by Cuban Women.* Vancouver, Canada: Pulp Press, 1982.

Reclaiming Medusa: Short Stories by Puerto Rican Women. Translated by Diana Velez. San Francisco, CA: Spinsters, 1988.

Sistren Theatre Collective. *Lionheart Gal: Life Stories of Jamaican Women.* London, England: Women's Press, 1986.

Watts, Margaret, editor. *Washer Woman Hangs her Poems in the Sun: Poems by Women of Trinidad and Tobago.* Trinidad: n.p., 1990.

LATIN AMERICA

Agosín, Marjorie, editor. *Landscapes of a New Land: Fiction by Latin American Women.* Buffalo, NY: White Pine Press, 1989.

Agosín, Marjorie, editor. *These are not Sweet Girls: Latin American Women Poets.* Fredonia, NY: White Pine Press, 1994.

Agosín, Marjorie, and Cola Franzen, editors. *The Renewal of the Vision: Voices of Latin American Women Poets, 1940–1980.* Peterborough, England: Spectacular Diseases, 1987.

Agosín, Marjorie, and Celeste Kostopulos-Cooperman, editors. *Secret Weavers: Stories of the Fantastic by Women Writers of Argentina.* Fredonia, NY: White Pine Press, 1992.

Castro-Klaren, Sylvia Molloy, and Beatriz Sarlo, editors. *Women's Writing in Latin America: An Anthology.* Boulder, CO: Westview, 1991.

Crow, Mary, editor. *Woman Who Has Sprouted Wings: Poems by Contemporary Latin American Women Poets.* Pittsburgh, PA: Latin American Literary Review, 1984.

Erro-Peralta, Nora, and Caridad Silva-Nuñez, editors. *Beyond the Border: A New Age in Latin American Women's Fiction.* Pittsburgh, PA: Cleis Press, 1991.

Garfield, Evelyn Picón, editor. *Women's Fiction from Latin America: Selections from Twelve Contemporary Authors*. Detroit, MI: Wayne State University, 1988.

Hoeksema, Thomas, editor. *Fertile Rhythms: Contemporary Women Poets of Mexico*. Translated by Thomas Hoeksema and Romelia Enriquez. Pittsburgh, PA: Latin American Literary Review, 1989.

Hooks, Margaret, editor. *Guatemalan Women Speak*. Washington, DC: Epica, 1993.

Hopkinson, Amanda, editor. *Lovers and Comrades: Women's Resistance Poetry from Central America*. London, England: Women's Press, 1989.

Lewald, H. Ernest, editor. *The Web: Stories by Argentine Women*. Washington, DC: Three Continents Press, 1983.

Manguel, Alberto, editor. *Other Fires: Short Fiction by Latin American Women*. New York: Clarkson N. Potter, 1986.

Meyer, Doris and Marguerite Fernández Olmos, editors. *Contemporary Women Authors of Latin America: New Translations*. Brooklyn, NY: Brooklyn College, 1983.

One Hundred Years After Tomorrow: Brazilian Women's Fiction in the Twentieth Century. Bloomington: Indiana University, 1992.

Open to the Sun: A Bilingual Anthology of Latin American Women Poets. Van Nuys, CA: Perivale, 1979.

Partnoy, Alicia, editor. *You Can't Drown the Fire: Latin American Women Writing in Exile*. Pittsburgh, PA: Cleis, 1988.

Ross, Kathleen, and Yvette E. Miller, editors. *Scents of Wood and Silence: Short Stories by Latin American Women Writers*. Pittsburgh, PA: Latin American Literary Review, 1991.

Urbano, Victoria, editor. *Five Women Writers of Costa Rica*. Beaumont, TX: Asociación de Literatura Feminina Hispanica, 1978.

When New Flowers Bloomed: Short Stories by Women Writers from Costa Rica and Panama. Pittsburgh, PA: Latin American Literary Review, 1991.

Zapata, Celia Correas de, editor. *Short Stories by Latin American Women: The Magic and the Real*. Houston, TX: Arte Publico Press, 1990.

MIDDLE EAST AND NORTH AFRICA

An Arabian Mosaic, 1993. Translated by Dalaya Cohen-Mor. Potomac, MD: Sheba, 1993.

Booth, Marilyn, editor. *My Grandmother's Cactus: Stories by Egyptian Women*. London, England: Quartet, 1990.

Boullata, Kamala, editor. *Women of the Fertile Crescent: An Anthology of Modern Poetry by Arab Women*. Washington, DC: Three Continents, 1978.

Caspi, Mishael Maswari, editor. *Daughters of Yemen*. Berkeley: University of California, 1985.

Fernea, Elizabeth Warnoch, editor. *Middle Eastern Muslim Women Speak*. Austin: University of Texas, 1977.

Kadi, Joanna, editor. *Food For Our Grandmothers: Writings by Arab-American and Arab-Canadian Feminists*. Boston: South End Press, 1994.

Opening the Gates: A Century of Arab Feminist Writing. Bloomington: Indiana University, 1990.

Stories by Iranian Women Since the Revolution. Translated by Soraya Pakmazar Sullivan. Austin: University of Texas, 1991.

Twenty Stories by Turkish Women Writers. Translated by Nilufer Mizanoglu Reddy. Bloomington: Indiana University Turkish Studies Program, 1988.

SOUTH ASIA

Dharmarajan, Geeta, editor. *Separate Journeys.* London, England: Mantra, 1993.

Holmstrom, Lakshmi, editor. *The Inner Courtyard: Stories by Indian Women.* London, England: Virago, 1990.

Tharu, Susie, and K. Lalita, editors. *Women Writing in India, 600 BC to the Present.* New York: Feminist Press, 1991.

Truth Tales: Contemporary Stories by Women Writers of India. New York: Feminist Press, 1990. Originally published by Kali for Women, 1986.

Truth Tales 2: The Slate of Life. London, England: Women's Press, 1991. Originally published by Kali for Women, 1990.

We Sinful Women: Contemporary Urdu Feminist Poetry. Translated by Rukhsana Ahmed. London, England: Women's Press, 1991.

We Were Making History: Life Stories of Women in the Telangana People's Struggle. London, England: Zed, 1989.

Appendix V
Criticism

This list of books and articles is a mixture of items relating specifically to women's writing in the third world and more general works dealing with postcolonial literature or with feminist approaches to literature that offer useful critical insights for interpreting third world women's literature. For works relating to specific authors or literary works, see their entries in the text.

GENERAL WORKS

Adam, Ian, and Helen Tiffin, editors. *Past the Last Post: Theorizing Post-Colonialism and Post-Modernism.* Calgary, Canada: University of Calgary, 1990.

Aijaz, Ahmad. "Jameson's Rhetoric of Otherness and the 'National Allegory.'" *Social Text* 17 (1988): 3–25.

Aijaz, Ahmad. *In Theory: Classes, Nations, Literatures.* London, England: Verso, 1992.

Appiah, Kwame Anthony. "Is the Post- in Postmodernism the Post- in Postcolonial?" *Critical Inquiry* 17 (winter 1991): 336–357.

Ashcroft, Bill, Gareth Griffiths, and Helen Tiffin, editors. *The Empire Writes Back: Theory and Practice in Post Colonial Literatures.* London, England: Routledge, 1989.

Ashcroft, W. D. "Intersecting Marginalities: Post-Colonialism and Feminism." *Kunapipi* 11.2 (1989): 23–35.

Barker, Francis, et al., editors. *Europe and Its Others.* Colchester, England: University of Essex, 1985.

Bhabha, Homi K. "The Other Question . . . Homi K. Bhabha Reconsiders the Stereotype and Colonial Discourse." *Screen* 24.6 (November-December 1983): 18–36.

Bhabha, Homi K. "Of Mimicry and Man: The Ambivalence of Colonial Discourse." *October* 28 (spring 1984): 125–133.

Bhabha, Homi K. "Signs Taken for Wonders: Questions of Ambivalence and Authority Under a Tree Outside Delhi, May 1817." *Critical Inquiry* 12.1 (autumn 1985): 144–165.

Bhabha, Homi K., editor. *Nation and Narration*. London, England: Routledge, 1990.

Blunt, Alison, and Gillian Rose, editors. *Writing Women and Space: Colonial and Postcolonial Geographies*. New York: Guilford, 1994.

Brydon, Diana. "The Myths that Write Us: Decolonising the Mind." *Commonwealth* 10.1 (1987): 1–14.

Brydon, Diana. "Commonwealth or Common Poverty? The New Literatures in English and the New Discourse of Marginality." *Kunapipi* 11.1 (1989): 1–16.

Chow, Rey. " 'It's You, and Not Me': Domination and 'Othering' in Theorizing the 'Third World.' " *Coming to Terms: Feminism, Theory, Politics*. New York: Routledge, 1989. 152–161.

Christianson, Barbara. "The Race for Theory." *Feminist Studies* 14.1 (spring 1988): 67–79.

Cixous, Hélène. "The Laugh of Medusa." *New French Feminisms*. New York: Schocken, 1981. 245–268.

"Colonial and Post-Colonial Women's Writing." *Kunapipi* [Special Issue]. 7 (1985).

Donaldson, Laura E. "The Miranda Complex: Colonialism and the Question of Feminist Reading." *Diacritics* 18.3 (1988): 65–77.

During, Simon. "Postmodernism or Postcolonialism?" *Landfall* 39.3 (1985): 366–380.

During, Simon. "Postmodernism or Post-Colonialism Today." *Textual Practice* 1.1 (1987): 32–47.

Ferguson, Marshall, et al., editors. *Out There: Marginalization and Contemporary Cultures*. New York: New Museum of Contemporary Art, 1990.

Gardiner, Judith Kegan. "On Female Identity and Writing by Women." *Critical Inquiry* 8.2 (winter 1982): 347–361.

Geiger, Susan N. G. "Women's Life Histories: Method and Content." *Signs* 11.2 (winter 1986): 334–351.

Grewal, Inderpal, and Caren Kaplan. *Scattered Hegemonies: Postmodernity and Transnational Feminist Practice*. Minneapolis: University of Minnesota, 1994.

Griffiths, Gareth. "Imitation, Abrogation, and Appropriation: The Production of the Post-Colonial Text." *Kunapipi* 9.1 (1987): 13–20.

Harlow, Barbara. *Resistance Literature*. New York and London, England: Methuen, 1987.

Hassan, Ihab. "Pluralism in Postmodern Perspective." *Critical Quarterly* 12.3 (1986): 503–520.

Hitchcock, Peter. *Dialogics of the Oppressed*. Minnesota: University of Minnesota, 1993.

hooks, bell. "Choosing the Margin as a Space of Radical Openness." *Framework* 36 (1989): 15–23.

Jameson, Frederick. "Third-World Literature in the Era of Multinational Capitalism." *Social Text* 15 (fall 1986): 65–88.

JanMohamed, Abdul R. "The Economy of Manichean Allegory: The Function of Racial Difference in Colonialist Literature." *Critical Inquiry* 12.1 (autumn 1985): 59–87.

Jayawardena, Kumari. *Feminism and Nationalism in the Third World*. London, England: Zed, 1986.

Johnson-Odim, Cheryl. "Common Themes, Different Contexts: Third World Women and

Feminism." *Third World Women and the Politics of Feminism.* Bloomington: Indiana University, 1991. 314–327.

Juneja, Renu. "Pedagogy of Difference: Using Post-Colonial Literature in the Undergraduate Curriculum." *College Teaching* 41.2 (spring 1993): 64–69.

Jussawalla, Feroza F., and Reed Way Dasenbrock. *Interviews with Writers of the Postcolonial World.* Jackson: University Press of Mississippi, 1992.

Kaminsky, Amy. "Issues for an International Feminist Literary Criticism." *Signs* 19.1 (autumn 1993): 213–227.

Kaplan, Caren. "Deterritorializations: The Rewriting of Home and Exile in Western Feminist Discourse." *The Nature and Context of Minority Discourse.* New York: Oxford University, 1990. 357–368.

Kaplan, Caren. "Resisting Autobiography: Out-Law Genres and Transnational Feminist Subjects." *De/Colonizing the Subject: The Politics of Gender in Women's Autobiography.* Minneapolis: University of Minnesota, 1992. 115–138.

Katrak, Ketu H. "Decolonizing Culture: Toward a Theory for Postcolonial Women's Texts." *Modern Fiction Studies* 35.1 (spring 1989): 157–179.

Kirpal, Viney. "What Is the Modern Third World Novel?" *Journal of Commonwealth Literature* 23.1 (1988): 144–156.

Lionnet, Françoise. *Autobiographical Voices: Race, Gender, Self-Portraiture.* Ithaca, NY: Cornell, 1989.

Liu, Tessie P. "Race and Gender and the Politics of Group Formation: A Comment on the Notions of Multiculturalism." *Frontiers* 12.2 (summer 1991): 155–165.

Lugones, Maria C., and Elizabeth V. Spelman. "Have We Got a Theory for You! Feminist Theory, Cultural Imperialism, and the Demand for the 'Woman's Voice.' " *Women's Studies International Forum* 6.6 (1983): 573–581.

Mani, Lata. "Multiple Mediations: Feminist Scholarship in the Age of Multinational Reception." *Feminist Review* 35 (summer 1990): 24–41.

Mitra, Indrani. "The Discourse of Liberal Feminism and Third World Women's Texts: Some Issues of Pedagogy." *College Literature* 18.3 (October 1991): 55–63.

Mohanty, Chandra. "Feminist Encounters: Locating the Politics of Experience." *Copyright* 1 (1987): 30–44.

Mohanty, Chandra Talpade. "Cartographies of Struggle: Third World Women and the Politics of Feminism." *Third World Women and the Politics of Feminism.* Bloomington: Indiana University, 1991.

Mohanty, S. P. "Us and Them: On the Philosophical Bases of Political Criticism." *Yale Journal of Criticism* 2.2 (spring 1989): 1–31.

Parry, Benita. "Problems in Current Theories of Colonial Discourse." *Oxford Literary Review* 9.1–2 (1987): 27–58.

Peterson, Kirsten Holst, and Anna Rutherford, editors. *A Double Colonization: Colonial and Post-Colonial Women's Writing.* Mundelstrup, Denmark: Dangaroo, 1986.

Said, Edward. *Orientalism.* New York: Pantheon, 1978.

Said, Edward. "Intellectuals in the Post-Colonial World." *Salmagundi* 70–71 (spring-summer 1986): 44–64.

Said, Edward. *Culture and Imperialism.* New York: Knopf, 1993.

Schipper, Mineke, compiler. *Unheard Words: Women and Literature in Africa, the Arab World, the Caribbean, and Latin America.* London, England: Allison and Busby, 1985.

Sharpe, Jenny. *Allegories of Empire: The Figure of the Woman in the Colonial Text.* Minneapolis: University of Minnesota, 1993.

Slemon, Stephen. "Monuments of Empire: Allegory/Counter Discourse/Post-Colonial Writing." *Kunapipi* 9.3 (1987): 1–16.

Slemon, Stephen. "Magic Realism as Post-Colonial Discourse." *Canadian Literature* 116 (1988): 9–23.

Slemon, Stephen. "Post-Colonial Allegory and the Transformation of History." *Journal of Commonwealth Literature* 23.1 (1988): 157–168.

Slemon, Stephen, and Helen Tiffin, editors. *After Europe: Critical Theory and Post-Colonial Writing.* Sydney, Australia: Dangaroo, 1989.

Smith, Sidonie. *A Poetics of Women's Autobiography: Marginality and the Fictions of Self-Representation.* Bloomington: Indiana University, 1987.

Smith, Sidonie, and Julia Watson, editors. *De/Colonizing the Subject: The Politics of Gender in Women's Autobiography.* Minneapolis: University of Minnesota, 1992.

Spelman, Elizabeth V. *Inessential Woman: Problems of Exclusion in Feminist Thought.* Boston, MA: Beacon, 1988.

Spivak, Gayatri Chakravorty. *In Other Worlds: Essays in Cultural Politics.* New York and London, England: Methuen, 1987.

Spivak, Gayatri Chakravorty. "Can the Subaltern Speak?" *Marxism and the Interpretation of Culture.* Urbana: University of Illinois, 1988. 271–313.

Spivak, Gayatri Chakravorty. "The Political Economy of Women as Seen by a Literary Critic." *Coming to Terms: Feminism, Theory, Politics.* New York: Routledge, 1989. 218–229.

Spivak, Gayatri Chakravorty. *The Post-Colonial Critic: Interviews, Strategies, Dialogues.* New York: Routledge, 1989.

Spivak, Gayatri Chakravorty. "The Burden of English." *Orientalism and the Postcolonial Predicament: Perspectives on South Asia.* Philadelphia: University of Pennsylvania, 1993. 134–157.

Spivak, Gayatri Chakravorty. *Outside in the Teaching Machine.* New York: Routledge, 1993.

Tiffin, Helen. "Post-Colonial Literatures and Counter-Discourse." *Kunapipi* 9.3 (1987): 17–34.

Tiffin, Helen. "Recuperative Strategies in the Post-Colonial Novel." *Span* 24 (1987): 27–45.

Tiffin, Helen. "Post-Colonialism, Post-Modernism, and the Rehabilitation of Post-Colonial History." *Journal of Commonwealth Literature* 23.1 (1988): 169–181.

Trinh T. Minh-ha. *Woman, Native, Other: Writing Postcoloniality and Feminism.* Bloomington: Indiana University, 1989.

Trinh T. Minh-ha. *When the Moon Waxes Red: Representation, Gender, and Cultural Politics.* New York: Routledge, 1991.

Visel, Robin. "A Half-Colonization: The Problem of the White Colonial Woman Writer." *Kunapipi* 10.3 (1988): 39–45.

AFRICA SOUTH OF THE SAHARA

Appiah, Kwame Anthony. "Out of Africa: Typologies of Nativism." *Yale Journal of Criticism* 2.1 (fall 1988): 153–178.

Bazin, Nancy Topping. "Feminism in the Literature of African Women." *The Black Scholar* 20.3–4 (May-July 1989): 8–17.

Berrian, Brenda F., editor. *Critical Perspectives on Women Writers from Africa.* Washington, DC: Three Continents, 1990.

Blair, Dorothy S. *African Literature in French: A History of Creative Writing in French from West and Equatorial Africa.* London, England, and New York: Cambridge, 1976.

Blair, Dorothy S. *Senegalese Literature: A Critical History.* Boston, MA: Twayne, 1984.

Brown, Lloyd W. *Women Writers in Black Africa.* Westport, CT: Greenwood, 1981.

Bruner, Charlotte. "Been-To or Has-Been: A Dilemma for Today's African Woman." *Ba Shiru* 8.2 (1977): 21–30.

Burness, Don, editor. *Wanasema: Conversations with African Writers.* Athens, OH: Ohio University Center for International Studies, 1985.

Busia, Abena. "Silencing Sycorax: On African Colonial Discourse and the Unvoiced Female." *Cultural Critique* 14 (winter 1989–1990): 81–104.

Carusi, Annamaria. "Post, Post and Post: Or, Where Is South African Literature in All This?" *Past the Last Post: Theorizing Post-Colonialism and Post-Modernism.* Calgary, Canada: University of Calgary, 1990. 95–108.

Christian, Barbara. "Alternate Visions of the Gendered Past: African Women Writers vs. Illich." *Feminist Issues* 3.1 (spring 1983): 23–27.

Clayton, Cherry. "Post-Apartheid, Post-Feminist: Family and State in Prison Narratives by South African Women." *Kunapipi* 13.1–2 (1991): 136–144.

Coulon, Virginia. "Women at War: Nigerian Women Writers and the Civil War." *Commonwealth Essays and Studies* 13.1 (1990): 1–12.

D'Almeida, Irene Assiba. *Francophone African Women Writers: Destroying the Emptiness of Silence.* Gainesville: University of Florida, 1994.

Davies, Carole Boyce. "Finding Some Space: Black South African Women Writers." *A Current Bibliography of African Affairs* 19.1 (1986–1987): 31–45.

Davies, Carole Boyce, and Elaine Savory Fido. "African Women Writers: Toward a Literary History." *A History of Twentieth-Century African Literatures.* Lincoln: University of Nebraska, 1993. 311–346.

Davies, Carole Boyce, and Anne Adams Graves, editors. *Ngambika: Studies of Women in African Literature.* Trenton, NJ: Africa World Press, 1986.

Daymond, M. J., J. U. Jacobs, and Margaret Lenta, editors. *Momentum: On Recent South African Writing.* Pietermaritzburg, South Africa: University of Natal, 1984.

Eke, Ebele. "Beyond the Myth of Confrontation: A Comparative Study of African and African-American Female Protagonists." *Ariel* 17.4 (1986): 139–152.

Flewellen, Elinor C. "Assertiveness vs. Submissiveness in Selected Works by African Women Writers." *Ba Shiru* 12.2 (1985): 3–18.

Frank, Katherine. "Feminist Criticism and the African Novel." *African Literature Today* 14 (1984): 34–47.

Frank, Katherine. "Women Without Men: The Feminist Novel in Africa." *African Literature Today* 15 (1987): 14–34.

Grandqvist, Raoul, and John Stotesbury, editors. *African Voices: Interviews with Thirteen African Writers.* Sydney, Australia: Dangaroo, 1990.

Gray, Stephen. "Women in South African Theatre." *South African Theatre Journal* 4.1 (May 1990): 75–87.

Holloway, Karla. *Moorings and Metaphors: Figures of Culture and Gender in Black Women's Literature*. New Brunswick, NJ: Rutgers University, 1992.

Hunter, E., and C. MacKenzie, editors. *Between the Lines II: Interviews with Nadine Gordimer, Menan Du Plessis, Zöe Wicomb, Lauretta Ngcobo*. Grahamstown, South Africa: National English Literary Museum, 1993.

Ibrahim, Huma. "The Autobiographical Content in the Works of South African Women Writers: The Personal and the Political." *Biography East and West: Selected Conference Papers*. Honolulu: University of Hawaii, 1989. 122–126.

Iesue, Renata. "Romance and Reality: Popular Writings by Nigerian Women." *Commonwealth Essays and Studies* 13.1 (1990): 28–37.

Izevbaye, Dan. "Reality in the African Novel: Its Theory and Practice." *Présence Africaine* 139 (1986): 115–135.

Jama, Zainab Mohamed. "Fighting to Be Heard: Somali Women's Poetry." *African Languages and Cultures* 4.1 (1991): 43–53.

James, Adeola, editor. *In Their Own Voices: African Women Writers Talk*. London, England: James Currey, 1990.

JanMohamed, Abdul R. *Manichean Aesthetics: The Politics of Literature in Colonial Africa*. Amherst: University of Massachusetts, 1983.

Lambrech, Regine. "Three Black Women, Three Autobiographers." *Présence Africaine* 123 (1982): 136–143.

Lewis, Desiree. "Myths of Motherhood and Power: The Construction of 'Black Women' in Literature." *English in Africa* 19.1 (May 1992): 35–51.

Lockett, Cecily. "South African Women's Poetry: A Gynocritical Perspective." *Tulsa Studies in Women's Literature* 11.1 (spring 1992): 51–61.

MacKenzie, Craig, and Cherry Clayton. *Between the Lines: Interviews with Bessie Head, Sheila Roberts, Ellen Kuzwayo, Miriam Tlali*. Grahamstown, South Africa: National English Literary Museum, 1989.

Mugo, Micere Githae. "The Relationship Between African and African-American Literature as Utilitarian Art: A Theoretical Formulation." *Global Dimensions of the African Diaspora*. Washington, DC: Howard University, 1982. 85–93.

Nasta, Susheila, editor. *Motherlands: Women's Writings from Africa, the Caribbean, and South Asia*. New Brunswick, NJ: Rutgers University, 1992.

Ngcobo, Lauretta. "The African Woman Writer." *A Double Colonization: Colonial and Post-Colonial Women's Writing*. Mundelstrup, Denmark: Dangaroo, 1986. 81–82.

Nichols, Lee, editor. *Conversations with African Writers*. Washington, DC: Voice of America, 1981.

O'Barr, Jean F. "Feminist Issues in the Fiction of Kenya's Women Writers." *African Literature Today* 15 (1987): 55–70.

Ogundipe-Leslie, Molara. *Recreating Ourselves: African Women and Critical Transformations*. Trenton, NJ: Africa World Press, 1994.

Otekunefor, Henrietta, and Obiageli Nwolo, editors. *Nigerian Female Writers: A Critical Perspective*. Lagos, Nigeria: Malthouse, 1989.

Peterson, Kirsten Holst. "Unpopular Opinions: Some African Women Writers." *Kunapipi* 7.2–3 (1985): 107–120.

Roberts, Sheila. "South African Post-Revolutionary Fiction." *The Commonwealth in Canada: Proceedings of the Second Triennial Conference of CACLALS, Univer-*

sity of Winnipeg, 1-4 October, 1981. Calcutta, India: Writers' Workshop, 1983. 203–215.

Sam, Agnes. "South Africa: Guest of Honour Amongst the Uninvited Newcomers to England's Great Tradition." *Kunapipi* 7.2–3 (1985): 92–96.

Schmidt, Nancy. "African Women Writers of Literature for Children." *World Literature Written in English* 17.1 (1978): 7–21.

Smith, Sidonie. "Self, Subject, and Resistance: Marginalities and Twentieth-Century Autobiographical Practice." *Tulsa Studies in Women's Literature* 11.1 (spring 1992): 11–24.

Stratton, Florence. "The Shallow Grave: Archetypes of Female Experience in African Fiction." *Research in African Literatures* 19.2 (1988): 143–169.

Stratton, Florence. *Contemporary African Literature and the Politics of Gender.* London, England, and New York: Routledge, 1994.

Taiwo, Oladele, editor. *Female Novelists of Modern Africa.* New York: St. Martin's, 1985.

Veit-Wild, Flora. "Creating a New Society: Women's Writing in Zimbabwe." *Journal of Commonwealth Literature* 22.1 (1987): 171–178.

Veit-Wild, Flora. *Teachers, Preachers, Non-Believers: A Social History of Zimbabwean Literature.* London, England and Harare, Zimbabwe: Zell/Baobab, 1992.

White, Landeg, and Tim Couzens, editors. *Literature and Society in South Africa.* Harlow, England: Longman, 1984.

Wilentz, Gay. *Binding Cultures: Black Women Writers in Africa and the Diaspora.* Bloomington: Indiana University, 1992.

Wilkinson, Jane, editor. *Talking with African Writers: Interviews with African Poets, Playwrights, and Novelists.* London, England: James Currey, 1991.

ASIA AND SOUTHEAST ASIA

Barlow, Tani. "Theorizing Women: *Funu, Guojia, Jiating* [Chinese Women, Chinese State, Chinese Family]." *Genders* 10 (spring 1991): 132–160.

Bennett, Bruce. *A Sense of Exile: Essays in the Literature of the Asia-Pacific Region.* Nedlands, Australia: CSAL, 1988.

Bruneau, Marie Florine. "Learned and Literary Women in Late Imperial China and Early Modern Europe." *Late Imperial China* 13.1 (June 1992): 156–172.

Chow, Rey. *Woman and Chinese Modernity: The Politics of Reading Between West and East.* Minneapolis: University of Minnesota, 1991.

Chow, Rey. *Writing Diaspora: Tactics of Intervention in Contemporary Cultural Studies.* Bloomington: Indiana University, 1993.

Chung Ling. "Sense and Sensibility in the Works of Women Poets in Taiwan." *Worlds Apart: Recent Chinese Writing and Its Audiences.* Armonk, NY: M. E. Sharpe, 1990. 78–107.

Duke, Michael S., editor. *Modern Chinese Women Writers: Critical Appraisals.* Armonk, NY: M. E. Sharpe, 1989.

Gerstlacher, Anna, et al., editors. *Woman and Literature in China.* Bochum, Germany: Studienverlag, 1985.

Goldblatt, Howard, editor. *Worlds Apart: Recent Chinese Writing and Its Audiences.* Washington, DC: M. E. Sharpe, 1990.

Hou, Sharon Shih-jiuan. "Women's Literature." *The Indiana Companion to Traditional Chinese Literature*. Bloomington: Indiana University, 1986. 175–194.

Hsin-sheng C. Kao, editor. *Nativism Overseas: Contemporary Chinese Women Writers*. Albany, NY: SUNY, 1993.

Kintanar, Thelma B., editor. *Women Reading . . . Feminist Perspectives on Philippine Literary Texts*. Quezon City: University of the Philippines, 1992.

Knapp, Bettina. "The New Era for Women Writers in China." *World Literature Today* 65 (summer 1991): 432–439.

Kristeva, Julia. *About Chinese Women*. New York: Urizen, 1977.

Laifong Leung. *Morning Sun: Interviews with Post-Mao Chinese Writers*. Armonk, NY: M. E. Sharpe, 1993.

Larson, Wendy. "The End of 'Funu Wenxue': Women's Literature from 1925 to 1935." *Modern Chinese Literature*. 4.1–2 (spring-autumn 1988): 39–54.

Lim, Shirley. "Voices from the Hinterland: Plurality and Identity in the National Literatures in English from Malaysia and Singapore." *World Literature Written in English* 28.1 (1988): 145–153.

Lim, Shirley. "Semiotics, Experience, and the Material Self: An Inquiry into the Subject of the Contemporary Asian Woman Writer." *Women's Studies* 18 (1990): 153–175.

Lim, Shirley. "Up Against the Nationalist Canon: Women's War Memoirs from Malaysia and Singapore." *Journal of Commonwealth Literature* 29.1 (August 1993): 47–64.

Ling, Amy. *Between Two Worlds: Women Writers of Chinese Ancestry*. New York: Pergamon, 1990.

Liu, Lydia H. "The Female Tradition in Modern Chinese Literature: Negotiating Feminisms Across East/West Boundaries." *Genders* 12 (winter 1991): 22–44.

Longxi, Zhang. "The Myth of the Other: China in the Eyes of the West." *Critical Inquiry* 15 (autumn 1988): 108–131.

Manlapaz, Edna Zapanta. "The Canon of Early Filipino Poetry in English: A Feminist Challenge." *Philippine Studies* 39.3 (1991): 337–350.

Manlapaz, Edna Zapanta. "Our Mothers, Our Selves: A Literary Genealogy of Filipino Women Poets Writing in English, 1905–1950." *Philippine Studies* 39.3 (1991): 321–336.

Manlapaz, Edna Zapanta and Ruth B. Cudala. "Wrestling With Maria Clara: Filipino Women Poets in English, 1905–50." *Philippine Studies* 38.3 (1990): 316–356.

Martin, Melmont, editor. *Modern Chinese Writers: Self Portrayals*. Armonk, NY: M. E. Sharpe, 1992.

Yue Daiyun and Carolyn Wakeman. "Women in Recent Chinese Fiction—A Review Article." *Journal of Asian Studies* 17.4 (August 1983): 879–888.

CARIBBEAN

Aandaye, Eintou. "The Caribbean Woman as Writer." *Sturdy Black Bridges: Visions of Black Women in Literature*. Garden City, NY: Anchor/Doubleday, 1979. 62–68.

Abruna, Laura Niesen de. "Twentieth-Century Women Writers from the English-Speaking Caribbean." *Modern Fiction Studies* 34.1 (spring 1988): 85–96.

Balutansky, Kathleen M. "Naming Caribbean Women Writers." *Callaloo* 13.3 (summer 1990): 539–550.

Bassnett, Susan, editor. *Knives and Angels: Women Writers in Latin America*. London, England: Zed, 1990.

Benitez-Rojo, Antonio. *The Repeating Island: The Caribbean and the Postmodern Perspective*. Durham, NC: Duke University, 1992.

Bruner, Charlotte. "A Caribbean Madness: Half Slave and Half Free." *Canadian Review of Comparative Literature* 11.2 (1984): 236–248.

Campbell, Elaine. "The Dichotomized Heroine in West Indian Fiction." *Journal of Commonwealth Literature* 22.1 (1987): 137–143.

Cliff, Michelle. "Caliban's Daughter: The Tempest and the Teapot." *Frontiers* 12.2 (summer 1991): 36–51.

Collins, Merle. "Themes and Trends in Caribbean Writing Today." *My Guy to Sci-Fi*. London, England: Pandora, 1989. 179–190.

Condé, Maryse. "Beyond Languages and Colors." *Discourse* 11 (spring-summer 1989): 110–113.

Condé, Maryse. "Order, Disorder, Freedom, and the West Indian Writer." *Yale French Studies* 83 (1993): 121–135.

Cudjoe, Selwyn R., editor. *Caribbean Women Writers: Essays from the First International Conference*. Wellesley, MA: Calaloux, 1990.

Davies, Carol Boyce, and Elaine Savory Fido, editors. *Out of the Kumbla: Caribbean Women and Literature*. Trenton, NJ: Africa World Press, 1990.

D'Costa, Jean. "Expression and Communication: Literary Challenges to the Caribbean Polydialectal Writers." *Journal of Commonwealth Literature* 19.1 (1984): 123–141.

Esteves, Sandra Maria. "The Feminist Viewpoint in the Poetry of Puerto Rican Women in the United States." *Images and Identities: The Puerto Rican in Two World Contexts*. New Brunswick, NJ: Transaction, 1987.

Fenwich, M. J. "Female Calibans: Contemporary Women Poets of the Caribbean." *Zora Neale Hurston Forum* 4.1 (fall 1989): 1–8.

Fido, Elaine. "Radical Woman: Woman and Theatre in the Anglophone Caribbean." *Critical Issues in West Indian Literature*. Parkersburg, IA: Caribbean Books, 1984. 33–45.

Harris, Wilson. *The Womb of Space: The Cross-Cultural Imagination*. Westport, CT: Greenwood, 1983.

Harrison, Polly F. "Images and Exile: The Cuban Woman and Her Poetry." *Revista Interamericana* 4.2 (summer 1974): 184–219.

Kirpal, Viney. *The Third World Novel of Expatriation: A Study of Émigré Fiction by Indian, West Indian and Caribbean Writers*. New Delhi, India: Sterling, 1989.

Luis, William, editor. *Voices from Under: Black Narrative in Latin America and the Caribbean*. Westport, CT: Greenwood, 1984.

Morris, Ann R., and Margaret M. Dunn. " 'The Bloodstream of Our Inheritance': Female Identity and the Caribbean Mothers'-Land." *Motherlands: Women's Writings from Africa, the Caribbean, and South Asia*. New Brunswick, NJ: Rutgers University, 1992. 219–237.

Olmos, Margarite Fernandez. "Survival, Growth, and Change in the Prose Fiction of Contemporary Puerto Rican Women Writers." *Images and Identities: The Puerto Rican in Two World Contexts*. New Brunswick, NJ: Transaction Books, 1987. 76–88.

Ramis, Magali Garcia. "Women's Tales." *Images and Identities: The Puerto Rican in Two World Contexts.* New Brunswick, NJ: Transaction Books, 1987. 109–115.

Salgado, Maria A. "Women Poets of the Cuban Diaspora: Exile and the Self." *Americas Review* 18 (fall-winter 1990): 227–234.

Savory, Elaine. "Caribbean Women Writers." *Tibisiri: Caribbean Writers and Critics.* Sydney, Australia: Dangaroo, 1989. 30–39.

Shea, Renee Hausmann. "Gilligan's 'Crisis of Connections': Contemporary Caribbean Women Writers." *English Journal* 81.4 (April 1992): 36–41.

Smilowitz, Erika Sollish, and Roberta Quarles Knowles, editors. *Critical Issues in West Indian Literature.* Parkersburg, IA: Caribbean Books, 1984.

Smith, Faith L. "Coming Home to the Real Thing: Gender and Intellectual Life in the Anglophone Caribbean." *South Atlantic Quarterly* 93.4 (fall 1994): 895–923.

Waldman, Gloria Feinman. "Affirmation and Resistance: Woman Poets from the Caribbean." *Contemporary Women Authors of Latin America.* New York: Brooklyn College, 1983. 33–57.

Wilentz, Gay. "English Is a Foreign Anguish: Caribbean Writers and the Disruption of the Colonial Canon." *Decolonizing Tradition: New Views of Twentieth-Century "British" Literary Canons.* Urbana: University of Illinois, 1992. 261–278.

"Women Writers from the Caribbean." *Spare Rib* 124 (1988): 18–22.

Zimra, Clarisse. "Negritude in the Feminine Mode: The Case of Martinique and Guadeloupe." *Journal of Ethnic Studies* 12.1 (1984): 53–77.

LATIN AMERICA

Andrist, Debra D. "Non-traditional Concepts of Motherhood: Hispanic Women Poets of the Twentieth Century." *Letras Femeninas* 25.1–2 (1989): 100–104.

Bassnett, Susan, editor. *Knives and Angels: Women Writers in Latin America.* London, England: Zed, 1990.

Berg, Mary G. "Rereading Fiction by 19th-Century Latin American Women Writers: Interpretation and Translation of the Past into the Present." *Translating Latin America: Culture as Text.* Binghamton, NY: Center for Research in Translation, 1991. 127–133.

Berry-Bravo, Judy. "Guatemala's Younger Women Poets." *Confluencia: Revista Hispánica de Cultura Y Literatura* 6.1 (fall 1990): 141–152.

Beverly, John. "Through All Things Modern: Second Thoughts on *Testimonio.*" *boundary 2* 18.2 (1991): 1–21.

Beverly, John. "The Margin at the Center: On *Testimonio* (Testimonial Narrative)." *De/Colonizing the Subject: The Politics of Gender in Women's Autobiography.* Minneapolis: University of Minnesota, 1992. 91–110.

Buarque de Hollanda, Heloisa. "Parking in a Tow-Away Zone: Women's Literary Studies in Brazil." *Brasil/Brazil: Revista de Literatura Brasiliera* 4.6 (1991): 6–19.

Castillo, Debra A. *Toward a Latin American Feminist Literary Criticism.* Ithaca, NY: Cornell University, 1992.

Dawes, Greg. *Aesthetics and Revolution: Nicaraguan Poetry, 1979–1990.* Minneapolis: University of Minnesota, 1993.

Fox-Lockert, Lucía. *Women Novelists in Spain and Spanish America.* Metuchen, NJ: Scarecrow, 1979.

Franco, Jean. *Plotting Women: Gender and Representation in Mexico.* New York: Columbia University, 1989.

Frederick, Bonnie. "In Their Own Voice: The Women Writers of the *Generación del 80* in Argentina." *Hispania* 74.2 (May 1991): 283–289.

Garfield, Evelyn Picón. *Women's Voices from Latin America: Interviews with Six Contemporary Authors.* Detroit, MI: Wayne State University, 1985.

Gautier, Marie-Lise Gazarian. *Interviews with Latin American Writers.* Elmwood Park, IL: Dalkey Archive, 1989.

Hahner, June S. "The Nineteenth-Century Feminist Press and Women's Rights in Brazil." *Latin American Women: Historical Perspectives.* Westport, CT: Greenwood, 1978.

Kaminsky, Amy K. *Reading the Body Politic: Feminist Criticism and Latin American Women Writers.* Minneapolis: University of Minnesota, 1993.

Kerr, Lucille. *Reclaiming the Author: Figures and Fictions from Spanish America.* Durham, NC: Duke University, 1992.

Klingenberg, Patricia. "Latin American Women Writers: Into the Main-Stream (At Last)." *Tulsa Studies in Women's Literature* 6 (1987): 97–107.

Larson, Catherine. "Playwrights of Passage: Women and Game-Playing on the Stage." *Latin American Literary Review* 19.38 (July-December 1991): 78–89.

Laughlin, Miriam. "Mayan Women Playwrights." *Belles Lettres* 7 (winter 1991–1992): 45–47.

Lewald, H. Ernest. "Two Generations of River Plate Women Authors." *Latin American Research Review* 15.1 (1980): 231–236.

Lindstrom, Naomi. *Women's Voice in Latin America.* Washington, DC: Three Continents, 1989.

Lobo, Luiza. "Women Writers in Brazil Today." *World Literature Today* 61 (winter 1987): 49–54.

Luis, William, editor. *Voices from Under: Black Narrative in Latin America and the Caribbean.* Westport, CT: Greenwood, 1984.

Masiello, Francine. *Between Civilization and Barbarism: Women, Nation, and Literary Culture in Modern Argentina.* Lincoln: University of Nebraska, 1992.

Masiello, Francine. "Subversions of Authority: Feminist Literary Culture in the River Plate Region." *Chasqui: Revista de Literatura Latinoamericana* 21.1 (May 1992): 39–48.

Meyer, Doris, and Margarite Fernández Olmos, editors. *Contemporary Women Authors of Latin America: Introductory Essays.* New York: Brooklyn College, 1983.

Miaz, Magdalena, and Luis H. Pena. "Between Lines: Constructing the Political Self." *A/B: Auto/Biography Studies* 3.4 (summer 1988): 23–36.

Miller, Beth, editor. *Women in Hispanic Literature: Icons and Fallen Idols.* Berkeley: University of California, 1983.

Miller, Yvette E., and Charles M. Tatum, editors. *Latin American Women Writers: Yesterday and Today.* Pittsburgh, PA: Latin American Literary Review, 1977.

Molloy, Sylvia. *At Face Value: Autobiographical Writing in Spanish America.* New York: Cambridge University, 1991.

Moore, Rachelle. "Our Women Don't Write." *Revista Interamericana de Bibliografía.* 40.3 (1990): 416–420.

Pinto, Magdalena Garcia. *Women Writers of Latin America: Intimate Histories.* Austin: University of Texas, 1991.

Price, Greg, editor. *Latin America: The Writer's Journey*. London, England: Hamish Hamilton, 1990.

Quinlan, Susan Canty. *The Female Voice in Contemporary Brazilian Narrative*. New York: P. Lang, 1991.

Randall, Margaret. *Risking a Somersault in the Air: Conversations with Nicaraguan Writers*. San Francisco, CA: Solidarity, 1984.

Randall, Margaret. *Sandino's Daughters Revisited: Feminism in Nicaragua*. New Brunswick, NJ: Rutgers University, 1994.

Rodriguez, Ileana. *House/Garden/Nation: Space, Gender, and Ethnicity in Post-Colonial Latin American Literatures by Women*. Durham, NC: Duke University, 1994.

Rosman-Asket, Adriana. "Out of the Shadows: Two Centuries of Argentine Women's Voices." *Critical Matrix: Princeton Working Papers in Women's Studies* 2.1–3 (spring 1986): 70–100.

Sadlier, Darlene J. "Making the Difference: Brazilian Women Writing." *Fiction International* 19.1 (1990): 37–50.

Shea, Maureen. "Latin American Women and the Oral Tradition: Giving Voice to the Voiceless." *Critique* 34.3 (spring 1993): 139–153.

Sommer, Doris. "Not Just a Personal Story: Women's *Testimonios* and the Plural Self." *Life/Lines: Theorizing Women's Autobiography*. Ithaca, NY: Cornell University, 1988. 107–130.

Sullivan, Constance A. "Re-Reading the Hispanic Literary Canon: The Question of Gender." *Ideologies and Literature* 16 (1983): 93–101.

Taylor, Martin C. "Women Intellectuals in Chilean Society." *Latin American Women Writers: Yesterday and Today*. Pittsburgh, PA: Latin American Literary Review, 1977. 18–24.

Waldman, Gloria Feiman. "Three Female Playwrights Explore Contemporary Latin American Reality: Myrna Casas, Griselda Gambaro, Luisa Josefina Hernandez." *Latin American Women Writers: Yesterday and Today*. Pittsburgh, PA: Latin American Literary Review, 1977. 75–84.

Wilson, S. R. "Art by Gender: The Latin American Woman Writer." *Revista Canadiense de Estudios Hispánicos* 6.1 (1981): 135–137.

Yeager, Gertrude M. "Women and the Intellectual Life of Nineteenth Century Lima." *Revista Interamericana de Bibliographía* 40.4 (1990): 361–393.

Zapata, Celia de. "One Hundred Years of Women Writers in Latin America." *Latin American Literary Review* 3.6 (1975): 7–15.

Zee, Linda S. "Spanish American Women Poets: An (Almost) Hidden Tradition." *Romance Languages Annual* 3 (1991): 649–653.

MIDDLE EAST AND NORTH AFRICA

Accad, Evelyne. *Veil of Shame: The Role of Women in the Contemporary Fiction of North Africa and Arab World*. Sherbrooke, Canada: Naaman, 1978.

Accad, Evelyne. *Sexuality and War: Literary Masks of the Middle East*. New York: New York University, 1990.

Accad, Evelyne. "Sexuality and Sexual Politics: Conflicts and Contradictions for Contemporary Women in the Middle East." *Third World Women and the Politics of Feminism*. Bloomington: Indiana University, 1991. 237–250.

Accad, Evelyne. "Sexuality, War, and Literature in Lebanon." *Feminist Issues* 11 (fall 1991): 27–42.

Ahmed, Leila. "Between Two Worlds: The Formation of a Turn-of-the-Century Egyptian Feminist." *Life/Lines: Theorizing Women's Autobiography.* Ithaca, NY: Cornell University, 1988. 154–174.

Ahmed, Leila. "Arab Culture and Writing Women's Bodies." *Feminist Issues* 9.1 (spring 1989): 41–55.

Arebi, Saddeka. *Women and Words in Saudi Arabia: The Politics of Literary Discourse.* New York: Columbia University, 1994.

Baron, Beth. *The Women's Awakening in Egypt: Culture, Society, and the Press.* New Haven, CT: Yale University, 1994.

Booth, Marilyn. "Biography and Feminist Rhetoric in Early Twentieth-Century Egypt: Mayy Ziyada's Studies of Three Women's Lives." *Journal of Women's History* 3.1 (spring 1991): 38–64.

Cooke, Miriam. *War's Other Voices: Women Writers on the Lebanese Civil War, 1975–82.* Cambridge, England: Cambridge University, 1988.

Dwyer, Daisy Hilse. *Images and Self-Images: Male and Female in Morocco.* New York: Columbia University, 1978.

Gün, Güneli. "The Woman in the Darkroom: Contemporary Women Writers in Turkey." *World Literature Today* 60.2 (spring 1986): 275–279.

Kabbani, Rana. *Europe's Myths of the Orient.* London, England: Macmillan, 1986.

Lazreg, Marnia. "Feminism and Difference: The Perils of Writing as a Woman in Algeria." *Feminist Studies* 14.1 (spring 1988): 81–107.

Malti-Douglas, Fedwa. *Woman's Body, Woman's World: Gender and Discourse in Arabo-Islamic Writing.* Princeton, NJ: Princeton University, 1992.

Marx-Scouras, Danielle. "Muffled Screams/Stifled Voices." *Yale French Studies* 82 (May 1993): 172–182.

Milani, Farzaneh. *Veils and Words: The Emerging Voices of Iranian Women Writers.* Syracuse, NY: Syracuse University, 1992.

Mortimer, Mildred. "The Feminine Image in the Algerian Novel of French Expression." *Ba Shiru* 8.2 (1977): 51–62.

Mortimer, Mildred. *Journeys Through the French African Novel.* Portsmouth, NH: Heinemann, 1990.

Ostle, Robin, editor. *Modern Literature in the Near and Middle East, 1850–1970.* London, England, and New York: Routledge, 1991.

Roche, Anne. "Women's Literature in Algeria." *Research in African Literatures* 23.2 (summer 1992): 209–216.

Tahon, Marie-Blanche. "Women Novelists and Women in the Struggle for Algeria's National Liberation (1957–1980)." *Research in African Literatures* 23.2 (summer 1992): 39–50.

Woodhull, Winifred. *Transfigurations of the Maghreb: Feminism, Decolonization, and Literatures.* Minneapolis: University of Minnesota, 1993.

SOUTH ASIA

Alexander, Meena. "Outcaste Power: Ritual Displacement and Virile Maternity in Indian Women Writers." *Journal of Commonwealth Literature* 23.1 (1989): 12–29.

Ash, Ranjana. "The Search for Freedom in Indian Women's Writing." *Motherlands: Women's Writings from Africa, the Caribbean, and South Asia.* New Brunswick, NJ: Rutgers University, 1992. 152–174.

Chavan, Sunanda P. *The Fair Voice: A Study of Indian Women Poets in English.* Delhi, India: Ajanta, 1984.

Cowasjee, Saros. "The Memsahib at the Writing Table: Women Writers of the Raj." *Encounter* 75.1 (July-August 1990): 53–56.

Daruwalla, Keki. "Confessional Poetry as Social Commentary: A View of English Poetry by Indian Women Poets." *Indian Horizons* 35.3–4 (1986): 15–24.

Desai, Anita. "Indian Fiction Today." *Daedalus* 118.4 (fall 1989): 206–231.

Kanitkar, Helen. " 'Heaven Lies Beneath Her Feet': Mother Figures in Selected Indo-Anglian Novels." *Motherlands: Women's Writings from Africa, the Caribbean, and South Asia.* New Brunswick, NJ: Rutgers University, 1992. 175–199.

Khan, Naseem. "Private Spaces to Public Places: Contemporary Asian Women Writers." *From My Guy to Sci-Fi.* London, England: Pandora, 1989. 165–178.

Kirpal, Viney. *The Third World Novel of Expatriation: A Study of Émigré Fiction by Indian, West Indian and Caribbean Writers.* New Delhi, India: Sterling, 1989.

Kirpal, Viney, editor. *The New Indian Novel in English: A Study of the 1980s.* New Delhi, India: Allied, 1990.

Lakshmi, C. S. *The Face Behind the Mask: Women in Tamil Literature.* New Delhi, India: Vikas, 1984.

Mani, Lata. "Contentious Traditions: The Debate on Sati in Colonial India." *The Nature and Context of Minority Discourse.* New York: Oxford University, 1990. 319–356.

Mukherjee, Bharati. "Mimicry and Reinvention." *The Commonwealth in Canada: Proceedings of the Second Triennial Conference of CACLALS, University of Winnipeg, 1-4 October, 1981.* Calcutta, India: Writers' workshop 1983. 147–157.

Nelson, Emmanuel S. *Reworlding: The Literature of the Indian Diaspora.* New York: Greenwood, 1992.

Paranjape, Makarand. "Distinguishing Themselves: New Fiction by Expatriate Indian Women." *World Literature Today* 65.1 (winter 1991): 72–74.

Paxton, Nancy L. "Disembodied Subjects: English Women's Autobiography Under the Raj." *De/Colonizing the Subject: The Politics of Gender in Women's Autobiography.* Minneapolis: University of Minnesota, 1992. 387–409.

Poynting, Jeremy. "East Indian Women in the Caribbean: Experience, Image, and Voice." *Journal of East Asian Literature* 1 (winter-spring 1986): 8–18.

Rajan, Rejeswari Sunder. *Real and Imagined Women: Gender, Culture, and Postcolonialism.* New York: Routledge, 1993.

Rustomji-Kerns, Roshni. "Expatriates, Immigrants, and Literature: Three South Asian Women Writers." *Massachusetts Review* 29.4 (1988): 655–665.

Sangari, Kumkum, and Sudesh Vaid, editors. *Recasting Women: Essays in Indian Colonial History.* New Brunswick, NJ: Rutgers University, 1990.

Seely, Clinton B., editor. *Women, Politics, and Literature in Bengal.* East Lansing: Michigan State University, 1981.

Suleri, Sara. *The Rhetoric of English India.* Chicago, IL: University of Chicago, 1992.

Viswanathan, Gauri. *Masks of Conquest: Literary Study and British Rule in India.* New York: Columbia University, 1989.

Index

About the Author

BARBARA FISTER is Bibliographic Instruction Librarian and Associate Professor, Gustavus Adolphus College. Her earlier writing has appeared in the *Journal of Academic Librarianship, Research Strategies, Choice*, and *RQ*.